ISRAELI DEMOCRACY

ISRAELI DEMOCRACY

The Middle of the Journey

Daniel Shimshoni

THE FREE PRESS
A Division of Macmillan Publishing Co., Inc.
NEW YORK

Collier Macmillan Publishers
LONDON

The Free Press
A Division of Macmillan Publishing Co., Inc.
866 Third Avenue, New York, N.Y. 10022

Collier Macmillan Canada, Inc.

Printed in the United States of America

printing number

1 2 3 4 5 6 7 8 9 10

Library of Congress Cataloging in Publication Data

Shimshoni, Daniel
  Israeli democracy.

  Bibliography: p.
  Includes index.
  1. Israel—Politics and government. I. Title.
JQ1825.P3S44   1982   320.95694   81-71151
ISBN 0-02-928620-4   AACR2

Contents

Preface

THIS BOOK IS A STUDY of the ways in which public policies were formed in Israel from independence, in 1948, until the elections of 1977 brought the country's first major change of ruling party, ending Labor's long domination of political authority.

Since 1977 there have been dramatic events, primarily the first legitimating recognition of Israel by an Arab country in the peace negotiations with Egypt. There is not yet, however, the perspective needed to analyze these events or their impact. The story is still at its beginning. What I hope to present is a kind of bench mark from which to study the social and political changes which will unfold.

As will become evident, the characteristics of the political system had their roots in the experience and beliefs of Diaspora communities, in the several streams of the Zionist movement, and in the process of settling and developing the country under Turkish and British rule; and I have tried to show some of these origins and their implications.

It is now almost 100 years since the ideas of modern Zionism began to be expressed in organized settlement. In the fall of 1980, Degania, the first *kvutza*, was seventy years old. Many of the political and social aspects of the early dreams are a reality, but many are elusive or seem irrelevant. The return to a national home was to be accompanied by a social and spiritual renaissance. Indeed, to many, a national home is an impossibility without it.

The arguments and the problems of action have concerned the depth, the nature, and the extent of the change needed in the Jewish people. To some, "normalization" would be enough—the Jews would have their own land and be involved, like other nations, in the full spectrum of human life—their own hewers of wood and drawers of water, policemen, criminals, and productive workers. To others, only the forming of a unique society would make the enterprise worthwhile, or even feasible. Ben Gurion expressed these two desires thus: "Two basic aspirations underlie all our work in this country: to be like all the nations, and to be different than all the nations. . . ."

In any democratic country, policy formation can be considered from the points of view of its democracy and its effectiveness, and these are the parameters with which I am principally concerned. In following this study, however, I hope that the reader will keep in mind, as I have tried to do, that there are larger goals involved, and that Israeli society seeks to express dual needs—for the unique and the universal, for supranational as well as national goals, and for a renewal of the spiritual contributions as well as the political condition of the Jews.

Acknowledgments

BECAUSE OF THE SCOPE of the work, many data come from the works of others, to which the notes and references give acknowledgment. I apologize for any omissions and absolve all others from responsibility for errors. Most of all, however, "I dwell among mine own people," * and a principal source has been my experience during the first thirty years of the state. But the material is in no sense autobiographical. It is impossible to acknowledge hundreds of conversations, incidents, interviews, and confrontations which gave some understanding. Some specific sources include the following:

Chapter 2, "The Search for a Constitution," was written jointly by Allan E. Shapiro, a member of Kibbutz Degania Aleph and lecturer in law and politics at the University of Haifa; Eliahu Salpeter, editor, foreign correspondent, and columnist for *Ha'aretz*; and myself.

In Chapter 3, the sections on municipal government and national-local relations make use of experience as a member of the Herzlia City Council and in local party branches. Hazza Natour provided very helpful material on Arab Israeli voting behavior.

In Chapter 4, "The Nation in Arms," the discussion on civil-military relations was assisted by experience in the Air Force and the General Staff. The material is based on published documents. Much benefit was gained from the

---

* 2 Kings, 4:13.

research of Meir Pa'il on the development of the Haganah in the Yishuv. Richard Smoke, Graham Allison, George Quester, Aharon Yariv, Jonathan Shimshoni, and Nathan Yanai read an earlier draft and made very useful comments.

Chapter 5, "The Political Economy," draws on experience as chairman of the Herzlia municipal finance committee, as chairman of the board of a private corporation, Advanced Technology, Ltd., and from membership on the board of El Al Airlines and on many public commissions. Gudmund Hernes, Mendes Saks, and David Kohav read an earlier draft and raised useful questions.

Chapter 6, "The Welfare State," developed partly from consulting to the Ministry of Education in the period 1966-73. Of great value were discussions of the work in progress with Herman Stein and Julian Wolpert, and comments by Israel Katz on a later draft.

Chapter 7, "Science and Policy: Knowledge and Power," reflects experience as the first Director of the National Council for Research and Development (1959-65) in the Prime Minister's Office, with David Ben Gurion and more briefly with Levi Eshkol. Among the founding scientist members were Israel Dostrovsky, Ephraim Katzir, Solly Cohen, Alex Keynan, David Ginsberg, and Moshe Priwess. The engineers were Alexander Goldberg, Bill Reznick, and Shimshoni. We were joined by three senior civil servants: Teddy Kollek, Director-General of the Prime Minister's Office, Ariel Arieli, Director of State Revenue, and Simcha Soroker, Director of the Budget. In the first year of the Council there were lively weekly discussions, through which we learned and developed our understanding of science policy. Some of the analysis is also based on a study made in 1975, with the support of the NCRD and the Bathsheva de Rothschild Foundation. Joseph Ben David, S. M. Lipset, and Herbert Bernstein read and criticized earlier drafts.

Chapter 8, "The Physical Environment," drew on a study which we made at Advanced Technology in 1972-73 for the new Environmental Protection Service, working with Moshe Arens, Lionel Kestenbaum, and others. Also useful was service on the Herzlia Town Planning Commission. Shalom Reichman and Bill Arad made very helpful recommendations.

David Vital first suggested the enterprise of this book, an act which my family regards with mixed feelings. Joseph Beilin and Ruth Shereshevsky were stalwart assistants. Shorter but very helpful assistance was given by Yehuda Carmi, Dalia Cohen, Ilana Kaufman, Zipporah Lefkowitz, David Naveh, Sylvia Bernstein, and Dan Keren. The figures and maps were drawn by Tamar Soffer.

At the Center for Advanced Study in the Behavioral Sciences, Mary Tye typed one draft and improved my spelling; Carol Treanor helped make sense out of confusing economic data, Miriam Gallaher edited an earlier draft of Chapter 4, and Pamela Gullard was an encouraging critic. The Center's help was invaluable. When my term as a fellow was interrupted by service in the Yom Kippur War, Met Wilson and Preston Cutler arranged for me to still have a full year at the Center, and my stay overlapped that of two groups of stimulating colleagues. In addition to those already mentioned, I want to thank Patrick Crecine, Michel Crozier, Bill and Scarlett Epstein, Alex Inkeles, Robert Merton, and Robert Putnam for their discussions. Jim March, Aaron Wildawsky, and Marty Lipset were sources of great encouragement. A final review was made possible at the Rockefeller Foundation's Bellagio Center.

I am greatly indebted, at The Free Press, to Gladys Topkis for her faith that I would finish, and to Kitty Moore and Laura Wolff for their editorial help during the last stages of completing the book. Finally, I owe an incalculable and principal debt to Rose Shimshoni as secretary, editor, researcher, and critic.

Herzliya   D.S.
January, 1982

List of Figures and Tables

Tables

PART I

The Forming of the Political Community

In the last 180 years, a momentous change has occurred in the social condition and the political role of the Jews. At the time of the Napoleonic Wars, the Jews as a people were peripheral. Most lived in semiautonomous defenseless communities or in ghettos, isolated from the mainstream of general political and economic development. By World War I, large numbers of Jews were participating in important ways in the general economic, social and intellectual development of advanced Western countries. In 1948 the sovereign state of Israel gained independence, and by 1974 its Jewish population exceeded that of the Soviet Union. Today the majority of Jews are thus citizens of democratic countries, whose economies and societies are open and developed.

The change was the result of the most extensive migration of any people, and of the Holocaust. In 1800, of the 3,300,000 Jews in the world, 83 percent lived in Europe, primarily in Poland and Russia, and 15 percent in Iraq, Syria, the Yemen, and North Africa. Only 8,000 were in North America, and 45,000 in Palestine. In 1939, of the 16,650,000 Jews, more than half lived in Europe, and more than 5,000,000 (31 percent) in North America. In Palestine there were already 476,000, or 3 percent. By 1948, the Holocaust had reduced the total number to 11,314,000. In 1976, of 14,260,000 Jews, 6,000,000, or 46 percent, lived in North America, and

1

3,000,000 (21 percent) in Israel. Emigration had virtually depleted the ancient communities of North Africa and the Middle East.

The Return

Throughout the period of exile some Jews lived in Palestine. Return on any scale, however, began in the nineteenth century, initially more from the Islamic countries. In 1882, when the modern immigrations began to gather force, Sephardic Jews were a majority of the Jewish population in the country. At that time about 20,000 Jews were living in the old towns of Safed, Hebron, and Tiberias. In Jerusalem, Jews were a majority of the total population of 20,000. Most depended on alms, fulfilling the *mitzva* of living in the Holy Land. By contrast, most of the modern immigrations to the Yishuv, as the prestate settlement was called, came as a part of the Zionist endeavor to create a Jewish life in a national framework.

Beginning in 1882, and continuing, with interruptions, until World War II, there were five waves of European immigration (*aliyot*). These came mainly from Russia and Poland until the 1930s, when German and Austrian Jews came in larger numbers as refugees from the Nazis. At the same time, immigration continued on a modest scale from the Islamic countries and, after World War I, from the Western democracies. Symbolic of the future, the first organized immigration from the Yemen also took place in 1882, when 150 left Sana for Jerusalem. After World War I, the British ruled under a Mandate from the League of Nations to foster the creation of a national home for the Jewish people in Palestine. The right to immigrate was constantly curtailed, however, in the face of Arab opposition. In 1939 a British White Paper drastically reduced immigration, which was virtually stopped during World War II; and it became free and legal only with independence.

The Origins of the Political System and Culture

In 1948 the state did not start *de novo* with independence. Although without sovereignty, the organized Yishuv enjoyed authority.[1] As a "state within a state," it solved most of its problems through voluntary or civic organizations. Now these could no longer handle the scope of the problems, and many tasks were thrust upon the new government. The country was invaded on the first day, and immigration from European refugee camps and from backward countries soon challenged the feasibility of political and social integration.

Nonetheless the institutional endowment from the Yishuv was impressive: a Western legal system left behind by the Mandatory government, along with stringent emergency regulations in the colonial tradition, and Moslem, Jewish, and Christian religious laws and customs. Public bureaucracies, appointed largely on a party basis, arrangements for civilian direction of the armed forces, and extensive trade unions and health and educational organizations continued in the new state from the Zionist movement and the organized Yishuv.

It was a society which formed a state, and not a state which set out to form a society. The political life in the local Jewish communities of the Diaspora and the intensive social organization and political culture of the Yishuv and of the Zionist movement abroad provided the political and social experience which made it possible for an initial population of less than 600,000 to receive more than a million immigrants within the period of a quarter of a century, and to do this without serious social conflict and within democratic norms.

In Part I of this book, the origins and basis of the polity are examined from three points of view. Chapter 1 shows how the political culture and beliefs of the Diaspora and the Yishuv found their expression in political parties and social movements, and how the Israeli forms of parliamentary, pragmatic socialism developed to become, for decades, the predominant mode. At all stages, the relations between ideals and reality are found to be important in determining the nature of the ideologies at work and in mobilizing and organizing the society for great efforts. With time, however, a growing disparity between ideals and reality is seen, which impedes the ability to find new directions or to generate renewed efforts.

The constitutional response to the rights and burdens of the new sovereignty is considered in Chapter 2. Although sovereignty solved many practical needs, the exigencies of being a majority in an independent state forced the community to face up to problems and divisions which in the past were accommodated by the creation of enclaves or separate areas of action, or by not deciding at all. While the voluntary nature of the Yishuv had helped to check authority, in the state individual rights needed the protection of formal sanctions against the growth of state or sectoral power. Decision making based on mutual agreements among groups declined, while reliance on statutory authority grew.

The role of the courts and their developing relations with the legislature are considered in Chapter 2. The courts enjoy high status and authority, though judicial review of legislative action is very limited. The press, a very important force, is seen to have traversed a difficult path. In the Yishuv it was an active arm of the struggle for independence. In the Jewish state it became a virile critic of the government. Problems remain, however, of access to executive information, and of the management of the publicly owned broadcasting system.

In Chapter 3 the integration of new immigrants and of Arab Israelis into active political life is analyzed. Most of the immigrants to the state came from countries which provided very little experience with democratic politics or participation in organized social action. Moreover, their political cultures were usually not congruent with those of the Eastern European politicians and Western jurists whose influence had predominated in forming the institutions with which the state began. The political integration of immigrants is seen to have been impeded by their initial settlement on the periphery, by the dependent character of local governments, and by wide gaps in educational attainment. The degree of congruence of political and associational divisions is examined. Among Jews, it is not found to be a critical problem. The political integration of Arab Israelis, however, is seen to be at a crossroads, and its direction and the chances for success are still uncertain.

Part I thus describes the political and constitutional settings, as a basis for the study of the development of public policy, which follows in Part II.

CHAPTER 1

Ideals and Reality

A SERIOUS OBSERVER of Eastern Europe in the late nineteenth century could sense the inevitability of change. In the Russian and Austro-Hungarian Empires, national minorities dreamed of independence and revival of their national cultures, while underground socialist groups worked for revolution. In the darkness of the Russian Pale of Settlement, the condition of the Jews was at a nadir, and the conviction spread that the solution lay outside of Russia. Although Palestine was a remote and impractical haven, by the end of the century the impact of the Zionist idea touched many more than the few thousand who actually joined the movement.

Zionism was the outcome of the interaction between the social ideas and movements of nineteenth-century Europe and the distress and disillusion of the Jewish situation. In a time of despair it offered hope, not only for the few who actually went to Palestine, but also for the masses who remained in Eastern Europe or migrated to the West. Throughout the centuries of exile, the return to Zion, or *Eretz-Israel*, had been a central image of the eventual Redemption, kept alive in the national-religious customs and liturgy. For the majority, however, living traditional religious lives, the return was an ideal concept, not a tangible political goal.

The symbolic appeal was inevitable; the practical steps were problematic. In the late nineteenth century, Palestine was an extremely impoverished country, subject to the vagaries of Turkish authorities, who opposed immigration.

Most rational Jews chose other destinations. Between 1882 and 1914, more than 2 million left Russia or Poland for the West, but only 60,000 went to Palestine, and many of these did not remain. Those who were to take part in founding the new polity were exceedingly few.

Future-oriented, even utopian, the Zionist movement was directed toward a social transformation. It was seen as a way to solve the problems of the Jews as individuals and of the spirit of the Jewish people, through the re-creation of the Jewish national home and the restructuring of Jewish society.

While most Zionists agreed on this central aim, many questions remained unanswered. What was the national home to be like? How was it to be attained? Would it be enough simply to have a home, like other peoples, whatever the social order, or would the creation of a unique society be an essential part of the goal? If so, what would be its nature?

In retrospect, it seems very possible that the upheavals of the nineteenth century and the many beliefs then in the field might well have led to a very different regime and culture than those which actually emerged. In tracing some of the more important developments, I will of necessity simplify what were in fact complex struggles and events.

The sources of the character of the polity are found in the Jewish communities of the countries of exile, particularly those of Eastern Europe, and in the changes which were taking place in community life in the nineteenth century; in European liberalism and nationalism; and in the many kinds of socialist ideas. These influences were transmitted and transformed by the early immigrants. Each immigration, and within it various groups and individuals, brought different experiences of political organization and came from different historical, intellectual and philosophic milieus. Some were organized in groups with explicit ideologies; others came as individuals.

Everything lay ahead, and to each group its ideals seemed not only possible but essential. Nonetheless, there was flexibility. In the early *aliyot*, many immigrants were young and single, mobile in body and spirit. Their experience in Palestine was to be their political university. Those who were politically active encountered the demands of new situations and the ideas and strengths of other groups. In the process, they modified the beliefs and goals which they originally brought with them, in this way developing the political culture and institutions with which the Yishuv endowed the new state.

The Diaspora Community as a Polity

The Jewish communities in Russia and Poland and the changes within them which took place in the nineteenth century determined the environment from which the early Zionist immigrants came. The Moslem countries were then remote from the political ferment of Europe, and their Jewish communities were neglected by the European Zionist leaders. The political impact of the Asian and African Jews came only later, after the mass immigrations to the state.

The attempt to rebuild a national home followed centuries of experience in local self-government under difficult circumstances. The Jewish community in the Diaspora expressed the traditional Jewish concept of the unity of religion and nation.[1] Virtually autonomous in its internal affairs, it had most of the functions of a religious city-state: the administration of religious offices and of the law, of education and welfare, of taxes and finance; and the mediation between the community and the constantly separate and frequently hostile outside environment. Indeed, the levying, within the community, of the exorbitant taxes imposed by outside authorities was a principal task of community government, as was the special pleading with outside authorities, called *shtadlanut*, to mitigate the effect of fines, expulsions, and violence.

The political culture of the Jewish community in Russia and Poland characteristically embodied contradictory strands: liberal values and oligarchic and antiliberal practices and distrust of the masses; equality and hierarchy; theocracy and secular rule; individualism and a desire for social justice. Its political structure was essentially theocratic and republican rather than popular. By present-day standards often autocratic and frequently oppressive, the typical Jewish community in Eastern Europe was well advanced, particularly in law, in literacy, and in social justice.*

The community was usually governed by an oligarchy of men of substance, chosen by an electorate limited to men having a prescribed minimum of means. This group administered affairs, elected local rabbis, and maintained relations with other Jewish communities and with gentile authorities. The rabbinate determined the qualifications of its own members and was the judiciary in all questions covered by religious law—and in almost all of the differences occurring between Jews in secular affairs. A widespread respect for the law and for learning led to a voluntary submission, even in lay matters, to rabbinic jurisdiction or arbitration, and to the ability of a community to enforce judgments.

Rabbinic authority was frequently reinforced by the support of the lay oligarchy. Differences between the rabbinate and the lay leaders could prevent community authority from being monolithic, but when rabbis and lay leaders acted in concert, heretical ideas and their proponents could be put down. Opposition to rabbinic or civic authority and innovations contrary to tradition were frequently squelched. The arbitrary power of outside authorities in matters of taxes and concessions and the patronage and favor which they dispensed could be a corrupting influence on those leaders through whom they dealt with the community.

---

* In the seventeenth century (that of the Bloody Assizes in England), the most extreme penalty imposed by a Jewish community was excommunication—and that rarely.

Despite the oligarchic structure, important restraints aided equality and liberty. These derived from the religious concepts of justice as social justice, of the value of human life and dignity, and of a higher law. The rabbis were independent in their judgments, studying, interpreting, and applying Talmudic law, whose written sources were available and uniform throughout a Jewish world in which there was a high degree of literacy. Although the rabbis were a religious elite and as judges very often rigorous and autocratic, the law was public, widely known, and studied and argued by laymen. "A strong critical spirit prevented blind obeisance to any mortal authority."[2] Nor was there an ecclesiastical hierarchy, for a Jew as an individual could relate directly to God. In formal worship, he could join with any other nine men to form a "ten," or *minyan*. If he asked a rabbi to intercede with the Almighty on his behalf, he did so of his own choice. Local oligarchies could therefore be controlled by the continual surveillance of the community, the sometimes countervailing force of the rabbinate, and an appeal to the law.

Education was an important source of equality. Scholarship was not directly class-restricted, although parental resources influenced the use which could be made of available opportunities. Learning was able to counter the prestige of wealth and allow for the advancement of the more intelligent members of the community. Moreover, a general sense of the insecurity and ephemeral nature of status and wealth reinforced the respect for learning and intelligence.

In response to outside pressures, members of the communities drew closer together. Communities felt a strong sense of responsibility toward all of their members and developed comprehensive voluntary systems to provide for education and charity and religious needs. The ability to organize was more obvious in the formation of small groups than of large ones. Extensive social organization provided further opportunities for community members to participate in self-government. Social cohesion and mutual dependence thus limited the power of the oligarchic leaders. At the same time, these mutual dependencies limited the degrees of freedom of voluntary groups and their members; and the voluntary organizations of the Yishuv later reflected this characteristic. The penchant for pluralist voluntary organization is seen today in the Jewish communities of the United States, which are very much at home in the organizing culture of America.

Changes in the Old Order

The general political character of the communities in Eastern Europe persisted, in some places, until the Nazi conquest. During the eighteenth century, however, and more rapidly in the nineteenth, a traditional order which had seemed immutable began to change, at first in content and eventually in form, as the cohesion of the communities and their ability to meet the needs of their members were diminished by forces from the outside and from within.

In the West, the role of the community declined rapidly in the aftermath of the Enlightenment. The emancipation which followed the Napoleonic Wars centered on the importance of the individual, and was conditioned on his becoming part of the national civil society. For Jews, religious and political identity became separate, and the Jewish community as such did not achieve a basis of equality with other ethnic groups, which pursued nationalist goals within their own countries. The result was the erosion and eventual disappearance of the community as the political focus of Jewish life.

For Jewish communities in nineteenth-century Russia, by contrast with those in the West, destructive forces came from a reactionary outside government. It made direct attacks on the legal basis of community organization. Oppressive policies led to both economic catastrophe and physical danger, and undermined the functions of the community's leaders. During the first half of the century, a program to force Jewish assimilation, by making life intolerable, included attempts to compel secular education, to impose government-approved rabbis, and to make the community governments illegal. These efforts were countered with some success through informal organization and subterfuge. Other measures, however, had a more serious effect. The government forced the community to collect increasingly onerous taxes; to be responsible for large public debt incurred through past wars and pogroms; and to deliver up youths, often as young as twelve years, for twenty-five-year terms of compulsory service in the armies of the Czar. These repugnant tasks diminished the legitimacy of the community leaders.

Jews were expelled from rural areas and confined to certain towns within a "Pale of Settlement," so that by the end of the century more than one-third of the Jews of Russia lived in communities of more than 10,000, making up more than 30 percent of the Russian urban population.[3] After a period of modest liberalization during the reign of Alexander II (1855–81), increasingly harsh measures were introduced, whose severity was mitigated only by the government's inefficiency. As Russia began to industrialize, Jewish artisans were excluded from the mechanized factories, while the freeing of the serfs began to take from the Jews their middleman and artisan status. Stringent restrictions on residence and occupations, rules of *numerus clausus* in secondary schools and universities, and officially sanctioned pogroms deepened the fear, poverty, and unemployment of the Jewish masses and blocked the opportunities of the intellectuals. Privileges and tax concessions widened even further the gap between the wealthy or, as they mainly were, *petit bourgeois* and small capitalists, and the masses, to whom the community leaders began to appear as an incompetent oligarchy of wealth, unable or unwilling to help. Class consciousness intensified.[4]

The widespread pogroms of 1881–84 confirmed the conviction of hundreds of thousands that the Jews could not survive in Russia. By the last decade of the century, most of Russian Jewry was destitute or on the move to the West. Under these conditions, the *status quo* was untenable, and local community government was often a façade. For a growing minority, neither tradition nor traditional leadership could make the social condition acceptable. The society had passed its peak of intellectual greatness, and fragments of it could only be creative by going new ways, as they did in Palestine and the West, where the pent-up ideals and energies of generations burst forth in a hundred directions.

The Search for a Way Out

Questioning of the old order had begun early in the nineteenth century. Following the emancipation in the West, for the first time, more than an isolated few could ask what it meant to be a Jew, and whether religious, cultural, and national identity were indeed one and indivisible.[5] The Enlightenment had a natural appeal to Jewish respect for reason and human dignity, and the newly available secular learning held great intellectual attraction and social promise. Increasingly, Jews began to question the role of organized religion, the authority of leaders and rabbis, the quality of Jewish society, and the necessity to remain passive in the face of oppression.

From the 1820s onward, the idea of reforming Jewish life from within began to spread in small intellectual circles in Eastern Europe. A movement called the Haskala (Enlightenment) advocated Western knowledge, the revival of Hebrew as a modern literary language, and a liberalism which would free the Jews from the rigor and narrowness of the small religious communities. The benefits of the promising secular world would be combined with those of the Hebrew culture.[6]

Many of the early members of the movement believed that a liberal Russia would evolve, in which Jews could maintain a separate culture, while at the same time taking part in Russian culture and public and economic life. Severe repression dashed these hopes and those of a solution through self-improvement, as it did the hopes of non-Jewish Russian liberals. Yet the modernist, Hebraist approach made the ground fertile for Zionism. The Hebrew language, indeed, was to be the principal unifying symbol of the national return, and its overwhelming revival was the first great national success.

Those who sought a way out through the non-Jewish movements for change, whether national, liberal, or revolutionary, sooner or later suffered disillusion and disappointment. The search, inevitably, turned to separate Jewish solutions. In the Russian Empire, little opportunity existed for assimilation—and even less desire, in view of the cultural attainments prevalent in the environment. Nationalist movements of the non-Jewish minorities were inhospitable, indeed often anti-Semitic. The Russian intelligentsia was an unfriendly milieu for assimilation, and in periods of pogroms, non-Jewish liberals were disappointingly neutral at best.

Developing out of the social tragedy of Czarist Russia and the growing class consciousness and secularity in the Jewish communities, another alternative was revolution. With their ideals of social justice and utopianism, it was small wonder that young Jews were caught up in revolutionary and reforming zeal. It is estimated that between 1884 and 1890, one-seventh of those serving prison sentences in Russia for political offenses were Jews.[7] Many Jews believed that the Jewish problem did not need separate action, but would be solved in the course of the impending general social upheaval.

As it turned out, the non-Jewish Russian socialist movements tended to reject those who tried to maintain a Jewish identity, and by the end of the nineteenth century most Jewish Marxists were members of specifically Jewish movements. The most noteworthy of these, at that time, was the anti-Zionist, Yiddish-culture Bund.* Other socialist-Zionist parties—the Poalei Zion, the Z.S. (Zionist-Socialists), and Tzeirei Zion—enlisted much of the Jewish working class, until they were eliminated by the Bolsheviks. Liberalism had been the hope of midcentury Russian protest; revolutionary social and political change was the goal at the turn of the century.

Zionism, which became an organized movement in the 1880s, had its modern origins in the struggle for liberalism and modernism early in the nineteenth century. Only later, in the immigrations to Palestine of the early twentieth century, did collective endeavor and socialism become central components. The result was a political culture which has strong collective as well as individualist elements, and in which parliamentary liberalism exists together with procedures and an organizational culture derived from experiences in Eastern European socialist parties.

The Watershed of 1881

For the many who needed to be convinced of the futility of the Russian Jewish situation, the tragic pogroms of southern Russian in 1881–84 furnished proof. In many places, spontaneous organizations of Zionist-minded youth protested the inaction of community authorities and tried to strengthen a national spirit and self-respect. The Hibbat Zion (Love of Zion) movement, developed as the grass-roots organization of early Zionism. By 1885 about 14,000 were members in more than 100 local groups. As was often to be the

* The Bund, or General Jewish Workers Union in Lithuania, Poland, and Russia, was founded in 1897 to seek a recognized, separate, Yiddish cultural life within a future socialist Russia. Its relative strength in early socialism is seen in the fact that in 1889, twelve out of twenty-nine Russian delegates to the Second International were from the Bund. Eventually, the Bund became a semiindependent component of the Social Democratic Workers Party, the forerunner of the Russian Communist Party. At the famous Second Party Congress, the Bund voted with the Mensheviks, whose oblivion they shared after the October Revolution.

case, events and reactions to them preceded analysis, planning, and rational organization.[8] Organized Zionism was the "response of a multitude of individuals and circles to a situation which they regarded as intolerable," with as yet "no preponderant leader or clear formulation of the aims."[9]

Ideas developed independently in Western and Eastern Europe. The immediate needs as well as the organization, numerical strength, and emigration to Palestine came first in the East. Emigration was already under way before a manifesto appeared, which, particularly for the Russian Jews, was the most influential statement of the situation. In 1882, in a passionate reaction to the helplessness of the Jews in the face of the pogroms, Yehuda Leib Pinsker published a pamphlet called *Autoemancipation*. It analyzed the cause of the abysmal conditions and issued a call for a national solution. Its ready acceptance showed that a consensus had developed among Zionists concerning central, basic propositions, if not courses of action.

The heart of Pinsker's diagnosis was that in every country of exile the Jews were a distinctive element which could not be absorbed. They were foreigners, yet foreigners who had no home country of their own. Because of their unique combination of culture and nationality, the Jews could only become a part of the countries in which they lived by abandoning their own culture. If that path was rejected, as it was by the Zionists, or not feasible, as was often the case, then the only alternative was the re-creation of the national home, in which the Jews would be a nation, equal and similar to any other nation.

Anti-Semitism was seen as a constant characteristic of the environment, which could not be changed. The causes and cures, however, were to be sought not only outside but within Jewry as well. Autoemancipation thus provided a solution in which Jews would cease to be a foreign and defenseless people. Inherent in this process was the idea of a social transformation, through which the Jews would begin to lead normal lives.

These attitudes and beliefs became the common denominator, the accepted challenge. Pinsker's pamphlet proclaimed a general national goal without defining how to get there. As immigration began, the creation of new settlements forced many issues and revealed the complexity of the problems which the Zionists faced.

Between 1881 and 1903, 20,000 to 30,000 emigrated from Russia and Rumania to Palestine, in what is called the First *Aliya*. They came mainly as individuals, not as organized groups with a specific ideology or plan.* The settlements of the First *Aliya* were able to sustain themselves only precari-

---

* Exceptions were a Rumanian group which settled in Zichron Ya'akov, and the Biluim, a few dozen young people who saw themselves as a social *avant garde*. The word *Bilu* is an acronym from the Hebrew *Beit Ya'akov Lechu Veneilcho* ("O house of Jacob, come ye and let us walk in the light of the Lord") (Isaiah 2:5). The Biluim had a concept of mission and social beliefs antedating many of the ideals of early labor Zionism: Jewish labor and the return to agriculture, social justice and an absence of exploitation; pioneering and collective endeavor. They succeeded in founding one small settlement, Gedera.

ously, depending on financial aid from abroad. Baron Edmond de Rothschild and others gave a large part of this support, but under the condition that the settlers be under the professional and administrative tutelage of his agents. Although the foundations for a political society were still remote, a Hebrew-speaking Yishuv came into being, and the return to the land had begun. By 1900 there was a rural Jewish population of more than 5,000.

Zionism as a Political Movement

In the late 1890s, however, the Zionist movement seemed to be making little real headway. The results of the early immigrations and of the Hibbat Zion organization in Russia were very modest. If Zionism was to become a broad-based national endeavor, it needed leadership and a program of action, a clarification of political goals, and the promise of a social transformation.

By the first decade of the twentieth century, it was well on the way to having all of these attributes. The change occurred through a combination of the needs and the characteristics of the Jews of Eastern and of Western Europe. Political views and organization of wide scope from the West were joined with the fervor, social consciousness, and "populist Jewishness" of the East.

The contrasting condition of the Jews in the East and the West was one source of differences in approach. Although the few Western Jews who then became ardent Zionists also made an analysis similar to that of Pinsker, their demand for a national emancipation came from a very different kind of experience. Like the Eastern Jews, they had before them the examples of the national movements, of the *risorgimento*. Pressure to act in the West came not from danger and distress, however, but from the frustration and disappointment with the failure of emancipation to eliminate anti-Semitism, and from the conservative reaction against liberalism, a cause in which the Jews played an ardent role. Long after other groups which through liberalism had succeeded in social advancement became conservative or reactionary, Jews continued to strive for the ideals of the Enlightenment. In an increasingly polarized Europe, this was often expressed through socialism, which men like Leon Blum saw as seeking to preserve the Enlightenment and the French Revolution, as well as the Judaic call for social justice.[10] Moreover, whatever his achievements and contributions in the arts, professions, or business, the Western Jew remained marginal to the society in which he lived. Exposed to prejudice and discrimination, he had to face them without having the backing or the sense of identity which life in the traditional religious community and orthodox belief had given his parents.

The initiative and political imagination of the West, together with the almost single-handed fervor and genius for public relations of Theodor Herzl, created a political focus for the movement in the Zionist Congress, whose first meeting was held in state at Basel in 1897. The Congress became the sovereign body of the World Zionist Organization. It decided both on the relations with the powers and on the allocation of resources to the Yishuv. The First Congress thus "established a precedent—and the principle—of unity, bringing together all of the very diverse strains of the movement: romanticists and pragmatists, orthodox and secularists, socialists and bourgeois, easterners and westerners, men whose minds and language were barely influenced by the non-Jewish world and those who were largely products of it...."[11] Its unity was derived not only from the appeal of common goals and symbols but from the constitutional, parliamentary way in which the Congress, and, from that time on, the movement were organized. A simple form of voting for party slates by proportional representation was used, and has continued in the state. This form of voting permitted the coexistence of groups holding widely differing beliefs, and ensured the representation, and often the conciliation, of small groups holding divergent minority views. It also encouraged the emphasis of ideological differences, strengthened the oligarchic tendencies of the leadership groups of different movements within Zionism, and fostered coalitions. Basic differences in conceptions led to divisions over practical programs as well as over theoretical analyses.

Before World War I, a most important question, later to be a cardinal political issue and a source of division cutting across the spectra of social and religious beliefs, was generally ignored. Few then considered the possibility of serious or lasting opposition on the part of the Arabs to a Jewish homeland. In the early years other questions were dominant.* What would the future home be like, and how, in practice, was it to be gained? Was the way through great-power diplomacy, as Herzl saw it, or through gradual and persistent settlement and development? Would the form of the future country be capitalist, socialist, or theocratic, or was this a question to be settled much later, after the return was established? If Zionism meant not just a home but a reformation of Jewish society, in what historical order should this come about? Should human change and development, as Achad Ha'am saw it, precede political and social organization, or was it essential to proceed as fast as possible with practical settlement and political persuasion?

The advocates of compatible views characteristically organized in

---

* Basic early writings include:

(a) On the overall aim: Moses Hess, *Rome and Jerusalem*, Leipzig, 1862; Yehuda Leib Pinsker, *Autoemancipation*, 1882 (English translation of *Autoemancipation* and of other writings in Arthur Herzberg [ed.], *The Zionist Idea*, New York, Atheneum, 1973); Theodor Herzl, *The Jewish State*, New York, 1904, *Old-New Land*, New York, Bloch, 1941, and *Diaries*, ed. by R. Patai, New York, Herzl Press, 1960.

(b) On the question of spiritual Zionism (and on many others): Achad Ha'am, *Nationalism and the Jewish Ethic*, Hans Kohn (ed.), New York, Herzl Press, 1960.

(c) On Labor Zionism: Baer Borochov, *Selected Essays in Socialist Zionism*, S. Levenberg (ed.), London, Rita Seal, 1948, and *Ktavim* (Heb.) (Collected Works), Tel Aviv, 1955; A. D. Gordon, *Kitvei* (Heb.) (Collected Works), 6 volumes, Tel Aviv, 1930; Nachman Syrkin, *Essays on Socialist Zionism*, New York, 1935; J. Ch. Brenner, *Kol Kitvei* (Heb.) (Collected Works), N. Posnansky (ed.), Tel Aviv, 1955.

separate movements, or *tnuot*, of which many were to be far more encompassing than political parties. To varying degrees, movements debated and
disseminated ideas and ideologies, campaigned in the elections of the World
Zionist Organization and the organized Yishuv, raised funds, recruited and
trained immigrants, and secured their right to settle. Each movement formed
its own economic and social institutions and fought for their survival and
growth. In these movements, members found strong bonds of association and
belief. The system reached its full flower between the two world wars, when
political mobilization was intensive both in the Yishuv and abroad. As the
Yishuv grew, so did its political weight, compared with that of the Diaspora,
until the Holocaust destroyed the European branches and leadership, and the
Yishuv remained as the center.

The spectrum of Zionist beliefs and movements later found expression in
the parties of the state, although, as will be seen, the old labels now conceal
many changes. There was no simple left-right ordering or homogeneity of
belief on many major questions within a movement or party, nor were the
parties, let alone the general groupings, monolithic in their organization.
Broadly speaking, two of the principal movements saw specific kinds of
society as the Zionist goal: Labor and the religious movement. The center and
right secular parties put most of their political emphasis on first gaining the
homeland and only then deciding its character. On one goal all movements,
except the Aguda, were agreed: the centrality of the Hebrew language in the
national revival.

These trends led to political organization before World War I. The following is a great oversimplification of the principal organized approaches, as a
rough guide until the discussion has been developed:

> *Labor* saw the essence in social organization and in the transformation of
> the Jews into a working people.
> *General Zionists* sought a national home with a pluralist and liberal base.
> To the extent to which they concurred on a social ideology, it was that
> of development through private enterprise.
> *The Mizrachi* sought a national home in which the rabbinic law and ortho-
> dox observance would be the law of the land.

Later on, after World War I, the *Revisionist* movement developed. Concerned mainly with the political aims of Zionism, it demanded the official
implementation of the original Mandate, including the territory of Trans-
jordan,* and full assistance by the British government in the achievement of a
national home, including large-scale immigration and colonization. When it

---

* Sloughed off from the original Mandate territory by Winston Churchill in the early 1920s, Jordan was created to give the Hashemites a kingdom in place of Syria, which had been promised to
Abdullah but was not at the disposal of the British, since it had been allocated to French control in
the postwar settlements.

became clear that the British were blocking these aims, the Revisionists went into active underground opposition to them.

At first, the General Zionist trend was the most prominent. At the First Congress, most delegates belonged to the educated middle class, and several decades passed before Labor gained power. In the Yishuv itself, however, regardless of its elective strength, Labor was to be the most important in developing the political culture and institutions. Combining a superior ability to organize with ideological appeal, Labor drew its strength mainly from having members who were organized and active in the country. The compositions of the Second and Third *Aliyot* were necessary conditions for Labor's eventual political success. The direction of Zionism was to be determined by the Yishuv more than the Diaspora.

Labor Zionism

Early Years of Experiment

A unique aspect of the way in which the beliefs of the Labor movement developed was the process of learning and change through experience in meeting actual problems and in seeking political power. The years of experiment and innovation in the Yishuv extended roughly from 1905, with the Second *Aliya*, until the mid-1930s, when Labor gained the political leadership of the Zionist movement. The Second *Aliya*, a small number immigrating between 1905 and 1914,* and the Third *Aliya*, which came in the years just after World War I, developed the ideologies, built the institutions, set the modes and provided most of the principal leaders of national politics in the Yishuv and the state.

The realities faced from the beginning belied the revolutionary theories and debates of prewar Russia. Soon after an immigrant of the Second *Aliya* was handed down from his ship to a small lighter off the shores of Jaffa, he confronted unexpected hardships. Young and alone, unused to hard labor, frequently unemployed and hungry, many suffered a general feeling of orphanhood and bewilderment. The most influential ideological teacher of the Labor movement, Berl Katzenelson, later was to recall that "of those who came in my boat, three remained."[12] Those who stayed on were self-selected, possessing the stamina, the inner resources of the belief in Zionism, and the desire to recast the Jew as a productive worker which were necessary to survive.

Disappointed by the failure of political Zionism in its appeals to the great

* There was also in this period a small but important *aliya* from the Yemen. (See Chapter 3.)

powers as well as by the failure of the Revolution of 1905 in Russia, disillusioned by the rejection of Jews by Russian revolutionary movements, many young immigrants felt that they were among the last of the Zionists rather than the first of a great movement. Once they reached Palestine, however, the political activists carried on without a break.*

By 1906 there were three rival Labor parties with a total of about 500 members. These intense rivals in ideology and style were the Marxist-Zionist Poalei Zion; the non-Marxist Hapoel Hatzair, strongly Hebraist and populist, emphasizing the remaking of the individual and the return to physical work on the soil; and a third group which called itself the Non-Partisans, although it had many characteristics of the other parties, especially the Poalei Zion. Each group tried to provide an encompassing way of life, with social services for its members, help in employment, sick funds, soup kitchens, and newspapers. For many years, the parties remained small, and personal relations and personalities were critically important to the directions which evolved.

In the new setting, party traditions brought from abroad were upset. Experience led to a distrust of blueprints and specific utopias. Abstract Marxism and what Katzenelson later decried as "the Talmudist and pedantic discussions of Europe" were largely set aside. If the differences among the beliefs of the groups seemed at the time to be tremendous, they were tempered by the need to put them into practice. Another source of flexibility was the plurality of beliefs that existed in Russia, from which the Second *Aliya* originated. In contrast to the more determinist atmosphere after World War I, from which the Third *Aliya* came, post-1905 Russia was a "crossroads of ideologies."[13]

While many early points of division now seem unimportant, there were strong underlying differences of concept. The nature of the debate is shown by two questions: first, whether or not the success of the class struggle was a necessary prior condition to the emancipation of the Jews; and second, whether change in the society would come about mainly through new social organization or, as A. D. Gordon and others believed, through the inner development of the individual. In other words, would individual efforts, sacrifice, and experience determine the social system, or would the system determine the qualities of the people in it? More orthodox socialists continued to believe in the primacy of the system, but it was the more pragmatic, humanist, and individual mode which eventually took root and flourished. Looking back, it now seems ironic that a sense of failure in achieving the ideals was an inevitable outcome of undertaking the awesome task of changing the character of individuals.

Although it was oriented toward the future, the Labor movement came to be more concerned with the practical way in which things were to be done

---

* Only months after he arrived, Ben Gurion, at the age of twenty, was a member of a small committee of the 1906 Ramle Convention of Poalei Zion, which issued a declaration of aims redolent of the European class struggle as seen in Marxist terms—concepts from which Ben Gurion and most of Labor later turned away.

than with utopian goals.[14] It tried, in the Yishuv, to build a movement (or, as the leaders saw it, a nation) with a broad social base, made up of practical institutions, which could also influence and indeed determine the direction of the non-Labor sector. The emphasis on institutions and organizations came from social theory, practical needs, and an understanding of political power. The Labor mainstream, later to abandon the concept of a class war as the motive force, was nonetheless influenced by Marxist thought in believing that the roots of changes in power and ideology are to be found in the economic and technological structure of a society.

The practical reason for the development of the economic organs of Labor was the need to create settlements and organizations in which the workers would provide their own work opportunities and services. In a country without developed capitalism, the immediate challenge was to create a working class rather than to conduct a class war.

The important struggle of the Second *Aliya*, of a class nature, was for the right to work as hired hands for the Jewish farmers of the First *Aliya*. There was no industry, and the limited Jewish agriculture of the time used cheaper Arab labor, at first refusing to employ the less experienced and more demanding Jewish immigrants. This struggle, which never really ceased until the Arab insurgency of 1936, was for jobs—to fill an economic need and to build a Jewish working class, but not for the displacement of the private Jewish farmers.[15] The first unions, formed before World War I, were regional organizations of agricultural workers.

Many years were to pass, however, before the leaders of the Labor mainstream abandoned the concepts of the class struggle. Haim Arlosoroff was to say to the 1926 convention of the Hapoel Hatzair, "Why is there no class struggle? Palestine was a colonial country. It is not a normal economy and imports capital. Since workers really started the economy and owned the production means, they are appreciated. We have a socialism of producers, not of consumers. We are not building a strategic base for a class war, but the opposite. We are creating social ways of life which will be such that we will not ever have a class war." With the merger in 1930 of Hapoel Hatzair and Ahdut Ha'Avoda to form Mapai, such views became widespread, eventually predominant but not universal. Belief in the class struggle was central to the views of many of the older Labor leaders, such as Tabenkin, and was particularly strong among the younger groups. The class view was reinforced in the 1930s by the spread of fascism and opposition to it in Europe, and exacerbated the struggles with the Revisionists in Palestine.

The early practical outcome, which was to change the whole nature of the Yishuv and the state, was that Labor turned to the creation of jobs, as well as fighting for the few that were available. On this overall goal the several factions of Labor could agree.

The forming of autonomous, voluntary working settlements, of which the *kvutza* and the kibbutz are the principal examples, shows how practical needs as well as beliefs in equality and community led to important social innovation. The initial idea of the Second *Aliya* immigrants had been to find work as employees, either for private farmers or on farms administered for the Zionist movement, originally set up for training purposes. It was only after administrators and tutors failed in the human relations of management that the workers acted in 1911 to form Degania, the first *kvutza*, or small agricultural communal settlement, next to the Sea of Galilee.[16] Other groups settled at about the same time. In the nineteenth century, there had been many proposals and some experiments with small communes in Europe and America, and knowledge of these must have influenced the early kibbutz settlement. But the forms which it took in Palestine, its diffusion and success, and the basic principle by which agricultural workers are cooperative owners' rather than administered employees came out of the specific demands of the situation. The idea of the *kvutza* could have been planned, but in fact it was not. Significantly, the World Zionist Organization supported the communes, tipping the scale in the direction of the future. Another development of lasting influence in that period was the way in which the unions of agricultural workers organized social services for their members—a forerunner of the comprehensivity of the Histadrut.

Over and beyond the many shades of differences, before World War I the common denominator of Labor beliefs began to emerge. The focus was on changes both in the society and in the individual Jew, whose precarious role as a middleman and fringe member of other societies would be abandoned. The Jews could only gain national independence through resettlement of the land and the revival of the Hebrew language, and individual independence through participating fully in the basic productive work of society. The personal ideal was *hagshama*, accomplishment, and *halutziut*, pioneering, in which the individual is willing to go anywhere and do anything to advance the cause, finding fulfillment in the group's achievements. People would do their own labor rather than exploiting others. There would be mutual help for all social needs and no class war as such, since labor would predominate and society as a whole would adopt its values. Land, particularly agricultural land, would be nationally owned, and settlement was to be voluntary and cooperative.

By the time immigration was interrupted by World War I, the mainstream of Labor ideology had developed patterns "strong enough to leave their imprint on most of the later ones."[17] Equally if not more important, there was a cohesive cadre of professional politicians whose vocation it was to form the Labor movement. Young, active, intelligent, they were able to learn from the organizational failures of the prewar period—in which only a small fraction of the workers joined the parties. Within two decades, they and those of the Third *Aliya* had gained for Labor political dominance of the Yishuv.

The 1920s: Years of Innovation and Organization

In 1917 the Balfour Declaration promised the Jews a national home in Palestine. The award of a Mandate to the British by the League of Nations made a national home seem feasible, giving new life to Zionism. The goal seemed within reach. Other national movements had achieved independence in the postwar agreements, and to socialists of all convictions, the possibilities of a new world at first seemed to be heralded by Soviet Russia. Lincoln Steffens could say, "I have been over into the future and it works."[18]

In this atmosphere, immigrants of the Third *Aliya* (1919–24) were more hopeful than those who came in the aftermath of 1905. They numbered about 35,000. Like those of the Second *Aliya*, they were young and unattached, but many were better educated than those of the Second *Aliya* and more fluent with ideas. Faith in socialism was widespread, and many of those who came, particularly toward the end of the period, had been exposed to the political culture and organization of the Eastern European socialist parties.* Discussion and intergroup rivalry were common, and there were intensive and diverse experiments in forms of settlement, ways of life, and organization.[19] In the 1920s even more than before the war, ideas were not abstract philosophies, but became strategies of how to settle the country, build a society, and organize for political resources and power. As often happens, experimental development and pioneering in the field went on at the same time as struggles over organizational form and for power at the center.

From the beginning, Labor's most influential innovation was the organization of the Histadrut. The form which developed served, at one and the same time, the goals of national development, of Labor enterprise, and of a trade union and social services. Not least, the political and economic control of the Labor movement by Ahdut Ha'Avoda was facilitated by the unique relation of the parties to the Histadrut.

From the first, there were serious threats to survival from the lack of work, land, and capital and from Arab opposition. Employment was perhaps the most pressing need. Paid work in agriculture was hard to find, and the purchase of land for cooperative settlement proceeded slowly. Although the Mandatory government had begun to build roads and other public works and there was some private building, industry was still rudimentary. Labor replied by creating its own cooperatives, firms, and agricultural settlements, and by hiring out cooperatively on government public works projects. When private building and manufacturing began to make city jobs available, Labor fought for the control of work opportunities and conditions by means of

---

* In the generation of postrevolution emigration, the Zionist-Socialists (Z.S.) and Tzeirei Zion were prominent, bringing with them knowledge of the organizational and political concepts of the postwar Communist Party, which were to influence the organizational forms and culture of the Labor movement. Also, they tended to see a more central role for the class struggle than did many of the leaders from the Second Aliya.[20]

strikes, pressure on employers, and occasional violence, and by operating its own employment exchanges.

The Labor movement's own enterprises could only be made viable, however, through large injections of capital. These came mainly from funds raised abroad by the World Zionist Organization, in which Labor at first was a small minority, joining the leading coalition only in 1926. Even so, Labor became the channel for a substantial part of the national capital investment, partly because of the tenor of the times but mainly because the labor organizations and their members were actually on the scene, ready to do the work. Zionist leaders of other movements favored the ideas of settlement on national land and physical work and pioneering, in which organized labor was taking the lead.*

In this situation, the central objects of political activity within the Zionist movement were the control of resources: the flow of national investments, the recruiting and training of adherents abroad, and securing their immigration. To build human and financial resources by finding jobs and establishing control over economic organizations became the practical purposes of the internal politics of Labor; through doing these things, the competing groups and factions hoped to achieve their larger social aims.

Party organization and the Histadrut provided the means for achieving these goals. In 1919 the Non-Partisans and the Poalei Zion merged to form Ahdut Ha'Avoda. Hapoel Hatzair remained independent until 1930, when it merged with the others to form Mapai. Figure 1.1 shows the alignments in the prestate Labor movement.

In 1920 Ahdut Ha'Avoda took the initiative in founding the Histadrut, together with Hapoel Hatzair. The Histadrut, or General Federation of Workers, was formed as an independent organization; it included all of Labor's trade-union, economic, settlement, and social activities. Formally separate from the parties, the Histadrut was, from the first, controlled by representatives nominated by political parties and elected by Histadrut members under a nationwide proportional-representation system similar to that of the World Zionist Organization. It rapidly became Labor's primary political instrument and power base, with the organized potential for building a large number of the institutions of the Yishuv society. In maintaining control of the Histadrut, Ahdut Ha'Avoda and later Mapai ensured themselves the eventual political leadership of the Yishuv and thus of the many social and

---

* Even Justice Brandeis, who opposed the proposals for national investment capital as approved in 1920 in London, had written earlier, "The utmost vigilance should be exercised to prevent the acquisition by private persons of land, water rights, or other natural resources or any concessions for public utilities. These must all be secured for the whole Jewish People. In other ways, as well as this, the possibility of capitalistic exploitation must be guarded against." Quoted in Jacob deHaas, *Louis D. Brandeis*, New York, Bloch Publishing Company, 1929. For the conflict between Brandeis and Weizmann over national versus private investment, see Chaim Weizmann, *Trial and Error*, New York, Harper, 1949, pp. 261–70; and A. T. Mason, *Brandeis: A Free Man's Life*, New York, Viking, 1946, pp. 758–64.

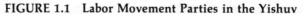

FIGURE 1.1   Labor Movement Parties in the Yishuv

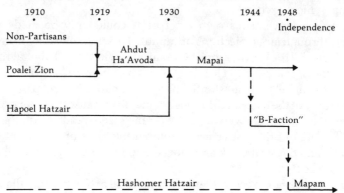

Hashomer Hatzair (Young Watchman)—A Marxist youth movement which developed the Kibbutz Artzi, one of the three principal national federations of kibbutzim.
Hashomer Hatzair did not see itself as a party until, after independence, it joined
with the former "B Faction" to form the Mapam Party.

"B Faction"—A faction bsed on the Kibbutz Me'uhad (United Kibbutz Settlements),
split from Mapai in 1944 in protest against Mapai's endorsement of partition plans
and immediate demands for a state. Forerunner of the new and different Ahdut
Ha'Avoda, 1954.

Ahdut Ha'Avoda—formed from the union of the Non-Partisans and the Poalei Zion.
The dominant Labor party of its period and forerunner of Mapai (acronym for
Israel Workers' Party).

defense activities which the Mandatory government did not provide.
Without denigrating the essential work of other groups in social services and
investment, the Histadrut was rightly called "The State in the Making."

The decision to found the Histadrut was the outcome of practical politics
and economic reality as well as of ideology. The economic imperative was to
present a united front of the Labor sector in order to secure national investment funds from the World Zionist Organization, which would be hard to obtain if several groups were to compete. The practical aim was to gain for
Ahdut Ha'Avoda the political leadership of the Labor movement. The party
had originally hoped to encompass within it all of the social services,
economic activities, and settlement programs. For this, however, it needed to
enlist the immigrants of the Third *Aliya* and, in addition, to serve as the channel for the transfer of national funds from the Diaspora. But many new immigrants were reluctant to join a party and formed their own unions to meet
their immediate needs for services and employment. In addition, organized
political groups among the immigrants, such as the Zionist Socialists, or Z.S.,
and Tzeirei Zion, had their own ideas, both on the structure of the Labor
movement and on the roles which they desired within it. The organization
served the needs of relatively apolitical potential members from among the
rank and file, as well as providing an effective political *modus vivendi* between the older leaders (then in their early thirties) and the new groups. The

Second *Aliya* leaders retained the central political and policy roles, while members of the new groups became leaders in organization and settlement. The transfer of social and economic activities to a common Histadrut and their formal separation from the parties were in line with the ideas of the Z.S., who then joined Ahdut Ha'Avoda, giving it electoral control. This electoral authority, as we shall see later, made it possible for Ahdut Ha'Avoda and later Mapai to control Labor's economic and organizational resources—a pattern which the Labor Party continued in the state.

These practical motives served a grand vision of "constructive socialism," of what a united labor organization could accomplish. It resulted in one of the most comprehensive and unique labor organizations in the world, providing all of the educational, cultural, health, and social services that the parties had previously tried to supply for their members, as well as employment exchanges and trade-union activity. Most unusual among the world's labor movements was the scope of the Hevrat Ovdim, the Workers' Holding Company, formed in 1923, through which the Histadrut owns or controls cooperative-labor economic enterprises, financial institutions, and manufacturing and contracting companies.* The Histadrut was seen not simply as the provider of services and employment, but as the vehicle through which the labor economy would be built and which could transform and lead the society. While serving as the first Secretary to be elected by the Histadrut, Ben Gurion said,

> The Histadrut . . . is not a trade union, it is not a political party, . . . a cooperative, or a mutual aid society . . . . The Histadrut is a union of people who are building up a new home, a new state, a new people, new enterprises and settlements and a new culture; it is a union of social reformers . . . rooted in the common destiny and tasks of all its members.[22]

Like the Histadrut, other major experiments of the 1920s were often more premeditated than those before 1914, and involved more comprehensive political or ideological considerations. Outstanding among the innovations of the 1920s were the large kibbutz and the *moshav*, or smallholders' farming cooperative, which today are principal forms of rural settlement.[23]

The *moshav* idea was conceived by *kvutza* members who sought more individual initiative and expression, based on the family as the social unit. In the *moshav*, in contrast to the kibbutz or *kvutza*, each family lives separately and works a small farm allocated to it from nationally owned land. Marketing, purchasing, finance, and some production are cooperative, but a family's income depends on its own efforts.

---

* The fact that labor owned industries from the first was a large part of the reason that nationalization of production was not important in Israeli labor ideology. Meir Avizohar says, "The fundamental difference in development of the ideological approaches to the public economic sector between Britain and Israel stems from the fact that in England the issue concerned reform of an existing economy, whereas in Israel a new economy was actually being created."[21] If you can't find an employer, become one. (Histadrut details are in Chapter 5.)

The large kibbutz was an outgrowth of the Gdud Ha'avoda, or Labor Battalion, which was an attempt to form a countrywide egalitarian commune, "shock troops of labor" who could go anywhere and take on any needed task in the "conquering of work." In 1924, some of its members founded Kibbutz Ein Harod in the Valley of Jezreel, which was to be the prototype of the large kibbutz. At that time, a small *kvutza*, such as Degania, produced only one crop and was therefore vulnerable to the vicissitudes of weather and markets. Personal relations in the small *kvutza* were very close, and critical to the continuity of the group; and the great dependence of a few people on each other required unusual individual efforts and devotion to work, making it difficult to absorb new immigrants or to allow members time for cultural pursuits. The large kibbutz was planned to have a diversified, integrated economy with mixed farming and marketing. Since it could expand in size, it would be open to new members, while allowing for individual fulfillment through the provision of a choice of cultural and work opportunities. From the *kvutza* were retained the principles of public land and financing, collective production, consumption and education, and an egalitarian life style.

The Labor Battalion and Ein Harod had political aims which went beyond the direct substance of their work. Some of the founders of Ein Harod saw their kibbutz as the headquarters of a larger political force which could get priority in the use of national resources. The Labor Battalion, receiving funds from the Histadrut for kibbutz settlement, diverted part of the money to other purposes, such as to help communes which formed for work in the towns and for road building. At that time, the idea of a labor battalion as a national force in the building of the country for and by socialism and of the commune as the predominant form—and indeed, the idea of the country as "one big kibbutz"—had a great symbolic and theoretical appeal to Ben Gurion and other leaders from the Second *Aliva*, as well as to its direct proponents. But the leaders of Ahdut Ha'Avoda were caught in two dilemmas. These ideas were not feasible on a national scale. They were not acceptable to the city workers or even to most agricultural workers, and the leaders did not have the sovereignty, power, or will "to force people to be free." Nor were they convinced ideologically that there was no other way to achieve Labor's goals.

If the resources had been made available to them, it is possible that part of the program of the *Gdud Ha'Avoda* could have survived as one of several modes of organization. Some members of Ein Harod supported the idea of the kibbutz as the center of a national commune. What they proposed, however, was a semi-independent organization which would have the right to use funds received from the Histadrut as they saw fit; in other words, having the same relation to the Histadrut that the Histadrut had to the World Zionist Organization. The leaders of Ahdut Ha'Avoda would not accept this deviation from the "controlled pluralism" they had in mind.

The party, on grounds of control and ideology, backed that group within Ein Harod that would restrict resources to use within the kibbutz itself. Funds to support the Battalion were thus cut off. This, together with internal ideological splits and the objective difficulty of holding together a countrywide commune, brought the experiment of the Battalion to an end, and it finally disbanded in 1927.* [24] Ein Harod continued to benefit from Histadrut favor, and spun off other settlements on the principles of the large, open-membership kibbutz. These eventually joined together in Hakibbutz Hameuhad, or United Kibbutz Movement. The end of the Battalion determined the marginality of the far left in Labor Zionism. It showed, as well, the methods by which the central leadership group in the Labor movement gained and used authority and control.

In the early days, settlement meant rugged physical pioneering, many years of hardship in reclaiming land and building, and often, before the state, settlement by stealth in the face of Mandatory government prohibition. It took many years before a new settlement was self-supporting. Access to resources was mainly through allocations of the party-controlled national institutions. To gain support, recruit new members, and further common beliefs, several settlement movements developed, and each was characterized by a different emphasis in beliefs, life style, and political aims. Under vastly different circumstances, new settlement under political-movement auspices continues to this day.

By the late 1920s, the kibbutzim and *moshavim* had formed into national federations, and through youth movements in the country and abroad began to recruit and train cadres of new members. These movements became important sources of party and national leadership, while their separate existence preserved factionalism within the Labor movement.

By 1930, when Ahdut Ha'Avoda and Hapoel Hatzair united to form Mapai, a period of unusual social creativity had produced institutions which are still the base of Labor's social resources. To the members and to a large part of the Zionist movement, the beliefs which the institutions embodied and represented assumed a tangible and detailed form through their incorporation in living organizations. By this time, however, the parties and the Histadrut were becoming complex and highly developed, operated by increasingly dominant organizations with well-defined modes of operation and directions. As will be seen, these dual characteristics gave the Labor movement the potential both for impressive achievement and for eventual stagnation. Long years of leadership in the Yishuv and unbroken terms of office in the state were to be inimical to the early forward-looking *élan* even as they fostered the growth of organizations and resources. These characteristics developed significantly during the period of the Fourth *Aliya* after 1924.

Many of the 82,000 immigrants of the Fourth *Aliya* were middle class. They were largely from Poland; there were also some 9,000 from the Middle East. Although their capital and their management experience were usually

* Ironically, after the Battalion dispersed, some of its leaders on the far left returned to the Soviet Union, and it is believed that most of them disappeared under Stalin's rule.

modest, they provided considerable impetus to small- and medium-sized industry and commercial activities and to the growth of the cities. Between 1923 and 1926, Tel Aviv grew from 16,000 to 40,000. As the number of urban jobs grew, the towns became the foci of Labor politics and Histadrut activity. A period of severe unemployment, beginning in 1927, followed a short-lived boom. In these straits, Labor's organization gave good service, enhancing its status in the eyes of employers and workers. Indeed, when Diaspora leaders of the World Zionist Organization tried to intervene directly in local decisions by cutting Histadrut support, the nonsocialists of the Yishuv stood by their Labor fellow Palestinians against the attempt for Diaspora control.

Ahdut Ha'Avoda's leaders reacted to the growing importance of the middle-class sector by recognizing the role of the private economy, while nonetheless trying to maintain control of the direction of the economy and access to jobs. They wanted to "ensure that socialists direct the private economy," as Berl Katzenelson put it, "without owning it." The official ideology was gradually modified by the requirement of appealing to city workers, who were less collectivist than the agricultural settlers, and by the need to stimulate the often laggard Histadrut organizations.[25]

The growth of party bureaucracies was, in part, the result of sophisticated party control of Histadrut organizations, in which party officials were employed. The way had been prepared for Labor's predominance in the polity far beyond the scope of the working class, through a broad-based appeal and by the formation of coalitions, but there could also be sensed a divergence from many of Labor's original ideals—particularly those of equality in rewards and of self-work, or performing one's own labor, rather than employing others. Although in the field a tremendous amount of pioneering was in progress under difficult and challenging conditions, political leaders were increasingly unable to ensure that officials in the Labor bureaucracies applied these same ideals to themselves.

"From a Working Class to a People": Mapai Becomes the Dominant Party

The 1920s saw both great innovations and the origin of Labor's characteristic modes of political organization. In the 1930s, these crystallized; and beyond its dominant role in the Labor movement, Mapai developed the political appeal and the broader relations which enabled it to lead in the Yishuv and the state.

The 1930s began inauspiciously. After severe Arab riots in 1929, a British White Paper drastically curtailed Jewish immigration and land purchase. With the rise of the Nazis, national survival became—and has since remained—the main challenge. From 1936 to 1939 a state of virtual war existed, with frequent Arab attacks. A central issue in 1937 was a British proposal, later withdrawn in the face of Arab opposition, to partition the country, providing for a tiny Jewish state, which at least would have had the sovereignty needed to admit many refugees. In 1939, on the eve of the war, a second White Paper stopped immigration almost entirely. In the 1930s only about 220,000 had come, in what was called the Fifth *Aliya*, of whom 40,000 were from Germany. The Holocaust cut off the sources of pioneering immigration through Hehalutz and Hashomer Hatzair and other European movements, which, together with the Yishuv's youth groups, had provided most of the new kibbutz settlers.

From 1933, when it polled 44 percent of the votes in the Zionist Congress, Mapai led the World Zionist Organization governing coalition. From 1935 until 1963, Ben Gurion was the national leader. In the Yishuv and the state, from 1930, Mapai and later Labor were in office for forty-seven years. Ben Gurion had been Secretary of the Histadrut from its formation in 1920. In 1935 he became Chairman of the Jewish Agency Executive. He led the state as its first Prime Minister from 1948 to 1954, when he briefly retired, and again from 1955 to 1963. He was thus at the center for more than four decades, leaving an incalculable imprint on the political system and culture. (For more details on the Agency, see Appendix F.)

After taking the lead, Mapai broadened and strengthened its base of support through coalitions and organization. In addition, it modified its ideology to become more general and less class-oriented. In 1929 Ben Gurion had talked of the aim of going "from a working class to a working people," reflecting the idea that the whole society, through the work and political lead of the Labor movement, would become socialist in its way of life. By 1935, when he was Chairman of the Jewish Agency Executive and represented the whole nation, he spoke of going "from a working class to a people."[26] The nation would not go through the stages of capitalist development, to be followed by socialism as the outcome of a class struggle, but directly to being a working people. In this, Ben Gurion's concept was somewhat like Lenin's; but the change would come without coercion or a class war. The Labor movement would be the cornerstone of Zionism, but it would work for, and with, the whole people and not just one class. Labor's historic role was to bring about Zionism and socialism as two sides of the same coin.[27]

In the eyes of the other Labor leaders, at least, this did not mean that Labor would forgo partisan control or, in the phrase then in use, "the hegemony of the workers." Labor's organization and way of life would predominate in a society of plural cultural and economic modes, and with a minimum of class conflict. As frequently occurs, the partisanship of followers exceeded that of some of the leaders who were involved in the larger national concerns; and it persisted after the leaders of factions were reconciled as they grew closer through interaction as members of a governing elite. In 1935 Ben Gurion was able to gain approval, over ideological objections, for the beginning of the long alliance with the orthodox Mizrachi, but there was no cooperation with the Revisionists, except for a short-lived defense alliance with the Revisionist military arm, the *Irgun Zvai Leumi*.

The relations which developed in the 1930s continued for decades in the state: a continuing coalition of Labor and the religious (Mizrachi) movements, Labor cooperation on many endeavors with the General Zionists, and fierce political competition with the Revisionists. The Revisionists had left the official Zionist organization early in the 1930s, facilitating Labor's political primacy. The Mizrachi and the General Zionists accepted Labor's political predominance, and in return were helped toward their own social goals.

The case of the employment exchanges is one example. These were initially party owned. Hapoel Hamizrachi and the Revisionist parties operated their own exchanges, while Mapai effectively controlled the Histadrut exchanges. Unemployment was often very serious. In 1927, for example, 40 percent of the workers in Tel Aviv were unemployed. Boycotts, threats of organized violence, and clashes at worksites were frequent as the Histadrut tried to force employers to accept it as a monopoly supplier of labor, and other groups fought back.

A common enemy was the British, to whom unemployment proved that immigration should be cut because of the country's "limited absorptive capacity." From 1927 the Histadrut cooperated with Hapoel Hamizrachi, who agreed to Histadrut primacy in return for a share in jobs and employment exchange management. Fierce and occasionally violent rivalry between Labor and the Revisionists continued.

In 1934 Ben Gurion unexpectedly reached an agreement with Jabotinsky, the Revisionist leader, to resolve the differences between the Revisionist labor organization and the Histadrut. It would have provided for abstention from violence, arbitration of strikes if approved by 25 percent of the employees concerned, and joint multi-party exchanges. Although favored by a majority of the Mapai central committee, the issue, particularly the anti-strike clauses, threatened to split the party since many city unions and Hakibbutz Hameuhad were opposed. A specially elected party convention proved indecisive and a referendum of the whole Histadrut membership rejected the pact by a large majority of those voting. Ben Gurion accepted with some grace, acknowledging the "legitimacy of democracy."[28]*

Organization as an Art

Coalitions in which Mapai predominated would not have sufficed without effective organization and appealing symbols. The pioneer ideology

---

* By the end of the 1930s, exchanges were joint efforts of the Jewish Agency and all principal sectors except the Revisionists. The management and allocation of work were divided according to a party "key" in which Labor's share was to be 60 percent.

and its symbols and institutions were essential to Labor's primacy as a source of broad public sentiment and support. But the forte of Mapai was the development of organization to a fine art. Its leaders were thus prophets armed, and prophets who were patrons.

Almost from the beginning, Labor's ability to organize was clearly discernible: success in building, penetrating or controlling central social, economic, and political institutions, and gaining access to national resources; vision, yet with flexibility in beliefs to accommodate different orthodoxies as well as nonbelievers; a division of labor between leaders who deal with policy and organization men who ensure political support; and the ability, through programs, symbols, personalities, organization, and patronage to mobilize supporters and gain legitimation for its leaders from outside groups.

Politically based power over resources and economic and social organizations was the heart of the system, beginning, as we have seen, with Ahdut Ha'Avoda's success early in the 1920s in controlling the Histadrut, the inflow of national resources, and a large proportion of immigration certificates. A necessary condition was election success; but this was followed by more detailed, effective, and self-perpetuating means of authority.

An important electoral arena was the election of delegates to the biennial World Zionist Congresses. These decided the leadership of the Agency Executive, which organized immigration, public investment, settlement, the conduct of foreign affairs, and eventually self-defense. Within Palestine itself, the principal elections were those to the Va'ad Leumi. Representing the groups and movements in the Yishuv, the Va'ad Leumi, or National Committee, had direct influence in education and social services; in voting for municipal councils, notably in Tel Aviv (where Mapai was consistently second to the General Zionists); and in the internal Histadrut elections. It was in the Histadrut that the Labor Party institution building, patronage, and party machinery first came to flower; and it is worth considering the system in the Histadrut and in Mapai in some detail because it formed the background for much of the political culture of the country.*

A majority in the Histadrut elections means virtual control of the key appointments; for example, it means nominating the executives and boards of directors of Histadrut-owned companies, the editors of *Davar*, the Histadrut daily paper, and the leaders of the trade-union department. By being in on the ground floor when new organizations are formed or penetrating existing groups with loyal supporters, the leverage can be made much greater than the election results would indicate. The result is not only executive control but extensive patronage for the faithful, ensuring their continued support and maintaining a reserve force of political workers and election funds.

Throughout the hierarchies, there are many levels of elected governing bodies and bureaucracies in workers' councils, local works committees, the

* The present tense is used because the description still applied to Labor and the Histadrut in the middle 1970s. For details of the Histadrut organization, see Figure 5.8.

health service, cooperative transport, marketing and purchasing, settlement movements, party branches, and national unions and pension funds. Most of those elected to the boards of economic organizations or of party institutions are on the payroll, usually in some kind of executive capacity, working in organizations which are headed by party leaders.[29] Labor activists thus earn a living from politics in a hierarchy in which they look up to patrons and down to clients instead of seeking open electoral support or operating in a more "horizontal," independent bargaining manner.

Since election procedures are democratic and candidates are duly nominated and elected, it is necessary to control nominations in order to dominate the system. Control is made possible through voting *en bloc* for slates chosen, not in primaries but by nominating committees. The system is usually closer to appointment than to election, despite attempts to make nominating committees "representative" in their composition, the pressures exerted by interested groups, and an electorate's formal right to change the list of candidates presented to it. Ethnic and other special-interest needs for representation are considered informally in the nominating process, but the result is top-down, or appointed, representation. The process is rationalized, unconvincingly, on the grounds that it ensures broader sociological and interest representation than would result from "open" nominations or primaries.

With variations, the way in which the top leadership is chosen is "pyramidal." A large group—say, the national membership—elects a smaller one which meets every few years in a convention. To meet at closer intervals, the convention then elects a still smaller forum, which has formal power of decision and is called an "executive" group. This group, in turn, tends to abdicate its power, choosing a still smaller group, and so on. While the largest group—for example, the membership—is "sovereign," in the end the smaller the group, the greater the power. Indeed, in the past a very small group of leaders within the Mapai machine could decide the principal management appointments in the Histadrut enterprises and unions by gaining the majority of the Mapai representatives on the Histadrut Central Committee. The Mapai representatives, in turn a majority of the whole committee, could then put through the decisions of the smaller group.

An example of central control through nomination and voting procedures is the selection of the Labor Party Central Committee.* In 1969 there were more than 3,000 convention delegates. They were offered a single slate of candidates for the 600 seats on the Central Committee. The slate was prepared by the convention standing committee, which was directed from behind the scenes by a handful of party leaders.[30] Nomination of the Knesset candidates

---

* Between conventions, the Central Committee has the authority to decide party policy and personnel changes. Constant pressure for group and faction representation increases the size of the membership—for example, from 600 in 1969 to more than 800 in 1977.

by the Central Committee is done in a similar way—from above, by a small committee in closed session. In the Histadrut, the party leaders have even more say, since members all over the country vote directly by proportional representation for the huge entire slates of convention delegates. These are presented by the several parties, which then have a free hand in choosing the Executive and Central Committee members.

There are many democratic elements in this hierarchical, oligarchic, and closed system. The elected bodies act according to specified parliamentary procedures, and the principle of representation is observed. Rival bureaucracies (whose aims and motivations spring from a complex of beliefs and ideologies, group and individual leadership interests, and coalition tactics) can provoke confrontation on important issues, but only a very large and organized internal opposition can achieve changes. Once decisions are taken, however, opposers are expected to accept them. Historically, opposing minorities that would not accept central rule, or could not reach an acceptable bargain with the stronger groups, soon got short shrift, and splits resulted. The struggles usually comprised, at one and the same time, aspects of power and belief. Examples were the disbanding of the Labor Battalion in the mid-1920s (discussed earlier), the split of the "B Faction" in the 1940s, and the brief separate existence of Rafi in the 1960s.*

An enduring division of opinion within Labor, as in the whole Yishuv, was over the territorial aspect of Zionism. In 1944, the so-called "B Faction," or Sia Bet, left Mapai. In 1942 the Zionist movement officially endorsed the specific aim of an independent Jewish sovereign state, which then implied accepting a partition which would limit the areas of settlement. For Hakibbutz Hameuhad and its supporters, settlement was the central goal, and also the way, rather than political fiat, to establish the boundaries. It was therefore opposed to declaring the aim of statehood, and argued as well against what it called "an overweening party bureaucracy."

With the Sia, Mapai lost most of the members of Hakibbutz Hameuhad, and with them many of the younger potential party leaders. There were several effects of the split. The loss of leadership potential disturbed the balance of the age groups within Mapai, which in the closed, hierarchical system led to years of internal strife surrounding the succession to power. In losing the membership of many kibbutzim, Mapai was deprived of much of the "amateur" kibbutz participation which had counteracted the impact of the more permanent and job-dependent members of the party or Histadrut

---

* Rafi, led by Ben Gurion, Dayan, Peres, and other followers of Ben Gurion, split from Mapai just before the 1965 elections. Rafi won only ten Knesset seats and had no organized economic base, sources of support, or influence in the Histadrut; nor, despite an emphasis on electoral reform, party democracy, technology, and *mamlachtiut*, did Rafi have major ideological differences with Mapai. In 1968, the Rafi Central Committee voted by a small majority to merge with the new Labor Party.

bureaucracies.[31] The kibbutznik, like a successful lawyer, could enter and leave politics without personal loss. At the same time, the proportionate weight of urban workers and voters continued to increase, and their value in the party is seen in the nomination of people like Golda Meir and Levi Eshkol, before the state, as Secretaries of the Tel Aviv Workers' Council.

Mapai in the State—Mamlachtiut and Partisanship

With independence, the leaders of Mapai became the leaders of Israel, and for decades they were closely identified with the way in which the state met the challenges to its security and society. The specific developments are the subject of most of the chapters which follow. I show, here, for future reference, the evolution of Labor movement party alliances and splits in the first thirty years of the state (Figure 1.2), and indicate only one of the important divergences of approach within Mapai—that over the priority given to the overall interests of the state, as compared with loyalty to party organizations and ideology. This Ben Gurion called *mamlachtiut.*

Party mergers and splits served to strengthen and perpetuate Mapai's partisan methods of organization and control. Other parties sought to emulate them; and in later discussion of the hierarchical political culture in Chapter 9, I speak of Mapai and other Labor factions interchangeably. Events were to increase the importance of the organization and the shift in emphasis from

FIGURE 1.2   Labor Movement Parties Since 1948 (for the Yishuv, see Figure 1.1)

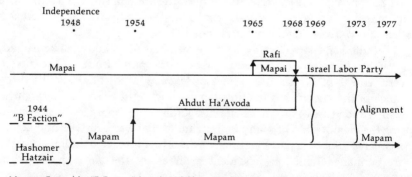

Mapam—Formed by "B Faction" (mainly Hakibbutz Hameuhad) and Hashomer Hatzair movement.

Ahdut Ha'Avoda—Split from Mapam in 1954, mainly because of Mapam's (then) pro-Soviet stance. Not to be confused with Ahdut Ha'Avoda of the 1920s, the forerunner of Mapai.

Rafi—Followers of Ben Gurion leave Mapai with him in 1965, rejoining with Ahdut Ha'Avoda and Mapai in 1968. Ben Gurion and a small following remained as the independent "State List."

Alignments—Electoral lists and Knesset delegations comprising more than one party and campaigning and voting in the Cabinet and Knesset according to an agreed platform. In 1965, Mapai and Ahdut Ha'Avoda; in the 1969, 1973, and 1977 elections, Labor and Mapam.

agricultural pioneering to the city, originally to solve the problems of the city worker and eventually to gain the strong support of the middle class.* Because of changes in the composition of its membership, Mapai could more readily become less ardently socialist in symbols and ideological tone, and its leaders were freer to advocate a clear alignment of the new state with the West.

The transfer of authority to the state accentuated a divergence which had begun to develop among the Mapai leaders and between age groups in the party. In an oversimplified way, the difference was between *mamlach-tiut*—the devolution of responsibility and loyalty to the state and its institutions, above party or particular interest and with a rational and constitutional approach—and the more partisan view, in which the interests of party and ideology are central and need to be considered at all times.[33]

As Prime Minister, Ben Gurion seldom used specifically socialist terminology; increasingly he used national and biblical symbols. Over the span of his political life, the language and content of Labor beliefs and the basis of debate became completely transformed from the "class struggle" of the early days of the Poalei Zion to national concerns. In place of voluntarism, or the performance of the social tasks by sectoral and partisan organizations, he advocated *mamlachtiut*. The concept was associated with the vastly changed circumstances which prevailed once the state was declared. The prewar trickle of immigration had become a flood, and few of the newcomers had previous indoctrination in any political movement. Formal state action was needed to meet the vast new problems of defense and development. In the difficult search for unity, loyalty to the country needed to be placed above sectoral loyalty, and formal legal and economic rewards and universalist criteria began to replace most of the volunteer impetus. National economic functions moved to the government, where the Labor leaders attempted to exercise the same kind of central control they had developed in the Yishuv.

Although the voluntary institutions prospered, they became more and more symbols of a pioneering past, their internal nature often contradicting the ideologies through which they were founded. The kibbutz remained an example and an important educational force. Its relative weight in the economy and in politics declined, however, and it was in *moshavim* that most immigrant farmers settled. The Histadrut continued to be the basis of Labor's political resources, but its contribution to social development became less

* In 1941, about one-third of the Mapai membership was urban; by 1946, one-half; by 1956, 85 percent! In 1938 the United Kibbutz Movement supplied two out of seven members of the Mapai Secretariat; by 1941, four out of twelve; and in 1942, ten of fifty-two members of the Executive Committee of the Histadrut. Including former kibbutz members or agricultural workers, the vast majority of Labor's leadership came from the cooperative working settlements until well into the years of the state.[32] In the state, kibbutz representation was less. In the First Knesset, eight kibbutz members accounted for 19 percent of the Mapai delegation. At the time of the Eighth Knesset elections in 1973, of the total Labor Party membership of about 300,000, 7.4 percent were from kibbutzim and there were seven kibbutz members in a Knesset delegation of forty-four.

unique. As the ranks of the founding generations thinned out, the old terms and symbols came to have less meaning to most Israelis.*

The more partisan always kept in mind the need to maintain and enhance political influence through symbols, and particularly through organization and the appointment of loyalists and the denial of political credit and appointments to opponents. The partisan view, in the persons of the leaders, was reflected in the ideological terms of debate. Among their followers, it expressed itself mainly in organizational orthodoxy and loyalty.

In actuality, motives were mixed. Some followers of Ben Gurion believed in *mamlachtiut* in a technocratic way, seeing party activities, ideologies, and political bargaining as hindering the sophisticated conduct of affairs by an elite; others saw in it the ideal of rising above partisan interest and a sign of maturity in national independence. Similarly, some adherents of sectoral or partisan loyalties sought mainly organizational power or personal advantage, while others were more concerned with the preservation of ideals. Clearly, this divergence was related to the extent to which the people concerned related the Labor movement to the idea of class. But at the second level of the party's functionaries, whatever their allegiance, organization and personalities began to come first.

Another development which became accentuated in the state was the division of labor between the party's bureaucrats and its political leaders. As Ben Gurion concentrated on national security, he left the management of internal party affairs to others, while the party's full-time organization workers concentrated on nominations, party finance, vote getting, and patronage.[34] The central machine gained a very high effectiveness in organization and in providing absolute and loyal support for the party leaders, while remaining almost completely divorced from policy considerations. The hierarchical political culture and *mifleget hamanganon* (party of the bureaucracy) reached their peak under this informal arrangement, and the dominance of the organization reinforced the inherent Mapai trend toward pragmatism. The importance of the organization became clear when Ben Gurion, running on the Rafi ticket in 1965 against the Mapai organization, got only about 9 percent of the votes for the Knesset.

Stagnation Follows Great Achievements

The Labor parties had a central role in the achievements of the state, but development was eventually followed by a stagnation of thought whose causes were more profound than the problems deriving from sovereignty, on the one hand, or the importance of party organization on the other.

* In 1953 when Mapai agreed to abolish the separate Labor school system, a large minority in the Histadrut agreed only on condition that parents of the children in a given school could decide whether or not to continue the socialist symbols, such as Labor songs and the display of the red flag on May Day. By the late 1950's May Day parades and red flags in schools were almost unknown in Mapai and its affiliated kibbutzim.

Given its grand aims and constitution as the heart of the Labor movement, the Histadrut, even in the Yishuv, began to become a focus for the conflicts between ideals and reality. Equality, physical self-work, voluntarism, and the Histadrut's aims for social change became less urgent. Even in the Yishuv the principle of equality had to be modified seriously in the towns.[35] The availability of many unskilled Arab workers made it hard to maintain a minimum wage level for the unskilled or newly arrived immigrants. The Histadrut agreed to large differentials in pay between the skilled and the unskilled out of fear that the highly skilled would leave the unions. In the 1950s the issue arose again over the question of a special pay scale for professionals, and again the decision was in favor of differentiation to forestall the defection of skilled workers. The record of the Histadrut in the 1960s and 1970s indicates that it fights for the more highly paid workers more than for those who are unskilled or lack positions of unusual leverage.

Once a pioneer, the Histadrut has since ceased to innovate. When its central leaders attempt to support national economic policy or to advocate equality, they lack the legitimate authority needed to confront parochial trade-union demands. Although its own giant firms experiment with worker participation in management, they normally follow what they see as their economic interests, which are hard to differentiate from those of other profit-seeking, rationally managed organizations. Deeper and more corrosive problems came from the use of Histadrut resources in politics.* The Histadrut faces not only the problem of trying to maintain a volunteer and innovative spirit in an organization with nearly a million and a half members, but the inherent human problems of an achieving and consuming society where, as de Tocqueville said of the Americans, many people are "brooding over advantages they do not possess."

In the state in the 1950s, Mapai under Ben Gurion was the almost unchallenged arbiter of policy and internal differences. In the 1960s, after Ben Gurion retired and the Lavon affair split Mapai,** the role of the party began to decline until in the 1970s even a united Labor Party which included Ahdut

---

* This misuse occasionally led to financial corruption. For example, in 1975 a former head of Solel Boneh, the large Histadrut building firm, was indicted for using his position to help a failing bank whose owner had apparently been of financial help to Mapai. David Hacohen, a retired Mapai leader and also a former head of Solel Boneh, then wrote in an open letter to the Secretary-General of the Histadrut, "It is hard to maintain both public probity and loyalty to one's benefactors at the same time." Hacohen did not see how someone who had been put into his job by Labor leaders, his patrons, could refuse to do their bidding, or reform the system overnight.

** Pinhas Lavon was Defense Minister in 1954 when Israeli agents were imprisoned and convicted in Egypt of sabotage intended to create friction between Egypt and the United States. An inquiry committee, appointed by Prime Minister Sharett in 1954, did not entirely clear Lavon of direct responsibility, and he resigned. In 1960 Lavon said that new evidence and documents cleared him and asked Ben Gurion for "rehabilitation." Ben Gurion refused to take a stand, and the Cabinet decided to appoint a ministerial committee, which decided that Lavon was not to blame. Ben Gurion attacked the procedure, demanding a judicial inquiry. Before the 1965 Knesset elections, the affair divided Mapai very seriously, accentuating and exposing its internal differences and leading immediately to the forming of Rafi by Ben Gurion. The Lavon affair was a crucial development in the history of Labor.

Ha'Avoda and Rafi seemed to function mainly as an organization for the nomination of candidates and for election campaigns and, in the election campaign of 1977, to function inadequately. The circumstances of this electoral debacle are presented in Chapter 9.

Foremost among the internal causes for this decline were the internal party system and the freezing of the development of beliefs. The dependency of the members of elected party forums in the "party of the bureaucracy" eliminated the political significance of the elected internal party institutions, while the lack of new ideas, combined with the difficulty of entry at the middle levels of politics, made the party unattractive to the young or to the new professional and managerial groups. For years there was little change in the forms of organizations, the modes of politics, or the persons of the leaders. While the political behavior of younger men trying to climb the ladders of power resembled that of their elders, it was not always accompanied by the same sense of history and direction. Twin challenges were thus posed: the Labor movement needed both ideological creativity and party democracy in order to regain genuine national leadership.

Religion and Politics

Over the centuries the Passover Seder has ended with the call "Next year in Jerusalem!" For most, this was a Messianic hope, to come true in God's own time; yet the Zionist movement owed to religion not only the longing for Zion but the belief in the congruence of nationality or "peoplehood" and religion, a congruence from which basic questions of the relation of religion and the state derive.

For Jews in the Diaspora, nationality and religion were indivisible. To the orthodox, a purely secular Jewish state on the Western liberal model seemed impossible. Religious and national symbols and culture were one. In the Moslem countries, the concept of separation of religion and nationality did not exist and the synagogue remained the center of community life much longer than it did in Europe. The interaction with modern Western culture, in which nationality and religion are seldom identical, came to the Jews of the Islamic countries much later than it did to those in Europe—indeed, many from remote areas had their first contact with the West when they came to Israel.

One source of disparity and malaise regarding the question of the role of religion in the state is the characteristic of Jewishness as a nationality. Even Jews who opposed formal religion saw themselves or at least were seen by others as having a common Jewish culture, with its own literature, language, and modes of social relations. To the religious believer, Judaism as a religion was a faith that people lived by. At the most, for the very orthodox it involved a life style in which almost every detail of behavior from the cradle to the grave was prescribed by the *Halacha*—rabbinic interpretations of the Talmud, recognizing that morality requires concrete form and practice in order to have meaning. At the least, Jews shared a common history and a future.

In the orthodox belief, this history is the working out of God's will through his people. The Jewish condition is an existential one, not one of belief alone separated from reality and action. "The Jew is that person caught in the grip of Jewish history with its unique traumas, its dangers, and its glories. The religious Jew in this perspective . . . acknowledges and accepts that situation as a charge." The history of the Jews is not neutral but "one of promise and fulfillment." [36]

In the despair of Eastern Europe, many orthodox individuals were drawn to the Zionist idea, although the rabbinate saw Zionist activism as a deviation from the Messianic belief and the concepts of history, and as strengthening the secularism that was threatening the unity and continuity of Judaism. The much-feared secularism was seen to be everywhere—in the Haskala movement and in the socialist and revolutionary groups. Secular views had spread among the Western Jews with the Enlightenment following Napoleon's liberation of the ghettos, and secularism was therefore to be feared within Zionism. Indeed, the majority of the members of the Hibbat Zion, the first organized Zionist group, were secular-minded intellectuals, although there were some orthodox members.

As the Zionist movement grew, so did the number of orthodox members. Those to whom the religious character of the future national home was of great concern formed the Mizrachi movement, the forerunner of the National Religious Party (Mafdal) in the state. Despite the constant need for compromise, the Mizrachi and its successors have been in almost every executive coalition of the Jewish Agency or the Cabinet since 1935. The motives for this participation were comprehensive—a genuine belief in active Zionism as a solution, a defensive action to prevent complete secularization of the Zionist movement and of the national home, and the wish to participate in the exercise of power and the use and allocation of resources. [37]

A second religious political movement was the ultra-orthodox Agudat Israel, whose aim, like that of the Mizrachi, was a *Halachic* state. Unwilling to compromise on this question, the Aguda approach was to seek autonomy for the ultra-orthodox in life style, religious and legal authority, and separate education, if possible with public support. The Aguda remained outside of the Zionist movement, and only became part of the organized politics of the Yishuv shortly before the end of the Mandate. As the Holocaust deprived the Labor movement of most of its reservoir of pioneering immigrants, it also wiped out the centers of orthodoxy. The Aguda in particular was left without its Diaspora support. Although non-Zionist, with the imminence of the state and the constant threats to national survival, it joined the polity and publicly accepted the existence of a secular state.*

As a result of Aguda separatism, the Mafdal in the state, like the Mizrachi in the Yishuv, was usually the sole representative at the Cabinet level of the religious point of view. Indeed, the Mafdal's share of power and resources has exceeded by far the proportion of the religious Jews which it actually represented in the world and eventually in Israel. The party controls the direction of the national religious schools and the appointments and administrative procedures of the rabbinic courts, and for decades it has headed such secular ministries as Interior and Welfare, in addition to the Ministry of Religious Affairs. Within succeeding Cabinets, the strength of the Mafdal came from its having, until the 1967 Six Day War, one central interest for which it could bargain support on other issues; from the power of its identification with the historic religious symbols; and from the threat of potential shifts in loyalty by some Labor constituencies if religious sentiments were affronted. In the 1977 Begin Cabinet, the Mafdal's strength was further enhanced by its identification with the Likud's foreign policy and by its heading the Ministry of Education.

The religious parties and issues have been influenced greatly by the beliefs of those who do not actually vote for them. Until 1977 electoral support for the Mafdal and the Aguda, taken together, has been consistent over the years at 13 to 15 percent in national elections (election results are presented in Appendix B); yet surveys show that only about half of the voters who see themselves as religiously observant actually vote for the religious parties. One cause is lack of support by Asian and African immigrants, although they are religiously observant.[38] This has been ascribed to the neglect of the Eastern communities by the prestate Zionist movement, and to limitations to political competition resulting from the circumstances in which the large early immigrations were received, discussed in more detail in Chapter 3, "Political Integration."

Labor, on the other hand, entered into the arrangement with the Mafdal for reasons which were broader than the simple needs of power. Like most Jews, the leaders of Labor have believed that religion, or religious practice, was responsible for the survival of the Jews as a people throughout the centuries. The Hebrew language, Jewish history, major holidays, and the Bible are symbols around which all the people could unite, and around which the Zionist movement rallied. There was a common wish to preserve these central elements of the culture; and their importance to a very large proportion of the people meant that a cultural schism might result if complete secularity were to be enforced by a political majority. From another point of view, the beginning

---

* The Aguda became faction-ridden after the death of its leader, Rabbi I. M. Levine, in 1972. Each of the four Aguda Knesset members in 1975 represented a different faction. Their public approach, however, has been consistent on religious questions, seeking and achieving a great deal of autonomy in separate neighborhood enclaves, schools, and rabbinic courts.

of the coalition (dating from 1935 when Ben Gurion became Chairman of the Jewish Agency Executive), can be seen as part of a conscious movement of Mapai and the Labor movement toward broader support and national leadership. In this, as in other moves from sectoral to national concepts, Ben Gurion's personal authority was important in overcoming ideological commitments in the interest of national unity.

In the thirty-year Cabinet coalition which resulted, the Mafdal consistently secured the backing of state power for the religious bureaucracy in enforcing rabbinic-law authority on agreed questions. Compromise is inherent in such an arrangement within secular politics. While the ultimate goal was a *Halachic* state—that is, one in which the rabbinic law is public law—compromise for the short term was defended and rationalized as necessary for participation, which alone could prevent or deter secularization. Through long association with day-to-day politics, the Mafdal's political culture, aside from its central religious interest, became as instrumental as that of the secular parties. This characteristic was accentuated by the fact that the party has been an agglomeration of factions and individuals who found little common ground on issues other than religion. After the death of Mordechai Shapiro, Minister of the Interior until 1969, the Mafdal had no dominant leader who could bring real unity.

In its stance on religion and the state, the Mafdal is caught in the crosspressure between the ultra-orthodox, who can accuse it of selling out in order to share in power, and the intense opposition by Mapam and a great many in Labor and in the liberal center to the use of legal power to enforce religious regulations.

After the Six Day War in 1967, a new dimension was added to Mafdal policy—advocacy by some of its factions of the retention and settlement of Judea and Samaria on religious and historical grounds as the land of the forefathers, promised by God to Abraham. The "young" faction became prominent in this cause, advocating a firm line on territorial questions in peace negotiations and a hardening of the accepted policy on official enforcement of religious observance. Its members include elements in the Mafdal which had supported the national efforts in kibbutz settlement and in defense. The older leaders and their followers continued to man most of the party bureaucracy, conducted the ongoing interparty bargaining, and managed institutions controlled by Mafdal; but the younger group continued to gain support and in 1976 became predominant, following some intricate interfaction alliance forming. As a result, the Mafdal as a whole became affiliated in the 1977 coalition with the Likud's foreign policy.

The direct involvement of religious interest groups in secular politics raises questions of individual rights and the distortion of the system of political decision and representation by the "arrangement." The constitutional aspects of these questions are analyzed in Chapter 2. A more fundamental problem is how, and with what legitimacy, specific organizations such as the Mafdal and the Aguda represent the religious sentiments not only of Israelis as a whole (most of whom vote for other parties) but also of millions abroad; and, indeed, what are the implications for the development of religious ideas and practice of such political involvement and of an hierarchy in the rabbinate (which is almost unknown in the Diaspora).

From another point of view, the general polity suffers the distorting effects of the compromise worked out between Labor and the Mafdal which has consistently given Labor (and in 1977 the Likud) a majority it did not earn, and has suppressed possible conflicts between the value systems of liberal democracy and orthodoxy.

The involvement of religion and its organized interests in secular politics leads to compromise, to the development of interests which in turn affect beliefs, to the involvement of the rabbinate in party considerations and of the parties in the selection of the rabbinate and in its decisions. The participation of orthodoxy in politics is a natural outgrowth of a system in which political action was necessary for any group that needed to protect its interests and gain resources, and in which ideas were embodied in institutions to such a great extent. Still, the major questions of religion are those of belief and culture, of what Judaism and the Jews could be. If the involvement of religion with secular politics were to cause many people to move away from religious concerns or to see them in a distorted light, Israel's contribution to Judaism could be greatly diminished.

The Revisionists in the Yishuv, Herut in the State

Led by Vladimir Jabotinsky (1880–1940), the Revisionists were the most important dissident party in the period of the Yishuv, and Herut, their successor, was the leader of the opposition in the state until gaining office in 1977, as a partner in the Likud. In the early years, the Revisionists, unlike the Labor movement, were more concerned with the creation of a state (within the original boundaries, which included Trans-Jordan) than with the details of the kind of society to be created.[39] Jabotinsky saw the early kvutza, kibbutz, and moshav as small-scale experiments to determine the optimal forms for the large-scale colonizing to follow.

The Revisionists wanted the Zionist movement to officially seek a state rather than a vaguely defined "national home," and to colonize on a grand scale on both sides of the Jordan. They saw the Mandate as a constitutional obligation on the part of the British to be active in colonization—to open the country to mass immigration and to provide arms for security and adequate educational and social services and economic aid. Mass immigration would rapidly achieve a Jewish majority, while large-scale development of agriculture and of the water supply would bring economic viability. This approach would make Palestine a more effective refuge for the already threatened European Jews. Should the main effort be put into fighting for a political solution, for large-scale immigration, pressing settlement as rapidly as possible, or, as large segments of Labor saw it, into building gradually through selection and intensive training? While immigration was in any case limited by the British, these divergent views were very important both within the Labor movement and in determining the priorities of Zionist political activity.

Originally the Revisionists were largely a cadre of political leaders and their close followers, with little organization for the immigration of members or for economic activity. In the mid-1920s, however, they founded a youth movement, Betar, which began to gather recruits in Europe and Palestine. In 1926 some of the Revisionists who had been imprisoned by the Bolsheviks for Zionist activity were released from Siberia and reached Palestine in a Revisionist "Second *Aliya*." Little Revisionist settlement or economic enterprise developed, however. Middle-class economic support went primarily to the General Zionists. Most of the middle class in the Yishuv saw the Histadrut as the coming establishment and, while lukewarm to socialism, supported the pioneer image. Like Labor, they were gradualist, while the Revisionists sought a rapid, major effort toward a comprehensive future goal.

In 1933, when the vote went against them on the issue of whether, as they believed, a Jewish state *per se* should be the declared aim, the Revisionists left the official Zionist movement, and in 1934, they formed their own labor organization, with social and employment services and unions; but it was too small an effort and too late to have a strong attraction for workers, nor could it compete effectively in getting jobs or plant representation against the strong (and often strong-armed) Histadrut. It was therefore natural for the Revisionists to propose that the Histadrut give up its political role and become simply a trade union. From this period stems the association of the Revisionists with the right. Opposing strikes, they sought compulsory arbitration in labor relations in a "national interest" which to some (in the atmosphere of the 1930s) was reminiscent of Mussolini's corporate state. Many early Revisionists were former prisoners of the Bolsheviks and therefore strongly antileft, while Labor reacted vigorously to attacks on the Histadrut. Members of the Betar youth movement paraded in paramilitary formations at a time when Europe was torn by fascism. Feelings ran very high; they were ameliorated somewhat from 1936 on by the common concern over increasing Arab warfare.

As the British closed the gates of immigration in the 1930s and Arab attacks intensified, the Revisionists began an active fight against the continuance of the British Mandate. Jabotinsky foresaw the European "social earthquake," the "tangible momentum of irresistible distress." The Revisionists split from the Haganah, forming the Irgun Zvai Leumi, an underground force that did not accept the authority of the elected internal political government of the Yishuv. When the state was declared, Ben Gurion forcibly disbanded the Irgun as a military force. Its leaders, under Menachem Begin, formed the

Herut Party when the older Revisionist politicians denied them access to leading roles. Jabotinsky, head and shoulders above his close followers, had left no obvious successor in the ranks of the Revisionist politicians when he died in 1940. The ascendency of the former underground leaders was aided by the legitimacy they had gained by their fight, which was believed to have had a great influence on the British decision to relinquish the Mandate. The "civilian" Revisionist politicians were pushed aside, and for years those who had not been active in the underground were outside the picture.

In the state, Herut, although in the Knesset, was in a sense "beyond the pale" for a long period. This status was encouraged by Ben Gurion, who became reconciled with Begin only at the time of the Six Day War, when Herut joined the Cabinet. Herut has appealed consistently to feelings of nationalism and social protest, campaigning intensively in the poor urban *shechunot* (neighborhoods) and in the early immigrant transit camps (*ma'abarot*), reinforcing the social dissatisfaction of low-income people, and particularly of immigrants from Islamic countries, whose experiences in their countries of origin also strengthened the appeal of Herut's nationalist stance.

Until the Six Day War, the ideology of "both sides of the Jordan," or indeed of any territorial changes, was academic. In 1965 Herut and the Liberals combined, without actually merging, in a joint election list called Gahal, whose election platform presented more moderate territorial demands. A long period as the "loyal opposition" and the association with the Liberals have modified many ideas. Even in opposition, leaders of Herut came, with time, to act and feel a part of the establishment on many questions. The days are gone when they could lead violent protests, as they did in 1955 against the acceptance of reparations payments from Germany, which was then being debated in the Knesset. While Herut still holds the position that the Histadrut should confine itself to trade unionism, the days of anti-Histadrut politics are past. Today Herut takes part in the internal Histadrut elections, in which its strength has been rising, although the party has not been in a governing Histadrut coalition. On social questions Herut has supported minimum-wage laws and national pensions and health services. Within the overall comprehensiveness of Jabotinsky's approach to Zionism, and it was considerable, the main thrust of Herut remains the central international question, and its involvement in domestic affairs was mainly in expressing social protest. The alliance of the Liberal Party and Herut, as well as the origins of the center parties, is shown in Figure 1.3.

The Center

The center is much broader than the membership or electoral support of so-called "center" parties shows. Israel is a middle-class country. Labor endorses a mixed economy, while nonsocialist parties have socialist affiliates, such as

FIGURE 1.3   Center and Right Parties

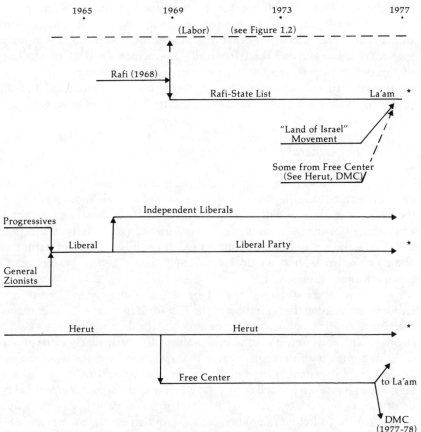

Likud, 1973: Herut, Liberals, State List, Land of Israel, Free Center
Likud, 1977: Herut, Liberals, La'am (The People's Movement)
*La'am formed in 1976 by State List, Land of Israel, some from Free Center.

the kibbutzim of the religious parties and the Independent Liberals. Parties of all hues are active in the Histadrut. Agreement on the goals of welfare, if not on the means, is very broad. Vested interests cause Labor to delay the nationalization of health services and pensions, while the desire to diminish Labor's political resources and the demands of its electors augment the Likud's efforts toward nationalization of health services and pensions, and for minimum-wage laws. Labor's electoral results have largely been a function of the extent of its middle-class support.

There are, however movements which embrace no very specific ideologies of the right or of the left. Their adherents generally believe in economic liberalism and pluralism and endorse a fairly broad spectrum of views on the future borders and on Israeli-Arab relations. These parties included, in the 1977 elections, the Liberals (although they moved to the right as partners with

Herut in the Likud), the Democratic Movement for Change (DMC), and, winning one seat each, the Independent Liberals and the Citizens Rights Movement. The three latter parties emphasized "good government" and constitutional procedures, protesting what they saw as the closed and authoritarian systems of Labor and the Likud. Ironically, the members and internal factions of the center parties, despite their espousal of abstract principles, lacked loyalty to their colleagues and to the needs of the organization, and this prevented them from gaining and keeping large numbers of adherents.

Liberals and General Zionists

The least ideological point of view, and one that was held before the state by most Zionists outside the country, was that of the General Zionists. Basically, they wanted a Zionism without "isms," a successful political and economic achievement of the national home. Most American and Western European Jews, like their non-Jewish countrymen, thought in terms of economic liberalism rather than ideological socialism and of a "general" rather than a specific form of Zionism.

The General Zionists and their Liberal successors have differed from Labor in advocating the limitation of the Histadrut to trade-union functions, thereby separating political and economic power. In addition, they have a stronger faith and interest in constitutionalism, and particularly in the importance of having a written constitution that clearly defines the separation of powers and interests and formally guarantees individual rights. Traditionally, Labor has taken a much more relaxed view of the separation of powers, or of "arm's length negotiations" while in practice having a considerable respect for the individual's political rights—and an even greater respect for those of a group.

Despite an orientation toward private initiative and the fact that most General Zionists in the Yishuv were involved in private business or farming, they cooperated with Labor in national enterprises, such as the defense forces (Haganah), and in other general institutions of the Yishuv. The Labor groups tended to predominate in national ventures, however, partly because cooperative institutions like the kibbutz could much more easily spare members for periods of national service. The General Zionists, on the other hand, consistently led in local elections in Tel Aviv and many other places. In local government, indeed, they were the leading party.

In terms of investment, employment, and production, enterprises formed with private capital were ahead of the Labor sector until World War II, while private agriculture led until the mid-1930s. There were outstanding private entrepreneurs and innovators in the Yishuv, such as Pinhas Rutenberg, who initially built the electric company, or the founders of the Dead Sea Potash

Works and such enterprises as the Nesher Cement Company. Why, then, did the so-called "bourgeois" parties in the Yishuv have a minor political role, dealing largely with local government, while Labor and the Revisionists were concerned with the national scene, as were many General Zionists abroad?

Part of the reason was the absence of organic and highly developed political youth or immigration movements which could cement contact with General Zionists abroad and provide a stream of politically oriented immigrants. There was no General Zionist youth group abroad which could compare to Labor's Hechalutz or to the Revisionist Betar. The General Zionists in the Diaspora, despite their numbers, had a much looser relationship with their *confrères* in the Yishuv. Then, as now, there was a lag in immigration and entrepreneurship from the Western countries. It was, and still is, easier to raise donations or sell government bonds abroad than to attract direct investment or immigration of people with some means of their own.

Although they conceived of growth as coming from private investment, General Zionists in practice supported the use of national capital for land purchase or investment. Most of the public funds went to build cooperative institutions or to buy the land on which labor settlements were formed. Despite awareness of ideological and interest differences between the General Zionists and Labor, the non-Labor groups did not develop a compelling system of beliefs and symbols or an organization that could attain power, attract adherents, or gain wide support. Labor, meanwhile, was able to enlist and inspire the help of many other groups in building the state.

In the state, the most direct descendants of the General Zionists of the Yishuv are the Liberals, associated with Herut in election alignments in 1965 and 1969 (Gahal) and in 1973 and 1977 (Likud). In election platforms the Liberal Party has come out for a general welfare-state policy, the limitation of government enterprise to essential infrastructure investments, and such policies as restrictions on cartels, the encouragement of competition, and a stronger constitutionalism.

The Independent Liberals originated with the German professional *aliya* of the mid-1930s and were later joined by people from other, mainly European immigrations. Within their organization, the Independent Liberals developed many of Labor's characteristics in miniature, such as ethnic blocs, subsidiary economic institutions, and party hierarchy. Generally supporting a Liberal view and yet joining nearly all of the Labor coalitions since the state, the Independent Liberals advocated constitutionalism, freedom from religious intervention in personal rights, equal access to information, and state guarantees of internal party democracy. Historically, their influence as a "conscience" was important, if limited. As a "permanent" minority coalition member, however, the Independent Liberal Party compromised on many questions, particularly those concerning religion and civil marriage. These compromises, internal stagnation, and the appearance of the Democratic

Movement for Change (DMC) led the Independents Liberals to gain only one seat in the 1977 elections. In 1981 they failed to gain any.* The small center parties (and, to the left of Labor, *Sheli* [Camp of Peace], which also failed to gain a seat in 1981) were important to parliamentary life. Enjoying more freedom of expression and more speaking time per member, they were able to keep minority views and matters of conscience before the Knesset.

In the 1977 elections the new Democratic Movement for Change won 15 Knesset seats, thus replacing the Independent Liberals as the liberal, constitutionalist center party. Its founding and initial electoral success were indirectly an outcome of the middle class protest movements after the 1973 war, and of long-standing dissatisfaction with Labor's modes and leadership. These protests are discussed in Chapter 9. After the demise of the DMC, Labor effectively included the majority of the center.

The results of Knesset elections, shown in Appendix B, and those of Histadrut elections, shown in Table 5.4, include elected delegations from parties whose origins have not been discussed. In Chapter 3, I analyze the failure of parties which hoped to represent Jewish ethnic groups, and also consider the gains shown until 1977 by the anti-Zionist communist party, Rakah. This party represents mainly the Arab nationalist sentiments of Arab Israelis, although in 1977 its delegation included two Jewish Knesset members. There are often, also, Knesset delegations of one or two members who usually represent a narrow sector or a single specific interest.

There have been two kinds of omissions thus far, presently to be corrected. First, the brief story of the development of the principal parties and political divisions in parliament and in the Cabinet obviously shows only a small section of the arena in which political power is lost and gained. The political interactions of the manifold subcenters and the bureaucracy will be analyzed in subsequent chapters, in connection with specific areas of policy. Second, one very large question has been dealt with only slightly, that is, the ways in which the Arab countries and a *modus vivendi* with them are perceived.

At first there was innocence of the possibility that the Arabs would oppose the re-creation of the Jewish national home; yet it was unavoidable that the return to Zion would confront the fact that Palestine was geographically a part of a Moslem Middle East that would try to reject a foreign, non-Islamic minority. While most twentieth-century inhabitants of Palestine were Arabs, at other times there had been relatively few. In nineteenth and twentieth-century Jerusalem, for example, Jews have been a majority. Under the

* In the 1961 elections, the Progressives and General Zionists joined to form the Liberal Party, gaining 17 seats, over a previous combined total of 14. A coalition agreement with Mapai fell through at the last minute when Ahdut Ha'Avoda agreed to join and Mapai no longer needed the Liberals. By this act, Mapai may have made possible the eventual electoral victory of the right, for in 1965 most of the former General Zionists, as the Liberal Party, joined Herut to form Gahal, and the Independent Liberals continued in the Progressive way. (See Figure 1.3.)

Turkish Empire the Arabs as yet showed little signs of nationalism, and those movements then active were not focused on Palestine. But the potential for tragedy was there, for both Jews and Arabs wanted to live in this same part of the world, and there seemed to be no way to fully reconcile the justice of both claims.

While not entirely insensitive to this dilemma, early settlers and the Zionist movement were mainly concerned with political negotiations with the powers, and with immigration and the development of the Jewish society. Herzl, perhaps fortunately for the *élan* with which he proceeded, seems to have ignored potential problems, as seen in his oft-quoted statement that Zionism would allow the movement of "a people without a land to a land without people." Achad Ha'am was, as usual, an exception. After his first visit to Palestine in 1891, he predicted the opposition by the Arabs, especially the city dwellers, once the Jews became numerous and offered competition;[40] but he saw the insurance of justice and equality for those Arabs already in the country as a prior condition for the success of Palestine as the spiritual center of the Jewish renaissance.

With time, the view of future relations with the Arabs went from ignorance and disregard to an initial optimism. The land, purchased mainly from absentee landlords, was to be won by work and settlement, carried out against the loose and corrupt background of the dying Turkish Empire. In the nineteenth century, the *fellaheen*, or peasants, had been leaving potentially fertile land of the plains along the coast and in the Valley of Jezreel, driven out by malaria, Bedouin predators, and the avarice of Arab landlords. Among the tribes and kingdoms of the Middle East, there were few signs of Arab unity, and the area of Palestine seemed minute compared to that of the vast other lands in which the Arabs lived. As early as 1916, Jabotinsky compared the (then) 35 million Arabs, living in an area greater than that of Europe, with the situation of the Jews, "having no corner of their own, wanting only one percent of the area of the Arab world." He went on to add that there would be no need to push out the Arabs of Palestine. There would be room for both.[41]

In the days before World War I, small-scale Arab attacks on Jewish settlements were seen as local robberies of professional predators or anticipated peasant opposition, akin to European anti-Semitism, against which the new Jew would defend himself. Many socialists foresaw reconciliation once the yoke of the *effendi*, or absentee landlord, was removed from the Arab proletariat. Borochov's is an example of a class-based analysis of Jewish-Arab relations.[42] He saw Palestinian Arabs as a people who had assimilated to every dominant culture which came to the area, lacking a real nationality. The *fellah*, or peasant farmer, would assimilate on a class basis and join a majority of Jewish and Arab workers. Belief in the *"effendi* theory" was finally laid to rest only after the Six Day War, when socialists from the Arab countries united to condemn Israel. The Communist Party in Palestine had always been anti-Zionist, and the belated realization that Arab left-wing intellectuals and socialists were anti-Zionists destroyed hopes that social reform or class solidarity could be a basis for understanding.

Even those who expected an emergence of Pan-Arabism were optimistic. Under a *Pax Britannica* the Arabs would have sufficient lands and states and would not begrudge Palestine to the Jews. Jewish immigration would raise property values and the standard of living, and all—Arab and Jew alike—would benefit. At the end of World War I, before the peace conferences, Chaim Weizmann negotiated with some success with King Faisal, the oldest son of the Hashemite "Grand Sherif of Mecca," for an arrangement in which the Jewish national home in Palestine would coexist with the large Arab kingdom which Faisal hoped to rule from Damascus, under British auspices. The plan became impossible when the French were allotted Syria and Lebanon in the postwar settlements.[43] Following the Balfour Declaration and the intensification of Jewish immigration, local Arab opposition crystallized. After 1936, sporadic riots became organized attacks. Many Jews, however, believed that expressions of good will, concessions, and a declaration for a binational state (which would, by nature, have an Arab majority) could lead to amity and acceptance. Leading intellectuals Martin Buber, Arthur Ruppin, and Judah Magnes, President of the Hebrew University, were among those who held this view; but their conversations with Arab leaders revealed little common ground. In the later years of the Yishuv, Hashomer Hatzair, the Marxist kibbutz movement, also advocated a binational state. Arab attacks led to a shift in Hashomer policy, and later, in the War of Liberation, many of the outstanding officers came from its ranks.

With the growth of Arab nationalism Jewish views became more pessimistic, or perhaps more realistic. In 1931, for example, Berl Katzenelson had advocated a binational state in which the differences between Arab and Jewish workers would eventually disappear. By World War II he was writing that the Jews should help the Arabs in their national aims on condition that they recognize a Jewish state in Palestine. "There is no doubt," he wrote, "that the Jewish State means full rights for the Arabs... [but] after all that has happened to us in the world, and that has happened to us in this country since 1936, we are entitled to say: we want to rule in this corner."[44]

As on other questions, Jabotinsky's approach to the Arabs was political. Prosperity would not make the Arabs see the Jewish state favorably, he wrote in 1933 and 1935; only the realization that the Jews and British together were determined to use power to establish it would gain acceptance for the state; if Zionism was moral, just, and necessary, it had to win, even against disagreement.

For the two decades preceding the Six Day War, events seemed to have resolved most of these questions. Rejecting the proposed UN partition, the Arab states invaded, and the 1948–67 boundaries were decided by the ensuing War of Liberation. Until the 1967 war, while there were differences of opinion on tactics and on the ways toward peace and deterrence, the major questions of historic rights, defensible borders, and the proportions of Arabs and Jews in the population were not really on the Israeli political agenda. Whatever the ideologies or hopes, in practice the borders were taken as given. The new borders of 1967 reopened the scope of available aims and options, raising anew many basic questions of the aims and character of the state and its borders and relations with the Arab countries.

From 1967 on, an inconclusive and frustrating internal debate has gone on. Until Sadat's visit to Jerusalem in 1977, Israelis debated the future borders among themselves. There was a very strong national consensus on a united Jerusalem as the capital of Israel, and on the need for long-term demilitarization of the West Bank, Sinai, and the Golan Heights. The creation of an independent Palestinian state in Judea and Samaria was widely opposed. It was feared that such a state would be irredentist, and could allow the positioning of threatening forces along the narrow pre-1967 borders. Further, it would not help Palestinians to return to their former homes in Israel. One form of proposed defensive settlement was the Allon plan, under which Israeli settlements and forces along the Jordan would provide a guarantee of demilitarization. This was, in fact, close to the pattern of Israeli settlement between 1967 and 1977.* In 1978 the Israeli-Egyptian peace agreement provided for autonomy of the West Bank Arabs in internal government for five years, within the Israeli security and economic system. At the end of that period, a permanent arrangement would be decided.

The issue of the borders is more complex and more deeply felt, and the differences are harder to bridge than would be the case if the questions were only those of defense needs or of compromises in the process of peace negotiations. Small groups represented the extreme views—those who would settle, by independent action, even without government approval, as a God-given right; and those who would withdraw unilaterally, without any Arab agreement or guarantees, as an Israeli initiative which could possibly lead to reciprocal Arab sentiment for peace.[45]

The desire that Judea and Samaria be part of Israel is strongly ideological. As part of the land of the fathers, they were included in the biblical promise of God to Abraham; and in modern times, they were included in the original Mandate as part of the promised national home, in which the right to settle applies as well as it does within the pre-1967 borders. Considerations in favor of eventual withdrawal involve not only prospects for peace but also the possible influence of a large Arab population on the character of the state. Since 1967 Jewish labor has shifted increasingly away from manual tasks, as tens of thousands of Arabs from the West Bank and the Gaza Strip joined the Israeli

---

* See Figure 4.1. Another very interesting idea was that of a "condominium" on the West Bank with Jordan, in which the residents could choose to be citizens of either Israel or Jordan, with full voting rights, etc., in the nationality of their choice. The authority of Israel and Jordan would be divided by function, not by territory, in the West Bank.

work force. A permanent incorporation, or an ill-conceived peace arrangement could lose for Israel either its unique Jewish quality, through a possible
Arab majority, or its democratic social character, if an attempt were made to
preserve the predominance of the Jewish population.

Views on these issues are far from congruent with party structure. The
greatest diversity is found within Labor; but even within Herut, particularly
among the leaders, there are those who would abandon ideological rigidity in
the face of pragmatic negotiating possibilities. Herut and the factions of Mafdal which became predominant in 1977 have strong ideological commitments
to the settlement and incorporation of Judea and Samaria. Mapam, which
had in the Mandate favored a binational state, is strongly for withdrawal,
mainly but not only on social grounds. The Liberal Party has moved closer to
Herut as a result of being its partner since 1965, but many Liberals do not have
a strong ideological commitment to keeping the West Bank.

Within the Labor Party and each of its component groups, there is no clear
right-left split on this question. For example, the former members of Ahdut
Ha'Avoda, generally more socialist than those of Mapai, take a harder line on
settlement. The differences of Labor and Herut also exemplify their political
cultures—Labor favoring a pragmatic step-by-step approach with modification along the way, and Herut favoring a comprehensive overall solution.

The specifics of the debate revealed underlying beliefs. Many people fear
the impact on the society due to demographic change, while others are greatly
concerned with the territorial aspects of Zionist beliefs. The most common
feeling is sorrow at an inevitable clash rather than enmity, of optimism or
pessimism rather than rancour. To those born in the country, the Arab's feeling that this was his home was understandable. Yet in comparison with the
suffering of the Jews and the vast other opportunities and resources of the
Arabs, the greater evil would be to deny to the Jews their own country with
secure borders, adding "with full rights there for non-Jews." Fear and hatred
of the Arabs were strongest among those who had suffered directly in Arab
countries. But even for the Israeli-born, there were memories of recent wars
and of the Holocaust.

The debate also shows the tendency of Israelis to project their own feelings
and way of thinking. The more pessimistic took the *amana*, or Covenant of
the Palestine Liberation Organization, with its aim of eliminating the state of
Israel as an expression of the long-run goal of the Arab states, with the PLO as
their agent or pawn. In this view, intermediate agreements and even peace
treaties can only be tactical Arab moves which do not renounce the long-
range aim of the end of Israel. In such a context, defense needs are much more
important than peace agreements, if the choice needs to be made.

In any case, there is the more remote possibility that a long period of
security or deterrence of war could lead to a change in the overall Arab aim.
Against this hope, there appears the increasing difficulty of deterrence, given
growing Arab resources and Arab war aims, which may not demand exten-

sive tactical success and which are asymmetric with those of Israel. Most Arab states seek an end to the state of Israel, and Israel seeks a viable defense which is not too costly in lives. For there is also asymmetry in attitudes to the deaths of soldiers. As one Egyptian said, "Man as a human being has not yet acquired that degree of importance for us. I was very shocked to see on TV that when prisoners of the October war were exchanged...Golda Meir and Moshe Dayan went to the airport to greet the Israeli prisoners...."[46] The more optimistic believe that eventually an important portion of the heterogeneous groups making up Arab politics will accept Israel's existence and that, as the Camp David agreements indicate, real progress is possible.

Present-day Zionism endorses seeking an accord with the Arabs, but one which ensures the security of a sovereign state having a Jewish majority. Continued tension or, on the other hand, unwise arrangements could impair the quality of the society—which is seen as the state's *raison d'être* as well as its source of security.

Ideals and Reality

Hopes for the future combining national and social dreams developed from the meeting of the social conditions and religious traditions of the 19th century Diaspora with the revolutionary currents of Eastern Europe and the spirit of the Enlightenment and Western liberalism. This meeting of beliefs and needs led to imaginative experimentation, to a symbiosis of ideology and organization, and to mobilization for great efforts. In the pluralist Yishuv society, volunteer enclaves permitted intense ideological rivalry and diversity, as well as a way of life in which belief was an integral part. The integration of belief into daily life which characterized the social religions in the Yishuv had also been a hallmark of religious Judaism in the Diaspora.

Well before independence, the political system was highly developed, rich in ideas, experience, and institutions. By the time independence was achieved, however, the close interdependence and interaction of ideals and reality characteristic of the early days had markedly diminished. Rigidities set in; experimental and pioneering roles and symbols merged with institutional interests and began to serve them. Pragmatism in decision and action increased, intellectual and ideological development slowed, and the beliefs and ways of life to which the different movements aspired were challenged with increasing severity.

In most party or institutional struggles, it is now almost impossible to unravel the linkages of interests, group or bureaucratic politics, personality, and beliefs. For decades, almost all of the debates concerning ongoing policies and organization were couched in ideological terms, while against this rhetoric were counterposed the practical questions of "will it work" and "what are the political implications." But the bureaucratic culture is not the main point in considering the role of beliefs in the Yishuv. If a hierarchical system gave importance to bureaucratic politics and to patron-client relations in the Labor movement, many other parties and movements also had access to the voters, even though Labor's resources were much greater. The culture, brought from the Diaspora and developed in the Yishuv, produced a functioning democracy through its concepts of the legitimacy of political opposition and procedural norms and freedom of expression. It was the belief in a future better society and the symbolic impact of actual settlement which gave Labor the appeal beyond its own members and the broad support needed to win the lead; and it was the ideas, interacting with the realities, which led to the initial social innovations.

Independence brought with it wars, the mass immigration of refugees, and the urgent need for rapid economic development and for national social services. In the new and rapidly changing environment, institutions which had grown to meet the needs and beliefs of former times were often inadequate, and the society reflected, to a diminishing degree, the ideals through which they had been conceived.

Independence did not mean the achievement of the ideal national home, or even of economic independence or physical security. What it did provide was the freedom to continue the struggle, under the advantages—and the responsibilities—of independent, legitimate authority. The chapters which follow study this endeavor.

CHAPTER 2

The Search for a Constitution

THE CONSTITUTION of Israel is not a written document endowed with superiority over ordinary legislation. But constitutionalism is sufficiently vital that democratic procedures are maintained while the country is still at war, and there is sensitivity to individual rights and respect for due process of law. The absence of a written constitution is not, however, mainly due to preoccupation with physical and economic survival. It is rather an indication of major differences that are not yet resolved, and of impediments to effective government which have not yet been overcome.

In a sense, a search is progressing on two levels. There is a desire to make government more effective in preserving individual rights and in ensuring fair political competition among representatives of many values and interests. On a larger scale, the search is for improved ways to bridge the major ideological differences which remain. Notable among these is the question of whether the state should be completely secular or partially religious—a division that has been resolved temporarily by postponing attempts to force a decision. Another important axis of division is over the role of borders and territory in the concept of the state, a question in whose resolution Israel itself has only limited autonomy. Third, not easily visible or sensed, is the continual

This chapter was written jointly by the author with Eliahu Salpeter and Allan E. Shapiro.

53

devolvement of new questions of how class, regional, and cultural interests should be represented, in view of the future development of the society and the economy.

In this chapter we examine the roles and relations of the principal institutions of government, locating the sources of authority, and the extent and nature of the separation of powers and of the provisions for the preservation of individual and minority rights. The roles of the several branches of government, and particularly those of the judiciary, show the sources of the strengths and limits of constitutionalism. Freedom of the press and of access to information are discussed in some detail because of the central role of the media in Israeli politics and government. Finally, we consider the need for more explicit rules and what the beneifts of a written constitution might be.

The Meaning of Independence

The problems of writing a constitution were first seen in the ways in which the challenges to setting up a government were met. In November 1947, the United Nations General Assembly voted to establish two independent states, one Jewish and one Arab. The date set for the end of the Mandate was May 15, 1948. From the beginning of 1948, as the British forces began to evacuate, attacks by Arab irregular forces from surrounding countries mounted. The provisional government of the Yishuv decided to declare the independence of the state, despite the imminent invasions of regular forces of the Arab countries and the probability that Britain and other powers might intervene on the side of Jordan.

It was necessary to adapt institutions and to create new ones overnight capable of solving pressing and ongoing problems. Sovereignty posed questions of legitimacy within the international order, and of internal legitimacy in setting up, in a voluntary pluralistic society, a legitimate government with the coercive, monolithic power of the state. In a continuing defense emergency and with the comprehensive scope of a centralized government, there is a constant challenge to provide for political competition, ensure a free press, and safeguard the individual rights of members of both non-Jewish minorities and citizens in general.

In contrast to the achievement of national independence in other dependent territories in the postwar era, the creation of the state of Israel constituted a devolution of power rather than a national revolution. Independence accomplished neither social upheaval nor a redistribution of political power within the indigenous Jewish community. It did not elevate a rising class or party to a position of dominance. It did not signify the victory of a political or social doctrine other than the Zionist ideal of a Jewish nation in the ancestral homeland, although many parties, of course, hoped that eventually their views would prevail. In the aftermath of the Jewish disaster in Europe, the termination of the Mandatory restrictions on immigration and land acquisition became a national imperative. The competitive and exclusive national claims of the Arabs, inside Palestine and beyond its borders, coupled with the abdication of responsibility by the Mandatory power, made political independence an act of national self-preservation. Hence the challenges of setting up a government derived from the fact of independence itself rather than from the need to confirm a new order within the community.

The question of legitimacy was central to the Zionist movement from its inception, and a legally recognized national home for the Jewish people was its declared objective. The issuance of the Balfour Declaration, its validation by the League of Nations, and its incorporation in the Mandate constituted the birth certificate of the political institutions of the Yishuv.* Zionist opposition to the policy of the White Paper of 1939, which prohibited Jewish immigration and land acquisition, for all the urgency it acquired from the Nazi Holocaust and the displacement of persons after the war, was essentially a demand for the fulfillment of a broken promise, a demand that a binding international contract for a legally recognized national home be honored and observed.

On May 14, 1948, Ben Gurion read out the Declaration of the Establishment of the State in the old Tel Aviv Museum (see Appendix A). The Declaration represented the common denominator of the goals and beliefs of the organized political system of the Yishuv—of Labor, the religious parties, the Progressives, and the General Zionists. It also complied with the terms of the United Nations Partition Resolution, which was a critical link in the chain of contractual obligations giving the new state its legitimacy in the international community.

The Declaration provided for the establishment of basic democratic rights. First and foremost, it guaranteed the rights of individuals and of religious and ethnic groups, allowing for freedom of conscience and religion. All of the exiles were allowed to return. Peace and cooperation with the Arab countries and adherence to the principles of the Charter of the United Nations were declared goals of the new state. Following the provisions of the partition decision, a Constituent Assembly was to be elected to frame a written constitution. In terms of political values, individual rights and constitutionalism were linked at the outset with the legitimacy of independence itself. This

---

* Issued in 1971 by the British government, it stated:

"His Majesty's Government view with favour the establishment in Palestine of a national home for the Jewish people and will use their best endeavours to facilitate the achievement of this object, it being clearly understood that nothing shall be done which may prejudice the civil and religious rights of existing non-Jewish communities in Palestine or the rights and political status enjoyed by Jews in any other country."

For the historical background, see Leonard Stein, *The Balfour Declaration*, New York, Simon and Schuster, 1961.

broad statement of individual rights, while not having the force of law, served as a general guide to future thought and action.

The Consent of the Governed

As in all democratic polities, in Israel the legitimacy of national sovereignty has meant a government based on the consent of the governed. A common denominator was needed that could serve as a basis of unity for the many ideological, political, and religious factions of the Jewish community, which at the same time would create a government capable of decisive action. The Declaration of Independence represented a minimal national consensus. Much was left unsaid, and there was a deliberate use of general language, as in reliance on "the Rock of Israel" rather than on God. The religious party members wanted the Declaration to express "trust in God," while Marxist socialists wanted no reference to a deity. The compromise was to say "with trust in the Rock of Israel." * Thus each party was free to interpret the document according to its own doctrines, setting a pattern of pluralism.

The acceptance of the authority of the Provisional State Council was based on its having been elected through the party system of the Yishuv—voluntary, ideological, and pluralist. In the state the pattern of universal suffrage and direct elections continued, along with nomination and representation through the organized parties. Wide basic agreement on the need for a parliamentary democracy and decades of experience with it did not mean a consensus on a model in which a ruling majority and a loyal opposition would alternate in power. At the time of the Declaration of Independence, Mapai had been the dominant party for sixteen years; but this had been accomplished by ruling through a coalition and not through a majority.**

A basic political assumption was that no "constructive" interest could be adversely affected without its consent in a matter which that interest considered to be of vital national importance. A legitimate government, therefore, would be one in which all legitimate interests were represented, or at the very least consulted. During the First Knesset, this concept included all parties except Herut and the Communitsts. Not only the arithmetic of

---

* For Ben Gurion's account, see David Ben Gurion, *Israel: A Personal History*, London, New English Library, 1972.

** In eighteen coalition Cabinets between 1948 and 1976, the most consistent partner with Labor was the Religious bloc. Nearly all coalitions, however, have been larger than needed for a mere majority.[1] This has afforded a comfortable Knesset voting majority, greater influence on committees, and increased legitimacy. With a broader coalition, Labor could balance contending forces and have the support on economic and social questions of the Religious bloc in return for maintenance of the *status quo*, while ensuring against possible threats of defection from the Alignment—as by Mapam or ex-Rafi Labor members (a cogent motive in the 1974-77 Rabin Cabinet when the Labor Party institutions abnegated much of their traditional role as a "supreme court" which decides internal party differences).[2] (See Appendix C).

multiparty government but a more fundamental intuitive sense of legitimacy gave substance to coalition building and coalition decision making.

The system could perhaps be accurately described not as coalition government, but as party federalism, with each faction enjoying limited sovereignty in its area of responsibility. Coalition agreements became treaties or covenants between autonomous centers of power rather than programs of action. Parliamentary approval of a government represented collective acquiescence to an agreed-upon division of functions. Consistent with this anti-majoritarian philosophy, as well as with a desire to enhance authority, Labor Party leaders have often affirmed that even if their party should achieve a parliamentary majority, they would form a coalition government.[1,2] Indeed, this has been the case in many public institutions in which the Labor Party has achieved an absolute majority.

Aside from the legal system and the pattern of primacy of the executive left by the colonial administration, the state began with the voluntary organizations and the social and political modes of the Zionist movement abroad and in the Yishuv. Needed unity was gained through the strength of the national symbols and by a political pluralism in which the various movements could ensure that their viewpoints would survive. The system included elections by proportional representation and the allocation of tasks and jobs according to relative party strength (the "party key"), determined by the votes in elections to the Zionist Congresses. Parties were allocated spheres of influence, and mutual agreements were made. A prominent example is the agreement between Mapai and the Aguda religious leaders to maintain the *status quo* in the relations of government and religion, which was to predetermine much of the political history of the state.*

The pluralist price of legitimacy prevented agreement on the drafting of a written constitution. The Constituent Assembly, known as the First Knesset, met from 1949 until 1951. Failing to agree to enact a written constitution, it began to function as the parliament, as subsequent Knessets have done ever since. The idea of a written constitution was not rejected, but the necessary general consensus was lacking on basic questions, such as the roles of religion and the state. In addition, there was a general wariness of upsetting sensitive power relations. The Legislative and Judicial Committee of the Knesset was instructed, by a resolution in 1950, to prepare a draft constitution and to bring each chapter for decision in the Knesset plenum. The chapters together would then form a written constitution. All of the Basic Laws passed by 1977, however, can be amended, as any other law, by a majority of members voting, except for Section 4 of the *Basic Law: The Knesset*, under which the

* The agreement was expressed in a letter sent by Ben Gurion in 1947 in his capacity as Chairman of the Jewish Agency Executive to Rabbi J. L. Maimon, leader of the ultra-orthodox Aguda, promising that the "status quo" would be maintained by a future government. He thus assured Aguda support for the new state. The text of the letter is given in Appendix A, translated by David Sommer from the original in the Zionist Archives (S/25/1446).

election system can be changed only by a majority of all of the 120 Knesset votes. The sections which prohibit the use of emergency regulations to change the election laws require 80 votes. These majorities are needed at every plenary voting stage, or "reading."

Aside from the immediate political arrangements of Mapai and the Religious bloc, the inability to reach a decision on a constitution came from a fundamental aspect of Israel parliamentary democracy: the system of concurrent centers of authority and the diffused veto power this implies as the operative constitutional resolution of the problem of pluralism. The result of this system was to institutionalize the process of avoiding decisions on basic matters on which consensus could not yet be reached.

The formal organization of the government, in broad outline, did not change during the first three decades of the state. Its principal institutions include: the Knesset or sovereign legislature, elected approximately every four years by proportional representation, the whole country being one constituency. Voters choose one of many party lists. The resulting proportion of the votes determines who the 120 Knesset members will be; a Cabinet, or governing executive, responsible to the Knesset and largely composed of Knesset members, although only the Prime Minister, by law, needs to be a M.K.;[3] a Supreme Court and subordinate courts, constituting an independent judiciary, but without formal provision for judicial review of legislation; and a President, whose duties are largely representative and ceremonial but who has a role in the process of forming new governments.

The Capacity to Govern

The capabilities of the new institutions were immediately challenged by the War of Independence, as Jordan, Egypt, Syria, Lebanon, and Iraq attacked; by the massive influx of immigrants which followed this attack; and by inadequate agricultural and industrial production and employment opportunities.

The government now had the coercive powers of a sovereign state, but legitimacy required the rule of law, in addition to representation of individuals and factions. The vitality of the law was a central aspect of both the Jewish and the British political histories and cultures. In the Law and Administration Ordinance passed by the Provisional Council, the laws and authorities of the Mandate period were continued in the state until new legislation should be passed to replace them. The temporary government assumed the authority of the British sovereign and the High Commissioner, and was empowered to delegate authority to its members and to act as the "Executive Committee" of the state.

While the departure of the Mandatory government left many of the administrative services in disarray, there remained as an imposing legacy a functioning legal system to which Israel owes its common-law tradition.[4]

Although based on British law, the legal system also contains elements of Turkish law and of the Ottoman *millet* system, in which each of the various Moslem, Christian and Jewish groups had autonomy over a broad range of religious, personal, and family law. The authority of these groups in areas where religious codes apply received the backing of the authority of the state. The Mandate also left strong central supervision and control, which led to weak and dependent patterns of local government. In the Colonial Office tradition, there was a strong primacy of the executive.

Many of the particularist and voluntary institutions of the Yishuv became part of the state machinery and were eventually largely depoliticized. Defense was nationalized soon after the state began, as was education in 1953. In contrast, by 1977 there had been no final decision on the nationalization of health services or pensions. The rapidly expanding government bureaucracy was staffed at the start by party or personal loyalists. As in the Yishuv, separate parties were allocated spheres of influence, which were partially delimited (although there was to be considerable duplication of function) by ministries. Mapai (and later Labor) retained the key areas of defense, foreign affairs, finance, education, and agriculture, which represented the largest part of the budget. Despite a considerable decrease in politicization and the growth of professional criteria, in many ways the administration remains more a federation of separate bureaucracies than a unified system. (Details of the formal organization of government are shown in Appendix E.)

Elections and the Parliamentary System

Universal suffrage, with periodic national elections of a sovereign Knesset, or unicameral parliament, was embodied in legislation by the First Knesset.* Voters choose between national party lists, on which the candidates are listed in order of priority decided by internal party procedures. To win one seat, a party needs at least 1 percent of the vote. The 120 Knesset seats are distributed in proportion to the national vote. Surplus votes, that is, those insufficient to give each party (with at least one seat) an additional seat, are allocated in proportion to the number of first-round ballots received by each party, in a procedure which tends to work against the smaller parties. No one party or preelection alignment has ever won a majority. Although Mapai or the Labor Alignment consistently gained a large plurality until 1977, the result has been coalition government in which the leading party has had the authority to govern through the principle of collective Cabinet responsibility even though

* All citizens become eligible to vote at eighteen years of age and can be elected at 21 years of age. Members of the Knesset have legal immunity, and convicts or the mentally ill can vote or hold office. Among those excluded as candidates are civil servants, judges or military officers who have not resigned at least 100 days before the election, and practicing clergy. Voting participation is high (78.6 percent of those eligible in 1973).

no party had a majority in the Knesset. The many lists on the ballot represent nearly all shades of beliefs and opinions. A large shift in voting is needed to change the dominant minority party or even to make a major change in its coalition partners and thus in national policy. Marked changes due to elections occurred only in 1951, 1955, and 1977.[5]* (Details of election results and Cabinet coalitions are shown in Appendixes B and C.)

The system of coalition government challenges participatory democracy and constituency representation. The bargaining process by which coalition agreements are made supersedes the platforms offered the voters by the several parties. In this way voters are at least once removed from the choice between platforms, as they are from the nomination of candidates. Indeed, a very critical feature is the closed internal procedure by which parties make up their lists of candidates. In 1977, a very modest increase in the openness of party nominations occurred, influenced, perhaps, by the Peres-Rabin contest in the Labor Party, and by the open nationwide primary of the Democratic Movement for Change.

The closed nominating process leads to the domination of the Knesset delegation by party leadership, limits individual entry and political competition, and is a principal source of a hierarchical and dependent political culture. Relations are more complex than simple dependency, however, and are not constant over time. Interest and associative cultural and religious groups are represented in the Knesset delegation, and there is thus an internal legitimacy to party lists. Candidates are often "pushed up" from below, or selected by constituencies, as in the case of leaders of settlement movements.[6] But on balance, selection is made by the party leaders who control the nominating process. The list-voting election system provides the framework, but it is mainly the nominating process which has kept the system closed. Although parties receive support and election expenses from the national budget, there is no legislation regarding internal party election or nomination procedures.

From the beginning, Ben Gurion tried to change the election system to one of constituency representation. Among justifications advanced were a search for authority and a clear mandate to go along with the responsibility of the dominant party; the image, probably idealized, of the relations which Israelis believe to exist in Britain between the majority and a loyal opposition, and between members and their constituencies; and that constituency representation would increase the responsibility of the candidates to the voters and attract more outstanding people as candidates.

---

* In 1951, dissatisfaction with the economic-austerity program led to a swing to the right. The General Zionists went from 5.8 percent (1949) to 16.7 percent (1951) and joined the Cabinet in 1952. In 1955 defense concerns brought left-wing activists (Ahdut Ha'Avoda) into the Cabinet, as the right-wing-activist Herut rose from 6.7 percent (1951) to 12.5 percent (1955). In 1977 Labor fell from power, the Labor Alignment polling less than 28 percent, compared 35.4 percent for the Likud.

The *Basic Law: The Knesset*, codifying proportional representation, was not passed until 1958, with most of the delay due to Ben Gurion's hope that election reform could be achieved. Dissenting from this reform were other parties fearing majority tyranny, or "majorization" by Mapai, the decline of their own representation, or possible political demise. Elimination of proportional representation was seen as threatening the implicit agreement on pluralist participation from which much of the state's legitimacy was derived. On theoretical grounds it was argued that the small size of the country as well as the importance of sectoral and ideological representation made the old system best. The system was also favored because it avoided the need by individual candidates for campaign financial resources which is so characteristic of British and American politics, and because the quality of most local government did not inspire confidence in regional elections.

After 1968, the movement to change the electoral system was revived again and gained ground. Support for reform was promised to Rafi in the agreement under which Rafi joined with Mapai and Ahdut Ha'Avoda to form the Labor Party in 1968. Action was postponed until after the 1969 elections because of the Ahdut Ha'Avoda–Mapai agreement which formed the 1965 election alignment. In 1972, a private bill to change the system, calling for thirty members to be elected by national list voting and ninety from regions, was introduced successfully (by sixty-two votes). By 1977, however, it was still held up in committee. The Liberal Party went from support to vacillation, and Herut and the religious parties remained opposed. Yet the tendency toward change grew stronger.* There was broad support in the intellectual community. Defense and economic pressures increased the desire and necessity for a more responsible government, and there was more confidence outside of the Labor Alignment that the danger of complete Labor domination or majorization had diminished. Regional elections constituted a main plank of the Democratic Movement for Change in the 1977 elections, one on which the diverse elements of the party could agree.

The Roles of the Knesset

The Knesset, as the supreme elected political authority, in turn delegates political power to the Cabinet, contingent on Knesset support. The Cabinet, as the executive, is responsible to the Knesset. It needs Knesset approval

---

*Municipal election reform, voted in 1976, was also on the initiative of ex-Rafi members. A mayor is elected directly by gaining 40 percent of the vote in one or two election rounds, and serves for four years regardless of the composition of the elected city council. The law confirmed a marked informal trend in which many local elections were determined by the personalities of candidates, regardless of national party trends. Before the new law, direct elections were held for municipal councils, which then convened to elect one of their number as mayor, to serve until the next elections, or as long as the council supported him or her.

before taking office and continued Knesset confidence to remain in office. As in the British Cabinet system, the Cabinet is a part of the Knesset.
The Knesset has several possible roles:

To act as an electoral college, choosing the Cabinet and Prime Minister
To provide a forum, national conscience, or sounding board expressing the broad spectrum of opinion, feelings, and interests
To develop policies and detailed legislation for their execution
To control and supervise the executive

As an electoral college, the Knesset's role is mainly formal. Rarely does a politician begin as a backbencher, make his name as a parliamentarian, and thus enter the inner group of leaders. In the nomination-election system, Knesset membership and activity *per se* are less important than an individual's external group support or his relation to the leaders of his party. The Prime Minister, on assuming office, takes an oath to carry out the decisions of the Knesset, and the Cabinet is responsible to it; yet Israelis often see the Knesset as merely carrying out the decisions of the Prime Minister and the Cabinet. Knesset members can feel like Rosencrantz and Guildenstern in *Hamlet*—on the sidelines in a large anteroom outside the court, seeing the entrances and exits, hearing the rumors and decisions, occasionally playing their own roles, but often feeling more like instruments directed by someone else.[7]

A visitor to the Knesset restaurant, seeing there most of the country's better-known political leaders, could believe that he was observing the very center of things. Yet, as an institution, the Knesset has had a minor role in most ongoing issues. If individual members are politically powerful, it is not usually as a result of their Knesset membership. The proportional-representation election system, collective Cabinet responsibility, and majority rule in party caucuses have made very rare the occasions on which an individual member from a large party can cast his vote purely as his own personal decision.

As a public forum, the Knesset is much more successful. It allows public self-expression and possibilities for political advancement by occasional speaking opportunities and committee work. Members from small parties, indeed, have more opportunities to speak than do backbenchers from the large delegations. The smaller groups can stay closer to the specific ideologies of their constituencies, and are heard on moral or general issues beyond the proportionate strength of their numbers. But the semicircular seating arrangements, formal time-limited speaking from a rostrum, and the allocation of individual speaking roles by the party caucus remove most of the interest and spontaneity from the debates. In public attention and exposure, the Knesset is increasingly overshadowed by the press, radio and television.

The more an issue is of wide public concern or a matter of conscience, however, the more the Knesset comes into its own as a reflection of public feeling. It is often closer to the people than the small leadership group, and more sensitive to opinion. Minority parties can espouse unpopular but deserving causes for whatever reason. The Knesset may be "the last to know" of an impending event if it is a foreign crisis (as in the Sinai campaign) or "the first to know" if it involves the broad public, as on the eve of the Six Day War when the Mapai Knesset caucus gave its frank opinion to Eshkol, telling him to step down as Defense Minister. But the Knesset caucus was, in this case, more a gathering of senior party members than a Knesset function *per se*. While there has been no showdown in the Knesset chamber comparable to the attack on Chamberlain in the House of Commons in 1940, its lobbies have served as the physical locale for the stirrings of members in their party or Cabinet capacities.

In the initiation of policy, however, or in the control of the executive, the power of the Knesset is weak. The source of weakness is the dependent relation of the Knesset members to party leaders, which is strengthened by the formal relation of the Knesset to the Cabinet. Most of the bills are proposed by the government, and their general outlines are decided in the Cabinet before they go to the Knesset. Under the principle of collective responsibility, a Knesset delegation must support the decisions of the Cabinet if the ministers of that delegation are in the governing coalition. Decisions of a Knesset party caucus bind the votes of individual party members. Members can leave parties without resigning from the Knesset; but this means joining another delegation—or starting a new one.

Bills which successfully pass in the plenum on the first reading are referred to a standing committee for detailed analysis and revision. In committees, discussion and decisions are more open except on crucial bills, when the full weight of party influence may be felt. The two most important standing committees are Finance, and Foreign Affairs and Defense. Appropriation bills go to the Finance Committee, which in addition approves many executive financial decisions, such as the transfer of funds during the fiscal year from one budget heading to another; but the Economics Subcommittee of the Cabinet is the real focus of economic decisions. The Knesset Foreign Affairs and Defense Committee has no executive authority, but it is kept relatively well informed. One indication of the lack of impact of these bodies is that few changes, if any, are ever made in the proposed budget law in the period between its approval by the Cabinet and the time, some six months later, when it is finally voted into law by the Knesset; nor does the Knesset effectively block the frequent supplemental budgets or the increases in government financial obligations, beyond the budget, through such measures as underwriting of loans by the government.

A further reason for the weakness of the Knesset is that it simply lacks facilities for knowledge and analysis which in any way compare with those of the executive. Committees usually have staffs of only one or at most two professionals and have seldom, if ever, commissioned serious works of policy analysis. Individual M.K.s have no staffs of their own, and in 1976 it was considered a step forward when one part-time secretary was assigned to every two Labor Party Knesset members. Knesset committes thus cannot match the much more extensive staff work and data at the disposal of the individual ministries, and have to rely on the personal knowledge and intuition of their members.

Still, in the post-1974 Eighth Knesset there were signs of growing independence and of more individual action by M.K.s. Several young members began to act as one- or two-man investigating committees into public scandals or crimes. Within delegations, members were less amenable to party discipline, and the Finance Committee accepted Ministry of Finance dictates far less readily than in the past. It was a period when Labor Party internal activity and cohesion were at a nadir and party influence was less helpful to the Cabinet in handling the Knesset delegation. The party leaders had neither the personal authority of Ben Gurion and Golda Meir nor the organizational influence of Pinhas Sapir. Above all, it was a time when the big issues of national boundaries and settlement policies cut across party lines and divided the Cabinet. Nonetheless, the underlying nature of the Knesset dependency on the Cabinet had not changed.

The Cabinet as the Executive Committee

The locus of formal decision making and the "Executive Committee" of government is found in the Cabinet, called in Hebrew *Hamemshala,* or "the Government." All of the political heads of ministries are members, and there are usually one or more ministers without portfolio. There is no formal limit to the number of members; in 1948 there were twelve, and in 1976, twenty-one. The influence of ministers depends as much on factors outside the Cabinet as on internal relationships and personal qualities, since most ministers are Cabinet members because they are leaders in parties or factions.

Members are selected and approved by their parties, often by a vote or at least with the approval of a senior party council; and their continued service in the government depends upon retaining the confidence of their party. In his or her own party, the Prime Minister has a considerable though not absolute influence on the initial choice of Cabinet colleagues, and, by custom, a power of veto. At one and the same time, a Cabinet member can head a large and complex ministry, be a candidate to head a more important ministry in competition with his colleagues, a loyal follower (or strong opponent) of the Prime Minister, and a colleague of other members in deliberations on any and all domestic and foreign problems. He is usually a member of the Knesset, but he may not be a member of a Knesset committee. While increasing the public responsiveness of ministers, these multiple roles reduce their effectiveness as executives.

The Cabinet has great authority, but its effectiveness in developing and deciding on policy has serious fundamental and technical limits. Representing a coalition, the Cabinet seeks a common denominator, while a dominant minority party, on all but the most crucial issues, takes on the authority of a majority. Labor's actual authority was usually much more effective than its proportion of offices or Knesset seats would indicate. The Prime Minister's Office, Defense, Finance, Education, and Agriculture were (until 1977) Mapai or Labor ministries, except for Defense under Rafi in 1967–68.

In parallel, an absolute Labor Alignment majority in the Histadrut gave it control of the material and organizational support and patronage of the whole complex of Histadrut economic and social institutions.

Yet Labor, as perennial Cabinet leader, itself often had serious internal divisions, especially on major international issues. In periods when the Cabinet is not dominated by an outstanding personality, as it was in Ben Gurion's time, or when the party in power has not resolved its main internal personal and policy differences, as was the case in the Rabin government in 1976–77, the Cabinet becomes "representative." Lacking will and resolve, it assumes the character of a senate or upper house of the legislature rather than that of an effective executive committee.

A further outcome of coalition government is that smaller coalition parties often enjoy considerable autonomy in their own ministries. These ministries can become fiefdoms which resist attempts to achieve a coordinated policy. While nowhere in the world are campaign promises meticulously honored, in Israel this malpractice is aggravated by coalition agreements.

The elections deal out the cards to the parties, giving each a proportion of the Knesset seats and initial bargaining resources. Negotiations for the formation of the government then determine the size of the Cabinet and the allocation of membership in the Cabinet and ministries to parties and individuals. Personal or party problems can be solved by the appointment of ministers without portfolio, and occasionally at this stage ministries are created or combined as part of the bargain. General policies are agreed upon for the next four years, and limits may be placed on the autonomy of the government on specific questions—which, it is agreed, will not be decided without a new election or some specified procedure. One example was the entry of the National Religious Party into the government in 1974, with an agreement that there would be no commitment on withdrawal from Judea and Samaria without new elections or NRP approval, and to appoint a committee to reinvestigate legislation defining Jewish nationality as it affects registration and the "Law of Return." On many points, such agreements may be far from the platforms on which the parties ran; yet they bind the general policies of the governments. In this way, the coalition process increases the distance between the platforms presented by the parties in order to get the vote and the program actually carried out.

Another fundamental problem is that the individual roles and responsibilities of parties in the coalition are often unclear because of the collective
responsibility of the Cabinet. In order for there to be effective government at
all, a large minority party assumes authority by means of collective responsibility and party discipline in the Knesset and by having a majority in the
Cabinet. Under the principle of collective responsibility, the entire Cabinet
stands behind a majority decision of its members and is politically responsible
as a whole to the Knesset for any of the acts of government and their consequences. This principle was developed and enforced by Mapai and finally
enacted into law in 1958 in the *Basic Law: The Government*. In Ben Gurion's
time, the enforcement of collective responsibility was the main focus of
Cabinet crises leading to new Cabinets. (See the summary of Cabinet crises in
Appendix D.) Further power came from the control by the dominant party
over resources—through the Ministry of Finance, the budget, the capital
market, government corporations, and the Mapai (and later the Labor Alignment) majority in the Histadrut. Because of the ideological differences between them, the other parties in the Knesset only once united to outvote Labor
on a government bill, although on the issues of the future boundaries and the
forms of peace negotiations an entirely new alignment is possible.*

The collective responsibility of the Cabinet also obscures the responsibility of the individual minister to the Knesset. In the law, the minister has to
answer formal questions and also appear before the appropriate Knesset committees. Thus both individual and collective responsibility exist side by side.
While in theory "the . . . individual responsibility of a minister for operations
of his ministry is a part of our constitutional conception of the relations between the executive and the legislature,"[8] in practice the only formal sanction
possessed by the Knesset is a vote of no confidence in the Cabinet as a whole.
There are many conceivable political sanctions against a minister by colleagues in his party or the Cabinet; but when the Cabinet stands by a minister
and exercises collective responsibility, there is no provision for formal action
against such an individual.

Other procedural and technical limits to Cabinet effectiveness derive from
its large membership, the shortage of time available to deal adequately with
most questions, and the priority given questions of defense and foreign affairs. In approving any strategic or major policy decision, the Cabinet has
neither the staff nor the resources needed for policy analyses. The Cabinet can
be asked to decide on actions on which consensus has already been reached in
smaller governing groups, or which may even be already under way. The
Sinai campaign of 1956 was revealed to the Cabinet only when it was about to
begin, an improbable situation today; yet the Cabinet was the focus of deci-

---

* In 1951, the Cabinet resigned when the Religious bloc (together with the General Zionists)
voted in the Knesset against the government's proposal for the way in which religious instruction
was to be presented in the immigrant camps. Ben Gurion accepted this as a vote of no confidence
and the Cabinet's term ended.

sion on the eve of the 1967 Six Day War. In defense matters the Knesset Foreign Affairs and Defense Committee often has more current information, while the Cabinet is far too large a group to act as an executive committee for ongoing questions of defense and foreign affairs.

The Cabinet is less often the leader of the system than it is the outcome of the workings of the political system—the resolution of opposing forces which has taken place within the parties and through the elections.

With all of these limitations, the Cabinet as a whole is the center of authority and responsibility. When a major disagreement cannot be bridged within it, the need arises for a new alignment or definition of power relations within the Cabinet, a new party composition, or new elections.

The Prime Minister and the Cabinet

Interaction of forces and the resolution of problems within the Cabinet depend on the situation, the coalition, and, above all, the Prime Minister. As the chosen leader of the government, the Prime Minister is, first of all, elected to the Knesset and is the leader of his party. Under the *Basic Law: The Government*, the Prime Minister is a member of the Knesset who has been asked by the President to put together a Cabinet which can receive a vote of confidence from the Knesset. The Cabinet then continues in office until the next Knesset elections, until it receives a vote of no confidence, or until it resigns.

Whether approved at the polls or coming to office between national elections, the Prime Minister, until 1977, was the candidate selected by Labor (or earlier by Mapai). Until Begin's election in 1977, no Prime Minister gained his first term as a direct result of a national election. Ben Gurion was Chairman of the Agency Executive when the state was declared in 1948 and began as Prime Minister of the provisional government. Mapai chose Sharett to succeed Ben Gurion when he retired in 1953, and returned Ben Gurion to office in 1955. Similarly, Eshkol was chosen by the party when Ben Gurion retired for the last time in 1963, as was Golda Meir when Eshkol died in office in 1969. When Mrs. Meir's Cabinet resigned in 1974, Rabin was elected by a small margin over Shimon Peres as the Labor Party's candidate in an unprecedented open vote in the Party Central Committee.

Formally, the Prime Minister is "the first among equals" and Cabinet decisions are made by majority vote. His main statutory advantages are that he can force the government to step down by resigning himself, and that he can publish documents which it would otherwise not be legal to reveal. On the other hand, he does not have the authority to disperse the Knesset, decide the timing of an election, or dismiss a minister.[9] * Even within his own party he

---

* In 1981, the *Basic Law: The Government* was amended to give the Prime Minister the authority to dismiss a minister at will.

may dismiss a minister only with party acquiescence and at the risk of a party rift; and the choice of ministers from coalition parties rests with those parties. His power is thus far more limited than that of a British Prime Minister, while his office lacks the coordinating staff of an American President. At an early turning point, Ben Gurion rejected the suggestion that the Bureau of the Budget be in his office, and it is now an important part of the Ministry of Finance.

The nature of leadership and the modes of work have been characteristically different for each incumbent and in each set of circumstances, but the most important source of power has always been political rather than statutory. To enhance their effectiveness, prime ministers have worked with small inner groups, which work out policy and decisions before the formal Cabinet meetings. These groups also arose from a desire for secrecy on security questions and for cohesiveness in discussion and decision, and from the desire of the dominant party to control Cabinet proceedings. Indeed, at every level in the political hierarchies, there are preliminary small-group caucuses before issues are brought before the formal elective bodies. In the Cabinet the roles of inner groups depend mainly on the Prime Minister and on his personal and party relations.*

Much of the character of the political system and the political culture was shaped under Ben Gurion as the political leader of the organized Yishuv and of the country over three decades. From 1946, two years before the state, and throughout all his years as Prime Minister, he held the Defense portfolio and was the architect of the defense forces, as well as civilian leader in the War of Liberation. From 1948 to 1953 and again from 1955 to 1963 he led, unchallenged, charismatically, "head and shoulders" above the rest. From 1953 to 1955 he was in attempted retirement in the Negev but in close touch with developments. Although experienced in organization and practical economics, he deliberately left party organization to the leaders of the party machine, economics to the Ministers of Finance Eliezer Kaplan and later Levi Eshkol, and concentrated almost single-mindedly on defense and foreign affairs.** In his view, "an Israeli prime minister must also be his own foreign minister."[10]

Formally respectful to the Cabinet, Ben Gurion consulted more with an inner group, which included his defense staff, close personal aides Nehemia Argov, Teddy Kollek, and Yitzhak Navon, and, in the first years, Moshe Sharett.*** But as Ben Gurion saw it, the strategic decisions were his and the

*Party based inner groups, known as *Havereinu* (our comrades), including the Secretary-General of the Histadrut, and *Sareinu* (our ministers), for many years were the Mapai forums which met regularly to develop policy before it came before the Cabinet.

**Notable exceptions were his efforts to nationalize education and to encourage integration of immigrants from many lands.

***Sharett, who had been head of the Political Department of the Agency and a leader of Mapai, was Foreign Minister under Ben Gurion from 1948 to 1953, Prime Minister from 1954 to 1955, and again Foreign Minister until ousted by Ben Gurion in 1956. From 1948 to 1953, Ben Gurion and Sharett worked in harmony, with Ben Gurion's strategic ideas dominating.

tactics were usually left to others. He would usually work out his own ideas and, if necessary, bring them to the Cabinet for approval. (See Chapter 4, "The Nation in Arms.")

When ministers are in major conflict, Cabinet meetings can become the locus of confrontation and clarification. For example, the Cabinet was the central arena when Sharett was Prime Minister (1953–55). Serving as both Prime Minister and Foreign Minister, Sharett had highly strained relations with Pinhas Lavon, who was Minister of Defense, and lacked control over defense policy. When Ben Gurion returned as Prime Minister in 1955, he and Sharett were on a collision course, opposing each other in the Cabinet and in Mapai until the party, as arbiter, agreed to Ben Gurion's demands to oust Sharett from his Cabinet post as Foreign Minister. This incident exemplifies one of Ben Gurion's main concerns—the need to secure the acceptance of collective Cabinet responsibility and loyalty.

When Ben Gurion suddenly resigned in 1963, Levi Eshkol stepped into the place of a founding father who had become the symbol of the achievement of independence, and whose personality, popular support, and party backing gave presidential stature. Eshkol came in with wide support in Mapai and an impressive record in negotiation and action as head of the Settlement Department of the Jewish Agency and as Minister of Finance. In personality and in method, however, he was more of a chairman than a leader, often seemingly indecisive and pondering. Small inner groups of party forums became the loci of decisions. After the Six Day War, when Dayan replaced Eshkol as Minister of Defense, the Cabinet and its Defense Committee became important, particularly in the "National Unity" government of 1969–70, when the Liberals and Herut were in the Cabinet.

In Golda Meir (1969–74), a more authoritative image of the Prime Minister returned. Consulting with an informal and *ad hoc* "inner circle" of advisers, Mrs. Meir firmly stated and authoritatively imposed her own views on what she held to be basic. Working through a few ministers in fields which she saw as important, she relied heavily in security questions on Moshe Dayan as Minister of Defense and on Israel Galili, Minister without Portfolio. The larger Cabinet followed her lead.

The Rabin Cabinet of 1974–1977, notable for its lack of cohesion, had the manifestations of an interregnum. Minister of Defense Shimon Peres and Rabin differed somewhat on policy and much in personality, and were rivals for leadership. In the grave economic crises following the 1973 war, the system for managing the economy, which Pinhas Sapir * had developed, was in disarray, and a new system had not yet emerged. In his first years in office, Rabin appointed several advisers who seemed initially to be intended as an Israeli version of a White House staff. These advisers, however, generally found themselves without resources and with very limited authority. It was a

* Minister of Finance, 1963–68 and 1969–74. (See Chapter 5, "The Political Economy.")

time when the fabric of the organization of the older parties was unraveling and the almost unchallenged small-group leadership ceased to function; when, after decades of stability, contests for the succession to the pioneering founders and groping for new modes took place in the public arena and no longer within the older closed party circles. The executive remained the supreme branch of government, but without cohesion, popular legitimacy, or the power to innovate. The concrete expression was the resignation of Itzhak Rabin (and thus of the Cabinet) in December 1976, which moved the 1977 elections up from November to May—the Cabinet continuing to serve as an interim government until the elections. As change seemed imminent, the courts provided more and more the image of stability and authority.

The Courts and the Constitution

Israeli law has its roots in English common law, from the Mandate, a system which has parallels in the case-law approach, to the interpretation of the Talmud. The common law is important not only in concepts of equity and procedure but also in the roles of creation and interpretation which it gives the courts, and in precedent and tradition which it affords in the absence of a written constitution.

There are three tiers in the judicial system—magistrates courts, district courts, and a Supreme Court. The district courts have unlimited jurisdiction (except that Supreme Court justices must be a part of a district-court bench when it tries capital offenses).* The Supreme Court serves as the Court of Appeals from judgments of the district courts and also as a High Court of Justice (*Beit Hadin Hagavoha Letzedek* or *Bagatz*), to which a citizen can turn as a court of the first instance for relief against the misuse of authority by a public body.[11] As a High Court of Justice, the Supreme Court decides most questions of public law. If there should be a court decision with which a majority of the Knesset disagrees, however, there is no formal barrier to new legislation to change the laws according to the Knesset's will.

Judges have permanent appointments and a retirement age of seventy. At all levels they are appointed by the President on the recommendations of a standing committee of nine, representing the Knesset, the Cabinet, the Bar Association, and the Supreme Court.[12] In the process of judicial recruitment, the Minister of Justice has played a key role, particularly as the dominant member of this committee. The selection process is designed to provide a nonpolitical judiciary.

Clearly, however, the proposal by a political leader of appointments which have considerable policy implications and political rewards can hardly be called nonpolitical. Indeed, appointments to the highest court have

---

* Continuing the Mandate tradition, there is no trial by jury. District Courts sit with one or three judges, depending on the case.

generally reflected the federative principles operative throughout Israeli political life. The justices are individuals whose views are seen to be well within the national consensus of social and political beliefs. To a great extent, appointments are "representative," although the suprapolitical image of the court prevents any strict or obvious application of the party key. A factor in the selection of Supreme Court justices may be the candidates' conception of the court as active or passive in the process of making the law and the constitution, although the attitudes of justices after their appointments are not always predictable on the basis of their past expressions.

The High Court of Justice is particularly concerned with such questions as unlawful detention, the misuse of authority by organizations performing public functions, and the limits of jurisdiction of other courts. The approach to questions of the use of authority is more like the British than the American, and the emphasis is on whether authority has been exceeded rather than whether the action involved was consistent with the attainment of the policy aims for which the authority was given. In the absence of clearly defined administrative standards, the responsiblity of the executive, in the formal expression of the courts, is to use its authority in ways which do not injure rights and to comply with the powers given to it by the legislature. Since the government is "in the Knesset" and responsible to it, the Israeli minister, like the British, is *politically* rather than judicially responsible for the "wisdom" of his administration, as long as he acts within the law—or so the court can say when it wishes to avoid an issue of political consequence.

For example, in investigating the conduct of the beginning of the 1973 Yom Kippur War, the Agranat Committee followed this distinction. It saw ministerial responsibility as a political question when an issue lies within the exclusive competence of a coordinate branch of the government (see *Jabotinsky vs. Weizmann*, 4 Psakim 399, 1951). It was thus not the proper subject of the committee's quasi-judicial role. The public did not accept this fine distinction, particularly in the case of Dayan, an authoritative Defense Minister and former Chief of Staff who was known to intervene in operational questions.

The Political Role of the Supreme Court

No institution wielding governmental authority, faced with decisions of basic importance, and constantly forced to choose between competing political values could fail to have political significance. Yet it is precisely a "nonpolitical" mystique that supplies the foundation and support for the supreme court's political importance. The court's role must be considered against the background of a somewhat fluid situation in which the search for a constitution is in midstream, in which there is an aura of the primacy of the executive, inherited from the Mandate, and in which the Knesset is legislatively supreme.

Roles have yet to be firmly worked out. The court's pronouncements on matters of fundamental importance are authoritative but not conclusive. The political role of the judiciary, in a country without a written constitution, and in which the political system in the Yishuv developed independently of the British Mandate courts, is evidence of the strength and weakness of constitutionalism in Israel's political culture. Its decisions can be reversed by the Knesset, as in the *Shalit* case (see page 79), or nullified by government action, as in the Bir-Am controversy.* But the government and the Knesset endanger their legitimacy when they do so, because of the high status of the courts and the law.

The source of the political strength that the court enjoys derives from the fact that it is perceived as both national and nonpolitical. It is a national institution in the sense that it is not constituted on the basis of sectoral representation. Like the Army, it stands above the conflicting currents of coalition politics. It institutionalizes the apolitical value of national survival. Its decisions are not the product of compromise, but of the perception of justice, not the resolution of forces, but the search for principle.

The development of the court's constitutional role has been aided by its generally low political visibility. This could reflect a lack of saliency of questions of basic rights in a society preoccupied with issues of defense and foreign relations, immigration and economic development. In the federative division of governmental authority, the court's administrative partner in the subsystem of law, the Ministry of Justice, was, until the early 1960s, assigned to a minor party (the Progressives, forerunners of the Independent Liberals), and its function was conceived as technical in nature, to be consigned to professionals with little political power, actual or potential. From the early 1960s until 1977, however, Ministers of Justice have been leading political *confrères* of the Prime Minister, in addition to being professionally prominent.

"Justiciability" and Judicial Review

The role the Supreme Court assumes is seen in the kind of cases it decides to consider as being "justiciable" and, when it decides a case, in the opinions themselves. Where the intention of the legislator has been clearly stated, it is incumbent upon the courts to follow it; but intentions are not always explicit, nor can they be in all cases. The interpretation of the courts thus makes law, and in the process the court can, at one extreme, limit itself to filling in the lacunae left by the legislator; or, at the other extreme, it can arrogate to itself the role of defining what the higher law is. That is, it can endeavor to impose

---

*Bir-Am and Ikrit are Arab villages near the Lebanese border. In the 1948 war, the area was cleared for military actions and the inhabitants were told that they could return later. This was not allowed, however, and they were given land in another location. In 1951 the Supreme Court gave a judgment that the return should be allowed "in the existing circumstance."[13] The Minister of Defense then changed these circumstances, using the Emergency Regulations to close the area and prevent return. In 1973 the appeal of residents to return was endorsed by much of Israeli public opinion, but the *status quo* remained.

its own views of what the society and polity ought to be and assume the role of constitution maker.

Direct accessibility prevents easy avoidance of jurisdiction, and the mandate of the Supreme Court is broad, to "decide in matters in which it considers it necessary to grant relief in the interests of justice and which are not within the jurisdiction of any other court or tribunal."[14] Still, it seems to have developed rules of access which allow it to work within what it sees as a national consensus, husbanding political strength by avoiding sensitive or controversial areas, and fashioning methods of institutional self-defense against the dangerously controversial issues increasingly presented to it for decision. One method has been a highly discretionary shifting of the rules of standing, which determine access to the judicial process. A strict interpretation of "standing," to include only those claiming injury as a person or as a member of a carefully defined class or group, has been used to preclude the hearing of claims of a "citizen" in the more general "public interest," and to avoid issues which could lead to a major social or political rift. Other approaches include the previously mentioned strict delineation of executive responsibility, which considers mainly whether the authority existed for the protested action, and the exclusion from judicial consideration of acts within the political discretion of a distinct branch of government rather than of legal justice.* The court is reluctant, also, to strike down subordinate legislation or to substitue its judgment for that of an executive department, even considering the weakness of parliamentary supervision, except in what it considers an extremely unreasonable procedure.**

On those questions which the court has seen as justiciable, its political involvement varies within a lower, or conservative and passive, limit and an upper, or "brinkmanship," limit. On the one hand, it has, as in the *Bergman* case,[15] arrogated to itself the right to nullify ordinary legislation contravening an "entrenched" provision of a Basic Law. Legislation as been proposed which would legitimate and formalize this judicial *coup de main*. In disallowing the election list of a party that was seen as opposing the existence of the state, the court, in the absence of statute, decided that it had jurisdiction over what is a political question.*** On the other hand, it has refused, despite explicit urg-

* See *Jabotinsky vs. Weizmann* (4 Psakim 399, 1951).

** See Justice Shamgar in *Bagatz* 156/75.

*** A 1969 law provided for financing by the government of parties in election campaigns to an amount proportional to their representation in the *outgoing* Knesset. Bergman brought suit, arguing that this was unfair discrimination and inequality, based on Section 4 of the *Basic Law: The Knesset*, which specifies "general, national, direct, equal, secret and proportional elections." Not only did this seem unequal, but the new law (1969) had been supported by less than the sixty-one required in the "entrenchment" provision of this section of the Basic Law. The court decided that the 1969 law was in violation of the provision for equality. Equality was thus defined more broadly than the concept of "one man, one vote." The court, in effect, saw equality in the election process as justiciable.

In the *Iredor case* (1965), 19 P.D. (III) 365, 387, the court accepted the disallowment of a list of candidates which included people with a stated intention of undermining the basis of the state, although there is no statutory prohibition. (See mention of the *Al Ard* cases in the later section of this chapter which discusses freedom of the press.)[16]

ing, to assume a general power of judicial review of legislation on the basis of what it conceives as values basic to a free society. This is precisely what it has often done, however, in the broad area of the review of administrative action and in legislative interpretation. Thus, in the second *Kol Ha'am* case (1953),[17] *Bergman, Iredor,* and *Shalit,* the court came close to an upper limit of deciding values on its own; whereas in the 1970s the court adopted a much more passive policy role. The possible influence of social theories espoused by individual judges can include a sensitivity to the limits of consensus and its implications for the role and power of the court.

Most Israelis would agree that, even in the nonreligious sphere, there is some form of a higher law, and that, if any one institution were to decide what this law is (in the absence of a written constitution), the one most likely to be respected would be the court. But the status of and respect for the court are maintained in large part because it is within the consensus of opinion and in many ways a reflection of it.

In Israel the limits of judicial power may be determined more by the fear of division in society than by the absence of formal legal authority. Problems of legitimacy and consensus can restrain court decisions which might split the society, just as the many "arrangements" which characterize the community can often prevent sharp confrontations, decisions, or arm's-length competition. The court most often can lead by seeming to follow, or at least to be above the political struggle, even in a period of flux when a new society is being formed. Within the modest limits which the court sets for itself of judicial decision on the higher law, there has been a consistent development of principled standards of governmental action, suprastatutory norms appealing to fundamental concepts of ordered liberty. This is the important role of the court in the search for a constitution.

The Rights of Individuals and of Minority Groups

The cultural and religious life of minority groups and the rights of individuals are, to a great extent, respected in practice, although there is not a bill of rights to constrain the lawmaker or to force the judges to weigh these fundamental questions. There are many obstacles: a defense emergency for over three decades; a large Arabic-speaking minority (about 500,000 out of 3,500,000 in 1976) whose loyalty it was natural to question in the early years of the state; an immigrant population (and therefore government officials) coming mostly from cultures and regimes in which the rights of the individual have little meaning; the ideologies and experiences of Eastern European socialist movements which provide persistent examples of closed, small-group leadership and a "tutelary" press; and a very complex relationship between religion and nationality.

The record is, nonetheless, encouraging. The gap between actual practice and the law and the cohesiveness of many groups and communities often work against the quality of life, but they also often help to preserve rights. A Western political and cultural orientation, a common-law tradition,[18] the role of the Jews in the liberal movements of the West, and the dignity of the individual in the Jewish religious experience (despite the subordination of the individual to the law)—all these, on balance, have been helpful. Yet continuing vigilance is needed. Only a few main areas are considered here to illustrate the questions: the problems of minority groups, the questions of "intermediate authorities" (as in religious law or the cooperative movements), and, at greater length, freedom of the press and expression.

The Arabs and Other Non-Jewish Minorities

The Declaration of the Establishment of the State says that the State of Israel will "ensure complete equality of social and political rights to all its inhabitants." Individuals of all races, creeds, and cultural associations are equal before the law. The government supports pluralism in the areas of religion and education.* Discrimination has occurred, however, because of the unequal impact of equal laws, the disadvantages deriving from belonging to a social minority, the suspicions or prejudices of individuals, and differences in the initial social and economic endowments of separate groups.

One of the few cases where the law actually discriminates is in requirements for acquiring citizenship. The law is designed to make it easy for Jews to immigrate and become citizens, in contrast with the former Mandate restrictions, while others go through a much more demanding process. Under the Law of Return (1950), a Jew and his or her spouse and children, whether Jewish or not, can immigrate and receive citizenship at once or become permanent residents while "opting out" of citizenship. Others are required to have been born in Israel (if the father or mother are not Israeli nationals), or to become nationalized, which requires a period of five years from arrival, some knowledge of Hebrew, and the status of permanent resident. Security checks and requirements for employment, where *bona fide*, impinge more on Arabs; and the Arabs, unlike the Jews and Druze, are not subject to the draft. The Arab and Druze minorities could not but be affected by the political changes and the ongoing war of the Arab states against Israel, or by the changes in sentiment and the relations between the state and the Arabs living in the occupied territories; nor could the ongoing emergency fail to exaggerate the suspicions of the majority.

* Under the law, Arabic constitutes an official language. It is the language of instruction in public schools attended by Arabs, and there are official Arabic translations of laws. Arabic is occasionally used in the Knesset. Facilities for the practice of Judaism, Christianity, and Mohammedanism are supported by the state.

If the Arab in Israel naturally feels an internal conflict of national loyalties, the Jew has an inner conflict between desire to have a state in which ideal equality prevails, and what is often seen as the *raison d'être* of Israel as the Jewish national home. The United Nations Resolution of 1947, indeed, called for two states—one, Israel, to be "Jewish" and the other "Arab" in their majority culture and national aims. Each was to provide for the individual and cultural rights of the minorities within its borders.

The most sensitive aspects of the rights of members of minority groups are restrictions which for many years were imposed for the purposes of security, and lack of opportunity in civil-service or defense-related employment. Although the objectionable security restrictions and land acquisitions were phenomena of the early years of the state, their memory still rankles and leaves a feeling of discrimination.

In the first two decades of the state, security within the borders was often a matter of first priority. The War of Liberation had taken place well into what is now the center of the country, and Jewish settlements were attacked by local Arabs as well as the invading armies. Other local Arabs remained neutral or fled, while the Druze assisted the Israeli forces. In the years before the Sinai campaign of 1956 and again in the mid-1960s before the Six Day War, terrorists raided civilian targets far into the country. In actuality, however, Israeli Arabs have given almost no help to terrorist groups. Measures such as the requirement of military travel passes to enter and leave specified areas, revoked completely by 1966, were to a large extent unnecessary, although covert investigation on the part of the government and fear of anticipated legal recriminations were undoubtedly a part of the reason for internal quiet in the early years of the state.

The continuation of the Emergency Regulations of the Mandate* restricted individuals' movements, allowed administrative detention, and permitted the government to close off and use private areas for security reasons. These regulations provided for the continuation of a Military Administration after the fighting stopped in 1949. The scope of its power was relaxed after the Sinai campaign and was revoked completely in 1966. In largely Arab areas, the usual government services were performed by the regular civil authorities, but the military, though very few in number, had a very considerable administrative influence. Since 1967, complete freedom of movement has made possible an extremely wide range of interaction for Israeli Arabs. Open bridges from the West Bank to Jordan have encouraged

---

* The Emergency Defense Regulations of 1945, originally passed by the Mandate government in order to keep law and order, were used mainly against the defense and immigration efforts of the Yishuv. They were continued in the state by the Law and Administration Ordinance (1948). The ordinance authorizes a minister to issue regulations needed for defense, public safety, or essential services and supplies. These regulations need to be reaffirmed by the Knesset at three-month intervals, and are in effect in any case only as long as an emergency exists. The state of emergency, declared in 1948, is still in effect. The military censorship, control of foreign currency, and court injunctions for strikers to return to essential work are examples of the powers conferred.

contact with people from other Arab countries, and within the country there is increased contact between Arabs and Jewish people.

In addition, there are laws which are unequally applied or whose outcome is discriminatory toward Arabs,[19] such as the national military-draft laws, that apply to all on paper but do not yet apply in practice to Arabs. Inequalities include certain rights or services given to Army veterans, such as the National Insurance children's allowances, which are higher if a parent has served in the Army. There are very few instances where laws related to acts of private persons specifically *prohibit* discrimination.* Laws giving benefits to new development towns do not benefit old Arab (or Jewish) towns. On the other hand, income and other taxes are less rigorously collected from Arabs.

To Arab Israelis, land is an important political symbol, as well as a necessity for living and farming. (See Chapter 3). The sources of political conflict lie in the extent to which land was acquired from the Arabs who remained in Israel after the 1948 war, in the early 1950s under laws which were not very generous in compensation arrangements;** and in a general opposition among the Arabs to the acquisition of private land for public purposes, even for their own community needs.***

While land was acquired without due regard for individual or property rights and without adequate compensation, most of the acres thus acquired belonged to those who joined anti-Israel forces or to those absent for other reasons. Others lost land because of minor border shifts, or were kept off their land because it was in an area closed by the Military Administration.****

* Here are two examples: (a) the Employment Services Law (1959), specifically prohibits the service from discriminating on grounds of sex, age, religion, nationality, etc., providing, however, for the applicability of security checks where the job requires it; (b) the Council for Higher Education Law (1958) withholds academic recognition from universities which discriminate on national or religious grounds in making appointments. But a private employer or landlord, for example, is not prevented by law from discriminating on grounds of age, sex, or religion.

** Legislation under which land is, or has been, acquired by the government includes: (a) Law on Property of Absentees (1950), providing for acquisition from one who during the War of Liberation (1947 to end of emergency) was a citizen of a country at war with Israel, or was in one of those countries, or was away from his permanent home in Israel in a place then outside the borders or controlled by enemy forces; (b) Law for Acquisition of Land (1953): land not in use by owner on April 1, 1952, and which was used since the state for defense, essential development, or settlement between 1948–1952, and is still needed for one of these purposes, could be acquired, with compensation per value in January 1950; (c) Land Ordinance (Mandate, 1943), since revised in state (1964), together with Law of Planning and Building (1965), Law for Building and Vacating Rehabilitation Areas (1965). Minister of Finance can acquire land needed for a public purpose.

*** In contrast to the Jewish sector, in which most land is nationally owned and used on long-term lease, Arab land is largely private. Most of the 375,000 acres of private farm land are owned by Arabs or Druze.

**** See footnote on Bir-Am and Ikrit near the Lebanese border (p. 72), which were in areas closed by the Military Administration. Villages like Taibe, on the former Jordanian border, lost much land because they were in Jordan until the 1949 Armistice Agreements moved them into Israel, some of their land remaining in Jordan and some being requisitioned under the 1950 Absentee Law. The original motive in acquiring border land was to settle Jewish groups for future border defense.

The inequities in the impact of the law now seem to be recognized, and efforts are being made to close the gap. Overall, the picture of Arab-Israeli civil rights shows some past mistakes. Nonetheless, there is now general equality of Arabs and Jews in civil rights if not in equality of access to all of the supports and benefits which are the outcomes of the political system.

Religion and the Individual

Under the Mandate, the Knesset Israel, the organized Jewish religious community, was a leading example of a voluntary organization which could to a large degree regulate the lives of its members. In the state, the religious community received the backing of state law in the enforcement, where Jews were concerned, of many aspects of religious law. There have been other attempts to enhance the authority of other voluntary groups, such as the kibbutz and *moshav* movements, but these have been unsuccessful. Conflict between individuals and the religious authorities over the freedom to believe or to practice religion has not been acute. The right to practice nonbelief, however, is more limited, as, for example, in the fact that public transportation and entertainment are halted on the Sabbath.

Religious authority impinges on an individual's rights in several different ways. First of all, religious law, backed by state law, decides to which community a person belongs. This means that the individual who is a member of a given religious community is subject to its religious laws and thus the decisions of its authorities which relate to important personal questions, including marriage and divorce. Of secondary concern are public funds given to the religious groups and used in any way the religious authorities see fit. This community organization derives historically from both the culture and practical coalition politics. The Turkish Empire, the Mandatory government, and the society of their times did not differentiate between the national and religious aspects of Judaism. Under the Turks, and with minor modification under the British, each *millet*, or community, was autonomous in matters of personal status, education, and charitable trusts, as well as religion. In this conceptual world, the question of whether the Jews constituted a nation or a religious community could not be answered because it could not be asked. The idea of the secular nation-state, in this context, was irrelevant.

Under the Mandate, membership in Knesset Israel was voluntary. A notable separatist group was the very orthodox Agudat Israel, who even now have independent rabbinic courts, places of worship, and schools. While the demands of national unity in a period of struggle kept the vast majority of Jews, including agnostics and atheists, within the fold, there were cases of defectors who did not accept a religious authority. Their personal status was ambiguous and was never defined under Mandatory law, while their existence represented an element of fluidity and freedom within the system.

In 1948, the state was superimposed on what had been a voluntary community, and the jurisdiction of the religious authorities and their interpretation of religious law in certain matters became mandatory for all Jews. Since
the sovereign power of the state permits no opting out, definitional questions
became important political issues. Can a person be a Jew from the point of
view of national identity but not of religious affiliation? Is Israel a secular
nation-state in the Western sense? If so, religion and state could be separated.
Or is Israel simply a sovereign *millet*? If so, the question lacks relevance.

The case of *Rufeysen*,[20] or "Brother Daniel," showed that a distinction was
possible in the standard for membership in the secular and religious communities, a separation of the state and the *millet*. Rufeysen, born a Jew, was a
survivor of the Nazi Holocaust who sought citizenship under the Law of
Return even though he had become a Carmelite monk. Taking a common-
sense and common-law approach, the court decided in 1962 that within the
national consensus, Rufeysen was not a Jew, although under religious law he
could claim to be one as the son of a Jewish mother. Eventually he became a
naturalized citizen as a non-Jew. The *Shalit* case (1970) made the separation of
the state and the *millet* a reality in deciding that the law for the registration of
the population should be interpreted narrowly.[21] Thus neither the Minister
of the Interior (nor his agent, the Registrar) nor the court would decide the
question of "who is a Jew." Aside from its broad historical and philosophical
interest, the question of "who is a Jew" has practical implications, as in the
process of becoming a citizen, eligibility for aid as an immigrant, or the right
to marry a Jew in a religious ceremony. In the *Shalit* case a Jewish immigrant
won the right to register his children by a gentile mother as Jews. (The mother,
as an athiest, had refused conversion to Judaism.) The court realized that the
case necessitated a sharp constitutional decision and hoped the government
would repeal the registration law, which it did not. Although the case was not
"ripe" from the viewpoint of constitutional consensus in a political and
historical context, the court reached a five-to-four decision, in which the
"religious law" test, specifying that only children of a Jewish mother are Jews,
was discarded.

Such a decision increased the fears of a culture war. The Knesset quickly
enacted legislation reversing the court, amending the original Law of Return
definition to say that a Jew is one who is "born of a Jewish mother, or has been
converted, and does not belong to another religion." It thus made the test of
religious law not the position of a theocratic minority, but the expression of
the government. The decision represented the national bargain, not the national consensus.

Many practical questions, however, have not been solved. Couples coming from Eastern Europe are often partners in mixed marriages in which no
religious conversion ever took place, while immigrants from the West are
often partners in mixed marriages in which conversion was performed by a
reform rabbi, making the conversion unacceptable to the orthodox Israeli

religious authorities. In the coalition negotiations after the 1973 elections, the Mafdal (NRP) demanded that the word "conversion" be construed to mean conversion by orthodox rabbis only. The demand was rejected, perhaps largely because of the potential injury to the unity of Israel and the western Diaspora, where most Jews are of reform or conservative persuasion.

By the fall of 1974, the Mafdal had joined the coalition on the promise that within a year a solution to the question of the definition of Jewishness, especially as it regards the Law of Return, would be worked out. By 1977 there was still no agreed solution and the larger constitutional question of the relation between membership in the state and membership in Knesset Israel remained to be resolved.

The most sensitive area in the relation of religion and the state has been that of personal status. For Jews, the rabbinic courts apply standards of religious law to such personal questions as marriage and divorce. The population is denied many public services on the Sabbath, and services of a religious nature, such as burial, are a monopoly of the orthodox. The political agreement to maintain the division between religious and secular authority originally came out of the alliance of Mapai and the Mizrachi; and the agreement concerning observance and separate education came from the *status quo* agreement, originally made with the ultra-orthodox Aguda (see Appendix A and Chapter 1.)

It was a gesture, perhaps later regretted, to secure Aguda support in a critical period and to demonstrate broad solidarity in the struggle to establish the state. Disclaiming authority for the decisions of a possible future elected state government and stating clearly that the imminent state was not to be a theocracy, the "status quo" letter states that the Sabbath would be the official day of rest. In personal law, all would be done to avoid a rift in the house of Israel. The laws of kosher food would be observed in all official establishments, and each "stream" would be free to manage its own educational system, after meeting minimum established requirements in secular subjects.

The concept of *status quo* has lived on. It is taken to mean broadly that no steps will be taken which would mean a gain for theocracy or for secularism, while on specific questions of authority or observance, arrangements which existed under the Mandate will be maintained. For example, there is bus service in Haifa on the Sabbath but not in Tel Aviv. The application of religious law can be seen to injure individuals, as in preventing or delaying their marriage.* It can discriminate on a class basis, for example, in favor of those who can afford private cars or taxis and thus travel on the Sabbath; and it arbitrarily decides what kinds of entertainment will be allowed. Nightclubs are per-

---

* Some examples of forbidden marriages are the following: descendants of the priests (the *Kohanim*) may not marry divorcees; so-called "bastards" (*mamzerim*) may marry only other bastards or converts (using the biblical definition of a bastard as the child of a married woman by a man other than her husband); and marriages between people of different faiths cannot be performed by religious or secular authorities. The non-Jewish communities, in turn, impose their own religious restrictions on their members.

mitted to remain open because they affect relatively few people, while legitimate theaters, which attract more people, are closed.

Considerable ingenuity has been shown in the pragmatic circumvention of religious rules. For example, secular courts recognize marriages which have been performed in foreign countries. Nonetheless, the solutions which the courts can provide are not always adequate. One approach has been to seek legislation which would permit nonreligious solutions in those cases where the *Halachic* law as it is now interpreted does not help. Such attempts have been successfully blocked by the *status quo* arrangement, as in 1976 when the so-called "Hausner Law" was defeated in the Knesset through all-out Labor Alignment voting discipline in enforcement of the 1974 coalition agreement. The object of that law was to permit civil marriage for those whom the religious laws prevented from marrying. The public and the Knesset were surprisingly acquiescent, probably due to preoccupation with the economic crisis and defense.

Other hoped-for relief could come through reform of the clerical establishment, or at least breaking the monopoly of the orthodox hierarchy. Nine recognized Christian communities, as well as the Druze and the Moslems, have religious courts; yet reform and conservative Jewish rabbis have no official status or authority. The institution of a chief rabbinate is in itself unusual and seldom practiced in the modern Diaspora. As on other questions, much will depend on external events. Larger immigration from Western countries, which have large reform or conservative congregations, could bring the orthodox monopoly under increasing pressure, as could demands by many Soviet immigrants for individual solutions. Faced with growing pressure, the orthodox hierarchy could adapt the substance of the law to human demands posed by the changes in Jewish life. But this is unlikely, since the day has long passed when religious law interacted with all facets of life and could develop like common law; nor, for more than a century, have the institutions of orthodoxy had the capacity to do so.* Religion is an area where a major confrontation has been systematically avoided, but the time may come when this is no longer possible. The nondecision and continuing federative agreement show the inability of the political system to bridge the differences in the basic values which are close to the central and most sensitive nerves of the society, and indicate that the balance is tenuous.

Freedom of the Press and the Public's Right to Know

Despite the ongoing emergency and the existence of restrictive formal legislation, belief in freedom of the press is well entrenched in the political culture. Although officials and politicians who express strong belief in the need for a

---

* Some form of *Sanhedrin*, or rabbinical legislative body, would in theory be required to change religious law.

free press do not always behave accordingly when specific incidents affect their interests, their attitude is not mainly lip service. On balance, there is an informed democracy and the press provides a continuous critique of the government and the society which, in scope and depth, although not always in accuracy, surpasses the criticism and analysis of the parliamentary opposition parties.

"Agreements" and the Law

The limits to the freedom of the press, as well as the protection of freedom of information and expression, are in practice mostly informal, a consensus or complex of "agreements" which depend more on custom and beliefs than on law. The forces for both restriction and liberalism and the outcome depend on the security situation, complex group and personal relations, and tradition. As in other public questions in Israel, the gap between life and the law is a source of potential tension.

For the early Zionist leaders, newspapers were ideological platforms which, in the tradition of the reform movements of the late nineteenth century, sought more to influence by argument than to transmit facts. To the older generation, the press was a mentor expressing social and political goals, and editorials and polemics were often more important than news headlines.

In the Yishuv, the press was an integral part of a united front in the struggle for liberation, with broad editorial consensus on outside affairs and self-censorship in the national interest. An "Editors' Committee of Response" coordinated a joint stand of the press in political matters *vis à vis* the Mandate and the world at large. The sense of being an insider in the struggle was reinforced by the conspiratorial and underground atmosphere of the period.

Some of this secrecy and self-censorship continued in the state and resulted in voluntary institutional arrangements whose effect is to restrict the flow of information. These include the Daily Newspaper Editors' Committee, the Censorship Appeals Committee, the Press Council, and informal meetings of the chief editors.[22]

The Editors' Committee is convened to hear officials or unofficial groups that wish to be heard. Closed meetings of chief editors can be requested by the Prime Minister, the Defense Minister, the Chief of Staff, or the Foreign Minister. They can ask for voluntary censorship where formal action would be illegal or politically undesirable. There is extensive off-the-record background briefing, and the voluntary censorship is not restricted to military matters. In this atmosphere of national participation, the committee, in the first decade of independence, agreed to withhold publication of news of the immigration from Arab and communist countries. The government believed that publicity could endanger the continuation of emigrations, and during the 1960s, the editors agreed to formal censorship concerning the import of oil, immigration, and certain foreign loans. The agreement came as a result of several days of discussion of the issues with Prime Minister Levi Eshkol.

The Press Council is a voluntary body representing the Reporters' Union, the Editors' Committee, the publishers, and the general public. Its formal *raison d'être* is to provide redress against publication of an item which is unfair to a person or group without costly and lengthy libel procedures. In practice, the Council more often hears complaints from government officials who feel that they do not have a strong enough case for the courts. It also votes from time to time to put certain subjects out of bounds.

Reporters also feel themselves citizens of a country under siege, and in critical periods it is only with difficulty that they disassociate themselves sufficiently to criticize those who are engaged full time in defending the security of the country, or expose to world view weaknesses which might aid enemies or deter friendly assistance. Reporting is often strongly influenced by situations and by the moods of the country. Finally, many reporters depend heavily on politicians and officials as sources of information, as these officials in turn depend on the newsmen to help them form their public image. Still, individual reporters act with more skepticism and degrees of freedom than the editors. There is thus a delicate balance between the confidentiality common to most Western countries, with their "off-the-record briefings," and newsmen's seeming to act as spokesmen for the government. Comment in many papers can strongly oppose individuals and policies, and many issues have received public review and change through muckraking exposés. The problem in the Israeli situation is that frequently the press itself feels that it could be giving aid and comfort to the enemy, so that self-restraint, combined with insider relations, may tip the scales in a form of self-censorship.

The complex informal limits are abetted by the potential if not actual use of restrictive laws, most of which are a continuation of Mandatory regulations and of the former powers of the Crown and the High Commissioner. The State Security Ordinance (Emergency Regulations) is the most important and effective source of restriction, as the basis for authorizing pre-publication military censorship of news to be published locally or dispatched abroad which could "endanger the defense of Israel, or the well-being of the public, or public order." Appeals of the Censor's decisions are heard by a committee of three, representing the press, the military, and the general public. Unanimous decisions are final, while majority decisions can be appealed to the Chief of Staff. The committee also hears complaints against papers that have violated censorship regulations, and can, in such cases, recommend punishments. These are usually small fines or a very brief suspension of publication. The committee's action and its right to punish are based on custom and not on law, through agreements reached between the Editors' Committee and the Defense

Ministry.* Material appearing in a foreign publication can be freely quoted in Israel, a procedure of which full advantage is taken. Direct telephone dialing abroad also reduces the effectiveness of predispatch censorship of outgoing news.

The 1933 Press Ordinance of the Mandate, still in effect, requires initial licensing of publications and authorizes the Minister of the Interior to close down papers after the fact for incitement "endangering public order." This authority has been rarely used, and in all cases appeals to the courts brought instant redress. Despite general dissatisfaction with this formal restrictive power, no really new press legislation has been enacted. Indeed, the Broadcast Authority Law and the *Basic Law: The Knesset*, which gives the requirements and conditions for open debate, are the only laws which incorporate a positive statement of freedom to publish.

Another law that could impinge on press freedom is the Libel Law of 1965 (amended in 1967), which extends into the political realm by recognizing the defamation of ethnic, national, or political groups as criminal libel and in which truth and "interest to the public" are not deemed to be sufficient defense if the information "exceeded the limits of what was necessary," as determined by the court. In its first decade the law was not used in connection with press freedom. It had, however, indirect results in changes in the political scene. Dov Joseph, the Minister of Justice who had strongly pushed the unpopular 1965 law, was dropped from the Mapai list for the 1965 elections, and Uri Avneri, maverick editor of the weekly *Olam Hazeh*, who had expected much use of the law in his case, formed his own party list and won two Knesset seats—and with them the right to reprint with impunity whatever he himself might say in the Knesset.

In the *Basic Law: The Government* (1968), Cabinet and Cabinet committee proceedings are deemed secret if they concern foreign affairs, defense, or anything declared to be secret by the government. The Prime Minister, however, may decide to release material for publication. Under treason and espionage legislation, the Cabinet, with the approval of the Knesset Foreign Affairs and Defense Committee, can define material as secret and its revelation as treason and espionage. A final potential legal restriction is the power of judges to hear security matters *in camera*.

To this depressing array of restrictive legal possibilities and informal arrangements are added a history of attempts at further restrictions and the existence of a national monopoly for broadcasting, whose executive is appointed by the government. Yet the country enjoys a very high degree of freedom of information, deriving less from formal guarantees than from a culture in which the right to speak out and criticize is part of the tradition and of the

---

* First in 1951 and again in 1966, when the phrasing of the original agreement was liberalized to specify that censorship was not applicable to "political matters, opinions, interpretative writing, evaluations . . . except for defense information which helps the enemy or injures national defense."

self-image of a Western democracy. The right to know is not provided in law and is not very widely endorsed but exists *de facto*. It is furthered by the very close interaction of people from many circles, which makes the spread of knowledge a common and accepted phenomenon.

The Courts

Because of the "arrangements" and self-restraint of the press and the government, there have been few opportunities to test the laws in the courts, and in these cases the courts have acted both for and against the right to publish and to know. The second *Kol Ha'am* case,[23] in 1953, and the *Sumeil* case of 1962[24] were notable endorsements of freedom of information, while in the case of *Al-Ard*, the courts followed a general national consensus heavily influenced by the emergency situation, ignoring the *Kol Ha'am* interpretations.

In March, 1953, *Kol Ha'am* (The Voice of the People), the Communist Party Hebrew daily, and its Arabic edition, *Al-Ittihad*, were suspended for ten days.[25] They had stated that Abba Eban, Israel's Ambassador to the United States, had agreed that "in the event of war in Korea, Israel would place 200,000 soldiers at the side of the Americans." The paper defended the Soviet Union's "dedication to peace" and attacked the Ben Gurion government as "speculating in the blood of Israel's youth."

Sitting as the High Court of Justice, the Supreme Court was asked to decide whether the Minister of the Interior was acting within his authority to suspend the publication because it was "likely to endanger the public peace." There were two possible interpretations of "likely":

> one, the so-called "bad tendency" test, which would justify suppression . . . if the offending words showed some, even if only a remote, tendency to produce the prohibited result; the other, the so-called "probability" test, which would require the minister, before suspending any newspaper, to be satisfied that it was at least *probable* that the words contained in the publication would endanger the public peace.[26]

The court decided that the "probability" approach would better express the intention of the legislature. Referring to the Israeli Declaration of Independence and saying that "the law . . . must be studied in the light of its national way of life," the court went as close as it felt the statute permitted to the Holmes and Brandeis "clear and present danger" test, and revoked the suspension. It did this mainly as a matter of values, saying that it was "called upon to define the relationship that exists between the right to freedom of the press on the one hand, and on the other, the power held by the authorities . . . to place a limit on the use of that right," and that the law should be interpreted "in the light of the basic ideas of a democratic regime."

At the time, it was hoped that "the clear and present danger test would be used in the future to mark the limits of free speech in Israel,"[27] but subsequent history has not borne out this forecast. In the 1960s, "clear and present danger" was ignored in the cases involving the Arab nationalist group Al-Ard.[28] In a succession of actions, the group was prevented from incorporating in order to publish a newspaper, and finally its attempt to present a list of candidates for the Knesset was stopped on the ground of its "intention to injure the existence of the State of Israel," although there is no legislative disqualification for seditious activities.

In the *Sumeil* case in 1962, in which a newsreel showed the expulsion of residents of Sumeil, a condemned Tel Aviv slum area, the producers sought an order from the High Court of Justice to prevent the Council for the Criticism of Films and Plays from ordering them to eliminate passages which showed police carrying out a woman whose clothing was in disarray. The Council claimed that the pictures were in poor taste and that the report did not properly represent the totality of the problem. The court authorized the showing, Justice Landau saying that the Council had not considered

> the right of the citizen to distribute and receive information on what is going on around him, in the country in which he lives and abroad. This right is strongly anchored in the right of freedom of expression and therefore belongs to those basic rights "which are not inscribed in a book," but which come directly from the character of our country as a democracy seeking freedom.[29]

Secret arrest and trial of the editors of the sex and scandal weekly *Bul* (Bullseye) a few months before the 1967 Six Day War was a rare instance when issues of civil liberty and freedom of the press merged in a crucial test of the strength of democratic concepts. In December 1966, *Bul* published a story implying Israeli involvement in the affair of Ben Barka, a former Moroccan leader kidnapped in France under mysterious circumstances, in which the press implicated the French security services. Authorities confiscated most of the copies of *Bul* after they left the printers, two of the magazine's editors were arrested, and the state obtained a court ruling of secrecy regarding the arrests, the trial, and the sentences. The fact that both editors were tried and sentenced to one year in prison under the treason and espionage laws was not made public. The government convened the Editors' Committee to explain and justify its actions. At that meeting only *Ha'aretz* protested, but abided by the secrecy ruling.

Foreign reports reprinted in Israel soon brought the case to public knowledge. In February, editorials in *Ha'aretz* (independent) and *Al Hamishmar* (Mapam) strongly criticized the government's handling of the case. Papers in the West reported "growing unrest and uneasiness" in Israel over the issue. Criticism of the lack of press freedom mounted, and the President of the Bar Association, Dr. Rotenstreich, denounced "the mistake of the juridical authorities in imposing a veil of secrecy over the sentence." Domestic politics were involved, in attacks on Justice Minister Shapira for mishandling the case.

During this time, the two editors continued to edit the magazine from their prison cells, and their names remained on the masthead. In March, possibly to alleviate growing criticism, Prime Minister Eshkol recommended pardons, which were speedily granted. Nevertheless, criticism continued to be voiced by the public and the Bar Association and in the Knesset.

Six months after the height of the excitement, the Press Council, the supposed guardian of press ethics, anticlimactically published its findings. It avoided the question of whether the imprisonment of the editors really affected press freedom, by stating that the rights of a journalist as a citizen *per se*—for example, protection against unfair process of law—were a separate question from the right to publish. The only case in which the Council thought that the two kinds of rights coincided would be where a journalist was prosecuted for refusing to reveal his sources. The Council leaders attacked *Bul* as being a scandal sheet which ignored the ethics of the Israeli journalistic community. *Ha'aretz* attacked what it considered to be the hypocrisy of a statement by the attorneys of the Press Council to the effect that refusing to reveal the names of those arrested preserves their rights. This approach was said to be particularly irrelevant in this case, when what was kept secret was the final verdict and sentence. Moreover, it was the prosecution that wanted secrecy, not the defense.

In this incident, the clannishness of the daily press, dating back to the Mandate and symbolized in the Editors' Committee, worked against the freedom of the press. *Bul* and its editors were outsiders who did not play the game according to the rules of the club and were not entitled to its protection. Moreover, in handling the case, the authorities panicked, possibly because of the concurrence of elements involved: secret operations, relations with the French security services, and the sensitivity of the ruling Mapai group, at that time under attack by Rafi, and with recent memories of the Lavon affair.*
Public opinion, not burdened by the group considerations of the press or the sensitivity of the Mapai leaders, displayed a keener passion for press freedom than did the press itself and kept the issue alive, appealing to a sense of fairness and of proportion between *Bul*'s action and the government's reaction. It reinforced those journalists who opposed the line taken by the Press Council,

---

* Pinhas Lavon was Defense Minister in 1954 when Israeli agents were imprisoned and convicted in Egypt of sabotage intended to created friction between Egypt and the United States. An inquiry committee, appointed by Prime Minister Sharett in 1954, did not entirely clear Lavon of direct responsibility, and he resigned. In 1960, Lavon said that new evidence and documents cleared him, and asked Ben Gurion for "rehabilitation." Ben Gurion refused to take a stand, and the Cabinet decided to appoint a ministerial committee which decided that Lavon was not to blame. Ben Gurion attacked the procedure, demanding a judicial inquiry. Before the 1965 Knesset elections, the affair had divided Mapai very seriously, accentuating and exposing its internal differences and leading immediately to the forming of Rafi by Ben Gurion.

ultimately forced the government to the defensive, and probably was an important factor in the early pardon of the editors.

Radio and Television

Before 1965, the broadcasting service was a branch of the Prime Minister's Office. In 1965, the Law of the Broadcasting Authority set up a national service with a three-tier management, each level appointed by the government. In 1968, the law was amended to include television and radio under one authority. There are no commercial stations, and the only alternative source originating within Israel is the Army's radio station, Galei Zahal, although foreign radio broadcasts are easily received, as well as television from Jordan and Cyprus.

A Plenum of thirty-one members oversees general policy, an Executive of seven makes ongoing management decisions, and the Director-General is in charge of executing the policy of the Authority. Operations are financed by receipts from listeners' license fees, approved annually by the Knesset Finance Committee. The Plenum is appointed after consultation with representative public bodies, such as organizations of writers, artists, teachers, and universities. Still, the ultimate authority for its appointment lies with the government, so that the independence of the Authority is not fully guaranteed by law.

The Plenum is required to meet at least six times a year. The Executive meets as frequently as once a week. Two of its members are civil servants, and all seven are part-time members. (Since 1977, the Chairman works full time.) The Minister of Education is the "responsible minister," and a minimum of ten Plenum members can ask him to appeal a Plenum majority decision to the Cabinet.

The Authority, says the law, is "to broadcast educational, entertainment and information programs, in the areas of policy, society, economy, culture, sciences, and arts, in Hebrew, Arabic, and other languages, for the needs of the population in the country, and for Jews in other countries; and to express in an adequate manner the image of Israel. . . ." It is to "give appropriate expression to the attitudes and opinions existing in the public, and to broadcast reliable information."

The Authority is still in its formative period, compared with the BBC or commercial organizations abroad, yet certain characteristics are already discernible. Although the Plenum and the Executive are charged with working in the national interest, the actual influences brought to bear on the Authority are more political than public. The charter to express "the attitudes and opinions . . . existing in the public" does not exactly denote an independent journalistic role. By custom the seven members of the Executive represent the political streams of the coalition, and the Authority is dependent on the Knesset for its budget and the level of listener fees to be charged.

The advent of television in 1967 led to an enormous increase in political interest. Politicians had no personal experience in broadcasting, although many were close to journalism as writers of political articles. Radio seemed to them a medium of lesser consequence because it left no record; but they saw that appearing on television could have an extremely powerful impact, which would clearly be in their best political interests. The increased political efforts of this period were exerted mainly at the top level of the Plenum, the Executive, and the Director-General. Drawn from the second or third level of party loyalists, such as those with a borderline chance to be elected to the Knesset, Executive members are potentially amenable to political pressure. But the interventions of the Executive have come as much from differences between the concepts which Executive members and the Managing Director had of their roles, and from a desire that the medium represent the majority consensus, or self-image, as from direct political demands. The Executive has tended to see its role as that of an "Editor-in-Chief," while successive directors would have preferred that the Plenum and Executive act as representatives of the public, the arts, and the sciences.[30] In the early period of the Authority, the Executive successfully stopped many programs which centered on criticism of the government. Knesset members and individual ministers focused more on attempts to exert influence at the working levels within the Authority. Genuine independence of television is not helped by the fact that it has taken many years to develop a strong nucleus of competent professionals. There are still serious problems in fashioning an organization in which technical and budgetary efficiency and coordination are combined with creativity and independent and competent journalism.

If one compares the Israel Broadcasting Authority with an idealized image of an independent public broadcasting authority, the customs of political appointments to the Executive and appointment of the Director-General by the government, as well as dependence on the Knesset Finance Committee for budget renewals, seem to work against it. Equally important constraints are the sensitivity of both the audience and the professionals and managers in the Authority to the public image of their country and to what they see as the bounds of a generally accepted consensus.

The Right to Know

Unlike Sweden or the United States, Israel has no laws providing citizens with the right to obtain official information;* nor is there, on the other hand, a comprehensive "Official Secrets Act" like that in the United Kingdom. There

* The courts have upheld the executive prerogative. In one case (*Shalom Cohen vs. Minister of Defense*, 17, P.D. 1023), the court upheld the denial of the status of accredited military correspondent to a reporter whose criticisms were unpalatable to the Ministry of Defense, saying that Army information services are for the good of the Army and are extended to journalists at its discretion.

are, however, several statutes, aside from espionage and treason laws, which limit access to government documents or knowledge. The *Basic Law: The Government* (1968) provides for control of information about Cabinet proceedings. Under the concept of collective responsibility for the coalition, Cabinet secrecy is designed to protect the decision-making process; but the difficulty of maintaining confidentiality in the deliberations of over twenty ministers from several parties and factions leads to recurring attempts to impose severe penalties. Periodically, there are suggestions (which, fortunately, have not been accepted) that the Secret Service be allowed to tap the telephones of ministers and, more practically, that the government create formal and informal kitchen cabinets where detailed and decisive debate of the most important questions will take place.

Knesset proceedings are open unless thirty members ask that they be closed. They offer, through questions, possibilities of exposing or confirming information—often following leads given by the press. Court trials are public. Under civil service regulations,[31] officials agree to keep confidential any material used in their work. Officially, only the spokesman or the director-general of a ministry meets the press, and approves all interviews with subordinates. In practice there is much informal communication, particularly with specialist reporters and through controlled or uncontrolled leaks. These leaks are particularly important in the internal factional and personal competition at the Cabinet level and are also used as trial balloons or as diplomatic communiqués. A serving government official, or one who has left the service, can publish information received in the course of his work only if a special Cabinet subcommittee will agree that publication would not affect security or the public interest.

The press must bear much of the responsibility for the practical limits to the right to know. There is a general spirit of confidentiality, and of information as an object of value and a bargaining counter. Reporters, feeling that they are insiders, have instinctively acted to preserve their share of the monopoly on news, and they have not fought as much as might be expected for the public's right to know, except in the case of the Cabinet restrictions of the 1968 law and subsequent attempts to impose severe penalties on the press for printing Cabinet leaks. Government officials, as a major source of news, use information to further policies and persons, on the one hand, or see it as a property of their ministry which can be dispensed *ex gratia* and not as a right.

Despite rampant curiosity in a country which is, in effect, a small community, the belief that the citizen should readily be able to gain information at will has only recently begun to be part of the political culture. This is due to the continuation from the Yishuv of a mode of "confidentiality," to the lack of development of concepts of the right to public knowledge in most Western countries (let alone many of the countries from which Israeli immigrants came), to the ongoing emergency, and to the limited extent to which adversary proceedings are used in public policy determination.

At a more sophisticated level, and perhaps more serious for policy, is a marked imbalance of the analysis made by the government and by its critics. Knesset committees, with staffs of one or two, cross swords with the dozens of economists and statisticians of the Ministry of Finance, or with the large bureaus of the General Staff. Opposition-party task forces of two or three try to counter the proposals of entire departments. A lone journalist or maverick backbencher occasionally succeeds, particularly when the government also "shoots from the hip." Within the ministries there has been little development of adversary procedures for the consideration of alternatives. No policy-analysis organization operates on any adequate scale outside the government. Bureaucrats use consultants readily on specific or technical questions but keep as their own province the analysis and development of policy and strategy and the synthesis of information and large systems.

Tendencies and Trends

In the early years of the state, most criticism of government secrecy came from the left. Until the Soviet policy of anti-Zionism became clear, there were frequent attacks on real or supposed agreements with the United States and the pro-Western tendency of the government. In the first year, dissident groups on the right and the left posed a threat which was hard to imagine in 1977,[*] and economic and social difficulties increased the scope for criticism. In the 1950s, however, the public still saw defense as sacred and was therefore quite ready to accept or even demand restrictions on military news.

The initially inexperienced censorship organization went through a period of learning during which there were many arbitrary decisions. Over time the gap narrowed between the press view that censorship is essentially voluntary, and that of the Army Censor, that it is more simply the application of the law and authority. The closing of several papers for periods of one or two days led in 1951 to the original agreement between the Editors' Committee and the Defense Ministry, followed by a long period with relatively few clashes. The definition of defense news, as distinct from political news, was clarified during this period, while with time the government's initial extensive mixing of political and military secrecy declined.

In 1960–61, the political ramifications of the Lavon affair, which began as a defense incident, led to a complex situation in which the press was reluctant to accept the dicta of the Censor. In the mid-1960s there was a notable clash between the press and the Censor, led, as was frequently the case, by Ha'aretz, over publication of a decision to develop missiles for Israel in France. This resulted in a new "agreement" between the editors and the Ministry, with clearer definitions of censorable material. The relationships in the late 1960s,

* See Chapter 4, "The Nation in Arms."

however, tended to show a general characteristic of the system: censorship tends to expand its scope to include the political, and the political scope of censorship and its activism tend to grow if the government of the day feels insecure.

The trend from the 1967 Six Day War until 1977 was for more public knowledge of purely military matters,* along with an increase in secrecy regarding international political relations. In the period of waiting on the eve of the Six Day War, the whole country debated what should be done. There was a great rise in public interest in questions in which defense, local, and international politics were mixed. At the same time the nation in arms and its families had acquired extensive knowledge of military details, there was greater sophistication about the nature of security, and thus there was more freedom to publish technical data.

Following the Yom Kippur War, freedom to reveal and to criticize defense policies markedly increased. In the first days of the war, a curtain of secrecy over the perilous situation led to a sharp drop in the public's faith in official announcements and to a demand for more information. At the same time, the sharp rise in financial needs in the aftermath of the war made it necessary to reveal more of the defense budgets and procurement policy as part of the process of gaining public support and sacrifice. The press felt much less ready to be limited, and the force of the self-imposed restrictions declined.

International trends were felt as well. In the United States, the Vietnam War created outstanding precedents of an absence of censorship. It was the period of the Pentagon Papers. (In Israel it is still highly unlikely that a ministry would commission the writing of a "Pentagon Paper" analyzing its own actions.) Internal Cabinet rivalry and a sense that social authority was weakening led to increased attempts at government secrecy and at the same time caused these attempts to fail. Cabinet rivalry increased the use of leaks, and the extensive network of subordinate centers of power was no longer a cohesive, unified system whose component members deferred to the alleged need for confidentiality in pursuing their interests.

The trend is clear. In 1949 there was no publicity regarding the background for the Sinai-Gaza withdrawal. In the 1957 withdrawal, after Suez, publicity was directed to help gain public acceptance; and the post-Yom Kippur period saw the publication of the Agranat Report on the conduct of the war, and details of the 1975 Sinai separation agreements.**[32] Until the Yom Kippur War, there was little if any public discussion of major defense issues and the concept of the Bar Lev line, as opposed to a more mobile defense along the Suez Canal, was discussed and decided wholly within the defense

* Still, in 1970 the censor held back publication of the movement of Egyptian missiles up to the Suez Canal in violation of the cease-fire, allegedly because knowledge of such movement would justify to the public the opposition of Gahal (Liberals and Herut) to the cease-fire.

** Only a preliminary summary was published. By 1981, the detailed report had not been released.

establishment. In 1979–80, contrasting views within the Army and the Defense Ministry on such questions as that of a separate, unified ground-forces command or the building of a new Israeli fighter plane, were publicly aired in some detail.

An Informed Democracy?

This most complex and troubling question concerns the extended and complicated interrelations of the government, the press as an institution, and the responsibility of individual reporters in limiting the flow of information. These relationships take place on several levels. The most extensive and formal are those between the Editors' Committee and the Censor, and the editors and the government, with the editors often acting as the voice of the government and as an active part of the national effort.

Over time, the number of daily papers has declined.* There has been a tightening of the formal or legal restrictive arrangements, such as changing from one to three the number of votes needed in the Editors' Committee to veto a decision to maintain secrecy.

The importance of the informal, even conspiratorial mode was demonstrated by the sharp reaction of the editors when the Rabin Cabinet, in 1976, asked the Knesset to approve the use of treason laws against newspapers publishing secret Cabinet discussions, messages from foreign governments, or reports of meetings with representatives of countries with which Israel does not maintain diplomatic relations. Press and parliamentary reaction quickly killed the proposal. This reaction was not a categorical rejection of the principle of censoring such news, but the editors' disappointment over not having been consulted ahead of time on the limitation, and the repugnance of the proposed drastic use of the Treason and Espionage Act.

At another level, there are extensive patron-client relationships of mutual dependence between reporters and politicians. In its relation with the administration, the press can collude in maintaining the monopoly value of having news and of being on the inside. More generally, pride in the national im-

* The approximate 1975 daily circulation of the largest Hebrew newspapers was:

	Weekday	Friday (weekend)
Ha'aretz (independent, early morning)	55,000	70,000
Davar (Histadrut, i.e., Labor Alignment, early morning)	40,000	44,000
Ma'ariv (independent, late morning)	145,000	225,000
Yediyot (independent, late morning)	145,000	225,000

Daily papers published by Herut and the General Zionists (Liberals) ceased publication more than a decade earlier. In 1975, there were twenty-seven dailies, fourteen in foreign languages, of which the most prominent was the *Jerusalem Post*. Three Arabic dailies are published in East Jerusalem, taking a basically anti-Israel stance and enjoying the greatest press freedom of the Arabic press in the Middle East. Two other Arabic papers were government-inspired, and Rakah (Communist) had a twice-weekly paper.

age and sensitivity to deviations from ideals lead the public to demand that the press, radio, and television remain within what they see as the national consensus, and news limitations are seen to be justified by the ongoing emergency.

The external threat, the potential of draconian laws, and the web of emotions and arrangements conspire to restrict information and expression in subtle and complex ways. For while consensus is important for national action, the ideas for the direction which should be taken may come from outside it. The enervating absence of legitimate alternative information could result in what Irving Janis calls "group-think"—a general chorus which reinforces opinions already held—but this now seems unlikely. The acceptance by the press and the public of the concept of a completely effective Israeli deterrence before the Yom Kippur War is an all too recent example.

There is some distance between the law and the actual situation, in which Israel can be said to be an informed democracy. Israelis usually know what is going on, but it is not because the right to know is spelled out. The censorship agreements, defects in the Law of the Broadcasting Authority (and the custom of appointing its Executive on a party basis), and the lack of positive legislation on the right to know are countered by the growing awareness of citizens that they should be allowed to find out what the government is doing about public questions. The high concentration of information in the government is associated with the dense growth of government activities. Information can be controlled in a host of ways—by simply withholding it, by off-the-record briefings, and by working through "insider" journalists. Neither in the Knesset nor in independent nongovernmental groups are there resources and organization for effective analysis and presentation of alternate policies. When, as they did after the Yom Kippur War, academics went down, as Theodore Roosevelt said, into the muck and mire of the arena, they did not last many rounds.

Still, many elements help to preserve freedom of news. The symbolic acceptance of the norm of press freedom gives journalists a feeling of security from prosecution. Because their status is high, they have a broad acquaintance with people who have access to knowledge. The value which people place on knowing creates demands on the press to find out and to publish what is going on. Extensive readership of the foreign press and the independent ownership of the local press of the highest circulation are important, as are the common-law traditions of the courts. The many ties to other countries make concealment difficult, and it is virtually impossible to withhold knowledge in the closely interacting and highly concerned general community. Growing depoliticization of the civil service and a decline of party control in general could lead to more regular, above-board sources and channels of information on public business, and to more openness and recognition of the public right to know.

In any period, citizens and the press get only the kind of freedom they demand. Their demands depend on a political culture of participation and knowledge that would be remarkable if it could always withstand the pressures of emergencies and the vagaries of public moods. Those in office, while publicly endorsing the norm of free information, may, when feeling threatened by opponents within or enemies without, withhold important information. It is then up to the press and the public to remind them that the strength of a country is in an informed public. Usually, they do.

The Search for the Constitution Continues

We now look again at the main constitutional challenges—the attainment of effective government which has the consent of the governed, agreement on what constitutes the higher law and on political and judicial processes which preserve it, and freedom of political competition.

The government has legitimate authority and is representative, but both criteria present problems. Legitimacy is seen in the fact that the political struggle takes place within the framework of the elective and parliamentary system. While there are many parliamentary weaknesses, general elections and appeals to the Knesset are the focus of broader political action, and the Knesset is effective principally as a forum in which the broad spectrum of national opinion is expressed. This is true even for extraparliamentary protests, which very often end up in front of the Knesset building. Indeed, there is a small, permanent sign across the street which says, "To the Demonstration."

A large part of the price of legitimacy is the continuing federative coalition, which, while ensuring representation, reduces the effectiveness of Cabinet government. The coalitions limit political competition and thus make representation imperfect. Agreements to form cabinets can ignore decisions that voters have made based on party election platforms, and the federative system and fears of social rift often prevent the confrontation of sensitive problems. Closed internal party nominating procedures and proportional representation in a single national constituency limit entry into politics, help to develop a hierarchical political culture, and seriously impair the independence of the Knesset.* The ability of the Knesset to control the executive is further restricted by the collective responsibility of the Cabinet and party voting discipline, which are natural corollaries of the coalition system. Other factors that restrain competition are the advantages gained by the largest parties from the way in which public funds are allocated for election and interim political expenses, and from the method of distribution of surplus votes in the Knesset elections.

* The development of party organizations, or *manganon*, is discussed in Chapter 1.

At best, the law in Israel lacks explicit guarantees of the right of the public to government information. At the worst, the laws are potentially very restrictive. Yet the press is essential, because of the inadequacies of the political competition which the election institutions can provide, and in particular those due to weakness of organized opposition in the Knesset. The ways in which the press exercises its role shows how strengths and limits depend much more on custom and on the web of relations in the community than they do on written or formal arrangements.

Another aspect of political competition is the separation of powers. While the legislature is weak in relation to the executive, the judiciary has far more effect in restraining executive power. Even though the courts work within a context which leaves little scope for judicial review, their political role is important. Much of their influence comes from having high status and respect as being above politics, from the independence of judges once they have been appointed, from the background and flexibility of the common law, and from the ready accessibility of the High Court of Justice. Symbolizing respect for the law and consensus on the common denominator of values, the court, in its composition, is less "representative" of political ideologies than it is of trends in the judicial view of its role as active or passive in the making of the constitution.

The role of the court seems to be limited by the absence of formal provision for judicial review of legislation, and by the use of standards of "authority" rather than of "administrative policy" in reviewing executive action. Looked at more deeply, however, the Court has, in the past, decided on fundamental or sensitive issues on occasions where it feels that there is consensus. On the other hand, it tends to avoid issues which could split the society, or which the political system itself cannot yet bridge. Despite an inherently passive approach (some say too passive), in which it may be "making haste slowly," the court effectively applies common-law constitutionalism. In this lies its political effectiveness, whose limits are defined by an aloofness from basic political controversy. This non-political stance is an important source and limitation of the court's strength.

Individual rights are preserved, despite the continuous state of emergency, a population coming from diverse political cultures, and the transition from what has been a small community to a larger, differentiated society. At the same time there are stringent emergency regulations on the books—although no terrorists have been executed, and the only person executed by sentence of a civil court was the Nazi Adolf Eichmann. There is a gap between the strictness of law and more flexible practice, which is bridged by custom and by the courts.

In this situation it is natural to ask whether a constitution, as intended when the First Knesset was elected, should not now be written, and if so, how it should be approved.[33] The constitutional validity of the Basic Laws already enacted and in preparation and of the "entrenchment" provisions is questioned by legal scholars, mainly on the grounds of the legitimacy of the making of what is intended to be a higher law by people and through a process not specifically chosen for this purpose. Various procedures have been discussed, such as requiring large majorities, calling special constitutional conventions, popular referenda, and requiring that constitutional provisions or amendments be reenacted in two successive elected Knessets.

Leaving procedure aside, is there already a consensus on values sufficient to give real force and meaning to a written constitution? For if there are differences in values that the political system has not yet bridged, is the time ripe to draft the written rules of the game and the guidelines of the higher law? If so, it could be argued that such a written document may be superfluous; yet if there is not already a social agreement, a written constitution could be meaningless, a classic dilemma of many countries.

Indications are that there is a growing consensus of opinion which could reach acceptable and legitimate guidelines and institutional reform. If this is so, the limits to successful constitution writing will be due not to disagreement on social goals, but to the backwardness of the state of the art of designing political institutions, and to the inevitability of unintended consequences when provisions are made for the guidance of human behavior. Questions of religion and the state, however, are another matter. These will remain divisive for some time, although, at the very least, the human-rights aspects can be resolved.

The extent of government involvement in the society develops new challenges to individual rights. The problems are not so much those of expounding general ideals, but of actually attaining them in the real world. Many people believe that the formulation of agreed and explicit guidelines for individual rights and of institutional provisions intended to guarantee entry into politics and competition would serve two needs. They could create a more tangible set of rules of the game which the developing society could strive to observe; and they could help (and force) those whose job it is to develop the meaning of a constitution from day to day—the executive, the legislature, and the courts—to face up to the more basic social implications of the many specific decisions which ongoing life in a complex society demands.

CHAPTER 3

Political Integration

THE POLITICAL SYSTEM of the Jewish Yishuv was already highly developed when the state was declared. Institutions of government and law functioned from the beginning; Mapai was the dominant party, and Ben Gurion the unchallenged leader of the nation. New immigrants and children growing up in Israel after 1948 found what seemed to them a world already made, replete with symbols of authority, patterns of leadership, and beliefs and institutions to which they were expected to adapt.

The vast majority of immigrants to the state, as well as Arabs and Druze who grew up under the Mandate, had not participated in the politics of a democracy. Despite this lack of experience, political integration is at an advanced level, as seen in the high degree of participation in politics and in the fact that power and resources are allocated through parliamentary and electoral processes. I inquire, therefore, into how the new citizens were introduced to politics, and indeed to the country; what unites people of diverse cultural origins, and to what extent political divisions are related to social attributes, such as religion, ethnicity, or socioeconomic status. The starting point is to consider who the people are, their origins, and the circumstances under which they joined the society.

The People

Most of the Jews living in Israel are immigrants, or the descendants of recent immigrants, although a small minority are descended from those who returned to the country in different centuries under Arab, Mameluke, or Ottoman rulers, and reestablished such communities as Safed, Tiberias, Hebron, Jaffa, and Jerusalem. Indeed, there were Jews in Palestine throughout the centuries of exile. At the end of the War of Liberation in 1949, there were about 750,000 Jews and 180,000 non-Jews. At the beginning of 1980, of 3,836,000 Israelis, 618,000 were non-Jews, mainly Arabic-speaking, including 481,000 Moslems, 88,000 Christians, and 49,000 Druze and other groups.

Between 1939 and 1948 more than 100,000 illegal immigrants were brought in, mainly from Europe under the British blockade. After 1948, immigration was freely allowed and actively aided. As the refugee camps in Cyprus and Europe emptied, most of the Jews in Islamic countries emigrated to Israel. By 1973 those of Asian or African origin and their children constituted more than half of the Jewish population. Other major immigrations came from Eastern Europe in periods of political thaws. From 1969 onward, most immigration was from Soviet Russia, including more than 25,000 Georgians. Comparatively few came from the Western countries. (See Figure 3.1 and Table 3.1.)

FIGURE 3.1   Sources of Increase (Jewish Population)

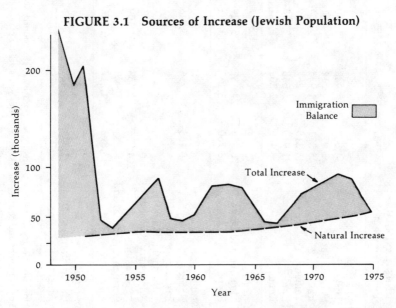

Based on Figure 2, *Israeli Society—1980*, by permission of the Central Bureau of Statistics.

TABLE 3.1. Principal Immigrations, 1948–75

Continent and Main Countries of Origin	1948–51	1952–54	1955–57	1958–60	1961–64	1965–68	1969–71*	1972–73**	1974–75**
Asia									
Turkey	34,547	942	3,960	1,969	4,793	n.a.	n.a.	n.a.	n.a.
Syria-Lebanon	2,913	614	761	1,341	1,401				
Iraq	123,371	1,934	654	401	541				
Yemen	48,315	867	127	171	704				
Iran	21,910	5,838	2,068	7,793	8,889	5,324	4,385	1,226	369
India	2,176	2,209	1,727	1,444	2,940	5,009	4,853	1,034	967
Africa									
Maghreb and Libya	76,338	24,137	88,529	12,362	114,265	n.a.	n.a.	n.a.	n.a.
Egypt	8,760	3,157	13,281	1,083	1,233	n.a.	n.a.	79	n.a.
Europe									
USSR	8,163	756	5,946	7,041	4,646	6,085	17,631	65,087	25,331
East Europe: Poland, Rumania, Bulgaria, Hungary, Czechoslovakia	294,736	7,468	41,109	35,785	70,760	6,048	3,674	140	n.a.
Germany, Austria, and France	13,892	1,217	1,176	1,265	2,288	2,699	3,682	2,409	714
America									
United States	1,711	428	416	708	2,102	2,066	1,583	1,464	***838
Argentina	904	799	1,177	912	5,537	2,155	2,102	2,841	805

* Does not include about 6,000 already temporarily in the country who changed their status to that of immigrant.

** By continent and country of residence (other years are by place of birth).

*** About 5,000 additional from the U.S. came in status of "potential immigrant."

Sources: C.B.S. *Annuals*, 1974, 1975, 1976; *Immigration to Israel, 1948–72*, part I, Special Series No. 416, C.B.S., Jerusalem, 1973.

Each immigration* was given a different reception in the new land, due mainly to changes in economic conditions, settlement policies, and employment opportunities. In addition, the groups varied widely in the social condition of their members, cultural heritage, and skills and expectations. The war had denied the Europeans the education and experience of the German refugees of the 1930s, but they had learned the arts of survival, or survived by chance, in the Holocaust. Although almost the entire Yemenite and Iraqi communities were brought to Israel in daring operations, some other communities at first sent mainly their disadvantaged and few of their elite. In 1954 the problems which this imposed led to a policy of selective immigration, confined to families which had at least one breadwinner and no chronically ill. At that time the society was overburdened with the simultaneous tasks of beginning industrialization and starting agricultural settlements, receiving large immigrations, and defense. Selectivity was quietly stopped in 1959, in a period of full employment.

Table 3.2 indicates the change which took place in the original occupations of immigrants over the first two decades of the state. There were many professionals in the more recent Eastern European and Russian groups, as there were among the smaller immigrations from Western Europe and the Americas. Coming as individuals rather than *en masse*, the later arrivals could more easily gain recognition of their talents. Their opportunities were further enhanced by the rapid economic growth following the 1967 war.

TABLE 3.2. The Occupations of Immigrants in Their Original Countries*
(as a Percent of Those Who Stated Occupations)

Occupation	1950–51	1961–64	1969–71
Professional, scientific, technical, and related	9.2	15.9	32.6
Managerial and clerical	16.6	17.0	17.8
Trading and sales	21.0	9.4	10.8
Agriculture and fishing	5.8	1.2	1.0
Transportation, communication, construction, mining, crafts and workshops	43.4	50.4	32.6

* For the origins in a given period, see Table 3.1. The data should be considered as of qualitative rather than quantitative accuracy; only about one-third declared their occupations, while others perhaps reported inaccurately.

Sources: C.B.S Annual, 1976; *Immigration to Israel, 1948–72*, Part I, Special Series No. 416, C.B.S., Jerusalem, 1973.

* The word "immigration" (*aliya*) is also used as a noun to designate those coming from a specific Diaspora community, or in a given period.

Differences in political culture and experience were also substantial. In the prestate period, young people often spent years in preparation and waiting for certificates of immigration, and once they reached Palestine, more time passed before they could be given land for settlement. Many dropped out, and those who remained were largely self-selected. Few of the postindependence refugees from Europe had the ideological approach or the political preparation of the many immigrants to the Yishuv who came under the aegis of political movements. More of the immigrants from Eastern countries than from Europe came directly from settled communities. Their longing for Zion was very strong, but more as an integral part of traditional Jewish life and religion than of the political and social ideologies which then predominated among those who received and taught the immigrants. Many of the differences in the general culture and skills of immigrants from Europe and those from Islamic countries are due to the fact that modernization, for Eastern European Jews, began many decades before it did for those from Asian or African countries.

Mass Immigration and Political Integration

Becoming immediate citizens under the Law of Return, many immigrants were soon involved in politics. In the beginning they were merely clients and, in return, voters. More genuine integration developed, however, in local Histadrut and town organizations, and eventually extended, in lesser degree, to the national institutions. Even if most of the immigrants had come from modern countries, political integration would have been difficult because of the problems inherent in the act of migration itself. It was made even more intractable in the Israeli context by the difficulties deriving from the scale and nature of the migration.

Several factors were to have a lasting imprint on the political culture and system. Among these were the dependency of the immigrants, coming without capital or professions and facing very difficult conditions of housing, employment, and accommodation to a new society; and the tutelary attitudes toward them of the veteran population in general and of political leaders and agents of immigrant absorption in particular. The arrival of very large groups fostered the development of stereotyped perceptions of immigrants as members of ethnic cultural groups, and the development of mass rather than individual solutions to their needs. Because the immigrants were sent to settle outside of the metropolitan areas, and to a lesser extent on their peripheries, the cities could play only a minor role in bringing the newcomers into fuller participation in the society. Almost from the first, there developed a congruence of country of origin, the level of social and economic skills, and location, a phenomenon which continues to be important in social relations and in politics.[2]

For many, the initial period was traumatic. Great expectations were disappointed, previous status was incongruent with new conditions, old skills were obsolete, and family authority was forced to give way to that of outside bureaucrats or new peers. Entry to a new society forced the immigrant to restructure his self-image and to form a new social identity. In the Israeli society, the Eastern immigrant faced the need to develop a more individual, separate ego, as opposed to a previous self-concept in which the individual was first of all part of a family.[3] Some of the older cultures were denigrated by the host society, and immigrants often observed modes of behavior which seemed strange and inferior. This was true not only regarding the veteran settlers of the Yishuv but also people from other developing countries with whom they interacted for the first time. Friction among immigrants from different countries was often exacerbated by competition for jobs and housing. As the country's general standard of living rose, later immigrants were given better conditions, incurring the jealousy of some who came earlier.

Early settlers and newer arrivals fell into the error of excessive generalization about each other. The major and most influential classification has broadly divided Israelis in terms of their characteristics into those who came from Asian or African countries and those of European or American origin. This approach has some basis in fact. To varying degrees, in recent times, Jews in the Islamic countries were second- or third-class citizens living in decaying feudal societies. The influence of the surrounding societies was often seen in the existence of rigid and premodern occupational structures, the organization of life in extended families and kinship groups, a leadership which was based more on wealth and status than on ability, and a lower level of technical skills than in the West. In recent times their communities were less autonomous and less organized internally than those of Eastern Europe. Nonetheless, these communities were highly integrated, and life within them is now remembered as based on the warm enjoyment of Jewish culture and close family life, and as having an honored intellectual tradition.

Eastern immigrants and their children do not usually see themselves, however, as belonging to a comprehensive *edat mizrach*, or "Eastern ethnic group," but rather as part of an *eda*, or group, from a specific country or more rarely from a part of a country. Differences between groups, and indeed within them, support these feelings. The differences between individuals or local communities in the Asian or African communities have been as great as within any other group. A Moroccan Jew could be a professor at the Sorbonne or live in a primeval cave village in the Atlas Mountains. A stereotyped view injured the process of social and political integration on both the national and the individual level. It caused injustice to individuals, in denying them the conditions and opportunities most appropriate to their personal talents and skills; it contributed to the mass approach to the reception of immigrations; and it enlarged the areas of possible misunderstanding between one immigrant group and another, and between veterans and new immigrants, even when both came from the same country.

Many long-resident Israelis, once immigrants themselves, have difficulty remembering the strangeness which the newcomer experiences, and have not always appreciated the dangers some immigrants, for example, the Russians or Yemenites, went through in order to escape their native land; nor, in the case of the Russians, can they understand the seeming ingratitude of someone who had left what most Israelis perceive as a totalitarian hell. In the larger cities, veterans made little voluntary effort to help newcomers, not mainly out of prejudice but because they were preoccupied with their own burdens. Organizations dating from the Yishuv, such as those started by Sephardic groups or Georgians, found little common ground with the later immigrants from their countries, and largely failed to make common cause with them.

Each *aliya*, even before the state, thus went through the feeling of being outsiders, and in a sense each integrated itself. Immigrants had to adjust to each other, to the new society, to a new language, to the differences between their self-images and the way they were perceived by others, and between their often utopian expectations and the reality which confronted them.* To all of these were added the basic economic needs: new skills, work, and housing.

The section which follows attempts to give a sense of the unity and diversity of some of the principal immigrations and their experiences; for, despite great internal diversity, each immigration had a history of its own, and its members often shared cultural characteristics which affected the process of political integration.

"There I Was a Jew—Here I Am a Moroccan"**

Moroccan Jewish communities have existed since antiquity.[4] Arab tribes penetrating Morocco in the seventh century met Jews already living there, and some Berber tribes are reported to have been converts to Judaism. The descendants of the earlier settlers, or *toshavim*, were reinforced after the expulsion from Spain in 1492 by many Spanish Jews, called *megurashim*, or "those who were banished." The descendants of these two groups maintained separate institutions well into the twentieth century.

Local communities were spread over a vast territory, and they were influenced by Berber, Arab, Spanish, and French cultures. Contributing to and benefiting from the high level of the Arab culture of the Middle Ages, the Jews

---

* Thus, depending on the extent of their Jewish background, Russians could expect to find in Israel a theocracy or an economic "America," and some American immigrants a utopian spiritual center. A school principal could come under the crossfire of American parents asking for open classrooms and self-expression, and of Russian parents demanding more discipline, neatness, and order.

** In the countries of origin, many aspects of the culture of a community which differentiated it from the surrounding society were seen as being "Jewish." In Israel, these same customs were perceived as characteristic of the specific countries of origin—Yemen, Morocco, or America.

in more recent times were affected by the backwardness and decay of their surroundings. Assimilation to the secular cultures of their neighbors was greater than that found in Eastern Europe, and local customs and belief in the supernatural influenced religious practices, particularly in the more remote villages.

Although it is difficult to compare the political cultures of these *kehillot* (communities) with those of Eastern Europe, since much less has been written about the life in Islamic countries, some comparison can be made. In both areas the rabbis were the judges, adjudicating questions of religious law or civil issues between Jews. Small, self-selected oligarchies of *gabaim* (leaders), men of wealth and status, administered local affairs. As elsewhere in the Diaspora, local communities were independent, and each provided for the indigent, for the elementary education of boys, and for the services required by religious precepts, carrying out the precarious relations with outside authorities through *shtadlanut*.* Perhaps even more than in Eastern Europe, religious practice was an integral part of all aspects of life.

Still, the cultural factors which could counter authoritarian or oligarchic strains appear to have been weaker in the Islamic countries than among the Russian and Polish Jews. The organization of the Moroccan *kehilla* (community) seems somewhat less complex but more formal. The customs of *hazaka* (the vested right to perform a service or to share an income) and *serara* (the hereditary or family right to an office, often associated with relatives of community leaders) were common. While male literacy was almost universal, the education of boys usually stopped at a lower age than in Europe. Literacy was less among girls, and in smaller villages, girls often were given in marriage in childhood. Overall, the members of the community seem to have been more deferent to community leaders and rabbis than were the Jews of Europe (as the women and children were more deferent to the father at home).**

In 1980 there were more than 220,000 Moroccan-born Jews in the state. They and the Rumanians are the largest immigrations from any one country. The Moroccans' difficulties and aspirations have been the most noticed, and their political role the most important. The experience of the Moroccans as Israelis shows the influence of the history of the communities, the changes in their social condition under the French protectorate, and the way in which they were received in Israel.

The French protectorate of Morocco (1912–56) brought more physical security and accelerated contacts with European culture, although the Jews

---

* The *shtadlan* was a community representative to non-Jewish authorities, a role also found in European communities.

** Contrast the apparent chaos found in some Ashkenazic synagogues, where often each person proceeds through the service with a style of his own, to the decorum and authority felt in many Sephardic congregations. The detailed histories of specific communities show changes from time to time in the authority relationships, but these broad differences still prevailed.

remained under the governance of the Moroccan Moslem authorities. But the transition from religious feudalism to modernity brought little amelioration of the social condition of most of the Jews. Although it was no longer mandatory for urban dwellers to live in the closed ghetto, or *Mellah*, many were forced by circumstance to remain, living in conditions of incredible overcrowding and poverty, with a consequent decline of family life and mores.

For most urban Jews, the problems of adjusting to a modern society had begun before they left for Israel. Those who fled the *Mellah* or migrated from a village to a newer part of a town and began to adopt European ways found themselves to be neither French nor Moroccan. The acculturation to French modes was difficult and in many cases superficial. The confrontation was more with a colonial facsimile of France than with the deeper manifestations of French culture. The depth of Jewish learning and culture had also diminished, and assimilation had begun among the educated. Acculturation weakened family and community ties, stimulated intergenerational conflict, and led to a decline of religious and social cohesion.*

As modernization led to decreased community autonomy, the role of the leaders became more that of enjoying an elite status than a leadership occupation; nor, under the changed conditions, did the rabbinate offer much social or Zionist guidance. Before the state, the world Zionist movement failed to develop strong ties with the Jews of the Maghreb, or to encourage their participation.

Urbanization was rapid, and by the end of World War II 60 percent of the Jews lived in the cities. Adopting European culture much faster than the Arabs, some Jews initially played an important middleman role between the Arabs and the French. These opportunities diminished, however, as the Arabs advanced and displaced many of the Jews, most of whom remained impoverished artisans or peddlers. The steep rise in the proportion of the poor, together with the decline of a sense of community responsibility among the bourgeoisie and the notables, led to the neglect of the needs of the numerous poor. The vast educational needs were not met, and only a minority of the children received a modern education at the Jewish Alliance schools or in the French system.

Beyond the relatively small numbers of the members of Zionist youth movements, the return to Israel initially attracted mainly the poor and disadvantaged, many of whom were encouraged to emigrate by their home communities. From the towns, most of the highly educated, more than 30,000,

---

* It is said that one of the traumas of the Moroccans (as well as other Asians or Africans) in coming to Israel was a decline, in the new milieu, of the father's authority and of family solidarity. In actuality, the solidarity was beginning to break down in Morocco. Often it was a determined mother who kept the children in school while the father retained symbolic authority and the administration of punishment. Obedience patterns had been the general rule in family training instead of the internalization of mores.

went to France.* Local leaders who reached Israel seldom maintained their high community status, since they were either not helped by the political parties, who tried to develop their own loyalists, or lacked specific abilities needed in the new setting.

Moroccan Jews had endured the simultaneous stresses associated with a decline in religious belief, a lowering of prestige of old occupations, the foiling of aspirations to reach the social status of the French middle class, and the frustrations of being outside the political struggle. Alienated in the general Moroccan society, they had strong associations among kin and friends. In contrast to the messianic return of the Yemenites or individual solutions of the Europeans, Moroccans sought in Israel majority status, economic deliverance, physical safety, and equality as Jews.

For many Moroccan immigrants, expectations and realities were far apart. The shock of marked changes in personal and family situations and the immigrants' level of education, skills, and often health did not allow full exploitation of the opportunities in the new land. While their *absolute* standard of living eventually rose, and, for most, the conditions of sanitation, housing, and medical care surpassed those in Morocco, their *relative* status for the most part declined, and Moroccan Jews felt themselves to be at the bottom of the social ladder. The social condition was aggravated by the fragmentation of extended families and communities in the new land. Middle-class Moroccans were included in the general stereotype of the "Eastern communities," and in the early confusion of mass immigration, usually obtained fewer job or housing choices than those with comparable skills who came from Eastern Europe. More skilled or better-educated people were often dealt with together with the unskilled. There was thus downward job mobility. A further handicap was the relatively large proportion of dependents. Moroccans often worked in lower manual occupations, in which they were not compensated by having a Labor Zionist belief that manual work and cooperative enterprise were noble or liberating, and from which they could not advance in a society which needed technical specialization. Many who had lived only in remote rural areas experienced the further shock of living in a heterogeneous society of strangers.

Frustrated by the distance between the realities and their high expectations, some Moroccans reacted in a manner seen by others as aggressive. Like the Russian Jewish immigrants in New York in the early part of the century,

---

* In the 1960s a movement called Oded ("Encourage") was formed under Ben Gurion's aegis, to bring academically trained Moroccan Jews from France to Israel. Several hundred came, a few directly from Morocco and others from France, and began to help advance the community as a whole. Until the Yom Kippur War, Oded was active in social and educational community programs. For a few years these activities were quiescent, and in 1977 Oded joined the Democratic Movement for Change, having important roles in the internal activities but gaining only one member of the Knesset delegation in the DMC internal 1977 primary elections. Subsequently Oded again became independent.

Moroccans were believed by many to have more than their share of criminals, and some reacted to what seemed like a rejection in the new country by believing that they were inferior persons.

The Moroccans as a whole thus did not have a very stable base from which to face their new challenges. The frequently superficial assimilation to French culture, the fact that many leaders did not immigrate, and the nature of the initial reception in Israel increased the vulnerability to the new problems of identity and self-esteem. For many, self-regard grew dramatically after the excellent performance of the children of Moroccans in the 1967 Six Day War; yet protests and strong feelings of discrimination still continued in the 1970s, primarily in those development towns and neighborhoods where poor conditions, low income, and ethnic origin seemed clearly to overlap. The Moroccans have the principal role among the Asian/Africans in preserving ethnic politics and in pressing social demands. This role derives not only from their experiences and the sensitivities they developed, and the large size of the North African immigrations, but also from a considerable ability to organize.

On the Wings of Eagles

After centuries of isolation as the lowest-status group in a remote and medieval caste-structured country, the Yemenite community came to Israel—some with incredible difficulty—in the nineteenth and early twentieth centuries. The first sizeable group came in 1882. The majority were brought shortly after the 1948 war, messianically, "on the wings of eagles," by a mass airlift.* In the period of the Second *Aliya*, a Yemenite immigration was encouraged by Labor activists who hoped this would help in the more rapid creation of a Jewish working class and increase the acceptance of Jewish labor by employers, but these early Yemenite immigrants and their children were not given opportunities equal to those of other early settlers, and their tribulations and their contribution in that early period are not adequately appreciated.**

As "unbelievers" in Yemen the Jews had been separate, a low but "protected" caste. A patriarchal society, occasionally polygamous, they were in many ways the intellectuals of Yemen. Almost all males were literate, and the Jews performed the mechanical arts for the Moslem *fellah*, soldier, or large trader. The town of Sana had a large community and a complex of synagogues, but many Yemenite Jews lived as isolated minorities in hundreds

---

* See Deuteronomy 32:11, "As an eagle stirreth up her nest, hovereth over her young, spreadeth her wings, taketh them, beareth them on her pinions."

** A leader of the Second *Aliya*, Yavnieli, went to Yemen in 1911–12 to encourage immigration. He later resigned from activity connected with it in protest against the inadequate integration of the Yemenites, whom he saw as being used as hired laborers, but without receiving the help of the community for social advance, or the opportunity for independent settlement. (Shmuel Yavnieli, *Massah Le'Teiman* (Heb.) (Journey to Yemen). Tel Aviv, Aynot, 1963.)

of small Moslem villages. In contrast with the Iraqi, Moroccan, and other communities, the Yemenites had little contact with colonial powers or their cultures. Their community was apart, turned inward toward Jewish life. Of the large Eastern communities it was the most integrated, socially and culturally.

In Yemen, rabbis played a strong leadership role, enhanced by the fact that they received no salary, earning their living from a trade. The lay leaders were chosen from the comparatively wealthy. One in each community had the dubious and dangerous distinction of being the negotiating representative to the local Moslem rulers, who could imprison him at a whim or convert him by force. An ambivalent and sometimes jealous attitude toward the *shtadlan* was later transferred to Israel, where Yemenites often looked on their political "ethnic representative" as an appointed rather than elected leader, not to be completely trusted to get a fair deal for his compatriots. Community mores were enforced initially by the family and on a wider scale by the "shaming" of deviants by the local community. Both of these forms of control deteriorated markedly in Israel.

The Yemenite leaders, although they came with the communities, usually could not function effectively in the new setting. The rabbis lost status by joining the government payroll. They were of little help to people facing a mystifying array of specialized bureaucrats. The Yemenites settled in Israel in a few local concentrations. Extended families or *hamulot* which had lived in Yemen at a distance from each other suddenly intermingled and competed. Factional and clan strife were often turned into local party rivalry, and factions or families could appeal in important matters to outside politicians, who in turn exploited them for their votes.

In Israel the previously autonomous communities tended to become dependent. Yemenites as a group faced some regression in the social conduct of the youth, associated with a persistently low social and economic status, a weakening of social control, and a lack of adequate new leaders and leadership patterns, although occasionally, as in the Jerusalem corridor, some autonomous settlements developed cohesion and new leaders. The problem was often exacerbated by the unemployment of the head of the family, whose skills were not usable in the new setting and whose authority was further injured by the importance, in the Israeli society, of activities which in Yemen were thought to be "womanly"—such as welfare, health, and education.

Many individual Yemenites enjoy outstanding success. In the general society there is a positive stereotype of the Yemenite, but on the whole the community is only slowly achieving social and economic equality. As a group which came with a messianic Zionist urge to return to the homeland, the generations of the immigrants accepted lower status with much less visible protest than the Moroccans; yet their difficulties, particularly in the pre-state Yishuv, were real and deeply felt. Present-day youth are actively seeking equality.

Some Other Aliyot

The Iraqi community also came almost in its entirety from a somewhat more advantaged background than those from most other Moslem countries, although with a lower average of skills and education than the Western *aliyot*. The history of the Diaspora in Iraq goes back more than 2,500 years. In modern times it was a homogeneous and stable community, living mainly in Baghdad and under a considerable Western influence through the British Mandate (1921–32). Occupations of Iraqi Jews included the professions, railroading, finance, and the civil service, as well as small trades. Women's education was developing, although a traditional subservient role for women in the home continued, and only in Israel did the Iraqi women begin to work outside their homes.[5] The Iraqi Jews were exposed to a British colonialism which attempted far less cultural absorption and domination than did that of the French in North Africa. The more benign experience of acculturation in Iraq affected mainly the more educated, for the Iraqi community had a more clearly defined and stable hierarchy and separation of classes than most of the other Eastern communities, and it was perhaps the only Eastern group in which there were communist intellectuals. The transfer of this class structure in Israel contributed to a comparative lack of organizational cohesiveness and mutual assistance among Iraqi immigrants.

Under the anti-Allied regime which took power in 1941, the Iraqi Zionists worked as an underground movement, organized by missions from Palestine. In 1950, Jews were allowed to leave if they renounced Iraqi citizenship and their possessions, and by the end of 1951 nearly all had reached Israel in a daring and organized exodus by air. In Israel a much larger proportion of Iraqis than of other groups settled in the metropolitan center, where they are strongly represented in accounting, insurance, and finance and include professionals, police officers, judges, consuls, and politicians. Their settlement had less geographic concentration than that of other groups, and Iraqis have assimilated more than other Asian/Africans into the general community, although at some cost. Little of the history and culture from the old country has been passed down to the next generation. Most of the poetry and stories were in Arabic, and much of the literature was ignored by the schools and the society for being part of a seemingly inferior or unknown Eastern culture. Another cost of the assimilation of the better-educated and of the continued class structure has been a lack of internal community solidarity or leadership, so that the economic and educational advantages of many Iraqis have not served, as much as they could, to advance the larger numbers of the less advantaged.

I have dwelled at some length on the people from Eastern countries because it is assumed that the reader is more familiar with the cultures and experiences in the more developed countries, and because of the importance of these immigrations to politics in general and to social policy in particular. Among the European/American immigrants, however, there has also been a tremendous variance in the societies from which they came and in the personal experiences preceding their *aliya,* which have depended mainly on the time of their immigration and their age. In the middle of World War II, children whose parents were left in Europe were brought via Teheran and settled and trained in kibbutzim. Polish Jews who came in 1948 had survived concentration camps or spent the war years in hiding or passing as "Aryans" outside the ghettos. Warsaw ghetto fighters, trained as members of socialist settlement movements, also came with the beginning of the state and founded kibbutzim, as did groups of American, English, and South African university graduates. Younger Jews, coming from Hungary or Poland ten years after the state, may have been bureaucrats in communist governments, professionals, or university professors, most often with little background or previous identification as Jews. Georgians succeeded in maintaining religious orthodoxy and individual enterprise in a province of the USSR and, having overcome the Russian bureaucracy, set out to take on the Israeli. The initial variety of personal experience and world outlook among the Westerners has been, if anything, greater than that among those from Islamic countries. Western immigrants, however, eventually assimilated to each other and became less diverse than those from the Eastern countries.

Generally, the Westerners were much more able than were the people from the Asian and African countries to interact with the bureaucracy and with the party representatives.* The fact that they were more highly regarded and had more schooling inevitably affected their opportunities. Immigrants from North and South America and from Western Europe have had little political influence, while their impact on science, the universities, and engineering has helped to lead the country rapidly into the front ranks of science and technology. The Western immigrants' small numbers, professional preoccupations, lack of fluency in Hebrew, and unfamiliarity with the ideological divisions and culture of the political system contributed to an inconsequential political role. The political impact of Western professionals, however, was not far less than that of many Israeli-born professionals and intellectuals.

Settlement on the Periphery

Together with the manner of immigrant absorption and political socialization, the peripheral location of settlements had a very great impact on political integration. The settlement of immigrants made spatial distribution both essential and possible, and it prevented the metropolitan center from

* Josephtal, for example, saw the Easterners as lacking in cohesion and organizing ability. "The main difficulty is that the immigrants have no leadership ... around which they can unite. There is little social cohesiveness ... there are no social nuclei." By contrast, "In all the Ashkenazi ma'abarot, a local committee emerges after about six months."[6] In more recent experience, the ability to organize has been no monopoly of the Westerners, as shown, for example, by the port workers of Ashdod, of whom a majority are of Asian/African origin.

being overwhelmed. Population distribution, always an ideological goal, was as much a necessity as it was a virtue. Dispersal, however, had an important cost measured in terms of education and social condition.

Nearly half of the immigrants to the state came in the first six years. Between 1948 and 1951, annual immigration was as much as 20 percent of the country's population. At first, abandoned buildings in such towns as Jaffa, Lydda, and Ramle and in former British army camps were filled, mainly by European refugees. By 1950 the influx from the Islamic countries was in full force, and in the hard winter of 1951–52, well over 200,000 people were in temporary quarters, many in tent camps, exposed to the elements and waterlogged by the winter rains.[6] Camps were soon replaced by *ma'abarot*, or transient villages, built of prefabricated huts. Although there was less physical distress in the *ma'abarot*, the feelings of strangeness and separateness from the society remained strong. Immigrants of later periods were spared these experiences, and within a decade less than 15,000 people were without permanent-type housing.

The temporary *ma'abarot* were located with the hope that there would be access to employment in agriculture or in adjacent towns, and these early decisions often determined the permanent location and indeed demographic composition of new towns or of peripheral urban quarters, or *shechunot*. In 1952 the transfer of new immigrants directly to new agricultural settlements was begun, and from 1953 on, the founding and growth of new towns and the development of old ones were greatly accelerated.

Figure 3.2 shows the location of new and old development towns, Figure 3.3 the striking differences in population and density, and Figure 8.1 the spatial distribution of agricultural land, ports, and mines. Even today, the periphery lags markedly behind the center in economic and cultural activities, in the standard of living, and in social and educational services and attainments. This lag will be more understandable in the light of the experience of settlement of new *moshavim* and development towns.

From the Ship to the Farm

In the early 1950s Levi Eshkol, then in the dual role of Minister of Finance and head of the Settlement Department of the Jewish Agency, put through a decision to set up more than 400 new *moshav* settlements.* By 1954 as many as half of the immigrants were being taken, with no previous training, from the ship to the farm. The need to provide housing and work, to meet food shortages, and to close defense gaps in sparsely settled areas make the daring deci-

---

* See Chapter 5. Just as Sapir later saw himself as the "industrializer of the country," so Eshkol had the imagination and could organize the political support for large-scale settlement of inexperienced, untrained, and often unmotivated newcomers.

sion seem in retrospect to have been almost inevitable. Villages based on private holdings were not ideologically desirable, nor did individuals have funds to invest. The communality of the kibbutz form had little appeal to people without an understanding of what was involved, and the essentially elitist kibbutz movements did not believe that undedicated nonbelievers could succeed. Of nearly 1 million immigrants in the first ten years, less than 2 percent went initially to kibbutzim, including children who were sent for schooling. Many more settled in moshavim.*[7]

The sites were allocated by party agreements at the top—some 80 percent of the settlements to be under the auspices of the moshav movement, affiliated with Mapai, and 20 percent with the religious settlement movement. Such an experiment on so large a scale would not have been possible without political mobilization. The location of a group thus determined its political auspices and the allegiance of the members, at least for the first few years.**

In contrast with most moshav settlers in the Yishuv, few of the new settlers were volunteers or experienced in the cooperative procedures and self-government which are central to the moshav idea. That the new moshavim succeeded at all is remarkable, for even those formed in the Yishuv or by veterans now have problems and paradoxes. Among these are the feasibility of maintaining the principle of performing one's own work without the aid of hired labor, of preventing moshavim near the large cities from becoming commuter suburbs, and of preserving cooperative purchasing and marketing. Social and political development were to prove the greatest challenge to the new moshavim.[8]

After the tutelage of the immigration administrators, the settlers came under the supervision of instructors sent by the Settlement Department of the Jewish Agency and chosen according to the agreed party key. Their encompassing task was to lead the new farmers in all matters of economic organization, cooperative self-government, agricultural practice, and social relations—the aim being to achieve an economically independent moshav on the classic cooperative model.

---

* In the first six years of the state, some ninety new kibbutzim were formed, largely by European immigrants and native Israelis. These, together with the new moshavim, increased the Jewish rural population from about 100,000 in 1948 to nearly 300,000 in 1955.

** Dov Goldstein (Ma'ariv, March 15, 1974), interviews Aharon Ozen, Minister of Communications (later Minister of Agriculture). Ozen, the first poststate immigrant Cabinet minister (in 1974), recalls that once he did not know the difference between a kibbutz and a moshav, although formerly in Tunisia he was a member of the Revisionist youth movement. (Only a small minority of the new moshavniks had any movement background or volunteered for agricultural settlement.) Arriving from Tunis in 1949, Ozen at first tried to join a moshav which was under religious auspices. He was rejected because he did not show outward signs of religiosity, such as wearing a skull cap—a common occurrence, he says, among Tunisians. Eventually, he heard of an opportunity in a Mapai moshav, and thus his future political allegiance was determined. Such a decision was more likely to be made by chance in the case of immigrants from the Eastern countries, where the religious culture was relatively diffuse and boundaries between the religious and the secular much less sharply drawn than in Europe.

FIGURE 3.2 Israel's Development Towns, by Size of Population, 1979

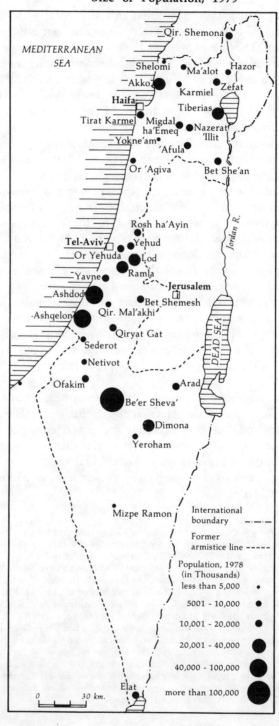

FIGURE 3.3 The Distribution of Population (Population Density by Natural Regions)

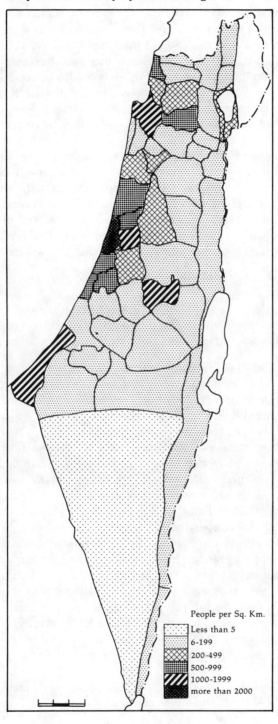

People per Sq. Km.

Less than 5
6-199
200-499
500-999
1000-1999
more than 2000

The assignments would have taxed the most outstanding leaders. Many early sites were not economically feasible. The new settlements often lacked roads to markets, electricity, and adequate housing. Until 1955 the government frequently assigned people of different origins to the same *moshav* in the hope that this would further integration. As a result villagers from a remote Maghreb countryside might find themselves living with Jews from India and a few Moroccan urban middle-class families; or rival clans from the same community could be located together. Heterogeneity often led to strife and unhappiness.

The country's suddenly expanded needs caused a shortage of instructors, and many of those enlisted were neophytes. A number came from outside the *moshav* movement; others were young people just out of the army who had volunteered for a year of service. Many were devoted, but success was mixed. Villagers and instructors had incongruent perceptions of each other. Instructors often tried to motivate the villagers through ideological explanations and by comparing their situation and roles with the heroism and trials of the founding fathers. But

> most of the immigrants...wished to maintain...the way of life transmitted to them, or to achieve a way of life to which they had aspired before immigration... [while] the field staff saw the village development as part of the system of action of the larger society in formation.[9]

In the crossfire of political movements, with friction among settlers, and the reality of hard economic facts, new settlements took years to reach economic independence. Nonetheless, they were more successful economically than in fulfilling the ideals of cooperation and self-government with which the *moshav* movement originally started. By 1976 more than two-thirds of the new settlements had reached income levels which made them independent of Agency support. Most were socially stable, in that population turnover was low and settlers lived in amity. In many new *moshavim*, however (and some old ones), cooperative managing, purchasing, and marketing organizations had the form but not the scope or content which were hoped for in the cooperative ideology.[10]

At the national level, most of the substantive roles in agricultural planning continued to be held by farmers from the older *moshavim* or from the kibbutz movements. Yet members of the new *moshavim* have gained much practical experience in the management of affairs, in relations with national institutions, and in the operation of large marketing and purchasing cooperatives at the national, regional, and local levels. However imperfect, the institutions afforded the forms and experiences from which a great deal was learned. By 1976 the Minister of Agriculture was an immigrant from Tunis, from a new *moshav*.*

* See footnote on page 113.

The Development Towns

Beginning in 1953, new towns were established and immigrants were also sent to old towns, such as Safed, Tiberias, and Beersheba. By 1974 more than 341,000 people lived in twenty-three new development towns, and 239,000 in seven old ones. Jerusalem was the only major city which received a proportionately large number of immigrants, although some development towns are not far from Tel Aviv and new neighborhoods or quarters often were built to provide public housing in peripheral areas of established cities.*

It was often decided to build a new town on the site of an existing transient camp, or *ma'abara*, or in an agricultural region far from the metropolis, and settlers' destinations were often decided by the coincidence of the date of their arrival in the country with building and settlement schedules. Early attempts were made to achieve a planned mix of settlers, but because of the unpredicted arrival of large groups needing housing, a neighborhood or small town was frequently settled by people mainly from one country.

Exigency and the vagaries of administration often put people together who were from the same country but whose needs were very different, and localities settled with people of a single origin often failed to develop social independence. An example is Rosh Ha'ayin (population 12,000 in 1977), a Yemenite settlement near Petah Tikvah. Here, suddenly placed by themselves in a new environment, the settlers had no close neighbors from whom they could learn, or through whom they could integrate into the larger society, so that progress was slow, and *hamula* (clan) politics persist. Eventually, settlements were planned to be composed of different groups, each living in a relatively homogeneous neighborhood. A successful example of this approach is Kiryat Gat (population 22,400 in 1977), a town between Tel Aviv and Beersheba, populated with people from more than half a dozen countries.

A central problem of the new towns has been their inability to reach a critical size which would support the services, variety, and amenities which could attract and hold people. By 1977, only seven of twenty-three new towns had a population of more than 15,000, and only four—Beersheba, Upper Nazareth, Dimona, and Kiriat Gat—had more than 19,000. Few of the new towns became in any sense regional centers. It was originally believed that the location of a town or a village at the center of a subregion would lead to its integration as a regional center for services to an agricultural hinterland. The kibbutzim and the older *moshavim* preceded the towns and were technically, politically, and educationally more highly developed, having their own service organizations. Regional services were set up on a cooperative basis between settlements, with little relation to the town except occasionally to hire

* See Figure 3.2. In Jerusalem (population 189,000 in 1965) there were 37,600 Asian/African and 23,800 European/American immigrants; Tel Aviv (386,000 in 1965) had 55,500 Asian/African and 82,000 European/American immigrants. See C.B.S. Special Publication 267, Table 24, pp. 62–65.

labor. Indeed, the development towns were seen as nonpioneering, nonagricultural, and not particularly wanted; and the agriculturalists, who later became industrialists as well, developed their own regional government and educational systems.* Another factor was the short travel time from most settlements to metropolitan centers, which made a hierarchical system unnecessary. The large number of new towns, all competing for industry and resources, reduced the chances of success for each one, and left most without an adequate economic base.

At first, almost the only available work was public relief employment, such as ground clearing or forestry, or day labor in kibbutzim or *moshavim*. The first industries established, such as textiles and food processing, added mainly unskilled workers. It was not until the mid-1960s that the periphery began to provide opportunities for more highly skilled work. However, despite substantial incentives given to industry to locate in development areas, in recent years economic growth and the increase in the sophistication of industry, paradoxically, have favored the center. Investment in the outlying areas was frequently capital-intensive, particularly in the exploitation of mineral resources, so that manufacturing jobs increased less rapidly than the growth of investment. Lower per capita income in the outlying areas caused a lower level of demand for services, while the center developed headquarters, warehousing, finance and sales, and other services at a rapid rate. The new port of Ashdod, for example, while making that city grow, probably brought an even larger number of jobs to the Tel Aviv area. Technical sophistication brought the need for highly skilled manpower, so that investors in high-technology industries resisted the financial inducements of the periphery in order to benefit from the services and manpower pool of the metropolitan area.**

Even when industry developed, many managers, teachers, and professionals commuted to their jobs in the new towns, making progress slow in developing any firm base of local community leadership or social fabric. Population turnover was rapid as a result of subcritical size and a lack of social or economic attraction. Negative selection left the weaker families rather than the stronger. Settlers who were more skilled or aggressive, many of whom came from Western countries, moved to larger or older towns, and their places were taken by new immigrants. For example, in Ma'alot, a town near the Lebanese border with a population of 5,400 in 1973, more than 20,000 *different* people lived at one time or another between 1957 and 1972. The objective difficulties in new towns were thus very great. Local social and political development lagged because many of the resources and conditions needed for them were lacking. The admixture of people did not lead to

* In many kibbutzim, in 1977 as much as half of the income came from industry.
** These trends are seen in the decline from 1967 to 1971 in the proportion of all of the subsidies and loans which were given in the periphery under the Law to Encourage Investment—from 80 percent to 60 percent.[11]

autonomous social and cultural development. There was little of an intelligentsia, and few opportunities or amenities to attract or keep them.

Local Government and Political Integration

These many disadvantages to the contrary, new and old development towns have been more important in political integration than the cities or even the new *moshavim*. In the larger cities, an upper layer of the veteran population and established party functionaries had things in hand. Immigrants living in the poorer city neighborhoods, or *shechunot*, had for years little representation in the city government or direct influence on it. Neighborhood committee chairmen (in the early years an Israeli variety of ward heeler), originally sponsored by parties or city hall, served as brokers for demands and votes. Only in the late 1960s and 1970s did unsponsored leaders begin to emerge, and neighborhood organization to develop.

In contrast to the cities, in the development towns the first veteran administrators constituted a very small management group, so that the contact of the immigrants with local government was more direct. The path to participation thus had many fewer obstacles. Even so, it was many years before there were acknowledged local leaders who were both of the place and selected by its people, and not merely coopted or appointed from above. This lag was due to the unusually dependent nature of Israeli local government in general and of the development towns in particular, to the way in which the towns were initially established and managed, and to the overall national process of absorption. The advances which eventually occurred were possible because of the existence of political and social institutions which served as avenues of political learning and integration. These aspects will be considered in turn.

Local government is dependent on the center for the direction of new immigrants to a town, for locating or expanding industry or government offices, for public housing (more than 90 percent in most development towns), health services, and for police and employment exchanges. The Welfare Bureau and the schools are nominally under the local council, but, as with the other services, their funds and policy come largely from the national government.

Local taxes, loans, and budgets are authorized at the center. The district commissioner of the Ministry of the Interior approves budgets, much as in the days of the Mandate. In a new town, such as Kiryat Shemona in northern Galilee, city taxes and fees in 1969–70 covered only 16 percent of the budget, and in the port city of Ashdod, 38 percent.[12] The central government collects a large proportion of land taxes directly and sets the ceiling for local property and business taxes, gives grants and consolidation loans, and underwrites borrowings. Wide variance in the proportions of this support results in extensive pressure and negotiating activity by municipalities. When a town council is in serious financial or administrative difficulties, the Minister of the Interior can appoint a "Called Committee" to manage the town and put its affairs in order.*

Social and educational services in the development towns often are less advanced than those in the older communities, more because it is hard to attract and keep good teachers and social workers than for lack of funds. Per capita grants for social services given to a community have depended on the decisions of an interministerial committee. Towns are classified into categories of priority, which determine the general levels of salary, tax, and investment subsidies which may be given in order to attract people and industry. Just as an industrialist's success was often due to an administrative decision on the terms of his "approved enterprise" status, so a town was more likely to benefit from the classification of the level of its social or industrial grants than from constructive enterprise or administrative economies.

In practice, center-periphery relations have been more complex.[13] The rules of the game in allocations and budgets are not completely spelled out, and this allows considerable scope for bargaining and for political and economic dealing. The loyalties of local and sectional party leaders and local bargaining power and initiative have been crucial, leading to marked differences among towns. As towns were established, the central authority for each was allocated, by agreement, among ministries controlled by different parties. Thus Moshe Sharret of Mapai was long a patron of Beersheba, and the town of Arad was built and managed by the Ministry of Labor. Kiryat Gat and its surrounding area were planned and developed by the Agency's Settlement Department; and Carmiel, in the 1960s, by the Ministry of Housing.

As part of the 1961 coalition agreement, housing became a separate ministry, under Mapai, and came to have the major say in the development of new towns and neighborhoods. This predominance was mitigated to some extent by the requirement, in the 1965 Law for Planning and Building, that plans prepared by the Ministry of Housing for building on public land go through the regular local and regional town-planning procedures for approval. The Ministry of the Interior, which has oversight over municipal government and physical planning, has been led by the Mafdal (NRP) since 1963; and thus had less influence on planning than the Mapai ministries. The managers and local workers of state agencies, which give services according to laws and regulations, were initially hired on a party basis. And even when associated with the same party, separate agencies could be part of different national ministries whose policies might not be on identical courses. This system, in recent years

---

*For example, Yaakov Schribaum, the City Controller of Jerusalem, has had a distinguished career acting as a "receiver," appointed by the Minister of the Interior to head "Called Committees" to clean up in towns in the wake of such shenanigans as unauthorized borrowing, inflated expense accounts, handouts, contracts without tenders, charges for services which people should have received free, or plain incompetence. After the committee restores order, it serves until new elections are held.

somewhat less politicized, complicated approaches to the center and encouraged the skills of *shtadlanut*.

Center-periphery relations within parties have been another source of dependence. Even now, local party and Histadrut leaders frequently see their present jobs and future roles as dependent on decisions of central leaders, and are therefore compliant. A personal veto by a party center leader could thwart a local mayoralty aspirant, or determine the factional composition of delegations to party conventions or central committees.* [14] A further source of central concern and control has been the instability of individual and group relations in many local party branches or town councils. Concerned for party unity, national party headquarters often intervene or arbitrate in the internal disputes of local branches.

Related to its condition of dependence, local government has been fundamentally ineffective. Many local authorities, even in the long-established and more prosperous communities, have lacked self-sufficiency and a resourceful spirit. Many mayors, in rebuttal, would ascribe the ineffectiveness of their regimes to their dependence on the center for specific allocations of resources—which, they say, denies them control or rationality of decisions. But this is only part of the story. Local administration has been highly politicized, often with little distinction between administrative and representative functions, since local coalition agreements usually provide the participating parties with paid jobs for elected councilmen as deputy mayors, each with control of departments. Even the second largest city, Tel Aviv, in 1973 had nine elected deputies who headed forty administrative departments. Thus the effective control of the mayor is strongly undercut. Lacking some of the civil service restraints of the national government, municipalities can go further in politicization, hire inadequately trained people, and design their organizations more to satisfy demands for office and patronage than to provide public services.

And pecadillos have been common. Sheer carelessness or worse in the granting and enforcement of sanitary and building inspection and licensing arrangements, the collection of taxes or fees, and the granting of permits has been characteristic at one time or another of most of the local governments. Town councils are often the providers of plums, and the parties of a *parnassa*, or livelihood. In some localities, office was sought (and to a lesser extent, still is) as the way to benefit the candidate and his associates. Many elected officials have not refrained from making decisions in which there was a conflict of interest.

In some ways the local scene thus seems to be an exaggeration or distortion of the national. The party names are the same, but they may stand for the tem-

* In the elections to the Labor Central Committee in 1969, for example, Sapir and the "Gush," or the central Mapai machine, instructed loyal local party secretaries to cut down the ex-Rafi representation in the new party center in the expectation that the new center would soon, as it did, vote for Golda Meir's successor and perhaps also vote on policies for future boundaries.

porary allegiance of cliques or factions, with little division on questions of belief. Personal antagonisms loom larger in the close local quarters, the politicization of administration goes deeper, and petty irregularities seem much more blatant, yet somehow more forgivable.

Another national phenomenon which reinforced the dependent condition of local government was the way in which immigrants were received. Citizenship was taught and learned in an instrumental, tutelary, and ethnic manner.

The process began before the immigrant came to the town, even before the town was founded. Agreed-upon party proportions were used in selecting the Agency emissaries who organized the emigration abroad, or who interviewed or made assignments to living quarters while the immigrants were still on the ships or in transit camps. Consequently, the immigrant was often unable to distinguish between the partisan and the substantive roles of the many officials who dealt with him.

Competition for the political loyalties of the immigrants by the right-wing parties, Herut and the General Zionists, was restricted by the arrangements and by the party key appointments. On arrival, all people were given membership in the Histadrut and its health fund, Kupat Holim, in which Mapai predominated. Welfare and educational bureaucracies began to minister to their needs under what were essentially party auspices. Employment for most was at first mainly on public works programs. Uncertain about his future work, location, or housing, and unacquainted with the political system or the complexities of ideological differences, an immigrant could feel almost wholly dependent on party-nominated officials or intermediaries. In the minds of many newcomers, the images of the state and of Ben Gurion and the other Mapai leaders merged. These factors contributed to stability in the balance of national political support, seen in election results which over the years showed little change as a direct result of the large immigrations.

Local government in the new towns was politicized from the beginning. Mapai's potential influence in housing, employment, and health was extensive. The NRP (Mafdal) usually had its agreed proportion in the appointed municipal council and among the Jewish Agency representatives, while at the same time it dominated the Religious Council and its services. "Who gets what" was influenced by both local and national bargaining. Thus Mapai and to a lesser extent the Mafdal had more to offer concretely to the voters than other parties, and represented the government to the newcomers.

Party functionaries at the center were more concerned with national patronage and machine building than with the integration of immigrants.[15] Indeed, the Mapai central machine was left to operate autonomously by the national electoral leaders, and from the early days of the tent camps it went all out as a "contractor for votes."* National parties, despite their sectoral and

* Josephtal complained in 1951 of some of his Mapai colleagues that "during the election campaign we did considerable harm in the settlements and *ma'abarot* by making insubstantial promises and buying votes..."[16]

ideological programs, adapted to what they saw as the local demands, catering to specific secular needs and pressures. Politicians were often seen initially as exploiters, whose sensitivity to people's needs increased remarkably as election day drew near. This in turn reinforced the pragmatic approach of the immigrants, who soon learned to manipulate the system and to choose their political affiliations on the basis of the hoped-for satisfaction of their needs.* Through the combination of politicization and dependency, the people started by learning to take, not to give or participate.

A second important characteristic of the process of absorption was the tutelary approach of the veterans—the mentors, officials, and political leaders. The common use of the term "absorption" rather than "integration" is revealing. It was the immigrant who was expected to change. As he was absorbed into the society, he would become modern and at the same time adopt the social values of the Yishuv. In the process, he would transform his premodern culture and role and be "resocialized."[18] The mentors, and academicians who later studied the process, were often at a loss to understand the values of the "premodern" cultures, or the importance of traditional and historical continuity in modern societies. The result was a depreciation of self-esteem, dilemmas regarding identity, and an acceleration of the inevitable decline, begun with immigration, of the influence and authority of the immigrant parents.

It was far easier, as has been seen in the new *moshavim*, to achieve economic modernization than to develop new social ideals or to foster political integration. This was only partly due to the attitudes toward immigrants. The society as a whole was diverging from its previous ideological modes of politics. For all neophytes, the political system was a relatively closed one. Of the immigrants, however, an even more extended apprenticeship was demanded, in the course of which political participation would be passive rather than active. Even veterans were required to progress patiently through the ranks of the political guilds, and this applied much more to the newcomers. When those who adapted most rapidly were incorporated into the lower ranks of the political hierarchy, the rest of their group or neighborhood could be left without leaders with the potential of developing political independence or with the ability to represent needs which could seem to conflict with the goals and norms of the veteran society. The emphasis of the veterans was on patience, on maintaining the older values until the training had become accomplished. Integration was seen to mean adaptation and absorption.[19]

A third aspect of the mode of integration was the fostering, by the national parties, of an ethnic mode of politics, of working with people as groups rather than as individuals. Ethnic politics has always been more legitimate locally

* For example, in a study made in the late 1950s, in the new town of Or Yehuda, 40 percent of respondents said they joined parties because of their aims, 40 percent for expected personal benefits, and 20 percent because of expected general social benefits.[17]

than nationally. It was natural for ethnic and neighborhood subgroups to have common interests which formed a basis for cohesion and political demands. Many immigrants held strong stereotyped views of people from countries bordering on their former homes, of whom there might be groups in the new town. Cultural differences, minor to an outsider, could irritate and lead to strong neighborhood antagonisms.

The national parties bear much of the responsibility for the early ethnic hue of local parties. In some *moshavim*, for example, clan-based *(hamula)* politics was encouraged where it might not have emerged spontaneously.[20] In doing so, the parties may have impeded rather than advanced integration. It was easier to view new people as a homogeneous group, and it was convenient for the national parties to work through apparent leaders of ethnic groups or neighborhoods acting as brokers, whose influence depended to a great extent on the patronage which they could deliver. The selection of leaders was at first often made from the outside, with inadequate understanding of the internal structure of the community. Ethnic politics "came naturally" to the parties: to Mapai, which organized on an ethnic basis nationally, just as its matrix organization came to comprise most other groups as well—youth, professionals, women, the kibbutz and the *moshav*, trade unions, and minorities; to the Independent Liberals, in encouraging Rumanian and other national groups; to Herut, which from the start concentrated its campaigns among the disadvantaged, and as a party of opposition urged that their plight was the fault of the establishment; and to Mapam, which sought to convince the "social underdog" of the class origin of his troubles.

In Beersheba, for example, Mapai developed a kind of feudal structure based on the leaders of several groups—the *vatikim*, or "veterans," workers of Solel Boneh,* and ethnic groups (from Persia, Hungary, India, Morocco, Iraq, and Rumania).[21] This oligarchy for years made the decisions, allocated patronage and economic advantages, and chose candidates, while the mayors had little control over these "organizational" aspects.

While national ethnic election lists soon disappeared from the Knesset (there were five in the First Knesset, three in the Second, one in the Third), locally they persisted much longer.** Perhaps the strongest factors working against ethnic politics at the national level are the strong belief in the unity of the Jews as a people, and the symbols characteristic of the proportional-representation national campaigns. In local politics these questions have not been germane. The unimportance of ideology in local issues and a "pressure group" approach made ethnic groups mobile and the local scene fluid—the group could readily switch its support to those promising actual or symbolic

---

* Solel Boneh, the Histadrut's contracting firm, did a large share of Negev building; workers wanted representation to advance their employment interests.

** In 1973 elections neither of two "Panther" lists achieved a seat. In 1977 and 1981 Charles Biton, a former member of the Panthers, was elected on the Rakah list, mainly through Arab votes for the list. In 1981 Tami, a religious-ethnic list (split from the Mafdal) gained three seats.

rewards. If disappointed, it could return to the fold. In addition to local parties with ethnic-group names, many lists were for years known to represent certain groups strongly. Thanks to the pragmatic nature of the local system, these lists could readily shift local coalition allegiance from one national party to another.

Local, regional, class, and religious interests soon took over as the formal basis for organization.* In local campaigns, as in national elections, blatant ethnic appeals largely lost their place and legitimacy. Comparing two consecutive election periods in a new town, it was found that problems were stated in socioeconomic terms much more in 1969 than in the more ethnic campaigns of 1965.[23]

Ethnic consciousness is still very much alive. But as social needs become more complex, people of different ethnic origins begin to feel that they are interdependent, and organize to solve their problems more along lines of the common needs of an age group, economic sector, or class, or even of class-related culture. Functional elites emerge in the towns and *moshavim*.** In places where the group political ties remained strong, a "consensus" politics developed. In a sort of mutually agreed consortium, the several groups that sought representation, participation, and rewards rather than control often unite to back a candidate in order to get larger rewards for the whole community.

Local Institutions and Integration

Within the general pattern of absorption, it was the center which established new towns and made substantial additions to the housing and population of the old ones. In both cases, the institutions common throughout Israel were provided, together with their managers. The new immigrant, facing a broad and confusing array of services and agencies, was at first dependent on central emissaries and their local representatives to negotiate with the varied and complex bureaucracies. At the same time, this variety and the possibilities of town life gave a potential for independence and participation beyond that which was conceivable in the totally dependent relation in the camps and *ma'abarot*.

From the start, the government, the Jewish Agency, and the national par-

---

* In 1965 there were thirteen ethnic lists in local elections, and in 1969 only eight in the whole country, although there were 112 lists with no national party link in 1965 and 70 in 1969, many of which represented local ethnic groups. In 1973, local lists won in twelve smaller municipalities. Nearly all had strong candidates and "local interest" or "good government" platforms.[22]

** In a study of an immigrant *moshav*, for example, it was found that "the political structure features the central position of the *mazkir* (secretary) vis-a-vis the other families of the *moshav*."[24] That is, his function in this case was more important than his group connections. On the other hand, there are cases in some new *moshavim* (and in Arab or Druze settlements) where the office is the means by which a clan, or *hamula*, gains control of resources.

ties designed the local institutions and put them into operation. Workers in dispensaries or in the cooperative stores, teachers and senior municipal workers, were veterans from the center. Many served devotedly for years, and the administrators often did much to teach their clients.[25] Sometimes the leader was originally from the same country as the immigrants but had previous administrative experience and had been in Israel longer. Veterans often identified with the town, or saw their service as a step in a political career. They organized institutions according to the models from the center—principally the town council, party branches, especially of Mapai, the Histadrut Workers Council, and the religious council (for the administrative aspects of *kashrut*, ritual baths, burial services, marriage, and synagogues). These institutions and the local national administrative services were increasingly manned by local people—at first by appointment and eventually through more genuine local choice.

A town council was initially appointed by the Minister of the Interior, its partisan composition arranged at the national party level. When a town was considered "mature" by the ministry, elections were held and its council became the senior local institution, the channel through which most national funds were passed on to the town, and often a principal source of employment and other benefits or patronage. The workers' councils have been no less important. Fostering trade unionism, neighborhood organization, and cultural and sports affairs, they provided many opportunities for elective and paid positions.

Local party branches, except for Mapai and occasionally the Mafdal, have been quiescent between elections. Like the town councils, but to a lesser extent, they have been the ground on which groups and factions compete, where new people can be brought into the system, and where the relative influence of individuals and groups is tested. Often, there is much overlap, and many people are at the same time party activists, members of the workers' council, and municipal employees or councilmen. Local Histadrut organizations offered the most ready avenues for experience and for the emergence of locally bred leaders. The workers' council could influence employers in giving jobs, particularly when jobs were scarce. The council had staff jobs for adherents and resources and people for extensive political activity, reinforced at campaign time from the center. With closer ties to the work places and requiring less professional knowledge, the local Histadrut activities often overshadowed those of the municipality in their potential for political socialization. Election to a works committee was frequently an immigrant's first political step.

Most of the veterans who led the new towns in their early years were eventually voted out of office, and at first replaced by local protégés of national politicians, usually in the internal party nominating process.[26] In time, the local leaders came to be chosen more by their peers, or at least approved by them, and as the party branches grew in size, their bargaining position vis-à-vis the center improved. The feudal type of *shtadlan* fared poorly at the hands of young voters. The clients of the former patrons developed more economic and social independence. The proportion of elected officials who were on party or movement payrolls declined, although it remained high. Immigrant youth learned Hebrew, went to the Army, and gained experience on works committees, on workers' councils, and in lesser jobs in the municipalities or in business. Often new leaders got their first chance in a reform swing, in the aftermath of administrative failure by the previous incumbents.

Local development was not the only reason for an increased local voice in the choice of leaders. After Ben Gurion left the office of Prime Minister in 1963, much of the impact of his symbolic appeal was lost to the central Mapai bureaucracy, and new local groups had more opportunity. Still, political sanctions and control of resources continued to give the center *de facto* veto power over many local nominations.* This was mitigated by a trend toward rationalization in the allocation of resources from the center, although the ministers still seemed to act vigorously to meet local needs only when awakened by a serious challenge.**

National control begins to decline as the Labor Party cells in the local works committees tend to disappear, as central Histadrut influence over the local workers' councils decreases, and as non-Labor parties gain adherents and split-ticket voting on national and local elections becomes more common. In the Labor Party, the growth in membership of some local branches and the formation of regional councils (there were more than 12,500 members in Beersheba in 1973, for example) are beginning to give more leverage to the periphery. The direct election of mayors (rather than their choice by the town council), passed into law in 1975, promised to strengthen the position and legitimacy of the mayors *vis-à-vis* the center. Local influence in the election of workers' councils also increased.***

Even though local authorities have been unusually dependent on the center, the institutions afforded experience in the exercise of electoral and deliberative proceedings, and, within a modest but increasing scope, in the allocation of resources. Through their activities, indigenous leaders emerged, as a whole new generation came into politics, learning to work within the institutions and electoral systems.

The local spirit, also, began to become more independent. There is a local desire for self-expression, a sign of coming of age. "Are you asking us before

* The central Labor Party machine was dormant, however, for most of the period of the 1973–77 Rabin Cabinet.

** In the protests after the massacres by Arab terrorists at Kiryat Shemona and Ma'alot in the spring of 1974, ministers and their representatives immediately appeared on the scene; projects which had ground to a halt or were delayed mysteriously speeded up; and budgets increased remarkably overnight; but things went back to normal. The towns soon felt again that they were forgotten.

*** Until 1977 there was only a national ballot in the Histadrut elections, and seats on the local workers' council were allocated in the same party proportion that a given locality voted in the national election. From 1977 there was separate balloting for local and national party lists.

you decide, or telling us?" ask the members of the Labor Party branch council in a development town, of an official from headquarters who is discussing with them a new national wage policy, which, they had good reason to believe, had been decided before the meeting.

Under-Representation

These are harbingers of progress, and not yet fully the real thing. Despite these changes, there is a cultural lag in the social and geographic periphery, that is, in the development towns and the *schechunot* in the cities, marked by a feeling of political inefficacy and dependence. This lag derived from the initial endowments of the immigrants, from the trauma of migration, and from the way in which the immigrants were received and introduced into the communities, as has been shown. Its concrete expression is found in the under-representation of the periphery in the Knesset and in the bureaucratic forums where major decisions and allocations are made. The broader the scope and the greater the apparent power of a position, the lower the probability that the incumbent is of Asian or African origin, or comes from a *shechuna* or development town. These groups are numerically under-represented at the higher levels of government.[27]

In view of the Israeli belief in the inherent unity of the Jewish people, it may well be asked, why the calculation of sociological representation (i.e., the proportionate participation of ethnic cultural groups in political and management roles) should be made. The question itself shows a lag in political integration. Were integration felt to be more complete, it would be assumed that a person was chosen for his individual characteristics. The knowledge of his origin would add little to the ability to predict his electoral or administrative opportunities. This situation, however, is still far off.

The calculus of sociological representation is made both by political leaders, who coopt and nominate, and by members of ethnic groups. Politicians seek election lists which are "representative," through the inclusion of candidates who can draw votes and support, by association, from a broad population. They also thus attempt to show that their party embraces the ideals of national unity. Those who feel part of an ethnic entity often believe that, without the participation of their own people in the exercise of authority as well as in symbolic status, their needs will not be understood, nor will they get a fair share of resources or status.* Less than proportional representation

* Glazer and Moynihan indicate another possible reason for the strengthening of ethnic association in a welfare state, as a more coherent and specific focus of political award than the broader concept of "class." On the one hand, ethnic organizations press for the interests of the members. On the other, those deciding on resource allocation receive more identifiable political credit than they could get from allocation to a more general or "class" category. "Why Ethnicity?" *Commentary*, 58, No. 4, October 1974.

can give a feeling of belonging to an inferior class of citizens, and works against political cohesion and legitimacy.

On at least three counts the mere presence on a list of persons of specific ethnic origins is not always convincing. A history of top-down nominations can give voters a feeling that these are not really representatives. Second, voters are cognizant of the difference between genuine power and symbolic roles, and are not impressed with those which give more honor than authority. Third, on balance, voters give priority to the quality of national leadership rather than to associational considerations. For such reasons, the inclusion of "representatives" in Knesset election lists has not in itself gained a party many votes.*

As the level of administrative or policy authority of an institution increases, the proportion of its participants of Asian/African origin decreases. At the level of the Prime Minister's informal "inner Cabinet," there were, by 1977, no Asian/Africans. There have usually been two or three Asian/African Cabinet ministers, but not in the most senior ministries or as yet in such jobs as Chief of Staff of the Defense Forces, Governor of the Bank of Israel, president of the largest government corporations, or Mayor of Tel Aviv, Haifa, or Jerusalem. There have been two or three Asian/African directors-general of the large ministries. In the three highest civil service grades below the directors, the proportion of Asian/Africans is only about 4 percent; it grows higher rapidly as the rank goes down.[28]

The Knesset has had a larger proportion of Asian/Africans than the higher civil service, growing from 10 percent in the early years to about 20 percent in 1956–69. It was 15 percent in 1969–73, 20 percent in the Eighth Knesset (1973–77), and 16 percent in the Ninth (1977–81), when the second-place Labor Alignment list included 23 percent. Similarly, more than 25 percent of the membership of its Central Committee was of Eastern origin in 1977, a larger proportion than in the central Histadrut bureaucracy. Nationally as well as locally, the Histadrut has offered more opportunities than government. In 1975 the Labor Party Central Committee reported 123 of Asian/African origin out of a total of 577. Within the party "bureau" or leadership forum, there were then three of Asian/African origin out of 29 members.**

While people of Asian/African background are represented in most bodies of power, participation is broadest at the local level of the Histadrut,

---

* In 1977 the Alignment presented more Asian/African candidates than the winning Likud. Mordechai Ben Porath, a former Alignment M.K. and supporter of Dayan, who had been a leader in the evacuation of Jews from Iraq in the early 1950s, formed his own list, yet did not get one seat.

** In 1976 prominent roles occupied by those of non-Western origin included, inter alia, Chairman, Knesset Foreign Affairs and Defense Committee; Speaker of the Knesset; Chairman, Knesset Labor Committee, Ministers of both Agriculture and Communications; Minister of Police; Treasurer, Histadrut; President of the State. In the 1981 Begin Cabinet, David Levy was Deputy Prime Minister and Minister of Building and Housing.

and in local government. Indeed, in the 1975 elections, non-Europeans won 40 percent of the mayoralities, mainly in the new and small towns. Three out of every four development towns elected Asian/African mayors, and 37 percent elected Asian/African secretaries of local workers' councils.

Underrepresentation in national roles raises the following questions: To what is it due? What may be the future trend? What is its importance? Underrepresentation is partly due to the existence of a structure and political culture which create discriminatory situations even though there is no discriminatory intent. Elections depend more often on "nomination" than on voter appeal.* There are the effects of the top-down system of appointments, longevity in office, and a tendency to "choose people you know" or at least whom you can easily "check out." These practices work against all newcomers, as does the initial concentration of many immigrants on the periphery—the national party bureaucracies and nominating power have in the past been based in the largest cities and their environs.[30]

Other reasons are the less than perfect process of political socialization, and the lag in educational attainments of Asian/Africans, who are not nearly as well represented among the country's high school and university graduates as they are in the population as a whole. Lesser educational attainment is also highly correlated with being the child of manual laborers and with living on the periphery.[31]** People in elite roles and in the most important administrative and elected positions at the national level are drawn from the higher civil service, industrial and financial management, and professional and scientific work, which usually require academic qualifications. The trend toward higher educational qualifications is seen also among elected leaders and in the Histadrut bureaucracy.

A necessary if not a sufficient condition for increased Asian/African "sociological representation" at the national level is therefore the closing of the educational gap. The trend is in this direction; the endeavor has behind it a considerable priority in the resources given for education. Direct election of mayors, enacted in 1975, will help, but even more important would be a less hierarchical character and increased accessibility of the party systems (for people of all backgrounds) and a marked qualitative improvement in local government.

The Asian/Africans are not alone in feeling that they have a disproportionate political representation. Other *aliyot*, such as those from English-speaking countries and the large Russian immigration of the 1970s, have also

---

* Increased political competition (for example, elections held following party splits) and periods of protest increase the proportion of Asian/African nominees.[29]

** This question is analyzed in more detail in Chapter 6, "The Welfare State." At universities, the proportion of Asian/Africans of a given age cohort was about one-quarter of the proportion of European/Americans in the same age group (C.B.S. *Annual*, 1976). Note the starting line of family education: in 1964 the percentages of immigrant women without any schooling were as follows: the Yemen, 85; Tunis, 49; Morocco, 48; Persia, 68; Iraq, 61; and Turkey, 41. For most of these countries, 80 percent of the women had seven years of schooling or less.

experienced it, and few English-speaking immigrants have been politically active. By 1976 Soviet immigrants were beginning to hope for at least symbolic representation on party Knesset lists, although most of them, like many Western immigrants, are nonpartisan in that the devotion which motivated their immigration was to the idea of Israel as a whole and not to one segment or specific ideology.

Eastern European immigrants, particularly in earlier years, had found themselves in a familiar milieu of ideologies, personalities, and parties. Thus the late Moshe Sneh went from the Polish Sjem, or parliament, and Zionist movement directly to the highest councils of the Yishuv; while the middle-class Germans who came in the 1930s and the Americans who immigrated after 1948 came into a partisan environment in which their political effectiveness was very limited in comparison with their central and outstanding professional and economic roles.* However, the German *aliya* of the 1930s resulted in the Progressive Party, forerunner of the Independent Liberals (which later incorporated strong Rumanian groups). "Liberal center" groups could provide political modes and ideologies more like those in which most English-speaking immigrants were educated. Such groups, however, have shown little growth. In the 1977 elections, the Independent Liberals were left with only one seat, and in the 1981 elections they gained none.

Political Integration: Unity and Division

The analysis thus far has emphasized the way immigrant populations and their children entered a democratic and parliamentary system, developed attitudes toward government, and now play active roles in politics and administration. For the immigrants and others on the geographic or social peripheries, the process of entry appears at first to contrast with the guild-like recruitment and progress of the veteran population, closer to the party and administrative centers. It is, however, a special and more acute case of the general approach to political apprenticeship, whose procedures delayed the active participation, not only of immigrants from developing countries but of those from the West and of much of the native Israeli intelligentsia as well.

Another aspect of integration is now briefly considered—the connections among beliefs, associations and interests. Potential lines of political segmentation are those dividing Jews of Eastern and Western origin; proponents of a religious state and those wanting a secular national culture; adherents of ideologies of the right or the left on both domestic and international issues;

---

* Their important contribution to agricultural settlement is less known. English-speaking groups have founded more than thirty settlements, and individuals have done much in private farming and citriculture. See Y. Morris, *Pioneers from the West*, Jerusalem, World Zionist Organization, 1953. For the German *aliya*, see Beling, *Deutsche Einwanderer in Israel*, Frankfurt, Europaische Verlagsaustalt, 1967.

and those holding opposing concepts of the future borders of the state and of the territorial nature of Zionism. These differences among Jews, although far from trivial, are much smaller than the distance which separates the religions, cultures, and national feelings of the Jewish majority and the Arab minority. A separate section later in this chapter discusses the political integration of Arab Israelis.

Despite the diversity among the 3 million Jews, and the closeness and intensity of interaction, the forces which unite are greater than those which divide. Religion, language, and ancient history are shared. There is a widespread feeling of association with the other Jews of the world, and Western civilizations are common reference groups. Along with constant outside threats there is awareness of the dangers of internal Jewish division, and fear of disunion has an important influence on policy. The congruence of class and ethnic-group membership with beliefs is limited, and historic developments have minimized the class struggle. In local politics, ethnic-group loyalties to parties are not consistent from one locality to another.

The role in the polity of the Jews of Asian or African origin, now a majority, has been shown to change with historical circumstances. From the experience of other countries, it can be expected that a strong ethnic undertone will continue for some time. Social integration and equality are greatly desired, but not yet at hand.* [32] This is seen in the limits of sociological political representation and in the cognizance of it as an issue; and in the large proportion of those of Asian or African origin among the people in the lowest income deciles, with the lowest education and in the poorest neighborhoods. Social and geographic mobility, while advancing a feeling of unity, leave residual concentrations of the less able.

Yet social assimilation is both desired and advancing. Physical differences among Jewish ethnic groups are more obvious in Israel than in many other countries. Differences in physical appearance among Jews show the result of centuries in different countries of the Diaspora, yet these differences are much less noticeable than those between major ethnic groups in Europe and the United States. In Israel there is no overt ethnic discrimination against individuals in jobs, housing, or political rights, partly because of the central place in the ideology of the absorption of immigrants and the experiences of discrimination Jews have had in other countries. Those of all origins see themselves first of all as Jews and Israelis.

There are two kinds of asymmetry, however, in the mutual perceptions of people of Western or of Eastern origin. The first is in what is called "social distance." Easterners accept Europeans, and want to be close to them, more than Europeans accept those of Eastern origin. This observation, however, needs two modifications. Easterners want social closeness only on condition

* Chapter 6, "The Welfare State," analyzes the questions of present and potential equality.

that it is accompanied by mutual respect; and Westerners tend to be ignorant of the existence of their own prejudice or to suppress their awareness of it.

Seeing that there are no formal social barriers, and perhaps unaware of the infrequency with which people of different origins or occupational and educational levels interact for purely social purposes, Westerners underestimate the extent of prejudice against Easterners, even as Easterners overestimate it. Europeans tend to ascribe the lag in the educational achievements of Asians and Africans to inferior home and neighborhood environments and to their origins in backward countries. But in many cases, they have a negative stereotype of the Eastern groups. Such feelings, indeed, are shared by some non-European parents who look for schools where the children of Westerners predominate, or by leaders in development towns who ask that more Western immigrants be sent so as to create "a less homogeneous population." A feeling of inadequacy among Asian/Africans is combined with a belief that the cause of the difference is not inherent in permanent characteristics, but derives from history and the absorption process. Thus there is often a diffuse, imprecise consciousness of congruence of class and ethnicity.* The class feeling, however, is generally nonideological, and is tempered by economic advance. Indeed, most of those questioned about this subject reply that, in the foreseeable future they expect all differences to disappear.

Some Asian/Africans are less concerned about discrimination in the allocation of benefits than they are over the support and dissemination of culture. When the Mapai faction of Labor put Ephraim Katzir in as President of the State (in a last-minute vote in the Party Central Committee, and for partisan, not for ethnic reasons), the first reaction of the defeated Sephardic candidate, Itzchak Navon, (he was elected to the Presidency in 1977), was to mourn Israel's lost opportunity to have its first Sephardic President, saying, "You only want to give us your culture, not to take of ours." ** Navon, coming from a learned Sephardic family which had lived in the country for several generations, was more likely to endorse cultural pluralism than one less educated. In the period following the mass immigrations, the poorer and less educated Asian/Africans often denigrated their own backgrounds, agreeing

* An example: housing for immigrants of the 1950s, at the peak of the Asian/African immigration, was built in small units. Families grew, and conditions of crowding resulted. By the late 1960s and early 1970s, when immigrants were coming from Russia and Western countries, standards had risen. The new apartments were much larger, while the new families were smaller. Many Asian/Africans saw in this discrimination in favor of Westerners. In some early years there was. Many European immigrants of the late 1950s were given much more choice of location and, as professionals, more individual treatment and better quarters; or, more commonly, the universally small apartments were occupied by both small Western and much larger Eastern families.

** Navon, formerly Ben Gurion's aide, had joined him in Rafi (Chapter 1). In 1972 the feeling of ex-Mapai in the Labor Party was strongly against ex-Rafi members. Beyond its recognition of his scientific attainments, the move to nominate Katzir was a move against Rafi. In 1977 Navon was elected President.

with others that they lacked modernity. As Asian/Africans advanced in the economy and society, more interest developed in the traditional cultures as a source of pride. Indeed, these feelings are now growing in scope.* There is a demand to teach more of the history and content of Eastern cultures, and the contributions of the Eastern communities to the return to Zion, so as to help children appreciate their heritage. "I would wish," says Navon, "that society would be Western from the point of view of government and science, Jewish from the point of view of tradition, and that the different cultures would develop individually and freely."

At the same time, assimilation, or rather the synthesis of an Israeli culture, advanced rapidly. As far as the broad differences between East and West, it may soon be too late to preserve or develop distinctive Eastern cultures. European immigrants were also cut off from sources of Western Jewish culture, but the Western culture was for years held in much higher regard, and predominated in the teaching in the schools. Most educated Asian/Africans, like their colleagues of Western origin, see themselves as part of an Israeli culture which is predominantly Western and modern.

The economic gap is narrowing faster than cultural or educational gaps. The income of many Asian/Africans is rising rapidly through enterprise and trade as contractors or technicians or as *moshav* farmers. They figure prominently among the "hard hat" occupations and as foremen and owners and managers of workshops, and as small business entrepreneurs, with a concomitant political advance in local union politics. These occupations do not require higher education, but the income they afford is often higher than the average in many professions.** The daily employment in Israel of tens of thousands of mostly unskilled Arabs from Judea and Samaria raises the relative status of partially skilled Israelis, even while it threatens the ideal of Jewish manual work.

Most important, however, are the expectation and desire of both groups for assimilation. The desire for integration is seen in the increasing number of marriages in which one partner is Eastern and the other Western. In 1972 more than 25 percent of the marriages of Israeli-born Oriental grooms were to Western-origin brides, as compared with about 18 percent of marriages where the groom was foreign-born. The proportion of "mixed" marriages has increased over the years; the proportion of marriages of Eastern men to Western women almost doubled in the 1962–72 decade.[35] Social integration will probably take place most rapidly where interaction is highest, among people

---

* About 70 percent of respondents to 1971 surveys wanted "all differences to disappear," while 83 percent expected to find "no differences" or "no substantial differences" in twenty years. Here again, there was asymmetry. More Orientals than Europeans (42 percent versus 23 percent) expected that "no differences will remain," while more Europeans (34 percent versus 24 percent) wanted cultural differences to persist.[33]

** It has been estimated that from the early 1950s to the mid-1970s, the standard of living of Asian/Africans improved twofold, rate of employment in professional and administrative jobs twofold, and high school and university attendance threefold.[34]

similarly placed, as in new middle-class neighborhoods. There are limits, therefore, to the medium-term integrative effect of mixed marriages.

Ethnicity and Political Division

The principal congruence of Asian/African origin and political attitudes is found in the ranks of the most disaffected and alienated and is thus expressed in social protest as well as in voting. Protest movements and riots involving Asian/Africans have been marginal in scope but important in their political impact because of public sensitivity to disunity. They have happened rarely, involved small groups, and did not spread through the communities. They were not riots *against* European ethnic groups, but protests against conditions and against the "establishment," which the protesters associated with those of European origin, even though the police involved in quelling the riots included large numbers, perhaps a majority, of Asian/Africans.

Protests have had little ideological content and leftist ideology has little influence among those in the lowest income deciles or among Asian/Africans in general; yet the potential threat of social unrest affects party nominations and government policies,* and the dissatisfaction of even small and extreme groups symbolizes the distance between the degree of integration desired and achieved.

Many lower-income Asian/Africans who do not feel alienated and who are part of the mainstream have a class feeling, seldom intense, which links their ethnic association with economic and social status. This class feeling, however, has little congruence with Labor institutions or beliefs. Until 1977 Labor was the establishment, and in the poor neighborhoods and development towns resentment was directed against the incumbents. Even before independence, Etzel, the Revisionist underground force, had a strong source of recruits in some of the older urban neighborhoods, such as Hatikvah in Tel Aviv, largely peopled by low-income Asian/Africans. Herut speakers in the early tent camps blamed Mapai for the poor conditions and accused the party leaders of dissipating each immigrant's "share" of the funds contributed for absorption. Herut reaped many votes over the years from those dissatisfied with the regime.

In addition to these social feelings, immigrants from Asian/African countries tend to endorse a more aggressive response to threats from the Arab countries and to be more alarmed by them. This kind of response is also found to be correlated with comparatively lower levels of education. Asian/African distrust of the Arab states could be expected, given experience in Arab coun-

* The role of protest behavior is discussed in Chapter 9, "On Democracy and Effectiveness," and details of the riots of Wadi Salib in 1959 and the Panthers in 1971 are presented in Chapter 6, "The Welfare State."

tries.* Their antagonism is accentuated by a rejection of their original association with what Israelis generally consider to be the less developed cultures of
the Islamic countries. Surveys have shown that distrust of the Arab states is
higher at lower educational levels. This distrust, where it extends to Israeli
Arabs, could be partly due to the greater cultural and economic threat which
the disadvantaged feel from the Arabs. But while differing views on the approach to the Arab states and the future borders are strongly held, and despite
the trends we have mentioned, opinions are distributed across social-
economic and ethnic groups, and to a considerable extent across party lines,
as was shown in Chapter 1.

Even more strongly held are views on religion and the state, and religious
practises have much more importance among Asian/Africans than in the
population as a whole. Yet the votes of Asian/Africans go mainly to the
secular parties, as do those of other Israelis.

The reasons for the limited Asian/African support for the religious parties
can be found in the limits to political competition at the time of the large immigrations of the 1950s, together with the dominant leadership of Ben Gurion
and Mapai, the appeal of Herut to the dissatisfied, and the neglect of the communities in Asia and Africa by the religious party politicians in the early years
of the Zionist movement. Thus, the Asian/African population, despite its
greater orthodoxy, has not given its overwhelming support to the clerical parties. Still, the potential for this support exists, and in all of the coalitions it has
enhanced the strength of the demands of the religious parties and has been a
factor in the stands taken by Labor and the Likud on questions of government
and religion.

Based on attendance at the religious schools, some 30 percent of all Israeli
Jews and a higher proportion of those of Eastern origin could be said to be
religiously observant, but the religious parties poll less than 15 percent in national elections. The political cleavage on questions of religion is only very
partially ethnic. The established Ashkenazic orthodox rabbinate has been
more legalistic and unbending than that of the Sepharadim, which takes
human frailty more into account. The sharpest cleavage of ideas and behavior
concerning religion over questions of religious and institutional autonomy,
state support, and public observance has been among those of Western origin.

Division on the Issue of Organized
Religion and the State

Views on the relation of the state and religion are intensely held. Their potential for division is greater than that of ethnicity and far more important than

---

* The remnant of Jews in Syria live in abject fear, virtually imprisoned in a small ghetto. The Jews
of Islamic countries, while they were not the objects of institutionalized murder as in the Inquisi-
tion or the Third Reich, were in constant danger and suffered many limitations and indignities.
See Davis Landes' picture of the condition of Jews under Moslem rule in Jerusalem in the 19th century in "Palestine Before the Zionists," *Commentary*, February 1976, pp. 47–56.

FIGURE 3.4.   Opinions on Government Enforcement of
Religious Observance

left and right social beliefs. The question is one both of the constitution and of
a way of life.* Many Israelis are somewhat ambivalent, seeing a need for national symbolism and observance but not wanting coercion of the individual.
There is, however, a polarization of feeling, as shown in Figure 3.4.[36] The intensity of feeling is related to the opposing concepts of a *halachic* state, which
is basically ruled by religious law, and of a liberal, secular state. At the national level, the conflict is largely confined on the surface to small-scale attacks from both sides on the *status quo*. These are carried on in the courts, in
the electoral-parliamentary process, and in attempts to extend patronage and
administrative control in the bureaucracy.

Social friction is often avoided through the development of orthodox
enclaves of residence in towns and rural communities. These enclaves,
although mainly urban, resemble in some ways the separation of many kibbutzim from the surrounding culture. Geographic separation can enhance the
felicity with which those who espouse very different life styles can live with
those of other beliefs in the same town or region, but it also perpetuates
distance and strangeness. Separateness is further encouraged by the religious
school systems, in which about one third of the Jewish children study, and the
exemption of orthodox girls and Yeshiva students from military service. The
religious parties are highly organized and institutionally self-sufficient. In
the manner of the "movements" in the *parteistaat* of the Yishuv, they own and
control economic, social, educational and settlement organizations.

In recent years, younger orthodox groups have made important advances
in modernization through the Yeshiva high schools, which combine prerab-
binic and secular education, and *Yeshivot Hesder* (Yeshivot of the Agree-

---

* The development of the political issues and parties relating to religion and the state, and the
constitutional questions, are analyzed in Chapters 1 and 2.

ment), whose students perform military service, often in elite combat units. The orthodox Bar Ilan University offers teaching and research at a high scientific level. Some of the female members of the Bnei Akiva youth movement serve in Nahal, the Pioneer Youth Corps of the Army. These organizations have furthered the national contribution and social participation, and broadened the patterns of interaction of the orthodox. The more modern orthodox youth, however, are if anything more determined in their religious-political views than their elders, although they believe that considerable patience will be needed to achieve the long-term aim of a *halachic* state.[37]

Weakness of Left-Right Dichotomy

The decline of ideologies and the growth of pragmatism have been described in Chapter 1. Surveys show that, in contrast to opinions on the state and religion, social beliefs are weakly held, and the proportions of people who say that they are "strongly capitalist" or "strongly socialist" are small. The great majority reply that their beliefs are "somewhat capitalist" or "somewhat socialist" (the opposite shape to that shown on Figure 3.4).

Parties of the right and of the left endorse the principal services of the welfare state. Hopes of mobility temper class feelings, and the weaker population had little or no Labor ideological indoctrination compared to that given in earlier years to many middle class children. The left is more egalitarian in its stated principles but not necessarily in actual policies. The demands of interest groups cut across a broad spectrum of beliefs, whose ideological importance becomes secondary. In the international scene, the anti-Jewish and anti-Israel policies of the Soviet Union have for nearly three decades prevented the mainstream of the Israeli left from supporting communist regimes and parties abroad.

There remain Jews who basically question the legitimacy of a Jewish, Zionist state. Their numbers are very small, and the people diverse; included are the extremely orthodox Neturei Karta, who reject a secular state and one set up before the coming of the Messiah; and supporters of far-left anti-Zionist groups. These people have little impact. Of more concern are those who, while considering themselves Israeli, feel alienated from the established society and express their dissatisfaction in crime, in avoiding military service, or in social protest. The fact that youth, however few, could grow up to feel alienated is considered to be a failure of the society. Limited somewhat by occupational mobility, alienation has been prominent enough to have, at least indirectly, a large impact on social policy.

The Political Integration of Arab Israelis

Arabic-speaking minorities have been marginal in national politics, although they are citizens, voters, and officeholders. The Histadrut, government ministries, and the parties have related to them as to ethnic-national groups rather than as individuals. They have been perceived and have seen themselves as a separate political sector whose interests are parochial and whose influence on general policy has been negligible.[38]

All this is changing. The sheer increase in population gives the minorities a feeling of solidarity and of potential political power.* [39] Their population is young, with a median age of 15.8 years in 1976, compared with a 24.2 national average, and its proportion of the electorate will grow unless immigration increases substantially. The social and educational level has begun to rise significantly after a delayed start.* Political organization is becoming nationwide in scope rather than local and is concerned as much with Arab nationalism and identity as it is with substantive social and economic issues.

Social changes achieved include urbanization, the modernization of villages with running water, electricity and access roads, better health, and the expansion of education. Unlike his father, the Arab Israeli is now more likely to be an urban wage earner than an agricultural laborer. In many villages, more than half of the work force commutes to work in town. Arab agriculture has become intensive and mechanized, and increasingly export-directed. Like their Jewish compatriots, Arab Israelis now employ Arab labor from Gaza and the West Bank.

Social and economic advance makes it possible to organize more effectively for political action, and stimulates it by constantly raising expectations. The ongoing conflict between Israel and the Arab states, increased interaction with the Arab world, and the experience of being in a minority accentuate the quandary in which the Arab Israeli finds himself regarding his identity and primary national loyalties. Any analysis of the development of minority political participation needs to consider the nature of local government, the impact of the social changes, the relations of the minorities with Israeli institutions, the interaction of Arab Israelis with West Bank Arabs and with Arab nationalism, and the influence of specific events and personalities in the Arab world.

---

* From 186,000 in 1949, the non-Jewish minority grew to more than 575,000 in 1977, including 38,600 in Nazareth. Of the rest, about 180,000 live in the so-called "Little Triangle" east of the central seacoast along the former Jordanian border, and there are 55,000 Bedouin tribesmen. Arabs live with Jews in the same towns in Jerusalem (100,000 of 376,000 residents), Haifa (14,700), Acre (9,000, or 25 percent of the population), Lydda (4800), Ramle (5,600), and Jaffa–Tel Aviv (7,700). Ma'alot (3,500 Jews) and Tarshicha (2,200 Arabs) are under a joint municipal council. Many Arab villages belong to regional councils, on which their representatives serve on an equal basis with those of the Jewish settlements in the region.

* Average life expectancy rose to seventy-two years in 1972 (similar to that of the Jews). The Arab Israeli has one of the highest annual rates of increase in the world—3.7 per thousand, compared to 1.55 among Israeli Jews. At the beginning of the state, only one-third of Arab children of elementary-school age were in school. In 1976 there were 90 percent. Between 1961 and 1975 the number passing the national matriculation exam each year rose from less than 100 to more than 800, and the number of university and other postsecondary students, negligible in 1949, was almost 3,000 in 1978, including more than 1,000 enrolled in postsecondary teacher or technician training.[40]

Local Government

Local government developed very differently in the Arab and Jewish communities. In the Mandate, only two predominantly Arab towns had municipal status, and the villages were led by the traditional leaders—the hereditary *muchtar* and other honored elders.[41] In the state, local elections were gradually introduced, and by 1975, except for Bedouin tribes, more than 90 percent of the minorities lived under elected local councils.** The many parties in these elections, whatever their names, have usually represented local clans or personalities, with the exception of Rakah and, in a few cases, groups more radical than Rakah. Elders have been reluctant to give their places to younger men, and when these were allowed to lead, it has been mainly due to their *hamula*, or clan, backing. There is much split-ticket voting, and clan loyalties are much less binding in national elections for the Knesset. The larger the town, the more the decline of the authority of the traditional leaders, due to the growing economic independence of wage earners and the extension of education.

Despite these changes, the major parties were insensitive to factors which increased the influence of Rakah or more radical groups. The younger, educated Arab wants to think for himself and no longer accepts passively the guidance of traditional leadership. In Nazareth in 1975 a left-nationalist slate made up of Rakah and a local "intellectuals" list gained office after many years of inadequate rule by Labor Party-supported traditional leaders. In other places as well, there is a trend towards a combination of nationalist, intergenerational, and *hamula* politics.

Local government and politics, however, have until now been less of a political training ground for Arabs than in the Jewish communities. Locally, *hamula*, personality, and the division of resources have been more dominant concerns than issues of principle. The village or town was not much enmeshed in national economic or political organizations, there was no serious attempt from the center to develop institutions or the local economy, and local men of property were also reluctant to attempt industrial enterprise. The tenacity of many elders has limited the learning opportunities and entry into local politics. Arab villages and towns have in many ways enjoyed greater independence in the conduct of their internal affairs than Jewish local governments. The dependency for budget support and infrastructure development has been at least as great as in the Jewish communities, but has worked through the local leaders rather than through grass-roots political activity;

** In 1975 there were fifty-five local councils, and twenty-seven villages were represented on regional councils. The role of the local *hamula* appears to have changed due to changes in patterns of economic organization. In the state, there have been far fewer large local or absentee landholdings than under the Mandate. The *hamula* organization was a natural way to organize for economic security or advantage, and offered protection against outside influence in local affairs. See Abner Cohen, *Arab Border Villages in Israel*, Manchester, Manchester University Press, 1965.

and in the Arab local councils, the problems of traditional authority and clan-based favoritism are added to all of the deficiencies which we have seen in the local government of Jewish settlements.

The Histadrut

Since 1955 members of minority groups have belonged to trade unions, and since 1959 they have been full members of the Histadrut. In 1977, more than half of the Arab wage earners were members. More than other central organizations, the Histadrut has advanced Arab political integration, but on a much more restricted scale than it does in Jewish communities. It started late, the scope has been modest, and most local activities have been run by a special Arab department at the national headquarters. Workers' councils in villages and towns were gradually established, but by 1976, these were few and not very effective. When an Arab village was attached to a larger Jewish council, the Arab members were not always active.* In the party lists for national Histadrut elections, minorities have been underrepresented.

Histadrut institutions afford administrative employment to young educated Arabs and provide some local political opportunities. There are more than 150 Arab cooperatives under its aegis. On a limited scale, the Histadrut has advanced Jewish-Arab interaction, and has been the only organization to make a comprehensive effort to do so; but it is still far from realizing its potential as an avenue for Arab political learning and integration.

National Elections and Parties

The symbols of Arab nationalism consistently gained in importance. In 1965 the New Communist Party, or Rakah, split from the Israel Communist Party and became largely Arab in membership and voter support. Affording an opportunity for Arab nationalist and anti-Zionist expression and political action within the law and in an organization which accepts the legitimacy of the Israeli political system, Rakah in 1977 achieved half of the total minority vote, and in some of the larger towns, more than 60 percent, declining to less than 40 percent in 1981. The election results are summarized in Table 3.3.

The Rakah increase from 1973 to 1977 can be explained in part by nationalist sentiment among the large number of young Arabs who came of

* In 1976 a Histadrut committee, noting the lag in local activities, recommended abolishing the central department and increasing the number and authority of local workers' councils. *Conclusions of the Committee on the Activities of the Histadrut in the Arab Sector* (Heb.) *(Maskanot Hava'ada Be'inyan Peulat Hahistadrut Bemigzar Ha'aravi)*, Tel Aviv, Histadrut Executive Committee, 1976. By 1980 little action had been taken on this report. For Histadrut politics and organization, see Chapter 5, "The Political Economy."

TABLE 3.3.   Voting in Minority Communities in National Elections to the Knesset (Percent of Voters Choosing a List)*

			Party			
Election Year	Labor** Alignment Parties	Affiliated Minority Parties (Labor)	Communists	Rakah	Non-Labor "Zionist" Parties Mafdal	Other
1961	25.0	45.5	23.2	—	4.0	3.0
1965	21.5	43.0	0.5	23.5	5.5	3.5
1969	13.3	41.6	0.5	29.5	8.5	5.0
1973	10.0	36.0	0.5	37.5	8.5	5.5
1977	11.0	20.8***	—	49.5	4.5	8.8

* Voter participation varied from 90 percent in 1955 to 74 percent in 1977.

** Includes Mapam as a separate list in 1961 and 1965.

*** Includes the United Arab list, and also, not formally affiliated, the Arab Reform Movement and Coexistence with Justice list.

Note: Appendix B shows the results in 1981, when the Arab Alignment candidates were included in the Alignment list. The results show: a decline in voter participation; a sharp setback to Rakah, down to 37 percent; and substantial gains for the Labor Alignment, to 29 percent.

voting age, eighteen, between 1973 and 1977. But the results also show the decline at that time in the attraction of the Alignment—the growing ineffectiveness of the Labor political machine in organizing voters, and a decrease in its ability to deliver resources; the devaluation of the image of the national leaders, seen in the resignation of Yitzchak Rabin before the 1977 elections, examples of corruption,* and other untoward events and the obtuse endorsement by the Labor Party of traditional protege-type leaders in its parallel Arab list. In the subsequent 1977 Histadrut elections, the Alignment Arab vote fell from 59 percent in 1973 to 53 percent, but Rakah gained little, rising from 31.9 percent to 33.3 percent. Arab voters deserted the Alignment in the 1977 national elections to a far greater extent than in the Histadrut campaign. One explanation is that the Histadrut elections are concerned more with economic than with national issues, and there was fear that Likud policies would lead to unemployment or abrupt changes which would hurt Arab workers.

The major parties make great efforts to attract the minority vote, both in their own names and, in the case of Labor, through parallel Arab parties. Traditional leadership and clans, machine politics, and contests based on issues and ideologies thus continue together. The relations of local leaders with the major national parties have shown much opportunism and

* See page 35, Chapter 1.

shtadlanut. As in the Jewish sector, these methods are becoming less popular, but although the traditional intermediary is becoming dispensable both to the voters and to the party centers, much of the substance of patronage in national resource allocation remains. *

Among the principal "Zionist" parties, Mapam was the first to offer full membership to Arabs, and one Arab has usually been in its Knesset delegation. Mapam integration of Arabs stopped short of encouraging kibbutz membership, but the party invested a very considerable effort in political training, and some trainees went on to prominence in Arab municipal politics as representatives of clan-based parties. The Labor Party admitted Arabs as full members only in 1969. The change in policy was gradual, and the first Arabs accepted were those who had military service. Although the party claims more than 10,000 Arab members, it has not been effective in organizing them. Labor encouraged separate Arab or Druze lists centered on prominent candidates and their immediate followers, hoping thus to gain family and local support from several quarters. Considering its religious and national ideology, the Mafdal has consistently received a surprisingly large proportion of the Arab vote, in some years equal to the 8 percent which it won of the Jewish vote. One explanation has been the Mafdal's patronage of towns through the Ministry of the Interior, and help given to Moslem religious functionaries through the Ministry of Religion. Another form of patronage is university education. Rakah gives scholarships for study in Warsaw Pact countries, and the Mafdal facilitates studies at Bar Ilan University. Mapam, despite its historically friendly ideology and its considerable efforts, did not succeed more than the Mafdal. As a "Zionist" party, its Marxism and the advocacy of Arab-Jewish conciliation could not compete successfully with the advocates of radicalism and Arab nationalism.

Political Issues

In the early years of the state, most Arab political participation was neither ideological nor focused on specific issues. Voters then felt obligated by clan or other dependencies, or vaguely intimidated by the security services toward voting for the establishment parties. The abolition of military government in Arab areas in 1966 and the open borders following the Six Day War suddenly afforded easy contact with the Arab world. The national decline of machine politics, the extension of education, and the growth of economic independence and resources among the Israeli Arabs combined with the rise of

---

* At a Labor Party conference at Beit Berl in 1976, the following exchange was observed: Zouabi, the former old-school mayor of Nazareth, blamed his defeat by Rakah on a lack of Labor Party (and government) support in patronage and budgets, asking, "Why don't you help your friends?" To this Minister of Defense Peres in effect replied that there was no longer room for brokers on material questions, even though there was, perhaps, on those of ideology.

Palestinian nationalism to bring about a substantial change in the political goals of Israeli Arabs and Druze. Not least in importance has been the growth in the proportion of young people. In 1976, 75 percent of Arab Israelis were younger than 30, as compared with 54 percent of the entire population. Both substantive issues and ideology are now important.

Because of the symbolic and cultural impact of the issues, there is no clear boundary between substantive issues and those of belief. The substantive questions which have been most important to Arab Israelis are discrimination against their interests by government policies, particularly in land use and development and in the way the national bureaucracies relate to them; barriers to political opportunity within the minority communities themselves; and limited career opportunities for the educated. For many of the intelligentsia, a general feeling of marginality causes more resentment than any specific problem.

Relations between Arab Israelis and the government began poorly. The period after the War of Liberation was one of mutual suspicion, terrorist raids into Israel, and great security concern. A Military Administration was established in parts of the country near the borders, in which most of the Arabs lived, imposing restrictions in certain areas where there were concentrations of Arabs, and requiring written approval for movement to the center of the country. These irksome measures increase both dependence on the Administration and suspicion of its intentions, and they enhanced social, religious, and economic separateness.

Government and the Histadrut organizations also encouraged separateness. Special departments were set up to deal with the affairs of Arabs. A multitude of agencies relate to the minority communities, and the Prime Minister's adviser for Arab affairs, the Ministry of the Interior, the Land Authority, and other ministries often follow different and therefore confusing policies. This pattern also exists in the Jewish sector where, however, unpopular policies are not seen as a national slight.

Since 1970 the affairs of the Druze have been handled on an individual basis by the general departments. The Druze are Arab in general culture and have an esoteric religion. There are more than 40,000 in Israel, living on Mt. Carmel and in the Galilee. Their life style and economy are similar to those of Moslem Arabs. The Israeli Druze belongs to a double minority: they are a minority of the whole Druze sect, most of whom live in Syria, and a minority among the Arabic-speaking Israelis. Along with some of the Bedouin and Circassians, the Druze fought on the Israeli side in the War of Liberation. Since the mid-1950s they have been drafted into the Army, and many remain in the career service or serve in the border police. In education, their progress has lagged, in a way comparable to the Moslem Arabs, behind that of the Christian Arabs. The strength of the traditional leaders and the *hamula* remain greater among the Druze than in the other minorities; and despite their military experience and achievements, the opportunities of younger Druze in their own communities and in the country do not fulfill their expectations. Numbers of young Druze now see far less distinction between themselves and Arabs than their elders do.[42]

Minority local communities, despite great progress, lag in public services and in educational resources and attainments. Although the Israeli Arab standard of living far exceeds that found in the adjacent Arab states and has grown faster than that of the Jews, it was low when the Mandate ended; and the general Israeli standard of living is constantly before the younger Arab, to whom the record of past progress is irrelevant. Beginning in 1961 and 1966, two five-year plans developed the infrastructure in most of the Arab villages.[43] The income of the average urban Arab family in 1977 was close to the national average, although, because of family size, per capita income was lower. Large families, little town planning, and the absence of any substantial public housing program for the Arab sector have led to a high living density.* As in other areas, there was no equivalent counterpart for the Arab communities of the massive government planning and development efforts which were made for the rest of the country. Arab local-government initiative has also been less, so that the feeling of dependency on the central government exceeds that in the Jewish towns, and causes resentment when local services are inadequate.

In the mid-1970s, land policy became a central issue, especially in the Galilee. Considerable acreage had been lost to Arab villages, particularly those near the borders, during and just after the War of Liberation, often under irregular procedures and with inequities in the dates which determined the values for compensation.** In succeeding years, land was taken for public purposes by due process, but the purposes could include the forming of new towns, such as Carmiel and Upper Nazareth in the Galilee, and for industrial sites, as part of the policy of population dispersal and for increasing the Jewish population of the Galilee.*** From 1965 to 1975, there was little change in the extent of Arab landholdings. In 1975, however, older plans for intensive development of the Galilee and the encouragement of settlement there were revived and updated. Although they involved the requisitioning of a considerable amount of land owned by Jews, mainly in the town of Safed, a substantially larger amount of acreage was to be acquired by the government from Arabs under eminent domain. Arabs were aware that the government's plans for developing the Galilee were motivated mainly by a desire to ensure a Jewish majority in the area, and they suspected development moves even

* In 1976, an interministerial committee recommended that housing subsidies be increased, additional building land be made available for public purposes, and special measures be taken to accelerate the completion of outline plans.[44]

** In an inflationary economy, delays in compensation inconvenienced Jews and Arabs alike, and in 1976 changes in the laws were recommended to permit immediate recompense.

*** With time, Arab agriculture became intensive, mechanized, and highly productive. Between 1965 and 1975, the extent of Arab land under irrigation doubled. At the same time, population growth increased the need for more yields.

when these were for the Arab sector; and there were also memories of land losses in the early years of the state. Land became a symbol and focus of protest in the Arab communities, and statements by the government that the intent was to "develop the Galilee" and not to "Judaize" it were not convincing. While remaining in the background, Rakah initiated the organization of a national "Committee for the Defense of the Lands," which protested to the Knesset and petitioned the Prime Minister against the plan. After the Cabinet approved the land acquisition plan, the committee organized a nationwide strike of Arabs, scheduled for March 30, 1976. Many Arabs opposed the proposed strike tactic, and the Committee of Arab Mayors preferred to try to negotiate a compromise plan. Still, the strike took place on schedule, with wide participation in many localities and little in others. Known as the "Day of the Land," it was the first large-scale Arab Israeli demonstration. Indications are that by the time of the strike, Rakah and the committee were no longer in control and that more radical groups were leading events. In some places, police and Army forces were attacked when they tried to enforce order. Many of the police, soldiers, and citizens were wounded, and six citizens were killed in the fighting.

Meeting later with Prime Minister Rabin, the Committee of Arab Mayors asked for a government commission of inquiry into the events and for revision of the land plan. Instead, the Cabinet responded by setting up a joint Arab-Jewish Council and a Committee of Ministers charged with advancing the integration and equality of Arab citizens. The strike was a signal that Israeli Arabs were beginning to associate their demands on internal Israeli policy with feelings of Arab nationalism, and that the process of the political integration of the Arabs was approaching an important and dangerous fork in the road. Yet the government's policy, aside from the new committee organization, showed little change during the remainder of the Rabin Cabinet's incumbency.

Arab mayors had organized a committee as early as 1974 to coordinate needs and demands on the central government. It also went into opposition on the land question, though advocating negotiations rather than strikes. Several of its prominent members are from Rakah, and the committee has continued to emphasize nationalist as well as substantive concerns—a developing characteristic of Arab politics in Israel—together with a growing Arab ability to organize on a national scale.

Another cogent issue is the demand for career opportunities for the youth. The young educated Arabs feel hindered in their job opportunities by the prejudice of the majority and by unreasonable security restrictions.[45] None of the special Arab departments in the government is headed by an Arab, except for those dealing with the administration of religion or religious law, and Arabs who are employed in these departments often say that they have not been given adequate authority. Arab civil service representation is disproportionately low for a combination of reasons: genuine security concern in some departments, or exaggerated security zeal in others; lack of awareness, or simply prejudice, and the fact that Arabs only recently began to complete secondary schools in fairly large numbers. The concentration of minority secondary school students in the humanities is another impediment, making it harder for Arab students to succeed in Israeli universities. A minority study for the professions or in technical or scientific fields, while the paucity of secondary vocational school training means that students who do not go to the "theoretical" secondary schools are destined for unskilled work.[46] These limitations to opportunity are exacerbated by a lack of entrepreneurship in the Arab communities or of attempts to develop it by the government. Official policy has been to create real opportunity for members of the minorities, but it has not been carried out with adequate priority or enthusiasm. Equal to the Jews in political rights and before the law, the Arab communities are unequal both in obligations (in not giving national or military service, except for the Druze and a few Bedouin, or in *de facto* taxation) and in effective claims on public resources.

The New Politics of Arab Israelis

Although the old politics of influence and favors, of the *hamula* and patrons, continues, its importance is declining relative to the politics of broader issues and beliefs. The new politics is more national and ideological and less parochial, instrumental, or deferential. There is more sophistication regarding political aims and strategies and the limits of permissible opposition to the state. Old ties are loosening and internal differences among Arabs, based on family or sect, are diminishing, resulting in an increase in individual independence and Arab national identification.[47]

Along with the changes in feelings, there is an increasing ability to organize on a national scale, demonstrated by Rakah and the Committee of Mayors.[48] These organizations have encouraged and focused Arab nationalist expression. In its manifestos, Rakah has accepted the existence of an independent Israel but asked for the creation of a parallel Palestinian state—in contrast to the demands of more radical groups, such as Bnei Hak'far, (Sons of the Village), who completely reject Israel's legitimacy. The trend of Arab politics is made more nationalist and radical by the existence of the extreme positions, and by Rakah's ability to involve other organizations and to work through fronts, in which other groups find themselves obliged to move toward a more radical public stance. Yet the left-national trend is not universal, and there is polarization between those who seek integration and those whose Arab nationalist sentiment predominates. This is shown, at least superficially, by the large numbers who voted, even in 1977 (and many more in 1981), for the "Zionist" or associated parties; and many Arab Israelis, and more of the Druze, might seek integration. A substantial minority of Arab

Israelis see their identity as both Israeli (politically) and Palestinian or Arab (nationally). It is conceivable that they could develop a satisfactory reconciliation of these two loyalties, in which both are effective.[49] But for moderates who wish to accept the status and implications of being Israelis, no wholly satisfactory organizational forms for political expression have developed.

The main sources of the Arab Israeli's dilemma of identity are the fact of his living as a minority-group member in a Jewish state, the influence of the conflict between the surrounding Arab countries and Israel, and the resurgence of religious nationalism. The idea of a Jewish state or national home implies a predominance of the culture and values of the Jews, who see the country as a spiritual home for the Jewish people. There they can work to fashion a society that will express and continue these values, which the Jews believe is not possible elsewhere on a permanent basis. This concept does not mean a monopoly for Jewish values or for the Hebrew language, but it does mean that Arabic culture, Islam, the Druze religion, and Christianity will not be predominant religions and cultures. Ideally, the several cultures and beliefs would exist together; but the violence of Lebanon or Northern Ireland and the problems of some of the larger cities in the United States show that this is not simple to achieve. Israel has been largely without internal conflict, and the beginnings of violence in occupied areas were stopped in a kind of "pax Israelitica"; but neither has there been very much interaction, aside from business relations, between the minorities and the Jews.

The Arabic-speaking Israeli is promised equal rights and cultural independence, and participation in the achievements of the state; but he could not be expected to share in the dream of a Jewish national home. His cultural and religious reference groups and national symbols are located beyond the borders, in countries which are at war with Israel.* The Jews, at the same time, are a reference group for modernization, technology, economic advance, social welfare, and democratic processes.

Contributing to the dilemma have been the expansion of education, contacts with the West Bank, and the growth of the relatively new concept of a Palestinian nationality. Education brings new opportunities, but it can also increase frustration and radical feeling. The educated Arab's diploma has not brought him the opportunities, power, or status in his own community for which he hoped. Indeed, he is resentful of the rule of the uneducated traditional leaders as well as the Israeli establishment. Comparing his progress with that of the Jewish academic, he is sensitive to real and imagined slights and condescension, and he often seeks nationalist or radical explanations for the sources of his malaise. Through periodicals and books, the Arab Israelis are in contact with the thought of Arab intellectuals abroad. The Arabic jour-

---

* If he were to be in those countries, however, he would probably feel more rejected by them, as a Palestinian, than he is in Israel as an Arab; much of the feeling of Palestinian nationalism has come from the poor experiences of Palestinians in the Arab countries.[50]

nals for which they write are a forum in which left and anti-Israel ideology are the accepted views, since the spoken and written thought of the Arab majority which surrounds Israel most often questions or denies Israel's legitimacy and tells the Arab Israeli that he is Palestinian, not Israeli. Radical sentiments which oppose Israel's legitimacy are widely held in the rapidly growing Arab student body in Israeli universities, boding ill for political integration. At the same time, the more educated can express the dissatisfaction of those whose advancement is restricted because they have little schooling.

After the 1967 war, Arab Israelis, for the first time since the establishment of the state, made close contacts with Arabs from Jordan and the West Bank. After an initial sense of pride in Israeli economic advance and modernity, they began to feel that the West Bank Arabs had one advantage—they could be politically active in a nationalist cause in an area in which they were the majority. Indeed, Israeli politicians who had not taken any particular interest in Arab Israelis in the past made numerous visits to West Bank leaders in the years following the Six Day War.

The political potential and needs of Arab Israelis have until now been largely ignored in the political calculus, except during election campaigns. Among Arab Israelis, independent and nationalist political activity has now begun in earnest, and is no longer marginal. On the question of how to achieve the political and social integration of the Arabs, Israel is at a fork in the road, and deciding the direction to take should be near the top of the agenda in the 1980s. If the question of their identity is a predominant dilemma of the Arab minority, the task before the Jewish majority is to find a way for more genuine participation and integration of the Arabs, a very difficult task, given the extent to which Arab-Jewish relations within Israel are dependent on the relations of Israel and the surrounding Arab world.

The Outlook for Political Integration

Regarding almost every question in Israel one can say, "Look how much has been done"; and one also says, "Look what has been done wrongly and needs to be done much better."

Masses of people from diverse cultures, lacking political experience, were introduced to democratic procedures and were afforded experience and political learning which made possible extensive political participation. The institutions developed during the Yishuv helped provide the framework of a going concern. Although limited in authority and resources, local government and local trade-union activity are giving broad experience. Immigrants are dominant in the affairs of the new *moshavim* and in most of the new towns are selected for office by their peers. A growing number of politically experienced and aware people are forming a base from which to achieve central roles. The problems lie in the differences between the form and the content of the processes, in which democracy and participation can be more formal than actual, and in the differences among groups in their access to political representation. These differences come mainly from the congruence of ethnic-group membership with educational attainment, living on the periphery, and social resources. They have also been related to closed and hierarchical party structures and to the dominance of the center over the periphery.

The stage was set by the manner of political socialization. The immigrant came into a world which was strange to him and administered by people whose goals often seemed at variance with his hopes and interests. Unprepared for the cultural and political changes he faced, his plight was aggravated by the often meager human resources and the time devoted to introducing the newcomers to the polity or to translating concepts and ideals. It was extremely difficult to transmit to thousands with no previous training a willingness, common in the Yishuv, for drastic change in personal roles.

In the state, facing at the same time demands of the new masses and of the new state apparatus, the parties and settlement movements did not rise to the challenge of political teaching. There were too few leaders available for the vast numbers attempting to settle under very difficult conditions, nor did the party leaders recognize the priority that integration should have. The Labor movement performed well in vote-getting and organizing roles, but party branches and trade-union local cells did little teaching in any depth. Practical political organization took precedence over social development, adult education, and instruction in ideas or cooperation. The parties' "ideal" role, in which the member was asked to contribute his efforts and in return was "built up" and developed by the movement, as if by agreement changed to one in which the member was mainly a voter and a gainer of benefits and patronage, or so it seemed to the recipients. The problem derives less from the political culture that the new immigrant brought with him than from the magnitude of the tasks of integration and the often instrumental, though well meant, way in which the immigrants were received.

Other agencies of social and political learning lost most of the importance they had in the Yishuv. The schools, along with an explosive growth in the number of teachers and pupils, have on the whole had a comparatively small influence on political socialization. Occasionally a source of young leadership was provided by a party youth leadership course or the rare arrival of a group trained in a youth movement abroad. The youth movements in the country, however, which had been of major importance in the Yishuv, lost most of their importance for secondary school pupils. They were not very active among working teenagers, and thus were of little help to many young immigrants.

Can the proportionately lower Asian/African representation at the center lead to alienation? Political socialization has indeed lagged behind economic gains. The slow advance of sociological representation may not in itself lead to increased alienation if visible social and educational progress is made.

What is the expectation for the advance of political integration, and on what does it depend? A necessary condition is a marked narrowing of educational differences among groups. Already advancing, this process will take a long time, even with the best will. But this is not enough, and a sufficient condition may be changes in the political system to allow more competition and freer entry into politics, as well as greater fiscal, financial, and management independence for local authorities, so that local politics can afford a much firmer democratic base for national political development. In a time of great economic stress and military threats, there is tension between the desire for direct popular representation and almost immediate participation, and the slow progress in the hierarchy of national politics and government which the present system allows. These contradictions reflect the tension inherent in a democracy between popular and elite government, and between social and political authority.

The desire for integration still exceeds the accomplishment. Ethnicity remains strong, and views on religion and the state, and on the territorial concepts of Zionism, are intensely held. Still, the political integration of Israeli Jews is proceeding, with difficulty, yet with great promise. That of Arab Israelis is a much more serious challenge and one not independent of the relations of Israel and the Arab states, and of developments in the Arab world. At the same time, political attitudes and behavior are increasingly the result of interests and values which cut across lines of association, ideology, and religiosity. This process, together with greater understanding and respect for cultural pluralism, shows the potential for political integration.

PART II

The Making of
Public Policy

From the beginning of the state, the political system provided legitimate
authority and the enforcement of decisions through the process of law. It
has not been easy, however, to build institutions with the capability of
solving substantive public problems. The job is far from finished, and this
part discusses the work in progress.

Security was the first requirement. In 1948 experts like George Marshall
and Viscount Montgomery expected that the invaders would crush the new
state within weeks, if not days. The possibility of survival became evident
after a few weeks, but there were eight hard months of intermittent battle
before negotiations could begin. These determined the 1949-67 borders,
ending the first major campaign of what was to be a continuing and
escalating war. In this first year, the patterns were set for the defense
organization and for civil-military relations.

In all periods, means available for defense have appeared inadequate to
achieve the ends, and have been vastly inferior to those of the Arab states.
In the fourth decade, however, there is a much higher *absolute* disparity
than before. This is seen in the levels of the forces and their destructive
capability, in the potency of Arab oil and economic weapons, and in the
size of the balance of payments and foreign debt. The difference of degree
is becoming one of kind as the interdependence within the more complex
society and the need for outside resources exacerbate the downside risks.

The continuing need for security has had a profound effect on the work of the government. In the informal dual system which developed, the attention of the Prime Minister and of the full Cabinet has been given mainly to security and foreign affairs. Although other questions are not merely residual, they have far lower priority on the central agenda. Most of the time, the economy and indeed most domestic policy have been guided by the Minister of Finance. The needs of social policy most often come into the forefront as the result of protests and threats of crisis, or during election campaigns.

Still, large resources are devoted to social services and economic growth. The nation seeks multiple goals at once—education, science, the services of a welfare state, the development of transportation, communication, agriculture and industry, and the absorption, housing, and employment of immigrants. The attempt to go forward on a broad front influences the way decisions are made and carried out. The strains on resources, the needs for capital import, and the rate of development reinforce inherent tendencies toward centralized government control. The ordering of priorities or the rational analysis of trade-offs is inhibited, since such clear-cut decisions could lead to the abandonment of important objectives.

The cognitive problems of policy are also immense. The scope of activities and challenges is that of large countries whose human resources for management and analysis are far greater. The pace of action, the importance assigned to it, and the impact of unexpected outside events have left little time or inclination to plan or to evaluate results.

There have been important demographic and social changes. In 1981 the population is more than five times as large as it was in 1948, and the trend is away from the characteristics of a community toward those of a society. The older ideologies are no longer realistic, and there is a decline in political authority, which formerly was supported by ideology and party organization. The expectations of citizens are at a higher level, not only for material well-being but for more participation in decisions, and at the same time for more authoritative government. Modes of action and decision which depend very much on informal organization, intuition, and the impetus of beliefs are confounded by the complexities of new situations.

Can the system of government adapt to the changes, create the strategies, and develop the participation and legitimate authority which will be needed? The chapters in this part try to provide some basis for thought on this question. Many of the substantive problems are outlined, and an analysis is made of the ways in which the government and the political system as a whole have reacted to them.

CHAPTER 4

The Nation in Arms

WITHIN THE MEMORY of most Israelis, the physical survival of the Jews has been the central concern and defense the most salient and immediate issue. In the 1948 War of Liberation, there were more than 5,000 deaths in a population of 650,000. In the October 1973 war, more than 2,500 Israeli soldiers were killed within only two and a half weeks, a number comparable to the proportion of Americans who died in the entire war in Vietnam. Nearly everyone lost a son, relative, friend, or acquaintance.

When parliamentary elections were held in December 1973, many first-time voters had fought in the Yom Kippur War and most of them were still on duty on election day. Many of their parents served in four wars since the state was declared and some were veterans of World War II as well. Most of the immigrants since the state had been members of minority groups in Arab countries or had lived in the Europe of the Nazi Holocaust.

Since 1946, periods of full-scale war have alternated with border raids, terrorist activities, and periods of comparative quiet. In Cabinet meetings, defense and foreign affairs have nearly always been first on the agenda. Even during a cease-fire the civilian population is inextricably involved. In 1977 more than one-third of the gross national product was spent on defense, and universal military service for men and women over the age of eighteen was required, with reserve duty afterwards for as much as forty-five days a year and much longer in emergencies.

Defense is an overriding concern because of the small size and closeness of the society, the experiences of the people, and regard for human life, combined with adverse and worsening ratios of the forces and equipment which Israel and the Arab countries field.

Within this context, the making of defense policy is considered from the point of view of the structure, development, and use of the armed forces. These are, of course, only a part of security. The search for peace depends as well on diplomacy and on the morale, human resources, and scientific potential of the society. But our concern here is with the effectiveness and democracy of the way defense policy is formed, that is, the relations of civil government and the armed forces, and, much more briefly, with the effect of the continuing conflict on the society.

For Israel, civil-military relations can be critical for several reasons. The readiness of the force has to be maintained because of war or frequent alerts. A second reason is the importance of the great powers, both as a source of arms for Israel and the Arab countries and as diplomatic influences. Third, defense makes enormous demands on available resources in people, funds, and the capacity for organized activity. Fourth, Zahal, or the Defense Forces, plays a symbolic role, giving military leaders unusual status and prominence. Finally, civil-military relations developed and have continued during actual conflict, and history shows that the problems of civil control in war are different in kind and much more acute than in peace.

Threats to democratic or social values could appear in several forms. A militarist or violent society could develop, and resources and attention could be withheld from social and human needs. Democratic processes could be endangered either through the alienation of the military from the polity and society, or through the politicization, involvement, or exploitation of the forces or their leaders in the contest for political power.

The democratic character of civil-military relations is allied to effectiveness. Neglect of social needs can impair the national potential of human will and resources. A disproportionate concern with the military aspects of security could lead to a neglect of diplomacy, or to inadequate questioning of the demands and strategies of the military establishment.

The discussion in this chapter will go along the following path: First, the strategic context is outlined, and with it the development of military concepts and forces and their use in the conflict. The roles of the powers and Israel's perception of them are discussed. I then restate, more specifically, the most pertinent questions regarding civil-military relations. To look for answers, the political-military system is analyzed in its historical development in the Yishuv and the state, and some conclusions are drawn. Finally, I address the question of the impact of the conflict situation on public attitudes about the use of armed force and toward the Arabs as people.

The Military Odds for Survival

Comparison of the military potential of Israel and the Arab countries shows Israel to be at a serious disadvantage in quantities of arms and men, funds for procurement, geography, and topography, and in the implications and importance of military and civilian casualties.

The approximate force ratios in 1978 were as follows:

TABLE 4.1.   Approximate Armed Forces Ratios, 1978[1]

	ARAB STATES*	ISRAEL
Combat aircraft	3.5	1
Helicopters	4	1
Tanks	3	1
Artillery	5	1
Missile boats	2.5	1
Personnel (mobilized)	7	1**

* Include Syria, Iraq, Jordan, Saudi Arabia, Egypt, Lybia, Kuwait.
** Closer to 3:1 when Israel reserves are called up.

While not exact, the ratios shown are indicative. Projected a few years into the future, they understate Arab numerical superiority. The opposing forces rival in size and modernity those of large European and Warsaw Pact countries, and their combat strengths compare to those at Stalingrad or the Battle of Britain. In addition to the potential of the Arab countries bordering Israel— Syria, Lebanon, Jordan, and Egypt, there are growing quantities of sophisticated Western arms in Saudi Arabia, Libya, and Kuwait. Other forces include the terrorists of Ashaf (PLO) and other groups, used for political ends throughout the world and against civilian targets in Israel.*

Escalation on both sides and new technologies increase the destructive potential of war, the economic burden, and dependence on the superpowers. The quantities involved cannot be replaced from local production, nor can the expense of stockpiling for long campaigns be sustained.**

* In recent years, the impact of terrorists within Israel has been minimal. In 1970 they were expelled from their bases in Jordan, and they have not had active support from West Bank or Israeli Arabs. Their activities in the rest of the world, however, such as hijackings and the murder of members of the Israeli 1972 Olympic team, have gained notoriety. The inability of the PLO to operate from the West Bank and Gaza has been ascribed to "effective security and intelligence, restoring normal life patterns and increasing people's stake in tranquility by improving their material well-being, and firm actions against those supporting or helping the P.L.O."[2]

** In 1973 Egypt and Syria lost more than 2,500 tanks and 500 airplanes in less than eighteen days. Initially, Israel puts more tanks in the field than France and Britain do together today, but by contrast cannot attempt to replace combat losses in men and materiel as they occur, in other than a very short campaign.

Geography also handicaps Israel, except for the short internal lines.[3] The maps which follow (Figures. 4.1 and 4.2) show the lack of strategic depth or room for maneuver, particularly within pre-1967 borders. The length of the many fronts is evident, as is the topographic importance of the Golan Heights commanding the northern Jordan valley, and of the high ridges running north

FIGURE 4.1   Distances and Flight Times from Israel for Arab Military Aircraft

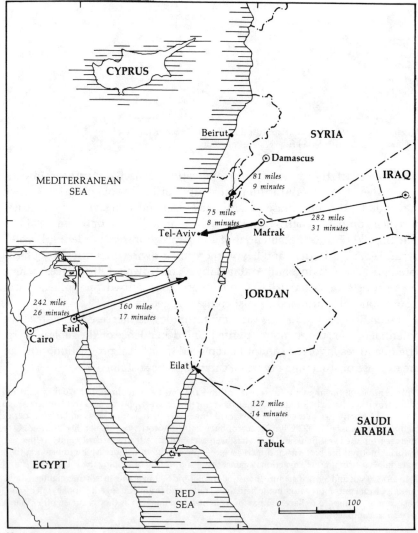

Note: Distances shown are in miles, and flight times are in minutes, assuming an average speed of 550 miles per hour.

FIGURE 4.2 The Allon Plan

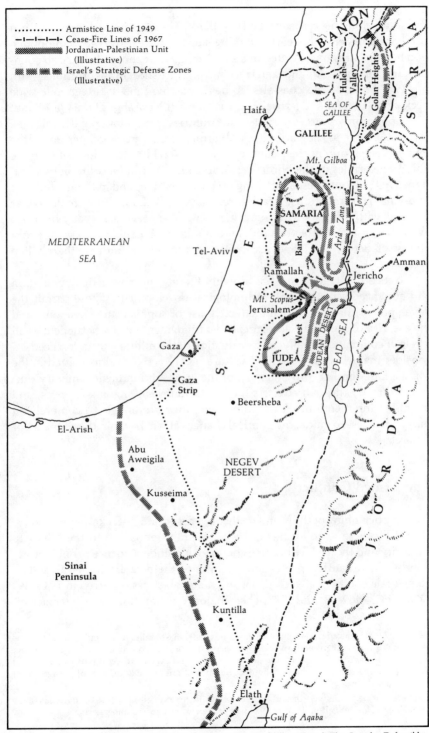

············ Armistice Line of 1949
—ı—ı—ı—ı- Cease-Fire Lines of 1967
▓▓▓▓▓▓▓ Jordanian-Palestinian Unit
              (Illustrative)
▓ ▓ ▓ ▓ Israel's Strategic Defense Zones
              (Illustrative)

and south along the center of the West Bank. These are important not only in combat but as effective early-warning sites.* Strategic targets and population in Israel are concentrated in a small area, while those of the Arab countries are dispersed. Air and land warning times are short in all directions. With pre-1967 borders, the coastal strip has a narrow nine-to-fifteen-mile-wide neck, and Tel Aviv and Jerusalem are within artillery range of the West Bank.

Population resources permit Arab countries to maintain regular full-time forces. As large as they are, the Arab armies are only a small percent of the military age group in their countries, while Israel has to induct all who are able.[4] The armies of the bordering Arab countries can be continuously stationed in the front lines, shortening preparation times and making it difficult to divine their intentions. Israeli forces have to be based on a small regular nucleus, with the rest of the available manpower serving as ready reserves. While the system is effective, the call-ups take time, could increase the probability of actual war, and are costly to the budget and to the civilian economy.**

To its advantage, Israel has a highly literate, homogeneous population and advanced scientific and technological development. These permit the development, production, and effective use of sophisticated weapons, and the exercise of ingenuity and independent judgment on the battlefield at all levels of command. Finally, any evaluation of the military situation needs to consider major world powers. They are highly active and interested in the Middle East conflict, provide most of the arms, and influence military outcomes directly through advisers (in Arab countries), ongoing supplies, and threats of intervention. At the same time, they are unable to comprehend fully, much less to guide, the political changes at work within the countries of the area.

The Armed Conflict

From the beginning of the Mandate there were sporadic attacks on the Yishuv. Originally these were local, but by 1936 Arab opposition to the Mandate authority and the Yishuv became countrywide. Independence brought invasion by the organized professional armies of the neighboring Arab states. Large-scale conflict between Israel and the Arab states occurred in 1948–49, 1956, 1967, 1969–70, and 1973. These major confrontations were interspersed

* The 1967 war reduced the length of defense borders from 616 miles to 406 miles. In 1975 Israel withdrew to the northern ends of the Sinai passes, and a U.S.-controlled civilian surveillance organization was installed to provide electronic warning. Egyptian forces on the eastern side of the Canal were supposed to be very limited, but indications are that this part of the agreement was violated.

** These considerations were important in delaying the reserve call-up before the outbreak of the Yom Kippur War. A call-up in May 1973 had proven expensive and unnecessary.

with terrorist raids into Israel and retaliations. Other parts of the Middle East saw frequent confrontations: Iraq against the Kurds, Egypt in Yemen, Northern Sudan against the south. Syria threatened to invade Jordan in 1970, and did intervene massively in 1976–77 in the Lebanese civil war, virtually ending Lebanese independence. Table 4.2 summarizes the principal campaigns and Table 4.3 the increase in weapons used.

The Forces and Their Methods[6]

In 1948 the new Army inherited the experience of small-group, underground, and guerilla-type operations, as well as that of the organized Allied forces. Most of the thousands from the Yishuv who volunteered for the British forces in the war were limited to technical or administrative duties because they were "colonials." A few were trained as pilots, however, and during the last part of the war permission was given to recruit a Palestinian Jewish infantry brigade which fought in Italy. The experiences of these Palestinians and the volunteers who came from abroad in the War of Liberation were to prove invaluable in organizing the training, logistics, and staff work of large forces.

At the same time, the Yishuv had developed its own doctrines of self-defense. At first the official defense arm, the Haganah, engaged in largely static defense of local settlements. In the mid-1930s it began to field small mobile units which learned to use guerilla-type infantry tactics—flexibility, mobility, and night cover.* These concepts found an institutional base in the Palmach, formed during World War II, in much of Zahal's later approach to tactics and leadership, and in the characteristic "attack" philosophy of Israeli defense.

The Army began the War of Independence with few well-trained men and a great inferiority in firepower.[7] There were barely enough rifles and virtually no armor or artillery.** For the Israelis it was an infantry war, costly in lives. Superior Arab firepower forced the Israelis to use indirect approaches, night cover, and dead areas to get very close to the objective, while in hand-to-hand combat, assault leadership and personal capability gave the advantage. While the headquarters of the brigades and of geographic areas set general objectives, most combat tasks were carried out by much smaller units.

---

* The first were Itzchak Sade's Field Companies, or "Posh," in 1936 and Orde Wingate's "Night Squads" in 1938. Most of the Haganah was composed of part-time volunteers. The Palmach, the full-time combat branch, began with British approval in 1941, when Rommel threatened to conquer Egypt. When the Germans retreated, the Palmach had to go underground, training and working mainly in the settlements of the United Kibbutz Movement and also in those of the Kibbutz Ha'artzi. At the end of 1947, it had 2,000 members in the field and 1,000 reserves. Drawn mainly from well-educated and ideologically motivated volunteers from youth movements or the kibbutzim, it was an elite which produced many Army commanders.

** Ben Gurion and the staff deliberated on where to use the four available artillery pieces. Two were sent to the north to help stop Syrian tanks, which were eventually deterred by the use of Molotov cocktails.

TABLE 4.2.   Principal Campaigns[5]

Period	Event
November 1947– May 1948	November 1947 UN decision on partition, to be effective May 15, 1948. British forces begin withdrawal, local Arab forces are joined by irregulars from other Arab countries. Jerusalem besieged but Jewish forces regain control of most of areas allocated to them in the UN decision.
May 15, 1948– February 1949	War of Liberation. Israel declares independence. Invasions by forces from Jordan, Egypt, Syria, Lebanon, Iraq. Invasions repulsed. Armistice agreements set 1949–67 borders, but peace negotiations fail and state of war continues.
1949–October 1956	Infiltraters from Gaza Strip and Jordan attack civilian targets in Israel. These are not stopped by Israeli reprisal raids on military installations, and escalation of terror and reprisal ensues. In 1954–55 British leave Egypt. Major Soviet arms supply to Egypt begins, 1955. Suez Canal nationalized by Nasser in 1956. French arms sales to Israel.
October 1956	Suez campaign. Israeli forces gain Sinai Peninsula, with French-British intervention on Canal. Israel then forced to cede territory gained, including Gaza Strip. UN forces stationed at Sharm el Sheikh and on Egypt-Israel border.
1965–67	Escalating terrorist raids from Syria and Jordan, guided by Syria, with Israeli reprisals. Egypt at war in Yemen.
May–June 1967	Six Day War. Egypt masses forces on Sinai border, closes Straits of Tiran (Sharm el Sheikh), secures UN forces' withdrawal. On June 5, Israel air strikes destroy most of Egyptian Air Force on ground. Jordan attacks. By June 11, Israel gains Golan Heights, Sinai, and Gaza, Sharm el Sheikh, the West Bank, and reunites Jerusalem.
1969–70	War of attrition on Canal, March 1969 to August 1970. Massive Egyptian artillery attacks countered by Bar Lev line fortifications, artillery, and mainly by Air Force. In January 1970 Israel bombs targets deep in Egypt. The USSR then builds extensive antiaircraft missile defense system. Russian pilots are involved, and several are shot down. After August 1970 cease-fire, Egypt returns antiaircraft missiles to Canal.
October 1973	Full-scale Syrian and Egyptian attack gains strategic surprise. Suez Canal crossed and Golan Heights entered with large forces, protected by ground-air missiles and infantry antitank weapons. Recovering, Israel has major military victory, crosses Suez Canal, cuts off Egyptian Third Army and penetrates deeply into Syria. Cease-fire imposed by U.S. and USSR, after USSR threats.
1973–74	Artillery war continues on Syrian front until cease-fire in spring of 1974. Israel cedes Kuneitra, remaining on most of Golan, with UN force separating Syrian-Israeli forces.

TABLE 4.3. Opposing Forces (Partial and Approximate)[1]

CAMPAIGN		ISRAEL		ARAB FORCES
War of Liberation (1948)		May	Dec	Iraq, Jordan, Syria, Lebanon, Egypt
	Brigades	6	9	17
	Tanks	3	15	50
	Soldiers	20–29,000	49,000	40,000
	Artillery	4	120	200
	Combat aircraft	Light planes	30	75

In May 1948, Israel had 22,000 rifles, 195 3-inch and 682 2-inch mortars, 1,550 machine guns. At that time, less than half of the Israeli soldiers were trained.

			Egypt	
Sinai (1956)	Tanks	200	600	
	Combat aircraft	125	250	

			Egypt, Jordan, Syria, Iraq	
Six Day War (1967)	Tanks	900	2,100	
	Combat aircraft	200*	575	

			Egypt, Syria, Iraq, Jordan	
Yom Kippur War (1973)	Tanks	1,700	4,600**	
	Combat aircraft	380	1,000***	

* Plus 40 Fouga jet trainers used in ground attack. Almost 400 Arab aircraft destroyed on ground.
** Ratio of Arab to Israel artillery more than 5:1. Equipment in use: Israel combat planes, Phantom F-4, Skyhawk A-4, Mirage III. Arab first-line aircraft, Mig-21 and Mig-23 reconnaissance (probably Russian-flown). Missiles: Israel, Israeli-built air-to-air (Shafrir) and U.S. Sidewinders, and Israeli sea-to-sea (Gabriel). Also stand-off air-ground weapons, such as Hobo, Walleye, Maverick. Egypt and Syria (all USSR), Styx (sea-to-sea), Komar boats and Kelt (cruise missiles), SAM 2, 2A, 3, 6, 7 ground-to-air. Antitank: Israel, TOW (U.S.). Egypt and Syria, Sager (USSR).
*** Includes about 300 planes in Iraq and Jordan not transferred to Syrian front.

In the three years following the war, the organization was adapted to the long-term needs of large forces. A system of universal service for all capable men and women* followed by many years of service in the ready reserves was introduced, creating a nation in arms. The universal reserve system was to be a cornerstone of defense capability. While before statehood the highest-level courses had been for platoon leaders, in the 1950s courses were begun for battalion and brigade commanders, and the organization of brigades and of higher headquarters was planned in detail.

In the six years between 1950 and the Sinai campaign, the Air Force had already developed and put into operation long-range plans for organization and training.[8] By 1956, on the eve of the campaign, the Air Force had grown

* Exceptions are made on religious grounds (very orthodox women and rabbinic students) and for Arabs, who can at present volunteer selectively. Druze have been conscripted since the mid-1950s. Ready-reserve service continues beyond the age of fifty.

from an original handful of pilots and a motley assortment of largely obsolete planes to a force of well-trained pilots, as yet inexperienced in combat, partially equpped with modern jet aircraft; yet whose potential was not yet recognized by the political leaders or the ground-force commanders.

In the ground forces, expansion to larger and more formal organization and the departure of some of the best wartime commanders brought a diminution in offensive spirit and imagination in combat. A solution was sought in special volunteer units, which kept alive the commando approach and eventually produced many of the generals of later years. The traditions of these units began in the reprisal raids of the years before the Sinai campaign and were marked by individual heroism and group solidarity in carrying out night infantry raids against military objectives over the Jordan and Gaza Strip borders. By the eve of the Sinai campaign, however, the raids had escalated in scale and were less effective because the repertoire was known to the enemy. Alternating predictably with the raids of infiltrating terrorists, the reprisals became too costly in lives and were no longer successful in deterring infiltration. The influence of the special forces lasted, however, and was even more important in raising the offensive spirit of the Army as a whole than it was in tactical development.

Deterrence on a small scale had failed, and the 1956 Sinai campaign, which followed large Soviet arms supply to Egypt, can be seen as a much more massive deterrent effort, an attempt to destroy the threat at its source. Israel, but not the Arabs, had accepted the outcome of the War of Independence. The Soviet-Czech arms greatly changed force ratios in quality and quantity of arms, and led to Israeli belief in the necessity, if not the feasibility, of preventive action. A preventive war was made possible, in Ben Gurion's view, when Britain and France decided on the Suez campaign, following the nationalization of the Canal. The allies' political aim—to bring down Nasser—failed. Under United States pressure, Israel's territorial *status quo ante* was quickly restored.

In the initial phase of the war, there was considerable deception, both as to the goal and the size and scope of the operation. Instead of Egypt, the Arabs expected the target to be Jordan, which had been the base for most infiltration and the object of recent reprisals. Israeli air and armored actions were initially restrained in order to give the impression that only another, if somewhat larger, reprisal was under way. Initial planning was for rapid movement, bypassing well-manned and fortified positions, which were expected to fall together with a general collapse of the defense. The operation as a whole was marked by the indirect approach.

The campaign, in which Suez was reached in five days, showed the skeptics what tanks and aircraft could do, even though these were still used mainly in supporting roles. The slower, less vulnerable tanks were able to progress faster than lighter vehicles, although there were then serious maintenance problems. Despite the strong advocacy by the early armor commanders for the concentrated use of tanks, armor was seen in the Sinai campaign as a support arm and deterrent. There were only one and a half armored brigades, and the rest of the tanks were distributed in the infantry brigades, which were the principal operating formations in the field.

In the decade between Sinai and the Six Day War, available resources were devoted to the all-out development of air and armor.[9] In the Armored Corps, discipline and the techniques of maintenance, gunnery, and maneuver reached a high level, as the armored brigades became the central arms of the ground forces. The Air Force was soon using all jet aircraft, and developed very effective systems of control, operations, and maintenance. Its training emphasized the initial gaining of air superiority, combat spirit, and the skilled use of tactics and weapons. These capabilities came out fully in the Six Day War. Zahal had been warned and took the initiative with surprise classic air attacks, which took the Arab air forces out of the war, producing the "clean skies" of almost absolute air superiority. In the succeeding days there was a race with time to reach the Straits of Tiran and to destroy the retreating enemy tanks. A war of movement was fought across the borders. The decisions of commanders in the field, at all levels, showed improvisation and initiative.

The division was the typical large field command unit, and armored brigades predominated. Each division operated in a different way, but in most of the larger armored thrusts, the attacks were direct and concentrated. This time it was usually the infantry which followed, supporting and cleaning up. At the cease-fire there were new borders on the Jordan River, the Golan Heights, and the Suez Canal.

Soon after the 1967 cease-fire, infiltration attempts from Jordan again reached serious levels, but were contained. Heavy Egyptian shelling of the Israeli side of the Canal led to the war of attrition, aimed at wearing out Israeli resistance through constant reserve call-ups and personnel losses. Israel dug in along the Canal, building the Bar Lev line, but suffered casualties which could not be borne indefinitely. The Air Force suppressed the massed Egyptian artillery and eventually bombed targets deep in Egypt, which led to limited Russian intervention. A cease-fire was reached in 1970. Ground-to-air missiles were used by the Egyptians for the first time, and after the campaign Egyptians and Russians completed a massive air-defense umbrella that included the whole spectrum of USSR missile performance.

The "Conception"—Following the Six Day War

The Six Day War had been purely defensive. No political goals had been set, nor was there, at the war's end, any developed or agreed-on political concept on the way to use the new border positions and the proven military superiority to gain a settlement that would give peace with security. The potential for a political role of Zahal in a possible peace settlement was enhanced, but no way was found to use it.

Swift and complete success in the war impeded the learning of strategic lessons. An image of invincibility and effective deterrence was reinforced by the statements of political leaders that "the enemy is not going to be able to fight for many, many years to come."[10] Paraphrasing Israel Galili, Golda Meir, and Moshe Dayan, the dominant view seemed to be, "Time is on our side. The Golan Heights, the Suez Canal, and the Jordan River give us favorable topography and some strategic depth, and these, together with Zahal as a deterrent, can prevent a war for a long time. In the meantime, new settlements, gradual integration of the West Bank population to our economy, and policies of extremely liberal rule and open borders to the West Bank and to Jordan will work toward peace and security." If the expected call from Hussein or Sadat asking for peace talks did not come, it still seemed as though there would be time for the liberal occupation, interaction between Jews and Arabs, and armed deterrence to do their work, and that the world would take on many of the problems, such as the great costs of resettling refugees, if, indeed, the Arab states could be induced to absorb them.

The conception that "it won't happen" thus became prevalent. Although Sadat said in interviews and speeches that he would soon go to war and the Russian build-up increased, it was widely believed that there would be no attack without both an impossible Arab air superiority and a unified Arab command. It was recognized that some forty-eight hours notice would be needed for the reserve call-up, but this amount of notice was assumed. In the worst case, given Israeli air power and the nature of Arab armies, it was believed that the relatively small regular forces could absorb the initial thrusts. In any case, Sadat seemed an improbable figure to lead a coordinated Arab attack. The more felicitous borders and the success of air and armor in 1967 had led to a more static concept of defense, [11] in which deterrence made the need for preemption seem improbable. Nor was it conceived that the Arabs would use a war of limited objectives, in which there would be only minor tactical success, as a political weapon with which to upset the *status quo*.

When the attack came, Zahal was for several days in the gravest danger, but mobilized reserves (in twenty-four hours rather than the planned forty-eight), soon counterattacked successfully, and took the war to the enemy's territory. The crossing of the Canal and the cutting off of the Egyptian Third Army showed a classic use of the indirect approach; and it was only intervention of the powers which prevented a more complete destruction of the Arab forces. Commanders in the field, often junior officers or NCOs who had survived their seniors, fought in the best tradition of the leadership examples of the past. Israeli commando capabilities had little scope, and after the war there was a call for the renaissance of their roles.

The Air Force could not follow the intended priority of first gaining air superiority over the battlefield because the still-mobilizing ground forces needed immediate tactical support. This was very costly, until the ground counterattack began and air resources could be devoted to the destruction of the missile launchers. The skies over Israel were kept clear, however, for an uninterrupted call-up of reserves, and Egyptian advances were held within their missile cover. Strategic targets in Syria were attacked effectively. In later stages, when the war became one of open movement, the Israeli superiority in air and tank combat came into play and most of the Arab tanks and aircraft were destroyed. The Israeli Navy, long considered an unimportant arm, came into its own, as its missile boats, using Israeli "Gabriel" missiles, countered the Russian-supplied "Styx" missiles and made a clean sweep of the Syrian and Egyptian navies.

The tactical surprise was minor compared to the strategic misjudgment. There was an unexpected coordination of the initial Syrian and Egyptian attacks, although the Syrians and Egyptians did not form a joint command headquarters. Nor were the tactical capabilities fully appreciated, and the serious Israeli losses in the first days were unexpected. Russian technology introduced massive use of new antiaircraft, antitank, and night-vision capabilities. The Yom Kippur War was the first large-scale encounter of air and armor with antiaircraft and antitank missiles. Following initially high Israeli losses, countertactics were rapidly developed. The new technologies had been known to be available, if not the scope of their deployment, through the experience of the war of attrition in 1970 and subsequent skirmishes, and countertactics had been planned. The tenacity of some Egyptian and Syrian units was remembered from previous wars. There were clear signs of the massing of force. Despite disbelief in an impending attack, in the last few days before the Yom Kippur assault the limited regular forces were ordered to be in readiness.

The strategic surprise was due less to a lack of specific intelligence than to the conceptual framework in which it was interpreted, particularly in the leaders' estimate of the situation. The shock came, not when the fighting started, but several days later when the initial losses and evidence of lacks in organization and problems of command showed that defeats were possible, that the belief that the regular force alone could prevail was not well founded, and that the Army was not a unique preserve but that it mirrored, as the nation in arms, the faults and virtues of the society as a whole.

The experience of the Yom Kippur War stimulated the search for the "ancient virtues." It is significant that the two generals appointed Chief of Staff in 1974 and 1978 were paratroopers. Efforts were made to expand the regular combat forces. The lessons of the war also sharpened the emphasis on two other elements: technology and borders.

An immediate lesson for the future was the need for integration of infantry, artillery, and armor in ground attacks, and of ground and air forces in eliminating missile launchers. The scale and scope of the air force was made more comprehensive to include, beyond air superiority and air defense, more explicit strategic, attack, and transport roles. And there was again a call, though unheeded, to develop sources of strategic intelligence which would report directly to the Prime Minister and the Cabinet, in parallel with the Defense Ministry's assessment.

Constant and Changing Concepts

The history of combat experience and force development shows certain underlying concepts which seem to continue to be essential under conditions of numerical and geographic inferiority, but also shows that increased scale, technology, and victories have from time to time seriously diminished their influence and application. It is clear that unusual qualities are needed in combat and in the effective use of resources. The most constant theme has been that excellence is the answer to the situation of few against many.* Reliance is to be placed not only on the use of arms *per se*, but on the quality of the society and its motivation. Leadership, imagination, and mobility count in combat. Officers go first (in the Zahal phrase, "follow me"), and in all campaigns they have suffered the highest proportion of casualties. In the field there is flexibility and independent judgment, since battles seldom go as planned.

An almost total use of national resources has been necessary even to maintain a 3:1 to 4:1 ratio of Arab to Israeli forces. Such ratios and the lack of strategic depth demand the use of indirect approaches, mobility, the ability to concentrate firepower, and, above all, fighting on enemy territory.** Once started, action has to be swift, because resources are limited and because the powers are expected to intervene at an early stage, particularly when things are going well for Israel.

There have been periods, however, when flexibility, the indirect approach, and initiative were somewhat neglected as military thought and planning were affected by large-scale organization, more favorable border positions, and the experience of success.*** In thirty years, field command

* Ben Gurion, introducing amendments to the Defense Service Law in the Knesset on March 5, 1951: "Our security is not only in the army. We cannot possibly build and maintain an army of such grandeur that its strength alone . . . will give us the desired security. Our security lies in the people—in the total ability of the people." In "Quality Versus Quantity," *Ma'arachot*, 254 (Heb.), February 1977, Yigael Yadin suggests, quoting the biblical example of Gideon against the Midianites, that fewness of numbers may make it easier to achieve excellence, both in spirit and in the use of arms. See Judges 7:8.

** The Agranat Committee, investigating the Yom Kippur War, asked David Elazar, the Chief of Staff, why he began planning the counterattacks at the beginning of the war, when defense was so critical. He replied, "Zahal has always sought to carry the fighting to enemy territory at as early a stage as possible on the assumption that the chance of winning depends on offensive initiative." Open letter of General Elazar to Prime Minister Rabin, *Ma'ariv*, April 20, 1976.

*** The Israeli military journal *Ma'arachot* published many more articles on strategic concepts in the 1950s than it did in the 1960s. In the sense of regard for techniques and knowledge, there is more professionalism in Zahal than in most other spheres of Israeli life, and this at some periods may have reduced strategic emphasis. That is, the efforts of some of the most capable commanders were devoted to reaching technical and tactical excellence. Still, the proponents of air and armor had to make their cases against great resistance, which stimulated operational thought on their part.

organizations grew to divisions and even armies, whose sheer size challenged the possibility of achieving unusual excellence, and whose logistical needs brought some of the disadvantages of bureaucracies, even though Zahal has a smaller administrative overhead than most other large armies.

There were years of delay and conservatism at the highest policy levels in understanding the roles of aircraft and tanks, although the faith of their practitioners never faltered. Once aircraft and tanks were adopted as the central forces, the greatest proportion of resources and thought went into their development, and the firepower which they provided at times decreased the emphasis given to strategic imagination in general and to the indirect approach in particular. As soon as battles were joined, however, initiative and improvisation were common at even the most junior levels of command.

The Complex Defense Challenge

Beyond the immediate tactical interface are the more complex problems of the longer-range impact of technology, borders, and the roles of the great powers. Technologies now on the horizon could be detrimental as well as favorable to Israel. Future warfare will involve precision guidance and automated aiming, remotely piloted vehicles and the dispersal of large firepower to small units and to infantry, and vastly more effective destructive capability.[12] Maintenance could be facilitated by the ready discard and replacement of components. Such developments could narrow the advantages of Israeli fighting men and technicians over their Arab counterparts. If technological change were to increase the relative effectiveness of defenders over attackers, a more static kind of warfare could develop, to Israel's disadvantage. On the other hand, Israel's unusual ability in technology, in fluid battle situations, and in the combat independence of small groups and individuals— all these could be used to take great advantage of new developments.

The danger posed by lack of warning and the manifest increase in destructive power emphasize the need for secure borders,[13] a question which is almost inseparable from ideology and politics. After 1967 the new boundaries and a sudden sense of independence seemed, for the first time since the debates in the Yishuv on the British proposals to partition Palestine, to open political and social options regarding the size of the country, the ratio of Jews to Arabs, the role of new settlements, and the way to peace.

The question of the military impact of the location of borders was inevitably mixed with beliefs about whether guarantees of the powers or peace treaties in return for withdrawals were meaningful; whether there was any change in what had seemed an underlying Arab strategic goal of eliminating Israel as a sovereign state; what relative weights the differing perceptions of the Israeli question in the Arab world would take now and with time; and whether the inclusion of many more Arabs in Israel would materially divert the society from its former goals if, as a result, the Jews were to relate to the Arabs as second-class citizens or leave manual labor to them. These complex questions turned much on beliefs and ideology and on broad assumptions about the nature of the Arab-Israeli relation. They made the analysis of defense strategy more confusing because it could not be discussed without intermixing political, military, and social criteria.

The 1979 treaty between Egypt and Israel meant withdrawal to the Sinai border of the British Mandate. Israel paid the price, not only in oil resources and loss of early-warning time, but also in giving up the settlements below the Gaza strip which blocked the historic path of armies attacking Israel from the south. The Syrian and West Bank borders allow far less flexibility, for reasons of distance (for example, the narrow neck at the center of the country between the foothills of Judea and the sea) and of topography (the Golan Heights, and the high ridges of Judea and Samaria).

There seems to be a general defense consensus in Israel that whatever the changes needed to achieve accommodation, Arab arms need to be excluded from the West Bank and the Golan for a very long time to come. Settlement patterns reflect the belief that there would not be effective demilitarization without an Israeli presence, and that the early-warning potential of the Jordan Valley and the ridges and the heights are important. It has been argued, mainly outside of Israel, that withdrawal and demilitarization could make possible the kind of warning given by the transfer of Egyptian forces to Sinai in 1967; and that effective control systems could be worked out for demilitarization, including graduated, defined, *causi belli*. In the limited area remaining to them, Israelis are understandably reluctant to undertake such experiments-given the ways in which the fundamental security relations with the powers and the Arabs are perceived. And for Israelis, secure borders are those which can be defended without a large loss of life.

The Great Powers

On many occasions, in different ways, Ben Gurion said, "It does not matter what the nations say; what is important is what the Jews do," yet "Peace will come to the Middle East when America and Russia want peace to come," thus expressing the need for self-reliance while recognizing the importance of the powers. Self-reliance is indicated both by the value of independence and by historical experience. The attitude toward the powers has been one of "respect them and suspect them," for they have larger stakes than the Middle East. Even those whose friendship is genuine can act in ways injurious to Israeli survival, and the changing games and roles of the powers reinforce caution. The relations between the United States and Israel have been unusually close, reinforced by ties of ideology and culture as well as the support of the large, free, and active American Jewish community. Israel is one of the few working democracies outside of Europe and North America. Yet the two governments often perceive their interests very differently.

Israel-Soviet relations were close for a brief period after the founding of the state, but from then on diverged. The USSR recognized Israel immediately after independence, allowed arms exports from Eastern Europe and saw in the new state a potential point of leverage from which to remove British influence from the area. It was soon apparent, however, that Israel would not become a satellite, and had in any case little to offer in comparison with the vastness of the Arab world. The USSR turned sharply from its pro-Israel stance. British hegemony was ending, and the Soviets could penetrate the area without Israeli help. Furthermore, a severance of ties with Israel helped to repress renascent Jewish nationalism within Russia. The USSR began to point to Israel and imperialism as a common external danger, using as examples the Suez campaign and American attempts (which, however, excluded Israel), to form regional alliances.

Arab involvement with the USSR began in the mid-1950s, at first indirectly. Rejected by the United States as the leader of a potential Arab-Western alliance, Nasser stayed out of the Baghdad Pact between Iran, Iraq, and Turkey and turned to the East for aid. Soviet relations with Egypt began on a large scale with the Czech arms sale in 1955, and from then on the Russian presence in Egypt, Syria, and Iraq increased, facilitated in 1958 by the fall of the pro-Western government of Iraq and with it of the Baghdad Pact.

The USSR continued to support its client states with massive arms, technicians, training, and even limited combat intervention; but it did not give them free rein. On the one hand, Russia has acted to prevent a complete Arab military debacle. On the other, it has stopped short of actions which could possibly lead to a world conflagration. Following Arab defeats, the USSR has repeatedly used threats of armed intervention to restore the balance and to reverse Israel's gains, and the possibility of Soviet physical intervention provides a convincing deterrent to Israel. After the 1956 campaign, Russian threats hastened the withdrawal from Sinai, and in 1967 the USSR's encouragement of Egypt was a major impetus to the Six Day War. Toward the end of the war, the Israeli decision to capture the Golan Heights was delayed and the advance in Syria was limited largely from fear of Russian military intervention.[14] The decision to bomb Egypt in depth during the 1970 war of attrition, to the extent that it was thought out, was partly influenced by a judgment that because the Russian presence existed in any case, "we might as well go ahead."[15] In the event, the bombings led to intensified Russian involvement, with a reported 15,000 to 20,000 Russian troops in Egypt during the spring of 1970 to support missiles and operate aircraft cover over Cairo.*

---

* Israel seeks to avoid direct military contact with non-Arab forces. Two exceptions: in 1949 British fighters were shot down when they crossed the Negev, and in 1970 Russian-piloted Migs were destroyed over Suez, in both cases without Israeli losses. The only known case of a request

Following the 1973 war, Russian influence in Egypt declined. Even before the war, Egypt was ill at ease with the Soviet advisory group, despite its tangible advantages. The Russians were seen to limit Egyptian independence, and their authority was resented by many Egyptian officers. Most of the military advisory operation was stopped in 1972. The United States was beginning to appear to Egypt as a source of diplomatic pressure on Israel and of economic and technological aid, as well as being helpful in improving relations with the Saudis. After the war, Egypt sought Western procurement of arms. The oil states began to buy large quantities of modern arms from the Unites States. These are readily transferable to the countries bordering Israel, and Saudi aircraft are within bombing range.

Israel has been committed to the West since shortly after independence. In the early 1950s the die was cast, as Israel came out strongly in support of the UN in the Korean War, and turned down an opportunity for possible relations with China.[16] In the first years of the state, hopes were for peace on a local basis, without identification with the strategies of East or West.* When this seemed impossible, at least in the short run, Western alliances were sought, or the guarantees of arms. Britain and the United States rejected these proposals, and the most that was achieved was the British-French-U.S. Tri-partite Agreement of 1950, to preserve the peace and sovereignty of the countries in the area.

By contrast with the role of the USSR, that of Britain in the Middle East was rapidly declining, and became negligible after Suez. In 1948, however, Britain was still the dominant power in the Middle East. She sought to make Jordan, with access to the Mediterranean, a major base and to preserve Suez bases as the lifeline of the fast-shrinking empire. Allied with both Jordan and Egypt, Britain supplied their arms and furnished the commander and most of the officers of the Jordanian Army. In the early 1950s, as the Western powers refused Israel's bids for firm commitments on arms, England withdrew from the bases along the Suez Canal without getting any political guarantees in return. Border infiltration into Israel from Jordan was followed by more organized *fedayeen* raids from Gaza, and the Straits of Tiran were closed to Israel. In 1954 and 1955, Israel felt threatened and isolated among the nations.

---

for physical intervention occurred before Suez. Ben Gurion, fearing attacks on population centers from the air, asked that French air cover be provided if needed. It wasn't.

* Pressure from the Israeli left was for complete neutrality or even Eastern association, but it diminished greatly in the light of the anti-Semitism of the USSR regime, seen, for example, in the Prague show trials and the Moscow doctors' trial at the end of Stalin's rule. In a lecture to the senior commanders in March 1953, Ben Gurion defined Israel as nonaligned, democratic, and concerned with immigration and the fate of Jews in the Diaspora. "But the extent of cooperation with other countries depends perhaps decisively on the freedom of action and movement of the Jews in those countries. . . . that is the first . . . reason why Israel cannot be part of the Soviet bloc . . . and still keep her identity." In addition to Russian denial of Jewish unity and Zionism, he explains, a second reason is that Soviet bloc membership requires subservience to Soviet political aims.

She was even advised by Britain to give up most of the Negev, as the way to peace.

Perceived common interests of Israel, France, and Britain in the defeat of Nasser made possible the Suez campaign of 1956. After the cease-fire, the Sinai Peninsula and the Gaza Strip were relinquished because of heavy pressure from the United States, with promises from Eisenhower to guarantee freedom of passage through the Straits of Tiran. A partnership with France began, epitomized by De Gaulle's welcome to Ben Gurion in Paris as a "friend and ally." Advanced arms, joint manufacture and R&D, and a nuclear reactor marked more than ten years of close collaboration, to end in the Six Day War of 1967 when De Gaulle warned Israel against a preemptive strike against the Egyptian troops massed on the Sinai border. By then, France had left Algeria and saw her interests diverging from those of Israel; procurement of arms and economic support from France ceased with a complete French embargo a year and a half later. The French alliance had provided technology as well as arms, helping to increase Israel's capability in weapons development. After the Six Day War, when De Gaulle's embargo made self-help a necessity, Israel was already designing and producing a broad range of high-technology weapons systems and components.

The inherently close ties of Israel and the United States have often been sorely tried. Upon independence, the United States recognized Israel at once, imposed an embargo on arms to the Middle East (which mainly affected Israel, as the British armed Jordan and Egypt), but tacitly allowed Israeli purchase of some surplus materials. In the 1950s the Middle East became a focus for the cold war, and both the United States and the USSR sought Arab alliances. Despite the Czech arms supply to. Egypt, American arms were not made available to Israel. In the decade which followed Suez, there was more compatibility of American and Israeli aims. Faced with Soviet penetration in Syria, Egypt, and, from 1958, in Iraq, the United States sought stability through a balance of power, and eventually became the principal foreign source of Israeli arms. The embargo which began in 1948 ended in 1962 when Kennedy agreed to the sale of Hawk antiaircraft missiles. After the end of the Israeli-French alliance in 1967, dependence on the United States escalated, and in the 1970s United States tanks, artillery, and aircraft were the major part of Israeli first-line equipment.

The swift and complete Israeli sweep in the 1967 war led both countries to hope that Israel's strength could lead to a settlement or, at worst, provide deterrence and stability. In contrast with the previous wars, the United States supported Israel's stance, linking territorial withdrawal to a viable settlement. Still, the Nixon regime became active in pressing both sides toward an agreement, trying, at one and the same time, to advance *détente*, show friendship to Arab countries, and support Israel. In this period, beginning toward the end of the 1970 war of attrition, the activity of both Russia and America in the area was greatly intensified. An important U.S.-Israel difference could be sensed: both sought a settlement to the conflict, but the United States emphasis was on a settlement *per se*, while Israel's primary concern was security.

This difference appeared more intensely during and after the Yom Kippur War. The United States sent Israel a very large resupply of arms and ammunition—but only after a painful delay, and after both Israeli difficulties and the massive Soviet airlift were obvious. It was believed that Israel could win handily without new supplies, and that too massive an Israeli victory could impede an American-sponsored settlement. At the war's end, the agreement between Russia and America on the cease-fire saved the Egyptian Third Army. The events dramatized the greatly increased dependence of both Israel and the Arabs on the powers, and the difference in U.S.-Israel priorities and security perceptions. For the United States, settlement was urgent. Sadat turned to America for economic aid, and as the power which could influence Israel toward a settlement that would be acceptable to the Arabs. The United States stance was both close enough and far enough from that of Israel to make this seem feasible. Indeed, the gap in American-Israeli perceptions was an essential element of Arab-American relations.[17]

The difficulties in the relationship of Israel with her closest ally point up the Israeli feeling of diplomatic isolation, and of the dilemma of the simultaneous need for independence and for support on a large scale. The United States repeatedly used arms and technology for leverage on Israel, as was evident in the negotiations with Nixon for aircraft in 1970, and in Kissinger's "reassessment" of needs following the failure of the Sinai negotiations in the spring of 1975.[18] Just before the Arab attack which began the Yom Kippur War, considerations of American support were important in the decision against a preemptive air strike against the Syrian missile system and Air Force.

Indeed, experience has associated security with the need for independence in political and defense actions. The Tripartite Agreement of 1950 failed to prevent aggression. France defected on the eve of the Six Day War, and President Johnson was unable to ensure the free passage through the Straits of Tiran which Eisenhower had promised at the time of the Sinai withdrawal after Suez. The cynically imposed Yom Kippur War cease-fire made the Israeli victory far less important than it might have been. Nor was there any evidence that ties of belief or kinship would, in a crisis, be stronger than perceived self-interest; for across the northern border of Israel, Lebanese Christians were seen to have been abandoned by the Western world.

These experiences reinforce concern.[19] Israel is denied European aid because of oil and is still isolated, diplomatically, from the Third World. In the month following the outbreak of the Yom Kippur War, a score of countries severed diplomatic relations with her. Relations with the USSR are impeded by the Soviet treatment of Jews and restrictions on emigration. There are substantial Soviet nonnuclear forces in the Mediterranean and the Indian Ocean; and whether or not the USSR would restrain or encourage an Arab attack, or even intervene, would depend only on her strategic calculus at the time. Despite the need for aid and an even greater need for allies, Israel for the present has sought independence of action and has concentrated on what is needed for defense in an Israel-Arab confrontation.

Physical security and peace have many imponderables. The 1973 war destroyed much of the optimism regarding the influence of elements in the Arab countries that would accept a lasting peace.* The Arab countries were seen as basically still opposed to the continued existence of Israel, although, tactically, they had aimed for much less in specific campaigns. Indeed, the likelihood of war was increased by the Arab integration of economic, political, and military warfare, and it has been suggested that Clausewitz's dictum was reversed by the Arabs, who made diplomacy the continuation of war by other means.[20] Stability in the area was diminished by competition between the Arab countries and by the continuing social and political disadvantages of the Palestinians living in them.

Israel thus sees the aims of the opponents as asymmetric, necessitating preparation for a "worst case" struggle for survival. The central goals was to change the Arab intentions, but this did not seem within easy reach by either political or military means. While Israel could not survive the loss of a major campaign, there does not seem to be an accepted concept in which a military victory *per se* would lead to a lasting peace with the Arab world. Partly as a result, there have not been specific political "war aims" beyond physical security. Impressive military victories in all of the campaigns (and notably the Yom Kippur War) have been followed by political retreats imposed by the powers. At turning points, such as that which occurred after the partition decision of 1947 (against which the Arab armies invaded) and following each succeeding war, Israel wanted to keep the new *status quo* while the Arabs tried as a first step to go back to the previous situations.

It has always been a time to wage peace, and to be prepared for war. Defense forces are needed which could deter attack, and if this deterrence should fail, have the option of a preemptive action or, at worst, of an effective second strike. Changing conditions make it increasingly difficult to maintain this capability. The scale of forces, even to maintain the historical Israeli quantitative inferiority (see Table 4.1), continues to drain the economy and reduces independence. Costs, and their dollar components, seem logically to be approaching their limits of growth, while scale could work against excellence. Over time, social development in Arab countries, the growth of their arms, and new technologies could decrease the relative Israeli advantage, bearing in mind that by 1985 Arab forces and arms will exceed those of NATO in Europe.[21]

Defense policy aims to overcome this trend through strategic thought and the wise use of technology and of the potential relative advantages inherent in

* In the history of Zionism this had happened many times before. See Chapter 1, "Ideals and Reality."

the Israeli society, while maintaining Israeli political independence in the face of mounting material needs. Beyond this, there is a need to find a relation between military strategy and the political goal of establishing normal relations with the Arabs. If another war were to be forced upon Israel, what would be the alternative military objectives, beyond immediate survival? That is, if there should have to be another campaign, how could it lead to a political settlement? The solution of these problems and the effectiveness of the defense-policy system depend a great deal on the quality of civil-military relations.

Political Authority and the Armed Forces

The problem of ensuring that force and the commanders of force are loyal and useful *servants* is an ancient one. Experience demonstrates that the relations between organized force and the civil government can distort democratic processes or lead to ineffective defense policies. Military rule is the most obvious nondemocratic form. By contrast, elected political leaders, such as Lincoln and Clemenceau, had great difficulty in finding effective commanders and in controlling them or even stimulating them into action. In recent times, problems of information, evaluating new technologies, and controlling vast, complex systems and the industries and bureaucracies which deal with them have become even more acute.

Models of civil-military relations, while not directly applicable, may give a useful perspective to the specifically Israeli analysis which follows.[22] Two forms, which are not imminent in Israel, are (1) praetorian rule, in which a military group takes over authority, or maintains civilian figureheads in power,* and (2) an extreme degree of politicization along ideological or class lines. As will be shown, the latter possibility was feared at the time of independence, but the separate or partly separate military groups on the right and on the left were soon dissolved and arms were nationalized.

An "ideal type," in which the military clearly accept and follow civilian authority, occurs when the officer corps follow professional goals and leave decisions on political aims and the employment of the forces to civilian leaders. Another model where the soldier accepts political authority is possible when the ideology of a state (or social movement or revolution) is ab-

---

* Attempts at forming a military-political elite within the Haganah failed early in the 1920s and later. Attempts by the generals in 1948 to force Ben Gurion's hand on questions of appointments came to naught because of his support by the other political leaders. In the waiting period on the eve of the Six Day War, military leaders were an active lobby but basically saw the limit of their role as attempting to persuade ministers. In Samuel Finer's terms (*The Man on Horseback: The Role of the Military in Politics*, London and Dunmow, Pall Mall Press, 1962), there is a "consensus on how power in the state is transferred, on where sovereignty lies, and there is a cohesive society held together by much more than the force of law." These factors tend to limit intervention to accepted means and channels.

sorbed by military persons who identify with the political goals and leaders. As in the professional case, although in a different way, the officers have a stake in the country—as part of its elite and in agreement with the leaders' ideology. Taking this model beyond the concept of a "class in arms," we have a "nation in arms" when the vast majority identify with defense needs and aims.

These models of effective civilian control are limited by the realities of bureaucratic politics, and by the difficulties of controlling forces once operations are under way. In Israel, therefore, there is continuing concern for civil control, because small-scale operations continue during the periods between the full-scale wars. In bureaucratic politics (the modern "wars of the Jews")* expertise, symbolic importance, and organization could give defense leaders unusual powers. Excessive secrecy could allow the Prime Minister or Defense Minister to employ the forces without adequate control by the other Cabinet members, who could be presented with a *fait accompli* which escalated actions or forced critical decisions. The hallowed aims and vast scope of the organization could make it an establishment, supported "because it is there," determining its own requirements and role.

Given the strategic context, the "worst case" model of a "garrison state" cannot be disregarded. Convinced of external danger, society becomes dedicated to defense and gives primacy to defense needs and to the experts in violence. Because sophisticated technologies and large material resources are needed, the preoccupation of leaders is less with physical violence, certainly not on a small scale, than with the defense-industrial-research complexes and overall control of the population. Coerced through fear and led by the experts in defense, the society gives up its underlying civil freedoms and becomes a modern form of garrison.

Two other adverse possibilities warrant consideration—alienation, and, obversely, a form of politicization that aims to exploit the military within a democratic parliamentary system. Separation of the military from the rest of the society could come about if the officers were to be wholly identified with a class, ideology, or ethnic group; if senior officers were to feel locked out of decision making; or if the government were to seem incapable of solving internal and external problems. Politicization could involve the exploitation of the defense organization by politicians to advance sectoral or partisan ends and to change political power relations. One form of distortion is for military action or outside threats to be used in ways not warranted by the situation, or for military promotions to be used for patronage. In another, partisan loyalty

---

*The reference is to Flavius Josephus, *The Jewish War*, G. A. Williamson (trans.), Harmonsworth, England, Penguin, 1960. The term is an Israeli cliché for organizational infighting, reminiscent of the internal struggles when Jerusalem was under seige by the Romans. For recent bureaucratic politics see Graham Allison, *Essence of Decision*, Boston, Little, Brown, 1971; and Morton Halperin, *Bureaucratic Politics and Foreign Policy*, Washington, Brookings, 1974.

or personal political ambition could influence decisions within the defense system, and reliance on outside political judges could replace professional or peer judgments of individual competence.

Applying these concepts, Israel will be found to have strong elements of a nation in arms, of identification of the military with national rather than class ideology, of the professional model, and of bureaucratic politics. In the continuing crisis, the prior and most relevant questions are the *effectiveness of decisions* and *public responsibility*, defined in terms of the following considerations: [23]

> Even though defense decisions are too critical to be made in the interests of parties or sectors or to be a crude outcome of bargaining, it is unrealistic to try to keep issues of such importance completely nonpartisan or to try to do away with bureaucratic politics. Indeed, many partisan differences are legitimate, and if they are understood, can make decisions more effective.
>
> The most complete information is needed beforehand and not after the fact. Multiple sources of information and interpretation are necessary, particularly at the highest organizational levels, which receive much of their information in predigested form.
>
> Alternatives must be developed, advocated, attacked, and weighed. All the relevant considerations—the implications of success or failure, the probabilities of alternative results, the extent to which aims and resources are congruent—need to be examined. Decision and advice groups should include both representatives of interests and independent critics.
>
> Those having the highest level of responsibility should make the major decisions and not be drawn into them through the momentum of actions at other levels. The real locus of responsibility for the large military and political decisions should be clear, recognizing that second-order decisions and the appointment of those who make them are integral parts of the political leader's public responsibility.
>
> The quality of information can be expected to improve with exposure. Public knowledge should be as complete as possible in each situation.

From these considerations, we ask:

> Is the defense-policy system effective? We expect to find that it usually is, despite the tragic surprise of 1973.
>
> Is defense under representative and responsible political control? We could expect to find that it is, but that the defense organization often has had an inordinate amount of influence on decisions; and we could expect to find that the dominance of one party, until 1977, led to some politicization of defense.

How do the recurrent crises, the primacy of defense needs, and universal
military service affect the political culture? We might expect to find that
violence, hatred, and fear are stimulated, injuring the democracy.

To look for answers, the development of defense organization in the
Yishuv and the state is described, and the characteristic relationship of the
defense system to the rest of the government is analyzed, within the overall
political system. It is found that the structure of the system does not explain
how it works; the process seems to lack elements which would be expected to
be necessary for political control or effectiveness. Yet there is very much of
both, and the explanation lies in the way the system developed, its political
culture, and its relation to society.

The System *

To participants, the defense enterprise is known as "the system," and those
who know what is going on are "on the inside" **—phrases reminiscent of
the small closed group of the underground days or the early years of the state.
In recent years the organization chart, budget, and senior appointments—
and since the Yom Kippur War many internal differences—are public knowledge. The enterprise has become large and complex, which has importance for
civil-military relations.

An examination of the system will presently show that, in comparison
with the experience of other democratic countries, in Israel military forces are
well subordinated to decisions of elected politicians; and that despite the
symbolic and bureaucratic importance of Zahal, grosser forms of politicization have not endured and those of militarism have not developed. These
results, however, are more the outcome of historical and cultural development than they are of effective organizational or constitutional design, and
there are important elements which need further attention. For this reason, I
will first discuss the historical and political roots of Zahal, before attempting
to analyze the working of the system in the state.[24]

The most important point is that, in contrast with many other nations
which achieved independence, in Israel civilian political leaders were in
charge of defense from the beginning, even decades before independence. In
the process there was politicization, in keeping with the *parteistaat* character
of the Yishuv. For historical reasons, however, in the State this did not take
the form either of political patronage within the military, on the one hand, or
of the dominance of class ideology, on the other. That those charged with
defense were chosen and guided by the party leaders was seen as the natural

* Hebrew, *Ha'ma'arechet*.
** Hebrew, *Betoch ha'inyanim*.

course of things. The political leaders, in turn, were limited in their authority over defense by the coalition and bargaining modes of the Yishuv.

Important elements before the state and in its first year include the decision in the Yishuv in the early 1920's that the defense organization would be part-time and voluntary; the beliefs and background of early Haganah leaders, the participation of both Labor and non-Labor leaders in the civilian control councils of the Haganah, the political socialization of the early commanders of Zahal, and the way Ben Gurion initially organized the Ministry of Defense.

As in other spheres, and simultaneously with the transition of Labor "from a class to a people," * defense experienced a transition from party control to party influence through the Histadrut, and eventually to control by the national institutions and thus by the state. Until the 1920s, defense was mainly a problem of guarding settlements against sporadic and local attacks, which were then only beginning to be motivated by Arab nationalism. Clandestine, guild-type Jewish defense organizations, such as the Shomer ("Watchman"), operated in something of the spirit of Eastern European underground movements. The Histadrut, almost from its foundation, assumed the principal responsibility for defense, forming the Irgun He'haganah, or Haganah (Defense). Ahdut Ha'Avoda, as the dominant party in the Histadrut, was faced with the following choice of decisions:

> Building on the Shomer groups, which had replaced the original Arab settlement guards with Jewish pioneers before World War I. The Shomer advocated combining settlement and political leadership centered on defense, and the development of a specialized ideological and professional "defense elite."
> Or, developing a very broad volunteer organization based on part-time, militia-type service throughout all the settlements of the Yishuv, with a minimum number of full-time leaders.

The decision was for a militia having a broad, part-time membership and against the concept of the Shomer. The defense organization, while it was forced to be clandestine, was from its beginning nonelitist and exposed to broad political processes and influences.

For subsequent civil-military relations, the beliefs and personalities of the early defense leaders were no less important than the structure. They reflected "practical Zionism," that is, winning the land through work and settlement rather than through international politics or force, and they generally agreed with the moderate democratic socialism of those who won the political struggles for the leadership in the Yishuv. Haganah leaders like Eliahu Golomb, Dov Hoz, and Shaul Avigur were nationalist, pragmatic socialists from the years and schools of thought which developed the kibbutz ideology. Their firm conviction of the need to subordinate force to politics may have come

---

* See the account of the political development of the Labor movement in Chapter 1.

more from their knowledge of the problems of nineteenth-century revolutionary movements than from Western political theory. In the Russian underground groups in the nineteenth century and the beginning of the twentieth, members whose role was violence seem to have dominated, often leading underground groups astray—not to speak of *agents provocateurs.* The experiences and literature from the period seem to have given early Haganah leaders a warning of the need for "civilian" control. Dostoyevsky's *The Possessed* was an example of their reading.

As individuals, the founders of the Haganah were of the highest caliber. But they were not the principal leaders of the national political struggle, although they were close to those leaders and of their stature. The defense enterprise was not the very first priority of the Yishuv until after 1945. The budget alone tells the story. Shaul Avigur reports a trip to Jerusalem to Jewish Agency headquarters in the early 1930s to get an appropriation to run the Haganah office; he returned to Tel Aviv crestfallen, with only £25. By 1942 the annual budget was £226,000, two-thirds of which was raised in the Yishuv from a self-imposed tax (*kofer hayishuv*) and donations. The rest came from the Jewish Agency.

The political leaders were always conscious of the potential importance of the defense organization for internal political control as well as for survival, but some years were to pass before defense became the main object of attention—this did not happen until World War II. From its inception, those who served in the defense organization were thus conscious that they were governed by political leaders and by developed civil institutions. These values were passed on to the younger men who went into the Palmach, the Haganah officers' courses, or the British Army, and who later, as the leaders of Zahal, trained the colonels and generals of the late 1970s. Before the state, there were thus present both the elements of civilian control and of ideological and political identification.*

The lag in priority assigned to defense, while limiting defense leaders to a secondary role, also made it possible for a younger generation of leaders to develop, through the experience of fulfilling important national tasks—first in the early Haganah, then, for the generation born in Palestine, in the Palmach and the British Army of World War II.

* The syllabus of a course for squad leaders, given in 1947, is enlightening. The course commander was Haim Bar Lev (Chief of Staff in 1968–72 and later Minister of Commerce and Industry). Taught in illegal underground circumstances at Kibbutz Dalia, the program called for 493 hours of instruction. Of these, 146 were devoted to "explanation and culture," to "the Zionist Movement," "The Diaspora," "Illegal Immigration and Escape," "Liberation Movements and Undergrounds in the World," "The Middle East," etc. Commanders of illegal immigrant ships spoke, and there were concerts, Sabbath songs, and poetry readings. Among the lecturers were Mrs. Golda Meirson (Meir), Itzhak Tabenkin (the ideological leader of Hakibbutz Hameuchad), Yigal Allon (head of the Palmach), Haim Bar Lev, and Itzhak Rabin, then a senior Palmach commander. While the higher Haganah leaders were mainly from Mapai, loyalties of the Palmach and especially of its commanders were more to the left, through the United Kibbutz Movement and the Shomer Hatzair.

Until World War II, defense was a subordinate need to diplomacy and to the problems of settlement and immigration. That is, although violence continually increased during the 1930s, sheer physical survival was not the Yishuv's single greatest problem, although eventually it became the main question for Jews as a people. The priorities were the struggle for immigration, for employment opportunities, for settlement, and the political help of the great powers. The methods of political decision and control, the institutions and their linkages throughout the society, were therefore highly developed before defense became central. Leaders came from nonmilitary institutions to organize, develop, and control the defense forces, instead of emerging from a military group which won the country's independence and which then tried to develop political institutions.

In 1929 there were serious anti-Jewish attacks, against which the British forces offered little protection. Participation in the political direction of the Haganah was broadened to include the non-Labor parties, which were given parity of representation on national and local "committees of control." The requirement that the leaders of the militia report to local groups which included politicians from both camps served to emphasize political control. Decisions of the control committees were achieved through bargaining, and it was years before the development of professional military staffs began a countertrend. Most of those who enlisted were politically oriented. Labor was the more highly organized movement, and kibbutzim and labor cooperatives were able to release people for the few full-time jobs involved. Thus it was that in practice the Histadrut had the most influence on actual operations and on the small full-time cadre which developed.

In 1936 a countrywide Arab revolt began, and in 1937 the British proposed partition of the country into Jewish and Arab states. Planning began against the prospect of confronting organized Arab armies. Although the partition offer was withdrawn, defense needs increased. The trend was toward more authoritative central control of the Haganah, encouraged by the need for central finance and by the operation of mobile units, the field companies, and Wingate's night squads. The Histadrut tended to favor central control and predominated in it, while the non-Labor General Zionists in the Haganah had more of their political strength in local government.

As a community which did not have formal sovereignty, the Yishuv showed a considerable ability to maintain a monopoly of control over the Jewish armed forces, but in the prestate period this control was not conclusive. As long as defense was largely local and did not face a major politically aimed and nationally organized Arab campaign, it was possible for groups which disagreed with the political policies of the elected Yishuv institutions to continue to belong to the Haganah. As the struggle became more broadly national and political, however, the Revisionists and others dissenting from the Zionist organization formed their own separate military forces. The principal independents were the Irgun Zvai Leumi, or Etzel (the Revisionist military group, headed by Menachem Begin), and the much smaller Lechi, a group which broke off from the Etzel when the latter agreed with the Haganah to suspend anti-British actions during World War II while the British were fighting the Germans. Etzel was the forerunner of the present Herut Party (Likud).

The ability of the elected Yishuv leadership to coordinate the actions and policies of these forces fluctuated with the situation *vis à vis* the British, the Arabs, and the progress of the war against the Axis powers. There were brief periods of cooperation. At most times, however, Etzel did not recognize the legitimacy of the organized Yishuv and in general followed a much more aggressive policy against the British, or in reprisals for Arab attacks, in contrast with the more usual Haganah policy of *havlaga*, or restraint. In 1944, in the so-called "season" the Haganah actually worked with the British to help find and arrest Etzel members. The rationale then was the need to subordinate the use of force to the political direction of the organized Yishuv,[25] which, in *havlaga*, tried to keep the Jewish struggle on a different level from that of the Arabs, by not using terror as a counter to terror.

After World War II, not only the Arabs but also the Mandate authority were in conflict with the Yishuv. Immigration, land sales, and Jewish arms were virtually prohibited, and the British government was no longer able to guarantee civil peace. The confrontation with the British led the World Zionist Organization to be directly concerned with the policy of arms use in the Yishuv, and the Jewish Agency took over the management of defense. As the conflict grew larger, the Haganah thus passed from a defensive role to become the political-military arm of national policy. The relation to political control at the end of World War II is shown in Figure 4.3.

The more politicized elements included the dissidents, Etzel and Lechi, who did not recognize the legitimacy of the central organization; and the Palmach, the full-time infantry forces of the Haganah, based to a large extent on the Kibbutz Hameuhad, or United Kibbutz Movement, politically to the left of Mapal. On the eve of independence, therefore, the most active defense organizations were politically oriented, Etzel to the right and the Palmach to the left.

Nationalization of Arms and Emergence of Zahal

By the end of World War II, the Yishuv had realized that it would have to solve its problems by itself, and that independence was the solution. Only release from the Mandate could achieve legal immigration, arms, and the freedom to organize defense against attacks from organized Arab armies from neighboring states. Defense finally became paramount, and in this period much of the character of the present Israeli defense organization was determined. Arms were nationalized and control was centralized, and, with the

FIGURE 4.3   Defense Organization, 1946

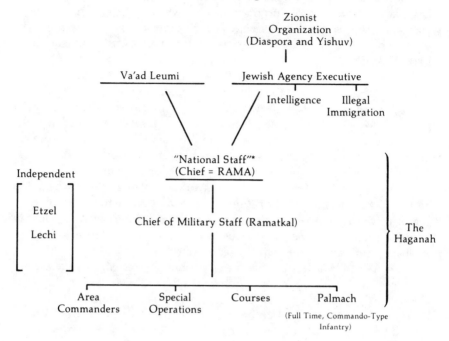

*The "National Staff" was political, each of its departments headed by two "civilians," one Labor and one non-Labor. Their work went into many of the details of the politically "neutral" military staff's duties. The development of the military staff was held back for some time because of the detailed activities of the political representatives.

state, authority was used to unite voluntary groups in a national Army. The essential present pattern of civil-military relations was worked out almost from the start.

As the struggle for independence gained in intensity and the Mandate drew to a close, an internal confrontation loomed over the continuing in- dependence or quasi-independence of sectoral forces. The outcome was the nationalization of arms, and the elimination of the direct influence, within Zahal, of the separatist trends of the right and the left. Decisions which sym- bolized this change include the abolition of the role of RAMA (Figure 4.3), the abolition of the separate command headquarters of the Palmach, and the inci- dent of the ship *Altalena*.

In 1947, Ben Gurion assumed the portfolio of Defense in the Zionist ex- ecutive and set about creating a central, nationalized, organized force. After intensive study of the defense problems, he took over completely, with the political backing of Mapai and the agreement of the General Zionists and religious parties. In the spring of 1948, a Minhelet Ha'am, or national, pre- state Cabinet, took office, with Ben Gurion as Chairman and Defense

Secretary. Referring to Figure 4.3, the "National Staff," which came between the Defense Secretary and the military, gradually ceased to function, and the present pattern of direct responsibility of the Chief of Staff, or *Ramatkal*, to the Minister of Defense was soon established. Ben Gurion abolished the intermediate role of the RAMA because he did not want to work through an intervening political person at the ministerial level—especially not Israel Galili, who represented the rival and farther left United Kibbutz Movement. In 1948 Galili, as RAMA, was acting much of the time as head of the military staff during a protracted illness of the first *Ramatkal*, Ya'akov Dori. Galili was popular with the generals, and his removal brought Ben Gurion into a head-on conflict with the senior military leaders and with his Cabinet colleagues, most of whom agreed with the generals. In the end, Ben Gurion had his way only by threatening to resign, almost on the eve of the War of Liberation.

The abolition of the separate headquarters of the Palmach came later in the war. Until the War of Liberation, the Palmach had been the principal full-time force. Most of its members, all volunteers, had a youth-movement background, and its units were based on kibbutzim, which gave an economic base through part-time work, as well as a cover for the illegal military training. In the war the Palmach was greatly expanded. Battalions became brigades and came under the operational command of campaign commanders and of the general staff. The Palmach headquarters, however, continued the functions of training, developing military doctrine, political and social indoctrination, and personnel. Many of the leading Palmach commanders were close to Mapam, which from 1948 included the United Kibbutz Movement as well as Hashomer Hatzair. Mapam thus had a larger "representation" in defense than it did in the electoral political system.[26] At that time, the party had a pro-Soviet orientation, and Ben Gurion feared the political indoctrination and the rival leadership potential of a quasi-independent Palmach, perhaps even more than its potential threat as a sectoral political-military force. At the same time, he felt the need for a more formal, professional Army, in the face of invasion by regular Arab forces which, in the case of Jordan, were British led. The Palmach fostered a style of informal, egalitarian, small-group leadership. Ben Gurion tended to favor officers with experience in the British Army in World War II.

Faced with the proposal to eliminate the Palmach headquarters, its supporters tried unsuccessfully to make the Histadrut the forum for decision. The Histadrut Executive Committee, indeed, met on the question, in what was perhaps the last occasion on which the Histadrut debated a military issue; but it had no influence on the outcome, and the separate headquarters were closed.

In the *Altalena* incident, the new government used force to establish its monopoly of arms. The ship *Altalena*, manned by Etzel and carrying a considerable cargo of arms, arrived during the first truce period of the War of Liberation and began unloading its cargo on the beach north of Natanya.

When units of Zahal approached with orders to confiscate the arms, the ship was moved to a position off the shore of Tel Aviv. Negotiations, in which the government demanded the surrender of all arms, were unsuccessful, and Zahal shelled the ship, which foundered and remained for some time an abandoned hulk just off the coast—a symbol of the end of Etzel as a separate military organization.

These incidents were part of the nationalization of arms, and of a major depoliticization of defense. In the place of the old *parteistaat* arrangements, however, came other forms of politicization, seemingly milder yet more complex. As far as the ongoing management and command of the forces were concerned, Ben Gurion succeeded in avoiding both separate sectoral armies and party patronage in the uniformed ranks. Since that time, parties have not been able to control or seriously influence lower- or middle-level appointments, or to use them to strengthen a party's base and control, thus advancing or weakening specific ideological or class trends. In this, Zahal was far from the "party key" formulas of the Yishuv, which some ministries and particularly the Jewish Agency continued in the state. The Army thus avoided the accretion of large numbers of incompetent officeholders.

A desire to avoid party-key management in the vital defense area partially explains Ben Gurion's insulation of defense from much of the general political process, setting a pattern of minimal direct party influence on defense administration. At pains to announce that partisan politics would have no place in the Army, Ben Gurion would be Minister of Defense "for all the people," and appointments and decisions would be made "without party dictates and without favor to party adherence." Party bargaining and loyalty would not determine policies or military office. For those within the defense system, the criterion of achievement did indeed generally prevail; and the defense enterprise, the first endeavor in the state to be fully nationalized, was effective beyond all comparison with those areas where the partisan management of the Zionist movement and the Yishuv still applied.

In other aspects, however, the defense organization was political. The civilian departments of the burgeoning Defense Ministry in the early days were deliberately staffed by Mapai or by apolitical (but personal) loyalists, referred to as *mishelanu,* or "one of ours." This was only partly in the ordinary party-key tradition, and was done mainly to ensure reliability in a period when the legitimacy of the government monopoly of arms had not been fully established and was still being questioned by Etzel and other groups. Later on, the need for thousands of new employees in the defense industries offered Mapai an unusual potential for patronage. This aspect has declined, together with a general decline in the politicization of local union activity, as is shown in the section on the Histadrut in the next chapter. In 1948, however, memories of the European class armies of the 1930s on the right and on the left, and of the internecine conflicts with the "dissidents," or *porshim,* in the underground were still vivid. Europe of the 1930s was then a very recent memory. The fear of a possible right-wing takeover by force was then still alive, as were the concepts of a Labor Army to oppose it. These thoughts were in the mind of Ben Gurion, Shaul Avigur, and others in the formative years.

In the first decade of the state, following the elimination of separate trends on the left and on the right, a nonideological form of politicization prevailed. We were not able to asses the extent of direct discrimination, but the fact is that the more ideologically minded Palmach commanders eventually left the Army, either by conviction or because their future careers seemed doubtful. Most of the military leaders of Etzel went directly into politics, where they displaced the "civilians" in the Revisionist Party, the reverse of the Labor movement experience, in which political leaders created the armed forces.[27]

So it was that the senior officers who remained in Zahal were mainly close to Mapai or politically neutral, accepting the general goals of the Labor movement, although they might belong to other parties or to none. Pragmatic rather than ideological, they conceived of the Army as a national, professional, and apolitical instrument of policy. They were personally associated with, or loyal to, the leaders of the new state, and to civilian control.

With time, the possibilities of other forms of politicization emerged, because of the expanded role and public image of Zahal, and thus of its commanders, beyond their purely military roles. These are discussed later, however, since it is necessary first to understand the unusual position of the Chief of the General Staff, or *Ramatkal*, his relations with the Minister of Defense, and the allocation of defense-policy roles among the elements of government. Until 1981 there were few fundamental changes in the formal overall arrangements, which are presented here as a preamble to a discussion of the variations that occurred in the working of the system.

The Minister of Defense and Zahal

The government's authority over the armed forces is exercised by the Minister of Defense on behalf of the Cabinet. What does this imply? As background, to the analysis, Figure 4.4 shows the overall defense organization. With variations, it is typical of the 1970s, and a direct development of the organization of 1948.

The Air Force and Navy commanders are directly responsible to the *Ramatkal* (an acronym for the Hebrew words which mean "Chief of the General Staff"). The forces thus are unified, but the Air Force and Navy are separate in the exercise of command and control, training, and logistics, so that each force has operational and administrative unity under a commander and his staff. In addition, the headquarters staffs of the Air Force and the Navy are the general staffs for air and sea warfare *per se*. Integration of the

FIGURE 4.4   Defense Ministry Organization

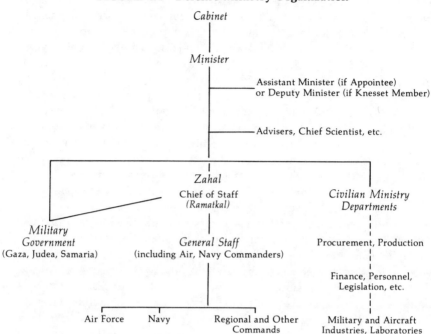

forces is done in several ways. There are common ranks and common general logistic and personnel services, and the *Ramatkal* is the commander of all the forces. He is advised by central operations, planning, personnel, logistics, and intelligence branches, whose heads, together with the commanders of the Navy and the Air Force, make up the General Staff. In its responsibility for questions specific to land warfare and the ground forces, the General Staff is parallel to the staffs of the Air Force and the Navy, while most of the direct operational control on land is carried out by area commands. These are supported by logistic corps which serve all of the forces.

Government corporations and departments in the Defense Ministry carry out research and development, the manufacture of aircraft, weapons systems and munitions, and procurement. The heads of all of these, the Chief of Staff, and the officers responsible for the government of the Gaza Strip and Judea and Samaria are under the minister's authority. The scope of the Defense Ministry is thus very broad, and responsibilities have to be delegated.

The modes of ministerial control and the organization of the armed forces developed from the early days of the long period when Ben Gurion was in charge. Indeed, they were the lengthening shadow of the man. Partly because of his unique status and will, partly because the Minister of Defense was also

Prime Minister for most of the first two decades, relations were not always formally defined. They "just grew" during the leaders' long service together.*

Ben Gurion's methods of work led to system characteristics which have continued—the primacy of the uniformed military in the making of decisions below the ministerial level, and the extensive delegation of authority to the level immediately below the minister. Ben Gurion chose not only the Chief of Staff but also the other senior officers. Reserving for himself the very major decisions, on the central issues he would "give himself a seminar" and study single-mindedly until he felt that he knew the crux of a problem. Other questions, where he felt that the priority was lower or that matters were under control, could be put out of mind completely, often to the frustration of protagonists unable to get a place for their projects on his agenda. Once a general direction was decided, those who had proven themselves to him, like Shimon Peres, who had the central role in building defense R & D and production, or Moshe Dayan, had a very free hand. The military forces, or Zahal, were Ben Gurion's focus at all times, and he developed a pattern in which the civilian components of the ministry were secondary. In the early years, the higher civilian staff was given second priority in the choice of personnel, and worked mainly to meet requirements set by the forces. But although he worked directly through the *Ramatkal* on all military questions, Ben Gurion helped insure civilian control and military effectiveness by keeping research, manufacture, procurement, finance, and conscription under civilian management. The third *Ramatkal*, Mordechai Makleff, resigned when Ben Gurion rejected his proposal to put most of these aspects of logistics under direct Army control.

Despite his authority and powers of concentration, Ben Gurion could leave questions of force structure and employment to trusted experts. Once he had established the organization, and when people in whom he had confidence were in charge, he could delegate authority to an unprecedented degree. Examples of this are the decision in 1950 to reject the Air Force's proposals for quasi-independence, and the decision before the 1956 Sinai campaign that armor would remain essentially in a supporting role. In neither case did Ben Gurion apparently study the problem himself in real depth, and the

* Ben Gurion was both Prime Minister and Minister of Defense from 1948 until he left office in 1963 except for a short break between 1953 and 1955, when Moshe Sharett was Prime Minister and Pinhas Lavon was Minister of Defense. Ben Gurion returned to Defense in 1955 and soon resumed both jobs. Levi Eshkol was also both Prime Minister and Minister of Defense for four years, until forced to nominate Moshe Dayan as Minister of Defense on the eve of the Six Day War. When Mrs. Golda Meir succeeded Eshkol as Prime Minister in 1968, Dayan stayed on as Minister of Defense, until Shimon Peres took over in the new Rabin Cabinet after the Yom Kippur War. Continuity was even more remarkable, when we consider that Rabin was Chief of Staff from 1964 to 1968, Dayan was Chief of Staff from 1953 to 1958, and Peres was Director-General of the Ministry from 1953 to 1959, Deputy Minister from 1959 to 1965 and Minister from 1974 to 1977.

Chief of the General Staff at the time (Yadin in 1950, Dayan in 1956) was the dominant voice in the decision.

In 1950 conflict between the Air Force and the General Staff over the role of and organization for air warfare came to a head. The Air Force was still small, depending on a few Palestinian Jewish pilots who had served in the RAF, a decisive contingent of volunteers from overseas, and the first few graduates of Israeli courses carried out during the war under primitive condi- tions in Italy, Czechoslovakia, and Israel. There were then more than 30 kinds of planes, which made maintenance exceedingly difficult. By 1950, however, the training command was regularly producing classes of highly trained pilots and mechanics and there was an effective staff and command system.

Zahal's General Staff, however, were all ground force officers who had lit- tle understanding of the potential role of air power in the region or of the organizational requirements of an effective Air Force. Both the Air Force and the ground forces agreed that there should be a unified command; but they in- terpreted the concept differently. The Air Force asked for its own integral organization under Air Force adminstrative, operational, and logistic con- trol—subject to the overall operational decisions of the General Staff. The ground officers wanted to integrate Air Force staff and command work within the General Staff. Then, as now, this staff was also the headquarters of the ground forces, an anomaly which the Air Force was among the first to point out. The debate also included strategic elements—whether the Air Force should aim first for air superiority or should come under the administrative and operational management of the ground forces, to be used mainly in sup- port. The debate raged between the young Air Force officers and the more established ground-force generals, with Ben Gurion looking on. A commit- tee, headed by Shaul Avigur, recommended a semi-independent force with its own political Undersecretary of Defense.* Ben Gurion, however, deferred to Yigael Yadin, then Chief of Staff, who asked that the proposal be shelved and integration made complete. Aharon Remez, the first commander of the Air Force, and one who had the vision of what it should become, then resigned.

The infantry commanders of Zahal had little faith in the young pilots; and after Remez, two infantry officers served briefly as commanders of the Air Force. Before they came onto the scene, however, the Air Force already had the organization, training methods, and military thought which were to become the basis for its later success, when resources became available.[28] The Air Force's staff and maintenance organization and its ability to train its own pilots, navigators, and technicians to a high level of excellence really decided the issue. Mahal, or volunteers who had served in the Allied forces in World

* Shaul Avigur was an important political leader of the Haganah, who headed illegal immigra- tion activity and the arms purchase in Europe during the last years of the Mandate. Retiring by nature, for many years he had a very considerable influence on defense in the state, even though he assumed no public office.

War II, together with ex-RAF Israelis, laid the groundwork. Succeeding generations of Israeli-trained officers developed air capability to major proportions and the Air Force gained the organizational independence it required. These developments resolved the question, although the General Staff continued to double as ground-forces and general headquarters. Only after Sinai did the Air Force get priority.

In addition to his personal immersion in selected problems, Ben Gurion frequently acted as a fatherly arbiter and held forums in which differing senior officers could press their views, but these meetings frequently had much of a ceremonial function. Ministers who followed Ben Gurion worked on a broader range of problems, but they did not have the kind of single-minded tenacity with which he studied the few questions he considered to be vital, nor did they encourage strong adversary proceedings between the General Staff and their office as a means of policy formulation. Becoming Minister of Defense after the Yom Kippur War, Shimon Peres appointed senior individual advisers, and the Planning Branch of the General Staff began to report to the Minister as well as to the *Ramatkal.* Peres' major task in 1974–77, however, was to restore to Zahal the organizational élan, confidence, and personal relations which had been shaken by the recriminations and the blame placed on the military, rather than on the political level, following the War.

One deterrent to confrontation is the desire of Defense Ministers to maintain the confidence of the forces as a means of increasing their influence over them. This is not as contradictory to the principle of civilian control as it sounds. Most of the expertise and data are within the forces, and confident relations are needed in order to make it fully available. While no one questions the primacy of political-level decisions on either the structure or use of the forces, a very considerable degree of delegation is an accepted aspect of the system. And as we will see presently, the support of the defense establishment is an important part of the political system through which the Defense Minister develops control; but the need for this support can limit his authority, and the need to maintain confidence and support and at the same time to confront, challenge, and question is one of the greatest tests of civilian leadership.

On its part, the Army closes ranks when threatened by intervention from outside the defense system in what it sees as central policy questions. Ministers have also come into conflict when trying to work directly with officers below the Chief of Staff. Chaim Laskov resigned as Chief of Staff in the 1960s when he could not prevent Shimon Peres, then Deputy Minister of Defense, from communicating directly with Laskov's subordinates. Ben Gurion backed Peres. Attempts by Pinhas Lavon (Defense Minister in 1954–55) to give orders bypassing the Chief of Staff were partly the cause of his downfall, which occurred after both the military and civilian leaders of the defense system, as well as the Prime Minister, ceased to support him. On the eve of the Six Day War, an important influence on Levi Eshkol to agree to step down as Defense Minister was the sharpness of the interaction in his meetings with the General Staff.[29]

If the primacy of the military is greater since Ben Gurion's time, one important reason has been that, although systems and technologies became more complex, no full-fledged policy or planning staff independent of the Army was developed. When Dayan was minister, the General Staff took over the R&D policy staff which formerly worked for the independent Chief Scientist, and a long-range planning branch was set up in the General Staff. Although the Directors of Planning and R&D have access to the minister, they are generals serving under the Chief of Staff. A crucial example of dependence was seen in the Yom Kippur War when the only substantial and "sole source" of intelligence evaluation available to the minister, and indeed to the Cabinet, was the intelligence branch of the General Staff.[30]

Defense-policy analysis by ministry groups outside of the armed forces could have been expected to enhance civilian control and decision-making ability. Indeed, it might have more impact in Israel than elsewhere because the defense system is integrated and has comparatively little direct parliamentary or other outside participation. Yet there has been no "MacNamara revolution" in Israel. For better or for worse, there are no important analytical staffs outside of the uniformed armed forces engaged in evaluating weapons systems or force structures.* Abortive attempts to form Rand-type institutions have failed to receive the essential government support. The monopolistic approach of the military, mentioned above, is only one of the reasons. The authority of the General Staff over all the armed services permits many questions to be settled internally, and the impetus for analysis due to inter-service competition is thus less in Israel than it is, for example, in the United States. Further, for many years the defense system had few procurement options. Many civilian defense leaders began their careers in times when only used or surplus weapons could be bought, usually by stealth, or even if purchased new, without the opportunity of choice. Still another cause has been the attempt to shield the Army from the political bargaining process. But perhaps the most influential reasons lie in a political culture in which complexity and the importance of unpredictable exogenous events are seen as the order of things.** This leads to skepticism regarding the ability of those not directly

---

* For the use of systems analysis or similar approaches to help base decisions on explicit criteria, such as cost-benefit ratios see Alain C. Enthhoven and K. Wayne Smith, *How Much Is Enough? Shaping the Defense Program, 1961-69*, New York, Harper & Row, 1971. On at least two occasions, ministers have appointed analysts, with a broad definition of duties, to make independent evaluations of force structure policies. Both had very brief tenure. Their failures are ascribed to the reluctance of the ministers to create confrontations by backing the analyst against the reluctance of Zahal to cooperate in this endeavor.

** In "Military Capabilities and American Foreign Policy," *Annals of the American Academy of Political and Social Science*, March 1973, Graham Allison discusses the limitations of analysis,

engaged in an operation to understand it or to analyze what should be done. Secrecy is a further impediment, so that those outside of the system, unless they have recently left it, do not have the knowledge or the credibility. For these reasons also, there has not developed in Israel a community of "defense intellectuals" with influence on strategic concepts.

The weakness of independent civilian analysis and knowledge compared to the strengths of the military staff affects relations within the ministry as well as those with outsiders. Within the Defense Ministry, the civilian branches follow policy rather than lead it, and they are at best referees of conflicts and bargains of the larger organizations within the system, for example, between the Air Force and the Aircraft Industries.*

In this situation, the minister has very limited civilian help in evaluating alternatives and making decisions. He needs to have self-confidence and intellect, supreme concentration, and strong political support; and he can get at the essentials of policy only if he is forceful, agile, and able to get data from several levels in the organization. Ministers who followed Ben Gurion have tried to lead in a system which was usually more suited to his unique personality and abilities, and to a smaller Army and simpler technologies. There has often been a dichotomy, therefore, between the personal characteristics of succeeding ministers and the system which Ben Gurion began. Even in Ben Gurion's time, however, the minister's control of policy weakened, particularly toward the end of the 1950s and in the early 1960s when Ben Gurion was more occupied with internal political questions and the Lavon affair.** Even earlier, however, once Zahal was a going concern and people that Ben Gurion trusted were in charge, important questions were left to military decision. Indeed, the priority which Ben Gurion gave to the military side of the Defense Ministry, in the recruitment of talented people, was later to be a source of weakness for civilian policy control.

The Chief of Staff (Ramatkal)

When he resigned, Remez was concerned with more than the Air Force, and he saw a serious threat to civilian control in the power status of the civilian parts of the ministry and in the burden on Ben Gurion as both Prime Minister and Defense Minister, which led him to delegate important questions to the

---

which derive from the complexity of decisions in defense and foreign affairs, the importance of political bargaining, and secondary effects of systems and decisions.

* Because the government owns most of the defense industries, the distortions of private profit in military-industrial decisions are largely avoided. On the other hand, ministry involvement in the organizational and economic success of its own units can distort acquisition and budget decisions. A feeling for the Israeli defense-industry proportions is obtained by considering a hypothetical state which has only the population of California but has an aerospace industry the actual size of that in California. In 1977 Israel Aircraft Industries employed almost 20,000 people.

** For the Lavon affair, see Chapter 1, note on page 35, Peter Medding, *Mapai in Israel*, and Nathan Yanai, *Kera Batzameret* (Heb.), op. cit.

military. Although the worst fears did not materialize, the *Ramatkal*, or Chief of Staff, has an unusually important and expanded role, due at least in part to the relatively great strength of the military as a source of knowledge and policy. The Chief of Staff has high public status and influence as the principal professional military expert, whose expertise is allied with his position, and whose access to defense information is superior to that of all others.[31]

The expansion and growth of independence of the role of the *Ramatkal* began during Ben Gurion's dual and concurrent service as Defense Minister and Prime Minister. When Moshe Dayan was *Ramatkal* under Ben Gurion (1953–57), the state was only a few years old, and organizational relations were in a formative stage. Personalities and party political relations counted more than they do today; and Dayan had been a political activist in Mapai. Then striving to increase the combat readiness of Zahal and also escalating antiterrorist reprisals, Dayan as Chief of Staff was given great confidence and considerable independence by Ben Gurion. Facing outward toward the Cabinet, party, and public, Ben Gurion was the spokesman and responsible authority for defense. Under his successors, however, the *Ramatkal* began to take part in the discussions at the political level.

When Levi Eshkol was both Prime Minister and Defense Minister, from 1963 to 1967, he began to bring the *Ramatkal* with him to Cabinet meetings dealing with national security. On many occasions the *Ramatkal* was present when important decisions were made, and the feeling grew that he was, in a sense, a partner in them. During the tense period of waiting on the eve of the Six Day War, Itzchak Rabin, as *Ramatkal*, at times felt that almost full ministerial responsibility was thrust upon him. Chaim Bar Lev, *Ramatkal* during the 1969–70 war of attrition, was close to Foreign Minister Yigal Allon and had access to Golda Meir's "kitchen cabinet." In the 1973 war, David Elazar was a full partner in the inner Cabinet meetings, where Mrs. Meir, who then gave him her full support, acted as virtual Defense Minister and Commander-in-Chief. The choice of *Ramatkal* is thus a key policy and political decision, and his orientations in policy and politics and personal compatibility with the Defense Minister are strong considerations over and above sheer professional ability. The role of the *Ramatkal* is also a function of the extent to which the Cabinet is united and has political strength. For example, in the 1970s, when Itzchak Rabin and Shimon Peres were opposed within the Cabinet, the independence of decision of the *Ramatkal* was greatly enhanced.

In this context the definition of authority becomes important. While there is little doubt in anyone's mind that the armed forces act on orders from the civil political authority, there has been a considerable lack of clarity regarding the chain of command and the kind of directives that the military commanders expect to be given by the politicians.*

---

*One common view in Zahal was expressed by a brigadier general who served on the Syrian front in 1973, in the following questions which he wants the political leader to answer: (a) What

Part of the reason lies in the Israeli form of Cabinet government. If a comparison were to be made to the American presidency, in Israel the Cabinet as a whole is the supreme commander. When the Agranat Committee investigated the conduct of the 1973 war, it found that the law was not clear on the division of authority and responsibility in defense matters among the Prime Minister, the Cabinet, the Defense Minister, and the Chief of Staff. The Cabinet, said the committee, had indeed approved the appointments of the Chiefs of Staff in the past; but there was at that time nothing statutory about this procedure. More serious for operational responsibility, they found confusion about who indeed was the Commander-in-Chief. The committee rejected the notion that a Minister of Defense is a "superior commander to the Chief of Staff," and took the surprising view, which public opinion later largely rejected, that the minister acts properly when he accepts the consensus of professional opinion which is presented to him.*

That, however, is not the way it is. Israeli Defense Ministers and Prime Ministers have been as prone as Winston Churchill was to decide on operational matters when they wanted to. In an open letter defending himself against the conclusions of the Agranat Committee, the late David Elazar, the *Ramatkal* of the Yom Kippur War, said, "In all the years since Zahal was formed, the *Ramatkal* and . . . Zahal acted on the basis of the subordination of the *Ramatkal* to the Minister of Defense in all areas . . . including operations. . . ."[33] Elazar was saying that the minister's authority is such that he should share any blame given to the *Ramatkal*.

The relations of the minister and the *Ramatkal* are not as clear as Elazar's statement implied, although usually a minister's instructions will simply be carried out. When the *Ramatkal* or other senior general disagrees with the minister, however, formal constitutional arrangements become important, as would be expected in a bureaucratic organization. Here the absence of a formally constituted Commander-in-Chief in the Israeli Cabinet system becomes problematic. In such a disagreement, if the *Ramatkal* insists, the Cabinet has the authority to decide. In practice, this most often means the Prime Minister, and occasionally a smaller ad hoc war cabinet, but the composition of this small forum is not specified formally and it varies with personalities and situations. In the Yom Kippur War, most major operational decisions, such as to call up the reserve before the war, to cross the Suez Canal, or how far to withdraw in Sinai in the first days of the war, were made by Prime Minister Meir, with the advice of a group which usually included Israel Galili, Defense Minister Dayan, General Elazar, and Yigal Allon. Mrs. Meir was, in fact, the

---

are the chances of war? With whom? How are the powers expected to act? (b) When and how could it start? (c) What are the goals? (d) How much time will we have?[32]

* The error of the Agranat Committee, however, was probably not due to a misperception of the practical realities, but to an overly "judicial" approach, in which the ministers were considered answerable only before the bar of political decisions, in the Knesset, and in elections. In fact, and so the public considered the committee's task, the aim was to determine what happened and who and what were responsible, whether elected politicians or not.

Commander-in-Chief, working directly with the Chief of Staff. The Defense Minister, in this case, had very limited authority. A further limit to his authority can be the need to give instructions through the military chain of command. Generals in the field have refused to obey instructions given them directly by the minister.*

When a situation arises in which the *Ramatkal* himself disagrees with the minister, constitutional arrangements are important, and a formally constituted relation between the Cabinet and the Minister of Defense is found to be lacking. The way in which such a difference is resolved depends on personalities, and on the political resources of the minister. It also depends, of course, on whether the minister is at one and the same time the Prime Minister and Defense Minister. While a minister serving in both roles would usually have considerable political backing and the ability to determine most Cabinet decisions, a Defense Minister having only that duty could presumably go more deeply into the issues and thus exercise more control.

The Commander-in-Chief is, constitutionally, the Cabinet, and at most periods, effectively, the Prime Minister—but giving actual orders to Zahal through the Defense Minister, or to the *Ramatkal* in his presence. The Defense Minister, in turn, usually gives commands to the forces only via the Chief of Staff—who has the option of appeal. On the other hand, the Chief of Staff may, most frequently, have the advantage in both knowledge and initiative, in the scope of the options and evaluations which he presents, and in the form which the translation of orders into action actually takes. The question of who gives the actual orders, while seemingly technical, is therefore very important. In ongoing operations, specific acts can affect important policy changes or outcomes.

In 1976 a *Basic Law: The Army* was passed, partially meeting the need for formal definitions. The Army is under the authority of the Cabinet and the *Ramatkal* is its commander. The authority of the Cabinet is vested in the Minister of Defense. The *Ramatkal* is appointed by the Cabinet on the recommendation of the minister. This is a provision intended to ensure that both are compatible, and its inclusion was probably influenced by reports that Dayan, in 1972, accepted Elazar's appointment against his will.[34] The new law can be interpreted to define the minister's role as a "superior Chief of Staff" for ongoing operational decisions. As has been shown, however, it is not that simple. The minister can have this role, effectively, only to the extent that the Cabinet and, in particular, the Prime Minister give it to him. The new law did not fully resolve the questions of command authority which arise because of the form of Israeli Cabinet government.

---

*During the 1973 war, when Dayan visited subordinate command headquarters, field commanders pretty much used their own judgment in accepting his suggestions. When, at the end of the war, Dayan asked General Tal, the Deputy *Ramatkal*, to begin an operation (which Tal saw as having political aims not to his liking), Tal insisted on either a direct written order or Cabinet approval. There the matter rested. On other occasions, generals have rejected ministerial recommendations on tactical and professional grounds.

The Defense Minister and the Political System

Military influence on policy derives from conceptions, forces in being, and the impact of large programs and organizations. The prospect of an enemy aiming to destroy the state or to use war as a diplomatic tool and the Israeli disadvantage in size of forces and borders demand efforts at deterrence and preemptive actions. In response, Zahal developed unusual capabilities, such as those of the Air Force and special forces. These abilities in turn helped determine policies adopted, usually legitimately or openly, as in the surprise attack on the Arab airfields in the Six Day War, or more subtly, as in bombing deep into Egypt in the 1970 war of attrition—a decision which apparently did not take into account many of the political variables and possible reactions. During the period which led up to the 1956 Sinai campaign, the military arm could specify what the available options were within a strategy accepted by the Prime Minister, but with implications of which the Cabinet was not fully aware.[35]

Because of the impediments which outsiders face in obtaining defense information and in controlling ongoing actions, and because of the advantages which the armed forces possess in initiating and specifying the options available for force development and operations, the actual authority of the Defense Minister is of central importance. He is the full-time link between defense and the political system, expressing in practice the political power over defense policy. Except in times of crisis, the ongoing management is in his hands. He needs to be an effective and authoritative member of both systems. The form of exercise of this power and the influence of the minister in particular depend on the extent and strength of the sources of support. This reinforcement determines the effectiveness of the minister's role in political control. The patterns are illustrated by the typologies shown on Figure 4.5.

These diagrams show the following kinds of relations:

(a) *Reinforcement of political support* prevailed during Ben Gurion's service as Defense Minister and Prime Minister from 1948 until 1953, when he retired temporarily, and from his return in 1955 until he lost much political support after the Lavon affair of 1960. At his peak, Ben Gurion had the full confidence and support of the Mapai Party machinery and rank and file, of the General Staff and the Defense Ministry bureaucracy, and of the populace. Ben Gurion did not always have his way in the Cabinet, but within the defense system the breadth of his sources of support, together with his personal characteristics, gave him almost complete authority, to the extent that he decided to use it.*

(b) *Almost no political control* was the situation in 1954–55, when Pinhas

---

* Examples: Yigael Yadin leaves as *Ramatkal* when B.G. does not give the Army the resources Yadin feels it needs; M. Makleff resigns as *Ramatkal* a year later when B.G. does not approve organizational changes incorporating civilian ministry tasks in the Army; in 1955, B.G. supports Moshe Dayan in decision to use tanks in support rather than as main arm; in 1958–59, B.G. backs Shimon Peres as deputy minister versus Chaim Laskov, the *Ramatkal*.

FIGURE 4.5   Defense Ministers and the Political System

(a) Complete Reinforcement of Political Support (1948-53, 1955-63)

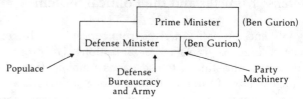

(b) Almost No Political Control of Defense (1954-55)

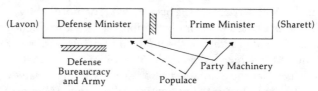

(c) A "Representative" Minister (1963-67)

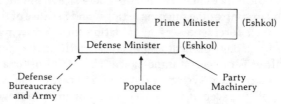

(d) "Balanced" Control (1969-74)

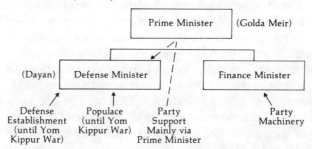

(e) Cabinet Rivalry—Professional Civilian Control (1974-77)

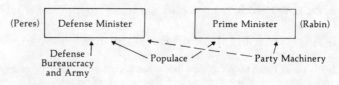

*See Chapter 5 for Sapir's role in the economy.

Lavon was Minister of Defense and Moshe Sharett was Prime Minister. The military and defense bureaucracy, whose appointments had been made by Ben Gurion before his retirement, turned their backs on Lavon (despite his sometimes excessive endorsement of their tactical reprisal proposals) and continued to confide in Ben Gurion in his retirement in the Negev. This period shows "false bureaucracy" in which the military might ask approval for a small reprisal raid, knowing that on the scene larger forces would be involved. Lavon saw himself as equal to the Prime Minister and did not keep him or the Cabinet adequately in the defense picture. While Sharett had much popular and party support, he had little involvement in the realities of defense operations, and trusted Lavon as little as Lavon trusted him. The system broke down rapidly, and Mapai as arbiter returned Ben Gurion to office as Defense Minister.

(c) *A "representative" minister.* Readers familiar with the history of the United States will recognize the behavior of a Secretary who shows great sympathy with the aims and methods proposed by the military leaders, often holding their affection or even respect, and in essence acting as their representative before the political leadership. An Israeli example is the tenure of Levi Eshkol as Prime Minister and Defense Minister, although some of his organization decisions—for example, in research, development, and procurement—showed him to be much more than a mere "representative." Relations with the Army were amiable and procurement and development extensive and successful, but functions were transferred from the civil offices to the military, and the real initiative was usually not in the hands of the minister or the deputy minister. Eshkol at this stage had the full backing of the Mapai machinery, but his popular support was moderate at best. The good will and the essential respect of the defense establishment for him was seldom if ever put to a test until the eve of the Six Day War.

(d) *"Balanced" political control.* At the time of the Six Day War in 1967, the offices of Prime Minister and Defense Minister once again became separate and have remained so.* A form of balanced political control resulted. Golda Meir, as Prime Minister usually had the support of the party machinery and the public and the respect of the defense enterprise. Dayan, as Defense Minister, had great popular support (most of which he lost after the beginning of the Yom Kippur War of 1973), along with that of the Army and defense bureaucracy. But as the Rafi faction leader, he got no help from the Labor Party organization, to put it mildly. Pinhas Sapir, the Minister of Finance, who differed from Dayan on both defense and economic grounds, had the support of the party bureaucracy. As a result, Prime Minister Meir emerged as the arbiter and principal source of party and Cabinet support of Dayan, with a very substantial say in all defense matters, including personal

---

* In 1980, on the resignation of Ezer Weizman, Menachem Begin became both Prime Minister and Minister of Defense. In the 1981 Begin Cabinet, Ariel Sharon was Minister of Defense.

approval of the highest-level appointments. Here she had no way, except her own very considerable intuition, to check what she was told.

In this period also, ministers occasionally worked in temporary coalition, thus preventing the opportunity for adequate policy confrontation. For example, an agreement between Dayan and Sapir on the size of the defense budget could minimize confrontation between treasury and defense officials at the working level, and thus lose opportunities for useful debate. Dayan's "expert" status, as a former *Ramatkal* and the Defense Minister in the Six Day War (although he was appointed just before the war began), was reinforced by Mrs. Meir's backing, which tended to insulate defense from detailed outside inquiry. Still, Dayan's lack of broader Cabinet support, together with his own work priorities, tended to diminish his effective administrative control. Within the ministry, he was occupied with what interested him most—some of the specific operational plans and, particularly, the relations with Judea, Samaria, and Gaza. The long-range questions of force structure, R&D, and the chores of ongoing management decisions were delegated. The scope of Defense Ministry responsibility worked against effective civil control.

(e) *Cabinet rivalry, together with professional, civilian control.* Minister of Defense in the 1974–77 Rabin Cabinet, Shimon Peres brought to the job decades of defense experience and extensive support from the defense industries, and research and procurement organizations which he had the major role, at the political level, in building. His relations with the *Ramatkal*, Mordechai Gur, were harmonious (he had, when Minister of Transportation, backed Gur's candidacy), and he made clear to Zahal that the Minister of Defense would take full responsibility. Peres had almost won the nomination as the Labor candidate for Prime Minister in 1974. The rank and file of the Labor Party was divided in its support for him and for Rabin, while the leaders of the decaying party machinery of Labor largely supported Rabin. The abilities, political backing, and ambitions of the two candidates led to an uneasy balance between their followers, together with formally correct but distant working relations between the leaders. As this rivalry divided the Cabinet, Peres retained a considerable measure of control over defense, largely because of high internal support and communication and his extensive personal knowledge and long experience. This control could be called, essentially, "professional."

Beyond Ministerial Control

These perhaps oversimplified models show how the internal authority of the minister depends on outside elements. But the political direction of defense involves much broader political considerations. It is not enough for a Defense Minister who happens to be a political leader to have authority. As international constraints become dominant and the influence of defense activity spreads throughout the society and economy, politics and strategy can no longer be separated. The forces have to be built and employed so as to serve the policies of the political leadership as a whole, an outcome which depends on the relations of the rest of the political system with defense. Within the defense system there remain vestiges of the divisions and loyalties of prestate days, as well as more recent personal and party loyalties. Nor can the centrality of defense permit it to be really "taken out of politics." I will return later to the possibility of politicization within the defense system, which will be found mainly at the level of the *Ramatkal* and his leading generals. The concern at this point is with the relation of the elected governmental institutions to defense policy.

"External" influence on the Defense Ministry is not easily evaluated. A friend tells how, when first elected to the Knesset, he had great expectations of helping to decide defense and foreign policy. Unaccountably, his information did not seem to improve after his election, nor did his chances to participate in serious debate on defense questions. His continuing loyalty was rewarded, however, and in a few years he became a member of the Knesset Committee on Foreign Affairs and Defense. Here he enjoyed presentations by the Foreign Minister and the Defense Minister, most often explanations of decisions already made, but after the novelty wore off, he realized that he had more information but he was still not deciding anything. He met occasionally with a small caucus of the committee, old-time Mapai members. Their gossip was livelier, but their information was not much better. Eventually he was invited to meetings of *Sareinu*, the Mapai ministers. But here too the point of decision seemed evanescent—near at hand yet slipping out of reach. It seemed that most important decisions were not being made in any formal, clearly defined forum. The Defense Minister and Prime Minister were constant factors, but others, sometimes with no official role, were also influential.

One reason the picture is confused is that the same people belong to many institutions, such as the party bureaus, secretariats, and policy committees, the Cabinet and ministerial committees, and the Knesset. The "wearing of several hats" and the multiple membership are not part of a charade, although some functions are ceremonial and honorific. Each forum has its own rules of the game. In each, different groups and forces are at play. As we move from one scene to another, we need to be conscious of the changes in roles and prerogatives, the differences in the rules and the games which are played in the different places, and the changes in the rosters of the teams. The fate of an issue can often be decided by the choice of locale. Still, the formal loci of decision are the Cabinet and the Knesset.

The Cabinet

As we have seen, the Defense Minister is the main point of interaction of the Cabinet and the defense system. A party leader, he has direct access to the public, and he has always been in the Knesset. The governing party, first of all, chooses him for the job, can remove him, and can dictate major policy to its representatives in the Cabinet. As the leader of the party, the Prime Minister has a major defense role. But because of the populist element of defense support, neither the party nor the Prime Minister can direct policy autonomously. The party feels the need for popular participation and support, at least after decisions are taken; and needs the agreement in the Cabinet of its coalition partners. Both of these aspects stood out in the extreme situation on the eve of the Six Day War when popular pressure was transmitted through the members of party institutions, and coalition and opposition parties all had determining roles. The Cabinet was able to decide and reach consensus after the interplay of popular and coalition party forces had made Dayan Minister of Defense, and added Rafi and Gahal to the Cabinet.[36]

Chapter 2, "The Search for a Constitution," evaluated the work of the Cabinet as the executive committee of the government. It was found that the effectiveness of the Cabinet is limited by its large size and by the coalition form of government, which have given it more of the character of an upper house than of an executive. There is an absence of staff assistance to the Cabinet in policy analysis or in coordinating the work of the government, and the agenda is crowded. Cabinet size makes secrecy difficult to maintain and prevents discussion of issues in adequate depth. The coalition partners and indeed the individual ministers want to take part in defense affairs, so that in most periods it has not been feasible to form a small, effective formal Cabinet committee for defense and foreign affairs. As a result, most important decisions have been made, or at least worked up, in small informal groups chosen by the Prime Minister.

There have been exceptions. When Levi Eshkol was both Defense Minister and Prime Minister from 1963 to 1967, there was an active Ministers' Defense Committee. At other times, as during the National Unity government, from the Six Day War to 1970, the full Cabinet was the central scene. Most of the time, however, an unofficial inner group of flexible membership usually has reached the ongoing decisions as a preliminary to full Cabinet discussion and formal decision. In ordinary times of cease-fire, no military operation, even on a small scale, is begun without the authorization of the Defense Minister and the Prime Minister.

Ben Gurion learned very early to discuss major projects with his principal colleagues, especially Moshe Sharett, before bringing them to the Cabinet. During the 1948 war, he brought a proposal for an attack in the Hebron area to a Cabinet meeting without talking first to anyone else, and it was voted down. Thereafter, until his deep policy break with Sharett in 1955, he apparently either tried to reach prior agreement or to act first and get Cabinet approval later, if the scope of the decision permitted. When Sharett and Ben Gurion were in agreement, they could swing Cabinet decisions, and it is believed that a similar relation prevailed in Mrs. Meir's Cabinet when she was in agreement with Defense Minister Dayan.

In the period leading up to the Sinai campaign, particularly after Sharett had been ousted as Foreign Minister, the Cabinet was not privy to the under-lying strategic trends. Except, probably, for Ben Gurion, Cabinet members saw the Israeli reprisal attacks on military objects over the border as straight-forward deterrent retaliation; yet the defense leaders, particularly Dayan, did not expect simple retaliation to work and intended, at least toward the end of the period, that escalation would lead to a large and effectively deterrent cam-paign. Ben Gurion himself decided to go ahead only at the last minute, while the Cabinet was kept in the dark until the Sinai campaign was under way. This type of use of the defense authority does not seem to have recurred, at least not in this elemental form.

After Mrs. Meir became Prime Minister in 1968, an inner circle of Labor ministers worked as a pre-Cabinet caucus. Generally included by Mrs. Meir were Dayan, Galili, Allon, Sapir, Eban, and, before he resigned in 1973, Minister of Justice Shapiro. Professional advice from senior civil servants and generals was given on an ad hoc basis. Invited on a personal basis by the Prime Minister, the caucus or other small informal groups made the principal deci-sions. On the eve of the Yom Kippur War, even the inner "kitchen cabinet" did not function as such. The possibility that Egypt and Syria would attack was discussed through informal consultations until almost the last minute. Once the actual fighting began, a small, still informal war council functioned. In an incident after the war of a terrorist attack on a school in the border town of Ma'alot, the Cabinet was found to lack preplanned organization for crisis management.

One lesson seems to be that at this point, the "informal organization" had become incapable of effective decision making. There is now wide agreement, in principal, that a small, formal, Cabinet-level group is needed to chart the relation between military and political problems, receive and weigh alter-native intelligence estimates and evaluations of situations, and decide on goals and strategies. This implies the need for a professional Cabinet staff and the strengthening of the Foreign Ministry's analytical capabilities. These could discontinue the monopoly of military intelligence on the interpretation of the capabilities and intentions of the powers and the Arab states. Recurring recommendations to this effect have had little impact.* In the Rabin Cabinet of 1974–77, there was no real improvement in the analytical resources of the Prime Minister's Office or the Cabinet secretariat, and a succession of frustrated individual advisers had no visible impact.

With all these limitations, the Cabinet is the locus of formal decision. It approves the appointment of the Director-General of the Defense Ministry, appoints the *Ramatkal* on the recommendation of the Defense Minister, and approves the budget and all other defense legislation before it is brought

---

* Examples: The Yadin-Sherf Committee (1963); Agranat Committee on the Conduct of the War (1974–75); Zadok Committee (1974).

before the Knesset. Declarations of war, the conclusion of peace treaties, and in fact all formal acts concerning foreign relations are prerogatives of the Cabinet. Its formal powers and role make it the center. When the chips are down, and given enough time, it can be the actual arena. The actions of the members of the inner groups are strongly affected by the Cabinet because "it is there" and because, despite the official secrecy of debates and votes, what happens in the Cabinet soon becomes known to the press and public.

Within the Cabinet, the most likely controversies are between the Ministries of Defense and Foreign Affairs and between Defense and Finance. Until the 1970s, the defense budget was determined mainly through an internal Defense review of plans, and of production and procurement opportunities. The rest of the national budget was a residue, after essential defense needs were met. Once the total defense and nondefense ceilings were set by an inner Cabinet group, the Bureau of the Budget in the Treasury delegated authority to the Budget Branch of the Defense Ministry for detailed review and "treasury control," thus sparing defense officials some of the most tedious arguments to be found in Israeli public service, and allowing members of the Army to be, in this respect, privileged citizens. Public confrontation of the defense budget first began in 1972, when defense had risen to 30 percent of GNP and social demands were particularly strong. The full Cabinet abnegated its authority to decide, and turned the Solomonic budget decision over to a committee consisting of the Prime Minister, Defense Minister, and Finance Minister.

Conflicts between the Defense and Foreign Ministries have arisen because of built-in differences in policy aims, Defense seeing diplomacy, most of the time, as a way to get arms; and because of the desire of both organizations to be the principal actor in important international relations. Conflict was stimulated in the past by differences in personalities and background between the Army officers and Foreign Ministry personnel, who often, in the early years, had more formal education and less practical leadership experience than the soldiers.[37] Populist support and the primacy given by Prime Ministers to Defense * have placed the onus on the Foreign Minister to struggle for participation and for the acceptance of his views. In this he has frequently been handicapped by the isolation of the people in the Foreign Ministry organization from an adequate flow of information and debate; and rarely has there been a feeling that there is a "defense and foreign affairs community."

In the handling of internal controversy, however, the Cabinet has been more like an executive than like an upper house. Adversary proceedings have been traumatic more often than they have been enlightening, especially when

---

* In the years immediately following the 1956 Sinai campaign, Shimon Peres, as Deputy Minister of Defense, conducted extensive diplomatic efforts to get French arms and technical backing. Mrs. Meir, who was Foreign Minister at that time, strongly objected to these infringements on the foreign-policy domain.

the differences were between members of the same party. The most critical of these were between Sharett and Lavon in 1953–55 and Sharett and Ben Gurion in 1955 (over whether Sharett's conciliatory peace policy could succeed, and whether the policy of retaliation was wrong). The formal Cabinet setting was used because these differences, and the personal feelings which they generated, could no longer be accommodated through informal give and take. Relations deteriorated to the point where foreign and defense policies were actively pursued in different and uncoordinated directions; and in the end Sharett had to leave. In this case, as in the rivalry between Shimon Peres and Itzchak Rabin, the ultimate decision was made within the Labor Party. Other controversies have been more manageable. The absence of confrontation within the Cabinet, however, reduces the importance of its role. The less consensus there is among the leaders, the more the meeting of the full Cabinet becomes the locus of actual decision.

The Knesset

The influence of the Knesset is more modest in defense than in other areas. The reasons include the Knesset's lack of power in the political support structure, the needs of secrecy, and the Knesset's lack of expertise. These have impeded the ability to mount an effective and knowledgeable opposition, and within the government the merger of Ahdut Ha'Avoda and Rafi into the Labor Party in 1968 accented the trend toward inner-circle decisions. Following the Six Day War, a growing sense of ease about national security made for more open discussion. The 1973 war and the strength of the Likud in the immediate post-war elections again prompted a demand for more public debate.

Mechanisms available to attempt to control defense policy include legislation, questions, motions on the agenda, the report of the State Controller, proposals for a vote of no confidence and voting approval of the government when it takes office, the budget procedure, and meetings of the Foreign Affairs and Defense Committee. Legislation has been comparatively meager, and covers the annual budget, military recruitment and service, the status of Zahal and the Defense Ministry, and a periodic continuation of the extraordinary powers given the government by the Emergency Regulations inherited from the British Mandate.* "Questions" are mostly used to raise issues of conscience, such as apparent injustices to individuals or groups. The report of the State Controller refers to management details and only very indirectly to policy. It serves, however, to unveil to the Knesset and the public a small part of the operations of the defense enterprise, and contribute to control. A much-delayed and technical check, it is nevertheless a "foot in the door."

The budget is prepared by the Defense Ministry and is coordinated in form

* Discussed in Chapter 2, "The Search for a Constitution."

and procedures by the Bureau of the Budget in the Ministry of Finance. The ceiling for defense has usually been negotiated by the Ministers of Finance and Defense, with the arbitration and active participation of the Prime Minister and occasionally one or two others of the inner circle. Until the 1970's, the total size of the defense budget was not published, and a joint subcommittee of the Finance and Foreign Affairs Committees went over it somewhat superficially *in camera*. Even so, when the total figure is available, Knesset members feel that they cannot really judge.*

The Foreign Affairs and Defense Committee is much better informed than the rest of the Knesset. It has a somewhat unclear role but an indirect effect, since the members of the committee are, after the ministers, important members of their parties and their opinions can have influence.** Membership is much sought after. Party membership quotas are proportional to the strength of the Knesset delegations, and the Knesset Organizing Committee can change the minimum size of Knesset delegation required in order to be given seats on the committee, thus eliminating the possibility of Communist or other splinter-party representatives. Most meetings are held *in camera*.

Formal Foreign Affairs and Defense Committee tasks include referral of all security and foreign-affairs bills, joint sessions with the Finance Committee on the budget at the most important second reading, and retroactive approval of mobilization within a given time limit, failing which it is canceled. The committee is similar in its powers and procedures to other Knesset committees. It can summon soldiers and civil servants as witnesses only via the ministers. Those appearing are not sworn in, nor are they compelled to testify. Thus the committee does not have the power or authority of a commission of inquiry, nor does it have an expert staff of its own.

Historically, the demands made by the committee or by opposition leaders have been mainly to ask for more access to witnesses and better information, or to give the committee the authority of a commission of inquiry, which none of the other Knesset committees has. All the time it was in power, Labor rejected these attempts, successfully confining the decisive debates to the party, the Cabinet, and the defense system, and arguing that explicit parliamentary control is not needed or desirable.

The committee's role can thus be expected to be general rather than

---

* In April 1972, for example, *Ha'aretz* reported "bitterness among members of the Finance Committee because of increases in the defense budget." It appeared that the formally approved budget of 5.3 billion lire was more like 6.3 billion, the difference coming from such sources as advances on the next year's budget and from a return payment of 150 million for Mirage aircraft impounded by France. A widely publicized 100-million-lire defense cut, made by a committee of Golda Meir, Moshe Dayan, and Pinhas Sapir, thus was called "fictitious" by some members. Adding to the resentment at being "out of things" was the use made of the defense cut by the Finance Minister to induce other ministers to reduce their budgets.

** After the unique change of regime in 1977, the committee was unusually strong in expertise, including a former Defense Minister (Peres), two former Foreign Ministers (Allon and Eban), three former Chiefs of Staff (Yadin, Rabin, and Bar Lev), and two professors of aeronautics with recent defense R&D experience (Moshe Arens and Joseph Rom).

specific, to legitimate and review rather than to initiate or even control policy. Of the past, Shimon Peres has said, "The committee is not decisive—but it did exercise influence, for example, in military government, on German policy, on attitudes towards Soviet Jewry's problems, and it united the nation around the army."[38] The committee has occasionally come close to being a political court of appeal. In the 1961 Lavon crisis, Lavon appeared before it and threatened to expose others and justify himself through documents said to be in his possession. This incident helped to precipitate the showdown within the Labor Party. Again, in a 1963 crisis over the German missile scientists in Egypt, Issar Harel, head of security, was to have come before the Foreign Affairs and Defense Committee to air his disagreement with Ben Gurion. He resigned before the scheduled appearance, partly, it is believed, in order to avoid it.

In the early 1960s, Knesset members advocated various forms of a security council. One proposal was to include retired defense experts and politicians who would review defense policy. Beyond the inherent Israeli doubt of the worth of opinions coming from outside an enterprise, one of the most potent factors against the proposal was the vision of a committee based on party representation meddling in the vital defense system. The debates on the mistakes of the 1973-war period revived such demands. Indeed, Mrs. Meir promised at least some form of security council in a 1973 campaign speech, but the logic of Cabinet government seems to give priority to a Ministers' Defense Committee, since the Cabinet already includes as members those directly involved.

By and large the Knesset has been important in its reflection of the general public feeling and conscience rather than in guidance of more specific defense and foreign policies. The broadest questions, however, such as that of the future borders and population, will be the prerogative of the Knesset, if not of a plebiscite or general election. Like most parliaments in the world, the Knesset is questioning its identity, and the frustration is perhaps greatest in matters of defense.

Parties and Defense

We have seen that following the nationalization of arms, a form of politicization developed in which extremes of right and left were avoided. While criteria of achievement were applied throughout Zahal, at the highest levels there were also criteria of loyalty to Ben Gurion's approach, or to Mapai, or to espousal of a purely professional military role.

Parties *per se* continued to be concerned with defense, however. For some years following independence, Mapam and Ahdut Ha'Avoda, whose kibbutz movements had been prominent in the Palmach, had "defense policy groups" with which senior officers met for discussions of policy and which sought to be of some influence. Officers close to Mapai were also members of party circles. But even though informal and personal party contacts continued still in the 1970s, there was no longer much of this form of political activity. An important source of change was the merger of Ahdut Ha'Avoda and Rafi with Mapai into the Labor Party in 1968, and the inclusion of Mapam in the Labor Alignment, from 1969. This lessened public opportunities for opposition, and Ahdut Ha'Avoda leaders became, as individuals, candidates for the political leadership rather than for lesser coalition participation. The new situation affected their behavior, stimulating debate within the party, since potential candidates in Israel are always campaigning and accentuating differences real and imagined.

Before Mapam and Ahdut Ha'Avoda were in the Labor Alignment, their differences with Mapai at times enhanced the defense debate. Because of their historic involvement in defense through the Palmach, and as socialist parties, they were "insiders" who could legitimately raise defense issues in public. As a party, Ahdut Ha'Avoda supported a firm international stance and raised the issue of arms dealings with Germany; but on balance its influence was through specific individuals who were formerly active in defense, such as Israel Galili and Yigal Allon.

Mapam historically advocated a conciliatory Arab policy and considerable withdrawal from the post-1967 boundaries, yet it accepted coalition discipline on these and on economic questions. Since joining the Alignment, Mapam has been able to vector policy toward more readiness for border concessions, particularly in the preelection platform drafting[39] and in 1974–77, by questioning the Cabinet's tolerance of the settlement of sites on the West Bank by unauthorized groups. Mapam's legitimacy as a partner or opponent in defense policy was weakened, however, by a continuing gap between its ideology and the realities of Cabinet decisions to which the party agreed over the years, despite its stated convictions.

Mapai, and later Labor, was until 1977 the final arbiter in defense, with the exception of the 1967 crisis of the Six Day War, when the coalition parties were very important. The role of Labor was, first of all, electoral—to decide who would be in charge of defense and to support him; to resolve major personal differences; and, to a lesser extent, to decide general policy direction.

The closer an issue was to the foreground of public opinion and, particularly, the closer it was to affecting the unity, image, and survival of the Labor Party, the more it was dealt with within the party. The role of the party was to elect, to choose the leadership, and to be a court of last resort when there were irreconcilable differences on issues or persons. As the dominant party, Mapai, and later Labor, was the arbiter in defense, mainly through its role in electing and supporting the Defense Minister. The party tended to avoid specific defense issues, in its pragmatic way emphasizing a choice of people rather than of specific policies, seeking, in the face of international uncertainty, leaders to meet the challenges.

The reduction and eventual abolition of military government in the largely Arab parts of Israel and the withdrawal from Sinai after 1956 were important questions resolved mainly within the party. While the conflict between Ben Gurion and Sharett, also decided within the party, was accompanied by intensely personal feelings, the issue was basically one of policy. Labor Party Central Committee debates on policy in the occupied areas, which preceded the 1973 war, were lengthy and inconclusive. After the war the differing positions crystallized, and policies, loyalties, and leaders were more clearly identified. The value of party unity and the need for Mapam's support against the growing strength of the opposition prevented a definitive and conclusive struggle. The broad spectrum of security views within the Labor Party has had the effect that potential voter support for bordering parties strengthens specific activities within Labor which are close to them.

The smaller coalition parties were important on only a few occasions, and their role has mainly been to reinforce control by Mapai and later of Labor. The Mafdal (NRP) was very influential in the decision to appoint Dayan on the eve of the Six Day War. After the 1973 war, the younger groups which strongly favor the settlement and retention of the West Bank became part of the Mafdal leadership, adding an important foreign-policy element to their previous concentration on religious questions.

Once elections have been over, the smaller coalition parties have had little defense influence; but they could bring down the government, secure new elections, or gain a "free conscience" vote in the Knesset on such major questions as boundary agreements, or even the choice of the Minister of Defense; but these are strong steps, to be threatened or used in extremity.

A Cloud No Bigger than a Man's Hand, or a Clear and Present Danger?

The broadest political decision has been—at the time of the foundation of the state—that defense is the most crucial issue and that it will be national and nonpartisan in its operation. As has been shown, one kind of politicization has been avoided—the use of military appointments for patronage. Another form which has been avoided in Israel is the partisan penetration of decision making, where partisan political motives could sway the internal decisions of the defense hierarchy, or military policy could be used to influence internal politics, a possibility whenever there is civil political control of the military.

A third kind of politicization would be the use of the authority and status of those high in the defense hierarchy to further a party, as in an election. In the first decade of the state, there were instances of electioneering in the Army, but they were not widespread. Zahal as a whole became highly professional, achievement-oriented, apolitical in form and in substance, with the military actions of serving officers remote from partisan politics, except for some at the highest level.

Nevertheless, in the 1970's, the relation of the parties to the Army came to have within it the seeds of a potentially insidious kind of politicization, and indications are that there are still some dangers. Events suggest a danger of politicization, or grounds for fear that a unique kind of politicization could develop despite the basic culture. On the other hand, as we have seen, the military is not a separate caste; the generals of the 1970's, or those likely to be generals in the 1980's, although lacking in political experience, were socialized to democratic values. They grew up in the age of ideology of the Yishuv or in the early years of the state.

In the past, a senior officer leaving the Army could expect to enter the highest management level of a large firm or the civil service, and a few have gone on to university careers. The higher management ranks today take longer to attain, and industrial management is becoming more professional. Until recently, officers as local level politicians or party organizers have been rare. Except for an occasional mayor, middle-level politics has not been attractive or hospitable to ex-officers, and the political bureaucracies tend to close their ranks against newcomers. The competition of the ex-officers is feared, and political incumbents are noted for their successful tenacity in office.

Recruiting at the Cabinet level is a different situation. When Moshe Dayan left Zahal in 1957, he was elected to the Knesset before becoming Minister of Agriculture. In 1968 the Chief of Staff of the Six Day War, Itzchak Rabin, decided to enter politics and was sent to Washington as Ambassador, with a promise of joining the Cabinet later. By contrast, in 1970 Ezer Weizman, who had been Deputy Chief of Staff, resigned from the Army and was immediately appointed by Gahal as Minister of Transport in the National Unity government. In April 1972, the outgoing Chief of Staff, Chaim Bar Lev, was appointed Minister of Commerce and Industry. The frequent invitation of the *Ramatkal* to the Cabinet can blur the line between political and professional decisions and personalities.

Some public unease was noticeable at the appointment of Bar Lev as minister, despite his high reputation.* There appeared to be an attempt to bring defense expertise into the Cabinet to counter Dayan's primacy, or to use the aura of Zahal to enhance the image of the older leadership. This image was a bit tarnished at the time of Bar Lev's appointment by a series of "affairs" in the economic arena, in which the Labor leaders showed carelessness and insensitivity to Labor's public responsibility in situations that could lead to

---

* An example is "Haminui" (The Appointment) in *Ma'ariv*, March 10, 1972, by Matthias Peled, in which party leaders are accused of using Bar Lev's standing to further their own goals. Others asked for legislation to prevent direct appointments to the Cabinet and other posts before a "decent" waiting period had passed.

misuse of public resources by predatory operators. Weizman's and Bar Lev's nominations also showed a bureaucratic or hierarchical aspect of Israeli political culture. Though undoubtedly popular, they were appointed, not elected, nor had they ever been elected to any office before gaining a powerful post in the Cabinet. In many ways, however, other non-Labor Party candidates with a military background showed ability as political entrepreneurs and were not simply appointed to a place on the lists. Ariel Sharon had an important role in bringing the Likud together in 1973; and although originally appointed, Ezer Weizman managed the Likud 1977 election campaign.

In 1973 the coincidence of war and a general election were important to the problem of politicization. During the war, Bar Lev served briefly in key Army roles as a reserve lieutenant-general, without resigning as Minister of Commerce. This was done with Cabinet approval, over the protests of the Minister of Justice. Generals Yariv (Labor) and Sharon (Likud) had appropriately resigned from government or Army service at least 100 days before the original 1973 election date, according to law, and were active Knesset candidates.* Sharon, indeed, had been the moving force in coalescing the heterogeneous Likud opposition list for the elections. Despite the law, however, both were recalled to central defense roles as reserve generals, and remained in service until just before the postwar elections of December 1973. Sharon commanded the successful bridgehead crossing over the Suez Canal and remained as a division commander within range of Egyptian guns, granting press interviews in which he derided his superiors; and Yariv represented Israel in the cease-fire negotiations.

By tacit agreement, the major parties abandoned a joint plan to legitimate the situation by legislation. In the face of public perplexity, things were left in their original state of constitutional confusion. After the 1973 elections, ex-colonels or ex-generals were in the Cabinet and Knesset—Rabin, Yariv, Dayan, and Bar Lev for the Labor Alignment, Colonel Meir Pa'il as the only representative of the farther left Moked. Ariel Sharon ** and Avraham Yoffe were elected for the Likud, and ex-General Shlomo Lahat became Likud Mayor of Tel Aviv in a personal victory over the large Labor Party machine. It is reported that when Menachem Begin left the "National Unity" government in 1970, several senior officers called to try to dissuade him,[40] and strong

---

* The *Basic Law: The Knesset* states that "Senior officers, whose rank will be determined by law, may not be candidates." The *Law of the Knesset: Elections* provides not only that "no officers of any rank in the permanent service "may be candidates" unless "discharged at least one hundred days before the elections" but also that "no candidate on the list will serve in the reserves from the day the list is published until the elections." A war situation like that of 1973 was not foreseen.

** In 1977 the Legal Counsel to the government stated that Sharon could not serve both in the Cabinet (as Minister of Agriculture) and as a general with a command role in the reserves. The Chief of Staff then relieved him of his command.

support for the appointment of David Elazar as Ramatkal in 1972 was said to have come from Yigal Allon, his old Palmach commander and a leader of the former Ahdut Ha'Avoda Party. Whatever legitimacy military rank could give was distributed over the political spectrum.*

The increased participation of ex-generals and the public reaction to these events is worth examining. One explanation could be the scarcity of talent among the middle generation of politicians, elbowing each other while waiting in the wings. This is not surprising. The closed party bureaucracy and the party list election system have been inimical, and many who would have been potential politicians, as well as kibbutz or industrial leaders, were more attracted to economic pursuits.

It is possible, therefore, that the prospect of a future political role could insidiously affect the relations of the top officers among themselves and with the political leaders while these officers are still in service. Bureaucratic politics and ambition for command can be disturbing enough by themselves without the exacerbation of political candidacy.

The political roles of former Chiefs of Staff have been significant. Of the first ten *Ramatkalim,* or Chiefs of Staff, six were elected to the Knesset and four of these were ministers. There are factors which could help avoid the dangers of politicization inherent in post-service political careers. The generation of politically socialized officers will soon all be civilians, and the number of political openings is limited. The growing number of retired senior officers available and the impact of the Yom Kippur War have reduced the attractiveness of military rank, *per se.* The development of more open entry into politics and of alternate leadership sources to the party bureaucracy and the military could be more important than the needed clarification of the constitutional position of direct appointment of ex-officers to the Cabinet.

Still another potential source of politicization is the relationship among defense, public order, and settlement in Judea and Samaria. During the period of the Rabin Cabinet, when unauthorized settlement occurred by groups from the Gush Imunim movement, the Army was assigned the task of preventing settlement or of removing the settlers. In one case, they were permitted to remain, but within the confines of an Army camp. In 1977, during the first months of the Begin Cabinet, it was proposed that certain new Gush Imunim settlements be permitted in Army installations in the capacity of reserve soldiers. Public opposition to this political use of military status quickly squashed the proposal.

* In 1977 Knesset elections, going from Left to Right, the following former senior officers were elected: Sheli (left socialist): Colonel Meir Pa'il; Labor Alignment: three former *Ramatkalim* Itzchak Rabin, Chaim Bar Lev and Moshe Dayan; the Democratic Change party, Yigael Yadin, former *Ramatkal* and two major generals, Meir Amit and Meir Zorea; the Likud: former air force commander Ezer Weizman and Brig. Mordechai Zipori; and on his own list, Ariel Sharon.

The Press

Until the Six Day War, confidentiality in the reporting of defense matters was ensured by both censorship and the heritage from the Mandate period, when the press took part in the struggle for independence. Since 1967 there has been a clear trend toward more open reporting of technical news and strategic debates, and toward criticism of the administrative efficiency of the defense organizations.* The government felt the need to explain the economic demands of defense to the Israeli, and indeed to the American, public. As the Middle East became a principal arms export market for the Western countries, many details became available, to be republished in Israel, from such journals as *Aviation Week*. Defense news, especially of accomplishments in R&D and production, has occasionally been timed for release to enhance the political standing of the minister or the government. With a nation in arms, news and knowledge of problems spread rapidly. Familiarity has dissipated some of the sacred aura of Zahal, while the reaction after the 1973 war legitimated the public criticism of defense policy. Still, the effectiveness of the press is limited by the modesty of the demand, in the culture, for the formal right to know, and by the paucity of independent resources for strategic analysis which could make press or parliamentary criticism effective. The press can indicate that a serious question is or should be on the agenda, such as whether or not Israel should design and build its own fighter aircraft; but it is seldom able to present arguments in depth. It has its greatest effect, perhaps, in determining and reflecting the public images of the minister and of the *Ramatkal*, which, as have been shown, are central elements in the quality of civil-military relations.

An Interim Summary of Political Control

The reader who has been looking for a convincing and formal process of political control over defense may by this time feel some disappointment. While institutions such as the Cabinet, Knesset, and Ministry of Defense have formal powers, in the totality of the system they have not been well organized to exercise them, and have lacked the knowledge and means needed to oversee the defense system. The views of the inner group of leaders, the expression of popular feeling through the parties and the press, occasional leadership rifts or actions of the great powers which bring issues into formal and open discussion—these factors, together with the kind of political support given the Minister of Defense and his ability to control "the system," have counted for much more. Some of the specific problem areas are as follows:

The authority of the political leadership has seemed to be clear on the

---

* For an analysis of freedom of the press, censorship, and the right to know, see Chapter 2, "The Search for a Constitution."

broadest questions, such as the decision not to call up the reserves early enough in the Yom Kippur War, or to make a preemptive start in the Six Day War; but its influence on the force structure and strategic-political concepts and, indeed, its capability in forming them are inadequate. Cabinet decisions have been made by a small informal forum without a policy staff; nor has there been a suitable prearranged operating procedure for crisis management. Further, the Cabinet has in the past depended on military intelligence and the General Staff for strategic evaluations. Parliamentary oversight, although improved, is superficial and belated, due to general political weakness of the Knesset as an institution, to the secrecy needs of defense, and to the technical aspects of the budget process, inadequate committee authority, or staff work.

The military as well as the Defense Minister may have too wide a scope of activity. A minister may be involved in the government of the West Bank, Sinai, and the Gaza Strip, in foreign relations, in the antiterrorist campaign, in general politics, and in issues of force structure, budgets, and military appointments. Some things are therefore neglected, leading, for example, to decreased scrutiny of the General Staff and of military readiness, accompanied by an expansion of the role of the Chief of Staff. The Chief of Staff thus has some policy and service responsibilities which in other countries are performed by civilian branches of the ministry. This serves to impair his effectiveness as the commander of the forces—at least in times of cease-fire.* There have thus been recommendations from time to time that the separate role of commander of all of the ground forces be established.

The effectiveness of the minister in managing defense has depended largely on personal and subjective control of an enterprise of extremely great scope. As the link between the political system and the defense establishment, the leadership of the minister has been due to personality and to the degree to which he achieved party, popular, and defense-system support. The system grew up, however, under Ben Gurion, who was also nearly always Prime Minister as well as Minister of Defense. More important, he was the leading founding father, who came to the defense job with unquestioned political support and the ability to concentrate and go deeply into what he saw as the cardinal questions. The system as Ben Gurion developed it was not suited to his successors; each continued it, however, if in his own way.

Adversary proceedings were inadequately developed, despite an inherently pluralist organization, because the ministry headquarters was not set up so as to be able to develop these processes.

The influence of the military on policy has been occasionally substantial, and not only or mainly because of the organizational lacks I have mentioned.

* The anomalies noted include the following: the General Staff (for all of the services) doubles as the staff of the ground forces as well; the Planning Branch of the General Staff and the R&D Department are simultaneously staff departments for the minister and for the General Staff, while only since 1978 has the Minister of Defense had his own long-range policy advisers.

Other reasons include the common perception of the situation and the resulting operating concepts which become accepted; the capabilities which come into being and therefore ask to be used; and the inertia of large programs, which once started are stopped with great reluctance.[41]

Despite these problems, the experience of three decades shows substantial achievements, and relations of the military to the civil government which are reasonably consonant with democratic criteria. That this is so, given some of the substantive and organizational problems, is due to the nature of the society, the way in which the defense system was developed, the ways in which the military leaders received their training, and their socialization to military-political relations; so that we now have to look beyond the formal arrangements and return to an earlier question—to the values of civilians and soldiers, and to attitudes and perceptions of the problems and of the outside world. We must ask whether closeness to violence breeds a gnawing hatred of the Arabs, whether wishful thinking distorts perceptions of the Arab world, and whether the great defense effort is leading to a militarized or technocratic society in which human goals have low priority. Operationally, we need to ask if deference to political leadership is a basic value in the military, and what the relation is between the military leaders and the political system and culture.

The Military–Political Culture

Whatever the machinery of government, effective political control depends on the political culture of the officers, particularly on the beliefs of the military about their own roles and their relation to civil authority. Separatism, from the society and from the political system, career frustration, and an absence of socialization to the legitimacy of the elected leaders in a democratic political system could lead to militarism—defined here essentially as acting on the belief that the use of armed force is the basic way to solve international problems, and that decisions on its use are made by and with the military. But there are other aspects of militarism, such as a vast array of customs, interests, prestige, actions, and thoughts associated with arms and wars, yet transcending true military purpose.[42] In Israel those things which transcend true military purpose are minimal. Officers seldom wear uniforms off duty. Only the highest-ranking reserve officers use their titles, and with some hesitation. Military rank in itself is a source of status only if it is very high, and there are limits to the extent to which there is a "diffused elite." A corporal in a daring volunteer unit can have more prestige than officers elsewhere, and even the carryover to civilian life is mostly limited to the approbation of one's peer group. The Army is far from being a separate caste, although because of the nature of its work, the demands on individuals can be unique, and group life intense and comprehensive. With a whole country in arms and each person serving for at least part of each year and for perhaps a good part of his early adult life, the Army cannot but reflect the society as a whole. Officers are recruited from a broad base, although kibbutz children are "overrepresented" in the volunteer units. A policy of short service careers and very early retirement, instituted so as to have young commanders, also works against the development of separatism.

The administrative tail of the Army is comparatively small, and there is affinity between technical and command roles. There is little separate garrison life, and the "expanded roles" of the military have brought it even closer to the society. One essential factor in militarism, a separatist military caste, is therefore missing.

Israel is in many senses still a community, and within this community, as in the British Army in earlier centuries, elite roles have been interchangeable. In the war of attrition of 1969–70, a farmer could leave his tractor, fly a close support-fighter mission, and come home for supper.

An amalgam of its own traditions and the national culture, the Army is a part of the society, even the much broader society of today; and the advantages and disadvantages of Israel's small size and the highly personal character of Israeli bureaucratic life are strongly reflected in the Army, partly because it is not too distant from the methods of personal leadership developed in the Palmach and continued in present-day NCO and officer training. As in many organizations which have grown rapidly, there remain in Zahal some of the informal systems of communication and relations characteristic of the earlier periods, many of which have important functions. The Army shows another Israeli "community" characteristic as well—the interpenetration and interlinkage of diverse groups, which serves to inhibit the development of separatist social movements. An example of this outside of the Army is that of university students, who as a group have parochial interests and no unique approach as students to national politics.

Because of Zahal's symbolic status and the public stance of outstanding generals, one must still ask whether the defense leaders do not form a separate elite which could become divorced from the values of the civil society. It would help, therefore, to see who the defense leaders are and to note their backgrounds.

In the 1970's most of the principal commanders were still in their forties. Those who had trained them and had recently left the Army were the last of the Palmach generation or were in the British Army in World War II, and the younger generals grew up entirely within Zahal. Even more than the younger officers, older groups did not come from any one social class in the sense of parents' occupations. They were born in Israel or came to the country as children, and are mostly of European and indeed Eastern European background. They took part in the creation of the state and were part of a small community which felt social and national ideologies strongly. Whether they are closer to the civilian community than are the successor generation of officers who spent all their formative years in a more professional and highly organized Zahal is problematic. One would expect to find that the older leaders lean more toward political careers when they leave the military, and are socialized more explicitly to accept political and civilian control. They do, in fact, feel themselves part of a national elite, and, like the British officers of previous centuries, they "have a stake in the country."

The values of the military elite which retired after the Yom Kippur War nevertheless range over a narrower spectrum than those of the population at large. The group selected itself originally by volunteering, and many of its older members were socialized in the Labor movement, the forerunner of much of the establishment during the first decades of the state. With Ben Gurion's leadership, members of the groups farthest to the right or left were filtered out. As we have seen, however, the views and political affiliations of officers cover a broad range within the overall national consensus, and they are not militaristic.[43]

Another possible source of military separatism is the closeness of personal ties which developed over the years, the long hours of work and common experiences, and close social contact. The effect is mitigated by the small size of the country, by the reserve system, which provides a broader meeting ground, and by early transfer to civilian life, which has been encouraged by the need for managerial talent in the expanding economy. The importance of the close ties is therefore most apparent in the elite roles of ex-officers after they leave the Army.

Still another possible danger to integration is that professionalization could make defense a closed system, where promotion to the top and thus into the national elite is done hierarchically, the officer emerging to public scrutiny only after he has reached the top Israeli rank of brigadier or major general. Given the leadership qualities of many such men, a "personality cult" could exist, even though the smallness of distance in Israeli life sooner or later tends to keep an individual from being taken too seriously by his peers.

Thus, increasing professionalization, the transformation of the community into a more differentiated society, and the passing from Zahal of the generation of the Palmach may increase separation of the permanent service after the generals of the 1970's have left the Army. Hints of separatism have been seen in the past, on occasions when the "honor" of Zahal is doubted as in the Lavon affair and ranks are closed. A good part of Ben Gurion's motivation in opposing Lavon was to preserve the prestige of Zahal. Another example was seen after the Yom Kippur War in 1973, in the dismay of the Army at what it considered a tragic and prematurely imposed cease-fire, and in its dissatisfaction when the Agranat Report on the conduct of the war blamed the military for the strategic surprise and not the elected politicians, including the Defense Minister. (But characteristically, while Army officers wrote or spoke publicly against the Agranat Report, they did not question in public the political decision on the cease-fire.)

Against possible separateness, however, are the transfer of officers to civil life at an early age, the early socialization they have had to other values, such as kibbutz membership, and the fact that, notwithstanding all the aura and success of Zahal, Jewish political culture is still somewhat skeptical of the hero, or *gibor*. The danger of separatism is still small, at least as long as the civil society remains open and growing, absorbing young retired officers, and is itself a vast reserve militia.

The question still remains of the way in which the uniformed military relate to politicians. At the beginning of this chapter I said that Israel in this respect, while having something of the "ideological army," is closer to the "liberal model" of the professional army and to a "nation in arms." This can be understood in the light of the history of independence. It was the politicians who developed the armed forces after they had laid the groundwork for civil government—and not, as often occurs, the military leaders who, having achieved independence, set up the government. Ben Gurion's nonideological politicization and the insulation of the forces from direct partisan influence followed.

Has the Intermittent War Made the Society More Violent?

One image of the new Israeli is a composite stereotype of the kibbutznik and the commando, and there are many cases in which these seemingly opposed characteristics appear in one and the same person. Yet Einstein is reported to have said, "When a Jew says that he likes to hunt, he lies." Like other stereotypes, these die hard and are not without some truth.

It is at first difficult to reconcile the history and folkways of the Diaspora Jew with the aggressive adapting of Israeli youth to physical danger. One asks whether impressionable years spent with possible death and combat do not engender a self-destroying hatred of the Arabs and a cult of violence. We can look for evidence, slender and impressionistic, in the way Zahal has fought when civilian settlements were involved, in public reactions to incidents involving Arab civilians, and in literature and interviews. In the wars since 1948, and in reprisal raids in the interim, there have indeed been occasions when civilians were killed by Israeli forces, underground or regular. Yet these incidents have been few and are in stark contrast to the essentially correct nature of the occupation of Judea and Samaria and the open bridges to Jordan after the Six Day War, which many Israelis consider to be an outstanding policy achievement.[44]

An examination of the known instances of Israeli Army attacks involving Arab civilians will show that they have been very few and that they very rarely involved cold-blooded violence. When they did, the news and protest spread rapidly in the small country, and official and judicial corrective action was swift. Government policies which seemed repressive have drawn considerable Israeli public protest. The motives of those protesting have been varied, but the impact has been significant and its influence on the leadership has been greatest when coming from "insiders" or from youth. Protests coming from "professional" protesters or from anti-Zionist groups have generally fallen on deaf ears. Although ministers have been interested in the good opinion of intellectuals, their actions have not been very responsive to the intellectuals' opinions where defense considerations may be involved. For example, in the spring of 1972, Mrs. Meir spent seven hours with a group of twenty writers, who asked that the Israeli Arab inhabitants of the border village of Bir-Am, who were sent away in 1948, be allowed to return. Despite very considerable public sentiment, the Defense Ministry case against the return prevailed. Another prominent incident, in which General Ariel Sharon was involved, was that of closing off the Bedouin lands at Rafiah, south of Gaza.* Despite the failure of such protests, Zahal, even in 1972, was far from sacrosanct, and on questions of conscience, at least, was exposed to public scrutiny. Until the 1973 war, however, little could be published of a technical nature, and much valuable criticism, for example, of the state of readiness of emergency stores did not appear in the press. This has now changed.

The symbolic and social role of Zahal, beyond that of being merely an instrument of defense, has not led to public militarism, although at some times it has contributed to overconfidence and to a lack of political sensitivity and concern. Israelis associate the Army with independence, nationhood, and a new image of the Jew.[45] It has been a symbol of national unity and embodiment of pioneering, above particular groups, interests, and parties. Besides its direct military duties, the Army has been important in education, agricultural settlement, the absorption of immigrants, and advancing management and technology.** The widespread identification with Zahal leads to feelings of

---

* Sharon was then commander of the Southern Command. The Bedouins in Pit'hat Rafiah were nomads before the Six Day War, afterwards settling near water holes and working as hired agricultural laborers. Some 14,000 acres were fenced off for agricultural-village development and the Bedouins were forced to leave. They appealed to the Red Cross, which approached Zahal. The Chief of Staff appointed a committee of inquiry. Protest from Israelis soon followed. Members of Hashomer Hatzair kibbutzim (Mapam) demanded the return of the Bedouins. The committee of inquiry recommended that the senior officers in charge be reprimanded for exceeding their authority but that the Bedouins not return for security reasons, members of the tribe having been involved in the killing of Israeli soldiers in Sinai. The Mapam Cabinet members who had previously protested did not oppose the recommendations. The real protest came from opponents of Dayan within the Labor Party. The affair culminated in an acrimonious showdown in a meeting of the party's leaders in which Dayan's attackers represented mainly the organized party machinery, and Golda Meir sided with Dayan. The Prime Minister was reported to have been particularly sensitive to a security question, saying, "I don't remember when a party newspaper talked in this way of a security matter, in the complicated situation in which we find ourselves. I know that such criticism is now very popular in the country."

** The Defense Service Law of 1949 provided for a year's service, mainly devoted to learning agriculture and cooperation and, for immigrants, Hebrew. Later the service period was extended to permit technical training, but new agricultural settlements continue to be started by Nahal, a corps of volunteers combining Army service and agriculture; and the high-school-age training corps, Gadna, was recently directed to emphasize work with marginal youth.

collective personal shame if it falters, and personal pride in its achievements. The Yom Kippur War in 1973 led to a more sober view of the Army and temporarily, in some cases, to an overly pessimistic reaction after the euphoria and self-confidence which had followed the Six Day War. The story of the extraordinary military victory against very great odds was told very late. Soldiers were seen not as supermen or saints, but citizens who reflected the society, warts and all; while failures in judgment of the political leaders, who had been idealized by the nation in arms, struck home to many who had identified with them. But although Zahal's idealized image and symbolic role have declined somewhat, both are still strong and important.

War and the Individual

Many impressions of the effect of war on Israeli values are found in literature. Writers such as Amos Oz, A. B. Yehoshua, and S. Yizhar depict the inherent tragedy of the land—that when the Jew finally finds a haven, he can abide in it in peace only through wars, at a cost both to Israelis and to some of the Arab peoples. Their writings express a feeling of insoluble dilemma, with no apparent way in which nationalisms can coexist in the same place, here, now, in this and the next generations; although living or at least working together of Jews and Arabs as people, if not as nations, has already proved to be feasible.

The literature shows consciousness of the injustice of war and dispossession, as it is felt and acted out among people, in their homes and villages, one man to another, whatever the historical merits and reasons. Amos Elon says of the literature, "Beyond speculation is the freedom of awareness of young artists and their public that is remarkable at a time when siege and war, terror and repression dominate all communications between Israel and her enemies."[46] And to youth brought up in an ideological framework in which history was seen to be acting out the destiny of a people, and the ideas for a brave new world were clear, the fact that ideologies cannot yet answer the human dilemma brings some malaise and revolt against the words and the beliefs on which they were raised.

Yet these beliefs were essentially humanist and egalitarian. The Israeli Army recruit is taught that the war is against the Arab armies, not the Arab people. He is not taught to hate, but is taught to use his weapons effectively. Formal training helps, but the culture and the ways of the Army passed on from one generation to the next are probably more responsible for these attitudes. The enemy is not dehumanized, nor is the recruit, and a destroying hatred of the Arabs has not developed.*

---

* The essential nonmilitarism of the youth is well shown in *Siah Lohamim* (Heb.) (*The Seventh Day*), Avraham Shapiro (ed.), Tel Aviv, Ihud Hakibbutzim, 1967.

Continued tension and war could, of course, ultimately change the society, and the feeling of pressure generated by the loss of time spent in the Army, problems of social adjustment, and economic struggle could possibly produce a generation of unreflecting, nondreaming, ambitious philistines. It would seem, however, that the totality of the situation of the country and of the Jew will do more to determine the culture than defense concerns alone. In the wake of the 1973 war, agonized soul searching accompanied national mourning for the fallen, as the community swung precipitously from the euphoria of the post-Six Day War period and the people asked themselves, "What have we done wrong? Were we surprised because we lost our ideals and became materialistic? Because we have not created a just society?"

Mourning and a biblical sense of guilt were heightened by the government's delay in publishing full reports of the striking tactical victories and of the courage shown in the war, and by the contrasting official silence or optimism at the start of the war, until the initial shock and confusion were overcome. At least for a time, the war seemed to have destroyed illusions of many kinds: that war could be deterred indefinitely; that time was necessarily on Israel's side, or, by contrast, that peace was within one's grasp if only territorial concessions were made; and that Zahal in its efficiency and mores, could be strikingly different from the general community of which it is so much a part. In the aggravated new strategic context, a new phase of defense was about to begin.

Some Questions

The overall picture is of a system whose sensitivity and effectiveness have been due more to the culture and strong community interaction than to organization or the way in which the formal political process works. The achievements have been unique in military operations against great odds, showing, at their best, flexibility and initiative, trained competence, courage, and decisive and independent command. Despite the importance and status of Zahal, there seems little cause for concern about the creation of a militarist or violent society or of a "garrison state," though there have been indications of politicization which should not be ignored.

There is a need to make the defense enterprise more open, controlled, and responsive, so as to increase its long-run effectiveness. The arrangements for parliamentary and particularly Cabinet supervision and for deliberation and development of alternatives seem to need urgent consideration. Economic constraints and the quality of the society are now integral aspects of security, and we need to gain a fuller understanding of this relation and apply it. Even more urgent is the need to relate military capabilities and political strategy, both in understanding and countering the combined Arab use of political, economic, and physical warfare and in developing a coordinated Israeli strategy.

Despite striking results in the past, the kinds of problems faced and the responsiveness which is needed to the defense situation require more than dependence on community and informal organization can provide. Among the questions which should be asked are:

How can the Israeli form of party-parliamentary-Cabinet government and the defense organization be made mutually adaptable to the needs of a clear line of command, on the one hand, and a more effective political strategy, on the other? That is, how can the political system become more effective in guiding defense policy? How can it overcome the unequal relations of today, where the civil organization for overall strategy does not have an organized potential for strategic thought comparable to that of the defense system? Would this depend on political changes that go beyond defense?

The change over generations, from leaders who grew up in the "amateur" or "partisan" days to those who were trained as regular professionals, is now completed, together with an increase in scale and technology, which can lead to bureaucratization. How can the unique advantages of the older "community" system be preserved while adapting to the new needs?

These problems, however, need to be addressed in the context of the war situation of "a nation in arms," which goes on simultaneously with struggles for economic and social development. These are analyzed in the chapters which follow.

CHAPTER 5

The Political Economy

ISRAEL'S ECONOMY faces the problems of industrialized and developing countries, of welfare states and countries at war. The situation is unique in the simultaneity of many challenges, in the scope of cooperative enterprise and the resources of the Labor movement, and in the decisive importance of exogenous forces—immigration, wars, and capital inflow. The economy can be described as "heroic." That is, it is often managed as though goals can be reached by sheer determination, despite apparent obstacles or impossible barriers. Or, in the Israeli saying, "There is nothing which can withstand a strong will."

The problems of organization and politics are those of an economy strained beyond its resource limits, yet having an unusual record of performance in most of the years since the state was declared. In this situation, the relations of production, that is, effectiveness in the use of resources, is of first importance. The political structure as well as the simultaneity of goals, however, can obscure the aims of policy. On the other hand, pragmatism prevents the economic blockages which could result from ideological rigidity.

In contrast with the organization for defense, the economy is political along most of its dimensions, and political aims are overriding. National needs of defense, immigration, and social equity are considered as independent variables in relation to the economy. Although defense is the most urgent, there is consensus on the need to support all of these aims, a situation

223

which increases the discretion of the Cabinet but at the same time limits its ability to make "hard" decisions which would explicitly lower the priority of any central aim.* General agreements are, therefore, followed by marginal negotiations.

Economic analyses based on theory are honored more than they are applied. The following examples illustrate the sources of skepticism about the value of formal or professional economic predictions. In 1920 the National Fund had an opportunity to purchase a large part of the Emek, or Valley of Jezreel. At the time the terrain was swampy and largely fallow. The price asked was high for those days, requiring large long-term credits. Apparently Zionists outside of Palestine opposed the deal after seeing the results of an unfavorable professional cost-benefit analysis. Whatever the analysis then showed, it is hard to imagine the achievement of independent Israel without the Emek, which today is the heartland of agriculture and the site of many leading kibbutz and *moshav* settlements.

Another instance occurred in 1927, when the Yishuv was suffering from a serious economic depression. The World Zionist Executive wished to reform the economic organization and management in the Yishuv, particularly in the Histadrut enterprises and the settlements. One proposal was that kibbutz settlement be stopped and replaced by the purchase of small farms by settlers with private means.

This kind of experience not only made for skepticism of expertise; it also led to an attitude, in all sectors of the Yishuv, of "give us the means and let us get on with the job." In Israel the belief persists that there is a difference in mentality between the Jews in Israel and those in the Diaspora. Thus Ezer Weizman (nephew of Chaim Weizmann and a former Air Force commander and Minister of Defense in Begin's 1977 Cabinet) said in 1973 to a twenty-fifth-year reunion of the Mahal (overseas volunteers of the 1948 War of Liberation), "It is good that you came, but in the end it is good that most of you left. We could then build an army suited to our mentality."

This chapter considers how the government has tried to manage the economy, and examines in some detail the organization for economic policy and execution. The political economy is shown to have an extraordinary degree of central direction, marked by a complex network of dependency, interest, and personal relations. This leads to hierarchical relations in the economy, in a system whose characteristic is control rather than regulation.

The following represent some of the principal developments:

There is a growing dissatisfaction with excessive central direction, despite widespread belief that the government is responsible for the state of the economy.

---

* A case which shows the impingement of several aims on an economic question was the decision to request and accept reparations from West Germany, based, in the end, largely on the belief that this capital inflow was essential for growth as related to defense needs.[1]

The resources of "subordinate" centers have grown and thus their degree
  of independent decision. Dependency has become more mutual, and a
  complex and secular bargaining mode overlies that of hierarchy and
  dependence.
Despite marked success over the years in achieving growth and technological advance, the realization is growing of the need to reform the
  structure of the economy if a substantial advance is to be made toward
  economic independence. Economic policy continues to be made,
  however, without due consideration of the economic impact of the
  social condition or of social and industrial organization.
The operation of the economy at or beyond the limits of resources restricts
  flexibility in the use of policy instruments, both of revenue and expenditure.

In order to understand the processes at work, we will take several steps.
First, a brief overview is given of the nature of political-economic relations.
The development of the main economic parameters is described, as well as the
structure of capital ownership and the substantive problems of economic
policy. We then see how the government, particularly the Ministry of
Finance, tries to control the economy, and we give attention to budget planning, the capital market, the Bank of Israel, and government corporations.
The authority of the executive is contrasted with the inadequacies of
parliamentary supervision and decision. The special role and identity of the
Histadrut are analyzed. Following this is a discussion of the beliefs of those
who influenced economic policy during the Labor regime. We then return to
the system as a whole, and attempt to answer the questions which were raised.

Politics and Economics

Nearly everywhere politics and the economy interlock on many planes. This
relationship can be found in national needs and goals, beliefs and ideologies
and institutions related to them, party resources which can maintain or increase power, and the method by which economic demands of individuals,
groups, sectors, trade unions, and social services are met. Local governments
depend on the national government for income and for the location of government facilities, industry, and services in their towns. Citizens, in turn, look to
the local authority for jobs, business permits, and other economic opportunities.

Political parties own or control economic institutions. Economic calculations and bargains reflect internal party struggles as well as relations with
coalition partners on noneconomic issues. While those who manage the
economy are pragmatic about means, an important residue of ideology regarding social goals remains. Whenever an institution or interest has em-

bodied important elements of the Labor Zionist ideology, as in the Histadrut cooperatives or the kibbutz movement, its claims have been strongly reinforced.

Political-economic relations, however, are most often motivated more by considerations of power than of ideology. As would be expected, politics and economics are most intimately connected when beliefs and ideology, economic interest, and political organizations are found together, as they are in the Histadrut enterprises or in settlement movements. In the Histadrut elections, internal appointments and the control of resources are based on party and faction strengths, with the strength ratios and even personal relations determined mainly outside the Histadrut, in the larger party sphere. Agricultural settlement movements, and to a lesser extent, transport cooperatives are party strongholds. Local workers' councils provide extensive organizational support in election campaigns and patronage in the employment of loyal supporters. Despite increasing generality and secularization, the Histadrut remains the organizational base of power for the Labor Alignment. The decline in the Alignment's Histadrut majority and in the party control of local unions increase the importance of the Histadrut as a focus of party concern.

Even the political opposition can be embroiled in the net of dependence, as shown by the Likud when Labor was in office. Economic institutions which could furnish support to opposition parties and to opposition parliamentary figures have felt in the past the need for restraint, in that they are also part of the interdependent government-led economy. Pressure groups in their turn are strongly encouraged by the political leadership to restrain parochial aims in the support of national goals.

In a system of central government control, almost every enterprise or institution at one time or another needs the government. Centralization is such that the ministers themselves are directly involved, particularly the Minister of Finance, who is seen as the leader of the economic system. Yet he is but one of the many points of intersection. Even the decisions of an all-active and powerful minister such as the late Pinhas Sapir * were only the visible part of the iceberg of a far-reaching system of political and economic interaction. By contrast, the Defense Minister and the Prime Minister have been virtually the sole points where defense and political activity interact.

Despite the centrality of politics, ongoing economic relations can be characterized more as dependent than partisan. In a mixed economy strong Histadrut, cooperative, private, and government sectors operate side by side, and firms are often owned jointly by more than one sector. Increasingly, managers are professionally trained in economics, business, and engineering. In practice, however, they devote a large part of their time and effort to seek-

---

* Minister of Commerce and Industry from 1955 to 1963, and Minister of Finance 1963–68 and 1969–74.

ing favorable government-directed actions or conditions on which the economic success of their enterprise depends.

In a continuing situation of peril, national goals have taken priority at the Cabinet level. But certain factors—the extent of government involvement, the small size of the country, the scope of government and cooperative enterprise, the frequent congruence of party and ideology with economic organization and interest, and the dependence of local government on the center—these logistic and structural features lead to a situation in which politicians and civil servants are more involved in ongoing economic activity and interact more with business managers or owners than in most other parliamentary democracies. But there are important and interesting exceptions to the partisan-dependent model: rewards and loyalties are not reserved for partisan supporters; control of the economy is not used mainly to reinforce party strength or sectoral power; and, during the frequent times of distress, national goals take priority over sectoral aims.

Some Questions

This brief overview raises questions about what this kind of political economy does to the nature of politics, about how effectively policy is made, and about possible developments:

Given the congruence of political authority and economic power, what restrains or limits the arbitrary use of this power to reinforce and maintain political resources, to reduce the economic base of the non-Labor sectors, or even the misuse of political authority for personal gain?

How does the dependency system of the economy affect the political system? Do interdependence and lack of "arms length" reduce adversary debate or public and parliamentary opposition? How do the dependency relations affect political culture and behavior?

Does the complex network make government "immobile"—a prisoner of its relations with interested groups and institutions, so that in serious situations it could not act with rigor and dispatch in the national interest even if in the process it would cause inevitable injury to sectoral interests?

Problems of national consensus and simultaneous goals have in the past been solved by growth and large-scale capital imports. When growth slows down, there is no longer "something for everyone." What characteristics has the system shown when external pressures increased, and how does the stress of reduced growth influence its effectiveness?

How effective is the system in the making of policy? Of economic strategy? Can it learn from experience, and can it change? Is the center overloaded?

What changes seem to be occurring in the system of political economy, and in the economy itself, and what effect could these changes have on the overall political system?

While far from being the only questions, these are worth keeping in mind, and we return to them later.

Some Parameters of the Economy[2]

In 1977, local resources were highly inadequate and foreign trade was out of balance, as they had been since the declaration of the state. Inflation was rapid, factors of production were fully employed, particularly labor, and real personal income increased. Service employment was proportionately very large. Growth depended on capital imports, because net saving within the country was negligible. Raw materials were few. The data in the following section show the elusiveness of economic independence despite notable economic growth.

From the beginning, the tasks appeared to require more than the available means. In 1949 the first Finance Minister, Eliezer Kaplan, considered it economically impossible to achieve the goals of the early years at the pace then demanded by Prime Minister Ben Gurion. After a very slow start in 1948–51, however, the economy grew rapidly and almost continuously, which was made possible by capital imports on a grand scale and a high rate of investment proportionate to the total available resources. Per capita gross national product rose to more than $2,100 in 1972, more than three times, in real terms, the 1950 figure, and became comparable to that of industrial countries in Europe.* Rapid growth, defense needs, supplying the services and income transfers of a welfare state, the absorption of immigrants, and the geographic distribution of the population are political goals whose simultaneous pursuit can load the economy beyond its feasible limits. Yet the immediate priorities vary, and stated aims have not always been the same as actions. For example, in the 1950s, the most frequently stated economic goals were "full employment, reduction of the import surplus, and geographic distribution of the population," while in practice, great emphasis was placed on expanding agriculture and the Labor sector, maintaining a high income in agriculture, and "inverting the pyramid," that is, trying to change the occupational mix from trade and services to "productive" labor.[3]

---

* The standard of living, however, is lower than in other countries with a similar GNP per capita because of the high proportion of defense expenditure in Israel (see Figure 5.1). Important elements in early growth were the technical effectiveness of agriculture, the demand (and eventually labor inputs) due to immigration, the rapid lessening of rigid rationing and administrative controls (after their failure in the early 1950s), and the regularization of the execution of monetary policy through the formation of the central Bank of Israel in 1954. From the mid-1950s, industrialization was emphasized.

The dichotomy between goals and objective conditions leads to recurrent economic crises. The paucity of raw materials makes the economy vulnerable to rapid changes in world prices, while the suddenness and intensity of the wars and unpredictable fluctuations of immigration strengthen the arguments of those who think that planning could serve only as background music to ongoing decisions. Also hard to predict are the adverse economic impact of external political and economic acts, such as the French arms embargo following the Six Day War, the attempted Arab boycott of certain international firms that do business in Israel, and the use of Arab oil as a lever to induce anti-Israeli economic acts on the part of otherwise neutral or benevolent countries. Indeed, well before the actual Arab attack in the 1973 war, Israel began to feel the effects of an economic siege.

Figures 5.1, 5.2, and 5.3 show some of the parameters. Figure 5.1 shows the emphasis on both defense and welfare, Figure 5.2, the history of inflation. Figure 5.3 shows the variation in the annual rate of growth. On the eve of the Yom Kippur War, expenses for social purposes had begun to exceed defense outlays. After the war, defense was on a new, much higher level. In 1976 the proportion spent on social services declined, although the level of income transfers was maintained. Beyond its immediate cost, the defense load appears to cause a reduction in the proportion of national income invested, and hence in growth.[4] A further result is a diversion of talent from social and economic tasks into both regular and reserve military service. At the same time, however, defense activity has advanced social integration, vocational training, and technological sophistication.

The postwar pressures resulted in overall dis-saving, a decline in the proportion of GNP which was invested, and increased foreign dependence.* Capital import rose from 18.6 percent of GNP in 1968 to 25.9 percent in 1972 and to about 33 percent of GNP in the postwar years. National saving declined from a peak of 12 percent in 1972 to –1 percent in 1974 and –7 percent in 1975.[5]

Before the 1973 war, one-way transfers of donations, grants-in-aid, and restitution payments were larger than loans, and together with exports covered most of the current deficit. Since 1973, the deficits have grown, and with them the foreign debt. The proportion of loans grew, and in 1975 less than 40 percent of the deficit was covered by one-way transfers or by exports. Table 5.1 shows this trend, which implies growing dependence and political vulnerability. Capital imports have usually covered the investment-saving gap. Thus in 1970 saving was 2.7 percent of GNP, investment 28.9 percent,

* The share of the United States government in long-term capital imports rose from 8.2 percent in 1969 to 35.1 percent in 1974 and 57 percent in 1975. From 1948 to 1970 the *total* of capital inflow from United States government sources was about 2 billion dollars, mainly as loans which were repaid. Following the 1973 war, U.S. aid in most years approached this sum, only partly in the form of loans.

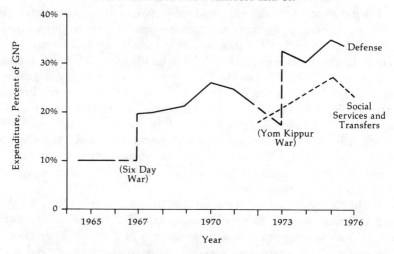

FIGURE 5.1   Government Expenditure, as a Percent of GNP, on Social Services and Transfers and on Defense

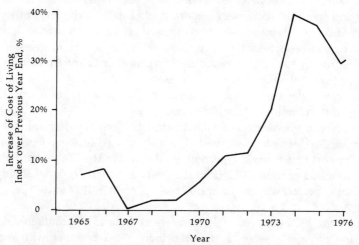

FIGURE 5.2   Annual Rates of Inflation

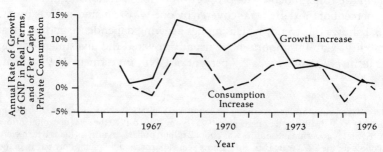

FIGURE 5.3   Growth in Production and Consumption

TABLE 5.1.   Balance of Payments and Foreign Debt[6] (Millions of Dollars)

Year	Current Deficit	Long-Term Capital Import	Of This, Transfers	Foreign Debt
1970	−1,234	1,231	649	3,598
1972	−1,114	1,795	1,059	5,678
1974	−3,397	2,356	1,718	8,223
1976	−3,316	3,284	2,224	12,120
1977	−2,560	2,598	2,005	13,634

and capital import 27.1 percent. More domestic saving was needed to permit growth to narrow the export-import gap.

As a result of the large and growing foreign and domestic debt, interest and debt repayment were 25 percent of the proposed 1977 budget—one-third of it in foreign currency.

An important trend in the first half of the 1970s was the growth in the exports of the higher-technology industries, agriculture, and defense, and the decline of the more traditional branches.[7] Between 1971 and 1975, total industry exports grew by 26 percent, while exports of technologically advanced industries and of defense each advanced almost 80 percent, as did agricultural products. Table 5.2 shows the composition of exports.

TABLE 5.2.   Share of Products in Total Agricultual and Industrial Exports, 1975[8]

Product	Percent of Commodity Exports
Citrus	9.6
Other agriculture	5.5
Minerals	4.6
Food, textiles, clothing, leather, plastics, rubber products	18.0
Polished diamonds (net of import cost)	29.7
Higher-technology products (chemicals, machinery, electronics, metalworking)	20.8

The proportion of workers in services is high and increasing. Indeed, it has been growing since the days of the Yishuv, and as a percent of total employment is comparable to that in the United States or Sweden. That in agriculture, while low (it declined from 17.6 percent in 1955 to 6.2 percent in 1977), provides nearly two-thirds of food needs and 15 percent of all commodity exports.[9] Unemployment was less than 5 percent in 1971–76, and in 1975, 65,000 Arabs from the West Bank and Gaza commuted to work in Israel. In this period, industry employed about 24 percent of the work force, while the proportion in public and community services rose from 24 percent in 1970 to 27.1 percent in 1975. It is an urban, industrialized, and service economy, in which ominously high service employment has been made possible only because of capital imports.

Economic Organization

Table 5.3 shows the division of ownership of economic organizations among the government, the Labor sector, and private industry. Many enterprises are jointly owned by one or more sectors or by more than one holding company. Each of the large banks is heavily involved in portfolio or direct investment, engaging in commercial and investment banking and securities trading. In 1972 the three largest banks together had more than 84 percent of foreign-currency deposits and 73 percent of public deposits. As elsewhere, ownership in itself is not necessary or sufficient for control, as the subsequent discussion of government corporations in Israel will show. There are many interlocking directorates, although only a thorough study could reveal them all and assess their implications. In most markets, three to ten firms together have a majority of sales.*

Government-owned industry consists mainly of mining, oil, heavy chemicals, power, transportation, and defense enterprises. In 1970 it represented 12 percent of national industrial production, three-quarters of mining, quarries, and oil, virtually all of water distribution and electricity, and only 2 percent of building construction, although in many years the government has financed or contracted for half of all new housing. As a consumer and employer, the government dominates the private sector, with public consumption or direct investment at almost half of the national product. Through its control and operation of the capital market, the govern-

---

* Industrial organization has had little attention from economists in Israel. For some analyses of concentration, consumer legislation, and the operation of the Cartel Law, see Lionel Kestenbaum, "Israel's Restrictive Trade Practices Law: Anti-trust Misadventures in a Small Developing Country," *Israel Law Review*, 8, 1973, 411. Also "Trade Practices Bill: Innovations and Deficiencies in Fair Competition and Consumer Protection," *Tel Aviv U. Law Review*, 3, 1974, 849; Yair Aharoni, *Concentration, Ownership Groups, and Ownership Interrelations in Israel: 1949–66*, Jerusalem, Falk Institute for Economic Research, 1970.

ment can direct the use of 80 percent of financial resources. Of commercial bank credit, about one-half is lent at the banks' own discretion and at market rates, and the other half is loans directed by the government. These are usually at subsidized interest. The government borrows by issuing securities which are linked to the cost of living or the dollar, and lends mainly in unlinked loans.

The Histadrut sector and the government and publicly owned services each employ close to one-quarter of the work force. The Histadrut share includes mainly members of cooperatives of various kinds, comprising kibbutzim, *moshavim*, and members of production or service cooperatives, who are, in essence, self-employed. In the Histadrut-owned firms where the Histadrut is an employer in the usual sense, the workers total only 4 percent of national employment. Government employees include national civil servants (some 7 percent of those employed) teachers, workers in local government and those in many medical and social services, and employees of government corporations.

Small-scale service functions, such as home repair or retail trade, are dispersed, while larger-scale services, such as power, bus transportation and agricultural marketing, civil industrial production, and defense industry, are highly concentrated. Agricultural production, as will be shown, is controlled through what are, in effect, government-led producer cartels. New industries are usually established by existing groups or at least jointly with them. There are thus, broadly, two types of economy which operate in parallel.

Rapid Growth Following Early Austerity

The development of the economy in the state began with little industry and inadequate food production. Moreover, borders were sealed, and Israel was unable to trade for industrial products or food with its surrounding neighbors. From the beginning, there was a large and growing import surplus, a chronic shortage of housing, and high defense expenditure. Stringent administrative controls were applied to imports, credit, and currency. Many foodstuffs, raw materials, and other goods were rationed. By 1951 it was clear that administrative measures could not stand against the pent-up economic and social forces. The election to the Second Knesset that year—the only one in which economic policy was the main issue—brought a swing to the right. The General Zionists, a party then largely representing business and private agriculture, received less than 6 percent of the vote for the First Knesset, but nearly 17 percent in the elections for the Second. Many administrative controls were abandoned or modified during the period, and extreme modes of administrative control have never been tried again.

Growth was greater in the first decade than it has been since then, averaging a compounded annual increase in GNP of 11.4 percent between 1950 and

TABLE 5.3. The Patterns of Ownership

Type of Enterprise	Government	Histadrut	Private	Comments
Major Banks	Bank of Israel (Central Bank)	Poalim (Worker's Bank, one of "Big Three")	Discount, Bank Leumi*	Government recently fostered mergers to create a fourth large, privately owned bank (First International)
Financial institutions (mainly for investment purposes)	Mortgage, shipping, agriculture, industry, development bank	- - - - -	- - - - -	Little or no investment banking; see section on the capital market
Provident and pension funds	National Insurance Institute	Workers' pension funds Insurance	Bank-managed provident funds Insurance Firms	Invest mainly in government-approved securities
Transportation Services	Air, rail, ports	Some shipping, Bus companies are Histadrut-affiliated coops Part owners in Zim firm	Shipping Internal and charter air lines	
Utilities and communications	Electric Corporation, post and telegraph	- - - - -	- - - - -	

	Government	Histadrut	Private	
Heavy industry	Mining, quarrying, heavy chemicals and fertilizer, petroleum and petrochemicals	Most heavy metalworking	Some	Histadrut reported about 17% of all industrial production in 1972, and plans to emphasize industrial growth
Light industry	- - - - -	Extensive kibbutz industry and in Koor Industries	Largely private	Recent growth of private and Histadrut share in electronics
Defense industries	Major, prime contracting, Aircraft industry, electronics, weapons	Part owner in electronics and other firms working for defense	Part or whole owners in electronics and metal working firms	
Housing and contracting	Ministry of housing controls subsidiary government companies	Shikun Ovdim, large housing builder, and Solel Boneh, largest contractor	Extensive private contracting and building	Histadrut (Hevrat Ovdim) 22.4% of output (26.5% of employment) in construction in 1972
Agriculture	Hula Authority, some others (a minor factor altogether)	Kibbutzim, Moshavim**	Citrus, some other branches Arab and Druze agriculture	Kibbutz and moshav— over 72% of agricultural product in 1972
Daily press	- - - - -	Davar, second largest morning daily; most foreign-language papers are Labor Party-controlled, except the Jerusalem Post.	Principal circulation is private (one morning, two afternoon papers); Mapam, religious parties have dailies	
Radio and Television	Broadcast Authority (Government monopoly)			

* A majority of the voting shares of Bank Leumi are held, indirectly, by the Zionist Organization.
** Moshavim are Histadrut affiliated, and have many cooperative aspects, but moshav farmers are to a great extent private farmers. (See the later section on agriculture.)

1958. The early need to house and employ great numbers of immigrants imposed a huge economic burden for social payments and emergency work provisions, followed by the expansion of agriculture and the housing and infrastructure costs of new development towns away from the Tel Aviv area. Agriculture benefited from large investments in water-resource development (more than 90 percent of total national water resources are used), and growing capital intensity increased productivity and maintained a high agricultural income. By the mid 1950s, industrialization was recognized as the way to further growth and employment. From this period on the government became the "banker" and the prime mover of industrialization, which was initially directed to import substitution and to providing work, however unskilled, as in textiles.

The New Economic Policy of 1962 and the Recession of 1966–67

Capital influx of reparations payments, U.S. grants-in-aid, contributions, and the sale of Israel bonds combined with deficit financing to create growth, excess demand, and inflation. A complex system of subsidies and incentives for export developed, with many concurrent official rates of exchange. Steeply increasing import surpluses, lower dollar reserves, and the administrative impasse of multiple rates and regulations led to a decision to devaluate from 1.80 to 3.0 lire to the dollar, beginning what was called the "new economic policy" of February 1962.

Export subsidies and high protective tariffs were continued, and a capital gains tax intended to curb land speculation was imposed. After the devaluation, the Histadrut, responding to the parties left of center, led a successful fight which neutralized much of the effect of devaluation. The impact of the devaluation and the new policies was largely negated by nonenforcement of the previously contracted linkages of mortgages to the exchange rate, by sharply increased conversion of foreign-currency balances, especially personal reparations, and by the linkage of wages to the cost-of-living index. It was a devaluation without deflationary measures, followed in 1965 by deflation without devaluation.

The absence of a firm follow-through in monetary and fiscal policy and in government wage agreements accentuated postdevaluation inflation. From 1963, the balance of payments continued to deteriorate. While one-way transfers and loans still more than covered the deficit, their sharp decline was imminent. West German national reparations were scheduled to end,* Israel bond sales declined from 33 million dollars in 1965 to 11 million in 1966, and foreign investment from 165 million dollars in 1964 to 113 million in 1965.

* The payments to individuals still continue.

At the same time, large development projects, such as the giant Galilee-to-Negev water carrier and the Dead Sea Works extensions, neared completion. A building boom peaked in 1963–64 and immigration fell from 55,000 in 1964 to 31,000 in 1965. The population growth rate slowed from about 4, to 3 percent in 1965 and 2.25 percent in 1966.

Despite portents of this decreasing demand, in 1964 the government decided to slow down the economy in an attempt to restrain inflation and reduce the import deficit. In the budget speech of January 1964, Finance Minister Sapir announced a policy of contraction. Building mortgages and material imports were to be restricted, and the development budget, capital imports, and the growth in the quantity of money were to be reduced. While demand fell, wages rose. For example, a large-scale attempt at a comprehensive "rational" job analysis as a basis for government wages resulted in government salary increases across the board much larger than those recommended—a rise of close to 30 percent prior to the 1965 parliamentary and local elections.

By 1966, recession was felt severely in building decline and in bankruptcies and unemployment. The sharpness of the downturn caught the government unprepared. Deficit financing began, and new development projects were eagerly sought, but were not found waiting in the files ready for action.

The recession left a deep mark, particularly in the development towns and among the unskilled workers, who were generally recent immigrants and whose unemployment rate was much higher than the national average of 7.4 percent in 1966 and 10.4 percent in 1967. At the time, the Cabinet did not realize or acknowledge the seriousness of the recession. Government spokesmen had continued to predict a rise of 6 to 7 percent in the GNP in 1966; in fact, it declined 1 percent per capita and gross investment declined 18 percent in 1966 over the previous year (see Figure 5.3).

These events were to have a long-term impact on the policy views of Pinhas Sapir, his advisers, and Labor Alignment leaders in general. Their lesson was that while the government could readily turn the economy downward, it could not decide how far and fast this trend would go. Second, it was learned that the general tools available to stimulate recovery are too crude to prevent the onus of a slowdown from falling on the disadvantaged. In May 1967, public investment and renewed immigration were only just beginning to promise improvement when the Egyptian armies came to the Sinai border, and the tense weeks before the Six Day War began.

Expansion and Sudden War—1967–73

After the 1967 war, the economy showed the impact of defense expenditures, the French arms embargo, Russian immigration, and growing demands for an attack on social inequality (see Chapter 6). Economic policy was expansionist, and deficit financing and capital imports were used to try to meet the needs. The imbalance of payments grew, the deficit on current account reaching 1.1 billion dollars in 1972. The results were soaring demand, overfull employment, and, eventually, sharp inflation. Indeed, the post-1967 period shows the importance of exogenous forces and resources, unanticipated social problems associated with rapid growth, and the results of seeking conflicting goals simultaneously.

After the 1967 war the rate of defense spending doubled to replace lost equipment and to try to keep pace with the flow of Russian arms to Arab countries. The Israeli commitment to armor, air power, and associated advanced technologies had begun earlier in earnest. From 1968 on, large sums went to fortifications and roads along the Suez Canal and to the costs of the war of attrition, from March 1969 through August 1970, in which heavy Egyptian bombardment of the Suez forces by more than 1,000 artillery pieces was countered with artillery and air attacks. In addition to huge foreign currency outlays, domestic defense production was intensified by the total embargo placed by France from 1969.*

By 1969, increased immigration, defense, and a soaring postwar mood had led to full employment, but the visible rise in the living standard since 1967 was clearly not distributed equally. The wage demands of the well-paid skilled workers in essential services were added to the protest movements of the strongly disadvantaged and newly married couples who needed housing. Not merely the result of protest, the ensuing policy changes, which emphasized expenditure on social needs, were a sharp reaction to the realization of the divergence of reality from the ideals of equality, which growth alone could not close.**

Before the 1973 war, the import surplus was covered by exports plus growing capital inflow. Its use, however, was not "under control," and much of the

---

* Defense industries designed and produced in depth advanced weapons systems, such as the Gabriel sea-to-sea missile and advanced air-to-air missiles. After the Yom Kippur War, Israel military exports became substantial, almost doubling between 1972 and 1976. A massive inflow of public funds was secured and guided by the entrepreneurial approach of Shimon Peres, as Undersecretary of Defense, and Moshe Kashti, director-general, who gave priority to growth and technical achievement over profit-and-loss calculations. The political strength of Ben Gurion and Eshkol as ministers had, over many years, achieved the needed resources for the defense system and kept it relatively immune from parliamentary or public intervention. It was an internal, closed, government-owned system, in which were concentrated most of the country's successful applications of highly sophisticated technologies. These achievements potentially could change the overall industrial-development strategy. Yet, as in other countries, the way to adequate commercial and export use of these unique capabilities is difficult to find.[10]

** In 1972, more of the budget for the first time went for social purposes than for defense, which was formerly an "autonomous" decision, with the rest of the budget as a "residue." From 1970 until the 1973 war, defense began to have to compete for resources. The 1973 budget, as it was proposed before the war, showed a small decrease in defense, a moderate increase in expenditure for economic development, and a 26 percent increase for social services. Even after the 1973 war, emphasis on housing, education, and health continued and marked the postwar budget of 1974. (See Figure 5.1.)

continued rapid growth in resources began to go into consumption or building and land speculation. In the period immediately preceding the 1973 war, nothing was done which curtailed demand or cost increases effectively, although exports were encouraged by increased premiums and lower interest rates and by a 20 percent devaluation, from 3.5 to 4.2 lire to the dollar in 1971.

The Postwar Economy

The sudden 1973 war put all previous considerations aside. The planned defense budget for 1973–74 had been a little over 6 billion lire. In the end it was 16.6 billion. Although the war's cost was hard to count, in March 1974 Pinhas Sapir put it at 7 billion dollars, or close to one year's GNP. The lost defense equipment was replaced with more modern arms, so that defense budgets remained at the new high level. Large income transfers were maintained, and public service overheads even increased. (See Figure 5.1 and Table 5.1).

In the year following the war, the economy regained momentum. A nearly catastrophic decline in foreign currency reserves was narrowly averted by devaluation from 4.2 to 6 lire to the dollar and by fiscal measures intended to cool the economy. These included increases of the indirect and capital gains taxes, voluntary and compulsory loans, and payroll taxes and loans. Subsidies of essential commodities were reduced, and the prices of government-controlled or regulated services, such as public transport and communication, fuel, water, and electricity, were raised.

While disaster was avoided, Israel paid a price. Inflation averaged almost 40 percent a year from 1973 to 1976, compared with 10 percent or less in most industrialized countries. Growth virtually stopped, and foreign investment dropped. Despite partial linkage of wages to the cost of living, employee frustration increased, and extensive labor unrest in 1976 and 1977 was manifested in slowdowns or "sanctions" in many of the essential public services. Government acquiescence to demands increased the unrest, which spread to other groups, enlarged the budget deficit, and further stimulated inflation. It was as though the problems of earlier days were seen through a magnifying glass—the same tendencies and general phenomena, but looming much larger, with quantitative changes which meant major qualitative differences.

There were many causes of the inflation besides the breakdown of wage-policy and the annual budget deficits.* World commodity prices rose, stabilizing only in 1976. Among the major imports, the price of oil rose four times and that of grains, two to three times. The large devaluation of 1974 was followed by many smaller ones, and by the fall of 1977, the exchange rate was

---

* In 1975, the deficit was more than 10 billion lire. In real terms, it trebled from 1972 to 1974. Some of the problems of budget legislation and control are discussed in the subsequent section on the budgetary process.

more than 10.30 lire to the dollar. The effects of indirect taxes, subsidy decreases, higher service charges, and wage linkage were abetted by continued public and private consumption demand. Public expenditure was partly financed by increased credits, while much private consumption came from savings, in anticipation of further devaluation or inflation. One of the more basic causes of inflation was seen in the misallocation of human resources to employment in public and commercial service overhead tasks, rather than in production and distribution.*

Severe inflation reduced industrial investment incentives, distorted calculations of management efficiency, and reduced export competitiveness. It hurt middle-income wage earners and pensioners, whose incomes were then only partly linked to the cost of living index, as compared with the almost whole linkage of government securities. It became increasingly difficult, politically, to maintain the level of educational and social services when they had to compete with outlays for transfer payments to maintain the incomes of the most disadvantaged. At the same time, the burden inflation imposed on the middle-income wage earners decreased public willingness to sacrifice.**

Several basic policy measures were introduced during this period. In the 1975 reform of income tax law,[11] the marginal rates of personal income tax were reduced, beginning at 25 percent and reaching a maximum of 60 percent. Provision was made for automatic revision of tax brackets with changes in the cost-of-living index. Calculations were made simpler and generally applicable, and most of a complex list of perquisites, formerly tax-exempt, were eliminated. The new plan was intended to provide incentives for additional work and earning and to encourage more honest tax reporting. It was to be accompanied by intensified tax collection efforts through requiring full accounting, and using stronger investigation procedures. By 1977, however, progress in these directions was disappointing.

A second change was the *a priori* authorization of "creeping devaluations" of up to 2 percent in any thirty-day interval, to be decided ad hoc by a Cabinet subcommittee. In 1976, an added-value tax of 8 percent was introduced. Its administrative success was impaired by the primitive bookkeeping arrangements of many small businesses. Cost-of-living wage increments were linked to 70 percent of the growth of the cost-of-living index, and became taxable. At the same time, the linkage of new government bond issues was reduced, first to 90 percent and then to 80 percent of the index.

Not accompanied by a reduction in public consumption or by balanced budgets, the reforms did not stem inflation. At the same time, the administrative problems of deepening tax collection were not overcome. Neither the fixed nor the human capital of the country was fully employed.

---

* See the discussion of the economy in 1975, in the Bank of Israel *1975 Annual Report.*

** In the 1977–81 Knesset, inflation reached more than 100 percent per annum. Wages, transfer payments, and tax brackets were eventually almost wholly linked, ameliorating the burden on individuals; yet adversely affecting the economy and public and private management.

Hidden unemployment and a decrease in the work devoted to production (and in its rewards) in proportion to that in the services reduced the ability to export and to reduce inflation.

One proposed solution was simply for the government to show determination in carrying out the declared policies, reducing private and public consumption to levels which resources permitted, and shifting resources, via incentives and changes in exchange rates, to more production for export. Critics of these policies, beyond disappointment with their half-hearted execution, questioned whether an economy stagnant in growth and investment would be able to shift its resources and change its structure, or whether a more drastic reorganization of the economy might not be needed to restore initiative and effectiveness. The sections which follow show, *inter alia*, the complexities of the economic organization which make such changes difficult—but not impossible.

Organization for Economic Policy

The formal organization of the government for economic policy is shown in Figure 5.4. A widely held perception of the informal relations is shown in Figure 5.5. Although it may be somewhat exaggerated, the "Sun King" is a reasonable approximation of Pinhas Sapir's role at the peak of his authority, from about 1969 to 1973. From then on, the role of the Minister of Finance diminished. In 1974, Itzchak Rabin became Prime Minister and Sapir was followed as Minister of Finance by Yehoshua Rabinowitz, who had just been defeated for reelection as Mayor of Tel Aviv. For twenty years, Finance Ministers Eshkol and later Sapir had been powerful and independent. Indeed, the government of that period has been described as a dual presidential system[12] in which the Prime Minister led in defense and foreign affairs, leaving the Finance Minister with almost complete autonomy in economic policy. In the spring of 1977, during an economic crisis and in an atmosphere of interregnum, much seemed to have changed, yet the basic modes and structure of the political economy still reflected the lengthening shadows of the ways of leadership of Sapir and of Eshkol before him. It will require some detail to understand the processes and possible directions of change. We start with the institutional arrangements and the foci of formal decision.

As in all spheres, the Cabinet has the ongoing authority. It approves proposed budget laws and all other economic legislation before it goes to the Knesset, all significant changes in fiscal and monetary policy, appointments to senior economic roles, such as the directors of ministries, the Governor of the Bank of Israel, or the Director of the Land Administration, and even such specific actions as the lease or sale of tracts of public land or the formation of government corporations or the sale of their shares to the public. In practice, the Cabinet's *Committee of Economic Ministers*, chaired by the Minister of Finance, makes most of the specific decisions.

FIGURE 5.4 Formal Organization—Economic Policy and Management, 1973-77

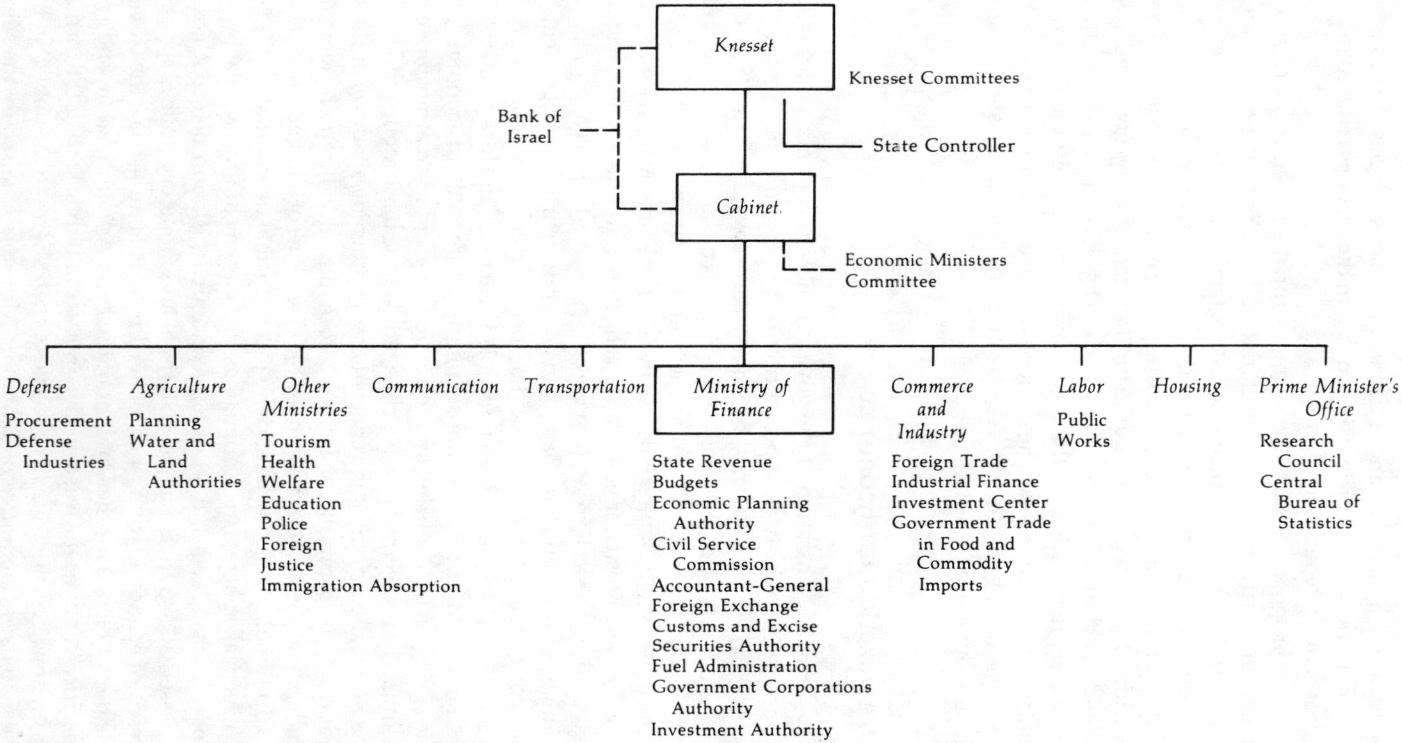

Knesset
Knesset Committees
State Controller

Cabinet
Economic Ministers Committee

Bank of Israel

Ministry of Finance

State Revenue
Budgets
Economic Planning Authority
Civil Service Commission
Accountant-General
Foreign Exchange
Customs and Excise
Securities Authority
Fuel Administration
Government Corporations Authority
Investment Authority

Defense
Procurement
Defense Industries

Agriculture
Planning
Water and Land Authorities

Other Ministries
Tourism
Health
Welfare
Education
Police
Foreign
Justice
Immigration Absorption

Communication

Transportation

Commerce and Industry
Foreign Trade
Industrial Finance
Investment Center
Government Trade in Food and Commodity Imports

Labor
Public Works

Housing

Prime Minister's Office
Research Council
Central Bureau of Statistics

FIGURE 5.5   "Le Roi Soleil"—Pinhas Sapir Circa 1972

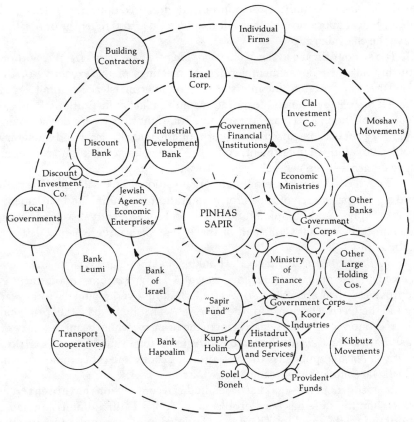

The *Knesset* votes appropriations, budgets, and fiscal measures, receives the report of the State Controller, and a report from the governor of the Bank when the rate of increase of the money in circulation exceeds a given amount. As in the British Parliament, the Knesset vote is the last of several stages in the legislative process.

Specific financial measures and the budget are the province of the *Knesset Finance Committee*, which handles the annual budget law and supplementary budgets during enactment, and is empowered to transfer funds during the year from one budget heading to another. In over 100 kinds of executive economic actions, such as government guarantees of corporate loans, the committee's approval is needed. After the Foreign Affairs and Defense Committee, membership in the Finance Committee is the most sought after.*

The *Knesset Economic Committee* works on legislation concerning nearly all economic activities, such as transportation, commerce, and agriculture,

* The Finance Committee has been compared to a "honey bottle"—full of buzzing bees. The entrance is choked with traffic. Those outside want to get in, while some inside are trying to get out, feeling that the work and time required far exceed the effectiveness of the members.

and general economic policy and planning. It lacks the operational authority of the Finance Committee for appropriation or taxation, and is therefore junior to it. Labor normally has felt that it could afford to let the opposition have the chairmanship.

The senior officials in the *Ministry of Finance* have very effective authority through their departmental roles, at meetings of the executive of the ministry, as advisers to the minister, and on interministerial committees or the boards of government corporations and financial institutions. The executives of the ministry are at the center of authority, where decisions are made or proposed in close to final form on the budget, fiscal and monetary policy, government investment, control of the capital market, and economic development—from general strategy to specific projects.

The *Jewish Agency* * is the main organizational link with the Diaspora and a principal source of funds for immigration and initial land settlement. Pinhas Sapir was a champion fund raiser, and consequently it seemed fitting for him to be elected Chairman of the Agency Executive when he left the Cabinet in 1974.

The *Bank of Israel* manages the banking and monetary system "in accordance with the policies of the government." The governor's appointment is approved by the Cabinet for a five-year term, thus overlapping the four-year period between elections to the Knesset. The bank has the principal macroeconomic research department in the country, while the main source of basic data is the *Central Bureau of Statistics* in the Prime Minister's Office, which, *inter alia*, publishes the cost-of-living index and other indicators on which wage and other agreements are based.

Independent policy-making or semijudicial commissions have been few in Israel, and their use has been problematic. A Bus Tariff Commission had a short and ineffective life. There is a Cartel Commission and a Consumer's Protection Commission and well-established local, regional, and national committees for land-use regulation. There are a host of interministerial committees of varying life span and authority, but these are responsible to political leaders,** and the political nature of the economy has effectively deterred the introduction of even ostensibly nonpolitical independent regulatory agencies that would diminish feudal ministerial authority.

Central Control: The Role of the Minister

In practice, economic policy is more centrally controlled than the organization implies, as indicated by the following list showing the ways in which the

* See Appendix F. Nongovernmental, the Agency is the principal operating arm of the Zionist Organization.

** For example, the classification of development towns, expressing the towns' "ability to pay" and deciding the proportion of local outlay borne by the central government, is decided by a committee headed by the Minister of Commerce and Industry.

government influences the economy. To use these means effectively, the Finance Minister has needed the backing of his colleagues in the Cabinet, of the Labor Party, and of a widespread clientele, much of which is nonpartisan. These are constituencies to be nursed assiduously and well, if programs are to be approved without serious clashes.

The Finance Minister depends, of course, on other Cabinet ministers, as they do on him. Each minister usually has political backing of his own, and the relatively independent spheres of influence which are allocated when coalitions are formed are able to redress to some extent the imbalance of power which favors the Minister of Finance. In this way, the semifeudal allocation to parties or factions of powers and prerogatives influences economic decisions and demarcates the feasible limits of intervention by the central authority.

Other practical limits are inherent in the wide scope of Ministry of Finance management. An illustration of this is the malaise of the supervision of government corporations, discussed later. As resources came to be more centrally controlled, the mutual interdependence grows—of borrower and lender, client and patron, follower and leader.

The organization and powers of the Ministry of Finance make it the focus of authority because of:

The role of the minister—in party affairs, the Cabinet, and the Economic Minister's Committee

The budget and the size and scope of government investment and consumption

The ministry's use of the civil service and the government's role as employer

Foreign-currency control

Control of cash flow by the Accountant-General and the State Revenue Administration

The ministry's determination of many factor costs—fuel, electricity, water, land, communications

Tax, customs, and excise management

Representatives on interdepartmental committees who accept the Finance view and bring back to the minister and the directors the opinions and situations in the other ministries

Representation on boards of directors, guidance of government financial institutions and of government corporations

Control and operation of the capital market

The most important source of authority for central direction and control, however, lies in the congruence of political and economic power. Sapir, and Eshkol before him, had strong support from the party machinery and indeed came to direct it. Particularly in Sapir's time, party support reinforced the formal authority of elected office, the statutory control of investment resources, and the detailed and improvisatory mode of intervention. These, together with the support of those he helped or could help in the future, created an incomparable combination of political, bureaucratic, and economic resources. The resulting dependency was based as much on a general "establishment" relation as on one directly of party.

In addition to party backing and government machinery, Sapir controlled overseas funds—from large-scale government loans to the more than 200 million lire of a "Sapir Fund," donations which he personally raised from Israeli industry and foreign donors, many of whom had dealings with him, as well, in the role of investors. These funds he directed to institutions or municipalities, reinforcing his interdependence with them. He was personally directly involved in the Gush, the machine of the former Mapai faction of the Labor Party. To those helped or hoping to be helped could be added the courtiers, drawn to the anterooms of power.*

These varied strands of power did not weave themselves. Indefatigable application and constant vigilance were needed to determine the membership representation of the Labor Party Central Committee, to make frequent and courteous appearances before the Knesset Finance Committee (in which he overwhelmed its members with mountains of data, read by the hour from briefs prepared in the ministry, which the committee could have little hope of checking or digesting), and to dominate the weekly meetings of the Economic Ministers Committee.

An important motive force in central government direction has been the entrepreneurial role concept shared by ministers and civil servants alike. Sapir, however, encouraged the entrepreneurship of others, as "the grand investment banker" of the country. He needed these clients to provide many of the ideas and to carry them out; and in his zeal to back enterprise with public funds, many entrepreneurs were helped to wealth, which came not always as the just deserts of the effectiveness of their enterprises. The rationale was to sow widely in the hope of success.**

---

* Brought to the Cabinet by Levi Eshkol in 1955 with a mandate to push industrialization as Minister of Commerce and Industry, Sapir moved to Finance when Eshkol became Prime Minister in 1963. In 1968–69, he was Secretary-General of the Labor Party, an experience which strengthened his hold on the machine and on nominations of candidates for the Knesset and party institutions, but also showed him at first hand the nature of politics in the development towns and other party branches. He practiced the mode of extreme personal intervention with extraordinary energy, from early morning until late at night, in the greatest detail and in literally thousands of brief, face-to-face encounters, as virtually anyone responsible for an economic enterprise of any size—industrialists, mayors, bankers, investors—came to his office or to his modest home in Kfar Saba, and as town after town, seeing him as a benefactor, conferred honorary citizenship upon him.

** The complex calculus of action was supported by Sapir's memory and a "little black book," and made possible by the dependence of business for its profitability on the government, through the facilitation of land use, water, low-cost credit, capital, and fast write-offs and tax relief under the law to encourage investment. Hundreds of "deals" (in which no one has questioned his personal integrity) created the culture of interdependence and bargaining, of personal microintervention and improvisation, which marked the relations of the government and the economy, extending even to influence over top-management appointments in private firms which had no government

In this atmosphere of growth, initiative, and intervention, it is not surprising that there was often little differentiation between party needs and the appropriate use of public funds and prerogatives. Within such a system, for a very few weaker individuals it was a small step from use of public resources or possible corruption for the sake of a party, to individual gain. Indeed, many of the very complicated arrangements were possible because of the intermeshing of so many elements of the economy, and the relation to it of political parties and their economic and financial institutions. Favors or help on one project could be rewarded through benefits on an entirely different front. Thus the support of another party for a Labor government measure could be traded for the award of economic support or rights to an institution related to the party or some of its followers; or the loss to investors on one project could be compensated by the conditions which provided profits from another.*

Continuity and Change: After the Yom Kippur War

In retrospect, Sapir's time is seen as an age of enterprise and entrepreneurs in which the administration's forte was its ability to generate capital investment, economic activity, and hope. Its weaknesses lay in the lack of strategy for movement, in the medium and long term, toward economic independence; in not encouraging the use of economic analysis; and in the dependence, politicization, and interventionist character of the system which was created. The adverse conditions that followed and the changes in leadership led to a period in which the civil servants and investment managers became "prudent men," lacking the confidence, the backing, or the authority needed either to make the economy move or to effectively channel or restrict activities. Nonetheless, the basic structure, despite some attempt at reforms, showed more continuity than change.

While the government financial system had taken form under the long

---

ownership. Sapir's reaction to his public image was to say, "I just work here. All day they come and ask you for things. I am the address for everything. I don't run everything. For example, I need the three big banks more than they need me." Three days before the postwar 1973 elections, while Sapir was under strong opposition attack for the state of the economy, full-page ads appeared in his support, signed by many industrialists and financiers from all parties, saying, "Few in the country have done more than Pinhas Sapir to advance the Israel economy. . . . It is hard to imagine the economy, which now withstood the tests of the War and the Arab boycott, without the contributions of Sapir . . . any economy would be blessed with his initiative and deeds."

*An example of a simple arrangement is one made with the diamond cutters. After the 1973 war, they had subscribed to 50 million lire of government bonds. The branch then came upon harder times and were granted as extension of five years in which to file the declaration of capital assets required by the Internal Revenue Department. Other arrangements, by contrast, have had a complexity often defying description.

reign of Eshkol and Sapir, in the short run its complex relations did not depend on personalities alone. When Yehoshua Rabinowitz was Minister of Finance, 1974–77, it was the adverse environment of the economy and the weaker domestic political authority of the Rabin Cabinet rather than Rabinowitz's personal style which revealed the strains in the economic order. In the deepening crisis, the need for change became apparent.

In the 1970s, the worsening economic situation did not allow for maneuvers in the old style, while it demanded overall changes in direction and method. A number of factors prohibited the kind of political and economic flexibility enjoyed by Sapir. The growing influx of foreign funds arrived in the form of official government aid or loans, allowing less discretion in their use than formerly, when donations or grants predominated. Resources available for investment were slashed by world commodity price rises, mammoth defense budgets, and the built-in requirements for income transfer payments and debt servicing. As the resources available for investment declined, growth paused.

The Minister of Finance and the Cabinet enjoyed far less political support than their predecessors. The Labor Party political machine, the Gush, was largely in eclipse, and Rabinowitz, once one of its leaders, was no longer able to gain broad support within the party. In addition, Labor Party leaders in the Histadrut became increasingly fearful of losing their majority position to opposition parties. Feeling the decline in the legitimacy of the central Histadrut leadership, they became less eager, or perhaps even able, to support reductions in government spending or to support wage-restraint policies against local union demands. The exposure of several cases of corruption connected with the Histadrut economic enterprises and government-linked corporations also inhibited initiative and the ability to make hard decisions.

It was an impasse both of means and of confidence. Although positive measures were taken which reflect Rabinowitz's perception of the need for change, he lacked the political support and determination to carry his policies through. As a result, the policies were not effective. The underlying system remained untouched and simply shifted into low gear.

Made with the help of economists outside the government, policy changes of this period included income tax reform, a value-added tax, and a greater degree of linkage of wage supplements. These, however, did not attack the larger questions of strategy or the structure of the economy. Discussion of economic analysis and macroeconomic parameters became more common and accepted, despite the fact that the government continued to attempt to direct microeconomic decisions as before. For example, civil servants continued to "ask the minister," although the longer time period required by the new minister, Rabinowitz, to make a decision gave an impression of vacillation in making unpopular decisions. The civil service, in its operations, took on a grayer hue. The economic centers which had developed considerable powers and resources of their own in the era of Sapir remained important,* and the capital-market arrangements which favored the Histadrut enterprises endured. In a time of liquidity pressure, due to inflation and of the drying up of investment funds and some sources of government procurement, many firms felt that they needed the government more than before. The principal change was the atmosphere, from an ambition for growth to a concern for survival, and from a willingness to take risks (since the minister would stand behind you if failure threatened) to a mood of hesitation and inaction, fearing that if trouble came, you would be on your own. The basic system continued, without either the leadership of Sapir or the means which had been at his disposal.

The Budget[13]

Each June or July, the Ministry of Finance begins to draft the budget for the fiscal year which starts the next April; by contrast, the lead time in the United States is nearly eighteen months. An advantage of the short lead time is that proposals are relatively close to current events and needs. As a result, however, the budget often gets to the Knesset too late to be passed before the start of the fiscal year, requiring voting on an interim budget. Unforeseen developments usually combine with inadequate contingency planning to make it necessary to pass additional budgets during the course of the year.**

Until 1973, each ministry built a line-by-line case, outlining its financial requirements, usually with no *a priori* departmental ceiling. While this practice allowed full scope for new ideas, it created broad gaps between available resources and demands and expectations. Such a system proves particularly frustrating during periods of inflation, when considerations of restraint take priority over those of the possible return on investment. Also, line-by-line examination can lead to tactical exaggeration of demands and to the embroilment of the Ministry of Finance, not very reluctantly, in myriad details including a host of detailed compromises. In 1973, a system of *a priori* block allocations to departments was introduced in the hope of reducing central intervention in detail, narrowing the gaps between proposals and reality, and reducing horse trading, although in the Israeli political culture, this is not easily done or always advisable. In practice, the Ministry of Finance continued to be occupied with details.

In July, the Budget Department in the Ministry of Finance sends the other ministries an overall budget forecast, showing a ceiling which forms the

---

* Among these, particularly the largest banks, the Histadrut economic enterprises, and major holding companies.

** There was an additional budget every year from 1966 to 1977; in 1975 it amounted to 15 percent of the original budget.

framework for each ministry's proposals.* Other background material includes a five-year forecast prepared by the Economic Planning Authority and a one-year "national economic budget" or "agreed economic forecast" prepared jointly by the Bank of Israel and the Ministry of Finance. While the ministries are working out their proposals, the referees in the Budget Department draw up independent estimates of what the ministries need. By September, if all goes well, parallel estimates are available, and the Budget Department can work out the budget goals and division by agency. In the nature of things, the proposed allocations cannot satisfy, simultaneously, ministry demands, national policy goals, and the fiscal and monetary restraints, so that revision and negotiation usually go on beyond the January target date on which a reasonably well-agreed-upon document should go to the Cabinet. The Cabinet debate, late as it comes, is in effect the last stage of negotiations which have been taking place on all levels during the fall and early winter. In these negotiations, the Minister of Finance tries to serve as the arbiter.**

From the Cabinet the bill goes to the Knesset—cloaked far less in secrecy than its British counterpart—where it is presented in a major budget speech by the Minister of Finance. The speech is comprehensive, outlining achievements, challenges, and goals, often painting a grim picture of the ability of resources to meet needs, calling for restraint in demands and efforts to accomplish goals, and presenting data showing that the government knows the problems and how the new budget will solve them.

After a general debate, and the first reading, the bill goes to the Finance Committee. In contrast to the very general policy attacks on the floor of the Knesset (where for the first time, in 1974, the opposition suggested an alternative budgetary approach), the committee goes into detail, knowing that the overall picture has already been decided. In practice, the Knesset has rarely if ever changed the budget as it was received from the Cabinet. Time constraints and the committee's backlog of current issues prevent a thorough analysis of the complex document and its implications. Also, the budget as transmitted is accompanied by statements of views and objectives but not by policy analysis. It has been suggested that the committee acquire a professional staff or study selected aspects in depth, throughout the year, in subcommittees; but it does neither. The total defense budget is public, but the classified, separate headings are discussed by a joint subcommittee of Finance and Foreign Af-

* In an earlier reform, the development, or investment, budget was separated from the ongoing budget. See Marver Bernstein, supra, p. 221.

** Major differences can be arbitrated by the Prime Minister or in an "inner Cabinet"; in the Labor Party, if it is a jurisdictional or personal question between two ministers; or by interparty negotiation if a coalition partner is involved. An experienced minister will prepare "hidden reserves" in his budget—what Haim Gvati, as Minister of Agriculture, called his "knipple," after the small reserve of her own which the Eastern European Jewish housewife used to stash away for an emergency (so her husband couldn't lose it).

fairs. Here too, time and security prevent thorough understanding or real control. Suggestions have been made that a defense study group hold continuous sessions throughout the year.

Less obvious, but a very real problem in the legislative process, is the fact that the budget presented to the Knesset does not show the whole picture of expenditure. It can understate the case, particularly when inflation raises linked wages beyond previous expectations, and be optimistic about revenue income. Important policy changes are caused by later decisions on operational questions, such as loans from the Bank of Israel to the government, rates charged by government-owned utilities, the underwriting by the government of corporate loans, the financial operations of government corporations, and the insurance by the government at highly subsidized rates of certain loans against changes in the rate of currency exchange; or, in the case of linked loans, against changes in the cost-of-living index. Most of the regular budget is "built in"—for example, statutory provision for schooling and transfer payments, debt servicing, or multiyear defense commitments—so that changes at the margin make the difference in most programs. These changes are often smaller than the "reserve" items which the Minister of Finance or the Director of the Budget can keep back for future needs, or promise as part of the resolution of the budget struggle. Given these limitations, the Finance Committee does not have an overall view of contending priorities and their expression in the budget. In these, the Cabinet and particularly the Ministry of Finance have the last word.

Over the years, the Budget Department has succeeded in attracting outstanding young economics graduates. Their general ability has more to do with its reputation than their specific training. In the decade or more since a quasi-performance budget structure has been in use, the common sense of referees and their detailed and energetic knowledge of the ministries has counted for much more than attempts at cost-benefit or other forms of analysis. One reason lies in the very uneven analytical capabilities of the different ministries, which hamper attempts to decentralize planning within "block" ministry allocations. Also, there is much more faith in the analysis of macroeconomic policy than in the validity of calculations of trade-offs of more specific programs. The allocation of tasks among ministries and the decisions on specific programs are political in their nature anywhere in the world. In Israel there is the added complexity of Cabinet coalition government and the consequent political allocation of tasks and resources among the ministries.* Indeed, most governments have serious difficulties in making clear choices between competing overall objectives and major programs intended to achieve them. It is much easier to approve incremental changes. In Israel, folk wisdom (over and above the fundamental difficulties of choice and

* For example, allocations can favor a minister representing a minor coalition party, whose particular faction within that party supports certain policies of the dominant party.

the inherent obstacles of coalition politics and lack of trained people) seems to have led to the failure of attempts to use PPBS or other analytical approaches in the ministries.* At the same time, the Budget Department intervenes excessively in the internal decisions of the ministries, thus working against responsible management.

There is progress, however, in developing macroanalytical frameworks. The government is well served with economic data by the Research Department of the Bank of Israel, the Central Bureau of Statistics, and the empirical research of the Falk Institute and others. Modeling of fiscal and macroeconomic parameters has been done at the Ministry of Finance since 1970. Attempts to enforce "rationalization" are often halted when the quasi-feudal independence of many ministries limits the use of the power of the purse and leads the Finance Ministry to exercise power through the less controlled parts of the process, such as subsequent transfers and allocation of "reserve funds." These ways, indeed, are more suited to the prevalent pragmatic bargaining in which the political power of personalities, factions, and coalition partners, and the use of symbolic or "cosmetic" appropriations come into play. Although the politics of the budget process in Israel has not been systematically studied, our experience indicates that the tactics and strategy are similar to those observed elsewhere.**

Planning

While economic planning should be part of strategic thinking directed toward accomplishing overall goals, where it exists, it is usually done partially, for a particular agency, sector, or project. For example, there is fairly comprehensive land-use planning at local, regional, and national levels. Multiyear plans are the rule in defense, as they are for many of the large basic projects in transportation and communication. In agriculture, producers and government control annual production levels, and these are coordinated with water allocations. The Ministry of Commerce and Industry publishes forecasts of industrial and export growth for five-year periods, and the Ministry of Finance produces five-year plans as well as a one-year national economic budget.

* Planning Programming Budgeting System. A budget format which attempts a clear definition of possible goals and the evaluation, through systems analysis, of ways to achieve them. See David Novick (ed.), *Program Budgeting, Program Analysis and the Federal Budget*, Cambridge, Mass., Harvard University Press, 1965.

** For example, no mayor of a town, in his right mind, would submit a balanced budget for the approval of the Ministry of the Interior. This, he would think, could show that his local tax base was adequate and lower the chances of additional support. For analysis of the U.S. repertoire of budget tactics and strategy, see Aaron Wildawsky, *The Politics of the Budget Process*, Boston, Little, Brown, 1964; and John P. Crecine, *Governmental Problem Solving*, Chicago, Rand McNally, 1969.

Most plans seem to fall into one of three categories. Overall economic plans are forecasts of what is likely to happen and what may be feasible, rather than plans. Although useful in raising questions, coordinating the estimates of separate agencies, and clarifying assumptions, they are not viewed by political leaders as a basis for making policy and remain in the background during policy discussions. The specific ministry plans, such as those for agriculture or the armed forces, are bases for decision, policy, and action. They often include considerations of the environments of the organizations, and of the relations of ends and means, that is, of strategy. Effective as bases of action for the time span and specific issues with which they deal, plans are largely uncoordinated with the rest of the economy, except after the fact. The third and most prevalent kind of planning is the design of specific projects, whose external impacts are very often inadequately considered.

The organization or structure of the economy is very rarely considered in planning. These questions have been widely discussed, and vary from pleas to allow a free market system to the need for a central comprehensive plan. On balance, professional opinion would probably seek stronger and more capable interdisciplinary and interagency national planning, in which more adequate consideration is given to market structure and organizational behavior as bases for feasibility and microdecisions. Plans would be directed toward strategic national goals, and toward an economic organization which made possible tactical decisions through market structure and administration.[14]

Both Levi Eshkol and Pinhas Sapir made abundantly clear their distrust of planning as a basis for policy decision. While generally a good listener and learner, Eshkol saw plans as specific programs, specifying, for example, how many tire factories to build in the near future—which is indeed the kind of decision in which Israeli Finance Ministers have always been involved. To Sapir, plans were the kind of forecasts which were made in his time at the Ministry of Commerce and Industry. He doubted, however, that forecasts could be a basis for hard decisions taken in advance. Who could know ahead of time that the dollar would be devalued, that the Egyptians would mass on the Sinai border in 1967, or that the Russians would allow even a trickle of Jews to emigrate? So how can you plan?[15]

The Central Planning Authority was set up by David Kohav in 1961 under Eshkol as Finance Minister, who transferred the Authority with him to the Prime Minister's Office. After a period the Authority was relocated in the Ministry of Finance, in keeping with the concentration of the Prime Minister's Office on foreign affairs and defense. The Planning Authority has not enjoyed resources, priority, or much policy influence, which can be ascribed to the reluctance of the ministers concerned to see the advantages in planning (a reluctance which they rationalized by the importance of outside events and the unknown future), or to their failure to comprehend that these very uncertainties increase the advantages and necessity of strategic thought.

A high degree of intervention from the center has thus been backed by a low level of effort in planning. The problems encountered by those who tried to develop planning show the effects of the strong beliefs of the political leaders in the potency of intuition, common sense, improvisation, and strong will in achieving goals, and of their reliance on "men of action." Also shown is a lack of appreciation by some professional economists of the problems inherent in resolving different claims of interests, and the need for realism in analysis. In a quasi-feudal coalition governmental structure, professional analytical or planning effort, which is not closely coupled with those who have the power for ongoing action, can have very limited effectiveness. Indeed, most of the variance from plans can be ascribed to the actions of the government itself.[*]

Monetary Policy: The Bank of Israel and the Government

The Governor of the Bank of Israel has limited independence in managing the country's monetary system. Appointed for a five-year term, the governor is not politically responsible, although his duties are defined as the management of the monetary system "in accordance with the policies of the government." This indeed is the way it works in practice. In a difference of opinion with the Cabinet, the governor has many options. He can mobilize public opinion and, on some issues, the influence of banking and industrial leaders. Professional opinion is usually on his side. The Research Department of the bank and the data which it generates are a principal arm of the bank in its policy struggles. The senior staff see the bank's role, in the policy debates, as representing "nonpolitical professional opinion," together with a "sense of the possible," in contrast with the universities, whose professional opinion (in the eyes of the bank) "seldom considers the possible." Leaders of commercial banking and Histadrut finance are on the bank's advisory boards. The governor has good access to the press and can report directly to the Knesset. But when the Cabinet's mind is made up on a major question, all this is of little avail.

The first governor, from 1954 until 1971, was David Horowitz, who had been close to the founding fathers of the country since the Third *Aliya*, in the early 1920s. Having immense prestige within Israel and in international development circles, Horowitz consistently took a prophetic stance, warning, as central bankers elsewhere, against the dangers of excessive monetary

---

[*] Haim Barkai suggests that, given the ad hoc nature of Israeli policy decisions, planners could be most effective by presenting ministers with the implications of alternate courses of action under discussion at a given time.

expansion, inflationary relations of saving, investment, and consumption, and deficits in foreign trade. Tending to avoid head-on conflicts with the government, Horowitz consistently advocated restraint of the economy and was very influential in the forming of economic policy without actually being able to take the lead.

Horowitz's successor, Moshe Sanbar, took office after a rapid career rise in the Ministries of Finance and of Commerce and Industry, in which he early became one of Pinhas Sapir's aides. In 1973 Sanbar shifted to a strong public stand against his mentor's policies, and recommended higher interest rates and restraint of the growth of the quantity of money, which could only be effective if government spending were to be slowed. Sanbar maintained his independent stance, only served one term, and thus had no political obligations for reelection. In 1977, he was succeeded by Arnon Gafni, the Director-General of the Finance Ministry, and a former Director of the Budget. Gafni rapidly entered into his new role, warning against overspending and deficit financing.

In the end, the government's statutory authority and its controls of the economy make its will prevail. Succeeding Cabinets have forced the bank to increase the money supply at a rate well in excess of the growth of the national product. The bank's governor, to be effective, has to find a way to speak his own mind, mobilize opinion, and yet to "join them" to avoid irreparable rifts.

The Capital Market

Through the capital market, domestic savings and funds from abroad are converted into investments by firms. In Israel the process is performed and controlled by the government, even when the bankers act as agents, rather than by independent investment banks or other institutions, even though these perform most of the technical financial functions, as shown in a simplified form in Figure 5.6.[16]

While commercial banks or individuals can lend at market rates, the source and uses of funds are restricted and regulated by such means as:

Requirements of liquidity and overall control of the quantity of money
Denying Finance Ministry approval for the issuance of nongovernment securities, except as part of an arrangement which predetermines the use or reinvestment of the proceeds
Requiring provident, pension, and insurance funds to invest in securities approved by the ministry*

* Under a 1954 agreement, Histadrut provident funds may invest about half of their deposits in Histadrut enterprises. The rest is held by the government, or in government securities. Other provident funds are required to deposit 92 percent of their deposits with the government or in government-approved securities. In 1980, the government decided not to renew this agreement, which had given Histadrut enterprises and Bank Hapoalim a considerable advantage in the capital market.

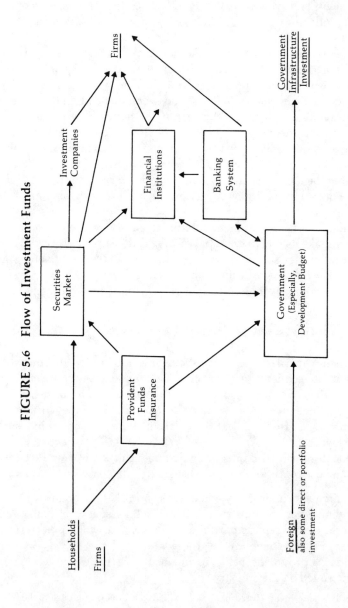

FIGURE 5.6 Flow of Investment Funds

Regulating foreign currency and foreign security holdings, and all borrowing or lending abroad

The positive or active modes of government investment stimulation are even
more important, however, in giving the government detailed control of the
capital market.

Most foreign loans, grants, or contributions come through the government or through financial institutions and large holding companies; foreign
investment in Israeli firms has been minor by comparison. The energy, success, and good will with which overseas transfer funds have been secured are
remarkable. At the same time, the relative absence of firm-to-firm direct investment means a loss in potential technological and marketing advance.*

When the government makes capital available for a specific firm, it sets the
conditions which, in effect, can determine the net profitability of the enterprise—interest rates, the tax structure, land costs, and occasionally monopoly arrangements. Loans "directed" by the government to specific firms are
given at interest rates far below the market rate, while the government insures
the linkage of principal to the cost-of-living index, subsidizes the interest rate,
and frees principal from liquidity restrictions. For example, in the early 1970s,
under the Law for the Encouragement of Investment a firm locating in the
highest-priority "development zones" could get 80 percent of the fixed capital
in loans or grants and 50 percent of the working capital at interest rates on the
order of 7 to 9 percent at a time when the market rate was 20 percent.** Other
benefits include fast write-offs, limits to income taxes on dividends, and local
tax and customs easement.***

The ability to secure government assistance can affect the growth and
profits of firms more than most other management talents. The consequent
dependency relations have been a major cause of the development of a
"bureaucratic political culture" and the complex interdependencies that make
"arm's length" an abstract notion. In his relations with the government, the
entrepreneur can find himself in many roles—claimant (as an industrialist) of
favorable investment conditions, contributor to institutions or board
member and fund raiser for charities or educational organizations which the
ministry wanted to advance, or collector or donor of political contributions.

As the government becomes more and more directly involved, it comes to

---

* Periodically, there have been elaborate "Economic Conferences," attended by potential investors, foreign industrial leaders, and Israeli counterparts. Aside from a new large holding company, the Israel Corporation, these conferences produced no advance in firm-to-firm relations in
marketing, technology, or finance, and little real increase in direct investment.

** These data refer to 1973. In 1977, the interest on directed loans was 17 to 20 percent, while commercial rates could exceed 30 percent. These were, of course, a function of the rate of inflation.

*** This generosity has been decreasing and the economic analyses and data requirements in order
to qualify for aid have been stiffened. Despite the abundance of voluminous spiral-bound reports
and proposals drafted by economists (who have much of the role in the Israel government that
lawyers have in the United States), there is skepticism about the extent to which investment decisions are actually determined by such a calculus.

depend more on its clients. Control, it was found, could be achieved without ownership. But in the end, the government, having widely sowed investment capital and benefits, is locked in and dependent on the managements' success. Failures or losses are often borne by the public purse, and frequently good money has to be sent after bad.

Having become directly involved with hundreds of firms, the government, perhaps partly by design, found a way to decrease its span of control. Mergers and the growth of large holding companies were encouraged. This can be related to a recognition of the impossibility of effectively controlling or directly supervising hundreds of managements. The interlocking directorates and personal relations involved would need, and should have, a special study. Large holding companies or conglomerates such as Clal (much of which is owned by the major banks), the Discount Bank Investment Company, the Histadrut's Koor Industries, the Wolfson-Clore Mayer Group, and the Israel Corporation (set up as a vehicle for foreign investment after the 1969 Economic Conference) are one way of reducing the Minister of Finance's span of control. Often they are headed by former Finance Ministry or other government officials who adopt new institutional roles as "economic men." Aside from the implications for economic power and competition, some conglomerates provide a modicum of effective decentralization. Their leaders, often former protégés or "right-hand men," tend to become surprisingly independent in their new roles and with their new organizational resources. In this process, the three largest banks (Leumi, Hapoalim, and Discount) became outstanding subcenters of power.

This gradual decentralization to several large economic centers, however, does not seem to be working in the same way for the government corporations. The next section will show that if, in private or Histadrut industry, the government can have control without ownership, of some public corporations, it can be said that there is government ownership without control.

Government Corporations

There are nearly 150 corporations in which the government owns all or a substantial part of the shares. Less than half of these are "pro forma" corporations, such as research laboratories which were incorporated for administrative convenience or to avoid civil service restrictions, or firms which provide basic services. An example is the Port Authority, which was incorporated so as to be qualified for a World Bank loan and with the hope, later disappointed, of raising capital in world markets. The "producing" corporations include the oil, mining, quarrying, and heavy chemical industries; the electric company and the national airline, El Al; and firms for the planning and distribution of water resources. The Israel Aircraft Industries is government-owned and autonomously controlled by the Ministry of

Defense, which also operates arsenals and laboratories as government departments.

Little ideological commitment to nationalization *per se* exists, partly because of the economic concentration available in the Histadrut enterprises. Labor governments in the last decade have shown no reluctance to sell shares in government firms. Such sales have often evoked criticism, not because of the principle, but because they were made at what seemed to the critics to be terms unfavorable to the government.*

Strong criticism is also aimed at the performance (and in some cases the probity) of managements and the lack of effective control; at the public costs from major losses, such as from the water company's overseas contracting firm, Vered, and from the civilian airplanes developed by the Aircraft Industries; and at the serious irregularities revealed in Netivei Neft, the Sinai oil-drilling company.

There could be several reasons why the government has not found the way to manage or control many of its own corporations effectively, despite the accounting and reporting reforms of the Government Corporations Authority in the Ministry of Finance (these formalities are about the extent of the authority of that office). The first is organizational; the boards of directors of the corporations are generally ineffective. Members serve on several boards and often lack the time or knowledge to consider policy adequately. Many are civil servants of the second rank, dependent on ministerial guidance but often lacking ready access to it. The independence and responsibility of the boards are seriously injured by direct intervention of civil servants and ministers in executive decisions, over the heads of the members of the boards.** [17]

Allied to the organizational problem is the lack of clear criteria for performance. There seems to be no overall strategy or rationale for setting up government corporations, for instance to bear unusual risk, to supply a function which is a natural monopoly, to create competition and technology, or to fulfill other aims where purely economic calculations might not be appropriate. When there is no defined goal or method of assessing management performance, the development and guidance of management becomes difficult if not impossible, and responsibility can be meaningless.

Finally, naiveté, inexperience, and a mysterious awe of the "doer" and the substantial investor combine with a disregard for the rights of "other people's money," where the "other people" are the taxpayers. Time and again the minister responsible will walk away from a public loss saying, "Well, you can't win them all." In entering partnerships, the government frequently puts

* For example, shares in the government-owned refineries were reportedly sold to the Israel Corporation at a loss. *Ha'aretz*, July 22, 1974.

** In the Israel Aircraft Industries, one of the largest firms in the country, the board of directors has virtually no say in major policy. The managing director in effect reports directly to the Minister of Defense, despite the scope of the minister's other responsibilities. D. Shimshoni, "Israel Aircraft Industries as a Planet," *Ma'ariv*, November 12, 1976.

up most of the money while receiving a minority of voting rights. This has been due to the naiveté of negotiators, overanxious to conclude the deal, or to the hope that the government's panoply of other controls will suffice. In some cases of a loss of net worth, the government has repurchased the shares from the original investors (who were often also substantial contributors) at par, with the public purse making up the loss.*

Regulation, Competition, and the Consumer

In contrast to the prevalence of intervention in decisions regarding production, prices, or investment, regulation means determining and enforcing the rules of the game: that is, setting the degree and forms of competition or market structure, the conditions under which goods and services may be offered for sale, and the safeguards to the public and the economy against unfair or discriminatory practices or the abuse of monopoly power. These safeguards can take the form of ensuring competition, inspection of the quality of goods and services provided, or, in the case of monopolies or essential public services, actually setting the rates and levels of service which are believed to be in the public interest, or developing market mechanisms through which they will be set.

Government intervention has been extraordinarily great, while regulation is unusually weak. Upon reflection, the situation is less surprising than it sounds. Control by rule making, while far from being "disinterested" or outside of politics, is still a very different situation from that in which complex dependencies and specific bargaining are the rule. The structure of the economy limits competition; efforts at consumer protection are feeble, and services are regulated through bargaining. Economic policy organization emphasizes investment decisions, and it is these which the government tries to use in order to stimulate and dominate the economy.

Legislation for the regulation of cartel agreements and for some aspects of consumer protection is less successful in providing regulating and enforcing machinery that works than it is in stating the aims and desires of the legislator. Attempts to use regulatory commissions for tariffs in public services, cartel regulation, or consumer protection have not been felicitous.

Given the small size of the domestic market, a high degree of concentra-

---

* Examples are those of Clal (on a large scale) and of the small Israel Research and Development Corporation. Clal was originally founded as a vehicle for investment by Latin Americans. After its founding, devaluation and recession reduced the value of its shares. Major banks and other investors, with government (i.e., public) help, and with eventual large capital gains, were enabled to buy the shares with no nominal loss to the original investors. IRDC was founded by the government as a venture capital firm to stimulate science-based industries. While the government put up most of the funds, substantial private American and Israeli investors had majority voting rights. After losses, the government bought out the shares at no loss to the original investors.

tion and occasional justification for monopoly naturally exist in many activities. A further stimulus to concentration is the need to compete in foreign markets against firms enjoying economies of scale. Still, the reasons for the lag in regulation lie deeper in the system of the political economy and its culture.

In the search for productivity and growth, the underlying concern and support are for the producer, and government departments which represent producers have primacy over those concerned with principles or the consumer. Because Israeli consumers are not well organized and lack belief in their potential influence, they show the inability to persist in organized, voluntary effort. This is common in Israel. Even American immigrants, fresh from civic activity and veterans of voluntary organizations, catch the local disease and lose interest, as they did soon after the Association of Americans and Canadians in Israel started a consumer rights group. When consumers' protection organizations have been set up, the government, or at least the Histadrut, has hastened to offer aid and support, so that even if successful, the organizations are not really independent. * The Histadrut has not been an effective countervailing proconsumer force, except on such general government issues as wage linkage, mortgage conditions, or price subsidies. The general consumer has second priority to the demands of the workers in the government-owned electric company, or to those of the driver-owners of the bus cooperatives, or to those of a foreign investor tempted by promised monopoly rights.

Another aspect is the high degree of concentration. The lack of an arm's-length relation, seen in the Histadrut's multiple interests, is found throughout the political economy. The large banks engage in commercial banking, investment banking, security transactions, the management of holding companies, and investment in property and industry. The formation and growth of conglomerates and holding companies has been encouraged far beyond the needs for economies of scale, partly through awe of size and partly to make it easier for the administration, so it was hoped, to direct the economy and to raise capital.

It is difficult for many government officials to conceive of the importance or even the continued existence of an entirely independent and self-directing group which is not subsidized in some way or connected with the government, a party or the Histadrut, or some other large public organization. Legislators or civil servants, when preparing legislation, seldom invest the efforts to think through how the process of regulation required by the new law will operate in practice, and what conditions are needed for the stated aims to be achieved. The rule-making mode is rare, and problems of implementation are neglected.

* Another example of lack of arm's length is Malraz, a voluntary citizens antipollution organization, much of whose financial support comes from firms (who are actual or potential polluters) and from the government.

As a result, much legislation remains of mainly symbolic value, except when the executive intervenes directly. Regulation is still a rare art.

Beliefs are an important reason for these conditions. Virtue is seen in size, and there is great respect for those who are actually building or doing, whether with other people's money and brains or with their own. A more basic cause, however, is the nature of the system. The economy is simply political, and those directing it behave accordingly. It would be unreasonable to expect a minister to abandon his prerogatives to an "impartial" public commission unless he felt that he could have the last word, or that at least those supporting him or his policies were intimately involved in the decisions. Neither beliefs nor organization lend themselves to changing the nature of the political economy.

Agriculture

The political economy of agriculture differs in important ways from that of industry. While government sees itself as the father, patron, and initiator of industrialization, in agriculture it regulates only marginal changes in a mature sector. After one hundred years of settlement and decades of the successful application of research, agriculture has a strong technological and economic base. While there are attempts to direct industry from the top down, the forces in agriculture in recent years come much more from the bottom up. Indeed, agricultural interests and government agricultural policy are often not really distinguishable.

Central to the Zionist ideology, agriculture has had unusually strong claims on support and resources, which are reinforced by the congruence of party or faction with interest. Mapam has its social and economic base in the Kibbutz Ha'artzi, the Ahdut Ha'Avoda faction in the Labor Party drew its main strength from the United Kibbutz Movement, and Mapai was dominant in the Ichud, or Union, of Kvutzot and Kibbutzim and in the *moshav* movement.[18] Since two-thirds of agricultural production takes place in *moshavim* or kibbutzim, most of the country's farmers belong to organizations with close political ties, even though as individuals they may be active in other movements or abstain from politics. This is more true in the *moshav* than in the kibbutz, where diversity is less common.*

In agriculture as in industry, the government controls the capital market as well as the artificially low interest rates of "directed capital," subsidies to consumers and producers, protective tariffs and export subsidies, and the rate

---

* While the marketing, capital, water, and purchasing of a *moshav* are cooperatively organized, the farmer is essentially an individual producer. Other private production includes most of the Arab or Druze farming and most citrus growing, which historically was important in the economic base of the General Zionists and their Liberal Party successors. In 1980, the Ichud and Hakibbutz Hameuhad (United Kibbutz Movement) merged.

of development and costs of land, power, and water. In agriculture, government decisions and support tend to be general, as for a region or crop, and the minister is concerned with setting the trends and conditions; whereas in industry, the leading officials or the minister can come to the aid of a large plant which is in difficulty.

The minister presides over stable political and economic relations, with well-developed institutions and rules of the game, both regarding "agriculture versus the rest" and within agriculture.[19] The resources given to agriculture and their prices have been outputs of the general political system, which regards agriculture as much more than an economic activity. Immigrant absorption, the dispersal of population, defense, and the return to individual labor and the land all reinforce the claims which are pressed before party leadership, Cabinet, Knesset, and bureaucracy. Aside from their beliefs, these groups have a more than proportional, if declining, representation of kibbutz and *moshav* members. Thus twenty-one kibbutz and *moshav* members were elected to the 1969 Knesset, or about one-sixth of the total membership and one-third of the coalition, while kibbutz and *moshav* residents were about 7 percent of the country's population.*

The overall goals have been the achievement of autarky in food, a level of income for agricultural work comparable to or higher than that of skilled labor in the cities, and the successful extention of cooperative settlement as a way of life. Autarky has neared its feasible limits; two-thirds of food requirements are produced domestically and exports total more than 300 million dollars a year. Farm income level is maintained by the control of production and the avoidance of surpluses, by capital intensity (stimulated by low interest rates and import duties on capital goods), by government subsidy of consumer and factor costs, and through the proliferation of kibbutz industries. The goals were achieved at some cost. A more "economic" calculus, combined with a dependence upon market mechanisms, could, in theory, have secured a more rational use of national resources, but it would also probably have fallen short of the general goals. For example, the large-scale settlement of immigrants from Eastern countries in *moshav* villages in the early 1950s required a considerable subsidy from the rest of the economy. Water, piped to the Negev from the north, is sold considerably below its cost. The cooperative way of life and the values of "do it yourself" labor led to emphasis on mixed farming and on small-family or kibbutz planting areas, since industrial crops planted on an economic scale would involve the deployment of large and mobile labor forces.** High capital intensity and extensive subsidies raise the farm income level, but may cause inadequate investment elsewhere.

---

* In 1973, some 100,000 kibbutz members lived in over 230 kibbutzim, with 83 belonging to the Ichud (and Noar Zioni); 75 in the National Kibbutz, or Kibbutz Artzi, Movement; 59 in the United Kibbutz Movement; and 13 in orthodox kibbutzim.

** Dorothy Willner, in *Nation Building and Community in Israel,* Princeton University Press, 1969, pp. 172 f., discusses the conflict of rationality and ideology in decisions in the early 1950s,

Within agriculture, the several sectors strive for a greater allocation of resources, usually but not always for distinctly economic reasons. Increased production quotas can also mean that a movement, region, or sector will have a larger work force and, therefore, extend its importance and way of life. Thus the representatives of kibbutzim and *moshavim*, of the "old" and "new" *moshavim*, of the regions,[20] and of the cooperative and private owners repeatedly reach a negotiated consensus on production and marketing which, in turn, leads to the allocation of resources, such as water, and of quotas within which input subsidies will be paid. These specific interests are related to the larger political sphere, as the organized movements seek influential roles in the agricultural bureaucracy, and seek to have the Minister of Agriculture appointed from their ranks. These contests are usually resolved amicably by mutual allocation of office, and by tacitly agreed rotation.

In planning and directing the agricultural economy, producers and government join forces in what are in effect producer cartels under government leadership. Their decisions are effectively carried out, reinforced by the government's ownership of land and water and by its machinery for price maintenance and export subsidies. The Minister of Agriculture is responsible for both the Land Authority and the Water Authority, which illustrates the absence of an arm's-length negotiating position in the allocation of resources. The result is a fusion of political and administrative decision. More than in other areas, a given group may act on an issue on grounds of "rational" analysis, partisan goals, and parochial interests all at once.

In the formal organization, the Minister of Agriculture is advised by a large staff, the Water Council and Water Commissioner, and the Planning Authority and branch Production Councils.* (See Figure 5.7.) In 1973 the ministry had more than 3,000 employees, nearly two-thirds professional staff, which operated extensive research facilities, field services, and technical services (such as veterinary medicine) and did economic planning. Within this

---

to settle new immigrants in the *moshavim* and not to set up larger-scale industrial-crop administered farms. She points out the relation of this decision to the sectoral political system of agriculture, in which parties and settlement movements agree on resource allocation and production. Eventually, she says, the bureaucracy of the Agency's Settlement Department dominated because of its professional and representational linkages, and through formal authority in resource allocation and planning.

* The Production Councils cover more than 80 percent of agricultural product value. Duties typically are defined to include (1) planning and directing production, (2) ensuring adequate farm income, particularly in difficult places, (3) organizing marketing, (4) managing branch funds to encourage export, ensuring minimum income, and (5) advancing technology and ensuring product quality. Some are "statutory," such as the Citrus Marketing Board; many are incorporated, with formal responsibilities defined. Government supervision in the statutory councils is essentially through membership on the boards of directors (including the chairman and deputy chairman of each council), and by decisions on subsidies and minimum prices, and approval of methods of setting production quotas. The total quotas for a branch are decided by the Joint Planning Center of the Ministry of Agriculture and the Jewish Agency), while the councils allocate the quotas within the branch.

FIGURE 5.7   Agricultural Planning and Policy

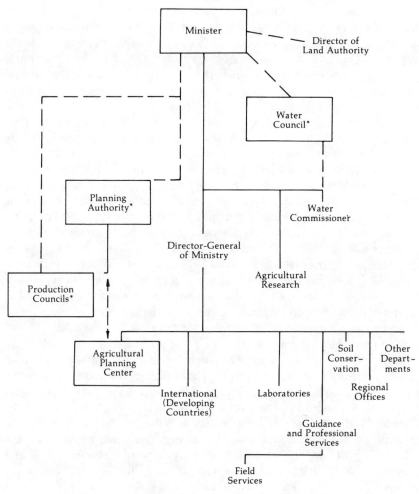

*A "representative" body operated jointly with the ministry, but outside it.

large organization there is ample scope for bureaucratic politics in addition to professional criteria and interest representation.

The Planning Authority is a "representative" body whose membership represents the interest groups. It is the focus of decision on the goals and inter-branch structure of agricultural development, the resources needed, and their allocation. The main input of economic and professional agronomic analysis is provided by the Planning Center staff, which has the help of other ministry departments, jointly with the Settlement Department of the Jewish Agency. Membership on the Planning Authority board is decided by a complex calculus, and it is often hard to distinguish between those "sent" (by the parties and organized movements) and those "appointed," as by the Agency or the government. The complex outcome of relative numerical party negotiating strength is determined mainly by party and faction strength in the Alignment, in the Labor Party, in the Histadrut, and in the agricultural movements. Representation includes the different kibbutz movements and the *moshav* movement (and through them, the parties), the Agency, regions, product interests, and the government bureaucracy.

While the Production Councils contribute to productivity and technological advance, their main role is to plan production and allocate quotas within a product branch. In this way they resolve the conflicting demands within their branch for greater shares of production and represent the branch's demands against those of other branches, for agricultural resources, such as capital and water. Farmers typically have 50 percent of the seats on a Council and the government 25 percent, but in practice both are stronger than these proportions show as against the influence of Council members who represent consumers and distributors. The farmers as producers are helped by the fact that Ministry of Agriculture civil servants identify with their needs: the civil servants have technical knowledge and experience and are the operators of the government's resources in subsidies and in the control of factor costs and their allocation. Indeed, their potent array of tools, the institutional arrangements, and the common desire to unite to advance agriculture's share "against the rest" help the professionally and politically strong civil servants and farmers to reach agreement. As in other kinds of cartels, there are problems concerning the realism of the assumed objective functions, and inequalities in political and bureaucratic influence can distort the allocations decided by the representatives on the quota committee of the Planning Authority and on the internal-branch Production Councils. But the political or power relations and the tremendous force of ideology are tempered by the strongly professional background of the several thousand people who are active in the civil service, in agricultural settlements, in the movements, and in research, development, and training.

The Histadrut

Before considering wage determination and industrial relations, more understanding is needed of the Histadrut, the General Federation of Workers in Israel. Far more than a trade union, the Histadrut (which means "Federation") has been called "the most important, most original, most problematic institution bequeathed to the State of Israel by the Yishuv."[21] The original name was "The General Federation of Jewish Labor in Palestine." Arabs have been members since 1959, and the name was therefore changed. It was from the first a broad, social, political, and national movement, "the state in the making." Many of its original functions are now nationalized, and indications are that the trade-union role is becoming predominant over those of social service and political mobilization.

The organization is vast and all-encompassing. The Histadrut is the only collective-bargaining representative, organizing more than 80 percent of the eligible labor force. In 1971 Histadrut economic affiliates produced more than 70 percent of the agricultural crop, 17 percent of industrial output, and over 22 percent of building and contracting. Of total domestic output, the Histadrut and government-owned sectors each produce about 20 percent and the private sector some 60 percent. Histadrut economic enterprises receive nearly half of the capital flow originating in its pension and provident funds. The extent of producer cooperative enterprise is unique, and over ninety industrial producers' cooperatives are affiliated with the Histadrut, while some 200 factories are owned by kibbutzim. One in four Israelis works in a Histadrut-affiliated firm or service, and its health services insure or serve more than 75 percent of Israelis. Growth has been rapid and consistent. In 1920, 4,400 members sent eighty-seven representatives to the first convention in Haifa. Between 1948 and 1977, the membership grew from 275,000 to nearly 1,400,000. About two-thirds of the Jews and half of the Arabs in the country are members of the Histadrut or belong to a member's family.

The formal organization, shown in Figure 5.8, includes three major activities: *social services* (particularly Kupat Holim—medical care and insurance), *trade unions*, and the *economic enterprises*, which are combined under Hevrat Ovdim, or "Workers' Company." Not shown in the chart but very important are the national political parties, which determine the leading personal roles and appointments within the Histadrut and the extent to which the internal groups have power of their own and independence from the central institutions. To understand the organization, it is important to remember that it is political and to analyze the relations of its political, bureaucratic, and economic elements.

The Political System of the Histadrut[22]

Belonging to a national movement rather than merely a union, the Histadrut member joins the national organization directly and pays his dues to it. He then is automatically a member of the union which represents the workers in his firm or occupation. Membership is not restricted, nor is it a prerequisite for employment. Israel has no "closed shop." All workers in an "organized" work place are represented by the union whether they join or not, and about 1 percent of the wages of non-members is deducted for this service. Many Histadrut members are not in unions—for example, those in kibbutzim or *moshavim*, housewives, or independent professional workers.

Several patterns of election and representation operate in parallel: (a) *par-*

FIGURE 5.8 Organization of the Histadrut—the General Federation of Labor

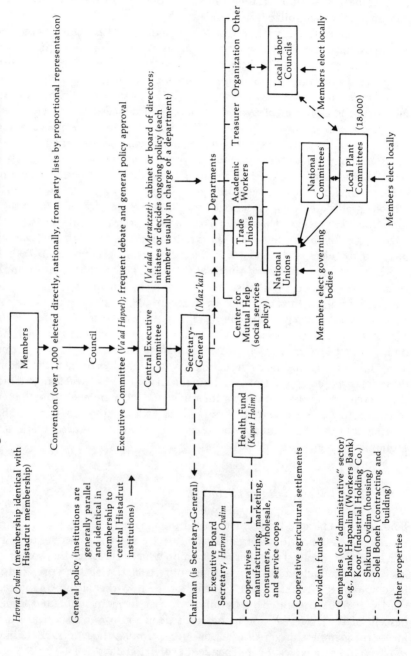

tisan or political, on the basis of the national parties and their local branches, which compete in national elections and those for local area workers' councils; (b) *bureaucratic*, and (c) *personal or nonparty*, found mostly in local plant union elections.

Every few years, nationwide elections are held for delegates to a convention (some 1,500 delegates in 1974) and for members of local workers' councils. As in Knesset elections, each member casts one vote for a slate, and the result is decided by simple proportional representation. Nominations to these slates are made by internal party nominating committees. The parties within the Histadrut parallel the national parties, to which they are, in principle, politically responsible for policies and decisions on appointments.

The convention elections decide the relative strength of the parties. Before adjourning, the convention elects a council which then elects an Executive Committee, or *Va'ad Hapoel* (167 members in 1974), that has authority between conventions and has the same party proportions as the convention.* The *Va'ad Hapoel* approves a Central Executive Committee, or cabinet, of 15–20 members. This committee, in contrast to the *Va'ad Hapoel*, includes only the parties in the Histadrut governing coalition. In a similar election, held on the same day as the national voting, a local area chooses its workers' council.**

Because of the immense scope of the enterprise and the bureaucratic power of the diverse management groups, it is the composition of the Central Executive Committee and the key administrative appointments (or, formally, elections by boards or councils) which determine who will have power in ongoing decisions. These appointments include the Secretary-General, members of the Central Executive Committee, the Secretaries of Hevrat Ovdim and of the Sick Fund, the managers of Koor Industries, Solel Boneh, and the Bank Hapoalim, the editor of the daily newspaper (*Davar*), and the heads of the Trade Union, Treasury, and Organization departments. Such appointments are determined or at least approved by the parties, outside the Histadrut, although internal backing and personal leadership influence the outcome.

Individual trade unions, such as those of the clerical workers, agricultural employees, building workers, nurses, and engineers, are national in scope and organized on an industrial or an occupational basis. Internal elections use the same system as do those for the convention, and relative party voting strength

---

* There is no requirement of a minimum percentage in order to achieve a convention delegation, and every delegation seated receives party expenses in proportion to its size, provisions which encourage splinter parties. In contrast to the Knesset, the Va'ad Hapoel members are not bound to support the line of the party representative on the Central Executive Committee.

** The local workers' council is in some ways a microcosm of the broad activities of the national Histadrut. Elected from local party lists by proportional representation, the council is the formal authority in signing contracts with local employers, and directs the Histadrut's social and political activities within the area assigned to it. The staffs are chosen by the local party branches, and owe much loyalty to them, although the national bureaucracy also has a strong influence on appointments.

decides the composition of a smaller Center, which then chooses a still smaller Secretariat.

At the top of the national hierarchy, the same people serve on the boards of directors of the major economic, trade union, and social services. Thus the Secretary-General, the leader of the Histadrut, is also Chairman of the Executive Board of Hevrat Ovdim (in keeping with the fact that membership in Hevrat Ovdim is coincident with membership in the Histadrut, each Histadrut member holding one share in the company). The boards of Hevrat Ovdim and its major subsidiaries are appointed with party authority and are political in aims and loyalty, as are the executive level of Kupat Holim and the pension funds and the leaders of the Trade Union departments.

Immediately below the level of top policy groups, however, bureaucracy prevails, and considerations in appointments include personal qualifications as well as party and personal loyalties. The motives and loyalties of the managers at these levels are often influenced as much by the economic or bureaucratic interest of their organizations as they are by party interests. Yet the Histadrut bureaucracy is politicized, and the staff members know well that they are party or even faction representatives.

The third pattern, that of *nonparty personal election*, is prevalent in the groups that are in the front line of labor relations—the workers' committee which represents the workers in a plant, and national committees which represent employees in multiplant organizations. Elections to the plant committee, or *va'ad*, are for individual candidates on a simple plurality basis. In the past, party "cells" were active within firms, putting up lists of candidates and trying to influence decisions of the *va'ad*. These cells became inactive for a variety of causes: the decline of the influence of the party bureaucracies, the amalgamation of the Labor movement parties, and the spread of a parochial approach within the unions.

In Chapter 1, we saw how party control developed and was exercised, and how Labor's political leaders, combining the resources of internal organization with control over much of the external inputs to the Yishuv in funds and immigration, gained dominant political leverage. As Table 5.4 shows, the margin of Labor Party control of the Histadrut has been declining since the state was established.

In this precarious position, Labor's Histadrut leaders are more responsive to internal demands, pressed urgently by the strongest union groups, in general representing the more highly paid workers holding jobs in critical services. The decline of party ideology and organization, the disappearance of local-union party cells, and the prevalence of nonparty plants' committees combine with a lack of representation of local unions at the center to reduce the legitimacy and effective authority of the central executive bodies.*

* In the 1974 convention, delegates from the work places were only 10.4 percent of the convention delegates, 8.4 percent of the members of the Executive Committee, and *none* of the members of the Central Executive Committee—a situation resulting from the election and nomination procedures described above.

TABLE 5.4. Histadrut National Election Results, Selected Years, % [23]

PARTY \ YEAR	1933	1949	1966	1969	1973	1977
Component groups—Labor Party	Mapai 81.6	Mapai 57.1	Mapai + Ahdut Ha'Avoda 50.9, Rafi 12.1	Alignment (Labor + Mapam) 62.1	Alignment (Labor + Mapam) 58.3	Alignment (Labor + Mapam) 55.3
Mapam	16.1 (Shomer Hatzair, Left Poelei Zion)	34.4 (includes Ahdut Ha'Avoda)	Mapam 14.5	—	—	—
Total Alignment Parties	97.7	91.5	77.5	62.1	58.3	55.3
Components of Likud	Not members	Not members	15.2	22.8	22.7	28.2
Liberal center parties	Not members	Haoved Hatzioni 3.8	Haoved Hatzioni 4.4	Liberal Labor Movement 5.7	Liberal Labor Movement 5.8	DMC 8 Independent Liberals (1.3), total 9.3
Others	2.3	1.7	2.9	9.4	13.2*	7.2**

Note: Ahdut Ha'Avoda was in Mapam 1948–54, and in the Labor Party since 1968. Liberal center parties first participated in the 1942 convention. Haoved Hatzioni was the workers and settlement movement of the Progressive Party, forerunner of the Independent Liberals. "Others," in 1973, included several small splinter groups and the Oved Dati, or "Religious Workers." For party development, see Figures 1.1, 1.2, and 1.3.

* Rakah, 2.4%; Moked, 1.7%; Panthers, 1.6%; Oved Dati, 4.3%.

** Rakah, 3.0%; Sheli, 1.1%; Oved Dati, 1.8%. See Chapter 1 for changes in party nomenclature and alignments.

Another centrifugal force is found in the separate aims of the economic organizations and the bureaucracies. The executives of Koor Industries, Solel Boneh, Bank Hapoalim, and Kupat Holim are conscious of the public and political aspects of their roles, but basically they pursue the aims which are characteristic of the managers of other large enterprises. In these roles they find themselves, as would be expected, in occasional quandaries as leaders in a federation which includes both employers and employees, but more complex and serious are the conflicts of management criteria with the political aims of the higher Histadrut leadership. These aims are expressed particularly by the essentially political executive board of Hevrat Ovdim. Some managers fear the exploitation of the resources of their firm for party ends, and the employment of pressure in this direction through the leverage of the Histadrut financial credit and investment resources. Their malaise is increased by the feeling that these party motives are inspired far less by ideology than they are by the organizational and authority needs of the leadership group.*

Motives are never as clearly divided as I have indicated. Internalized political and social values can strongly affect decisions. But heterogeneity of membership and a scope comprising a great variety of enterprises make it very difficult for the Histadrut to maintain the loyalty of diverse groups and remain the sole and legitimate representative of labor.

Against the background of internal differences, the relations of the Histadrut with a Labor government are often ambivalent and uneasy. Historically, the support which the Histadrut afforded Mapai, and later the Labor Party, has been immensely important. It facilitated election finances, gave the backing of the daily newspaper *Davar*, and recruited party activists and gave them jobs, especially through local workers' councils, spreading an extensive net in the local communities, neighborhoods, voting precincts, and plants.** Labor, as the controlling party, has been the principal beneficiary, which is why, for example, Rafi felt that it had to run in the Histadrut elections, although unprepared, shortly after it split from Mapai in the summer of 1965.

In their turn, Histadrut leaders owe their nomination and much of their standing to the party. In the complexity of their situation, however, they were torn between the will to support the policies of governments which the Labor party led and the need to counteract centrifugal forces and to stem the decline of the electoral support for the party within the Histadrut, as well as to main-

---

* This was in the background of the resignation of General Zwi Zamir as head of Solel Boneh, in 1976. Zamir stated, *inter alia*, that the politicized policy control of Hevrat Ovdim, reinforced by the financial leverage of Bank Hapoalim, together with the intervention of the unions in internal Solel Boneh decisions, prevented the exercise of effective management.

** In Chapter 3 the importance of workers' councils in local-level politics is discussed. In the Yishuv a council had labor exchanges, welfare services, and schools. In the state it lost many roles, but it still remains the basis of the local Labor political machine, a prime source of recruitment, the introduction of immigrants to political life and their absorption, and patronage.

tain their individual primacy. To these are added the differences which naturally arise because of a government and a Histadrut both of whose activities include almost every facet of economic and social activity.

In the Yishuv, the Histadrut had been the center. After the state was declared, the leaders of the Yishuv period moved on from the Histadrut to the power of the government, where they assured the prerogatives of their new institutional roles as earnestly as they had battled in the past for Histadrut independence—and the Histadrut took second place. At most times the Secretary-General and the other Histadrut leaders have accepted the role of junior partner more or less gracefully.* Caught between the demands of the membership and of national or party needs, they generally tried to avoid head-on confrontation through negotiation and peaceful bargaining. When this was feasible, there was a good deal of prior government-Histadrut consultation on impending changes in policy which affected prices or incomes, but there were several occasions where announced policies were greatly changed or their results negated after Histadrut protests.

At times in the past, depending upon personal relationships, the informal Mapai caucus of *sareinu*, or "Our Ministers," was expanded to include the Histadrut Secretary-General and was called *haveireinu*, or "Our Comrades."[24] Major questions, in any case, were discussed by the Labor members of the Cabinet or by an inner group of Cabinet leaders; and where the conflict was head-on and irreversible, the party became the final arbiter and the "supreme court."

In the Rabin Cabinet of 1974–77, however, the party's organizational influence was at a nadir, and institutions which previously could have served to adjudicate and resolve major differences were inactive. Within the Histadrut, the feeling of independence increased, because of the lack of an overall party authority to which to refer. It was a time of uncertainty regarding both relations and ideals.

A Trade Union or a Social Movement?

Encompassing, heterogeneous, and powerful, the Histadrut is at a crossroads in determining its future role. It faces fundamental problems of direction and identity. From its founding in 1920, it has been a political and social move-

---

* Histadrut Secretaries who demonstrated great independence were Pinhas Lavon (1956–61) and Itzchak Ben Aharon (1969–1974). Lavon's independence was based on considerable support within the Histadrut and many sections of Mapai. In the end it was impossible to separate Lavon's advocacy of Histadrut independence as a total movement, his beliefs, and the personal struggle with Ben Gurion. The Mapai Central Committee deposed Lavon as Secretary-General because of this struggle, aside from any differences in beliefs. Ben Aharon emphasized specific issues, voicing public opposition to government incomes policy. In the end, he was left without the support of the Labor Party machinery and fought the 1973 elections almost single-handedly. The rank and file continued to see in the Labor list a representation of the establishment. The Labor Alignment majority dropped to 58 percent and Ben Aharon resigned as Secretary-General.

ment, whose aim was to gain political power for the Labor movement, to achieve its social goals, and, through institutions, to help build the Yishuv. Initial success was impressive. Before there was industry on any serious scale, workers had job security, freedom from domineering supervision, and a voice in determining norms and welfare plans. Health insurance became almost universal.

The Histadrut added a strong organizational base to the resources of the new state. It could help in economic growth, in consensus, and in relative labor peace. The elective institutions were important in the political recruitment and socialization of immigrants, and to this day afford a way of entry and advancement in the political system.

With success, the membership became a cross section of the general population, and the economic organizations' centers of resources and power. With time, the influences of party organization and of ideology diminished, as did the legitimacy of the central leadership group. Far from being monolithic, the Histadrut membership now represents almost all of the partisan views and ideologies, and most of the parochial, regional, sectoral, ethnic, and occupational interests in the country.

Problems are now those of future identity. Once a striking innovator, the Histadrut is now an establishment whose trappings seem to exceed its real power; whose ideological call for equality of income, socialist cooperative enterprise, and mutual help falls on deaf ears of parochially interested union groups, or seems to counter the needs of national economic growth; whose leaders have diminishing legitimacy either as the leaders of a largely secular and all-embracing membership or as the guides and mentors of the way of life in the increasingly independent cooperatives and the economic centers belonging to Hevrat Ovdim; and whose capacity to initiate change is open to serious doubts.*

One future road for the Histadrut would be to become only a secular federation of trade unions. This, however, would mean avoiding the greater challenge. To remain a major social force, the Histadrut needs to create new ways and once again become a unique movement of social innovation.** In this it will be hampered by bureaucratic inertia and partisan conflict and

---

* The large (for Israel) Histadrut headquarters in Tel Aviv used to be called "the Kremlin." Reactions to this tangible symbol of the bureaucracy are varied. Moshe Sharett, in his autobiography, expressed shock on seeing the marble floors and costly building (which over the years was probably cost-effective). A new immigrant from Poland said to me, "This looks like what I came here to get away from." A politically ambitious youth might say, "This looks good, but it is no longer the way to the top."

** On a more specific level, there are serious proposals to change the representative base by having regional elections for workers' councils, and to elect representatives from plant committees to workers' councils and to the convention and the Executive Committee.[25] The Likud, as a strong minority in the Histadrut, opposes the proposal (adopted in 1981) for regional elections, seeing them as enhancing Labor influence by virtue of big kibbutz votes in the regions.

distrust, and the immensity of the conceptual problems, which involve fundamental questions of modern society which are not unique to Israel.

Labor Relations and Wage Policy[26]

Although it is highly developed, the system of industrial relations and wage determination has not yet succeeded in creating an atmosphere or norms of work relations which serve the urgent needs of the economy. At a very early stage, labor achieved unusually strong rights:* permanence in employment, seniority benefits, such as "last hired, first fired," severance pay, and a considerable amount of control or veto power over many management decisions. These prerogatives preceded the state and many of the provisions were later enacted into law.

An important constraint is the practice of linking wages in an occupation to the wages of other groups and to the cost of living. Initially, a large part of a wage was determined by the size of the family—"to each according to his need." (At present, children's allowances specified by law are paid by the National Insurance Institution, and give very great help to low-income families with many children.) Counteregalitarian forces soon arose, as the Histadrut tried to retain the loyalty of professional groups and highly skilled workers in periods of labor scarcity. The vertical wage differentials which resulted are often thinly disguised by complex fringe benefits and allowances.

The system is criticized for inequities and for an inflexibility which impedes the economy. The reward of industry and initiative or the discouragement of absenteeism or incompetence is often prevented by the rules. A strong plant committee (va'ad) can dictate or veto promotions, and job security can prevent the transfer or discharge of incompetents. Production workers have less favorable vacations, work hours, and job security than those in the services. In general, the strong, those in skilled occupations or essential services, are better represented by the Histadrut than the weak. Unions, particularly local committees, frequently demand renegotiation of work agreements before their term has elapsed. Critical services, such as ports and communication, are disrupted despite public opinion and the moderate sanctions provided in the law. Indeed, severe labor unrest has mainly occurred in services

---

* Among labor laws, Hours of Work and Rest (1951) provides for an eight-hour day, a weekly day of rest, and regulation of overtime; Annual Leave (1951) with pay; Labor Inspection (1954) provides for a safety and hygiene institute; and there are laws regulating the work of youth, women, and apprentices. A nationalized Employment Service has a monopoly. Its use is mandatory, and in practice private employment agencies operate virtually only for professionals and the performing arts. There are laws providing for government mediation of labor disputes and enforcement of agreements in special labor courts, and for the guarantee of wage and severance payments. In 1972, after repeated strikes in government services, the Labor Party backed legislation allowing labor courts to grant injunctions against unauthorized strikes in public services. In 1972 there were forty complaints, and injunctions were given in such areas as Social Security Administration, the national airline, El Al, broadcasting, and the oil pipeline.

operated by the government or by public corporations, encouraged by the leverage which their operators possess and by the feeling that public funds, in contrast to those of private firms, have no foreseeable limits. The institutional arrangements and the prerogatives for the conduct of labor relations were developed in a period when technological organization had not yet given the power of control to small groups of technical workers.

The Long Process of Wage Determination

Negotiations are complex, often ineffective because some roles are cere-monial, the actors seen on the stage are not those who in the end decide, negotiations drag on, and agreements when reached may not be kept. At the same time, the government, employers, and the Histadrut understand the need for cooperation in restraining inflation. In principle they accept the idea that wage increases, beyond changes in the cost of living, should be related to increases in productivity. In practice, however, overfull employ-ment, excess demand, and politics within and outside the Histadrut have made wages the outcome of local and sectoral bargaining strength and of a "political cycle" in which income levels tend to rise in the years before national elections.*

Every one to two years, a national agreement is negotiated between the employers and the Histadrut. Employers are represented by the Manufac-turers Association, which is the most important group in the Coordinating Office of the Economic Organizations. It includes, however, only part of in-dustry, and its members are not owned by the government or the Histadrut and are seldom firms owned by the largest holding companies. (The Histadrut constitution prevents its firms from negotiating with unions.) At this stage, the government, when it intervenes, usually does so on the level of general policy.**

In these national negotiations, limits are set for across-the-board wage in-creases in the new period. Minimum wages can be included as well as incen-

* A phrase used by Edward Tufte and Yoram Ben-Porath. Dividing each of the four-year Israeli election periods into periods of two years each, Ben-Porath found a much higher rate of economic growth in the two-year periods immediately preceding elections, and cites specific measures of encouraging economic activity before elections, and of restraint immediately thereafter. (Ma'ariv, February 1973). For example, only one of the major devaluations, that of 1957, took place in the eighteen months preceding an election. Edward Tufte found similar phenomena in most countries which have regular free elections.[27]

** To influence wage levels (in addition to such means as capital investment, its own employ-ment, and demand), the government can employ changes in income taxes and compulsory loans for employers and workers; factor costs, through service charges and import duties; price con-trols; the government's internal wage policies; and food subsidies. In 1970, a "package deal" was negotiated between the government, manufacturers, and the Histadrut, determining an overall tax-wage-price relation, which held for a short period, until excess demand overwhelmed at-tempts at restraint. A similar arrangement was proposed in vain in the spring of 1977.

tive pay. Arrangements for linking pay increases to the cost-of-living index were formerly complex and important points in bargaining, but from 1976, these were adjusted periodically to 70 percent of the increase in the index.* In recent years, severe inflation has made negotiations increasingly difficult.

The next step is the negotiation of specific branch agreements; for example, between the metalworkers and the metal industry, or the Civil Service Commission and the Government Workers Union. The rationale for separate agreements is that productivity and profitability vary from sector to sector. Branch agreements, in practice, may void the national decisions, whose provisions are often more of a floor than a ceiling. Eventually, often *sub rosa*, individual firms and even the government make added "arrangements" with unions or committees. These are often based on unique conditions, such as high profits, or the leverage of critical occupations. If necessary, national limits can be circumvented by complex paycheck additions—whose twists, turns, and fictions may threaten a serious decline in the national morality. "Additions" can be given for such items as professional literature, use of public transport, car mileage, work clothes, and "extra stress" or danger, whether or not in fact these exist.

There are other reasons for the subsequent distortion of the overall national terms. When the smoke of the rhetoric has cleared, it turns out that the real players may not be in the game, since the largest employer, the government, was not on the employers' side of the table in the "global" negotiations, and the President of the Manufacturer's Association represented only a minority of the employers. Nor is the Central Executive Committee of the Histadrut necessarily seen by branch unions or national or local committees as their legitimate and binding representative. Most often, union leaders have lacked even a spectator's role in the global negotiations, nor, as we have seen, do local plant committees or workers' councils have any direct representation at the center of the Histadrut. As specific branch negotiations drag on, the real power relations emerge.

Delay is another factor which aggravates relations. Most often, the overall national agreement is signed very late—after the beginning of the year in question, and the unions are not always eager to complete branch or local contracts. Wages in any one occupation are linked "horizontally" and "vertically" to the wages of other groups. This maintains both wage levels and differentials. It pays to wait, since agreements are retroactive. Because of these linkages and differentials, a small branch which represents a critical trade can hold up the whole country's negotiations. The government has also been accused of procrastinating in order to delay the outflow of additional cash from the Treasury.

* The 1976 global agreement provided an increase of 6 percent across the board for production workers (1976 maximum to be 6 percent, 1977 to be 3 percent); provision for pay differentials for individual productivity; decreased sick pay for short absences; and improved family rights in pensions of production workers.

The year is far along by the time branch agreements are signed. Only then do the individual firms and workers' committees begin their own negotiations. Here the government as employer can play several difficult roles. In corporations where it is a shareholder, it usually holds back in deference to direct management-union bargaining. When it is the direct employer and negotiator, the government is subject to the pressures of critical services and to the unions' perception of the Treasury as an inexhaustible source, in situations where measurement of productivity and profitability may be virtually impossible.

The influence of the workers' councils on the terms of work contracts and on the ensuing relations depends on the strength of the plant committee, or *va'ad*, at the work place. Where the *va'ad* represents a cohesive, large group, and particularly when a national committee represents the workers from several locations, council influence can be small. Still, it is estimated that more than 95 percent of disagreements are settled locally.[28]

Looking back at Figure 5.8 the plant committee is seen to report both to the local workers' council and to the national trade union, which is in turn coordinated by the Trade Union Department of the Histadrut. The emergence of national committees is related to the broad scope of the central Trade Union Department, which has difficulty in reconciling the demands of the different sectors, the need of the Histadrut leaders for internal support, and the requirements of national economic policy. Nor, given the election system, do the national officials have the legitimate authority enjoyed by the elected committees which directly represent the workers at the work places.

Making an agreement stick is often more difficult than getting it signed. In a great many cases, despite artful provisions, the branch and local agreements are formally bound by the overall national decisions which preceded them. One way of regaining room for local bargaining is to first sign the agreement and then bargain about how to keep it, or about what the interpretation of the provisions should be.

Once there is any serious breach in the overall wage levels, the demand for horizontal linkage takes over, and it becomes almost impossible to withstand the spread of demands, backed up by strikes and sanctions. This is what happened in 1976–77, an election year marked by what was then seen as a high rate of inflation. The government acquiesced to the demands and threats of specific groups until little remained of the original wage policy or, in the public sector, of labor peace.

Many specific proposals have been made for ways to improve negotiations and to ensure the continuity of essential services.* Changes are essential,

---

* These include extending the scope and use of arbitration, a national wage council, ensuring enforcement between agreements, disallowing payment of wages during sanctions, the avoiding of delay, and rationalizing the government's organization for employee relations. It is proposed that the government assume the central role in arbitration, which until now has usually been *de facto* the task of the Histadrut Central Committee or Trade Union Department.

but it is necessary for their designers to keep in mind that labor relations are part of the political system, and it is even more important to realize that in Israel the dimensions of labor involve, beyond material rewards or political and industrial power, the question of whether a new and independent working society can be achieved.

Beliefs

Because a small number of people participate in making the main economic decisions, it is worth considering how their ways of thinking have been reflected in their actions. Most of the politicians involved are practical men, unencumbered by economic theory. They are aided by civil servants who are usually well trained in economics. Much advice, often unsolicited, comes from foreign donors or investors, or from lending agencies, such as the World Bank, and from academics.

In 1977, Simcha Ehrlich, a Liberal, became Minister of Finance, and the other principal economic ministries, except briefly for Transport and Communications (DMC), also came under the control of ministers from the Likud. Their announced economic creed, *before* they had experience in office, was far different from that of Labor, and called for the disengagement of the government from the ongoing management of the economy. Indeed, at one point it was rumored that Milton Friedman would be the economic adviser of the new government. It is too early to assess the beliefs of the leaders as they are put into practice. Through most of the 1977–81 Cabinet, in any case, the principal civil servants continued in office.* We will therefore consider here the beliefs as they were expressed in word and action in the first twenty-nine years, until 1977.

Acceptance of the role of the state as responsible for the economy is widespread. Little remains, however, of doctrinaire socialism or belief in nationalization *per se* as a goal, for the sake of a principle; but there is also considerable skepticism with regard to complete reliance either on market mechanisms or on firm administrative controls. The failures of the austerity period of 1948–51 showed how social and market forces overcome excessively rigid administrative controls. Speaking of his own experience, Sapir said to the Labor Party Central Committee, "We have learned through many years that it is better to harness market forces than to direct an economy by administration." He was, however, referring to the market for consumer goods or for small-scale service functions. On the investment side intervention has been the rule, as has been shown. The causes for this approach are found not only in the obvious and pervasive political aims and methods through which the nature of the economy developed. There is a lack of understanding of the

* Economic developments from 1977–81 are briefly summarized in Chapter 10.

needs and methods of competition, or of the possible disadvantages of cartels and monopolies. There is little ideological basis or political demand for antitrust action. Bigness is seen as a blessing, not a curse, and there is awe of the large *konzern* and those who run it as there is inexplicable regard for the building contractor as a man who is actually building the country, or so it seems. The image of these people held by many civil servants or politicians is closer to that of the captains of industry of nineteenth-century lore than it is to "Wall Street against Main Street." When he meets overseas industrialists or potential investors, the Israeli knows that there is a difference between a promoter and one who worked his way to the top and actually understands an industry. But entrepreneurially-inclined civil servants or politicians continue to be impressed by the panoply of successful business, and respect for the producer and his role remains dominant. A politician or bureaucrat can revere the man of great affairs, whom in his heart he would like to be.

Those in office feel a need to be active, to make things happen in the real world, and are not as concerned with thoughts or policies. Led by the historic examples of Eshkol and Sapir, the central government enters into a host of detailed economic decisions whether or not it is capable of making them, and whether or not market forces or actors more directly involved would have better information, intuition, or strategies. To many bureaucrats and politicians, the idea of independence for most activities is difficult to conceive and actively discouraged.*

Professional economic advice is eagerly offered and respectfully considered. Though heard, its utilization has been problematic. Pragmatic reactions to social and political pressures, memories, experience, and the limited scope of the advice have limited its effective use. Most professional opinion has been concerned with macroeconomic issues, such as saving, investment, demand, and the supply of money, or the advocacy of increased use of general rules and of the price mechanism.[29] There has been comparatively little academic interest in market structure or in strategies of growth or export.[30]

Academic economists outside of the government have often felt that their recommendations are used selectively, the government adopting those which suit its plans and ignoring other, integral parts of the proposals. This was more true, perhaps, in the period before the 1974–77 Rabin Cabinet than since. For example, presented with fairly comprehensive programs of tax reform (the Zadok Committee of 1964, or the Asher Committee in 1973), the government adopted only some measures which seemed instinctively right or which promised political payoff, and avoided the "harder" recommendations.

---

* An example is an unsuccessful attempt by the government to control the Israel Foundation Trustees, an independent, nonprofit trust, where funds go mainly for social science research and education. These funds are mainly from nongovernment sources overseas. In 1968, the Deputy Minister of Finance earnestly tried to secure strong government representation on the board of trustees. Sources of overseas funds should not be independent of government, it was frankly said. Surprisingly, some scientists agreed, although they were a minority.

After the Yom Kippur War there was a swing to another extreme—the idea that expert committee recommendations should be adopted *in toto*. In contrast to the previous plans, the 1975 Ben Shachar Committee income tax reforms were immediately endorsed, almost blindly.* This approach was inspired more by the memories of the erosion of many major measures under the impact of group pressures than it was by the belief that the recommendations would be right in their entirety.

It is easier to discern the beliefs when looking back to the first quarter century of the state than it is to mark the trends that might develop in the next decade. For one thing, the 1977 elections marked the replacement of a large proportion of the Knesset members (48 new members out of 120).** Few in the Cabinet had been in a position of leadership in the 1950s or 1960s. And the lessons and modes of the past, seen in the actions of the founding generations, will in all probability, even if remembered, have less influence in the future. Until the Rabin Cabinet, longevity in elective office was the rule. In this, Israel was different from many other parliamentary countries, in which the civil servants remain and the ministers change frequently. In Israel's first twenty-five years, the ministers remained and the bureaucrats moved on. In this, civil servants in the Ministry of Finance resembled senior army officers—the rapid growth of the economy led them into impressive opportunities outside of the government, particularly within the establishment orbit of the Minister of Finance.

To the politician of the past, experience was the great teacher and planning a hazardous practice. Unexpected events could negate the best of forecasts, which in any case could not evaluate the potential of the mobilized will of the nation, capable of overcoming all obstacles. Exogenous forces were perceived as difficult if not impossible to predict. This feeling combined with an ambivalence toward analytical or professional economics to relegate planning and analysis to the background.

Heroic economics—the attempt to surmount all obstacles and venture forth on a broad front—and pragmatic experiment seemed to work. The approach was long on endeavor and short on analysis or strategy. The impression, during the time of Sapir as Minister of Finance, was that of an organist who, having pulled out all the stops, skillfully plays alone with incredible per-

---

* Possible reasons are the all-professional composition of the committee, which had no "representatives" of the bureaucracy or of interests; the fact that the basic approach had long been part of the beliefs of the professional community; the copious practical detail in the recommendations; and the timing of the report—in the spring of 1975, when the Cabinet had had no good news or initiative to offer the public since taking office almost a year earlier. At the time the report came out, the distortions of the existing tax structure were felt by the public to encourage lying and evasion, and a widely favorable reception gave the Cabinet little alternative but to act on the recommendations.

** The party nominees for the postwar 1973 elections were chosen before the war, so that 1977 was the first real postwar election. See Chapter 9.

sonal vigor. There is music on the rack before him, yet he is improvising rather than following it. Musicologists and composers sit nearby, frustrated in attempts to intercede, to get him to read the score or to adopt one of theirs, as they scribble on their own sheets, trying to keep up with what has already been played.

The source for such an approach was the underlying pragmatism of the Mapai attitude to life, and the concepts politicians and civil servants had of their roles and of their beliefs in the sources of economic growth.

Drawing a parallel from Israeli agriculture, the belief has been that many projects and enterprises need to be funded in the hope that some will succeed. Nor was it foreseen that the system of support and dependence which developed would lead to distorted goals and a false entrepreneurship carried out with "other people's money." There was wide tolerance of failure, perhaps come by honestly if looked at in the perspective of the story of economic growth of the developed countries.*

Experience also taught other lessons than the need for enterprise and determination and the immense difficulty, if not impossibility, of imposing strict administrative controls on the consumption side of the economy. The recession of 1965–67 seemed to show that while you could slow down an economy, there was no easy way to control the rate of decline or the ultimate consequences. It was concluded that great caution is needed in starting any downside movement and that any changes made in economic parameters should be gradual and incremental. Growth, and the success in securing large-scale capital inflow (in the face of professional warnings) promised to solve foreseeable problems. If socialist ideology was a very minor part of the economic calculus, the social values of equality and integration have been very important, and the crossfire of group pressures reinforced the beliefs of politicians that tangible rewards must be given to secure social cohesion. This is seen both in the reallocation of incomes and in the avoidance of restrictive measures which could lead to unemployment. A growing real personal income has been seen as needed for effective absorption of immigration without social unrest, to encourage professionals and executives, and to work toward social equality. Energy restrictions, inflation, and chronic unemployment and balance-of-payment problems threaten to shake established paradigms. In Israel, the faiths which formerly guided economic actions are challenged by quantum changes in defense needs and in deficiencies of foreign currency and capital, and by the inherent conflict between the policies needed for growth, to improve the balance of payments, and to limit inflation. It seems unlikely that the beliefs implicit in the old system can apply within the new order of parameters, yet the new course has yet to be developed.

---

* Regarding business failures as part of the process of economic growth, Brandeis said in a speech to potential investors in Palestine in 1923, "There has been hardly a single field of great business success in the United States which does not rest on a foundation of failures. . . ."

The Nature of the Political Economy

A first concern in trying to understand the political economy was with the question, *what restrained the partisan use of an economic power which is highly congruent with political authority?* In practice, the close relations of the economy, politics, and government tend to be more those of an "establishment" than of a purely partisan kind, and national goals are usually placed above sectoral demands. Some of the reasons are the following:

1. The circumstances are such that survival needs can overwhelm more partisan considerations and that immediate goals as well as means are often determined exogenously.

2. Institutions which embody or exemplify beliefs and which give political support are favored, at least when they can perform. The challenges and opportunities, however, exceed these capabilities, and other groups are given a chance. Thus, in the 1950s and 1960s, Labor governments would have given more advantages to the Histadrut enterprises had they shown greater entrepreneurship and effectiveness.

3. Following independence, most of the national roles of the Histadrut and the Jewish Agency began to pass rapidly to the state. Power passed, although not absolutely and not without struggles, to the government centers, where the leaders of the Labor movement conceived their roles as national. Although they strengthened Labor-controlled institutions, the new national leaders tried to keep some balance of power between the sectors. Compromises were carried out, accommodating other parties in specialized or subordinate roles within the system of power.

4. The "practical men" are pragmatists with regard to the way in which goals are to be attained, even though ideologically oriented regarding what the goals are. For example, in the second half of the 1950s, when it appeared that industrialization should get priority, to provide employment for immigrants and to stimulate economic growth, resources were shifted from agriculture to investment in industry, using entrepreneurial talent from many quarters. There was active encouragement of the growth of major financial and industrial empires which now rival the Histadrut enterprises in resources and entrepreneurial talent, providing competition and enhancing central government control. Itzchak Ben Aharon, on the ideological left within the Labor Party, has said, "In Israel there is no responsible public group that questions the legitimate place of private enterprise in the economy. . . ." The way has been generally open to alternative organizations and strategies of development.

Our next question was, *how does the system of economic relations affect politics?* In the main, it restricts political competition. Since most economic enterprise depends to a greater or lesser extent on the government and thus on the political center, the edge of political opposition is dulled. In turn, a bureaucratic political culture emerges in which the flow of ideas and initiative tends to be from the top down, and in which adversary procedures and debate of policy alternatives are discouraged. This condition makes the Knesset's already ineffective control even weaker, and reinforces the closed nature of the political system. A further effect is to discourage independent action by an individual because of the advantages which the system gives to being part of a group and thus "represented."

Further examination shows the growth of mutual dependency of patrons and clients and of the government, pressure groups, and subordinate power centers. Operations are both hierarchical and bargaining. Specific economic interests are involved directly in making decisions, because of the lack of understanding of the concept of "arm's length" and because the knowledge of interested people and their willingness to cooperate are needed. The degree of mutual involvement and the small size of the country work against attempts to avoid conflicts of interest.

The system of the political economy is thus a restrictive force, decreasing the openness and freedom of the political system and fostering a bureaucratic and dependent political culture, the reduction of initiative, passive loyalty, and desire for security. These also serve to preserve inequalities, such as that in which the political and economic influence of consumers is less than that of producers. Foreign investors can be encouraged at the expense of local tax-payers, and workers in critical services are much more powerful than the rest.

Do these close interrelations render the government immobile where hard decisions are needed? How well can situations be handled in which there is little increment of growth to be allocated? Social consensus, growth, and political stability have been associated with the ability to satisfy the demands of many groups. In 1975–77, zero growth coincided with a low point of the Labor Party's internal cohesion, its strength within the Histadrut, and the internal legitimacy of the Histadrut leadership. At the same time, there was a decrease in the authority of the government in the management of the government corporations and in its labor relations. Attempts at comprehensive central control were unsuccessful in coping with many extensive and complex endeavors. In a seeming paradox, as the central control of resource allocations increased, the ability to guide their effective use decreased.

The system imposed authority and decision through a constant process of compromise, in which responsibility is reduced by the extent of interconnection. Because of the interdependencies, reactions are incremental, and there is much bargaining *after* a policy is announced. This may be the most feasible method when there is little adversary opportunity or alternation in office, and when the legitimate form of *de facto* confrontation is bargaining and dependency. For years, the Labor Party carried the big stick—the congruence of economic resource control and political authority. Partly as a result, ongoing decisions are much more in the hands of the ministers than is the case elsewhere,* so that "hard" decisions are impeded when political authority wanes.

The ability to develop policy is another matter. Talents and information are available, but their use is not as effective as it might be because (a) reactions are anticipated, correctly or not, and intimidate. When planning steps are about to be taken, there is much consideration of possible resistance by entrenched organizations or groups, or by ministries which are thought to be interested parties or fiefdoms. (b) The arts of designing the execution and follow-up of policy are in a primitive state and receive little attention. This is also the case with the ability to decentralize decisions and regulate them. (c) As an output of the system, a strategic type of thought and action is rare. (d) Many of the benefits of debate and adversary challenge were not available, not to speak of the stimulating effects on a politician before 1977, of being out of office and having to try to return. The capability to meet future challenges with effective policy should be measured in these terms, rather than by looking mainly at the impressive record of achievement in the past.

What are conceivable future developments? It is difficult, if not impossible, to consider them outside of the context of the overall political system; however, some speculation might be of value.

One eventuality is the further growth of independent centers of organizational and economic power, away from the government. Protégés, or nominees, once they begin to feel their new authority, whether it be in the Bank of Israel or in a conglomerate, have been seen to become "their own men." It remains to be seen whether the trend toward independent control of resources will become steeper in the new regime. One great bond has now been untied—that of the Histadrut and the party in office, and another severance is planned—the separation of the Histadrut from much of its control of health services. Within the Histadrut, however, politics remains a predominant concern. Alternate trends are conceivable. Foreseeing an era of greater economic challenge and more open competition, the Histadrut leaders could try to strengthen the economic efficiency and effectiveness of Hevrat Ovdim. On the other hand, fear of losing control of major resources could lead to increasingly zealous political control.

While there seems little doubt that the general tendency toward the uncoupling of microeconomic decisions from government will continue, given the change in the parties in office, there are strong forces working against a major change. The political economy which I have described, with all of its problems of organization, has worked reasonably well without polarizing or splitting the society. Since all sectors have a stake in the present structure of

---

* In France, Michel Crozier has suggested that the politicians are weak while the bureaucracy is tough and makes the draconic decisions which are needed when things are particularly critical.[31] In Israel, the ministers have relatively more direct control.

the country, the economic establishment would probably join and follow any likely and reasonable political leadership which succeeded in meeting the needs of survival and individual rights. There is serious doubt whether the economic system could be uncoupled so as to gain benefits of increased initiative, adversary proceedings and arm's length, and effective system policy and management, without parallel changes in the political system itself. Alternatively, can the political system become more open and the political culture less bureaucratic without substantial change in the way the political economy works? The eventual answer will depend a great deal, as has economic development in Israel *per se*, on exogenous forces and outside challenges—but no less, as in the past, on the way institutions and ideas can adapt to new situations. In the past, failure of enterprise was not penalized. Since the 1973 war and in the crises of the world economies, this is no longer feasible.

The economic future could indeed look dark for a country dependent on the outside, locked in to defense needs, and isolated because of oil from nearly all fair-weather friends and allies. The resources available to overcome these obstacles include highly developed institutions, energy and enterprise, trained analytical ability, cohesion under outside threats, and a workable degree of freedom from ideological rigidity. An extensive system of education, a literate, energetic, and ambitious population, and developed science and technology can do much to overcome the adverse external situation and the inherent limits of a small home market, distances from overseas customers, and the diseconomies of essentially small-scale industry. The help which these advantages might give, however, is still to a large extent checked by the system characteristics and by inadequate strategic thinking directed toward the future. There is one resource, however, which is domestic and which in the end will decide the outcome—the capacity of people. The development of this potential force is a principal concern of social policy, which we now consider.

CHAPTER 6

The Welfare State

THE GOAL before independence was an ideal society in which social ills would be eliminated by productive work, full employment, and egalitarian rewards. The accent was on the youth, and the inconvenience of the elders was the lot of the transitory generation of the desert.* In reality, rapid economic growth, universal education, and comprehensive welfare services have eased but not eliminated serious social problems; nor has the ingathering of the exiles, through the simple fact of their rescue, led to their equality or to full social integration. Potential divisions emerged along ethnic and class lines, rooted in the congruence of social and educational disadvantage with community origins.

Decades after independence, the ideal image is confronted with a reality in which some children born in a Jewish state can grow up to be uneducated, alienated, or delinquent, and in which there exist substantial inequalities in life opportunities. There is fear that these conditions could endanger unity and cohesion, while external threats and economic crises bring a realization that only a sound society using all of its talents can stand up to the dangers inherent in the growing armies, wealth, and influence of the Arab states. This chapter considers the challenges, the response to them, and the beliefs and in-

* In Numbers 32: 11 and 14, Moses explains that none who were twenty years old or more when they left Egypt, except Caleb and Joshua, would enter the promised land.

287

terests which influenced social policy. There are four sections—a short summary of the social condition as it appeared in 1980; an overview of the development of social policy; an analysis of the experience in several of the principal areas; and a consideration of the ways in which social policy was determined.

The Challenge

From the first months of independence, the ideals of equality, and even of minimum living conditions, were tested by the great influx of impoverished and comparatively uneducated immigrant refugees.* The country could not supply the needed food, housing, and employment. As a result, economic growth—settlement, new industry, and the absorption of immigrants—preceded questions of income distribution. Within a decade, public housing, extensive new agricultural settlement, and the founding of industries had made the economy viable, and by 1959 the national product was more than two and a half times that of 1949. Few people were without some form of permanent housing. Virtually all had access to health care, and public health programs had largely arrested infant mortality and tuberculosis.

Social integration and education advanced much more slowly. The geographic dispersal of the population to development towns and to new agricultural settlements was achieved only at some social cost. The kinds of employment available in development towns offered comparatively little chance for technical or managerial advance, and the initial concentration of people with low levels of skill and education was increased by selective migration of those who were more enterprising or skilled, from the periphery to the center. This made it even harder for those communities to become self-sufficient in providing effective local government, social services, and cultural amenities. In the older towns, slum areas developed, with concentrations of rapidly growing families having low incomes and education. Conditions in these neighborhoods were in sharp contrast with those in nearby middle-class suburbs, increasing the feelings of deprivation and frustration.

Elementary education was compulsory and free after 1949. Within less than a decade, however, large differences were seen between the average attainments of children whose parents were born in Israel or came from Europe and America, and those from Asia and Africa. In a way similar to the experiences of large immigrations in the United States, the educational and oc-

* Even in the Yishuv the new immigrant was behind, as shown in a 1933 scale of daily building wages (approximate 1933 dollars):[1]

Skilled worker "A"	$3.00
Builder's helper	1.80
Unskilled worker	1.52
New immigrant	1.20

cupational mobility from the first generation to the second has been high, and more than one-quarter of all university students are children of parents who had only elementary education or less. This achievement, however, occurred mainly in families of Western origin. In 1975, the proportion of each age group which entered a university was still more than three times as high among European/Americans as it was among youth from Asian/African families.

The causes of this lag and the progress which has been made will be discussed later. The gap at the lower extreme is of particular concern. Of the 8 or 9 percent of the high school age group who do not study or work, the great majority tend to have the following characteristics: they are children in families with five or more children; their parents have less than an elementary education, and were born in an Asian or African country; and they live in crowded housing, in a poor neighborhood, or in a development town. Although more than 50 percent of all Jewish youth finish high school, substantial differences remain. The issue is seen as the central policy question of the educational system, and that having the highest claim on resources.

Arab education is still behind that in the Jewish sector, in facilities, in the proportion of teachers who are fully qualified, and in student attainments. Only 20 percent of Arab youth follow vocational studies, compared with nearly 50 percent among Jews. The gains have been impressive, however, and from 1965 to 1975 the proportion of Arab teenage youth studying in high school doubled. There remain underlying questions of an Arab education which, it is hoped, can at one and the same time support cultural pluralism, create understanding of the Jewish and Arab identities, and advance Arab social and political integration.

The Equality and Maintenance of Incomes

In terms of income, Israel remained egalitarian, compared with many other countries. Even relative poverty has not shown the sharp increase of inequality often associated with accelerated development. Broad income maintenance and housing programs have reduced the incidence of extreme want. Extensive national ownership of land prevented the growth of a class of landowning *rentiers*, and the costs of building, taxes, and interest have discouraged potential urban landlords. *Relative* inequality of current money income increased only slowly, due to institutional restraints on wages, progressive direct taxation, and transfer payments.[2] There was moderate success in teaching immigrants new skills and in giving them new occupational direction. The proportions of total income received by high-, medium-, and low-income families are similar to those in other Western welfare states. In a typical year the one-fifth of the families with the lowest incomes receives about 7.5 percent of the total income, and the highest one-fifth about 40 percent, after taxes and transfers.

The data, however, do not ease the sense of deprivation felt by those with the lowest incomes; nor have these ratios been very useful in policy analysis.* Inflation raises the nominal market value of the investments of those at the upper end of the scale, while for those with low or medium incomes, proportionate outlays on housing and food grow. A fairly small group accumulates large equity or urban real estate holdings, their capital gains often enhanced by legal or illegal tax avoidance. A self-employed middle-class population, working mainly in small businesses and personal services, operates in a cash-transaction economy whose extent seems widespread but is hard to quantify, and in which the collection of taxes is still ineffective.

Economic growth was accompanied, however, by acute differences in terms of *absolute* income, increasingly manifest in the close quarters of a small country. The disadvantages of immigrants from developing countries were exacerbated by the rapidity with which Israel became an industrialized, service-oriented society, where rewards go to those with training and achievement. Left behind were large families in which the head of the household was an unskilled wage earner, as well as those whose lack of earning power was limited by health or age. Stronger groups could successfully demand a larger share of the rising national income, while the aged, the less skilled, and those whose occupations were not critical to the operation of essential services had much less economic bargaining power or support within the Histadrut. Political relations and market forces thus enlarged the absolute gap, affecting mainly the children in large families in which the father was unskilled or not working.

The impact of these forces on differences in income is ameliorated by the extent to which income maintenance is guaranteed in adversity or old age. The National Insurance Institute (NII) collects payments from employers, employees, and the self-employed. The benefits paid cover a wide spectrum, including old-age benefits, insurance against work accidents, allowances for children under eighteen years of age, insurance against physical incapacity to work, maternity grants, unemployment insurance, and compensation for wages lost through Army reserve service. The extent of pension coverage and the levels of old-age benefits are inadequate, however, as are the provisions for the chronically ill and for geriatric treatment and rehabilitation. Income maintenance, because of the NII and the policy of income transfer, became a less critical aspect of social policy. There remained, principally, the question of the aged, a constant need for provision against the inroads of inflation, and the existence of specific sectors in which several dimensions of poverty are seen in the same family and in the same neighborhood.

---

* Particularly so because of the lag in data. From 1969 to 1976 there were no new survey data available on household expenditures.[3]

The Multiple Facets of Poverty

Among the weakest of the population, a single family may face poor living conditions—in crowded housing and in a poor social and physical environment—and cultural deprivation for its parents and children, who show low scholastic achievement. These have a cumulative effect which threatens the life chances of many children and thus the future of the society.

A landmark study, made in 1971–72, assessed the "multiple, simultaneous conditions . . . of poverty for children."[4] Using as indicators low income (less than 40 percent of the mean wage per person), very crowded housing (three or more per room), and a father with seven or fewer years of school, the data showed a very strong impact of poverty on large numbers of children, mostly in large families. For 22 percent of those below eighteen in 1969, at least two of the three conditions occurred simultaneously, and for 3 percent of the children, all three. In families in which the three conditions of distress occurred, one-third of those between the ages of fourteen and seventeen neither studied nor worked, compared with only 5 percent of the youth in families which had none of these attributes. Table 6.1 shows the conditions of children in the urban Jewish population in 1969, 1972, and 1977.

In 1969, 15 percent of all children and 21 percent of those of Asian/African origin lived in families whose income was below 40 percent of the mean. While these conditions are continuously being ameliorated, they are still found extensively in some areas, particularly in the development towns, and in poor urban neighborhoods, or *shechunot*. Most of these neighborhoods, in which there is a concentration of the facets of poverty, developed from the original location of transit camps, or *ma'abarot*, or from the relocation, together, of people who had lived in these temporary quarters and who were moved *en masse* in order to better their housing conditions.

The achievements in public housing have been dramatic. Many early solutions, however, were the seeds of future slums. In the 1950s, the government built small family apartments only 300 or 400 square feet in area, and often whole neighborhoods were constructed without adequate planning for services. The growth of large families eventually led to high densities and to geographic concentration of homogeneous poor populations. Intense overcrowding and neighborhood cultures of poverty were kept from spreading to catastrophic proportions only by continuous large-scale investment in public housing, and by the gradual improvement of planning and building standards. Yet most of the original smaller and substandard dwellings remained in use.

The criteria generally used to specify substandard housing are in themselves substandard: "Two or more, or three or more persons per room of the dwelling." Two to a room means, for a family of four children and two parents, an apartment of about 500 to 600 square feet, having two bedrooms and a living room. Such a family living three to a room would occupy a one-bedroom apartment.[6]

**TABLE 6.1.   Vulnerability Characteristics Among Jewish Children
(0–17 years old)**

	1969	1972	1977
Total Number of Children	891,000	952,000	1,056,000
Size of family			
Children in families with four or more children	355,700	369,800	341,000
(Percentage of total population of children)	(39.9)	(38.7)	(32.3)
Children in families with six or more children	160,200	168,300	102,400
(Percentage of total population of children)	(18.0)	(17.7)	(9.7)
Housing density			
Three or more persons to a room	232,100	191,900	94,300
(Percentage of total population of children)	(26.0)	(20.2)	(8.7)
Education of head of family			
Eight or less years of schooling	522,000*	503,500*	550,000**
(Percentage of total population of children)	(60.8)*	(54.2)*	(52.0)**

* From Habib and Katz.[5] Unstarred data in table are from Keren Ya'ar and Souery.[5]
** Estimated from *Statistical Abstract of Israel, 1978,* and Mosheh Egozi.[5] Table 12 in Egozi shows 46.5 percent of fathers of children in the first grade to have had eight years or less of schooling, versus 60.1 percent of fathers of the children in the 8th grade.

The improvement is impressive, but in 1977, 2.9 percent was nearly 24,000 families, and included a much higher percentage of the children of the country, almost 9%, since it is the large families which are crowded.* Family size is strongly related to ethnic group, so that those born in North Africa and

TABLE 6.2.   Housing Density

YEAR	% OF FAMILIES WHO LIVED TWO OR MORE PER ROOM	% OF FAMILIES WHO LIVED THREE OR MORE PER ROOM*
1959	56.9	22.9
1969	27.7	8.5
1974	20.4	5.2
1977	15.3	2.9

* By 1982, this criterion was obsolete.

* Lavatories and kitchens do not count as rooms. If additional criteria are applied, such as the need for repairs or private family baths or showers, the number of families in substandard dwellings could be 45,000 to 50,000 (1977).

Asia and their children formed a large part of the population with poor living conditions, although sharing, over time, in the general improvement in standards.*

Housing is not the only or, often, the most severe problem of poor neighborhoods, in which there is a high concentration of people with social problems—members of the weakest groups, who participate least in the society, whose children have the least chance for advancement, and who cannot make good use of the universal education and other services which the welfare state tries to provide. Outmigration of the more successful intensified the homogeneity of the weak population. In particular, these neighborhoods epitomize what may be the most serious result of the historical development of the concentration of poverty: a feeling of dependence, of having a right to be supported, and of a lack of efficacy in controlling their future progress, fate, or present condition. In many places, however, indigenous leadership has begun to develop, and is finding expression in the participatory arrangements of the urban rehabilitation projects begun in 1978.

Health Care

Medical care is now widely available, heavily subsidized by the government, and thus inexpensive. More than 95 percent of the population is insured for treatment, hospitalization, and medicines. Most of those who are not insured are either those of means or those who are provided with care through the social welfare agencies. About half of the hospital facilities are provided by the government, and most of the rest by the Histadrut's Kupat Holim, or Sick Fund, which also acts as an insurance agent for the medical insurance of Histadrut members. Most outpatient care is given through the clinics of Kupat Holim or those of other, smaller funds which care for about 10 percent of the population. The smaller funds, not having their own hospitals, send their patients to government hospitals, provide their own clinical services, and insure their members. The members purchase prepaid health care, which is provided as required and in keeping with the availability of facilities. Births and the treatment of accidents are paid for by the NII.

With more than one physician for each 500 people and extensive hospitals and insurance coverage, the broad needs of health care are met; yet there are sources of dissatisfaction. The problems of the system are mainly associated with its efficiency in the use of resources, with the lack of convenience for patients, with the quality of care for noncritical cases, and with preventive public health provisions. Insurance coverage is not uniform, and until 1975 many were not eligible because of age or previous disease. Urgent hospital-

* From 1970 to 1977, the percentage of families whose head was of Asian/African origin living three or more per room declined from 16.4 percent to 6.2 percent while the national average declined from 7.5 to 2.9 percent.

ization and surgery are always provided, but those whose cases are not considered critical often wait a long time for hospital treatment. In the general-practice clinics, relations are often impersonal and administratively irritating. Most specialists work full time in hospitals, while the general practitioners, who staff the clinics, have little connection with more advanced medicine and see themselves as second- or third-class professional citizens. Although nearly all doctors are salaried employees, they concentrate in or near the larger towns, while development areas are understaffed. Facilities for the chronically ill, aged, and mentally ill are inadequate, as are those for dental services. While public health statistics show the general health to be good, those living in crowded conditions suffer from deficient public hygiene. Intestinal disease, for example, is much above the average.*

The system tries to give superlative and sophisticated care to hard cases while providing minimal, adequate care for the greatest number, resulting in a generally low standard of comfort. Inconvenience and overcrowding are frequent. Cultural differences in expectations among people of different origins, and between those of doctors and patients, cause dissatisfaction. There are continuing ethical problems due to private practice, which staff specialists are allowed under certain conditions. Egalitarian wage policies have made it hard to reward excellence in the public systems or to attract and keep nurses, so that labor relations are repeatedly disturbed. The system is replete with major administrative problems which the Ministry of Health has not been able to solve. An almost singular move toward efficiency was an early decision to use general hospitals for military purposes, avoiding overlapping facilities. Other recommendations have been offered in vain, however, and serious organizational development will probably have to wait until the political questions are resolved, permitting attention to be directed to the more substantive and difficult problems of labor relations and organization.

Work and the Distribution of Occupations

The distribution of occupations is of concern for two reasons: the contribution of work to economic and social development, and the relation between social values and the kind of work people do. On both counts, the occupational distribution in Israel is questionable. The employment in service, white-collar and managerial roles, commerce, and finance is high in proportion to that in industry and agriculture, in comparison with other industrialized countries (See Table 6.3).[8] The rate of work-force participation is also lower in Israel (See Table 6.4).

* The incidence of diseases such as dysentery and stomach typhus has fallen continuously. There is no evidence of simple hunger in calory intake, but children in large families and the aged poor have a borderline intake of vitamins and proteins, for cultural as well as financial reasons.[7]

TABLE 6.3.   Percentage of the Work Force Engaged in Principal Sectors

	% IN AGRICULTURE	% IN INDUSTRY	% IN COMMERCE, FINANCE, MANAGEMENT, AND SIMILAR SERVICES
Israel	6.2	23.9	52.0
United States	3.7	22.4	47.2
Great Britain	2.5	32.6	43.1
West Germany	6.4	34.8	41.0
Sweden	6.1	26.5	50.8
Switzerland	7.7	37.7	38.2

TABLE 6.4.   Work-force Participation as Percentage of Total Population

	ISRAEL	U.S.	SWEDEN	ITALY	GREECE
Men and women	33.1	45.2	50.4	35.5	36.9
Men	43.9	55.9	57.8	52.2	54.3
Women	22.3	35.0	43.1	19.6	20.2

The differences in sectoral employment (Table 6.3) are ascribed to the imbalance of payments—with Israel as a heavy importer of capital; the supply of labor from Judea and Samaria and Gaza, which discouraged deepening the use of technology in production; the inflationary demand economy, which has allowed service costs to be passed on to the users; the greater return to financial and intermediary services than to production; and to an accompanying change in values regarding the desirability of industrial work as compared with the white-collar occupations. The occupational distribution reflects a character of economic activity which impedes progress toward economic independence.

The Response to Social Needs

The foregoing brief account of the principal parameters of social welfare indicates that many basic needs are satisfied. Recurrent protests, however, brought home what the data should have demonstrated: that egalitarian tax and wage policies, economic growth, and schooling did not eliminate want, nor did they rapidly reduce the inequalities of life opportunities. The protests were symptoms of the subjective dimensions of the social condition. These challenged the ideals of the new society, which sought a degree of integration beyond the elimination of want and the provision of education and health care. The following brief history will show how the social policy system developed, and why the welfare state is not enough.

The Yishuv had provided its own services. Voluntary and dispersed, they were rudimentary, except for schooling and medicine. Welfare then had low priority and meant mainly the charitable care of the residue who could not help themselves and were not expected to become able to do so.[9] In 1931, when Henrietta Szold set out to organize the Social Service Department of the Va'ad Leumi, or National Committee, she found the partisan and ad hoc welfare activities in a state of neglect and confusion. "Everything is chaos," she wrote, "and the chaos is static."[10]

There were soon more order and professionalism, helped by the work of refugee social workers from Germany. Organizations of national importance in social welfare were the Histadrut, the Hadassah Medical Organization, and the Va'ad Leumi. The Histadrut developed provident funds, health insurance, labor exchanges, unemployment relief, and housing assistance, a broad array of insitutions which outlined the essentials of a future welfare state. While these services were only for members, it was hoped that eventually the membership would include all wage earners and self-employed who did not employ others. Other political movements later began services on a smaller scale.

In the Yishuv, the Jewish community provided its own medical care. The Mandatory government had operated rudimentary facilities, used mainly by Arabs, as well as public health and veterinary services. Hadassah developed hospitals, research, clinics, and pre- and post-natal care, working mainly in Jerusalem, but also in Tel Aviv and the *moshavot*. The city of Tel Aviv and religious organizations in Jerusalem also initiated services. Founded in 1912, the Kupat Holim of the Histadrut was by far the largest medical organization by the end of the Mandate. In 1948 all health funds together enrolled 55 percent of the Jewish population.

The state was committed to welfare from the first. Labor governments in England and Sweden were influential examples, but the greatest impetus came from the obvious and urgent needs of immigrants for employment, guidance, and medical care.* Newcomers received an initial six months membership in Kupat Holim, and a new Ministry of Health took over public health and began to build government hospital facilities. The services of the Va'ad Leumi and the Mandatory government were incorporated in new Ministries of Welfare and Labor, and the Jewish Agency gave social aid in the camps under its charge and in new settlements.

From the groundwork of the welfare state, laid in the Yishuv by the

---

* For example, independence brought European refugees who had a high incidence of tuberculosis, and among the Eastern immigrants there was at first much infant mortality. Within a decade, tuberculosis was practically eliminated. The practice of giving birth in hospitals became accepted, and clinical services grew, as did family instruction. These dramatically reduced infant mortality from 51.7 per thousand in 1949 to 20.8 per thousand in 1974 among Jews. Among Arab Israelis it decreased from 62.5 in 1955 to 37.0 in 1974.[11] The Arab Israelis now have one of the highest rates of natural increase in the world, 3.7 per cent in 1977.

Histadrut and other voluntary organizations, there began a process of transfer to the state of the central social welfare functions. Education and employment services were nationalized, and a major and continuing commitment was made to public housing as a right; while nationalization of medical services and pensions was to be successfully opposed by the Histadrut. The scope of social services was extended, but their quality was limited by budget constraints, by the partisan dispersion of authority among different ministries (with the lesser coalition partners, generally, receiving the responsibility for health or welfare), and by the limits of the managment and financial capabilities of local government.

Before the War of Independence was over, an interministerial committee began to draw the outline for a welfare state.* In 1950 the Cabinet approved the general aims, but without details, of a program calling for medical insurance, pensions, unemployment insurance, grants to mothers, disability insurance, and children's benefits. The costs of insurance were to be borne by the employers, the workers, and the government. When it came to actual legislation, however, the provisions were attacked from many quarters. The Ministry of Finance feared the high costs involved in immediately guaranteeing full welfare services, most of whose recipients, as new immigrants, would not be able to contribute for some time. The Histadrut, and within it particularly the left, saw a national health service as inimical to the political and organizational appeal of Labor, and as going counter to the concept of providing services for members only. Decisions on the health services and pensions were deferred, to be investigated over the years which followed by a series of irresolute public committees. By the time of the 1977 elections, these issues had still not been resolved.

The most important positive result of the first Kanev Committee was a system of universal insurance based on the National Insurance Institute, founded in 1953. Beginning with survivors' and old-age benefits, work injury and birth expenses, the NII expanded over the years to become the principal agency for carrying out transfer payments on a universal basis. Under its first director, Giora Lotan, the NII developed a rational, apolitical organization that formed the basis for its later growth. As national needs and resources grew, benefits and premiums were increased, additional groups of people and types of risks were included, and eligibility was made more liberal.[12] **

---

* The committee chairman and moving spirit was Itzchak Kanev, who had been head of the Histadrut's Kupat Holim and a leading champion of welfare. He was, at the time, Director of the Histadrut's Research Department; and the fact that he could chair a committee of government department heads shows the blurred lines of those times. Other members of the committee, while civil servants, were strong party men. Histadrut leaders probably saw Kanev as their representative, at least until he recommended that health services eventually be nationalized.

** In 1977 premiums paid by employers and employees totaled about 20 percent of basic wages, up to a ceiling equivalent to a medium-level professional salary.

Wadi Salib: A Turning Point

In the 1950s it was widely believed that formal equality—in access to education and eligilibity for social services and work—would lead to equal opportunity and social integration. Before the end of the decade, these beliefs were seen as an illusion. A lag in educational achievement was already becoming apparent, but it required the occurrence of violent protest to dramatize the disparities which had developed and to place the social condition closer to the center of national concern.

The change was triggered by the 1959 riots in Wadi Salib, an old, decrepit section of Haifa, at the base of Mount Carmel. Abandoned by Arabs in the 1948 war, it was settled by the lowest-income North African immigrants, who soon saw themselves left behind by other groups in the general social advance. The area retained only the poorest. In July 1959, violent outbreaks were sparked by false rumors that police had killed a local resident under arrest. A few demonstrations in other towns followed.

In the Wadi Salib quarter, extreme personal and group frustration was prevalent. What appeared to the residents as political exploitation and politicization of services had not been accompanied by any sense of genuine political participation. The protests were specifically ascribed to the individual frustrations of the leaders, who felt that they were being used without concomitant recognition in status or political roles; but the reasons lay much deeper.

Initial official statements ascribed the events to political incitement, but the government recognized that there were underlying problems. To depoliticize the issue and also to search for causes, it appointed a commission of inquiry. This localized the issue and took it out of the Knesset and national politics. While the ensuing report drew attention to the marginality of the protesting group, it emphasized the seriousness of the deep feelings of discrimination which the protests revealed. At that period, when a "melting pot" theory was still widely held, the events seemed to show a failure of social integration, and their impact on policy was felt for some years.

In the 1960s, the demonstrated inadequacy of the provision of formal equality led to the introduction of compensatory measures. These were particularly evident in the formal education system, where expenditures in real terms grew 10 percent a year between 1962 and 1972, compared with an annual growth rate of 2.8 percent in the number of pupils. Extra resources were directed to schools and classes in which disadvantaged children studied. Structural reforms followed later, in an effort to advance integration and to extend the upper age limit of compulsory education. In 1968 an act was passed providing for a reform of the school system, in which there would be six years of elementary school, followed by six years of high school. Tuition was to be free and attendance compulsory through the ninth grade, and eventually through the tenth. In development towns, tuition was made entirely free, while elsewhere scholarships were provided according to need. The faith in formal education as a central arm of social policy was not diminished by evidence of the limited ability of schooling, by itself, to develop the society.

Throughout the 1960s, children's allowances and welfare services were extended. The professional training of social workers began, and research developed data which gave more meaningful evaluations of the conditions of poverty.[13] In 1966, a sharp economic recession hit hardest at unskilled and semiskilled workers. Unemployment was felt most in the development towns. After the 1967 war, economic growth and full employment resumed. The recession prepared the way, conceptually, for the later introduction of unemployment insurance and for the maintenance of income through payments rather than through emergency work projects. But in the economic boom, social euphoria began to disappear as equal aspirations were confronted with visible social differences. In 1971 the protests by the Panther group in Jerusalem and demonstrations for housing by young couples propelled the social gap to the top of the political agenda.

The Panthers were a group of marginal youth, some with records of juvenile delinquency. Their surroundings and life experience led to acute feelings of frustration and alienation. Most belonged to large, non-Ashkenazi families in Musrara, an old, poor neighborhood which until the Six Day War had been on the border of no man's land between Israel and Jordan, or in the Katamon neighborhoods. Many of the group had grown up together, dropping out of school at a young age.[14] Their organization as a protest group was encouraged by Jerusalem social workers who were dissatisfied with municipal policies toward community work and believed in neighborhood action. The wordings of the demands were general, asking for "equality" and "an end to discrimination." There were complaints about the better public housing given to recent immigrants from Russia, and there was a general attack on "the establishment," together with demands that "ethnic differences disappear."

Apparently the police initially mishandled the potentially violent group, denying permits for demonstrations and arresting some of the leaders—which in turn led to the use of force and to property damage, clashes with the police, and wide publicity. The national government intervened, tempers eventually cooled, and the group adopted quieter methods, such as parades, for which permits were given; requests to speak to ministers and Prime Minister Meir, which were granted; and formal political organization. Extensive reports in the press and in Knesset debates in the main decried violence but also agreed that there were root causes which needed attention.

Protest led to shock, and shock to inquiry, as it had after Wadi Salib. Scholars became champions, and their findings the basis of policy in the early 1970s before the Yom Kippur War, particularly the report of the Prime Minister's Committee on Children and Youth in Distress, which was influenced by data from the Research Department of the NII and from the Falk and Szold Institutes. Even though many of its recommendations were not used, the work of the committee was a milestone in Israeli social policy. Appointed following the Panther protests, the committee at first was asked to recommend policies to counteract juvenile delinquency. The chairman, Israel Katz, soon convinced Golda Meir that delinquency was only a symptom of the deeper problems of the social condition. The terms of reference were extended to include the overall conditions of children and the organization of the social services which affect them.

After more than two years of work, ten subcommittees including, in all, over 100 members brought out reports which painted a dismal picture of the multiple conditions of poverty under which a large proportion of the children lived. Recommendations were made for larger budgets and for universal rather than selective services, directed so as to be available and beneficial to those in distress. The organization of the social services would be rationalized, for example, in the unification of organizations providing income maintenance. The committee asked that a special group be appointed to follow up its recommendations and called for the development of an integrated social policy.

The overall result was more significant than the specific outcomes. The committee brought together many able and concerned people, who developed and presented a coherent definition of conditions, and issued a cogent demand for a social policy aimed at improving opportunity and social integration—not just at easing potential frictions and averting crises. Heightened public sensitivity to poverty led to recognition of the need for high priority in allocating resources and directing efforts toward alleviating it. A beginning was made at central policy coordination through a Ministers' Committee on Welfare and the new office of Welfare Adviser to the Prime Minister. Although an important start was made in central data collection and analysis, the effectiveness of these attempts was limited by the semifeudal Cabinet organization, and by the separateness of the paths along which social and economic policies are formed.

An outstanding development of the early 1970s was the extension of transfer payments, especially in the form of children's allowances and old-age benefits, resulting in the removal of many families from the selective relief rolls. Between 1969 and 1975, the percentage of all families which received relief money as their sole or partial support dropped from about 5.5 percent to 2.7 percent. About five times that number received help in kind, such as rent or tax reductions, institutional and home care, or the placement of children outside the home. More than one in seven people (with a considerable turnover) still had some connection with the welfare system.

Social service personnel (such as truant officers, workers with street-corner youth, community workers, and community-center leaders) increased rapidly during the first half of the 1970s. These services did not seem to go very far toward solving the major problems of the social condition. It is probable, however, that in many areas their activities prevented a serious decline.

The 1973 war slowed but did not stop the growth of social efforts. On the eve of the war, the proportion of resources used for defense was decreasing, reaching below 20 percent of GNP for the first time since the Six Day War. (Figure 5.1) Education was holding its own at about 20 percent of the budget, while the outlays for income maintenance were being increased. As an outcome of the war, defense outlays rose steeply to 40 percent of GNP, and by 1976 were still more than 33 percent. The principal reduction came in the investment for economic growth. Social budgets were cut proportionally less, but the effects were felt in the services rather than in the level of transfer payments. The extension of free and compulsory schooling through the tenth year and the expansion of the junior high school system were curtailed. University budgets were slashed in a conscious decision to favor support for the early school years, which would help larger numbers of children in the search to close the social gap. Social services given in kind were cut, but not as part of a master strategy. They were simply more vulnerable because their levels, in contrast with income guarantees, were not protected by legislation.

More than before, the period after the 1973 war showed the complex dependence of social effects on economic policy measures. Rapid inflation threatened the middle class as well as the lowest income groups. Economic steps, aimed at reducing overall levels of consumption through price increases or at restraining budget deficits, led to sharp reductions in the real incomes of middle-income and professional people, who had neither the linked capital assets of the better off, nor the transfer compensations of the poor. The trend was to more universality of income maintenance, with priority given to raising the levels of the poorest groups and to a relative reduction of the middle-income living standards.

More was done and more success was achieved in transferring money resources and providing for the physical needs of housing and medical care than in learning how to improve the cultural aspects of the quality of life; and there was great difficulty in organizing to provide social services effectively, or, indeed, to work out overall social policy and goals. Efforts were made to develop services which could teach people to avail themselves of the opportunities which were offered and to manage their family affairs; and there was more emphasis on adult education and the provision of services which fostered personal, family, and neighborhood development.

Changes in organization with a view toward rationalizing the delivery of social services proved to be impossible in the coalition Cabinets, with different parties leading the several social ministries. The Mafdal led the Ministry of Welfare, and Labor the Ministries of Education and Labor, until 1977. Attempts to nationalize health services and pensions were caught in the web of the relations of the Labor Party, the Histadrut, and the government, as will be shown.

Situational needs, interests, bureaucratic and party strengths, and beliefs determined the responses to the social challenge. As a guide to understanding these effects, the history of developments in several policy areas is analyzed briefly in the following sections. The discussions include employment and the maintenance of income: employment services, unemployment insurance, pensions, and transfer payments; housing; health care; education; and organization for the absorption of immigrants.

Employment and the Maintenance of Income

Nationalization of Employment Services

In the Yishuv, employment was a political as well as an economic necessity. Beyond its central place in the ideology, work was needed to prove to the British and the world that the country had the economic capacity to absorb more immigration.[15] In the internal politics of the Yishuv, recurring hard times enhanced the political salience of job patronage or work allocation.* Taking over the separate employment services of its component parties, the Histadrut initially sought a monopoly as the supplier of labor, and engaged in a bitter and occasionally violent struggle to this end against the Revisionists and the religious Hapoel Hamizrachi, who had organized competing services. Work opportunities were then a major attraction for membership and helped the Histadrut ranks to grow from about 5 percent of the Jewish population in 1920 to over 25 percent in 1936.

Gradually the Histadrut abandoned the aim of monopoly for a broader coalition in which the Histadrut, and through it Ahdut Ha'Avoda and later Mapai, would be dominant. In 1927 an agreement was made with Hapoel Hamizrachi in which the latter would benefit in return for recognizing Histadrut primacy, a step which neutralized the Mizrachi parties' possible political advantage in the employment field. A bitter but unequal struggle continued against the Revisionists, in whose ranks there were few private employers who had either the political conviction or the economic capability needed to resist Histadrut pressure. One reason that Labor did not achieve a monopoly was the importance of the General Zionist government of the city of Tel Aviv and of the Mandatory government as employers. The leaders of Labor were also becoming convinced that, in practice, by giving concessions Labor would continue to predominate in a coalition arrangement. By 1937 more "general" labor exchanges were established in Tel Aviv and the

---

*In 1927, for example, 40 percent of the workers in Tel Aviv lacked regular work. A severe economic crisis in the 1930s was due to the world depression and restrictions on immigration. In the early 1950s, the economy could not employ, in the short term, masses of untrained immigrants.[16] In the recession of 1966–67, as much as 10 percent of the work force lacked employment.[17] From 1970 to 1976, employment was full or overfull. During the 1976 civil war in Lebanon, Lebanese could work in labor-short factories in Israel without creating public or union protest.

moshavot, and by 1943 in the other towns, to include other groups, but not the Revisionists. From 1939 the Jewish Agency was represented in the control of the exchanges, and supplied most of the budget. In a type of "party key" arrangement, 60 percent of the jobs went to Histadrut applicants.

The trend toward nationalization, begun in the Yishuv, continued in the state. At first, the exchanges were really part of the local workers' council, collected Histadrut dues and pension contributions, and helped in the negotiation of agreements on the conditions of work. This sectoral form of operation was fought not only by the right. Mapam, when it headed the Ministry of Labor in 1948-49, also favored nationalization. Mapai soon regained the ministry, however, and by 1959 the government was providing 75 percent of the labor-exchange budgets. For many years Mapai was able to use the exchanges effectively as a political resource through patronage in staffing and work allocation.

Pressure for nationalization had developed among a broader public, and the 1955 coalition agreement promised "a just allocation of work, without discrimination, and on the basis of first come first served, seniority, and other rules which will guarantee fairness and efficiency in work allocation. . . ." The desire for equal access to work, to be shown by the removal of sectoral control of the employment service, coincided with belief in *mamlachtiut*, the national rather than sectoral approach, favored by Ben Gurion and many younger Mapai leaders, such as Giora Josephtal, who was Secretary-General of Mapai from 1955 to 1959.[18]* The motivations of the Mapai leaders were thus both electoral and ideological.

The Histadrut leaders agreed, if not wholeheartedly, with Ben Gurion, reassured by the Histadrut retention of the organizational strength of the health services, Kupat Holim. By that time, also, they were second-echelon followers, at best, rather than the leaders of Mapai.** The first rank of leaders, in their government roles, took more of an electoral and *mamlachti* view. Many in Mapai agreed to the change because they saw it as one of form rather than content. The electoral benefits of reducing overt party intervention could be gained without loss of control.

Other conditions were favorable for the change. The role of the exchanges in the social political system had diminished. Labor agreements were by then negotiated by the national unions, and the Histadrut had centralized other functions, such as the collection of pension-fund contributions. Employment

---

* The Knesset elections of 1955 brought a marked decline in General Zionist strength, and Ahdut Ha'Avoda and Mapam were candidates for the coalition. The Progressives were wanted in the coalition by Ben Gurion, as representing the liberal middle class and constitutionalism and as a counter to the left; and they made nationalization of employment a condition of joining the government.[19]

** Pinhas Lavon, who was still of the first rank, although defeated by Ben Gurion, followed Namir as secretary-general; but in other roles the party leadership had already gone over to the government. Namir, secretary-general until 1955, then became Minister of Labor.

was no longer the crucial problem it had been in the absorption of immigrants, nor as amenable to direct political, instrumental use. The advocacy of sectoral employment services no longer had much symbolic electoral appeal for the followers of Ahdut Ha'Avoda or Mapam, so that Mapai had little opposition from the left.

In 1959 a law provided for a national employment service under the aegis of the Ministry of Labor, to serve all equally. It was to be overseen by a national commission on which the "general public," the employers' organizations, and the Histadrut would be represented. The minister was given extensive powers to appoint the executive and senior workers of the service and to decide on the organization. Existing exchanges were transferred to the government.

Formal nationalization was part of a long development in which Mapai-dominated exchanges began to serve members of other groups as well. The change had been continuous rather than discrete. The politicization of the employment service did not stop abruptly with the transfer to the government, but it did decline somewhat along with the increasing professionalization of the civil service and the greatly diminished role of the employment service in the long periods of full employment.

Unemployment Insurance Results from Fiscal Needs— and Is Yet Untried

The question of income maintenance for those who cannot find work first arose during the large immigration of the 1950s. Emergency public works, in forestry or land clearing, were used as a short-run alternative. By the beginning of the 1960s they could be discontinued, as agricultural and industrial development had materially reduced unemployment. Work projects were preferred over welfare payments for ideological reasons.

The needs created by the recession of 1966, however, exceeded the possibilities of emergency work, and the government had no plans ready for projects which could have immediate effect. Although unemployment insurance was necessary, neither incomes nor government resources permitted the deduction of premiums from wages or the payment of unemployment benefits. By 1970, as employment and incomes increased, the Ministry of Finance looked for ways in which to curb inflation through wage restraint and other means of reducing consumer demand. The memory of the recession was still strong. In 1970 an agreement was made among the Histadrut, the government, and the employers on price and wage restraint, known as the "package deal." One of the provisions, not specified in detail, was for wage deductions and employer contributions for unemployment insurance. It was hoped that these would postpone purchasing potential to a time when it might be lacking. Overall economic considerations thus overcame the fears that payment without work would lead to social degradation.

Once this broad political decision was made, it was thought that only questions of method remained, and the problem was referred to a professional but representative committee, headed by Dr. Rivka Bar Yosef. Two controversial problems of principle then arose, however. The first was the possible elimination of the custom of severance pay owed by the employer—officially one month's pay for each year of service, but often more. The second question was whether unemployment payments should be at a fixed rate, the same for all, or vary as a proportion of the previous wage. The Histadrut was successful in retaining severance pay, as a "basic right of labor," even though pension rights, together with unemployment insurance, could eliminate the need for it. In the event of unemployment, compensation was to be wage-related. In the interests of mobility, some of the funds accumulated from the contributions of employers and employees were earmarked to finance retraining programs.

In 1950, when the Kanev Committee had first recommended unemployment insurance, the Histadrut, Mapai political leaders, and the Ministry of Finance were opposed. Twenty years later these stands had changed. The ideas of social policy, expounded over time by professionals and academics, the fiscal interests of the Ministry of Finance, the belief that mobility of labor would be needed for economic growth, and the impact of the 1966 recession all combined to change the prevailing views.

Pensions: A Histadrut Bastion Is Endangered

Before independence, the population was younger and there was less concern for security in old age than there is now. Some consideration for independence after the working years was shown in the goal of home ownership for workers, and in the founding of Histadrut pension funds; but in 1948, these funds enrolled only 65,000 workers. With time, pension and endowment contributions became a major source of investment funds for Labor enterprises, as well as a very important form of household saving, and the level of employers' contributions was an important point in negotiating plant work agreements.* By the midsixties, there were seven separate contributory funds within the Histadrut, each related to a major branch of enterprise.

About 80 percent of all wage earners in 1976 had some form of pension or retirement fund coverage, through Histadrut funds or other contributory arrangements or through the budgeted pension rights of local and national government. Only one-half of those insured, however, were insured for continuing income for their survivors, or for themselves should they become unable to work. Of those then over sixty-five, only a small proportion had

* Employers and workers contribute. In order to enjoy tax exemption, it is required that 92 percent of the funds be invested in government-approved securities, and of these, about one-half are invested in Histadrut enterprises.

pensions, and one-half of the elderly received welfare supplements to their National Insurance payments. Since 1974 these supplements have been paid automatically to those in need, bringing the income of a single person up to 25 percent of the average national wage, and that of married people with dependents up to 40 percent. Even though they are linked, these stipends alone offer a very meager existence.

Originally it was hoped that most workers would supplement National Insurance benefits with Histadrut pensions; yet by 1963, less than 3,000 were getting these pensions, compared to nearly 70,000 then receiving NII old-age payments. The coverage of the funds was seen to be inadequate, and other means were sought.

Another factor has been the actuarial condition of the Histadrut funds, threatened by the increase in the average age of the members, the generous benefits, and the division of the Histadrut programs into separate funds, which decreased their risk-bearing ability.[20] The aging of the population was accompanied by increased competition from other forms of saving, such as insurance or the provident funds of the banks. Younger people were reluctant to undertake to contribute for long periods, in some cases more than forty years, in order to receive a pension of 70 percent of their last wage.

As the average age rose, political sensitivity to pension needs grew. At independence only 4 percent of the population was over sixty-five; by 1975 the proportion was more than 8 percent.[21] The political impact of the greater numbers was enhanced by the existence of a pensioners' organization and by the diffusion of the belief that personal freedom is linked to individual economic independence.* At the same time, the pension funds and Kupat Holim remained the last great power bases of the Histadrut, aside from purely trade-union activity. In contrast, the NII, as a large, semiautonomous organization within the government, sought to make social transfer payments larger, less discretional, and more universal, and to perform these transfers through its facilities. The Ministry of Labor was interested in removing barriers to mobility caused by the linkage of pensions to specific work places, and the Ministry of Finance sought higher saving from wages while trying to keep the bill low; and both of these ministries wanted to strengthen control from the center. These considerations led to demands for national pension legislation, initiated by Almogi, then Minister of Labor, in 1968.

The Histadrut pressed for a public commission on which it could fight for the independence of the funds. In 1969 Chief Labor Court Justice Bar-Niv chaired a committee which included, in addition to leading civil servants, representatives of three separate parties in the Histadrut, which had tried but failed to have the terms of reference specify that any proposed system would use the existing funds.

---

* For example, even though all the needs of members are cared for as long as they live in the kibbutz, there is a demand for kibbutz pension programs to increase the dignity and freedom of the aged, and to give the feeling that they are remaining because they want to, not because they have to.

The main questions at issue were, and still are, who should control the flow and management of the pension funds, what the economy can afford, and who should pay. At one extreme, the NII advocated a national fund which would pay a large supplement, based on wages earned and NII premiums, paid universally. At the other, Mapam and Ahdut Ha'Avoda, within the Histadrut, sought more strongly than Mapai to limit the universal component severely, continuing the central role of the Histadrut funds. The Ministry of Finance, estimating an annual cost of 27 percent of the wage bill, wanted to lower the annual earned pension increment from 2 percent to 1.5 percent, thus requiring forty years of work to earn a 70 percent pension.

The Histadrut sought to reduce the importance of the universal, or NII, portion, thus increasing the incentive to join Histadrut funds. Further, it opposed a national coordinating body, as restricting the independence of its funds. The Manufacturers Association feared that compulsory insurance could force employees to join Histadrut funds and asked to found its own, partly as a source of investment funds for private industry.

The elderly themselves had far less influence in the debate than the large organizational interests. Those as yet without pension rights had no direct representation, since the Pensioners Association acted mainly for those already entitled to pensions. But the real focus of the struggle was the control of investment funds and the organizational resources which the funds gave as a "last bastion" of Labor strength. The public arguments, however, were stated in terms of actuarial prognoses, economic growth, and public finance. Thus proponents of nationalization asked for the actuarial safety of large numbers of members and adequate compulsory contributions, and cited additional benefits of job mobility through universally valid pension rights. Their opponents claimed, for the Histadrut funds, the advantages of closer contact with members.

The impasse reflected the difficulty in evaluating the costs, benefits, and feasibility of a universal system of adequate pensions. Politically, it was related to the division of opinion within the Histadrut and the Labor Alignment, in which the political power associated with the continued control of the Histadrut funds contrasted with social needs and electoral appeal. This impeded what would in any case be a hard decision of social priority. By 1977, despite committee recommendations, there was as yet no bill before the Knesset.

Income Equality and Income Maintenance

Welfare payments were originally conceived as a way of supporting the residue of the people who could not support themselves. They were seen as charity doled out by social workers according to needs, and in many cases, in practice, as a compromise between needs and individual and political pressures. Rather than help their clients gain the ability to advance on their own, social workers were compelled to dissipate their energies and abilities in an ameliorative and bargaining role. At the same time, there developed a comprehensive system of public subsidies, reaching into many areas, including public housing, essential foods, and public transportation.* The concept of welfare as charity gradually changed, and more universal methods were used, exemplified by the transfer payments of the NII.

The way to determine these benefits, however, was the subject of debate for some time. Throughout the 1960s, welfare and NII benefits were determined in nominal money terms, occasionally updated following changes in living costs and standards. The aged were particularly hard hit by this process, and their NII stipends dropped from 20 percent of the average wage in 1954 to 12 percent in 1970. By the end of the 1960s, full employment was achieved, but poverty remained. The demands of those left behind led to a reassessment of the egalitarian ideal. Those who saw economic development as the central aim tried to show that equality was in fact being achieved, while their opponents argued that whatever the indices, there were many unmet needs, and valid underlying causes for disaffection.[2]

One approach, which failed to be accepted, was to determine a minimum welfare budget for the least advantaged. It was hard enough to establish what the needs were or, ethically, to decide them for others; and such a budget, even if it met subsistence needs, would ignore the relative nature of poverty. Further, those who worked at less skilled occupations, families with many children, and many of the aged did not see themselves as the proper recipients of welfare; yet they had difficulty making ends meet without financial assistance in addition to wages or old-age benefits.

The approach eventually adopted—together with its larger political implications—was that of poverty as a *relative* concept.[22] From 1973, income guarantees and social supplements were linked to the average wage or, in some categories, to the changes in the consumers' price index. Children's allowances were introduced to assist larger families of low-skilled workers; but they were universally applied. Begun on a modest scale in 1959 for the fourth and subsequent children, allowances were later extended to the first three children of wage earners (1965) and of the self-employed (1970). By 1974 the children's allowances for a family with four children were more than 20 percent of the average wage, and 50 percent for a family with nine children. The effect was to reduce by 25 percent the number of children whose families

---

* Subsidies paid to the producers of such essentials as flour, oil, sugar, or public transport have been important aspects of income maintenance and price-stability policy. They are criticized for benefiting those not in need, for distorting consumption patterns, and for placing the budget at the mercy of fluctuations in world commodity prices. Arguments for subsidies have included the statement that money paid directly to needy consumers might find less beneficial use. The marginal benefit of money saved through subsidies is much higher for those with low incomes. Subsidy cuts raise the cost-of-living index and, in its train, wages and linked obligations, thus stimulating inflation, so that the net saving to the budget is considerably less than the gross subsidy cuts.

had an income below the poverty line. In the tax reform of 1975, children's "exemptions" were eliminated, while credits against the taxes owed were given for each dependent, with refunds in the case of overpayment of taxes. As such, they were a step toward a negative income tax.*

As it became the principal vehicle for the transfer and equalization of money income, the National Insurance Institute was successful as the advocate of liberalization of benefits and criteria for eligibility. In this its Research Department was particularly influential, as the principal source of data and analysis of the income and expenditure aspects of the social condition. The role of the NII expanded, also, because of the administrative ease afforded by its organization for collection and disbursement; and its universality meant that an increase of a fraction of a percent in obligations to contribute resulted in a large absolute cash flow.

Income transfer became a central element of social policy within a consensus regarding the government's responsibility to provide for a minimum standard of life, because it was easy to administer, while insurance payments absorbed part of the money supply, thus reducing the propensity to spend, and providing the government with an important source of cash flow. The system is somewhat regressive, because of a ceiling on the income on which contributions are based; but it went far toward equalizing money income and the ability to purchase basic necessities. In 1977, after taxes and transfer payments, the ratio of the average incomes of the top and bottom deciles was reduced from 22:1 to 8:1.** One critical consumption need, however, that of housing, has for many Israelis remained too costly to purchase or rent in the open market; so transfer payments alone do not provide an answer.

Housing: A Striking Physical Achievement Presents a Social Challenge

The response to immmigration, new families, and the need for housing has been massive public investment in building over the years. Public housing

* Assuming a "poverty line" which is 40 percent of the median disposable income, in 1969 about 15 percent of all children were members of families with an income at the poverty level or less after accounting for taxes and transfers. It is estimated that the incidence of a poverty income level in 1973 was 12.5 percent of families and 9 percent of children.[4,23] In 1975, about one-third of those over sixty-five were poor, and made up one-sixth of the poor people in the country. A critical shortage of facilities for those chronically ill or unable to care for themselves added to the problems of the aged.[24]

** For quantitative measures, see note 2. In the full employment of the 1970s, Lorentz coefficients were 0.30 or less. For a Lorentz coefficient of 0.0, each tenth or other arbitrary fraction of the population gets an equal share, while 1.0 means that the highest division receives all of the income. By such measures, Israel is comparable to Canada, Scandinavian countries, and the United States. These measures are limited by the consistency of inputs and by distortions, such as those caused by tax evasion and fringe benefits at the higher range, or by nonmeasurable transfers at the lower. Small changes in coefficients, particularly when not showing a consistent trend, may not be indicative. The most reliable input data are from the surveys of family budgets.[3]

starts have usually represented about one-half of new dwellings in the country, or one-third of the area built.* Another response was to attempt to clear and rebuild old neighborhoods under an ineffective 1965 Law for Building and Evacuation of Rehabilitation Areas. In 1978, the government initiated a large-scale urban rehabilitation program called Project Renewal, which aimed at changing the social condition in urban slums through a concurrent program of social and physical improvement, the measures taken to be determined through extensive resident participation in decisions and with an emphasis on community development.

Although the greatest part of the physical housing needs have been met, more complex problems remain—of the quality of the society as it develops in the environment of neighborhood living, and of flexibility in the use of the available stock of housing. As has been shown in the account of the integration of immigrants, public housing decisions have been a principal determinant of the social condition. The results, seldom foreseen or intended, often decided the character of, location of, and relations between groups in the shechunot and development towns. The quality of housing was related to the period in which people came. In the 1950s, needs were urgent and resources very limited. Typical family units were smaller than 400 square feet in area, and often less. In th 1960s, individual apartments were larger, but very often part of massive, long, four-story apartment buildings, which led to very high densities and proved difficult to enlarge or modify as needs and standards changed. In the 1970s, new public housing had reached typical apartment areas of more than 750 square feet, at a time when private housing norms were over 1,000.

In the 1960s and 1970s, many families, whose size had far outstripped the quarters they had been given on first leaving the transit camps (ma'abarot), were transferred to larger quarters. They found themselves, however, living with the same people with whom they had lived in the old neighborhood (and whom they often regarded as culturally deprived and, like themselves, stigmatized for it). They were now often in concentrations of very large families of similar background, in high-density buildings. Many remained in the older neighborhoods, which, like the new, were often characterized by social malaise, and which, in addition to high density, usually lacked amenities and adequate social and commercial services.**

As the children grew up, it was found difficult for young couples, particularly those who came from poor neighborhoods, to get housing of their own.[26] Little new rental property was available, and high interest rates and a lack of mortgage loans caused almost two-thirds of more than 30,000 new families, in 1975, to depend on social help in the form of public housing or

---

* More than 80 percent of the country's dwellings, some 850,000, were built between 1948 and 1974. Housing starts in some years were nearly twenty per thousand population.[25]

** Chapter 8, "The Physical Environment," and Chapter 3, "Political Integration," discuss settlement and population dispersal.

government-assisted mortgages. For many, inflation prevented these solutions from being feasible. At the same time, the total inventory of housing would have gone much farther toward answering the needs if ways had been found to make its use more flexible throughout the life cycle of families, and if the rents charged for public housing were high enough to allow maintenance to keep pace with physical depreciation.

Policy and Organization

Minimum adequate housing has been seen as a social right, not to be allocated entirely according to need (as is medical care), but on a minimum standard believed necessary to social and mental health. Where a family cannot find a solution on its own, there is a consensus that the government should step in. In practice, the economy of housing is mixed—both public and private. The state constructs new dwellings, plans new towns and neighborhoods and builds infrastructure, clears or rehabilitates slum areas, and subsidizes mortgages or saving schemes on a large scale.

Until 1961, housing was a branch of the Ministry of Labor, which then was the political ministry *par excellence*, comprising housing and employment services. From 1961, there has been a separate Ministry of Housing, until 1977 under Labor. The ministry operates a vast and complex organization, consisting of its own staff, seventeen government corporations, part ownership of mortgage banks, and subsidy programs for budget and development.* The government participates with municipalities in joint public corporations to build or renew areas; and through the public Amidar Corporation it manages, rents, and sells public housing. Most public construction is commissioned from the large building companies, owned by the government, the Histadrut, the Jewish Agency, and large private contractors. Allocation to new immigrants is determined by the Ministry of Absorption. For others, decisions are mainly at the municipal and regional level, by housing committees on which the different social ministries and local government are represented, but which the regional offices of the Ministry of Housing tend to dominate.

The recurrent policy questions are how much housing to build, of what types, and in which locations; and how to make it available to those who need it most. The decisions are complicated by the competing aims of population distribution, the locational desires of immigrants, and the need to set priorities among three large and important groups: immigrants, new families,

* The new ministry arose largely from personal and coalition changes. When Ahdut Ha'Avoda came into the coalition in 1961, Yigal Allon asked for the Labor Ministry, then under Josephtal of Mapai. The solution was a separate Housing Ministry under Josephtal, with Allon as Minister of Labor. The aegis over towns, typically, was also divided. Carmiel came under the Ministry of Housing, since Labor was developing Arad, while the Agency developed Kiryat Gat and the surrounding Lachish area.

and those living in substandard conditions. More recently, sensitivity to the social context of neighborhood life and to the importance of reducing social dependence have added a new and crucial dimension to that of housing *per se*.

A second kind of question is how to achieve the goals economically—for example, whether or not, and under what circumstances, rental property is the better solution, particularly for young couples,* and whether it would be better to rehabilitate older and more central areas than to develop new ones. These problems, and land-price policy, deserve far more attention than they have received from economists and government analysts. Similarly, progress in rationalizing building methods has been disappointing, considering that the Ministry of Housing, as the largest buyer and builder, could experiment and impose solutions with relative ease.

In housing as in the rest of the economy, politics, policy, and bureaucratic behavior are closely mixed. In new rural settlement, the Agency works through political settlement movements as it has always done, and location and population are determined by agreement among the parties and the agricultural and regional planners. Urban housing policy is not directly partisan, and reflects the demands of groups, national-regional settlement goals, the interests of the large public building firms, the needs of the economy, and bureaucratic politics. In the allocations to individuals at the local level, partisan patronage has decreased with time, compared to the impact of the demands of local neighborhood, ethnic, and other groups; and there has been considerable rationalization of procedures, such as the introduction of a point system to determine priorities.

Housing is very sensitive to public pressures. The organizations involved in building or managing housing have much to lose or gain, the resources involved are large, and the importance to the economy is great.** Economic and employment considerations are added to those of the social goals, and these interests are embodied in large and powerful institutions. Those who cannot get it easily with their own resources see housing as their right, a natural outcome, perhaps, of the system through which immigrants were supplied with their needs, administratively, on arrival. Substandard housing is the most visible evidence of a social gap, since it is concentrated in specific neighbor-

---

* Homes are usually built with short-term mortgages which cover less than a quarter of the costs. Seventy percent of all families owned their own homes. (In poor neighborhoods the proportion between owning and renting is reversed.) For old buildings, stringent rent controls from the Second World War were continued, leading to poor maintenance. The high cost of land, building, and money make it difficult, if not impossible, to get an adequate return from new rental property, since government subsidies or unusual tax benefits are not available.

** Building provides 10 percent of the employment in the country, plus that of peripheral industries. In 1976, a year of modest immigration, new housing was 5 percent of the government budget. The large housing companies are helped with low-cost capital and land and get additional rights to private building as a reward for building public housing. Strangely, public housing has followed the business cycle of the private housing developers instead of operating counter to it, and the impact of periodic shortages or surplus is thus accentuated.

hoods and among members of identifiable ethnic groups or young couples. Differences are often due simply to the timing of arrival in the country and to family size (which varies among cultures). Thus an immigrant from an underdeveloped country who came twenty-five years ago, living in a two-room apartment with eight children, could see a new immigrant arriving from the Soviet Union in 1975, with only three children, placed in a three-room apartment.

As on other questions, protests have stimulated housing action. Wadi Salib and the Panthers had a general impact, but a very specific and influential occurrence was a series of live-in strikes carried out by young couples in the same period as the Panther demonstrations. In the early 1970s, housing for immigrants (by this time of ample quality) and slum clearance had priority over housing for young couples. An attempt to organize as a national group resulted mainly in independent local demonstrations with parades or sit-in strikes in the offices of mayors or of the Ministry of Housing, or the unauthorized occupation of empty flats.

The young couples' demands were much more specific and substantive and the protesters more widely representative and less marginal than the Panthers. The government, in effect, was charged with having failed in planning resource allocations, and with discriminating against native youth in favor of new immigrants. The Cabinet's reactions to the protesters were mild and encouraging. Mrs. Meir acknowledged that "this is one of our most serious problems," but went on to add, "Since the State was founded, defense problems have always been first on the Cabinet agenda." Mr. Sapir agreed that "at today's prices, I wouldn't be able to buy a flat," and unfroze some 100 million lire for housing in a crash program to building additional units. Local authorities or representatives of the Housing Ministry negotiated with the protesters, finding partial ad hoc solutions or promising future programs. Local planning committees allowed zoning variances to contractors who would undertake to build price-controlled flats for newly married couples. The protests died down following government promises of higher priorities. An assessment of needs, compared to the availability of housing, was never clearly resolved. It is complicated by the uncertainties of predicting immigration and by locational immobility of those seeking housing. The reaction to the young couples was less one of hurt or bewilderment than that the problem was a rational one which could be solved by the use of thought and resources; and the events had a measurable and rapid effect on housing investment priorities.

The demands for housing work against the goals of population dispersal. New couples or crowded families resist moving to new communities even if it would improve their housing conditions; and professional immigrants naturally prefer the metropolitan centers. There is also some question about the chances of improving the overall urban condition unless the attractiveness of the periphery and its opportunities are substantially improved. Nor is the

Ministry of Housing, when deciding where to locate new construction, insensitive to the concentration of voters in the central areas, to economy in construction, or to the interests of the large building companies. In 1976 it was claimed that 35 percent of new building was on the coastal plain, 22 percent in the Negev and the south, and 11 percent in Jerusalem.

Beyond physical achievements, housing policy and organization show a high concentration of the control of resources and the power of the producer which characterize the Israeli economy and government. Until 1965, the Ministry of Housing could plan new neighborhoods without approval of the town-planning system. For decades, the criterion of success was the number of housing solutions provided for individual families.

In the planning of new quarters and of towns, there is now within the government more countervailing force than before. Since 1965, the ministry's town plans need municipal and district planning-authority approval, and the Land Authority itself seeks to make policy for land use. Together with such elements as more control, competition, and diversity of opinion, much more effort is needed in the analysis and rationalization of this central economic and social activity. The goal is not merely, however, that of economic rationality and flexibility in resource use, but the development of a system which could materially reduce the present unusual degree of dependence, greater in housing than for any other social need.

The Politics of Health Care

There is general agreement, among doctors as well as patients, that the provision of medical care for all is a public responsibility. The controversy, on the agenda since the early 1950s, is whether the policy and management of health care should be dominated by the Kupat Holim of the Histadrut or nationalized, like education. Related questions concern organization and criteria for effective and efficient service, and the ethical dilemmas which arise in a social medical system when some people are prepared to pay for more prompt or comfortable care or for the services of specialists of their choice.

From another point of view, the issue is not that of government or Histadrut control, but whether the service will be dominated by the experts and producers (the physicians) or by the consumers. Both the Histadrut's Kupat Holim and the Minister of Health are politically responsible. In practice, however, their response to the public is as remote in regard to health services as is the response of bureaucracies in other fields.[27] The question is thus far more complex than the language of the public debate shows. In thirty years none of the principal issues were resolved through the political system.

Like pensions, health care is only partly nationalized, and remains a major resource of the Labor movement, which has strong interests of ideology and power to keep things as they are. Since 1937, a Histadrut tax office, *Lishkat Ha'mass*, has collected dues and health insurance, at a high overhead cost.

The hundreds of office workers involved form a reserve battalion for political campaigns. For Mapai, and later the Labor Party, the vast organization of clinics, hospitals, and laboratories serving more than 2 million people provides extensive patronage and support. For the Histadrut, the medical service is a major membership attraction for hundreds of thousands, and guarantees the payment of union dues.* At the same time, the parties agree that medical services should be provided publicly for all. This explains the seeming paradox in which the right urges the nationalization of health, while the left tries to preserve the autonomy of the health-insurance funds. While Mapam has ideological reasons for strengthening the Histadrut as a class bastion of Labor, Labor's pragmatic interest has been in the political-resource potential of the organization. The Histadrut has been strong enough to prevent nationalization, but it has not been able to maintain autonomy and at the same time gain public financial support for all of the Kupat Holim requirements.

Time changed public values and the relative strengths of the interested groups. The Histadrut's overall position became weaker, while the hierarchies in government hospitals and of the medical profession grew stronger. Yet most, if not all, of the Histadrut's demands were entrenched in the proposed National Health Law, which was in committee in 1976. The history of the long impasse in the debate on health legislation shows these changes.

After independence, health was emphasized in the proposals for comprehensive welfare services brought to the Cabinet in 1950 by the Kanev Committee. It was an interministerial committee without interest-group representation, and despite their requests, doctors were not among the members. The report recommended eventual national health insurance after an initial phase in which there would be universal insurance through the existing funds.

Opposition was general, including Mapam and many in Mapai. Ironically, the Progressives (antecedents of the Independent Liberals, who were the principal advocates of a nationalized system in the 1976 Cabinet) voted against the measure through fear of injury to the smaller funds, which, like the Kupat Holim, were then politicized. In 1951 they still saw the political system as one in which they too could develop effective support through services and economic activity, not foreseeing that the dominance of the Kupat Holim of the Histadrut, together with professional and bureaucratic interests, would make the political importance of the smaller funds negligible. The Ministry of Finance opposed increased demands on the budget. Proponents of *mamlachtiut* (or of the overall state rather than sectoral interests), like Ben Gurion and Josephtal, did not press too strongly, in Ben Gurion's case probably due to realization of the political importance of the resources available.[28] In any event, it was feasible not to decide because the vast majority of the people had insurance coverage, and there was thus no acute or salient public issue.

---

* Amnon Barzilai, in a series of articles in *Ha'aretz*, July 1976, reports surveys made for the Histadrut in 1969, 1971, and 1974. In these there were two large groups of reasons given for being Histadrut members, both by about 25 to 30 percent of the respondents: (a) "for ideological or trade union reasons," and (b) "because of the health or social services provided."

In 1955 the guidelines of the new Cabinet had promised universal health coverage based on the existing funds. A second Kanev Committee was appointed in order to plan it. By now the Medical Association was much stronger, and three doctors joined the civil servants and representatives of the National Insurance Institute on the committee. The report, while favorable to the Histadrut position, recommended a National Hospitalization Authority. The existing funds would be represented on the governing council of the Authority in proportion to the size of their membership, so that the Kupat Holim of the Histadrut would probably dominate it. Yet the Histadrut rejected the report, seeing it as the beginning of nationalization and publicly questioning the legitimacy of a decision made by a group in which the Histadrut had no representation. Perhaps the Histadrut would have done well to endorse the proposal. Time was not on its side, and both the Progressive Party and the doctors opposed the proposals, as advancing, in their view, politicization and Histadrut dominance.

By the mid-1960s, however, Kupat Holim appeared to be more willing to give up some of its predominance. It was in growing financial stress, and beset with problems of labor relations with professional and service personnel. There were internal factional struggles related to the politicization of Kupat Holim, because of which the labor factions had not agreed on a party "key" allocating jobs in proportion to party strengths.* Partial nationalization was seen as a way out of these difficulties. The change in view was explained as being due to the needs created by changes in medical technology, the increased services demanded by the public, and the decline of voluntarism in the medical profession. In 1966 Abba Choushi, the Mayor of Haifa, was appointed to head a committee which was asked to recommend how best to give all of the people full coverage using the existing funds.

The committee, which had broad representation from the parties, the medical profession, and senior civil servants, was sharply divided on the issues. The majority advocated extending insurance coverage under the existing system, in which the tax offices of the funds would continue to collect the dues. A minority, representing the doctors, the Liberals, and the Independent Liberals, emphasized rational organization and, particularly, freedom of the insured to change from one fund to another. They recommended that dues be collected nationally by the NII and that membership in the Kupat Holim and the Histadrut be uncoupled—that is, membership in one would not be contingent on membership in the other—while hospitals would come under unified national management.[29] These polar differences were to remain central to the ensuing legislative struggle.

After the 1969 elections, legislative proposals called for joint management by the Ministry of Labor (insurance) and the Ministry of Health (hospitalization and medical standards). Continued insurance through the existing funds

---

* The classic mode of the Yishuv. See Chapter 1.

was proposed, with dues to be collected by their separate tax offices. Insurance funds and hospitals would be supervised by public boards, on which the funds would be represented in proportion to their membership. While in principal, it would permit members to change from one fund to another, the proposal provided no protection against the removal from Histadrut membership of a person who left Kupat Holim for another health fund.

Before the law could be drafted, opposition began to organize. A public committee headed by the President of the Bar Association, Joshua Rotenstreich, then published and attacked the proposals. Its critique was based mainly on the proposed dominance of a national body by the Histadrut's Kupat Holim, on the probable decline or demise of the smaller funds, and on the claim that the proposed supervisory Authority would create large overheads with few accompanying administrative benefits. Despite opposition, by 1976 most of the provisions had been approved in committee. The Labor Party, which led the Ministry of Labor, would be in a position of control, whatever the degree of nationalization. If the extent of nationalization were to be great, the Labor mainstream would be able to direct it, as it had other public services. If small, with Kupat Holim predominant, Labor influence would remain high.* Mapam was in more of a dilemma, ideologically committed to Histadrut predominance yet lacking control within the Histadrut, and seeking more authority for the Health Ministry, which it then led. In the end, Mapam was the strongest proponent.

By this time, public opposition was led by the Medical Association, with wide press coverage and support—and that in the Cabinet by the Independent Liberals. Opposition kept the bill in committee, while an acrimonious public debate focused on two main questions: the continued collection of dues by the tax offices of the funds, which would give a public function over to private organizations and add an estimated several hundred million pounds a year to collection costs;** and a clause which allowed an internal vote in an approved national organization or trade union to bind its whole membership to join a specific fund. While a member could change funds after a six-month delay period, an amendment was defeated which would have prevented the Histadrut from expelling a member who left its health fund. The Histadrut's attitude was understandable. Over and above the political resources involved, Kupat Holim was, for the Labor ideology, the most prominent example of the ideal of mutual help. The uncoupling of membership in the Histadrut and Kupat Holim would signal the transformation of the Histadrut from a social movement into a trade union.

The basic political issues thus remained vital to the groups concerned.

---

* In 1965, fourteen out of fifteen regional directors of Kupat Holim were from Mapai, and twelve of sixteen administrative directors of hospitals.
** The NII proposed to collect the insurance at an incremental cost of 0.5 percent of the dues; while the Ministry of Finance estimated that tax-office costs were more than 8 percent of the dues.

What had changed were the strengths and public roles of the groups. The Medical Association, once small and malleable, became large and vocal.[30] While the doctors opposed the extensive party politicization of the management of the Kupat Holim and demanded that doctors be given the leading administrative roles, they were also very critical of the ministry's inability to get resources for its hospitals or to give administrative leadership. The Ministry of Health's bureaucracy reflected the continued weakness of a minor alignment partner ambivalent about the government-Histadrut relationship and having less management or professional capability than the government hospitals (officially under the ministry's supervision) or Kupat Holim. Another question is the policy roles of physicians versus those of patients. Kupat Holim is governed by politicized boards that, in theory, represent the interests of consumers (patients). In practice the parties and the Kupat Holim bureaucracy tend to predominate.

Of course, the relations of beliefs, interests, and personalities were far more complex than I have been able to show here, and the Histadrut was no more monolithic regarding health than it was on other issues. Most of those on the center and the right, within and outside the Histadrut, would have accepted a nationally controlled and unified organization. For this they found growing acceptance, as the financial questions became more critical and dissatisfaction with the level and the convenience of services grew. The more closely the problems are observed, however, the more difficult the organizational solution for effective care appears. The issue called nationalization may be a misnomer. In recent years, the government has paid the bill. The questions are, how much control the government should have, and what form would enable it to make health policy most effective. For most of the public, concerned with the cost and accessibility of medical care, the political questions are not the issue.

The Fostering of Immigration: A Cornerstone Is Neglected

The advancement of *aliya* (immigration) and *klita* (absorption) has been less effective and has had less priority than its central place in the purpose of the state would imply.[31] In the 1973–77 Cabinet, it was not once on the full Cabinet agenda. The difficulties arise from the clash of modes and jurisdiction, of the Agency and the government; from the gap between the personal goals and needs of the recent immigrants from the West or the Soviet Union, on the one hand, and the goals and needs of the state, on the other; from the relatively low priority accorded to organizations, within the Israeli governmental system, which are engaged in advancing overall goals rather than specific services; and from the inability of the government to lead in tasks which require a large amount of voluntary action. The issue became salient after the Six Day War, when it was felt that the potential of Western *aliya* was not being realized.

Until that time, in the Yishuv and the state, the Agency had coordinated *klita* activities in Israel, as well as fostering *aliya* in the Diaspora—encouraging, selecting, and transporting immigrants, providing initial housing, settlement, and work. In the Yishuv both the organization and the selection of immigrants was done on a partisan basis, emphasizing recruiting and education abroad. In the state, the organization continued to be manned according to a party key, but the selection and encouragement of immigrants became largely nonpartisan, and the emphasis of the parties shifted to seeking the support and votes of immigrants after they arrived in Israel. In its work, the Agency preserved the complex and ineffective organization characteristic of the partisan system.

The period of the Six Day War saw a turning point in immigration. By then only small remnants remained of the Jewish communities in the Islamic countries, and immigrants came mainly from developed countries. Although lacking ideological preparation, most identified strongly with the Jewish state. Above all, they came as individuals, each with his own desires for location, life style, and work fulfillment; they were much more critical than earlier groups of the society and bureaucracy they encountered, and they expected to influence their surroundings and their personal situation. Many possessed higher education and professional expertise, and most were from countries to which they could return if they so desire. For many Western immigrants, migration to Israel lowered the standard of living, to some degree, but their status relative to that of others was high.

Only the Russian and other Eastern European emigrations were limited by their governments, but no developed country produced a large number of immigrants. The small number of immigrants aroused wide criticism of the Agency's operations abroad, while the disappointment of many immigrants after they arrived called into question the methods of absorption. These, it was charged, were a continuation of the "mass approach" used for the earlier groups from underdeveloped countries, and were no longer suitable, if indeed they ever had been. *

In 1967 and 1968, strong public criticism of the Agency developed in the Knesset and the press. The Agency reacted by trying to rationalize its administration and by unifying the departments concerned. The change was doomed from the start as party representatives insisted on maintaining the old feudal partisan arrangements.

Public salience led Labor to see *aliya* and *klita* as a party issue. The party was predominant in the Agency bureaucracy, and thus felt itself to be an ob-

---

* In 1966–67, the net balance of immigration was very low, partly due to the recession. Following the Six Day War, many in the West expressed an interest in immigration, but it appeared that this potential was not being realized. Of more than 7,000 who volunteered to come and work at the time of the war, less than 900 remained.

ject of dissatisfaction. If the government's role were to increase, it was important that the party decide how the new power relations would work. The government, it was said, could not abnegate responsibility for the success of *aliya*, which was both central to the Zionist ideal and necessary to the economy and the society. In addition, party leaders, among them both Yigal Allon and Lova Eliav, wanted to take charge of Absorption, in which each saw a personal challenge and opportunity.

In 1968 an internal Labor Party committee recommended that the functions of *klita* in Israel be taken over by the government, while the Agency continued the work abroad. The Cabinet decided to set up a Ministry of Absorption. As to how it would work, the decision said vaguely that "arrangements will be made for cooperation between the government and the Agency." Labor members of the Agency executive were successful in their protests, and secured an agreement that the Agency remain responsible for "initial *klita*," that is, the initial training, housing, and job arrangements. It was realized that Agency budgets were raised abroad, and that cooperation between the Diaspora leaders and Israel could be very important for immigration.

The new ministry began its work with Allon as Deputy Prime Minister and Minister of Absorption. The staff in the field came mainly from the Agency, while the central civil service leadership was recruited apolitically and set out to eliminate partisan treatment and individual patronage. Budgets came mainly through the Agency, as before, while the services actually provided, such as housing, continued to originate with the ministries concerned. In coordinating all of these to meet the needs of immigrants, the Ministry of Absorption has had an ineffective career, caught between the budgetary power of the Agency and the autonomy of the other government departments.

Under the unclear compromise arrangements, departments which produced the needed services in Israel felt relieved of responsibility without relinquishing authority, while the Agency's work abroad continued as before. In 1969, seeing the decline of the minister's role, Allon, the first minister, resigned when his demands for increased and well-defined authority were denied. His successors have not been more fortunate.

As "overall aims" or as a "goal and principle," *aliya* and *klita* face a disadvantage inherent in the matrix of the Israel government. Ministries which command the greatest resources and authority, and are headed by the most senior political leaders, are those which have the responsibility for the production or operation of specific services; ministries concerned with advancing principles or with coordinating for specific objectives are usually of a second order, particularly when they do not control the resources.*

The political system thus failed to react effectively to the demands of a new situation—the potentialities of Western and Russian *aliya*. The attempt at a

---

* Chapter 8, "The Physical Environment," illustrates in more detail governmental organization involving "principles," "production," and "coordination."

compromise between "apolitical" state management and the vestiges of the kind of organization which worked in the pioneering period of the Yishuv was only partly at fault. It is not clear how well a fully "state" system would work; for *aliya* can succeed only through the involvement of the Diaspora, and *klita* only through the efforts of Israeli society, organically.

Education: The Great Hope, Still Unfulfilled

There is widespread faith in the effectiveness of schooling and in the influence of teaching on culture and beliefs. Since the early days of the Yishuv, schools have been expected to transmit Hebrew culture and Jewish religious values, as well as the ideals espoused by labor or other movements, and to help absorb immigrants. More recently, attainments in formal schooling have been principal criteria of progress toward social equality.[32]

Many expect education to go far toward the development of an *am segula*, a people of unusual quality, or, a more modest and tangible goal, the achievement of scientific excellence. There is hope, also, that the education of Arab youth can lead to political integration, together with a healthy cultural pluralism. It is realized that education *per se* is not a recipe for the attainment of these goals, but there is sufficient belief in its potential to make it the object of great political concern.

In the beginning, hopes were unbounded. Public education, says the 1953 State Education Law, is to be based on:

> the values of Jewish culture and the achievements of science, of love of the homeland, and loyalty to the Jewish State and the Jewish people, on practice in agricultural work and in handicraft, on pioneer training, and on striving for a society built on freedom, equality, tolerance, mutual assistance, and a love of mankind.

The initial strategy was, simply, to make schooling compulsory and available. After nearly thirty years of experience, hopes are less sanguine, goals are more specific (yet broadened to include the Arab and Druze minorities), and strategies are more sophisticated.*

The question of "Jewish consciousness" illustrates the hopes. The schools are asked to preserve Jewish values in a secular world and to help close the distance between Jews in Israel and those in the Diaspora. More intellectual depth and understanding of Zionism, of Judaism, of the Bible, of the Talmud, of Jewish history, and of the Diaspora communities could, it is hoped, bring Israeli children into the stream of Jewish culture and experience.

Against this goal are marshaled the dominant culture of the secular

---

* The change is reflected in a plan for education in the 1980s, which averred that the system could not instill values not held or at least hoped for by the community outside. The humanities and Jewish traditions are mentioned as before; but goals are outlined in greater detail, with increased emphasis on social responsibility and on individual autonomy and participation.[33]

Western world; the rejection of the exile in many Zionist ideas; the desire to build a new Jew, and the political and cultural separatism of orthodoxy. For new generations, even the Holocaust seems a part of ancient history, as wars between France and Germany are for European youth. Emphasis on achievement and with it the seeking of equality of opportunity, or at least the universal attainment of minimum standards, has become of much greater concern than left or right ideology.

There is now a better understanding of the relation of means and ends, there are discussions of developing social responsibility among pupils, and of the need to give an individual the ability to teach himself throughout life. The atmosphere of the classroom and the need to involve the community in the school are on the agenda. Resources are directed to the preschool years, and to educating and working with parents, and there is more sensitivity to the relation of education and the general social condition.

Before independence, there was a comprehensive system of Hebrew education in which four autonomous trends were supported by the political movements and the elected Va'ad Leumi, or National Committee: Labor schools, managed by the Histadrut and the kibbutz movement; General Zionist schools; schools of the religious Zionist Mizrachi, and of the ultra-orthodox Agudat Israel. Secondary schools were private, modeled on the highly selective European *gymnasia*. Their Hebrew curriculum, together with active political youth movements and underground defense activities, gave many of the young a unique culture and sense of national participation. Teachers at all levels were deeply involved. The Teachers Association, founded in 1903, was then in essence a board of education, developing curricula and methods, and seeing teaching as a mission to further the national rebirth, rather than the trade union which it is today. In the towns, the Labor schools enrolled only a minority of the pupils. The Labor youth movements, however, developed cadres of future kibbutz members and leaders of the Labor parties, through intensive after-school activities.

With independence came explosive growth in the school population—from 100,000 elementary pupils in 1948 to more than 300,000 in 1953—most of whom could get little help in their studies from their immigrant parents and for whom qualified teachers were scarce. The ensuing decline from preindependence standards of teaching and learning was not foreseen at the time, and did not become an issue for some years. More immediate was a bitter struggle between Labor and the religious parties over the enrollment of the immigrant children. A 1949 law provided for compulsory elementary schools, divided into three separate trends—religious, Labor, and "general"—with the choice of trend left to the parents. Most immigrant parents, especially those from Eastern countries, were religiously observant; but they were confused by the many parties and ideologies and awed by the Labor government and the image of Ben Gurion. Confusion was increased when Labor started its own religious schools. In 1951 the coalition government broke up when the religious parties claimed that children were being forcibly enrolled, or at least enrolled by misrepresentation, in the Labor religious schools.

Searching for national unity and social integration, Ben Gurion tried to divert Mapai from the party rule of education. He was aided by the results of the 1951 elections, in which the General Zionists' representation increased from seven to twenty Knesset seats, following wide dissatisfaction with the economic-austerity program. The new coalition included the General Zionists, Mapai, Mizrachi, and Mizrachi Workers (Poalei Mizrachi), but not Mapam. By 1953 central national control of the schools was achieved, with only partial depoliticization. The separate Labor and General Zionist trends were combined as one option, and state religious schools were a second. Both were under the central control of the Ministry of Education. Since the law did not say exactly how the general and the religious systems would be supervised and coordinated, much scope was left for bargaining in future coalition agreements.

The 1953 State Education Law nationalized and centralized control in the Ministry of Education. State primary education is based on curricula prescribed by the Minister of Education and Culture, and state schools will not have "attachment to a party or a communal body or any other organization outside the government." The religious trend and the kibbutz and *moshav* schools retain cultural and ideological separateness under the ministry's aegis. The NRP controls religious teaching in state schools, while the ultra-orthodox Aguda receives state support without real supervision. Municipalities build and maintain schools, but elementary teachers are national civil servants. High schools are either private or municipal but follow centrally designed curricula, are inspected by the Ministry, and prepare for uniform government matriculation examinations.[34]

Circumstances had helped Ben Gurion's stubborn efforts toward nationalization. The principal enthusiasts for Labor schools had been the kibbutz and *moshav* movements, and these retained separate education under the new arrangements. The party-machine leaders foresaw little electoral impact. Many in Mapai believed that the social aims of Labor would be achieved in the national schools, since the teachers in both general and Labor schools belonged to the Teachers Union, part of the Histadrut since 1950; and in any case, a Mapai leader would be the Minister of Education. From the point of view of political control, the General Zionists, indeed, lost out; but from that of ideology, the system became "general." The expected transfer of Labor values and symbols to the state system did not come to pass; and in the secular state schools, in which two-thirds of the children study, the teachers came to represent a cross section of national beliefs.*

* Symbolically, the Mapai Central Committee voted in 1953 for the use in schools of the red flag and workers' anthem in the celebrations of May 1 and the Histadrut anniversary. Ben Gurion's influence and a threat by the General Zionists to split the coalition secured a withdrawal of this demand.

Through the new arrangements, the NRP (Mafdal) assumed control over the policy and organization for national religious schools. The party, first of all, remains on guard in the national coalition against what they see as creeping secularization. The Minister of Education is advised by a Council on Religious Education, which can recommend or veto the appointment of teachers in state religious schools. Religious-trend schools are supervised by a special branch of the Ministry of Education, which the NRP controls. The Mafdal did not gain a complete monopoly of all religious education in the field; the Aguda continues to operate its own independent schools, enjoying both autonomy and government support.

Social Equality Is Challenged

The new law, in itself, did not cause the divisions to subside. That between right and left did, indeed, gradually disappear, preserved only in the enclaves of the Labor agricultural settlements; while religious education continued to reinforce a principal division in the society. Soon after the law was passed, however, these questions were eclipsed by the gap in educational achievement found among the children of the mass immigrations. Many children were found to be lacking in the basic skills. A uniform curriculum and compulsory elementary schooling were not achieving equal opportunity, integration, or identification with the society.* Scholars began to question educational policy, and school results and protests (as in Wadi Salib in 1959) led to the realization that ten years after independence there was a lag in basic learning which was strongly congruent with ethnic origin. The ideals of the absorption of immigration and of equality were threatened; and the broad gap in attainment became, and remains, the greatest educational concern.

Originally, inequality in school achievement was accepted, as deriving from the natural distribution of abilities. Resources were concentrated at the higher stages of learning and research—whether in universities or, in the religious system, in the rabbinic studies of the yeshiva—as part of the quest for excellence. The correlation of attainment with ethnic origin was something else again. It touched a raw nerve—and it was at this point that the seeking of equality of opportunity began to have influence on policy.**

The first corrective steps affected "statistics rather than substance."[37] Children were automatically promoted with their age groups, and a lower

---

* For example, in 1957 Moshe Smilansky wrote, "Equal opportunity means the opportunity to benefit from a program adapted to the abilities, needs, and objectives of the individual and adapted to this environment, while formal equality in standards can keep many youth from getting the education they need."[35] Scholars, such as M. Smilansky and C. Frankenstein, then had a pivotal influence on policies for the disadvantaged.

** The question of equality and opportunity is considered on pages 340–343 below. See also the references listed in notes 35, 36, and 49 for discussions of concepts of opportunity and disadvantage.

standard was set for pupils of Asian/African origin on the survey tests, or *seker*, then used as a criterion for secondary-school admission and scholarships. The lag was cumulative, however, and the high school drop-out rate remained very high.

More fundamental measures were clearly necessary, and in the 1960s a whole array of compensatory measures were begun. Classes and schools having many disadvantaged children were given a higher claim on resources, allowing for smaller classes and more equipment. Typical programs are longer school days, boarding schools for gifted children from disadvantaged homes, inducements in housing and seniority for teachers who are willing to live and work in development areas, prekindergarten classes for three- and four-year-olds, and day-care centers.[38]

The main point of attack in the 1960s, however, was to increase the proportion of fourteen- to seventeen-year-olds in school by efforts directed toward making secondary school eventually compulsory and free, thus increasing mobility and overcoming geographic and ethnic segregation. From 1963 to 1968, the Minister of Education, Zalman Aranne, fought for and ultimately succeeded in introducing an "intermediate school" for grades seven to nine, with free and compulsory school initially through fifteen years, to be extended gradually to sixteen years of age. A public committee was charged in 1963 by the minister with investigating "the need and possibility of extending free compulsory education laws." In 1965, it recommended a six-three-three system, six years of elementary school, followed by junior and senior high school.[39]

The report gave public backing to Aranne's own view that formal structural change would be needed in order to make the compulsory addition of free years of school effective. He at once accepted the general terms of the proposal, while the Elementary Teachers Association rejected them and refused to cooperate with ministry officials in further discussions.*

Following the 1965 elections, Aranne made the reform a condition of his continuing in office. Because of the opposition of the Teachers' Association and wide public interest, an unusual parliamentary committee was appointed. Based on a party key, like that of the standing Knesset Education Committee, it also included nonvoting members from the elementary and secondary teachers' associations and from the ministry. Like other Knesset committees, it had no professional staff. The parliamentary committee voted two to one for six-year elementary and six-year comprehensive secondary schools.[40] Aranne's decision to fight in a special Knesset committee rather than within Mapai worked well. The Mapai Secretariat, in agreeing, was probably aware that the Elementary Teachers' Association, in its role as a trade union, did not have strong membership support for the use of such

---

* The teachers' motive was particularist. Most elementary teachers, who were not university graduates, would have to requalify to teach in the seventh and eighth grades. Further, the Association stood to lose influence in relation to the secondary school teachers' organizations.

measures as strikes in fighting an issue which the public saw as social and pedagogic rather than partisan. The Teachers' Association failed in all-out attempts to influence the parties and members of the Knesset, and strike proposals by the Association leaders were turned down by a majority of the members.

The NRP (Mafdal) voted against the bill, fearing that limiting primary school to six grades would weaken the religious school system. Mapam and some Ahdut Ha'Avoda members were also opposed, seeing an opportunity to gain political support within the Teachers' Association. But Aranne made good use of his strong support within Mapai (he was very close to Prime Minister Eshkol and the Mapai machine), and the public's feeling that education should be extended, to get formal Knesset approval for the structural change. In 1968, the reform became law. The victory showed considerable skill in the husbanding of influence and the use of public appointive committees.[41] A very important element was Aranne's success in displacing the focus of the debate from pedagogic questions, such as the qualifications of teachers in the intermediate grades or the need for improved curricula, in which the teachers' union could have a legitimate say, to that of integration and comprehensiveness.[42]

After an initial period of preparation, the reform began rapidly. Its impetus, however, soon waned. In the early years, 1970–74, about twenty-seven intermediate schools were introduced each year. By 1977–78, the rate had declined to fifteen. In 1977, 43 percent of those in the relevant age groups were studying according to the new system in the Jewish schools, and 33 percent of those in Arab schools. The teachers' union did little to encourage teacher retraining, and there were budgetary difficulties after the 1973 war. The mingling of students from broader catchment areas was frequently achieved, yet truer integration was less frequent, since the program was introduced more in homogeneous areas than in those with a heterogeneous population; and many schools succumbed to the easier road of directing less qualified students to lower-level classes or to vocational courses in the early intermediate grades.[43]

The Slow Advance in Narrowing the Gap

Structural change thus accompanied compensatory measures. The attainments, while encouraging, show how much more needs to be accomplished. The data in Table 6.5 show something of the rate of progress.

The participation of Asian-Africans in university education also advanced. From 1966 to 1974, the percentage of the age cohort of youth of Asian/African descent who qualified in the matriculation examination, or *bagrut*, increased from 3.1 percent to 7.4 percent, while that of those of European/American descent rose from 24 percent (1967) to 35 percent (1974).[46]

TABLE 6.5.   Educational Data—Jewish Students

(1) Of those aged 14 to 17[44]	1969	1978
Working	18.1%	5.0%
Studying	73.5%	86.3%
Not working or studying	8.4%	8.7%

(2) Participation of Asians/Africans * secondary schools[45]	1966/67	1976/77
As proportion of all in age group	49.9%	58.7%
As proportion of all secondary school students	35.6%	50.6%
As proportion of college-preparatory high school students	26.7%	36.1%
As proportion of vocational education students	47.0%	63.6%

* Born, or father born, in an Asian/African country. In statistical data the concept of "Asian/African," currently used, is losing its significance as an increasing proportion of children are born to parents who were born in Israel.

Absolute gains, however, have left a substantial relative gap, which becomes manifest at an early age and is cumulative. The differences are strongly related to the educational levels of parents. Pupils whose parents had no formal schooling, for example, have been found to be at a level of reading comprehension which is one year behind the national average in the second grade, and more than two years behind by the sixth grade. Differences in attainments in arithmetic, geography, and science are also substantial.[47] Parents' education, in turn, is associated with the country of origin. More than 95 percent of parents without schooling come from Moslem countries. Aside from the lack of ability to help which such limitations engender, parents without schooling tend to show less interest in the progress of their children in school, and to communicate far less with the children and their teachers about what goes on in school.[47]

The association of other than directly ethnic factors with a lower educational attainment is suggested by Table 6.6, keeping in mind, however, the

TABLE 6.6.   Father's Occupation and Secondary School Study (1967 Data)[48]

Father's Occupation	% of Those Aged 14–17 in Full-Time Studies	% of those Aged 14–17 Not in School
Professional	73.6	5.3
Managerial and clerical	64.5	3.8
Manufacturing workers	39.2	20.0
Building workers	31.7	26.7
Service workers	30.2	24.5

correlation of residence in a development town and nonprofessional occupation with the father's Asian/African origin.

Discrepancies are further aggravated by the markedly lower proportion of licensed teachers in the development towns, away from the center—in some cases less than 70 percent. Still, children from development towns, in small numbers, have been reaching the universities in larger proportions than those from the most disadvantaged big-city neighborhoods. The possible reason is the greater feeling of equality which prevails in the smaller towns, whose population is often more homogeneous. Students from both environments have benefited greatly from special post-Army preparatory courses, which give a second chance to those who did poorly in secondary school or who studied in a disadvantaged school environment. These courses have been one of the most successful compensatory programs.

On balance, most of the educational gap can now be seen as deriving from different social and economic starting lines, with a residue of culturally related differences still to be overcome. Intelligence tests, given in the early grades, show consistent differences between those of European/American and those of Asian/African background which decrease substantially but do not disappear when family social and economic criteria are held constant.[49] Such findings stimulate the search for more effective compensatory measures. They lead, as well, to go beyond formal schooling, and to concentrate efforts on the youngest age groups, and on improving family and neighborhood environments.

The desire for equality in schooling is ambivalent. On the one hand, the sheer growth in numbers has lowered the standards of most secondary schooling. The retention of the traditional *gymnasium* forms, national matriculation requirements, and separate trends of vocational education retain much of the previous selectivity. Yet most secondary schools now have the traditional form without the former quality of content. If selectivity could be justified in the Yishuv by a search for quality and by the development of a modern Hebrew high school curriculum, these considerations no longer apply. In the American experience, plural avenues of advance and the postponement of final career choice to as late an age as possible have in many ways removed the dichotomy between universal schooling and the need for excellence.[34] Israel may be headed toward comparable solutions, adapted to work under Israeli conditions.

Arab Education

As has been said, Arab education has not yet caught up with the scholastic achievements, or the facilities, in the Jewish schools. Progress, however, has been continual, as shown on Table 6.7. By 1975, of non-Jewish children, 88 percent of the boys and 64 percent of the girls were in school. Illiteracy among

TABLE 6.7.   Percentage of Age Group 14–17
in Secondary School[51]

	1964–65	1969–70	1974–75
Jewish education	60.5	72.1	83.8
Arab education	15.1	22.1	36.1

adult non-Jews was halved between 1964 and 1974, and there were more than a thousand university students, compared to virtually none before independence. By 1980, there were three thousand.[50]

The Mandatory government supported public schools, attended mostly by Moslem pupils. Only one-third of the children between five and fifteen years of age were in school, and of these, only 10 percent studied for more than five years. Christian Arabs had more schooling, mainly in church-supported schools. Seventy-two percent of the Arab boys and 50 percent of the Arab girls born in 1960 finished the eighth grade, compared to 97 percent of the Jewish children born in the same year. While minority secondary school attendance was also far lower, it grew rapidly.

During the 1948 war, the departure of most of the prosperous and better-educated Moslem town dwellers left few qualified Arab teachers in Israel. Other reasons for the disparity in Arab education are less support for coeducation in Moslem communities, and the parsimoniousness of local governments in villages and towns, which often give low priority to funds for education.* These towns also do not qualify for the special grants given to the development towns, or benefit from the special budgets for disadvantaged children. Also, many of the original inspectors in the Arab education system were older men who had been selected for office in the first years of the state, when few Arabs with academic qualifications were available. In some cases their continuity in office prevented the appointment of more qualified younger men; the ministry did not seem to be making very serious efforts at the reform of Arab education, and on the local scene *hamula* relations frequently acted to thwart appointment on merit.

More fundamental is the problem of setting the goals of Arab education in a state whose central theme is the rebuilding of the Jewish national home. Until the mid-1970s, Arab pupils, in the opinion of many, did not learn enough about their own heritage, although they studied in Arabic and received Moslem or Christian religious instruction. In 1975 a ministry task force on Arab education recommended a much stronger background in the modern history of the Arabs and fuller discussion of the Arab-Israeli conflict. It was hoped that a deeper understanding among the Arabs of their own identity and

* In a 1969 survey, similar priorities were found among Jews from Islamic countries, whose family expenditures on education were found to be a far smaller proportion (income held equal) than among those families of native-born or European/American origin.[51]

that of their Jewish neighbors would make it much easier for the Arab pupil to participate fully as a citizen.[52]

Changing Educational Policy

Experience showed that it is easier to think of changes in the system than to carry them out. One reason is the inertia of the large, centralized organization managed by a bureaucratic elite. It is guided by a minister who usually has strong political backing, who is prodded by the Knesset Education Committee, and who is seldom subject, on strategic questions, to grass-roots pressures.

By the 1970s, university research was beginning to have considerable influence at the top. A planning unit was started in 1969, and economists and sociologists began to work in the ministry, leading to much improvement in the data available. University scientists contributed to long-range planning, for which the internal bureaucracy of the ministry had little time or leaning.

Change is slow, and it often seems that only a major shock, as from Panther protests, can create noticeable movement and relate educational issues to underlying social demands. A minister, if he chooses a very few issues selectively, and if he sees the job as other than a stepping stone to higher office, can accomplish changes, but only slowly.

A principal impediment to change in the school system is that innovations have usually been tried from the top down. Parents do not participate very much in schools in an organized way, and parent-teachers associations are not very active. Local governments are responsible only for facilities, and in poor communities even these are paid for and decided at the center. Parents and local educational politics are concerned most often with the relative facilities given to religious and secular schools, delays in repairing buildings, and the boundaries of school districts, which determine the social composition of the classes. After 1978, residents in many Project Renewal neighborhoods were actively involved in attempting to improve the quality of instruction.

Education is a massive, centralized system which has become accustomed to central professional direction. For example, when the local schools were asked, in 1974, for suggestions and allowed to use up to 25 percent of their class time in projects of their own, few proposals were presented.

Following soon after the courts and defense, education was the first major service to be nationalized. It then ceased to be a specific election issue, but in the larger political sense beliefs on the teaching of religious tradition and the extent and nature of the autonomy of the religious schools within the national system have continued to have important implications.

From the beginning, until the Mafdal took over in the 1977 Begin government, Labor was in charge of the ministry. The ideological differences between the left and the right soon ceased to be an issue. Mapai, and later Labor, almost never intervened as a party, and refused to debate, in party forums, the proposed Reform Act of 1968. At the same time, social and religious beliefs had an important influence on the perceptions of political leaders and bureaucrats. Education continues to symbolize, to many different kinds of people, the way in which the institutions of the society can work to ensure the achievement and preservation of *their* specific and separate values. For this reason, the Knesset has more influence in education than in many other areas, as a public forum for the spectrum of beliefs. In the nationalization of education and in setting the goals sought through the reform of secondary education, the Knesset was expressing a national consensus. The Knesset Education Committee includes many former teachers. Its role has been to prod, as when it thought that Yigal Allon, as Minister of Education, was not advancing the reform fast enough; or as a watchdog, for example, in preventing the Treasury from cutting back on free ninth-grade education in an economy move in 1975.

The attitudes of the nonorthodox toward the religious school subsystem have been ambivalent. The religious-trend schools are seen as helping to preserve the national cultural and historical traditions, which are a principal source of the values and strength of the society. This goal is sought, in a different way, in the "general" schools.* At the same time, the extent of separation of the religious system has a potential for social and cultural division. The religious schools include a very much larger proportion of disadvantaged children. This is due, in large part, to the more traditional preference of Asian/African parents. At the same time, the religious subsystem is inherently more selective and elitist, seeking out the talented and investing a much larger proportion of the resources in their advancement, at the secondary school level. The establishment of Secondary School Yeshivot and at the more advanced stage, of *Yeshivot Hesder*,** has drawn off some of the most talented potential leaders from the ordinary local religious secondary schools, in many cases leaving them with a far less talented student body. The maintenance of separate schools and other facilities in small development towns leads to diseconomies, because of scale, further preventing adequate compensation for the disadvantaged.

The secondary school yeshivot, while they have not succeeded in integrating religious beliefs and philosophy in the actual study of lay subjects, have opened up the whole field of scientific and modern studies before those who previously would have confined themselves to the traditional preparation for the highest Talmudic studies. These institutions have had an important political impact within the Mafdal, drawing an elite of orthodox young

---

* Ben Gurion was gravely disappointed, when visiting a maritime academy, to find that the cadets were not well versed in the nautical events of biblical antiquity.

** *Yeshivot Hesder*, in contrast to the ordinary rabbinical training *Yeshiva*, do not ask for deferment from military service for their students, who combine military training with alternate periods of Talmudic studies, often serving in elite combat units.

leaders into the political and social activity of the country, through secular knowledge and professions and through their contribution to defense. They are a political cadre loyal to the values of the Mafdal on questions of religion and the state, but they have also been important in the emphasis of the Mafdal, and particularly its young leaders, on activist settlement in Judea and Samaria. At one and the same time, these institutions thus advance both modernization and separatism.

The importance of the values which education can help to transmit is, in the ongoing search for policies, overwhelmed by the demand that the schools further open greater equality of opportunity and individual mobility; and that unusual efforts be expended to encourage the most talented, so as to advance the country toward the achievement of excellence. It can be argued, with much justice, that the improvement of the present living conditions of parents and children is a necessary basis for education; and that narrowing the educational gap does not come at the expense of excellence because it enlarges the numbers of those who may possibly reach distinction. Nonetheless, the need to clarify alternative priorities and strategies and to choose among them remains.

The Politics of Social Policy

The foregoing observation of the developments in several policy areas shows how most of the elements of the welfare state came into being, and how many of the principal issues were settled while others remained unresolved. The most prominent change in organization was the transfer of the control of many social services to the state and to local government.

A second issue of organization concerned the internal working of the government. Here the problems have been to organize effective social services and to create a focus for the development of social policy and for its coordination. These attempts were at best only partly successful.

A third important question was the priority given to social policy, in resources and in its place in the order of public business. Pressing needs of defense and the concern with economic viability have usually come first; social issues have been resolved, most often, as an appendage or corrective to economic measures, whose implications for the social condition can often overwhelm the effects of specific social measures.

Finally, most important, has been the way in which national social goals were developed and the ways by which it was hoped to achieve them. A broad consensus on the general aims of a welfare state was not sufficient, once the attempt was made to define and achieve specific goals. Separate goals, on each of which there is some agreement, often conflict. The geographic distribution of the population is accomplished only at a considerable social cost. The payment of large children's benefits, as in Israel and France, can help the life chances of children and give a minimum adequate income to large families of unskilled workers—yet could work against participation of some in the work force. The long-range goal of equal opportunity demands different measures than the short-range needs for equality of income. Even if it were the most effective way, at the present time, central or tutelary administration of social services can conflict with self-determination and participation as an element of the quality of life. Programs which encourage the maximum personal advance of the most gifted individuals in poor neighborhoods can leave these neighborhoods without potential leaders or strata of self-reliant citizens. Most difficult of all in conception and resolution has been the integration of separate questions and policies as they affect the overall social condition and as they imply trade-offs between present needs and future opportunities, or between the different demands and benefits of particularist groups. Beliefs, interests, and bureaucratic politics were the principal determinants of the ways in which these issues were approached, and set the limits to their resolution.

The Political Context

As a part of the larger political system, the context in which social measures are decided reflects the characteristics of coalition government, partisan modes of allocation, and the bureaucratic politics of the larger institutions within the government and the Histadrut. The elements include groups and strata which have social demands, or revealed needs, or are affected by economic measures; the media, in amplifying, stimulating, or giving perspective to these demands; academic research, and the concepts and demands of professionals, such as the doctors, social workers, or teachers; groups, parties, and the leaders of a Histadrut which is far from monolithic; the government bureaucracies; and, on questions of settlement and immigration, the Agency.

On most issues, two overlapping systems formulated policy measures and decided how they would be carried out. One is the internal governmental system, in which the main protagonists are leaders of the bureaucracies and the ministers concerned (and thus, indirectly, their parties). The second is the relation of the Histadrut, the parties, and the government bureaucracies. These systems overlapped mainly through the Histadrut's interest in problems of income maintenance and the national control of services. These are areas in which the Histadrut saw its participation as a necessary condition for the legitimacy of a decision.

The effects of economic policies and conditions and the demands of groups and strata in the public impinge on these systems. The needs of the most disadvantaged have usually been presented by academics or by the media. This has been most effective when protest behavior, the media, and data reinforced each other. The demands of the more skilled workers or professionals have usually been made through wage struggles of local and national union organizations, and these interests have been represented through the Histadrut or in direct union-employer confrontation. The influence of these groups on the Histadrut leadership reflects the partisan needs of Labor within the Histadrut, as well as in the national electoral contest, although in the latter, the weaker groups may have slightly more impact than they do within the Histadrut.

Protests, abetted and stimulated by the media and academics (and occasionally by politicians) have been effective mainly because of the way in which they struck at the sensitive self-image of the society as one of equality and of social integration. Immediate reactions were strong and not always well thought out, but the subsequent long-term trend has reflected substantive changes in policy. In these changes the parties have reacted to specific demands instead of taking the initiative. The Likud, when in opposition, protested against social ills and benefited from dissatisfaction with the establishment, but it did not propose alternative social programs; and Labor and the Histadrut, while advocating welfare state provisions, have been mainly a conservative force. This paradox derives from the historical development in which Labor was already dominant at independence, so that the state began with a broad range of social institutions many of which Labor had developed, and Labor thus remained the heart of the establishment. Conservatism, in this sense, meant the maintenance of things as they were, not the least because of their relation to political power.* Another aspect of conservatism is in the inherent beliefs in work and in economic growth, so that the Labor Party and the Histadrut have not willingly represented those who, for any reason, were not working. But beyond these, the performance of the Histadrut has been greatly affected by its role as the basis of the economic and organization resources which to Labor seem essential to the aim of being dominant in a democratic political system. The control of these resources requires that Labor continue in political control of a Histadrut in which the Labor Party no longer polls a clear majority. The alignment of Labor plus Mapam received only 58 percent of the vote in the 1973 Histadrut elections and 55 percent in 1977. Labor leaders see this as reflecting increased social dissatisfaction, the decline of ideology, and the decline of party influence in the local union organizations, which increase the danger to continued Labor rule, at least without major concessions to possible coalition partners.

Reduced authority of the center over the local works committees or workers' councils, or indeed, over the national unions, thus combines with internal electoral needs to enhance the independence and influence of strong groups (usually representing workers who are skilled or in essential services)

* Thus in Britain unions fought for nationalization of pension funds, since these were run by the employers, while in Israel it is the unions which have the funds and the employers who would like to have them, or to nationalize them.

which are not restrained by ideological agreement or by the party hierarchy; while the power of the highly politicized managements of the Histadrut bureaucracies, such as the pension funds and Kupat Holim, derives from the size and scope of these organizations and from the importance of their resources to the Labor Party.

On questions of the nationalization of services, internal Histadrut divisions have been largely along the left-right spectrum, with the right supporting nationalization and with Mapam opposing on the grounds that the services and economic resources support the class political struggle and that the Histadrut should be a comprehensive movement, not a trade union. The Labor Party center is divided, weighing questions of organizational strength, political advantage, the financial problems, and the ideas of *mamlachtiut*. The determination of the economic and service organizations within the Histadrut to maintain their individual autonomy and authority is mitigated, however, by the growing needs for government financial support.

Overall, the Histadrut and Labor, while conservative, have supported welfare demands while opposing nationalization. Labor legislation and National Insurance coverage are comprehensive; and conceivably, the declining Labor electoral strength within the Histadrut could lead to a greater response to the needs of the lower-paid workers and the disadvantaged, and to a less conservative role in general. For although the Histadrut electorate is broadly identical with most of the voters in the Knesset elections, Histadrut election results are more directly related to social questions than are those to the Knesset. Another factor is the opportunity for the Histadrut leaders to assume a more independent role in a period such as that of the Rabin Cabinet of 1974-77, when the Labor party institutions were relatively inactive. Their political role is enhanced even more when Labor is in opposition to the government.

On the other hand, such an interrugnum and the desire to maintain the internal dominance could reinforce the need which the Histadrut leaders historically have seen for the support of the strong groups, and to strengthen their opposition to national control of social services.*

The employers, represented by the Manufacturers Association, have worked to restrain the increased costs of social benefits, even though these are often passed on to the consumer. The Association has also tried to have benefits embodied in legislation or national agreements so as to reduce the scope of collective bargaining and lessen potential friction. As a sector, employers benefit from the subsidy of firms through the low wage scale of the unskilled, supplemented by children's allowances, although as citizens there are manufacturers who question this characteristic of Israel policy.

Academics and professionals have had a considerable impact. Knowledge

---

* For example, the *moshav* movement at one point opposed increased children's allowances (the NII premiums of their members would have been increased). The Histadrut has successfully opposed a minimum-wage law, since it would reduce the scope of collective bargaining.

has been a powerful weapon when it concurred with social demand and protest, dramatizing and symbolizing social needs. If the academy does not agree on what should be done, it has helped frame social goals in tangible forms, as in the concept of relative poverty, or putting the spotlight on target populations. Academics have broken the rules of formal administration, going outside the hierarchy in presenting their case. An additional source of academic and professional influence has been the extensive government use of public committees, to which nearly all important policy questions have at one time or another been referred.

The inevitability of committees probably began with the need for Histadrut representation and participation in national social policy decisions. Indeed, the first major government committee, as we have seen, was headed by Kanev in his Histadrut welfare role. Subsequently, committees were needed to represent different views and groups within the Histadrut and the Labor movement parties, and to agree on policy before proposals went to the Knesset or the Cabinet. On "representative" committees on social questions, the Histadrut has enjoyed a considerable veto power, which means that separate parties or groups within the Histadrut can also have such veto power. As professional and academic groups grew stronger, they came to be represented, and with time took the lead. Committees served to bring out data, to sound out the sources and strength of opposition, and often to be a form of arbitration.* But while committees have been a bona fide source of expertise, they have often been used to delay or to advance issues in accordance with previous views of the ministers who appointed them.

In the early years, Mapai was a focus of decision on such basic questions as the nationalization of education, while Herut was vocal in social protest. Since the mid-1960s, neither has had a direct policy role, although political parties remain influential in the appointments in politicized organizations, such as Kupat Holim, the Ministries of Welfare and of Labor, and the Agency. The extent of support which a minister commands in his party is a principal determinant of his authority, as was shown, for example, in Aranne's ability to reform the structure of secondary education. Until 1977 Labor led the Ministries of Education and Labor, and the Mafdal headed Welfare. In both Labor and Welfare, politicization was considerable, and it continued, if to a somewhat smaller degree, in the Health, Education, and Housing Ministries.

In the 1950s Mapai was still a main focus of national policy, Ben Gurion was dominant, and the national approach of *mamlachtiut* had his political weight behind it.** Mapai leaders still hoped for a working society or Labor

---

* Seen in committees headed by "experts," where both (or several) sides agree ahead of time that the committee's reports should be implemented.

** Personalities have been, from time to time, decisive in differing ways and to different degrees. Examples, among others, include: Ben Gurion and the nationalization of education and of the employment exchanges, Aranne in school reform, Kanev in the welfare approach, and Israel Katz in dramatizing the social needs.

domination through the democratic process.* By the time the questions of pension and health nationalization were in committee in the 1970s, the decision capacity of the Labor Party was far from that of the early Mapai, and even Labor dominance in the Histadrut appeared tenuous, which could lead, with Labor in the opposition, to more resistance to any diminution in the Histadrut role.

The political system thus found the larger questions of national control hard to resolve. The impact of bureaucratic politics on substantive decisions was reinforced by the fact that the several ministries, in the coalitions, were often led by different parties. The debate on any given issue was motivated, perhaps to an unusual degree, more by motives of organizational advance and authority than by professional policy consideration. The bureaucratic interest is inevitably closely interrelated with concepts and strategies. Thus the NII exemplified the concepts of broader income maintenance on a universal basis, while the Ministry of Welfare carried out and emphasized the need for family welfare support and counseling on a selective basis, and struggled (with the Ministry of Education) for more scope in administering services in kind. It was, however, a "weak ministry with weak clients," while the Ministry of Finance was "strong, with strong clients." Finance could join with the NII in favoring a universal approach to welfare support on the grounds of administrative effectiveness, and in justifying larger and anti-inflationary payroll insurance deductions. Yet at the same time it could see selective transfers and the reduction of subsidies as steps toward economic efficiency and a spur to growth. The Cabinet, beyond other values, was interested in reducing sources of tension, and the Ministry of Labor, in increasing the mobility of labor. The Ministry of Housing, enjoying the power of producers who dispose of large resources, could point to the importance of its programs to the national economy and to employment, as well as to welfare and the absorption of immigration. All of these organizations thus tried to benefit from a strong reinforcement of interests by ideas. The existence of political fiefdoms magnified the importance of bureaucratic politics, exacerbating the difficulties of organization.

Dilemmas of Organization

It is hard in any regime to organize effectively to develop and carry out social policy. The complexities of behavior, the importance of forces and events external to the social services, and the limits of the state of the art are seen in the unintended consequences of policy decisions. In Israel, partisan and sectoral

---

* On most issues, the Knesset became the main focus of decision only after the major partisan question was settled. It lacked data and expertise, although eventually alternate public sources of knowledge developed in the universities, Falk and Brookdale Institutes, and the Bank of Israel.

forces are added to the more common dichotomy between local and national authorities, and the form of coalition government weaves partisan and ideological considerations into administrative decisions. As a result, there are serious problems in carrying out a coordinated policy, in changing to a chosen new direction, and in operating social services in an effective manner.

The impediments go beyond the primacy of security and economic issues which led decisions on social programs to be a residual, considered only after other questions; and beyond the low political salience of social questions, except in the face of protests. Attempts to formulate an overall social policy made little progress. At the Cabinet level, no effective focus for decision developed, nor was there adequate information for decision on the national or regional social condition, the inputs of resources, and the regional and sectoral impacts of activities. In this situation, Israel was not alone.[53] The allocation of the portion of the budget which remained after debt servicing and defense—about one-third of the total—was effectively determined, in considerable detail, by the Ministry of Finance, not by the social ministries or the Ministers Committee.

The lack of integration of economic and social policy was one of the most serious questions. Policies intended to have an economic result often affect the social condition more than specific social choices. Decreases in subsidies sharply increase the prices of basic foods and fuel. Income tax reforms alter relative incomes, while decisions on the linking of the cost-of-living index and pay supplements affect the proportion of workers whose earnings are below the threshold of poverty. A high rate of inflation has more social importance than any of these. Even more powerful are the qualitative aspects of economic development. An example, given previously, is the way in which the location of low-skill industries retarded the social advance of development towns. Conversely, the degrees of cooperation and motivation inherent in the social condition are principal economic resources and constraints.

Low political significance of welfare was seen in the allocation of the Ministries of Health and Welfare to minor coalition partners,* and the great infrequency with which social questions are on the full Cabinet agenda. In the Rabin Cabinet, a Ministers Committee for Welfare was appointed, as well as an Adviser to the Prime Minister and a Public Council on Welfare. The Ministers Committee met frequently, but more to discuss and learn, or to explore the situation, than to decide. For most practical purposes it was outside of the mainstream of the budget process. Despite the fact that its members were the ministers concerned, the important decisions were made elsewhere. After an initial impetus, Prime Minister Rabin gave little of his political leadership resources, in time, influence, and effort, to the social questions raised by his Adviser.[53]

The Knesset Welfare and Labor Committees, which had no staff, made

---

* For example, in 1974–77, Health to Mapam and Welfare to the Mafdal.

decisions only on the specifics of bills referred to them. Lack of policy resolution seriously reduced the effectiveness and efficiency of the social services. Organizational solutions, on which administrative and professional opinion could possibly agree, were not carried out because the political system had not achieved the necessary condition—the prior resolution of a sectoral, ideological, and coalition impasse. The multiplicity of national agencies on each local scene caused confusion, and resources were distributed into separate efforts which were each individually inadequate. In the field, multiple authorities employed different concepts and criteria, and often carried out policies with conflicting outcomes as they advanced their various ideas and organizational interests.*[54] Examples of issues which remained outstanding were the unification of income-maintenance services, and the merger of the departments in the separate ministries which deal with the same problems.

In the central government, the Ministries of Welfare, Health, and Absorption were relatively weak in professional and administrative authority. Although for many years the Ministry of Welfare had been staffed with Mafdal political loyalists and was far from being the center it should be of social service expertise, in the 1970s it began to recruit experienced young professionals and to acquire the ability to give guidance as well as funds to the local authorities directly responsible for the work. The Ministry of Health has had very little capacity to develop and direct the national hospital system. Its professional and policy analysis staff has been limited in scope, so that the ministry has not been an effective center for medical policy. In the government hospitals, it has been constrained by civil service and budget controls; while it could give little guidance to Kupat Holim, which receives large government subsidies and has great flexibility in the use of personnel and funds. Faced with these problems of providing medical care, the ministry has not been able to address the larger questions of policies for health.

Few local governments, which became responsible for the operation of welfare services, gained the maturity in politics or organization needed to manage services effectively or to resolve the conflicting demands of local groups. The pattern of local welfare operations was one of individual and group pressure, and politicization. Social workers, seeking to develop local activism and participation, naturally urged neighborhood leaders to demand more from city and national offices rather than to carry out improvements through local community actions. Welfare services thus depended on the quality of local government, which was often most problematic where the needs were greatest.

---

* For example, four organizations send poor children to boarding schools; seven try to help youth who are not working or studying. The Ministries of Justice, Police, and Welfare all work on questions of delinquency, while the NII, and the Ministries of Labor, Welfare, and Health all have rehabilitation services. The city of Herzlia is unique among local governments in organizing a unified Department of Welfare Services, including family and community social services, health, education, and cultural activity.

In this situation, political nonsolutions, lack of a central resolve, and local incapability impeded organizational or substantive change. Even in education, where the broad political questions seemed to have been largely resolved and where there was a strong central authority, changes proposed from the top moved very slowly, and there was little grass-roots initiative within the scope of the system. Many ideas developed in Health and Welfare, but the chance of their adoption or effective use was very limited, because of the frequent lack of adequate local organization in Welfare, and of national guidance in Health. The diversity of interests and actors and the organizational dilemma enhanced the importance of the ideas entertained by those involved and determined, to a large extent, their reactions to demands and events.

Ideas and Concepts of the Social Process

Charity was (and is) important in the Diaspora communities. Those well off took care of the poor, discretely, and with regard for human dignitiy. If there was equality of man before God, this was not true of the status ladder of the community or in the life chances of children; yet basic literacy and knowledge of the Bible and prayers were acquired by nearly all male children, and respect for learning allowed a brilliant poor youth to continue to study, especially if his talents became obvious at an early age.

In the Yishuv, the early Zionist immigrants found many Jews living on charity, mainly from the *halukah*, or allocations from abroad. The rationale of this widespread system of dependent poverty was that it supported the indigent in carrying out the *mitzva* of learning or of simply living in the Holy Land. In the beliefs of Labor, in particular, work and mutual help were to replace charity. Rewards for work would be a function of need, and mobility would prevent stratification, as would equalization of status resulting from the enhanced position of manual work. The practical expression of these ideals would transform the individual into a member of the newly liberated and productive society.

Even before World War I, there were contradictions between the historic and political aims of the return of the exiles in their masses, and the social goals of the new man in the new society, which demanded self-selected, dedicated individuals. When the Second *Aliya* encouraged immigration from the Yemen, it was found impossible to choose only the young and able-bodied for *aliya*, and welfare help was needed for those members of the extended families who could not work. Even young, unattached *halutzim* from Eastern Europe needed health care and hostels, or food in periods when there was no work. Still, relief was considered a temporary necessity and not a permanent policy. Social services helped to resolve the ideological conflicts inherent in large-scale immigration.

In the beginning of the state, it was widely hoped that the mere rescue of masses of people would permit their integration into the society and their social rebirth within a relatively short time. Schools, health services, and extensive public housing would afford minimum adequate conditions, and economic growth, through a general increase in living standards, would make the basic needs available to all.

As the founding fathers and older settlers saw it, the newcomers' lot was good and improving. They had come home to a democracy, to physical conditions which were better than those most of them had left; and the way was open, if not for the parents, then for the children. Most of the immigrants from the developing countries saw things very differently. Physical improvements over previous conditions were accompanied by a decline, both in status and in income, relative to others. They evaluated their condition, not on the basis of what it may have been before, but increasingly by how it compared to what they saw around them; their concern was more with current conditions than with the future, and parents were at least as important as the future opportunities of children. Benefits were looked upon as rights, and people rapidly became accustomed to the provision of their needs by a top-down administration; for the founding fathers and their followers, despite their optimism, were strongly paternalistic. It was hard to admit that the ideas and institutions of Labor Zionism permitted poverty and lags in education to continue, that there were conditions which threatened unity or the idea that the youth would overcome the distortions of the old society. In a 1971 May Day address, Itzchak Ben Aharon, somewhat cynically, paraphrased the thoughts of Labor leaders:

> How did it happen that . . . this movement which created kibbutzim and *moshavim*, and brought in a million Jews and made *menschen* out of them . . . how can they put shame and responsibility on us, of poverty and lack of education and of housing . . . and Panthers and an underworld and prostitution . . . To admit this —would be the hardest thing in the world to do.

It has been suggested by S. M. Lipset that Israel began with a belief in the equality of *results*, as seen in the welfare-state benefits of the European social democracies, while America began with the concept of equality of *opportunity*, and that these two points of view are coming closer together.[55] The Israeli emphasis on results has been, I believe, a political expedient as well as an outcome of the influence of the values of unity and integration. Thus, while the underlying belief has been in opportunity, policy has favored the satisfaction of present needs. Emphasis on results is found in the Labor ideology, in the "mutual assistance" of members, and in the more comprehensive welfare-state models. Yet the very ideals of immigration and integration imply a belief in social change and mobility and in the attainment of future goals; present needs and future aspirations are included in the system of beliefs.

If the United States consciously aims to be a plural society, Israeli society sees its plural cultures as being those of Jews, Arabs, Druze, or other minorities, while the Jews are, or eventually should be, one community. Threats to this unity arouse intense reactions, which tend to ignore the differences over many generations in the cultural environment of the various countries of the Diaspora. The desire for integration thus strongly limits the extent of the social gap that can be tolerated.* And there is another aspect, reflected in the internal politics of the Labor movement, seen particularly in the framework of the Histadrut. Much of egalitarianism in Israel, as in America, has meant the embourgeoisement of the skilled worker and the diffusion of a middle-class mode of living. Much, also, comes from the demand of one group to have the same benefits as another. This has long been the central thrust of Israeli wage bargaining, a process in which the more skilled and those in essential services are favored.

The disturbing stimulus of visible income differences has been blunted, if to a decreasing extent, by social custom. Elements of a relatively simple and modest life style have remained from earlier and more difficult times, reinforced by the continued existence of egalitarian islands in the kibbutz and other small communities. These mitigate the impact of increasing gaps in absolute income and consumption, just as the informality in the American manner and the image of mobility make differences in wealth more acceptable.** The feelings on this score in the Israeli society are mixed. Israelis can be ebullient, individualist, brash, and yet deferent to power, status, and learning and to the continuity of family culture. Yet alongside this deference, which somehow seems out of character, there is the egalitarian familiarity of members of a family who are both pleased with and envious of the success of relatives.

The emphasis on results has also been due partly to the difficulty of understanding the social forces at work. Economic growth, in the mixed economy,

---

* For this reason, the use of quotas for group representatives is not generally acceptable, except on political lists aimed at the electorate. It is not considered legitimate to appoint to jobs people who are less qualified than others simply because of their ethnic identification, except where specific experience or qualifications are not considered necessary. For example, in the 1950s, a lower standard, the "B norm," was demanded of pupils of Asian/African origin on the *seker*, or eighth-grade achievement test. This practice was later rejected as being pejorative, as well as opposed to the integrative concept. Instead of the B norm, a universal lowering of formal requirements was acceptable, as seen in the simplication (and the provision of the choice of examination levels) in the national matriculation examination. In 1977–81, there was some tendency to demand or stimulate politically more of a "positive action" approach, (for example, within the Histadrut, after its 1981 election, in which the Likud virtually retained its 1977 strength) but what is written here still applied to the majority view.

** There is, however, a surprising acceptance of status, or ascriptive inequality, seen in the greater rights and job security of white-collar workers. Profits from capital or professional services are also regarded with equanimity. As an extreme example, a Mapai leader and former Minister of Justice Ya'akov Shimshon Shapiro received extremely high fees for arbitrating a case involving public corporations, without enduring serious party obloquy. The Labor movement, indeed, has been ambivalent about property and income equality, and shows an unusual respect for property, for corporations, and even for unearned income, the latter rationalized by the need to encourage and protect household savings.

made the equality of rewards more and more impractical, as the bureaucracies of the government and the military grew and industrial scale increased, and with them, the rewards for training and talent. In the dynamics of the highly differentiated and achieving industrial society, relative equality of income and status need to be considered in terms of the access of the individual to opportunities for the acquisition of skills and in terms of the ability of people to acquire new capabilities. Social policy towards this goal has not so far been very effective.

Toward More Understanding

The system, however, has shown that it can learn. In the early 1950s, dissatisfactions in the immigrant camps did not cause a national crisis mainly because the problems were expected to disappear. Within a decade, new protests brought the realization that the melting-pot theory was not working—at least not yet.[56] Groups of Jews from different countries continued to show separate modes of behavior in their interactions with each other and the rest of the society, which remained a source of stress. The hope that growth would eliminate poverty was dispelled by events, along with the belief that universal schooling would of itself provide equal educational opportunity, and that the parents can be neglected without hurting the future of the children. Social processes, left to themselves, were not enough. It became clear that feelings of relative deprivation and a low opinion of one's self and one's origins contain more of a threat of social rift than do differences in income. The specter of delinquency and alienation led to a search for deeper changes rather than for ad hoc easing of crises, and for an understanding of the social process and the implications of policies. Perceptions changed, not only in reaction to events, but through the diffusion of academic and professional ideas from Israel and abroad.

Throughout most of the 1960s, there were many efforts, largely unproductive, to analyze the equality of incomes, or to estimate minimum household consumption expenditures. By the end of the decade, however, the combined influence of events, professional approaches, and newer data led to new concepts. Relative deprivation came to be seen as the central income measure of poverty, and the ratio of a family's income to the national average wage became an important criterion. It was realized that poverty is a result of multiple adverse conditions, which can create a trap that only major and intense intervention can release.[57] The idea was more and more accepted that universal services are needed and that "services for the poor are poor services," but also that universal services need to be designed and applied with sophistication. As Titmuss wrote, "The challenge . . . is not the choice between universalist and selective . . . services . . . but what particular infrastructure of universalist services is needed in order to provide a framework of values and opportunity bases within and around which can be developed socially accepted selective services aiming to discriminate . . . in favor of those whose needs are the greatest."[58] Neighborhood participation came to be encouraged, not only as a normative democratic aim but to enhance political support of demands, and to establish social needs from first-hand knowledge. Eventually, dependence was to be attacked by encouraging self-help and neighborhood responsibility.[59]

These changes in thinking were influenced by British thought and experience, with some lag in time. The American example was seen in the profession of social work and in the application of psychology. Schools of social work were started in the 1950s at the Hebrew University, and later at Tel Aviv and Haifa Universities. Itzchak Kanev, the early champion of universal welfare services, had studied with Beveridge at the London School of Economics. A later champion, Israel Katz, who was head of the NII from 1968 to 1973, and Minister of Labor and Welfare, 1977 to 1981, had close contacts with Titmuss, Crossman, and others. In the late 1960s, researchers at the NII published data comparing incomes to average wages, while studies for the Szold and Falk Institutes showed how widespread the occurrence of multiple conditions of poverty was among children. The Prime Minister's Committee on Children made these data tangible symbols of social goals.

The new beliefs failed to show much conscious concern, when translated into social policy, explicitly for Arabs and other minorities. The Prime Minister's Committee on Children merely stated that the matter should be given special attention in the future, without discussing the question. The Ministry of Education's long-range planning group in 1975 did carry out a thoughtful analysis and made some important qualitative recommendations, showing a concern for the role of education in the integration of the minorities in the society, and the advances in minority education have been impressive.

The preoccupation with defense and the economy, which have generally placed social policy low on the agenda, works even more strongly against social policy for the minorities. So does the kind of thinking that held the condition of poor immigrants as good because it was better than in their former country—and which, similarly, tended to be satisfied with the marked improvement in the standards of living and health among the minorities. Because social services are largely administered by local authorities, national neglect has been abetted by a low level of concern by the minority leaders themselves. Both minority and Jewish consciousness of these needs is rising, however, and it will be getting increasing political attention.

The conceptual approaches I have discussed can be described as those of applied social science, in that they attempted to understand the trends in the social condition, and the relations between these trends and policy decisions. Social science can influence the way in which the actors in the political system see the world; indeed, it is an integral part of the system; but these perceptions and the goals toward which they are directed are related to articles of faith more than to science. Beliefs which have been of great influence include:

The value of work. A person's role in society is expressed through his work. One implication: the highest priority should be given to getting people who are not working into the work force; and the social services should be organized around the concept of productive work.*

Optimism for the future and for youth. Youth growing up in the Jewish state will overcome the social ills and distortions of the past. Some implications: neglect of the parents in educational policy;[60] sensitivity and strong reaction to evidence of setbacks and gaps in educational attainment and in social integration of youth; possible neglect of social services in the early years of the state "because of the *halutzic* ideal of equality and romantic dreams."[61]

The value of social unity and integration. The ingathering of the exiles will result, eventually, in an integrated and unified Jewish community. Implications: sensitivity and strong reaction to symptoms of disaffection or alienation, or of divisions along ethnic lines. This sensitivity has had a very strong impact on social policy.

The right of welfare. The society has the duty to provide all individuals with a minimum standard of life and with health care in a manner which preserves their dignity. Implications: a broad program of social welfare and an emphasis on results.

To these beliefs should be added an important element of the political culture—the pragmatism, incrementalism, and compromise of the mainstream of Israeli politics, which fosters different simultaneous approaches; but which can, on the other hand, divert attention from the fundamental questions to current symptoms. The forms of practical expression of beliefs and social concepts depend a great deal on the way they are related to the organizations which plan and operate the social services, and to the political system of which they are a part.

Facing the Issues

We can now reconsider how interests, party and bureaucratic politics, and beliefs influenced the ways in which the principal issues were faced; how the nationalization of social services progressed; the need to organize to provide more effective services; the attempts that were made to develop an effective process of defining social goals and strategies; and ways to gain a high place for social issues on the national agenda.

In all of these areas, intentions were only partly achieved. The employment services and income-maintenance organizations were fully nationalized, and education largely so, although within the national educational

* To quote a press interview with Prime Minister Rabin in 1976: "The income of the individual should be constructed around the central axis of work. . . . The citizen . . . has a right to [public] help only if justified by unusual circumstances. . . . The aim . . . is employment for a person according to his ability, to help him develop his abilities through occupational training; . . . and only if he can't, or there are social circumstances, then help him via the N.I.I."

system there remains separatism between the religious and nonreligious trends. The debate on the nationalization of pensions and health care reached an impasse. With the nationalization of many services, politicization was diminished but not eliminated, and the ground was prepared for the advance of professional approaches.

Although the delivery of community services improved, in each locality divided and often redundant national authorities were active. Diverse agencies carried out the tasks, often with conflicting policy goals. At the Cabinet level, the Ministers Committee on Social Welfare and the Office of the Prime Minister's Adviser made only a modest advance toward becoming a focus for the formation of an overall policy; and in effect remained outside of the budgetary process. The Cabinet was characteristically a coalition of fiefdoms which, together with the de facto rule of the Treasury's Bureau of the Budget, prevented the development of an effective Cabinet machinery for social policy. Although there was a broad consensus on general aims, when it came to specific policies, particularist groups and bureaucratic interests could readily divert the course. But, beyond an inadequate knowledge of inputs and their results, perhaps the largest deficiency of the way policy was formed was the fact that economic policy and social policy were formed separately, with social policy a dependent follower.

As different issues arose, the relative importance of the elements varied, although all were present, even if in subordinate roles. In the struggles over the nationalization of services, political and organizational resources were a predominant factor; yet ideology retained importance. This is seen, for example, in the belief, or at least the rationalization, that the retention of health services and pensions within the Histadrut would preserve the concept of mutual help and also the broader Histadrut role, beyond trade unionism. In the issues which were decided in earlier years, such as education and the employment services, many who supported nationalization hoped that the influence and ideologies of Labor would be preserved, since the new leaders of the nation came from Labor. Looking back, it appears that Labor's influence, while it declined, survived its ideology. Some of the more orthodox left saw the nationalization of the Labor schools as the source of the end of ideology, and of "socialism without doctrine." In the compromise through which the schools were nationalized, the groups for whom doctrine was of the highest importance, the settlement movements and the Mizrachi, retained very considerable autonomy within the new system as did the Aguda outside it. Their separatism gained legitimacy and support from the fact that the broad public saw both the kibbutz ideology and traditional Judaism as essential in preserving the unique characteristics of the country. In the general schools hopes came to naught that most of the teachers belonging to the Teachers Union would internalize, and thus transmit, Labor values.

Politicization declined only gradually in the bureaucracies of important ministries. Until 1977, the Ministries of Housing and Labor continued to be the preserves of Labor, and Welfare and the Interior of the Mafdal. Profes-sionalization grew, however, in all of the ministries. Coalition allocation of ministries, the desire for political control and patronage, and the interests which the several organizations developed in the well-known modes of bureaucratic politics combined to create separatist organizations. To this was added the higher relative power of organizations which are producers and doers, as compared to that of those whose task is the development of prin-ciples. These characteristics of the system made it difficult to develop a coor-dinated policy, and even harder to carry one out. One could ask why Mapai, and later Labor, was not adequate as a focus or forum for policy resolution, even in the heyday of the party's power. One answer is that social questions provoke a very broad spectrum of often conflicting interests and beliefs, so that the party could not satisfactorily resolve them. An example is seen in the debate over educational reform in the 1960s, when the party declined the role of arbiter, even though the protagonists, the Minister and the Teachers Union leader, were both within the party.

Those who needed the social services were seldom represented directly, with the forceful exception of occasional strong protests. Although concern for the welfare of the aged grew, as the proportion of older people in the population increased, there was little effective formal organization of the elderly. Similarly, while the decision to pay children's allowances involved the incomes of the lower-paid workers, the National Insurance Institute and scholars were much more active in achieving them than the Histadrut. Academics and the providers of services became the champions of the in-terests of the recipients.

Indeed, the role of ideas and social concepts has been greater than is com-monly supposed. In Israel, as elsewhere, the state of the art of social policy making is limited by the meager available knowledge regarding the effects of social action. As a result, policy determination is based more often on norms than on empirical evaluation of ongoing programs. Further, the integration of beliefs with organizations and their purposes served to reinforce divisions created by the Cabinet allocation of fiefdoms and by loyalties to the aims and interests of bureaucratic organizations. This integration often contributed to the positive outcome of forceful and effective action by strongly committed people; but it also impeded change and limited the rationality of decisions and resource use. The impact of divisions was enhanced when there was public ac-ceptance of the ideological bases of the separate organizations, as was shown in the case of the separate trends in education; or, in the beliefs in the advan-tages of universal and equal services, which secured support for the univer-salist income-maintenance policies of the National Insurance Institute.

The principal roles of concepts and beliefs, however, were the develop-ment and acceptance of the commitment to welfare, that is, the responsibility of the state to provide for a minimum level of income for all, for medical ser-vices, and for housing. Second, the sensitivity of the leaders to the self-image of a people which believes that it is an integrated, just society caused many rigidities of the system to be overcome, and made it sensitive to populist as well as to bureaucratic influences and responsive to the absence or presence of active political leadership on social questions.

It was a congruence of forces—the protests of the alienated, the data and analyses of the academics (and the more learned members of the government), and the media which revealed the extent of inequality. These facts and sentiments acted strongly on the very sensitive national self-image, and led to action. It was a concurrence of interests, needs, and beliefs which moved the system; it was the rigidity and inertia of the system which made populist influence a necessary means of moving it.

And it was the general acceptance of the responsibility of the state for welfare which narrowed the areas of debate, mainly but not entirely, to means and organization rather than the overall goal, so that the debate was not clearly one between left and right. This consensus, like other elements of Israeli belief, was largely the outcome of the interaction of initial concepts with a reality that differed greatly from that which was originally assumed. Thus the belief, characteristic of the period of the Yishuv, that productive work in itself would be able to provide for most social needs, began to be eroded even during the Second *Aliya;* but the great change took place following the mass immigrations of the 1950s, when the ideas were rudely shattered that the simple ingathering of the exiles and the provision of formal equality would be enough to provide for an integrated society, or that the returned exiles would accept a long apprenticeship in lower status until real equality was achieved.

The system showed that it could learn. *Inter alia,* the lags in the achievement of educational and occupational equality and mobility led to a shift from the concepts of equality of output or current receipts toward the seeking of equality of opportunity. Beyond the establishment of the universalist welfare systems and the arrays of compensatory measures, these same experiences led, however, to a social system in which the provision of needs continued to be largely paternalistic, from the top down—whether in the provision of support and services to individuals, or in the gross dependence of local governments on the resources of the national government, or, most seriously, in the perception, by the less endowed population, that the system comprised, on the one hand, an establishment whose duty it was to fulfill the needs, and, on the other, the people, whose right it is to receive what they require.

However necessary and effective they may be, transferring funds or providing services may not lead to the kind of development of individuals, families and communities for which high hopes were held. Indeed, the dependence engendered may well have deterred these possibilities. There was much greater success in the basic maintenance of income or in providing housing—necessary but not sufficient conditions for well-being—than in developing human resources or an independence of spirit. Despite continuing international and economic crises, there is great concern for the social condition. Limited by serious constraints on resources, most of the material problems of welfare were met, and few were hungry or without housing or medical care. What remained to be done was much harder—to develop the qualitative aspects of life; and for the society to gain the ability to build itself from the ground up. These would require intensive social thought and much innovation in practice.

CHAPTER 7

Science and Policy:
Knowledge and Power

SCIENCE POLICY concerns both the advancement of science and technology and the impact of science in public affairs—how knowledge and thought influence power and its use, and how scientists and intellectuals, ideas and creative or analytical modes of thought relate to government. Just as economic thought and action in Israel have emphasized production more than marketing, so science policy has been more concerned with the performance of research than with innovation or with the use of science in making policy.* This chapter examines the relations between science and policy.

Science in Israel is Western, and closer to the United States than to Europe. It is evaluated by the usual standards of publications, discoveries, facilities, and the success which graduate students have in leading foreign universities. In applied science there have been areas of notable achievement, for example, in agriculture and aerospace technology. The Technion's concept of engineering is similar to that of M.I.T. or Cal Tech. Science is integral to university teaching, and basic research is done in universities, rather than in separate institutes as in France or the USSR.

---

* When Moses came down from Mount Sinai and told the people that he brought the Law, they pledged to obey, saying "Na'aseh ve nishma"—"We will do and we will listen" (Exodus 24:7). This is believed by Talmudic sages to show the faith of the people, in that they agreed to obey even before they heard the Law itself. Some Israelis now say, however, that the statement applies to present-day Israeli policy making, and shows an antagonism to planning or analysis, and that the mode of the culture is to act first and think later.

While noting the high quality of defense technology, medicine, agriculture, and "big league" basic research facilities, some observers have commented that Israeli research has been more effective in publishing results than in using them.*[1] There is ambivalence, also, about the role of knowledge and thought in the making of general policy, and the status of science is much greater than its influence. While two outstanding scientists, Chaim Weizmann and Ephraim Katzir, have filled the symbolic role of President of the State, it was only in 1977 that scholars or scientists first reached Cabinet rank. Science is revered, but policy is made pragmatically.

Questions of Science Policy

In a small industrial country, located far from world centers of learning, science policy is perplexed by the following kinds of questions:

How to be a successful province. In small countries, science follows world fashions, reference groups are located abroad, and research goals are often not related to local possibilities. There is an imbalance of technical payments; much more technology is imported as products or even as design and consulting work than is exported. The problems are how to be a producer as well as consumer of science, to become part of the center, and how to use science as a window on the world yet avoid merely following current fads.

How to overcome the disadvantages of small scale. Because of costs and a small home market, few areas or large projects can be developed economically. On this scale, market mechanisms which allow competition to decide are seldom effective, yet free play of enterprise and ideas is needed. It is very hard to manage a small science investment portfolio.

How to enjoy the advantages of a small science community while avoiding some pitfalls. Interaction and community of purpose may be easier, but the accentuated roles of institutional and personal relations can work against communication, cooperation, and scientific objectivity.[2]

How to keep the best people and enable them to enjoy their potential. A policy of trying for academic excellence and of giving each person a chance to go in whatever direction his talents take him risks the export of intellectuals, at least in the short term, when opportunities and numbers may seem out of balance. Indeed, a small surplus or deficit in the number of people with certain kinds of skills can become critical.

How to make science part of policy making and yet preserve the role of the intellectual as a critic. A small country has fewer people available to work on the same spectrum of problems as that of a large country. Scientists are close

* The number of Israeli scientists per 10,000 population who published in international journals in 1975 was 15, compared to 10 in the United States and 9.2 in Switzerland (*Scientific Research in Israel,* Jerusalem, NCRD, Prime Minister's Office, 1979).

to the establishment and often identify with it, and personal relations can work against objectivity.

Added to these are local peculiarities: a large immigration with a high and unpredictable variance of endowments; major developments in defense technology, whose results, as in other countries, are used in the general economy with difficulty; a critical attitude toward the state deriving from earlier times when the Jews, eminent in European science, were marginal to their societies, whereas now they are part of the majority and have strong identification with national goals. Israel is a society which has not yet learned to make its collective talents equal to the potential sum of those of the individuals.

These general problems, in the context of economic and military siege and of hopes that science and the quality of the people will substitute for wealth and numbers, lead to the following questions:

How effective has science policy been in advancing science and the contribution of the scientific potential of the country to the society, the economy, and defense?

How does the political system of science work, and what is the political culture of the scientist?

What are the roles of scientists and of science and technology in politics and policy, and on what do they depend?[3]

We shall now see how science grew at first without policy; how, in contrast to much of Israeli society, a pluralist higher education and research establishment emerged (not without the resistance of the old, established institutions), while dependence on government funds led to attempts to reach a more rational and authoritative mode of resource allocation and to a change in the politics of higher education and research. There has been a reasonably effective response to the short-range needs of science, yet far less success with the more strategic questions of developing excellence, or of using scientific potential in order to help meet problems and demands which are extraordinary in proportion to resources.

The Universities

At the turn of the century the idea of a university in Zion caught the imagination. Jews were eminent in European science, and Europe was still the center of the world. The Technion in Haifa was founded as early as 1912, and a university was endorsed by the 1913 Zionist Congress. In the middle of World War I, under the Turks, faith in the future led to the purchase of the Mount Scopus site from its English owners, and a cornerstone was laid as soon as fighting stopped in 1918. At a colorful inauguration ceremony in 1925, Lord Balfour sounded the themes, "The Law shall go forth from Zion" and "The genius of the Jewish people is shown in modern science." Achad Ha'am, who saw spiritual primacy as the main goal of Zionism, had written that the institution was to be:

> not a mere imitation of a European university, only with Hebrew as the dominant language, but . . . the true embodiment of the Hebrew spirit of old, . . . to shake off the mental and moral servitude to which our people had been subjected in the Diaspora.[4]

In actuality the results were more modest. At first the university developed on a European model.* The Technion made an early decision to become an institute of technology rather than a training school for sorely needed technicians.[5] These enterprises were, for a long time, very small, and the curricula selective; they offered only graduate degrees until the B.A. was introduced in the 1950s. Excellence varied from field to field according to which persons happened to have the motivation to go to the small and remote country, and it is now seldom remembered that in the 1930s some refugee scholars saw Istanbul or Buenos Aires as offering more opportunity than Jerusalem.

Indeed, in the short run they did. When Second *Aliya* immigrants left home before finishing the *gymnasium*, or the Third *Aliya* after somewhat more schooling, most in both groups sought to be laborers in the pioneering mode rather than professionals. Although in later immigrations the highly educated often lacked similar motivation, there were few alternatives to physical work or minor commerce, and professors *manqués* became high school teachers. The few secondary schools of the Yishuv benefited, successfully combining Hebrew education with the intensive curriculum of the European *gymnasium* or *realschule*. Today the academically selective form, if not the old quality, of the secondary school remains, while the status and training of teachers and the intellectual content of the studies are somewhat diluted.

Hebrew education shared priority with pioneering and national service. An ideological ambivalence regarding higher education was partially solved by pluralist and volunteer efforts—a mode which continued well after independence. Despite urgent practical needs, the Hebrew University, the Technion, and the Hebrew secondary school became, with the kibbutz, symbols of the national renaissance; and while the symbolic importance of the universities in creating the national home was widely recognized and never in doubt, to many of the most able youth in the thirties and forties, the *halutz*, or pioneer, was the ideal. National service in settlement or defense took precedence, and many went to kibbutzim or the Palmach instead of going to the universities. By 1977, only two Prime Ministers, Moshe Sharett and Menachem Begin, had been university graduates.

* In the Nazi period, says Joseph Ben David, the Hebrew University was "the last surviving example of the classic German university."

354   ISRAELI DEMOCRACY

These priorities probably made independence possible, but they caused a gap in the growth of new generations of scientists and engineers. This gap, and the loss to the immigrants of the thirties of many opportunities for professional experience, did considerable harm to the potential for scientific leadership.

In the state, science and the universities grew rapidly, without the benefit or hindrance of a national policy. The senior university staff (professors and lecturers) increased from about 120 in 1948 to more than 4,000 in 1975, and the number of students from 1,635 to 51,500.[6] Ambivalence toward academic training disappeared, and university study became the norm for those who passed the national matriculation examinations. The number of entering university students in a given year came to be only slightly less than the number passing the matriculation exams, allowing for two or three years of Army service between high school and college. Figure 7.1 shows the growth of university entrance, which paralleled the spread of secondary schooling.

Most of the increased enrollment was in the social sciences and the humanities, which are often less rigorous in their analytical demands than natural science or engineering. The rapid growth, particularly in the 1960s, for some time masked the fact that secondary school selectivity acts as a restricting factor, in access both to universities and to study of the sciences and technology. Most of those who pass the matriculation examination are

FIGURE 7.1   Growth of University Entrance

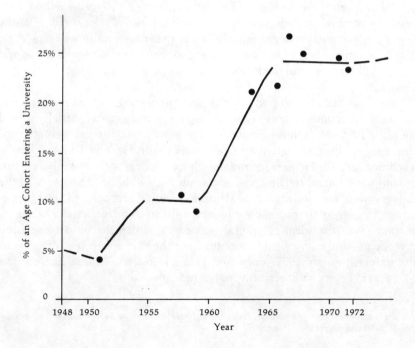

students of "theoretical" secondary schools, completing what corresponds to college-preparatory programs in American high schools, and these are less than 30 percent of those of high school age. Who the university students will be is thus largely decided by the choice of secondary school when the students are in their early teens or, in reality, at a much earlier age.[7] Of a given age cohort, the proportion of college students in Israel is less than half of that in the United States, but somewhat higher than that in Europe.

Pluralist Growth

In the 1950s, the challenge was to catch up with the changes taking place in Western social science and technology. In this period, immigrants from America and England were important in developing science. As the universities multiplied and became Americanized in form, the Germanic "Herr Professor" mode of one professor to a department gradually waned. While it still remained strong, however, the authority which the professors enjoyed helped, on balance, to thrust some older departments into new approaches, while new departments, such as aeronautics and computer science, growing *de novo*, faced fewer problems of internal resistance to change. This process, following the pioneer efforts of the 1950s, continued the introduction of more analytical or scientific modes of the leading Western universities.*

The reference groups for most scientists are now in Western Europe and North America. Many Ph.D.s are earned abroad. Professors spend summers at Woods Hole and sabbaticals at Michigan. Graduates remain close to their former mentors, and continue in their kind of science. Business schools look to Harvard and Stanford; medical schools, even though they include premedical training in a six-year course, are essentially "American."**

From the 1960s on, universities proliferated and competed, unlike most other public ventures, which were much more under centralized control. Haifa University, Ben Gurion University in Beersheba, and many junior colleges were founded. Bar Ilan sought to meet the needs of orthodoxy for a university combining religious values and secular learning.

The campuses are splendid compared to the primitive elementary and high school buildings. Local ambition could possibly have been directed more toward improving the schools or the inadequate public libraries. The displacement of effort was caused by the search for local prestige through the symbol of a university, as well as by fund-raising appeals which emphasized

---

* Some examples: economics, recast in the ei rly 1950s in an analytical mode largely by Don Patinkin; the study of modern sociology, firs developed by Shmuel Eisenstadt and Joseph Ben David; and the influence of Sydney Goldstei as Vice-President of the Technion, in instilling a scientific approach to technology. There a: others.

** Of immigrants joining the faculties between 1967 and 1973, about 60 percent came from the United States, 10 percent from Eastern Europe, and most of the rest from Western Europe.

buildings as memorials. The new universities have contributed more to creating regional and related ethnic opportunities than they have to developing new and diverse approaches. Haifa, Bar Ilan, and Ben Gurion University have been important in encouraging higher education among the Arab Israelis and Jews of Asian/African origin. The new pluralism, however, led to little heterogeneity in goals and methods. There is a trend to uniformity of approaches and standards—and students enroll mainly near their homes. Most new universities were originally branches of Jerusalem, which furthered homogeneity of approach.

Research and Development

Basic research grew with the universities and, until the 1970s, developed much faster than technology. Abstract thinkers are highly esteemed, if seldom listened to, and enjoy enhanced prestige and rewards. Men of action can be highly respected (and listened to) as "public men." Yet the academic establishment sees as inferior pursuits the attempts to integrate thought and action, as in applied research or policy analysis. In the historic Jewish condition, action is needed to stay alive; but to stay alive in order to pursue higher and more abstract goals, the "Jerusalem above." In practical affairs, it is believed that experience and straight thinking are needed more than theory.

Most of the growth in research until the mid 1960s was sparked by entrepreneurial laboratory directors, or by such an expert at organizing contributions as Meyer Weisgal of the Weizmann Institute. Large government financial commitments were made to match private donations, and extensive facilities were built in the universities and government institutes.* Industrial research then lagged, however, inadequate in scope, effort, and direction to the needs of the economy.

Still, there were impressive applied achievements. In the Yishuv new types of plants and animals had been introduced, pests were controlled, agriculture was made intensive, and new methods had been accepted. Medical research had then a sort of golden age, and serious tropical diseases were stamped out. In the state, medical research expanded, and the medical schools and associated hospitals gained strong support from basic science and a reputation for work on chronic diseases. In agriculture, defense, and medicine, the scope of demand led to more research and to the application of results. Agricultural research expanded and flourished. Its results, rapidly applied by

* From 1966 to 1977, overall R&D expenditure grew from about 1 percent of GNP to more than 2 percent (1.2 percent in nondefense R&D). In the 1970s important changes took place in the location of R&D activity and in the relative proportions of the funds spent on basic and applied research. In 1966, about two-thirds of R&D could be defined as "basic"; by 1978, two-thirds was defined as "applied." In 1966, only 11 percent of nondefense R&D funds were spent in industry. By 1978, this proportion had risen to 43 percent (report of Director, NCRD, November 1980.)

intelligent farmers who thought in economic terms, led to high levels of productivity. Since 1967 the Israeli Agricultural Field Service has led to important advances by the Arabs in Judea and Samaria.

Industry first developed to meet Allied supply needs in World War II. After the pause caused by the War of Liberation, a research council in the Prime Minister's Office founded government laboratories for applied research before there were industrial counterparts. Most of its small policy staff soon left to start government laboratories, and the original council acted mainly as the manager of several government labs, until the NCRD of 1959. These laboratories kept the country active in chemical and mineral technologies, and began work on physical standards, solar energy, arid-zone biology, desalination, textiles, chemical engineering, and geology. The Applied Mathematics Department at the Weizmann Institute spun off the government Geophysics Institute.

In the 1948 period, defense research had attracted some of the best scientists. Ben Gurion lent his support during the long years which then passed until the promise of high technology was achieved, mainly through long-term investment in people. After Suez, experience in cooperation with France in defense research gave technical leaders confidence in their capabilities and in the management of complex projects. After the Six Day War, De Gaulle's severance of these ties compelled and stimulated independent development and the growth of human resources. The Aeronautics and Electronics Departments, among others, at the Technion came to be very large and of high quality; and in some fields the country's capability now surpasses by far the proportions suggested by the national product or the population.

In most other industries, however, government attempts to stimulate R&D for a long time had only limited success.[8] Policy changes have been the priority given to applied science by the National Council for Research and Development (NCRD) from 1959; the establishment of the offices of a Chief Scientist and Research Authorities in several ministries after the Katchalsky (Katzir) Report of 1968; and in the 1970s, greatly increased government funding of development projects in industry.

Beginning its work in 1959, the NCRD became the first champion of industrial research. Increased government funds were channeled to cooperative research associations and government laboratories, and to matching grants for development projects in industry and the universities. These measures had only a small direct effect. Central laboratories, separated from market links, were not effective innovators. Industry, then still relatively undeveloped, had little readiness for risk investment in research, and the demand for matching grants was small. A public company for investment in new science-based firms was formed, but achieved little. Perhaps the 10 percent a year growth rate of the economy at that time gave an unwarranted euphoria, providing the hope of profits without investment in developing new technology; and it was not then well understood that development is not enough, and that innovation depends on markets.

As the principal outcome of the Katchalsky Committee (1968), responsibility for most applied research was allocated to functional ministries. In particular, the Ministry of Commerce and Industry took over the advocacy and funding of industrial research, in parallel with the large systems in Defense and Agriculture. It was hoped that the NCRD, freed from these specific tasks, would pioneer in new directions. In the 1970s, however, its role declined. Still, the essential need to use science as a national resource came onto the public agenda for a time, and the idea of technology and science-based industry as the source of growth was accepted as a belief. The Chief Scientist of the Ministry of Commerce and Industry made matching grants to industry for R&D on an increasing scale. By 1977, government was funding nearly 30 percent of civilian industrial R&D. Israel was catching up, in the proportion of research to industrial output, with leading European countries.

Public discussions of industrial research policy have been hortatory, and in recent years little new has been said. The patient is doing better than the doctors, however. Individuals and firms with initiative have exported highly sophisticated products in electronics, computer-based systems, and aviation. Hundreds of Israelis have worked successfully in engineering, production, and technical teaching in most of the Third World countries, and Israeli-designed plants are in operation abroad. With all this, a strategy for technology, a way for the economy to get major returns from the country's scientific potential, is still to be found.[9]

Government and Science:
I. The New University Politics

The government, as the provider of three-quarters of all research funds, is the natural focus of the politics of science; and outside of government it is the universities who are most active. By the end of the 1960s, growth and geographic dispersal had led the universities from an elite and selective role to one of mass education.* Their political support was beginning to come from local or regional interests and from the demands of a large middle class for the education of its children. Universities began to rely more on government and less on individual donors or organizations abroad to meet the increasing financial needs. Yet government resources, in turn, were limited. By the 1970s the days of largesse were over. The competition for the allocation of resources intensified, and its nature changed as well. The predominance of individual

---

* In 1975 Tel Aviv University had 12,250 students, Jerusalem 13,850, Bar Ilan 7,500, Beersheba 3,900, and the Technion 8,100. At the Weizmann Institute there were 550 post-graduate students. C.B.S. *Annual*, 1975, supra.

and institutional initiative, acting through the personal relations among donors, ministers, and institution builders, declined. In the new situation, resources for universities had to compete in the public arena with those for schools and other social needs; and bureaucracy, local demands, and national public opinion became the principal factors.

These changes led to a new politics of higher education. In the old politics an institutional entrepreneur could secure large gifts from donors of buildings or even parts of buildings, and from groups of "friends" of the institution. The Treasury would promise counterpart funds, often through complex Sapir-type arrangements,* sometimes involving other investments by the donors. An institution could get a subsidy from the Jewish Agency in return for limiting official campaigns abroad and for not competing with national fund raising. Particularly painful to the Treasury was the success of universities in running up huge deficits, which the government later covered. By 1966, for example, the Hebrew University of Jerusalem had a deficit of some 70 million lire. The President of the Technion, on the other hand, was criticized by his faculty for staying within the budget.

In the transition to a new politics, all of the institutions had more public resources, but they differed in the bases and sources of strength of their claims for support. Ben Gurion University in Beersheba could claim to further settling the Negev and dispersing the population, and the advancement of students of Asian or African origin. Tel Aviv had the advantages of a large potential student population, the political strength of the metropolis, and the entrepreneurial force of President George Wise, who had plans ready for building when the government finally decided to start to spend its way out of the 1965 recession. Haifa University benefited from the Labor strength of the city political machine and the needs of the northern region, while the Haifa Technion, far from the Jerusalem establishment and with high laboratory costs, asked for support which was based, not on student numbers, but on its contribution to national technology. By contrast, the older Hebrew University and the Weizmann Institute had thrived on the classic modes of the old politics.

As the government's outlays grew, it sought to rationalize the process of investment and allocation, while the universities, needing the help of the bureaucracy, sought the approval of the general public for their demands for resources. In the midsixties, however, there were no administrative arrangements to suit the new politics or the new complexities. The Minister of Education, Zalman Aranne, resisted Treasury pressure to act on higher education. He was ambivalent about the professors ("They are far from reality") and felt that priorities should go to helping the disadvantaged and to preserving Jewish cultural traditions; but he also recognized the political

* See Chapter 5, "The Political Economy."

weight and symbolic import of the university, and how hard it would be to enforce or even find criteria for allocations.

The universities desperately sought new resources while hoping to control their use. The deficits and demands created a mood of financial catastrophe, while, at that time, extrapolations of enrollment trends predicted a serious lack of places and prevented using the simple remedy of budget cuts. The Ministry of Finance sought "order," to be achieved through budgetary controls. In this atmosphere, the Sherf Committee on the Organization of Higher Education was appointed in January 1965.[10] The universities (but no students) presented testimony which contained little fundamental analysis. It did, however, include definitions of "academic freedom," which served as rallying points. Later on, when a Law for Higher Education was proposed, this was the only issue on which the universities all agreed. For there were differences between the new and the older institutions, and between all of the universities and the government. The established Hebrew University and the Weizmann Institute backed a weak central council under the Minister of Education, who, they hoped, would be preoccupied with other tasks. The newer universities and the Technion, having perhaps fewer independent contributors of their own, and each with a "rational" case for support, favored a strong national policy.

What emerged from the Sherf Committee was a proposal for a central Authority to decide on accreditation, budgets, and programs. On the Council of the Authority, independent scientists were to be in a minority to government representatives and university administrators, and final decisions would be made by the minister. After considering the report, a committee of ministers proposed a Law for Higher Education (1968) which would give the professors a majority on the advisory council.[11] The final say, however, even on accreditation, would be the minister's.

This visible threat to academic independence aroused little immediate concern among professors or students. It may be that knowledge of the proposal was limited, despite some press coverage, and the war of attrition in 1969–70 soon diverted attention. Vigorous opposition developed, however, among the leaders of the institutions. In private meetings, the heads of the universities convinced Prime Minister Eshkol that even if the law had the support of a Cabinet majority, there would be a major public outcry in the press and the Knesset if he forced the bill through. His problem then became, what changes to make in the proposal. Clearly the government had overstepped the line of academic freedom to which the universities could acquiesce, whatever their separate tactics.

By this time (1969), Yigal Allon was Minister of Education and Deputy Prime Minister. Unlike Aranne, he was willing to take responsibility for the universities and found in higher education less resistance to ministerial initiative than in the rest of the high-inertia educational system. The impasse on academic freedom was resolved through the appointment of a Budget Committee, subordinate to the old Council on Higher Education, which was predominantly academic. Four of the six members of the Budget Committee would be professors, and accreditation, in practice, remained an academic and not a political prerogative. By 1973, the issue was resolved. University budgets came under central review, and had to compete with other Ministry of Education budgets.

Thus, in the transition to the new politics, the universities had narrowly escaped coming under political control. The government's initiative had come from ministers whose styles were authoritative and bureaucratic rather than political-ideological,* and the danger was avoided when the institutions and a broad public found common values in an appeal for academic freedom. Decision on the resources for the universities was now in the public arena to stay. While remaining an establishment, the universities began more to seek public support, which, in the long run, is the basis for political and bureaucratic decisions.

The Imperfect Market for Research-Project Support

Aside from funds for development and the heavy government subsidy given to student fees (and thus indirectly for faculty salaries), the variable costs of university research are largely met by funds for specific projects. Their provision is insulated from national politics, is less dominated than capital investment by institutional considerations, and has plural external sources of support. Younger scientists often staff allocation committees, and the system is reasonably open to newcomers. The autocratic rule of departments had largely been eliminated in the 1960s.[12]

The political system of basic science is thus diffuse and pluralist, with several sources of support in the different ministries and in foreign funds. Internal independence could continue to flourish only if the scientists take enough of a continuing interest in policy to avoid the possibility of more bureaucratic and centralized direction of basic science and the universities.

The younger scientists, however, are more occupied with their work and needs than with questions of broader science policy. They have a common belief in the principle of academic control of science, and they understandably see this more in the perspective of freedom within an institution and department than would some of their leaders, who often value freedom from outside pressures more than they do internal democracy.

The interest of most practicing scientists in research policy has been ephemeral, except for questions related to their own research or institution; and "citizen" action has usually been in response to a sharply perceived threat,

* For example, Zeev Sherf, later Minister of Finance, and Ya'akov Shimshon Shapiro, Minister of Justice.

declining rapidly once the problem has been confronted. As has been shown, little protest was heard from individuals when the Sherf Report threatened academic freedom. There are few young Turks. In other countries, change is accompanied by struggles between generations. This has not been so in Israel, where most of the "citizens" or activists in national science policy are leaders of institutions or fields, who may have most of their scientific work behind them; and most of the politics of higher education is institutional.

Government and Science:
II. Applied Science and Technology

In technology, in contrast to higher education and basic research, it is the administrators, politicians, or commanders who decide what is to be developed. On a few rare occasions, groups of leading engineers became aroused enough to lobby energetically on a specific issue, joining with academics to protest an appointment or development decision. These incidents, however, occurred in areas like aeronautics or economics, in which there are consensus and group cohesion. While technology became a more integral part of government through the offices of Chief Scientist in the ministries, this did not bring the technologists who are responsible for development into policy roles (the nearest they came was in agriculture and defense). As in other countries, engineers work mainly in hierarchies, and their freedom and inclination to press divergent views are limited. Decisions on development have been determined more by the bureaucratic politics of large development and production organizations, and intraministerial competition, than by the professions.

On larger questions of science policy, there have been only a few examples of the spontaneous organization of scientists and engineers. After the War of Liberation, a group of scientists who had led the technical branch of the Haganah convinced Ben Gurion that Israeli science could produce new and advanced weapons systems and that the way to do this was with a civilian-led organization.[13] In this way the Weapons Development Authority was founded.

In another example, the National Council for Research and Development (NCRD) was formed in 1959, through a coincidence of interest, though stemming from different motives, of engineers, scientists, and a few civil servants and industrialists. Their common ground was a belief that science should be developed as a major national, social, and economic resource. Some of the leading scientists, already secure in their personal achievements, were concerned about getting more resources for science, while making sure that scientists should retain control of research policy; and they also saw science as developing the character of the country. Those experienced in industry and defense saw the exploitation of technology as the *sine qua non* of economic independence, and felt keenly the lack of emphasis on applied science. To the

Director of the Budget, science was a wildly growing plant which needed pruning, while to others in the Ministry of Finance it seemed an area in which a start could be made toward national planning. The Finance Ministry, therefore, sought control or at least rationalization based on expert advice.

In the Prime Minister's Office, then responsible for science, Ben Gurion and Teddy Kollek were sensitive to the importance of science in shaping the quality of a society, and had asked for a report evaluating Israeli science policy.[14] The main theme of the report was that despite Israeli capability for research, there was no policy for scientific activity or for using the results; nor was the country investing in research in proportion to the potential of its human resources. This situation was contrasted with the belief in science as the principal way in which a small country could close the gap between its challenges and resources.

The work of preparing the report served as a focus of the efforts of several ardent believers in the role of science, some of whom later formed the nucleus of the first NCRD board.* The civil servants in the group were instrumental in gaining the backing of Prime Minister Ben Gurion and Finance Minister Eshkol, thus leading to the cabinet decision to establish the National Council, with a mandate to advise the government on science policy.

In its first year, the Council was an active forum for national policy, and could command intensive efforts by the leading scientists and engineers of the day. As policy created the need for action, however, differences in motivation among its members and the difficulty of accomplishing change led to a decline in their interest. By the mid 1960s, when Levi Eshkol was Prime Minister, the Council came to be run largely by its internal staff rather than by the practising scientists, as had been the case at its inception. Even in the heyday of the Council, the mutual education of scientists and administrators, gained by working together, was not fully able to overcome their differences of culture and motivation. These differences were not, as described by C. P. Snow, gaps in the kind of things which they understood and appreciated; that is, it was not a difference in taste for the humanities as opposed to science, but rather a difference in values: the scientists sought effectiveness and creativity, and the civil servants, efficiency and control.

Trying to gain more resources for research, scientists were frustrated by the feudalism of the ministries, which prevented the Council from carrying out an overall policy. Civil servants, in their turn, were disappointed in the reluctance of scientists to seek "rational" organization. Expert committees, asked to investigate the potentialities of a given field, predictably recommended new institutions or more funds.

As long as the debate was on generalities, the support of the Prime Minister was notable. When it came to the struggle for resources, however, Ben Gurion was reluctant to intervene in the interministerial budget wars over

* See Acknowledgments.

what he saw as minor matters, compared to defense. Levi Eshkol, in his turn, looked with profound skepticism on predictions that investment in research could produce great economic benefits.*

In the absence of forceful leadership by the Prime Minister, the several ministries resisted central intervention. An R&D Committee of the Cabinet had a brief and ineffective life in the fall of 1965, probably initiated by Mapai and Ahdut Ha'Avoda as a countermeasure to the new Rafi Party's campaign emphasis on science. Since then the ministers' committee and the Council itself have seldom been convened.** Despite its decline as a voice of the scientific community in science-policy formation, the NCRD, through its civil servants, still helped meet some of the specific needs of the first half of the 1970s. Among these were the challenges to counter the decrease in resources from the United States government granting agencies, develop the diplomatic and technical possibilities of international scientific relations, form and spin off the Environmental Protection Service, and to help to find employment for scientists and engineers from the USSR. Perhaps its most important achievements, which came in its first years, were gaining acceptance for the idea that industrial research is essential to the economy, and getting policy for science onto the Cabinet-level agenda, even if at a very low priority. The broader questions of science policy, however, remained intransigent.

The Influence of Science on Policy

Consideration of the extent to which resources are limited, and of the "worst case" implications of failure, together with the impressive size and quality of the scientific enterprise, leads to the expectation that science would be of major importance in making policy more effective. Circumstances and political culture, however, have limited that role. Exogenous political, military, and economic forces cause many politicians to doubt the efficacy of forecasting and planning. Other factors which discourage the use of analysis include the close relation of beliefs and interests, and the influence of intensive interaction, characteristic of the small community.

Even in an ideal world it is not clear to what extent knowledge and analysis can or should dominate policy decisions. It can be argued that even if ex-

---

* Ephraim Katzir (then Katchalsky) tells of a long session with Eshkol in which Jerome Wiesner (who had recently finished his service as science adviser to Presidents Kennedy and Johnson), Katzir, and Shimshoni expounded before most of the Cabinet the theme of "Science as the Endless Frontier" and depicted the importance of research for economic growth and well-being. After some questions, the others left Eshkol alone with Katzir and Shimshoni, at which point Eshkol turned to them and said, "Now we're alone. Why don't you tell it like it really is!"

** In 1977 the NCRD was transferred from the Prime Minister's Office to the Ministry of Energy and Resources. In 1980, new members were appointed and the Council was reactivated. It soon stopped meeting when the Minister of Energy summarily dismissed the director for opposing his energy policy. Prominent members then petitioned for the return of the Council to the Prime Minister's Office. It continued in the Ministry of Energy after the 1981 elections.

ogenous forces were minor and the future more predictable, questions involving social values and goals could be resolved better by the play of wills and interests within a political system than by science. The relation of scientists and
intellectuals to policy is seldom simply rational or analytical, at one extreme,
or an expression of parochial interest, at the other; nor does the politician or
administrator see the scientist only as employing scientific methods or expertise. The scientist can provide specific expert knowledge or opinion; seek
resources and organizational support as an interested party; or participate in
decisions as a citizen. The intellectual can be used to lend legitimacy to a
regime, a candidate, or a policy; or he can be an outspoken critic of the social
order.

Intended and actual roles differ, and actions produce unintended effects.
The role of science is often determined by situational or system parameters,
such as the political system (as it operates in a given policy area); the political
culture of politicians, administrators, and scientists; the social relations
among scientists; and the relevance and state of the art (and therefore the
capability) of a discipline to help. Experience in several policy areas gives a
basis for analysis.

Foreign Relations and Defense

Three kinds of questions are indicative of the role of science: those involving
technology and defense systems; those of military and diplomatic strategies;
and the broader question of Israel and the Arab world.

Scientists and engineers have a substantial influence on decisions regarding specific programs. "Hard scientists" contribute to defense mostly in
an engineering role; that is, the "how" (as in R&D, in proposing new systems
and technologies, or improving the effectiveness of an existing approach).
Within the framework of defense planning and development, however,
engineers have broad scope. They head many of the technical, manufacturing, or operational bureaucracies, and their ideas and developments determine much of the perception and actuality of what can be done.

For the first two decades, most of the leading positions which controlled
defense production were not held by scientists or engineers, but by administrators in whose loyalty and capability the political leaders had faith. In
this way resources for science were obtained, and skepticism overcome. The
opinion of the broader scientific community was not adequately elicited,
however, and in a few major decisions there were substantial differences. In
1970 an electronics engineer was appointed as Director-General of the
Ministry of Defense. He was followed by an economist, and, in 1977, by
another electronics engineer. In 1977 an engineer was appointed to head Israel
Aircraft Industries, the country's largest technological enterprise; and an
aeronautical engineer, Moshe Arens, became Chairman of the Knesset Committee on Foreign Affairs and Defense. In the Rabin government the Director-

General of the Foreign Ministry was Shlomo Avineri, professor of political theory.

Scholars in foreign affairs, or strategic studies, have had little direct influence, as experts, on diplomatic or military strategy, although they are asked to prepare professional background studies. Eventually, ideas, theories, and the employment of graduates in these disciplines have an indirect impact, as they do in economics. There is, however, no general recognition of a professional status or uniqueness in these subjects, and "anyone with a head on his shoulders and the right experience can deal with them." The state of the art of theories of international relations has not inspired confidence; more potential is seen in specialized knowledge of the Middle East or other areas, and good use is made of it.

After the 1973 war, the Agranat Committee and the press demanded plural sources of ideas and of intelligence evaluation.[15] A Department of Policy Research was formed in the Foreign Ministry, and intelligence and general security advisers were appointed by Prime Minister Rabin. The effect of such measures, by 1981, was not substantial. The defense establishment continued to rely on internal staff work, while the Cabinet and the Knesset largely lacked internal or external resources for defense-policy analysis.

On the broader questions of Jewish-Arab relations, intellectuals, few in number, have stated important critical positions. In the 1930s, President Magnes of the Hebrew University, Martin Buber, and others formed a small movement called Ihud, or "Unification," which sought a joint Arab-Jewish state in Palestine. After the 1967 war, some intellectuals criticized what they saw as inadequate government efforts for a peace settlement. There was little consensus among scholars, however. Those without direct professional concern, such as economists and writers, were often more optimistic than the Middle East specialists, who were less sanguine about the possibility of an Arab willingness for peace. On specific questions, scholars held divergent views, so that Mrs. Meir could say, for example, that since the experts were not agreed, a layman could properly decide whether there was or was not a Palestinian entity. She decided that there was not.

Overall, on the basic questions, the views of the academic community were probably similarly distributed to those of the rest of the college-educated people in the country, although there are probably fewer scholars on the right. Academics comprise a high proportion of the strongest critics, and their views are listened to even if seldom acted upon.

Economic Policy

Economists have had more influence on economic policy than scientists in other fields have in their areas, except perhaps basic science and higher education.[16] The impact of academic economists was initially indirect, through the training of many of the higher civil servants, production of copious data, and dissemination of theoretical concepts. An analytical approach to the study of economics first came into practice at the Hebrew University in the early 1950s. Since then, hundreds of young economists have made their way to influence through the Bureau of the Budget and other departments. In time, Sapir, as an archpragmatist Minister of Finance, could be heard to extoll the virtues of market mechanisms in allocating and pricing resources.

The influence of academics on specific issues is rarer, but it is occasionally notable. Examples are some of the decisions to devalue the lira, and the reduction in government outlays which helped induce the recession of 1965. Economists have been members of a host of public committees, but only on a few occasions have these had a conclusive effect on public policy. A notable exception was the Ben Shachar Committee, which in 1975 proposed basic income tax reforms, and whose recommendations were adopted almost in their entirety.

As professionals, economists have often been missionaries or moralists. As the generators of public accounts, they had a basis from which to prophecy impending doom from lack of restraint in consumption, imports, or the quantity of money, from the ignoring of market forces, or from nonrational economic behavior; or to point to cheating and evasion.

This unusual influence may have several causes. Macroeconomic theory, by definition concerned with public policy, seemed to have the answers until the world economic crises of the midseventies. On many issues, marginal analysis, programming, and empirical tools were seen to be very helpful, although they have not been very useful in resolving questions of social and industrial organization. Questions of monopoly and regulation are orphans; and they are the kinds of questions in which the politicized economy would be most resistant to theory, in which the pragmatic approach of the politicians has the most sway, and which Israeli economists study least.

Within the academic community the economists have unusual consensus and cohesion. Many worked together over the years on public or academic projects, studied in the same schools in Israel and at Harvard, Berkeley, or Chicago, and generally agree on the basic paradigms. In contrast with defense technology, economists' professional knowledge and experience is acknowledged to be greater outside the government than within. The government (fortunately, most probably) does not follow most of the dictates of academe, and there are frustrations and mutual mistrust between scientists and politicians, as in other fields; but in economics there is more of a common language of discourse than elsewhere. And the social linkages which the economists developed enable them to work together in voluntary movements on questions outside their expertise.

Social Policy

Social scientists and academics in social work or other fields related to social policy work in a diffuse and pluralist area, in which policy is still in the process of being nationalized, in which the clients of the administration are weak, and which can get priority in Cabinet discussion mainly in response to crises. There are many examples in the world of welfare-state policy and a not inconsiderable body of theory, in addition to the egalitarian goals from the days of the Yishuv. There is consensus on the social-policy goals, but little agreement or coherence of thought on the means by which they are to be achieved. Social science has provided data and improved the sophistication of their use. For example, the main professional contribution of the Committee for Youth in Distress[17] was the shift in the analysis from the equality of current income to the distribution of life opportunities, expecially in the early years. Another example is the questioning by scholars of the hidden agendas of social policy, claiming, for example, that a system in which a gainfully employed parent of a large family needs welfare support (as, for example, in children's allowances) is one which gives a public subsidy to industry.[18]

Complex problems and the absence of shared paradigms limit professional contributions to specific and partial questions and deter the emergence of a cohesive intellectual community in social science and policy. Capabilities in national and local government are growing, yet the academic community still has greater professional strength than the practitioners.

In this situation, the roles of the scientists and professionals are more political (and indeed more intellectual, in the sense of probing and seeking change) than simply advocating a return to an accepted mode or morality or recommending a way to keep a system going. Professionals have acted as spokesmen and champions for weak clients and encouraged and legitimated protest groups, focusing and providing a rationale for the protests. They interpreted and dramatized situations and questioned beliefs and hopes in the melting pot or in growth as a guarantee of welfare. When their actions coincided with protest movements, such as the Panthers, or with those of young couples demanding housing, they reinforced the impact of the protests on very sensitive nerves. Thus, while they still cannot provide ready solutions, the social scientists and social workers have had an important part in getting the questions high on the agenda and in achieving a more rational debate. Although acting politically and in advocacy, they do not oppose the form of the regime, but rather specific policies or lack of them.

The educational system has been far more centralized than the social services. Despite central control, however, both control and possible change are limited by the inertia of the system, the long lead time involved in training teachers, experimenting, and gaining the acceptance of change; by the strengths of the teachers' unions; and by budget limitations. Of these, union opposition is less of an impediment than inertia and lack of people, as shown by the enactment of the 1969 educational reform bill over the union's opposition.

Research in education has had a considerable influence on the thinking of administrative leaders. In the wake of the post-Sputnik American curriculum-reform movements, prominent natural scientists began to devote themselves to curriculum reform in biology, mathematics, and physics.[19] Over time, this movement lost some of its glamour for scientific leaders. Other areas of academic impact are seen in the very broad scope of experiment in approaches to teaching the disadvantaged. Educational research first signaled the congruence of the lag in school achievement with ethnic association.

In practice, however, the openness of the administration at the top, to experiment and suggestion, has exceeded the ability to put ideas into effect or to ensure that experiment can keep up with the changes actually taking place in the schools. In contrast to the scientists' missionary and political advocacy in general social policy, in education scientists have acted more as professional experts, and in that role advocate changes in the system.

The Physical Environment

The struggle continues between the representatives of strong bureaucratic and business interests, and the noticeably weaker representatives of the principles of environmental quality and population dispersal.[20] Central foci of the discussion, if not of effective enforcement, are the National Council for Planning and Building, and the Ministers' Representatives Committee for Environmental Quality, whose staff work is done by the Environmental Quality Protective Service. These bodies are, on a general level, targets for the advocacy and proposals of scientists who are concerned with the environment, while the main public forum is the press.

We would expect to find that the scientific community exerts considerable and concerted pressure to help conserve environmental quality. Except on rare occasions, however, there seems to have been little cohesion or even professional consensus among those in the related technical areas. While some are *engagé*, others seem parochial in their advocacy of more support for research. Many give expert advice when called on or carry out professional duties, as in city planning, but take little public initiative. On the whole, outside of professional services, most architects and city planners seem to have tried very little to affect the social impact and aesthetic character of the environment, or to influence decisions when choice between environmental amenities and economic development or between private and public benefits needs to be made. Administrators and developers are more consistent in seeking economic goals.

Missionary devotion is seen more among government scientists and laymen than in academe. At the same time, the government has a difficult time finding good people to work in planning or on the technologies of environmental quality. This lack and the general dominance of producers and their interests over those of consumers greatly reduce the potential influence of scientists. For while the outside scientists and technologists may be professionally stronger, on the whole, than those in the government, their impact is limited by the strength and structure of the interests and priority system which they face, by the deficiencies of the state of the art when it comes to macroanalysis, by the structure of political representation in metropolitan government and on environmental questions, and by frequent subordination by professionals of citizens' motives to their own occasionally parochial concerns.

On Influence

An analysis of the patterns of influence shows that the *professional* influence of scientists on policy was greatest when the state of the art in their discipline was the most relevant to the problems encountered, when there were community and consensus within the profession, and when the scientists outside of government had much greater professional authority than did the professionals within the civil service. These conditions prevailed, for example, in the natural sciences and economics. They are, however, necessary but not sufficient conditions; for the most cogent and urgently needed policies can be ignored if the timing and perceived interests are unfavorable. When (as in the cases of the founding of the National Council for Research and Development of 1959 and the 1975 tax-reform bill) interests and timing were decisively favorable, the academics' recommendations were adopted at once.

Nor do the variables consistently affect influence in the same direction. For example, it might be expected that on an issue where power is diffuse, or pluralist, so that there are a good many centers of decision, the scientists' influence would be higher since there are more (and probably weaker) available "targets" for it. Yet in areas where control is centralized, like defense, influence on "how" things are done is high, and more important than in some areas where the organization is less centralized, as in social policy or the quality of the environment. This expectation is not fulfilled, however, in the case of social policy. Even though authority is diffuse, the impact of academics has been significant. They have helped to dramatize the issues and to get them onto the public agenda, to give legitimacy to protests and to provide the information (and ammunition) needed to develop policies.

Although there are serious limits to the direct and specific influence of science and scientists on policy, there has been considerable general impact. Politicians have valued the good opinion of academics and have been upset when policies were attacked, although this seems to have become less true in the late sixties and the seventies. Don Price has compared the high general status (and usually, low influence) of European science with that of the lower general status (if high professional respect) and greater influence of American science and technology.[21] As the numbers of scientists in Israel grew and science and technology became more familiar in government, the condition of diffused high status changed, moving toward the lower general standing but more concrete professional credibility and power characteristic of the American scientists. At the same time, some leading natural scientists still retained something of the old aura which caused them to be consulted on questions outside their field of expertise.

Politicians and administrators are ambivalent toward scientists—in the Hebrew, *kabdeyhu ve'hashdeyhu* ("Honor him but be careful of him"). For the management of an important technical or financial enterprise, the common practice in the first two decades of the state was to nominate someone you knew and could trust, who, usually, was not a scientist or engineer. Scientists were not coopted, like ex-generals, to political roles of power, although some of the more famous were sought by a politician to lend enhancement and legitimation—or, occasionally, as personal sources of general inspiration, to give him ideas and keep him abreast of what was intellectually new and interesting.

On a broader level, however, government often seemed concerned to have the good opinion of scientists, not only, or mainly, because the universities grew to be a constituency of many tens of thousands of students, teachers, and other employees. Politicians could be sensitive to the good opinion of scientists, intellectuals, *gymnasium* students, and kibbutz or youth-movement members because these were the people who should have believed most in the national goals and on whom the future of these goals depended. Politicians wanted them, of all people, to give their support and understanding. Many hours were given to listening to divergent views from such sources, even if there was little immediate practical effect.[22]

Considering the increase in the number of full professors from a score to hundreds, a decline in the awe of academics is not surprising, and it was one factor in making the influence of the culture of the administrator stronger than that of the scientists. Another was a change in the politicians. In older generations of politicians there may have been more dreamers, ideologues, and entrepreneurs. Now, or so it seems, there are more managers.

On issues related to their professions, the influence of scientists has often been indirect. One of the reasons is that in most areas the formal arrangements for policy analysis and staff work have been slight. This enhances the importance of the internalization of ideas and belief systems. Scientists have affected the views and beliefs of men in power or their constituencies, trained students who went on to government, and helped in creating a climate of opinion amenable to new ideas or actions.

The relatively few intellectuals who have temporarily served in the government, usually as advisers to ministers or as heads of important departments, have often reported considerable frustration. Their practical experience of how to bring about action and move the system has usually proved inadequate, and their hope for large and rapid, rather than incremental and gradual change has been unrealistic. The opposite kind of problem also exists: their advice could be adopted too readily, leading to decisions that were impractical to execute or to the "overkill" of a problem. Of this, however, there has been little evidence.[23]

Roles: The Intellectual and the Society

It is difficult to compare the roles of intellectuals in Israel with those in the other countries in which there is a developed scientific community. The movement for a national home, although it succeeded in creating and defending a sovereign state, is still in progress. Many of its goals are still to be achieved and consolidated. What were once social movements are now established institutions, but many of those who are still active in science, or at least in its governance, worked with the founding fathers and in the struggle for independence in a pioneering era when institutions were being created, and science and higher learning were only beginning. Now the professional and scientific community, which has grown enormously, faces difficult tasks. It strives to keep up with the leaders in world science despite the obstacles of scale, distance, and resources; to develop its own individuality; and to work out the roles of the scientist in the postindependence society.

One basis for the analysis of roles is the extent to which, in their relation to government, scientists act as citizens, as experts, or as interested or parochial parties. As could be expected, on questions not related to his own field or institution, the scientist is a citizen like other citizens of comparable backgrounds (and is no more active than they are), while on questions relating to his own field or activity, the relation is parochial, or professional, increasingly so with more administrative responsibility; but beyond a certain level of status, we would expect to find that "parochiality" and interest representation again decrease.[24]

The parochial mode is related to the concept of intellectuals as a class, which gained credibility with the rise in the numbers of educated professionals—lawyers, doctors, engineers, and university and other research scientists. Their influence grew, as has been shown in the case of the medical association and the national health service proposals. One important impact was to increase substantially the resources allocated for their projects and institutions—and thus, indirectly, to influence more general policy decisions. If not fully an establishment, science and the professions form a resource which can claim to be essential. They are a large and growing constituency, with strong claims to be encouraged and developed.

The Intellectual as Citizen and Expert

The growth in the numbers of academics and professionals did not lead to their more direct representation in politics and government. Lawyers are one example. In Israel they have little prominence in politics compared to their American colleagues. In the Knesset in 1975, there were 25 lawyers out of 120 members, and of these only 4 were in the Labor Alignment delegation of 51. As was shown in Chapter 2, the Supreme Court has little power of judicial review; and in the Israeli civil service, economists have much of the prominence which lawyers have in other bureaucracies. Yet the common-law tradition tends to counteract and somehow make viable what could otherwise be restrictions on individual liberty; and the judges, as well as journalists, have essential roles in restricting the power of the regime and of the majority, especially in the absence of a written constitution. Many concepts, such as that of conflict of interests, found their expression in court opinions rather than in legislation.

The highly educated have felt a lack of opportunities for personal participation and efficacy in influencing policy. The political system seems closed to entry in most parties, except at the very top or at the lowest levels. These feelings have been somewhat mitigated by the opportunities for face-to-face interaction with political leaders which the small size of the country affords, and by the needs and opportunities for direct professional contributions. Still, although the extent of serious alienation has been small, there has been continuing frustration regarding roles and the perceived disparity between the ideal and the actual. Such feelings explain the attraction of the Democratic Movement for Change for professionals and the better-educated in the 1977 elections, and their frustration with the results achieved in practice. In the Labor Alignment and the Likud, the influence of scientists and professionals has been small, and the feeling often has been that their prestige was exploited more for symbolic enhancement than to influence change.

The relations between science and power, expressed in the roles of the intellectual as expert and citizen, is critical for the future of the society. In analyzing the roles of intellectuals in the United States, Richard Hofstadter differentiates between "intelligence" and "intellect," defining intelligence as "an excellence of mind that is employed within a fairly narrow, immediate and predictable range . . . within the framework of limited but clearly stated goals . . . it seeks to grasp, manipulate, re-order, adjust," while "intellect . . . is critical, creative, contemplative, . . . it evaluates evaluations, and looks for meaning in a situation as a whole . . . ponders, wonders, theorizes, criticizes, imagines. . . ." [25] S. M. Lipset and Asoke Basu go further, and suggest a four-way classification in which the role, whether of intellect or intelligence, can be either "innovative" or "integrative." [26] (See Table 7.1.) Using this approach, the roles of Israeli scientists are seen to be on the whole much more those of "intelligence" than of "intellect," and their intellectual roles are more often "integrative" than "innovative."

In the "integrative" and "intelligence" roles intellectuals could make contributions of great value. Independent criticism of the existing values could be the beginning of a reconstruction of the goals and a restoration of social momentum; but there is little *fundamental* criticism leading to social creativ-

TABLE 7.1.   Roles of Intellect and Intelligence

	"Intellect" ↓	"Intelligence" ↓
"Innovative" →	Seeks to express new ideas on basic questions.	"Moralist"—interprets and improves modes and concepts within established goals. (For example, seeks reforms via application of professional norms and scientific methods.)
"Integrative" →	Reinterprets and integrates established values. Preserves goals and beliefs by giving them cohesion and clearer meaning.	"Caretaker"—expert in making the existing system work. (For example, furthers the achievement of specific goals through professional activity.)

ity. This is not said mainly in a negative sense. Given the position of Israel among the nations, the feeling of social responsibility is as great, or often greater, than that of intellectual responsibility in determining how the scientist acts as a citizen; and it is difficult for many intellectuals to look at the society from an outside vantage point. In this, writers have been more successful than the academic intellectuals, who have been, by and large, allies of power, or of one of the camps of power,* and thus experts rather than radicals. If there is a cult of criticism, there is none of alienation.

Another reason for conservatism is that potentially influential radical movements abroad oppose Zionism or indeed Israel's independent existence. The gods of communism had failed and the new left offered no positive social program. If there is not yet a new, coherent Israeli social dream, those of the Zionist movements are still very appealing, if even only part of the ideals could be achieved. For example, on the question of the social order, the calls are heard for a return to basic values. These values can be humanitarian, "constitutional," as for individual rights or party democracy, a return to the pioneer virtues of the Labor movement, or more simply those of civic probity. On another plane, the call can be based on professional paradigms, as in economics.

Often very critical but operating within the system, active scientists usually seek improvement as "moralists" or "experts"—their role varying from one issue area to another, as we have seen. Differences observed between the activities of those in different fields, and particularly between those in the

---

* Like ex-generals, Israeli professional intellectuals are found across the political spectrum. Examples: On the left, Matti Peled, a former general and a professor of Arabic literature; in Labor, A. B. Yehoshua and Yizhar Smilansky, who for many years was a Mapai M.K. and later served part of a Knesset term for Rafi. In the DMC at the time of the 1977 elections, there were Israel Katz, Amnon Rubenstein, Moshe Maoz, Yigael Yadin, and other professors, while Likud M.K.s then included author Moshe Shamir and Professors Yosef Rom and Moshe Arens.

social sciences and natural science, are somewhat less than would be expected from the experience in Europe and America. There are also, it appears, fewer major differences between the academics and others than would be expected. In general, the factors which tend to increase influence also seem to enhance the tendency to attempt a more active role. Thus professional consensus and strong group linkages can increase the feeling of efficacy and lead to heightened activity, although consensus could reinforce the conventional wisdom and impede a search for change. Personal links, cohesion, and consensus can not only increase the scientists' proclivity for action, but make their views more convincing to the politician.

The existence of a model of scientists' actions or of policy in other countries could encourage Israeli scientists towards similar actions; but this kind of influence is confined mainly to professional questions. The existence of strong interest groups or centralized control could be expected to deter activity; but while they reduce the scientists' influence, they can serve as a focus for it.

The historical setting of the scientists' life experience can also lead to important differences between generations of scientists. The generation who studied at the university in the late thirties and the forties has been much closer to the national liberation movement and to the government than those who studied in the fifties and thereafter. They generally feel closer to decisions, more effective, and more identified with the political system. In the Yishuv and early state, natural scientists and even engineers were more involved than the younger men of today, whose mode tends to be that of the professional and expert. With one or two notable exceptions, today's generation of natural scientists and engineers is seldom active in public questions, except on issues close to their professions; the older leaders, who were part of the independence struggle, are, with time, less active. But while the number of academics who have questioned the basic regime is very small within the organized groups which sought change, intellectuals have made up a large proportion of the leaders. Aiding these activities are the academics' control of their own time and their own and others' expectations of their roles; they are asked to speak out.

Among the few prominent instances of the activism of intellectuals are the Min Hayesod ("From the Foundation") movement in support of Lavon against Ben Gurion in the 1960s,[27] and the post-1973 protest movements which preceded the fall of the Labor Alignment in the 1977 elections. Before the 1973 war, most scientists had considerable faith in the ability of political leaders to conduct affairs sufficiently well, so that neither strong protest nor alienation resulted, at least where defense and international relations were concerned. The events of the war brought into question many aspects of the society. Much faith was lost; but few felt that they had a clear idea of what they, personally, could do to change things, or of what specific changes were needed. They demanded changes in the political system and its leaders, more openness and party democracy, and a revitalization of public responsibility.

The period following the 1973 elections seemed to bring no improvement. Following a period of puzzlement and passivity rather than of anger, a considerable number of professional people and academicians abandoned their support of Labor in the 1977 elections.*

Some Conclusions

The limits of present knowledge of science and the implications of its forms of organization and the changes going on in the system make it seem unwise to try to relate, directly, the achievements of science to its political system. A grand scientific infrastructure has been achieved, bringing Israeli science into the mainstream of Western science and technology. Yet quality is uneven, and in many fields greatness is elusive. As has been shown, the academic market still has imperfections, many of which are related to the country's size.

In some fields the Israeli scientist is as one standing on one of the spokes of a wheel, while other Israeli scientists in the same field stand on other spokes. These colleagues, in some disciplines few, face the hub, or center, of the discipline abroad, rather than forming a collegium together. In this way they maintain relations with the center, but they lose many benefits which could accrue from closer interaction among themselves; and the relative isolation of each scientist, as he regards the world scene, can diminish the participation in world developments. In this sense, some fields of Israeli science are still provincial; and in Emerson's terms, have yet to develop their own individuality and independence.**

The growth of the universities and research funds has thrown the question of resources for science, for good or ill, into the public arena, a change which could possibly endanger freedom of science if tendencies to seek control and efficiency are not offset by a continuing interest and participation by intellectuals in the politics of science; and if institutional dominance of the politics of science were to deter participation and representation. More positive signs are the democratization of departments and a growing openness of the peer-project system; but the existence of plural institutions could do more than it has accomplished thus far to create a genuine plurality of opportunity and of approaches.

The system has reacted well in a crisis—whether to a perceived threat to academic freedom, to an imminent decline in foreign research grants, or to the employment needs of academic immigrants. But in the main the span of interest has been limited to specific occurrences to the neglect of longer-range or

---

* The elections of 1977 and the role in them of professionals and academics are discussed in Chapter 9.

** In an address at Harvard in 1837, Emerson called on the American scholar to free himself from the constraints of disciplines as they were then defined, and from dependence on European scholarship.[28]

strategic questions. Like the politicians, scientists have not gone very deeply into fundamental causes or long-term trends or meanings of science policy.

One policy question is that of industry, where the complex relations of science technology and markets are now beginning to be understood and a strategy for economic and social development as they relate to technology is beginning to emerge. A second question, more important, is the role of the intellectuals in helping the nation understand its situation and chart its course, in contributing ideas and the needed creativity and belief; in posing new aims and challenges, and in fighting, not for lost causes, but for those which have not yet been won.

The role of the scientist is both that of a citizen and that of a professional. In this unique duality, if they were ardent believers in the importance of ideas and concepts, scientists could, it is hoped, initiate and delineate ideas and concepts which the society needs in order to understand and to restructure its goals and strategies.[29]

Before the state, the Zionist movement, as might be expected, enjoyed a much more intensive intellectual ferment than it has since independence, led more by thinkers and writers outside of academe. In the fourth decade of the state, the help of independent intellectuals and of those in the universities was needed in developing concepts and understanding to meet the new times.

CHAPTER 8

The Physical Environment

THE CHARACTER of the environment is the result of many influences—the spatial location of residence and economic activities, forms of settlement, the ways in which technologies are used, and, significantly, citizen behavior. The roles of the government can be to plan and encourage the dispersal of population and activities, to control building and land use, to pass and enforce measures intended to deter injuries to the environment, and to educate. While there is agreement on the general and vaguely stated goal improving "the quality of life and the environment," specific measures often run counter to private interests or to other public goals, and economic, bureaucratic, and cultural forces often lead to an outcome far different than that originally intended. In Israel the making of environmental policy has demonstrated the operation of bureaucratic politics under conditions of asymmetry of powers. Public awareness has been low, and the opportunities for full public information and adequate debate on alternatives have been limited.

The Quality of the Environment

The quality of the environment has been endangered by rapid change—the increase in population (from the immigration of Jews and the high rate of natural increase of Arabs) and economic growth, together with a great central metropolitan concentration. The country is beautiful, with variegated topography and vistas, flora, and climates; but there are also the crowding, traffic, and noise of Tel Aviv, high-rise apartments and hotels in Jerusalem, cement mills, chemical plants, and refinery smokestacks in Haifa, blocks of identical apartment houses in the new towns and suburbs, and unplanned and often jerry-built Bedouin dwellings clustered along stretches of the road in the Negev.

It was not always so. When Justice Brandeis saw the country for the first time, he wrote to Mrs. Brandeis:

> It is a wonderful country . . . it is a miniature California [he was writing in 1919] . . . contrasts of nature are in close juxtaposition, and the marvelous quality of the air brings considerable distances into it. . . . It was a joy from the moment we reached it at Rafa."[1]

But Brandeis was also seeing a country whose most fertile areas had been denuded over centuries, and the picturesque appearance of many older towns and Arab villages concealed intensely overcrowded and unsanitary homes and alleyways.* The most fertile lands on the coastal plain and in the Valley of Jezreel were largely uncultivated during the Turkish rule, mainly because of the malarial swamps and the attacks of Bedouin raiders on the Arab *fellaheen*. Land was readily available, but it was hard to gain subsistence or security.** Jewish settlers of the nineteenth century also found difficulties. In 1878 a first attempt to settle in the plains at Petah Tikva was defeated by malaria, and it was some years before a permanent settlement took hold on the site.

With the Mandate came an increase in relative security, capital imports, and, carefully limited, Jewish immigration. In the state, change accelerated. For many years growth was exponential, and resources soon were used to their limits. By 1973 there were only 0.35 acres of usable agricultural land per person in Israel, compared to 0.42 in Holland, 0.88 in England, and 5.25 in the United States.[2] Intense agriculture uses nearly all of the renewable water sup-

---

* Visiting in 1895, Pierre Loti wrote, "I traveled through sad Galilee in the spring, and I found it silent under an immense shroud of flowers. The showers of April were still falling, and it was no more than a desert of grasses. . . ." Another French visitor said of Jaffa, ". . . streets are nothing but vaulted passages, blocked up with garbage and filth, and resemble nothing more than sewers put to another use. Everywhere life seems immobile, stagnant, wounded at its very source"; while the Jewish quarter in the old city of Jerusalem was "a labyrinth of narrow, filthy alleys and dark, fetid hovels." (David Landes, "Palestine Before the Zionists," *Commentary*, February 1976, p. 47.)

** In 1800 there were only 300,000 people in the 9,000 square miles west of the Jordan. In the nineteenth century, Arab villagers from the Judean and Samarian hills began to come down to the plains and cultivate fields, staying in seasonal quarters, many of which eventually became permanent villages. On the higher lands, in the Galilee and on the plateau of the West Bank, were the bases of Arab rural life. These, together with some immigration from Egypt and other adjacent lands, provided the people for the newer Arab villages and the expansion of towns. See Abner Cohen, *Arab Border Villages in Israel*, Manchester University Press, 1965, for sources on Arab village settlement, and D. Weintraub, M. Lissak, and Y. Azmon (Chapter 1, supra) for Jewish settlement.

TABLE 8.1.   Jewish Rural Settlement

TYPE OF SETTLEMENT	NUMBER OF LOCALITIES		PERCENTAGE OF THE JEWISH POPULATION	
	1961	1975	1961	1975
Moshavim and collective moshavim	366	378	5.7	4.8
Kibbutzim	228	226	3.5	3.3

ply, and also large quantities of fertilizers, pesticides, and herbicides. Motorization and industry compounded the threats to environmental quality.

Tel Aviv became the center of a very large metropolitan complex. Somewhat ironically, an urban society in which the vast majority work in services or industry emerged from the great success of agricultural pioneering, which reclaimed swampy malarial ground and made desert areas productive. In 1973, 86 percent of the population lived in towns. Half of all Israelis lived within a short radius of Tel Aviv, and over 75 percent along the coastal strip running from Lebanon in the north to Gaza, and going inland from the Mediterranean to the Judean foothills.*

The timing of immigration and the associated settlement policies dominated the spatial arrangement. By the end of the 1950s, the pattern of location was already set, and most of the settlements of the 1970s were in place. The physical form, densities, and locations can be seen on the maps on Figures 3.2 and 3.3 in Chapter 3. Table 8.1 shows the slowing of new settlement formation within the pre-1967 borders. In Judea and Samaria, on the Golan Heights, and in the Jordan Valley, the Gaza Strip and Hevel Yamit, about four times as many settlements were added between 1967 and 1977 as were founded within the old borders.

While dispersal fell far short of the goals which were set, urban crowding and building on scarce agricultural land were partly checked.** The social and economic attractions of the metropolis were to some extent balanced by strong political forces acting for the preservation of agricultural land and by

---

* The extent of the change is shown by the following: In 1922 about 750,000 people lived west of the Jordan. In 1975 this same territory held 4,500,000 people, and within the boundaries of the state, 3,500,000 lived in less than 8,000 square miles. The use of electrical energy grew from only 500 million kilowatt-hours in 1950 to more than 8 billion in 1975. In the same period the per capita GNP nearly trebled.[3]

** Between 1966 and 1973, the Committee for the Preservation of Agricultural Land approved requests to transfer 27,535 acres from agricultural to other uses and refused requests for the transfer of 2,930 acres (the total of cultivated agricultural land in 1973 was about 1 million acres). The committee deals with land which had no building on it by 1968. Most unbuilt land authorized for nonagricultural use was not arable.[4]

TABLE 8.2.   Population Distribution

REGIONS	PERCENTAGE OF TOTAL POPULATION			
	1948*	1961	1967 (After Six Day War)	1975
Metropolitan Districts				
The Tel Aviv and Central Districts	50.0	50.7	47.5	46.4
Haifa District	20.5	17.0	16.0	15.0
Jerusalem District	10.2	8.8	10.7**	11.2**
Southern District (including Negev)	2.5	8.0	10.5	11.8
Northern District (including Galilee)	16.8	15.3	15.3	15.2

* November.
** Includes East Jerusalem.
Source: C.B.S. *Annual Abstract*, 1976.

the direction of immigration, although with time to a decreasing degree, to outlying areas. Since the mid 1960s, however, there has been little increase in dispersal except to the south, as Table 8.2 shows.

These data show more dispersal than in fact there was. Nearly half of the 15 percent of non-Jewish Israelis, mainly Arabs and Druze, live in the Galilee. It is due to their large family size that the north kept a constant proportion. In some central Galilee hill areas, Arabs comprise two-thirds of the population.

Regional differences in population density are striking, from about 5,600 per square kilometer in Tel Aviv, 500 in its surroundings, to less than 100 in Central Galilee and 17 in the Negev (see Figure 8.1). But it is in the availability of economic and cultural activities and in the standards of living and of social services that towns at the periphery lag behind the metropolitan center.[5] The quality of life is thus threatened not only by physical and social aspects of the metropolitan concentration itself, but by marked gaps in the social condition and life opportunities between the center and the periphery.*

The pattern of dispersal and spatial location thus became almost static. Within its constraints, town plans and building limitations are often violated. Injury to the environment and its erosion are prevalent. Building is frequently crowded and poorly maintained. To what extent are these conditions accepted, and what is done to correct them? That is, how are policies carried

* The social condition at the periphery is analyzed in Chapters 3, "Political Integration," and 6, "The Welfare State." While there are many tangible problems in these communities, the principal malaise is social. People feel dissatisfaction, not so much for themselves as for their children and their life chances, while the young say that "there is nothing to do here." Despite economic advances, there is a feeling of pessimism in some of the least successful towns and settlements.

FIGURE 8.1.   Location of Agriculture, Ports and Minerals

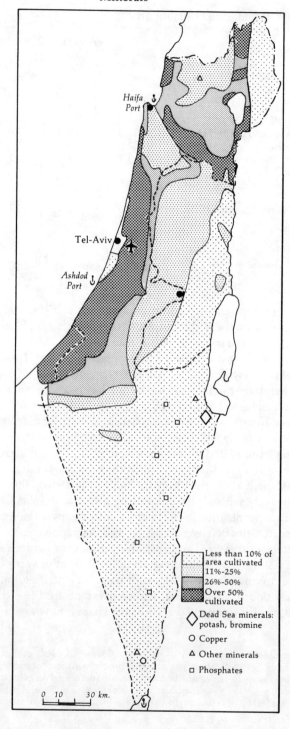

out, and perhaps more important, how are goals and policies determined? To look for answers, we consider first the background of beliefs, and then the organizational arrangements.

The Importance of Beliefs

Because of the power of the economic and bureaucratic interests involved, systems of belief might be expected to be of secondary importance in deciding environmental questions. Restrictions on land use, together with growth, make the right to use land a primary object for investment and speculation, and a focus of local, national, and bureaucratic politics. Yet beliefs have a strong influence, not only through the actions or decisions of individuals, but because of the way ideology is interwoven to an unusual degree with the formation of organizations. It remains a rationale and source of power even after the initial ideals have merged with or are replaced by organizational or economic interest.*

Environmental questions generally have low political salience. This is only partly due to the priority in the Cabinet and Knesset of defense and the economy. The roots of popular neglect go deeper. In the culture of much of both Eastern Europe and the Arab countries, the street or the "domain of the public" has not been felt by the individual to be his responsibility, and in Israel the growth from a community to a society was accompanied by a decrease in the effectiveness of social pressure on behavior.

Before the Yom Yippur War, in the early 1970s, the public reached an affluence and feeling of security in which concern for the surroundings rose in the national consciousness, to the point where the environmental issue could not be ignored by the parties facing the impending elections. A boom in building activity and in industry made evident the dangers to the quality of the environment. Israel was not alone in this. World concern, which led to the creation of the Environmental Protection Authority in the United States and the Department of the Environment in Britain, encouraged Israeli interest in the environment and gave examples of possible action.

Many policies and organizations important to population dispersal and to the environment are rooted in the central beliefs of the Zionist movement. Settling the Negev and the Galilee has always been a stated national goal. Defense concepts called for border-zone settlements, and the Zionist movement sought a return to the soil. In the political striving of the Yishuv, settlement on the land was seen as the way to win the right of legitimate possession, and land was to be nationally owned.** The city, as part of the ideal form of

---

* See Chapter 1, "Ideals and Reality."

** Most land is now publicly owned, although long-term leases give the occupants, under certain conditions, almost effective ownership. The Zionist movement early set up a National Fund to buy and own land nationally in perpetuity. The purpose, stated at the Fifth Zionist Congress in

the country-to-be, was largely neglected in these concepts,[6] nor was it foreseen that economic growth and mechanized, intensive agriculture would lead to such a predominately urban society. In the Yishuv, the collective settlements became a principal political base of the increasingly powerful Labor parties, while the cities were imagined as centers of the less politically coherent bourgeoisie, although in fact, Labor leaders over the years devoted great efforts to organizing political support and control in the cities. The Tel Aviv and Haifa Workers' Councils became very important sources of power,[7] and the Zionist Executive supported professional city planning.*

Indeed, because of the primacy of the agricultural ideal among political thinkers, it was mainly professionals who were concerned with the form of towns, and city planning was one of the few areas where there was considerable professional influence in the Mandate and the first years of the state. In the 1920s, Richard Kaufmann, a German immigrant who worked for the Yishuv institutions, and C.R. Ashby, an English planner, who was brought by the Mandatory government, helped transfer the European planning technology of the time. Considerable innovation was seen, for example, in workers' cooperative garden suburbs within the larger urban area, and in the design of Moshav Nahalal in the Valley of Jezreel.[8] In the 1930s, a group of planners advocated a hierarchical structure, in which there would be regional and subregional service and commercial centers. This approach was used later, in the siting of several of the development towns. As it turned out, however, regional centers did not develop, largely because of the accessibility of the larger metropolitan areas and the national form of organization of the agricultural settlement movements.

The influence of planners grew, until well into the 1950s, and then declined.[9] During World War II, the Yishuv began to anticipate the responsibilities of the state. A subcommittee of a National Planning Commission undertook, at that time, to begin a comprehensive land-use plan. At that time, planners were active in a "Circle of Reform," many of whose members joined the Physical Planning Department of the new government.

The years 1948 to 1952 were the heyday of authority of the central group of planners. They found a sympathetic ear, and their plans were taken seriously. Settlement was accelerating, and the planners were decisive in

---

Basel (1901) was "To buy with the gift of the people lands in the country of Israel to be the property of the people; to give it only as rental land which can be transferred as an inheritance both for working and for building; to permit the worker who has no capital to settle on the land; to insure Hebrew work; to insure proper land use; to stop land speculation." Large tracts were purchased in the Yishuv from absentee landlords, and by 1947, some 250,000 acres had been bought from larger private owners, 125,000 from peasants or smallholders, and 30,000 from churches and foundations, and 45,000 had been obtained by government concession.

* For example, an overall plan was commissioned, by the Yishuv, for the Haifa Bay Area, to be executed by Abercrombie, a well-known British planner. It provided for workers' suburbs (the *Krayot* of today) and industrial areas alternating with green belts, including areas for heavy industry. Other examples were Talpiot, in Jerusalem, and Afule, in the Valley of Jezreel.

locating new towns, kibbutzim, and *moshavim,* and in designating urban land limits. They were instrumental in securing the extension of Mandate legislation on which central planning authority was based.

Working originally in the Ministry of Labor, which in the first years was under Mapam, the planners were soon transferred to the Prime Minister's Office and then to the Ministry of the Interior. This ministry was held in most Cabinets by the Mafdal (NRP), to whom neither the environment nor agricultural land were the most important political commitments.

The underlying reasons why the planners' influence declined after 1952 are more basic, however. Many of the original group were leading architects who returned to private practice. The large enterprises of building and settling were under way; and the results of growth and industrialization soon overtook the planners, who lost influence to those who were actually developing and building. Political support for the planners withered, and with it their professional resources and budgets.

A dominant belief in growth as the answer to many defense or social questions led to awe of the *doer* who is *building the country* physically, whether as a bureaucratic entrepreneur or as a private contractor. In many ways, building has been for Israel what the automobile was for the economy of the United States, representing a large proportion of employment directly and in supplying materials, components, and requiring transportation. The big building companies, government, Histadrut, and private were like an establishment with a claim to be supported. The government could have been expected to invest in public housing in order to counter the effects of slack demand for private housing. In practice, however, government and private building have followed almost the same cycle of activity.

City council members who represent parties which have gone all out for the welfare state and union ownership of industry have shown surprising respect for private contractors or speculative builders, and awarded them unusual rights at the expense of plans and environmental quality. Because they had only limited influence in other matters, local government councils saw in allocation of building rights an unusual opportunity for discretionary behavior; and mayors were often not very anxious that town plans be completed, since this could reduce their potential authority and patronage.

The institutions which affect the environment thus grew in a climate of beliefs with many contradictions: belief in growth and industrialization as well as in agriculture, the return to the land, and the need for population distribution; belief both in socialism and in private entrepreneurship; belief in the need for professional theory and comprehensive planning as well as pragmatism and compromise; and belief in legislation, but with little concern for implementation, which, when it comes, is pragmatic. Once a policy is decided upon, it is sent floating out to seek its fortune against opposing demands and interests, which work themselves out in a milieu in which many large organizations are responsible for the development enterprise. En-

vironmental politics is therefore mainly bureaucratic politics—and we look
next at the operations of the organizational arrangements for coordination,
planning, and the setting of environmental standards.

The Formal Organization Is Comprehensive

The government owns or controls most of the resources and organizations
which determine the use of physical space. The instruments at its disposal include comprehensive zoning and planning of land use, control of the capital
market, water-resources development, pricing, and allocation, and indeed
the ownership of most of the land and the construction of half of the housing.*
All these would seem to provide means of control which are unusual in a
parliamentary democracy. Most citizens, indeed, do not feel themselves
serious partners in determining the quality of their environment. Yet the
government is far from having a coordinated or even authoritative control
over environmental use and conditions, nor has it shown a capability for enforcing planning standards which is in any way comparable to its formal
authority.

Figure 8.2 shows the institutional arrangements and the formal allocation
of authority. Table 8.3 outlines the roles of the organizations engaged in setting standards and enforcing them and in related economic activities. A considerable coordination machinery is seen, centered on the National Council
for Building and Planning, which is chaired by the Minister of the Interior (in
practice, by the director-general of the ministry). The staff work of the Council on land-use questions is done by the Planning Department of the ministry,
and on environmental questions by the Environmental Protection Service
(EPS).** These arrangement are more impressive in appearance than in practice. The weak authority of the central Planning Department and the independence of the operating agencies responsible for economic development

* In 1960 the National Land Authority was set up to take over all publicly owned land including
that of the Jewish National Fund, abandoned land, and government lands. The user pays a
ground rent to the land authority and holds a long-term lease which can specify permissible land
uses. The release of land for rental bidding, the sale of public lands, and the prices for land rent
could be important instruments in land-use policy. There are important private holdings as well,
particularly in citrus growing and some small farming, and including most Arab or Druze farming. Within the cities, particularly Tel Aviv and Haifa, private ownership was more extensive
than elsewhere, and land designated for residence is usually parcelled into plots no larger than a
quarter of an acre. Overall, in 1967, the Land Authority had jurisdiction over 5 million acres,
which was 93 percent of all land, and all mineral rights were publicly owned. The kibbutzim,
moshavim, and development towns are all on publicly owned land.
** At the end of 1975, the EPS was moved from the Prime Minister's Office to the Ministry of the
Interior, thus giving up some prestige, at least in the eyes of the uninitiated, hoping to gain integration of physical planning and environmental considerations. Time will show whether this
aim was achieved. During the first year of this arrangement, it appeared that there was an asymmetry of influence. At the start, at least, the influence of the environmental analysts on the approach to physical planning seemed to be small.

FIGURE 8.2 Formal Organization—Planning and Environmental Policy*

(See Table 8.3 for role of agencies.)

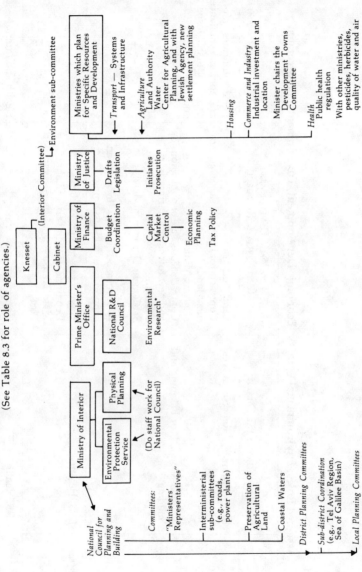

*Chart is as of 1976. After 1977 elections, the National Council for R&D, mining, and power were transferred to a new Ministry of Energy and Infrastructure, and the Public Works Department, from Labor to the Ministry of Building and Housing.

TABLE 8.3. Assigned Roles: Environmental Quality, Economic Development, Environmental Enforcement [10]*

AREA	ENVIRONMENTAL QUALITY	ECONOMIC DEVELOPMENT (AUTHORITY & RESOURCES)	ENFORCEMENT
Land Use Planning and building	EPS on Ministers' Representatives Committee National Council for Planning and Building	Land Authority Contracts for lease and sale of government lands. Housing Ministry Contract, lease, sale of public housing and new towns' or quarters' infrastructure. Settlement Department–Jewish Agency New rural settlements, location and support until self-sustaining.	Local authorities enforce building and zoning compliance through approval of plans, inspection, and the courts
Transport Infrastructure	EPS, Health	Highways—mainly Public Works Department—Ministry of Labor* Mass Transit—Ministry of Transport Ports	
Power	EPS, Health	Commerce and Industry* Atomic Energy Commission	Health and Interior—joint responsibility. Ministry of Finance—fuel quality.

Noise and Chemical Air pollution	Health and Interior, EPS Transportation—aircraft noise	Ministry of Commerce, Transport (Sources of pollution are power, manufacture, transport.)	Health and Interior have joint responsibility.* Commerce and Industry re factory impact statements, licensing.
Water Quality Drinking water = Lakes and streams and effluents	Health	Water Commissioner (Agriculture)	Health = Water Comm., by administrative action under Water Law.
Sanitation		Local authorities and Water Comm.	Health, through field services, and local authorities
Herbicides Pesticides	Health	Ministry of Agriculture	Agriculture
Food	Health	Agriculture and Industry	Agriculture and Health jointly, but mainly Agriculture
Beaches	EPS, Interior, Health, Transport (oil pollution off shore)	Local authorities, Ministry of Tourism*	Interior and local authorities; Transport
Quarries and Mining	Interior	Commerce and Industry (to 1977) Energy and Infrastructure (since 1977)	Licensing by Commerce and Industry (to 1977) Energy and Infrastructure (since 1977)

* As of 1976. After 1977, Public Works in Ministry of Building and Housing; Tourism in Ministry of Commerce and Industry; Mines and Power in Ministry of Energy and Infrastructure. (See Appendix E). From 1982, air pollution enforcement solely in EPS.

make coordination difficult. The Ministry of Housing and its subsidiary corporations, for example, plan, build, or contract for all public housing, or about one-half of all the housing starts in the country. In development towns or urban renewal projects, the ministry will most often build the infrastructure as well as the housing. The National Land Authority, which has the title to some 93 percent of all the country's land (but a very much smaller proportion of the land in the older cities), carries out the government's pricing policy for land use or sale and for contractual restrictions of benefits, and is beginning to be an independent and important proposer in its own right of land-use policy.

The Ministry of Transport is another major economic actor, with responsibility for the transport infrastructure, rail, ports and airports, mass-transit systems, and, together with the Public Works Department, highways. The ministries very often operate through government corporations or authorities which have specific tasks, such as operating ports or even building a new suburb or industrial complex. As entrepreneurs, these large organizations push for the advance of their particular mission and have the resources and incentives to try to force the hand of policy.

The Strength of Social and Economic Forces

In deciding how land is used, social and economic change and their agents tend to be stronger than plans and planners. The organization for physical planning, shown on the left-hand side of Figure 8.1, embodies the concept of *a priori* designation, in detail, of future land use. The approach resembles that used in British planning legislation in the period just after World War II. But in its actual operation the system has some similarity to American experience, in which development proceeds and changes under the continuous impetus of economic and social forces. The Israeli system is better designed to control the way in which the individual owner uses his plot than to foster integrated planning.

Under the Planning and Building Law of 1965, a national plan for population and activity distribution is approved for a period of about twenty years. The national plan is general, indicating the regional and district dispersal desired. It is a wish, a guide, but not cast in a very enforceable form, although the 1975 plan (for the year 1992) for the first time had the statutory status of a "guideline" for the ministries.

Within the framework of the national plan are outline plans for districts and for local authorities. Local town plans are the detailed specifications of these longer-range plans. If these have not yet been drawn up, local town planning committees have the authority to specify the limits of land use. If plans do exist and a builder asks to exceed or change their limitations, the local committee can recommend variances from these building limits to the district committee.

Town plans show in detail the use limits of every lot, even for parcels smaller than a quarter of an acre. In periods of accelerated immigration or growth, town plans and even outline plans rapidly become obsolete. The obvious economic incentive for the builder is to get the greatest land-use value from each plot. This combines with plan obsolescence to create tremendous pressures on town planning committees to recommend variances, and makes violations a worthwhile gamble for contractors.

Town planning committees are usually the elected town councils, which have strong political and financial incentives to allow variances and to agree to higher building densities. Building rights and city employment are the main available forms of local patronage, the need for which is exacerbated by the desire to reward each of the parties which are partners in the coalition on the town councils (which are elected from party slates by proportional representation). Further, a town gets a substantial "improvement tax" for its coffers when it approves changes which increase the value of a plot. In addition to local pressures, the town often comes up against the wishes of central government agencies. These are hard to resist, particularly when the agencies act as a coalition. Another source of the ministries' power is that they contribute to the costs of making plans for roads or sewage, or pay for the preparation of outline or town plans.

Instead of planning, local committees spend most of their time reacting to requests for variances from the existing plans. The changes recommended, and they are legion, are passed on to the district committee, which in its turn spends its sessions more on these requests than it does on regional planning. Somewhat ironically, local committees, which are strongly political in their representation and low in the strength of their professional qualifications, can take the time to debate each case in some detail, while district committees, which have stronger professional participation, must often dispose of masses of files in cursory fashion. The exceptions are decisions on major projects in which large government agencies are interested, for these agencies dominate the representation at the district, even as local politicians dominate the local committees. Influence is hard to measure, but the balance of decisions at the town level probably favors the contractors or developers or government departments which are building in that town. At the district level, the outcome depends on the relative strengths which the various government agencies can muster.

Arab and Druze communities are more laggard than most Jewish town councils in preparing outline and town plans, making it very hard to control the direction of building activity in these towns and villages. Much of the delay comes when factional or *hamula* politics prevents the achievement of consensus on the land uses which the public interest demands. Deference to individual property rights, as compared to public domains, makes it difficult to gain approval for plans which provide for the acquisition of private land for public purposes and puts in doubt the legitimacy of the right of government to tell an individual to limit building on his own land.

The picture of local planning would not be complete without noting that enforcement, which is the responsibility of local governments, is chaotic and generally ineffectual. In many towns, inspectors feebly try to cope with wholesale violations; yet even the results of their modest inspection often come to naught, and it is difficult to carry out court orders for demolition or to stop building. Showing great reluctance for enforcement, town councils seem impotent or unwilling to perform the police function regarding cleanliness or compliance with building regulations. They do so only when there are unusual and considerable pressures from the press or important civic groups, and relaxation of inspection has been used as a form of patronage. The vast number of requests for variances delays the whole permit-granting process. In the meantime, builders often try to establish facts by taking the considered risk that a building will be finished before any decision is made. At the worst, they expect to pay a fine and a land-value-enhancement tax. As in some other areas of Israeli life, and particularly where the environment is concerned, "law is one thing and life is another."

At the national level, the executing departments seem to have much more effect on the outcome than do the planners. Comprehensive planning is separated from the planning and execution for specific sectors, carried out by the principal executive agencies. One problem with this arrangement is that the executive agencies are not coordinated. It is hard in practice to achieve a coherent policy, even though the National Council for Planning and Building approves plans for highways, national parks and nature preserves, mass transit, and power-plant locations. Large projects, however, have a way of gathering momentum within the confines of the economic ministries, whose power to move rapidly and get projects onto the agenda exceeds that of the coordinating planners. Like trains on the track, the projects are often hard to stop once they have been started.

The planning staffs have, for many years, had difficulty in attracting outstanding people in competition with private practice or agencies of the economic ministries; projects are debated when they are already under way, and the resources controlled by the executive agencies, together with their closeness to the action, give them the initiative and a good head start over the planners, or indeed over those concerned with some principle of environmental quality, such as the Ministry of Health.* As it turns out, not by accident, the important operating agencies were controlled by the Labor Party or Mapai before it. Because of this imbalance of forces, the operating agencies were more important political foci than are the planners;** and as a center of

* Leon Peres points out, for Australia, the larger authority of agencies conceived with *principles* as compared with that of those concerned with *interests* ("Ecology, Conservation, and Politics," *Search*, Vol. 1.4., 1960).

** The Land Authority is an example. A Cabinet-appointed Governing Council in effect ensures that the Authority carries out the government's wishes. These, however, do not yet comprise a coherent social and economic policy for the use of land, and many basic questions are not re-planning decision, the National Council often lacked timeliness and political strength.

Setting and Enforcing Environmental Standards

By the 1970s, a long period of accelerated growth, industrialization, and settlement had placed the environment in danger of deterioration, much of it irreversible. The public and indeed the political system were slow to react; and the culture, priorities, and power relations all seemed hostile to the environment. Public interest for two decades had been too little and too late; it was sporadic, and there were few organized ways for citizens to participate or indeed to have advance knowledge or projects of changes afoot which could hurt the environment.

But as the standard of living and feeling of security grew after the 1967 war, public concern for the quality of life increased, the issue came onto the political agenda, and the public became more active and in some cases effective. The following are examples of public action: A decision to build aerating ponds for disposal of the Tel Aviv sewage near the town of Rishon aroused intense local opposition, particularly after initial attempts failed to eliminate pervasive smells, and the ponds became an important issue in Rishon city politics. Hanania Gibstein, who had led citizen opposition to the project, subsequently ran for major, defeating the Labor candidate. In another case, a proposal to use part of the national park on Mount Carmel as a quarry drew broad public opposition and was defeated, despite the support of organized labor in Haifa for the project.[12]

Cases which ocurred during periods of defense tension failed to get either genuine public support or adequate Cabinet or Knesset debate. For example, the issue of the large Reading Power Station addition in north Tel Aviv, notable for its high smokestack, happened to come to a head during the 1969–70 war of attrition. The press expressed "public opposition," but there is little evidence of public action, even in writing letters to the editor. As one of the Cabinet members put it, this was not the kind of issue over which to divide a Cabinet at that time.

In 1971, a temporary Knesset Environmental Committee was formed,

solved, such as the pricing policy for land at the center and the periphery and its relations to population distribution goals,[11] the preservation of open spaces and the sale of public land in the central regions, and the roles of land prices for public and private building as a factor in the cost of housing. The Authority, subject to constant and conflicting pressures, has attempted from 1975 to develop its own capability to make major plans and to initiate measures to make population dispersal more effective, as well as to be able to withstand pressures to release government land for building in the center of the country. In 1976, the Land Authority presented for public deliberation a program for the development of the Galilee which was very different from that prepared by the Ministry of the Interior, thus perhaps initiating a decision mode closer to open adversary procedure.

chaired by a leader of the opposition, as well as an Environmental Committee of directors-general of ministries. Some of the scientists who had a professional relation to environmental questions became active, and the recommendations of a joint study group of the Academy of Sciences and the National Council for Research and Development (NCRD) laid the groundwork for the formation of the Environmental Protection Service (EPS). The EPS, which grew out of the work of the NCRD, was formed with independent status in the Prime Minister's Office in 1973. The role and title of the Service were modestly stated—to be largely professional and advisory to the Cabinet, the ministries, and the central land-use planners on the impact of plans or projects and on what could be done about it. A Committee of Ministers' Representatives was set up to advise the Cabinet on environmental questions, and to guide the priorities of the Service. The EPS was started at a time when world interest in environmental protection was at its peak. The political salience of the issue in Israel had grown, and politicians, before the Yom Kippur War, saw it as an issue for the 1973 elections.

Looking again at Figure 8.2 and Table 8.3, we find that while there is no Cabinet member for whom the environment is a central responsibility, there are arrangements for coordinating environment and land-use questions, and there is formal statutory authority for setting and enforcing standards. The allocation of responsibility, however, is diffused and in several cases is divided among more than one ministry, with a deleterious effect on standards and enforcement and a reduced likelihood that decisive action will be taken (as in the case of noise and air pollution, assigned to both Health and Interior, where enforcement and even measurement have been ineffectual).*

Paradoxically, despite this diffusion, the responsibilities for economic or physical development in a specific sector often overlap with responsibility for the quality of the environment as it relates to that sector. Examples of the lack of separation of powers are seen in questions of water quality and of vehicle standards, and in the certification of pesticides. The effects of the concentration of powers are not only possible distortion of the allocation of costs and benefits, but also, and perhaps mainly, limitation to public knowledge and to the confrontations or debates which are needed for the allocation of values.

Air Pollution

The handling of air pollution shows the difficulties which can arise when responsibility for enforcement is divided; the way the environment can come off second best in the complex negotiating political mode; and how large projects which have important impacts often gather momentum before there is much public knowledge or debate.

---

* In 1982, enforcement was assigned wholly to Interior (EPS).

Under the original antipollution legislation (1961), named after Shimon Kanowitz, a former Knesset member, the Ministries of Health and the Interior share the responsibility for enforcement against noise and material air pollution. Both enforcement and the specification of enforceable criteria have been conspicuously inadequate, and the police and the ministries involved tend to blame each other. Until the 1970s, the courts found the law hard to enforce, usually claiming that measurable criteria or monitored data were absent. These now seem to be less of an obstacle, showing sensitivity of the courts to a changing climate of opinion.*

Vehicles and their routes are important factors in air pollution. The Transport Ministry licenses vehicles and approves traffic routing. It also sets technical specifications and examines vehicles for pollution compliance. Its clients include strong groups, such as the bus cooperatives and truckers, whose economic interests, as in routing or in truck overload limits, often run counter to the quality of the environment. Environmental considerations usually have a minor role in the complex net of relations in the transportation sector, which involve rates and earnings, public service criteria, and political and economic power.

Major projects have usually made much headway before there was any public awareness or questioning. Examples related to air pollution or noise are the Tel Aviv rapid-transit system and the new Tel Aviv central bus station, begun in 1969 and still unfinished in 1981. After a half-hearted Cabinet approval before the 1973 war, rapid-transit planning went into low gear during the postwar budget crises. Just before the war, the plans had been well along, with little public knowledge of the details. Pressure by the Minister of Finance for economies rather than public demand to know what was afoot resulted in the appointment by the Minister of Transport of a public committee to evaluate the plan. The mayors of most of the metropolitan towns bordering Tel Aviv did not know the plans, and the public committee was given four weeks in which to consider one alternative, which it approved. Subsequent economy moves stopped the project.

The controversial location of the Tel Aviv interurban bus station was decided during the recession of 1965-67. A large private contractor, who was able to finance much of the construction, happened to have assembled some lots in a particular place, thus determining the location, despite attempts by the Ministry of Transport to hold up the project until more thorough planning and evaluation could be carried out. The pressure of the Ministry of Finance to solve an immediate problem (in this case, fear of unemployment in the recession) and the political power of the Tel Aviv city administration won the

---

* The Reading Power Station case (1969) established the right of an *individual* to sue against a *public* annoyance. A 1971 decision (against Mekorot Water Co. and Dan District Municipal Union) found that antipollution laws could be enforced even when detailed regulations were not available.

day handily. In the cases of the bus station and of rapid transit, alternate plans were not presented, nor were public hearings held.

Water-Pollution Control

The preservation of the purity of water sources is an example of an integrated system with focused responsibility in which there is little outside public intervention or room for arm's-length negotiation or debate. Both in law and operation, water planning is comprehensive and thoroughly engineered, a situation required by the need to use water resources to their limits. The Ministry of Agriculture and its public corporations carry out nearly all of the activity and control over water planning and quality. Recovery, distribution, pricing, and allocation are managed by the Water Commissioner, under a Water Commission whose general policy is influenced primarily by the largest users of water, the agricultural producers.

There is one major water-resources planning organization, Tahal, a government corporation, and one water producer, transmitter, and distributor, Mekorot. The directorates of Tahal, Mekorot, the Water Commission, and the Ministry of Agriculture are strongly interlocked. Under a stringent Water Law, the Water Commissioner can initiate prosecution for any injury to the quality of a potential or developed water source. There has been very little litigation or prosecution of violators, and the principal impact of this power is expected to be felt in the approval of new factories.

In deciding on the approval of factory locations, the Water Commission works jointly with the Ministries of Health and Commerce. The Commission does not have the kind of linkage with industry that it has with agriculture. Even so, the prevailing economic nature of negotiation could be expected to benefit the larger interests when they come up against the Water Commission, although there is not yet sufficient experience from which to draw conclusions.

A trusteeship over water has thus been vested in the agricultural interests, with the possibility of override by the political system as a whole, perhaps most specifically by the Ministry of Finance. Those in charge of water policy, beyond an underlying belief that "what's good for agriculture is good for the country," see water quality, quantity, and allocation as problems which need to be dealt with by one integrated system, reasoning that this is necessitated by the technology. From the inside, the agricultural enterprise looks far from monolithic, and to its participants seems to offer sufficient pluralism and room for adversary proceedings. From the outside, however, it seems unlikely that the integrated system will allow alternative strategies to be advocated vigorously and in public. Still, the concentration of capabilities and the power provided under the Water Law can give positive enforcement and coordination results, as seen in the informal organization, under the Water

Commissioner, of the Kinneret (Galilee) Administration. By 1975, this group was able to coordinate land-use planning, waste disposal, research, and water use for the Sea of Galilee Basin.

The Sea of Galilee is one of the few cases where the impetus came from the public, in this case initially from part of the academic community. Dangers to the sea are seen from two sources—agricultural and town waste disposed in it, and the excessive growth of algae due to the nitrates which came into the sea from the Huleh Lake bed, north of the sea, which had formerly been under water and was drained to be used for intensive agriculture. Saving the quality of the sea had the symbolic appeal needed to stimulate serious efforts to overcome these problems, through changes in cultivation and the control of building and sewage disposal.

The Limitations of Population Distribution Policies

Measures intended to achieve a wider distribution of the population have gained a stand-off, at best. After mass immigration slowed, population dispersal continued to be an accepted national goal. It has been mentioned in the guidelines of almost every Cabinet since 1948, for example in 1948, "to prevent an exaggerated concentration in the cities"; in 1961, "continuing to populate the empty areas and to settle in the south and the Negev"; and in 1966, "to encourage immigrants and older settlers to go to the outlying areas." Ben Gurion gave a dramatic personal example when he resigned as Prime Minister and went to live in Kibbutz Sde Boker southeast of Beersheba. Like much of the outcome of antitrust legislation in the United States, however, policies for population dispersal in Israel achieved something of a draw.

From the end of the 1950s on, agricultural employment needs decreased, proportionally, and the development towns remained the basic vehicles for immigrant settlement and population dispersal. Among the measures available have been public housing with heavily subsidized rental or purchase conditions, income tax incentives to individuals, land-use planning and authorization, price policy for public lands, the siting of government installations, and, above all, directing new immigrants to the periphery. A Law for the Encouragement of Investment provides geographic and economic criteria for substantial aid in the form of subsidized loans or grants, fast write-offs, and tax relief.

Such measures have served to reduce somewhat the natural migration from the periphery to the center. As we have seen, they prevented an explosion of metropolitan population and the decimation of agricultural land. In time, however, these policies became less effective and were much less ardently pursued. Succeeding national plans were adaptations to an emerging reality and to the forces at work, rather than attempts to influence the future.

It seemed as though increased dispersal was an aim intended mainly symbolically, whose attainment was not wholeheartedly sought.

Dispersal suffered because of the decrease in population of the agricultural
hinterland, and the failure of the idea that new towns would become regional
centers. Highly skilled manpower and technical services were much more
readily available at the center, diminishing the impact of financial incentives
to industry to locate on the periphery. After the 1967 war, the opening of the
Golan Heights and other borders attracted willing settlers, diverting them
from the Galilee and the Negev; and the new towns lacked both social
amenities and economic activities which could attract and keep a varied and
skilled population.*

As each ministry or agency pursued its own goals, thought and action
were fragmented. Despite the declared concensus for the development of the
periphery, there are no effective mechanisms for unified action. Cabinet
pluralism, or indeed feudalism results in dispersed authority, so that services,
resources and planning in a region or development town are provided almost
independently by many different agencies, each of which sees its actions in the
region in the light of its national aims; and each, to make things more difficult,
has a different degree of decentralization of authority and resources. More
important than all of these factors is the fact that development of the Negev or
the Galilee has to compete with many other major national needs. The lack of
an administrative authority, and/or of integrated regional planning and action, makes it easier for other programs to push dispersal goals aside. Major
development at the periphery is unlikely without such a strong regional
authority, which could concentrate on getting the needed resources in competition with other national needs, and which could use them effectively.

For a long time the various ministries concerned with the new towns were
under different parties, which added political competition to the confusion of
services. Each town or village came, in its early and more dependent years,
under the patronage of a specific ministry or a specific central political figure.
Thus the late Moshe Sharret of Mapai was long a patron of Beersheba. At a
later time the town of Arad was built and managed by the Ministry of Labor.
In the coalition agreement after the 1961 elections, the Ministry of Housing
was formed, under Mapai, and came to have a major say in the development
of most of the towns. At this time the basic dependency mode of local government was already well established.

By the beginning of the 1960s, it was clear that not only coordination but
also more serious use of available powers would be needed if a great increase
in metropolitan concentration was to be avoided. By then, 75 percent of the
population already lived on the coastal strip. A ministers' Committee for
Population Dispersal functioned from 1961 to 1966, with disappointing
results. In 1963, the ministers appointed a committee, chaired by David

---

* Chapter 3 discusses local government and center–periphery relations.

Kohav, then head of the Economic Planning Authority, to recommend con-crete goals and ways to achieve them. The committee asked for comprehen-sive measures, with many more new immigrants to be sent to developing areas; priority would be given to the already existing development towns rather than creating new ones, to give the existing towns a chance to gain a minimum viable population; there would be strong disincentives to building and settling in the central region, such as taxation or not releasing public land for building, together with a substantial increase in the incentives for in-vestments in the periphery. Most important, perhaps, was a recommendation for a permanent task force to follow up implementation. The full report was not made public, nor were its stronger recommendations adopted.

Indeed, to carry out these recommendations would have required going from generally expressed, generally accepted stated goals (to be modified in practice by a host of conflicting pressures and requirements) to a clear-cut organization with specific aims and the authority needed to achieve them. This was a difficult solution for the system to accept, because of the con-flicting demands of economic growth and dispersal and because of the political weight of the country's center. A 1970 report[13] again recommended the concentration of effort on a few towns (seeing a population of 20,000 as the minimum for a successful independent town) and asked for a Ministry of Local and Regional Development which could plan, execute, and coordinate social, economic, and physical development. Years passed, but the problem remained. In the spring of 1975, Prime Minister Rabin was asking for sugges-tions as to how a single coordinating representative of the central government could function in a peripheral region, but no new steps were taken.

Over time, the policy of deliberate population dispersal thus became eroded. Immigrants were sent more and more to the central areas, mainly through the allocation of housing. In the early 1960s, the proportion of im-migrants sent to the periphery dropped to about 40 percent, while in 1957, for example, 57.3 percent had been sent to outlying areas and only 27 percent to the coast.[14] In the decade between 1965 and 1975, more than 50 percent of new immigrants were directed to the central region and only one-third to outlying areas, the rest finding their own arrangements. Some of the smaller develop-ment towns received no immigrants at all. In a rationalization it was said that the nature of the immigration had changed to one of more academically trained people from Western countries or the USSR. Their direction to the center had the effect of leaving a more homogeneous population in the development towns, characterized by lower economic status and having predominantly Asian or African origin.

Building also reflected government acquiescence to the trend to the center. Only in 1975 did the Ministry of Housing begin to give very large mortgages and price incentives in development areas. The first years following the Yom Kippur War showed little economic growth, however, and few new or in-teresting job opportunities developed at the periphery, so that young couples and crowded families who lived in the central region persisted in demanding solutions to their problems at the center, having no real inducement to move. Reacting to the political strength of these demands, the decisions of the Ministry of Housing were part of the trend to suburbanization and spread of settlement in the central region, where, taking both public and private building together, 70 percent of the national construction effort was under way.

Despite the incentives given to industry to locate at the periphery, recent economic growth and the increase in the sophistication of industry, paradoxically, have favored the center. Investment in the outlying areas was frequently capital-intensive, particularly in the exploitation of mineral resources,* so that manufacturing jobs increased less rapidly than the growth of investment. Lower per capita income in the outlying areas caused a lower level of demand for services, while the center developed headquarters, warehousing, finance and sales, and other services at a rapid rate. The new port of Ashdod, for example, while making that city grow, probably induced an even larger number of jobs in the Tel Aviv area. Technical sophistication brought the need for highly skilled manpower, so that investors resisted the financial inducements of the periphery in order to benefit from the services and manpower pool of the metropolitan area. These trends are seen in the decline from 1967 to 1971 in the proportion of easy-term loans given in the periphery under the Law to Encourage Investment—from 80 percent to 60 percent.[15] Dispersal policy, indeed, has been pursued with ever-increasing reluctance.

The Political System of the Environment

The foregoing brief analysis shows the complexity of the task of safeguarding the environment. The performance of the system can be considered on two levels. The first is more professional: the organized use of technology, law, and economics to meet specific challenges to the quality of the environment. The second, more general, is the ability of the political system to recognize and meet the hard decisions which arise when perceived economic and social needs and goals confront those of protecting the environment.

On the more technical level, much progress was observed, but also organizational and cognitive problems. Several paradoxes were noted. Budgets and the authority to act are dispersed among several ministries and authorities in the characteristic manner of Israeli Cabinet government; yet in many areas there is little separation of the powers to plan or to enforce or execute, nor is there opportunity to deal at arm's length. Extensive formal coor-

---

* Kohav had recommended that investment benefits at the periphery be linked more strongly to the provision of jobs than to the capital invested in physical plant.

dination arrangements are confronted by bureaucratic imperialism, so that for most development towns or areas, economic, social, and physical plans are imperfectly integrated. Legislation and stated policies are extensive and comprehensive; but in practice these often seem to be symbolic acts, whose consequences reveal an unusual propensity to neglect problems of follow-up and implementation.

The cognitive ability of the system—its capacity to gain and use knowledge in order to plan and to set and enforce standards—shows several deficiencies, particularly in the availability and use of professional resources and in integrating considerations of physical and social needs and goals. The authority for economic development projects has been divided among separatist ministries. In this situation, planning could be integrative, but it has far less impact than economic action. The professional strengths of environmental experts and planners were diffused among small groups, each of which had limited resources or political backing. Public knowledge, becoming more widespread since the founding of the EPS, is still available only with some effort. Feedback and monitoring have a long way to go in order to give a full picture of changes taking place and of the effectiveness of technologies and policies. Professionals and academics whose work is related to the quality of the environment have lacked skill and cohesion in their attempts to influence the political system, and enthusiasts for environmental quality are more likely to be found in government than in academe or private professional offices. When adequate knowledge is at hand, the organization, as well as cultural factors, as has been shown, makes it difficult to apply effectively.

On the broader level, the ability is needed to recognize and make the important decisions among values and strategies. Here the criteria are political: the public responsibility of those who make the decisions; the degree of representation and participation of the public; and the effectiveness of the system in setting its goals.

Public responsibility was found to be imperfectly focused. Town councils, which act as the local town planning commissions, as well as the Cabinet, which approves national land-use plans, assume "collective responsibility." Their election through proportional representation reduces geographic and personal accountability. As has been shown, there is no one minister whose political future could depend on changes in the quality of the environment. Where the planning, setting, and execution of economic goals are all carried out by one and the same agency, few if any outside groups are in a position to demand an accounting. In other cases, responsibility is weakened by dividing it among more than one ministry. The inadequate focus of environmental issues thus works against responsibility to the public, and this, in turn, reinforces their inherently lower priority.

Public participation and representation were also found to have notable limitations. One element has been that principles and the integrative environmental interest are represented by planners and environmental specialists, groups whose organizational weaknesses have already been mentioned. Only since 1977 has the EPS had a vote on district planning committees. While the public at large can register opposition to proposals coming before the district committees, direct political representation is limited to the presence of several mayors. These are often active logrollers, so that the specific interests of many localities may be considered very inadequately.

The diffusion of power within the Cabinet has had an important effect on participation and representation as well as on the process of setting priorities. Ministries which have the largest budgets and the greatest autonomy have an asymmetric degree of power to act. Thrown into the arena of bureaucratic politics, many issues are thus resolved within an operating ministry, or in the trials of strength between ministries operating alone or in coalitions. When "rational" criteria are applied, the economic trade-offs are given most weight, and less regard is given to meeting minimum environmental standards.

Public hearings are used very little. In the prevalent administrative culture, information is given to the public only grudgingly, and then only to those interested and informed enough to know what they want to know and where to find it. Public knowledge is sparse and gained late in the game, while public confrontations have an inadequate institutional base and occur sporadically, usually when pressures have reached a boiling point.

Protests by citizen's groups and editorials against new insults to the environment appear periodically, only to die quickly; and before the 1970s, there was no real popular feeling behind them.* The press and public usually take up issues at a late stage when decisions are firming or building has already begun. A feeling of inefficacy is widespread, and successes in opposing projects have been few. There are, however, harbingers of increased participation—the emergence of newer populations from a tutelary status, growth in the membership of voluntary organizations, and an increased sensitivity of politicians to public environmental demand, seen in the occasional overruling by district committees or the National Council of the still insensitive local councils in response to protests by affected citizen groups.

Lastly, we consider the *capability to set goals and values.* This requires the creation and diffusion of knowledge and understanding, a degree of salience which can get the issues onto the agenda, the confrontation and resolution of different wills, and the availability and consideration of alternatives. Goal-setting capability has increased, but on all these counts there remain serious problems.

It is in the creation and presentation of alternatives and the confrontation and the resolution of different aims that most thought is needed. Confronta-

---

* The organizations which have so far had some effect are Malraz, or the Public Council for the Prevention of Noise and Air Pollution in Israel, and the Nature Preservation Society, an Israeli "Sierra Club" with some 20,000 members. Malraz, which is partly government-supported, has been a focus for legal actions, and has achieved some important court decisions, but it lacks resources and financial independence.

tion is limited by the extent of public participation and interest, by limits to representation, and by a concentration of powers which reduces the opportunities for arm's-length negotiation or for the presentation of alternative programs and values. When it comes, confrontation is most often carried on between opposing groups whose resources are manifestly unequal. Organizations which represent principles, and thus in some sense the "general public," are weaker in organization and in political and material resources than those representing interests and economic missions and goals. When a principle, or ideal, is combined with or consistent with an organizational goal, the power and influence can be tremendous.

The quality of public debate is particularly important in a small country due to the large potential impact of large-scale projects. Some possible examples are the use and location of nuclear power plants, and a proposal to construct, from the Mediterranean to the Jordan–Dead Sea Valley, a saltwater canal and hydraulic power station, utilizing the large difference in levels. Other major decisions could be new plans and organization for the development of the Galilee and the Negev.

The critique given here is of conditions as they were in the first decades of the state. In the 1970s, the trend was toward greater consciousness of the importance of the public domain, and increased knowledge of the relations of social and physical aspects of the public and private living and working spaces. Time will tell whether the system will develop so as to be able to understand and solve the complex problems that appear once the more obvious technical questions have been overcome and the full impact of the conflicting effects of economic growth, population, and nature is felt.

PART III

A Working Democracy, with Much Unfinished Business

The experience of the first twenty-nine years affords a perspective on the ways in which policy has been formed, and suggests an agenda for the future. Chapter 9, which follows, considers what can be learned about the democracy and effectiveness of the methods by which diverse needs, aspirations, beliefs, and demands are resolved. The discussion is based on the way things were until the 1977 elections brought about the first major change in the parties in power. The circumstances of the change are discussed in some detail, since the first occasion in which a ruling party or group is voted out of office is a milestone in the history of a new democracy.

Observation of the complexity of political and social interactions and of institutional development shows a viable and thriving democracy. There are also, however, nondemocratic elements in the system and culture, and many sources of frustration. The difficulties are outlined, not with the intention of showing a balanced picture of the whole, but as problems which have to be faced and about which something can be done. The tasks would seem to require all of the available resources of the society, and more besides. In the recurrent crises, however, degrees of energy and cooperation are revealed which show that there are large unmeasured reserves. The possibility of overcoming the constraints lies in releasing more of the full potential of the society and in using it more effectively.

405

CHAPTER 9

On Democracy
and Effectiveness

IT IS A LARGE ORDER to try to analyze or to define the meaning of the democracy of a political system. To make it at all possible, several specific elements are considered. These include the extent and kinds of political competition; the ways in which people participate in politics and influence public affairs; the relations of authority and hierarchy and the limits to the use of authority; and finally, the responsibility of the government to the public.

Knowledge that is needed for analysis of the system can be found mainly in the policy-area discussions of the preceding chapters. The variation among areas is partly ascribed to their differences: in the salience of issues in national concerns, in the degrees of autonomy of Israel and the importance of exogenous forces and events, in historical developments and rates of change, and in the degrees of interdependence with other policy areas and the magnitude of the challenges. In nearly all cases, concurrent goals and needs make demands which are on or beyond the limits of action permitted by the resources available.

Following an assessment of democratic characteristics, effectiveness is considered. Somewhat less emphasis has been given to effectiveness because, seen as more practical, it is less neglected; because, subjectively, I give a somewhat lower priority to effectiveness as a criterion; and because the participative elements of democracy can have a profound influence on effectiveness.

Observers from within a system have difficulty in evaluating it. Instead of "handing out grades," an analysis is made of the factors which are believed to contribute to effectiveness in the context of the challenges. A successful governmental system needs the following abilities, *inter alia:*

To appreciate the challenges, through a realistic understanding of the environment and of people's needs and desires

To formulate goals and strategies—which involves learning; generating, exposing, and considering alternatives; and reaching decisions.

To mobilize toward the goals, and to exercise legitimate authority as well as some efficiency in carrying out policies

These abilities are seen to be related to political competition, the existence of alternatives, and participation.

People and Government

The central role of government in people's lives is reflected in the large proportion of voters who are party members, in high election participation, and in media coverage.* Few are the evenings when a Cabinet minister is not seen on the television news or in a special interview, and public affairs and personalities are perennially discussed at social gatherings. It is a spectator sport, however, and participation is more virtual than real. Individuals usually feel that they have little influence on the outcome of specific issues, but they are compensated by having a good seat from which to watch the proceedings.

Many local party activists keep up with what is going on at the center through information provided by patrons. Those active at party centers and people whose work leads to interaction within elites often feel that they are on the inside of things, since they can express opinions or rub elbows with those who decide or who hear things at first hand from those who do. Most citizens, however, are more in a "subject" type of relation where government services are concerned; that is, they seek to manipulate the system to get their due rather than to take part in decisions.**

The feelings (and the reality) of efficacy are much higher for persons as members of groups than as individuals, and the influence of members on government action is thus primarily through the group. Organized groups are well represented in party, Histadrut, regional, and sectoral institutions, and

* The percentage of those eligible who vote has been about 75 to 85 percent. In 1977, the Labor Party and Mapam, which together polled 430,000 votes, claimed over 250,000 members. The Democratic Movement for Change polled 207,000 votes, and had by then nearly 35,000 members, while the parties in the Likud, which polled 584,000 votes, reported a total of about 120,000 members. Membership figures should be looked at skeptically, however. They are seldom up to date and are probably exaggerated, if only because of the incentives to branches to overreport, in parties in which convention representation is based on branch enrollment.

** See the discussion in Chapter 3 of the dependency relations and political socialization out of which a "bureaucratic political culture" developed. The concepts of "parochial," "subject," and "participant" aspects of political culture are familiar from Gabriel Almond and Sidney Verba, *The Civic Culture*, Boston, Little, Brown, 1963.

their representation is preserved and encouraged by proportional representation and coalition procedures. A member can feel that the group is working to ensure his rights and needs and express his opinions, particularly when these relate to a group's parochial interests. *

Even members of institutions, however, often feel that they lack the opportunity for effective participation in solving their problems. Nor do Israelis often organize spontaneously to do so. Although they are only a generation or two removed from the highly self-organizing community dynamic of the Diaspora, Israelis lag in the development of voluntary organizations for political action or for social and community ends. "If an American," said Tocqueville, "were to be condemned to confine his activities to his own affairs, he would be robbed of half his existence." A counterpart statement for Israel would begin, "If an Israeli were to be condemned to be separated from his sources of information. . . ." But if the Israeli demands a good vantage point, he seldom goes down into the arena.

Independent civic organizations which seek to determine and advance the public interest have had little influence and are active in only a few specific areas. There are exceptional occurrences every few years, at election time, or when a particular interest is affected and frustration leads to strong protests; or when a national crisis is afoot, as on the eve of the 1967 Six Day War. Local party branches are generally somnolent, awakening to feverish action in election years.

Contributing to this condition are the centralization of functions in the government, the strength of hierarchy and control, the dominance of the center over the periphery, and the top-down way in which immigrants were received; that is, in the multitude of dependency relations which are the sources of a bureaucratic political culture, and in elements of the system which act against pluralism, such as the weak impact of parliamentary opposition.

Yet along with this highly organized and characteristically hierarchical system, there is a strong populist trend in which the people relate directly to leaders and events. Indeed, direct popular influence is stimulated and advanced, *inter alia*, by the closed nature of many institutions. Why this could be is seen in the ways in which popular will has been manifested in elections, in Cabinet crises, and in protests.

Political Competition

Elections and the Change of Regime

A necessary if not sufficient condition for democracy is that the people choose and replace those in authority. An important definition is that of *polyarchy*,

---

* I refer here to groups with defined social and economic functions and interests, such as kibbutz movements or clearly defined economic sectors.

in which there exist organized and legitimate oppositions "free to contest the conduct of the government in elections honestly conducted among a sizeable electorate."[1] In addition to competing in elections, oppositions also need to have a realistic chance to win from time to time.

For a new country, the ordering of succession to the founding fathers as well as a broader change of regime is a principal hurdle in the continuation of democracy, and the first change of regime is a major event in its history.[2] Before 1977, the possibility of a new regime in Israel was a matter for conjecture, and since it had never happened, there was no hard evidence that it could. Some observers believed that a new form of democratic change was emerging, in which a dominant party remained in office but changed its coalition partners and policies in line with the will expressed in elections.[3]* The possibility of this option decreased after the mid-1960s, when agglomeration resulted in the Likud and the Alignment, which are far less homogeneous in ideology and interests than their components were. The public thus had less opportunity to vote for specific groups or ideologies.

Until 1977, however, elections were effective mainly because they were there. Between elections, anticipated voter reactions affected policies, although electoral appeal competed unequally with internal party organizational and factional considerations in decisions on nomination lists and major policy issues. Continued election success reinforced the tendency to neglect the electorate most of the time.

Defeat of the Dominant Party

In 1977 Labor lost office after a rule of twenty-nine years in the state and fifteen years before it in the Yishuv.** Until then, the parties of the noncommunist left, taken together, had always won a small absolute majority.***

---

* Elections which produced notable changes included 1951 and 1955, and 1973 as a forerunner of 1977. In 1951 the General Zionists gained from seven seats to twenty, largely because of dissatisfaction with the austerity economy, while Mapam on the left and Herut on the right declined. A coalition was soon formed of Mapai, the General Zionists, the Mizrachi, and the Progressives. Control of the economy was liberalized. By 1955 economic growth had begun, yet the malaise of the early large-scale immigrations was felt. Arab arms were rapidly increasing, and security became central. The General Zionists lost seven seats, down to thirteen, while the activist Ahdut Ha'Avoda, split from Mapam, won ten seats, and Herut also gained. Mapai formed a coalition with Ahdut Ha'Avoda, the Progressives, and Mizrachi, and Herut began to emerge as the leader of the opposition. The Sinai campaign occurred in the following year. Details of election results and Cabinet coalitions are given in Appendixes B and C.

** As in other parliamentary democracies, most of the changes have taken place between elections in Cabinet or coalition reshuffles. The composition and circumstances of change of the Israeli coalitions are summarized in Appendix C.

*** The electoral success of Labor was that of Mapai. In 1959, its peak year as a separate list, Mapai polled 38.2 percent of the votes, compared with the entire Labor Alignment vote of 39.6 percent in 1973 and 24.6 percent in 1977.

Figure 9.1 shows continuity and change in national elections, for broad ideological groupings.

Many reasons have been advanced for the stability between the groups and the long dominance of Mapai. Until the agglomeration in the 1960s of the Labor Alignment and the Likud, voters could shift specific party allegiance within a broad sector without demanding of themselves a major change in outlook. Proportional representation was conducive to continuity. Labor's partnership over the years with the National Religious Party was an important prop, reducing the necessity for other coalition partners. But these factors only complemented underlying political and social conditions, and it was the larger context which determined events. The founding fathers of the Labor movement built the political and social institutions and were in office during the achievement of independence, the ingathering of the exiles, and the ensuing growth of the economy and the social services. Associated with the policies for national defense, which, like the law, seems above party, Labor and its leaders were the symbols of security and hope, identified with the rebirth of the nation.

FIGURE 9.1   Knesset Election Results

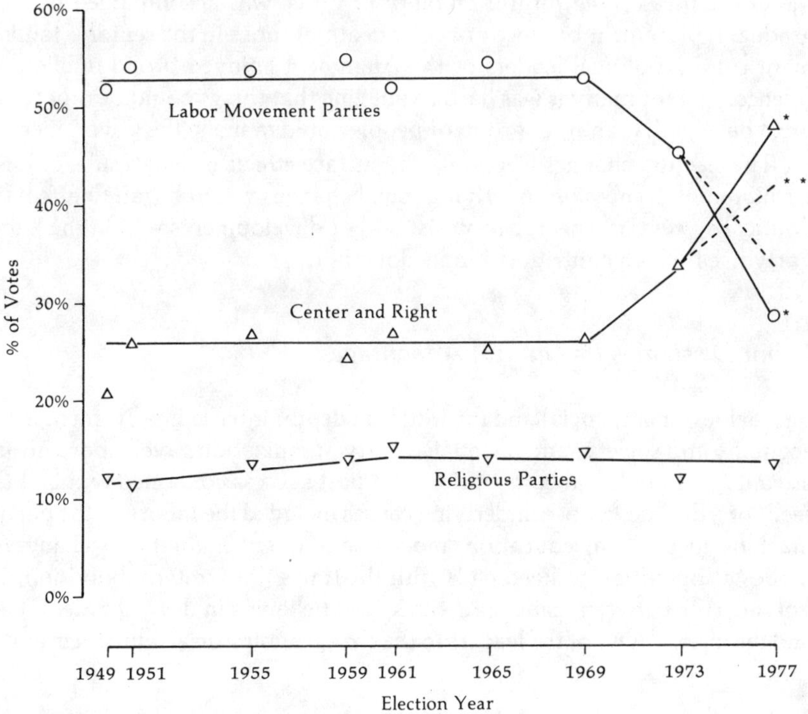

*If DMC is assumed "Center and Right"
**If DMC vote is assumed equally "Labor" and "Center and Right"

Predominant in Labor, and fashioning its character, was Mapai. The party's ideological demands were flexible and not class-bound, and it could aggregate and integrate, cutting through ethnic and class lines, incorporating a broad spectrum of new groups and interests. Party leaders directed the burgeoning governmental structures, and an extensive organization connected the roles of the party in the government and in the social institutions with party patronage and interest representation. The combination of the organization with leaders who had electoral appeal and could solve national problems held together a huge conglomerate whose members or well-wishers were at the center of the institutional activities of the society.

Client dependency relations accompanied the control over vast economic and social institutions, their resources, and employment and service opportunities. The Histadrut could be the image and the agent of social services and workers' rights, while organization provided the links to the bureaucracies and employment opportunities. All of these, together with the mode of interparty allocative agreements inherited from the Yishuv, limited political competition, especially during the years of large-scale immigration, and to a lessening extent into the 1970s.

To its leaders, and indeed to most other people, the party seemed invincible in the foreseeable future. Stability of office was accompanied by only gradual replacement because of age or death of those in the senior establishment roles.* Political leaders of the Alignment enjoyed broad public confidence, and for many it was hard to imagine that things could be otherwise, or to believe that another group of people could manage the government.

The election changes were only the surface effects or end results of long-term opinion trends, of underlying social changes which began to affect the political system, of specific protests, and of developments within the Labor Party itself which contributed to its downfall.

Labor Dissipates Its Natural Advantages

Past achievement, social and institutional depth, intense involvement in the economy and society, and unequaled party organization gave Labor unusual advantages in political competition. But past success contained within it the seeds of a decline, whose underlying causes included the failure of the party's machine in political education and its subsequent inability to change its modes of operation to keep pace with the times; deep internal division, involving rifts between leaders, factions, and believers in different ideologies; and the insensitivity of the leaders to the changes going on around them and to

---

* In 1973 Yuval Elizur and Eliahu Salpeter could publish an account of the biographies and personal characteristics of leading and promising Israelis in many spheres and only jokingly comment that perhaps it should be bound in loose-leaf form.[4] It might have been a good idea.

the decline of the ideals and images of the party. Operating as a closed political system, the party was unable to benefit from self-correcting actions which more open arrangements could have encouraged.

It will be recalled that early in the state, the surge of governing opportunities and responsibilities left the party machinery to people of the second or third level, on whose tutelage new immigrants and young people came to depend.* Political education and socialization were instrumental in nature and often failed to impart a deeper sense of values regarding political processes and goals, although the extensive development of institutions provided opportunities for experience in political processes for a great many people—who drew their own lessons. Divorced from policy considerations, the party bureaucracy was principally concerned with maintaining an organization whose strength derived from patronage and the images of the national leaders—and progressively less from the appeal of ideals or social goals.

The system of political control was at first held together by the pervasive influence and penetration of Mapai, whose adherents were placed in key positions. In time however, government bureaucracies, the Army, and private and public enterprises began to overshadow the Histadrut and other sectoral organizations. The proportionate economic role and membership of the kibbutzim declined, and they did not play much of a direct part as institutions in the absorption of the mass immigration of the 1950s. Many avenues of advance opened which had no party dependence. Bureaucracies which had originally been highly politicized began to recruit and promote on the basis of merit and professional qualifications. In trade-union locals, party cells which had once acted on the instructions of the political leadership ceased to function, and local works committees, elected on a personal basis, began to defy central Histadrut restraint. The parties in general and Labor in particular lost much of their role as intervening centers, through which the individual was active as a citizen of the polity and through which the demands of interests could be resolved. This development worked against one of Labor's principal advantages. As the conditions which had led to the ascendency of the organization began to disappear, the organization became far less capable of delivering the vote or ongoing public support than the leaders of the party imagined. By the time of the 1977 elections the fabled machine was a paper tiger. As though sensing the imminence of defeat, many local Labor organizations seemed to be merely going through the motions of a campaign.

Internal divisions were critical, facilitated by the broad spectrum of social groups and beliefs which Labor encompassed. The sources of rifts included differences of personality and of generation; loyalty to the interests of urban versus rural groups, or of the new *moshavim* versus the old established ones or the kibbutzim; diversity between the national, or *mamlachti*, view and the sectoral view; and, after the Six Day War, the questions of borders, peace,

* This process is described in Chapter 3, "Political Integration."

and security. All these differences, combined with personal rivalry for leading roles, worsened relations within the Cabinet.

In the first decade of the state Ben Gurion's personality and leadership style served to disguise the underlying rifts which became exposed with the reopening of the Lavon affair in 1960. As Ben Gurion began to advance those whom he considered to be the most promising, the party was split by a bitter generational, ideological, and personal struggle. The younger men, in whom Ben Gurion placed his trust were more experienced and concerned with national policy than they were with ideology, voters, or party machinery and its bargaining transactions. They followed his lead in endorsing national above sectoral goals, as these were embodied in sectoral institutions, such as the *moshav* or kibbutz. As Ben Gurion's followers struggled for leadership roles, his opponents accused them of lacking ideals and a sense of history. The promising younger activists, feeling that they were being held back, organized to advance their interests and views. As outsiders to the party machine, they called for more party democracy.

Ben Gurion's actions to advance his proteges was seen by the veterans as a threat to their own continuation in office and to the ideals of which they claimed to be the guardians or even the embodiment. The closed party system exacerbated the struggle for succession. A bitter split of Rafi from Mapai ensued.[5] In the 1965 elections the party-machine leaders remained loyal to Levi Eshkol and Mapai. At a time when organization was still far more important in an election than popular appeal, Ben Gurion suffered a serious disappointment at the polls. After a brief period as an independent party, most of Rafi returned (without, notably, Ben Gurion himself), joining with Ahdut Ha'Avoda and Mapai in 1968 to form the Labor Party.

Unification was to solve neither the ordering of the succession nor basic internal conflicts.* Ben Aharon of Ahdut Ha'Avoda, a principal advocate of unification, had envisioned a large, ideological social democratic party which would enjoy the practical benefits of Mapai's large-scale organization and Histadrut resources.[6] In actuality, the Labor Party became a conglomerate in which the common denominator was mainly historical experience in the Labor movement and ambition for common electoral success; and in which the greatest source of difference was the question of the future borders, although the importance of sectoral-ideological, as opposed to national, authority remained an issue.** Within the Labor party the former Rafi leaders had perhaps the greatest leverage because of their potential for popular support and the feasibility of their defection to the right.

---

* Moshe Dayan, then the leader of Rafi, immediately announced that he would fight from within the Labor Party to depose Pinhas Sapir and Levi Eshkol.

** Ahdut Ha'Avoda, based on the United Kibbutz Movement, remained strongly organized as a faction, while the Rafi leaders, at home again in the fracas of the party elite, sought to win former Mapai supporters, neglecting their former adherents in the local branches. There, as often happens, the distance between followers remained large, long after the national leaders, albeit without amity, had come together in the small group at the top.

Until the Yom Kippur War, the party seemed held together by Golda Meir, whose clearly expressed and firmly held beliefs called for a return to the socialism of the pioneering days, together with firm security views similar to those of Rafi and of most of Ahdut Ha'Avoda. After the war the party elite continued as though nothing had happened to disturb the tenor of the old modes. Although election results showed a marked decline for Labor and an advance for the Likud, these cannot be ascribed directly or mainly to the war. In many ways, the first postwar election was held only in 1977. The 1973 elections were postponed for a few months, but there were no changes on the lists of candidates, which had been drawn up before the war. The appointment of a public inquiry commission on the conduct of the war, the Agranat Committee, had defused the war as an election issue.

In 1974 the competition for leadership still took place within the Alignment. After the elections, the contest for the succession focused on the responsibility for the strategic surprise of the war and on the political stance which had not deterred the attack. As internal party attacks on Dayan mounted, Rafi used the principle of collective responsibility to support him, saying that "if there is to be a resignation, it should be of the whole Cabinet." Growing public protest and the publication of the preliminary Agranat Report in the spring of 1974 led to the Cabinet's resignation. In an unprecedented open election in the Party Central Committee, Itzchak Rabin was elected by a close vote to form the new Cabinet—with the support of Pinhas Sapir and the machine and most of the representatives of Ahdut Ha'Avoda. Peres became Minister of Defense, and continued Peres-Rabin rivalry marked the duration of the Rabin government.

On the surface a large and important change had taken place. In the new Cabinet, only Israel Galili represented the Labor old guard. Yet neither the renaissance in thinking which the more educated demanded nor the image of leadership sought by the broader public came about. Thinking about ongoing affairs stagnated, the importance of ideals continued to diminish, and intellectuals became much less involved. In the Yishuv the Labor movement had been a home for active thinkers, as well as for experts in organization and political maneuver. Kibbutz movements had been leaders in social development, defense, and politics, seeing themselves as an *avant garde* and the defenders of egalitarian and pioneering ideals. In more recent times, while many intellectuals retained strong ties to the ideals of Labor, they seldom felt that their participation was really desired except as window dressing. Many supported the Alignment in 1973 because "there was no other place to go." *

But the departure or rejection of intellectuals was more a symptom than a cause of the decline in the importance of thought and belief, a decline which would have been harmful in the best of situations but which became critical in

---

* One group calling itself "The Alignment, in spite of everything," supported Labor in 1973, with this kind of reasoning. In the 1977 Alignment Knesset election list, there was no candidate among the first fifty-five who had an academic or primarily intellectual occupation.

the face of the brooding dilemmas caused by the divergence of the society from the early hopes and by the enduring challenges to security. As we have seen, the Labor ideology had developed in its detail through interaction with real situations. Ideals thus came to be embodied in institutions. These, while symbolizing the beliefs, became political and economic centers of power and, as organizations, took on lives and interests of their own. Success in organization eventually led to a lag in social development and innovation. The role of ideologies became conservative, and for most people the symbols lost most of their meaning or the ability to call forth voluntary action or unlimited personal devotion in overcoming great obstacles. While it was still dominant, the questions asked in the Labor Party regarding a proposed course of action came to be, will it work, and how will it affect our political resources?

The insensitivity of the leaders to the changes taking place outside the party and to the need for internal renewal was related to a system which inhibited the entry and circulation of many who could have helped renew ideas and modes of action or understand the needs for change. Rivals acted as though their only problem was to triumph in the internal leadership struggle, and not to save the party's lead or to resolve major national social and economic questions. As in the old Democratic South, they saw nomination as equivalent to election. Nor did they understand the importance of the populist or electoral element in Israeli politics, the implications of the demographic and social developments, or the seriousness of the postwar protests.

At the same time, the division of labor within the party between policy and organization broke down, and both suffered. In previous governments, the specialists in organization had been followers of the policy leaders, most of whom they saw as head and shoulders above the rest: They were content and effective in operating and controlling the machine, the party appointments, and patronage, preferring this power over a place in the limelight. Party loyalty was compelling, and even a strong leader like Sapir could subordinate his own strong conciliatory beliefs, in international relations, to loyalty to Golda Meir. Rabin could not command this kind of loyalty. As a political neophyte seeking party backing, he brought several of the principal organization leaders into the Cabinet. In their new roles, they could not contribute to a renewal of the declining party organization, losing both their influence on internal party affairs and the ability to secure strong party backing for unpopular but necessary government measures. The party machine lost most of its ability to deliver votes or patronage, but even more serious was the decline of the party's function in resolving major questions of policy or personality. Meetings of the Central Committee or the smaller and more authoritative forums took place less and less frequently, seldom debating and never resolving the outstanding issues of policy. The meetings of the Labor Knesset delegation, or *siya*, became the only active formal party forum for policy debate.

While Rabin himself displayed sincerity, effort, and endorsement of the laws and public probity, there was no vision of a new future. Beyond the diminution of the leaders' images as the result of internecine rivalry, there occurred a series of cases of alleged corruption in high places, which were related to the historic involvement of the party and party funds in economic enterprises. In retrospect, the devaluation of the leaders' images and the inability of the party to resolve issues were more important to the impending electoral defeat than the decline of the machine; and in the absence of new thought, there was less and less of substance for the activists to sell to the public.

In 1977 Long-Term Trends Come to Fruition

The constant pattern of election results over many years concealed underlying trends in the society and its opinions, whose delayed impact was seen only in the 1973 and 1977 elections (Figure 9.1). Part of the delay was caused by limits to political competition in the early years of the state, when the Labor movement controlled the institutions of immigrant absorption and social services or acquiesced in the allocation of a share in their management to other parties on the basis of a well-controlled party key. Labor's domination of the national symbols of legitimacy was of great importance.

The process of national rebuilding was never without conflict or protest. Over the years, Herut had expressed and reinforced the malaise and nationalist sentiments of residents in the poorer areas in the large cities, in the development towns and, in the early years, in transit camps and *ma'abarot*. By the 1960s it was clear that Labor's more consistent supporters were, ironically, the middle class, the more established, those longer in the country, people living in the better neighborhoods, and more of European/American than of Asian/African origin. On social and economic questions, these people were naturally more satisfied with the regime; but their proportion in the population was decreasing. And within all groups, younger people did not as fully associate Labor with the founding of the state.*[7]

Still, it was considered possible that as they grew older and advanced economically, individuals would tend to identify more with the establishment, so that over time the predominance of Labor would not change substantially. The lengthening of the time that those of the large immigrations of the 1950s were in the country and the embourgeoisement of many did have an effect. Social and economic dissatisfaction, however, together with the growing legitimacy of Herut, were to be more powerful. In the recession of the mid-1960s, the development towns and the Asian/African immigrants in

---

* In studies based on polling districts for the elections of 1969 and 1973, the support for the Alignment came from neighborhoods with medium-level incomes, higher incomes, and lower-level incomes, in that order. Development towns, however, tended to vote more for the Alignment than did the poor city neighborhoods or *shechunot*.

general, as mainly unskilled or semiskilled workers, suffered the greatest loss of employment. The economic boom following the Six Day War served to accentuate absolute income differences and to stimulate social protest and concern, which were not fully alleviated by massive income transfers and other social programs. Indeed, by the year preceding the Yom Kippur War the government's popularity had reached a low point. Although its foreign stance was generally approved, the economic and social policies were decried.[8] As expectations grew, differences in income became more irritating, and a feeling of increased defense security led to greater attention to the problems of social inequality and discontent. At the same time, social gains began to remove many of the Labor Alignment's early advantages. Broad groups gained experience, administration became more meritocratic and depoliticized, and the role of the more partisan forms of patronage declined. Many people in the development towns and the *shechunot* began to feel more independent and free to express dissatisfaction and to vote against the government. Because of the trend toward nationalization, social welfare was no longer the administrative or ideological prerogative of the Histadrut, and protest against the establishment naturally found Labor as its target. Despite increasing defense outlays, the public grew accustomed to a rising living standard, while inflation, which in 1971 first exceeded an annual rate of 10 percent, created insecurity within the middle class no less than among the less advantaged.

These changes also set the stage for the decrease in Labor's middle-class support. Disillusion with Labor was accompanied by increased acceptability of Herut and the Liberals. In the 1965 elections mutual vituperation of Mapai and Rafi had injured Labor's image. Herut's membership in the 1967 National Unity government gave it a legitimacy hitherto denied, and it became possible for many more people to imagine Begin and his colleagues in important national roles if not actually at the helm. A decline in the importance of ideologies and their symbols eliminated most of the feeling of sacrilege which previously could accompany opposition to Labor or endorsement of the Right.

In 1977 an important delayed effect of the 1973 war was the crystallization of the postwar middle-class protest, whose strongest electoral manifestation was in the Democratic Movement for Change (DMC). We have noted the dissent of the poor urban *shechunot*, where economic and social disadvantage were often ascribed to ethnic discrimination, and the malaise of the development towns, which sprang more from a feeling of marginality and dependency than from acute distress.[9] The frustration of the educated middle class came from their sense of exclusion from influence in the face of the leaders' apparent loss of direction and ideals. The feeling was that the governing elite, no longer competent, would not listen, let alone permit participation.

After the Yom Kippur War, demobilized soldiers and citizens' groups in which academics were prominent demonstrated to demand the resignation of the entire Cabinet, and of Dayan in particular, calling for a return to the former ideals of the quality of life and the society. The protests, begun by a few individuals, soon gathered support, and they intensified following the publication of the preliminary Agranat Report on the War. Together with attacks from within the Labor Party, the protests led to the end of the Cabinet's tenure. Intellectuals, students, and other war veterans directed protests against the program and personalities of the government's leaders—questioning the legitimacy of the regime.*

In the large parties there was strong internal opposition, not always devoid of partisan or personal interests, against holding the elections in December, without a chance for new people to try for nominations. The opposition, the Likud, wanted immediate elections in order to take advantage of the protest feeling in the air, and the veteran Labor leadership did not want to throw open the lists to the vagaries of populist sentiment in the wake of the war. As a result the elections were held on December 31 with the original prewar lists. The protest had begun to develop when, in November 1973, shortly after the cease-fire, a reserve captain named Motti Ashkenazi began a sit-down strike outside the Defense Ministry in Tel Aviv, demanding that Moshe Dayan resign as the Defense Minister responsible for the preparedness failures of the war. Eventually he was joined by a host of others, many spontaneously and many organized by Dayan's political opponents (such as busloads of Mapam kibbutz members who came to join demonstrations, and a few anti-Dayan Labor M.K.s who encouraged Ashkenazi by visiting him during his protest vigil). Other reservists participated, and many academics. Said one of the protesters, a reserve colonel with a kibbutz background, "For years I had the naive feeling that there was someone on whom we could depend, that we lived in the shadow of the giants of the generation. . . . I didn't have a feeling of being needed. . . . I thought that, anyway, it wouldn't help to protest, but this is an argument that doesn't hold today. . . ."[10]

The essence of what was being said by the protesters was:

> *The leadership:* "The leadership group has been in office too long, some of them for decades. While estimable people, they are fatigued from the stresses of a long period in office in very difficult times, and lack the verve, flexibility, and openness to new ideas needed to meet challenges from without or to give solutions and leadership within." (A minority went further and saw the small group of veteran political leaders as characterized by factional and personal opportunism, and striving at all cost for self-preservation in office.)

> *The system:* "The political system is 'closed,' in that party oligarchies control the membership of elected bodies, including nomination to the parliamentary candidates' lists and Cabinet membership." Advocates of electoral reform added, "Because the Knesset elections are based purely on proportional representation, (1)

---

* Protests of the immediate prewar years, in contrast, had been mainly those of the greatly disadvantaged, and led to a substantial increase in the emphasis on social questions. The nature and outcome of social protests is analyzed in Chapter 6, "The Welfare State."

the voter has little if any relation to any one representative; (2) in the resultant coalition government's substantive platform, compromises are made, so that the voter feels no opportunity to affect policy; (3) new candidates and old owe their places to the leadership, which keeps the system closed and reduces parliament to a rubber stamp."

The society: "The society has 'lost the North Star.' In the euphoria and economic boom of the years before the Yom Kippur War, materialism and occasional corruption came to replace the old ideals of public service; and selfish individualism replaced the cooperative spirit. Worse yet, lost are the binding ideals of a Zionism which sought to create a new man and a new society despite all difficulties. The old ideologies and their symbols no longer seem to apply, nor have new faiths taken hold which can give the kind of spirit which alone can overcome incredible social and political adversity."

To many people, much of the critique inherent in these protests was justified by the style and the events of the period of the Rabin Cabinet. Yet nearly all of the protest movements soon died out, and it was mainly the Shinui, or "Change," movement which retained organizational continuity. Begun mainly by university lecturers, Shinui split in 1975. Some of the founders, following Amnon Rubinstein, continued the aim of a liberal center party, emphasizing electoral, constitutional, and social reform. Declining alliances with dissidents farther to the left, such as Lova Eliav, Shinui decided to become a political party and to contest the election. Its demand for more openness and responsibility in government received further stimulus from the exposure of cases of misuse of public or Histadrut office in the interest of party finance or even personal gain. In 1976 the Democratic Movement for Change (DMC) was formed when Shinui merged with a group formed around Professor Yigael Yadin, who for many years had advocated electoral and civic reform and who led the new party. They were soon joined by others.* Shinui's small, homogeneous, and cohesive national organization aided the rapid deployment of the new party as the principal liberal center party of the 1977 elections. The common denominator of the DMC's varied groups was the desire of the more educated middle class for reform and participation.

The DMC platform called for regional elections, the meeting of social needs, and an intermediate if somewhat vague stance on the future borders ("the Jordan as the secure line of defense; Israel as a democratic and a Jewish

---

* In March 1976, Shinui reported 1000 dues-paying members (*Ha'aretz*, March 31, 1976) while on the eve of the elections there were nearly 35,000 in the DMC. Many of these, however, were signed up *en masse* in an organization drive which preceded the party's primary elections in March 1977, as individual candidates and groups sought support for nomination. Among important groups that joined were former Labor members led by Meir Amit, a former head of the security services and managing director of the Histadrut's Koor Industries; the Free Center led by Shmuel Tamir; and Oded, an organization of ex-North African professionals, not previously active as a group in party politics. Many non-affiliated individuals joined, and for a time the party had a wealth of professional, managerial, and academic talent.

state"). Those dissatisfied with Labor or with the ineffectiveness of the small parties, but who could not accept the ideology or personalities of the Likud, were thus afforded a list which proclaimed social goals and was within a broad consensus on security. Many hoped, not for a complete downfall of Labor, but for a Labor-DMC coalition which would carry out the DMC reform program. When the DMC gained only 15 seats, however, Begin formed a Cabinet with the Mafdal, and the DMC eventually joined largely on Begin's terms.

Beyond the specific issues, underlying social changes increased the attraction of the liberal center. Despite the continued reliance of the economy on government, economic centers of power (and their managerial elites) were developing more independence. Nor were they able, in distress, to rely on the backing of a powerful Minister of Finance. The Cabinet was no longer reinforced, as in former times, by an authoritative and encompassing party organization. Economic stagnation, an interrugnum in government, and the declining role of the Labor Party seemed to make active participation and political expression both necessary and possible.

In the 1973 elections the Likud had made large gains, reaching 30.2 percent of the vote. In 1977 the Likud vote increased to 33.4 percent,* the Labor Alignment dropped sharply to only 24.6 percent, and the DMC received 11.6 percent. In 1977 the continuing growth in the numbers of younger voters, the less advantaged, and those of Asian/African origin (categories which can noticeably overlap) voting against Labor and for the Likud was reinforced by the representation in the DMC of the middle-class protest and by the internal decline of Labor. Underlying social and political changes which had been long under way and the more equal·distribution of legitimacy and of organizational effectiveness thus provided the necessary conditions for change.**

Yet despite its major sources of support among the less advantaged, the Likud did not, as some of its leaders believed, come into office as the spearhead of a vast social reform. Its Knesset candidates and its principal postelection officeholders came mainly from social backgrounds similar to those of the Alignment—with some variations, such as the virtual absence in the Likud of kibbutz members. No Jacksonian revolution swept into office many citizens from the poor city neighborhoods and development towns, who had given the Likud its plurality. These, as voters, waited to see what improvement the change in leadership would bring.

* To the Likud vote could be added 1.9 percent for Ariel Sharon's list, and 2.0 percent for one Plato Sharon, who ran by himself as a single candidate, appealing to the disadvantaged and in general supporting the Likud.
** The dilemma of many voters is shown by the relatively large number who were "undecided" until shortly before the elections. See L. Guttman, "Before and After the 1977 Elections" (Heb.), *Bulletin No. 45*, Institute for Applied Social Research, Jerusalem, August 1977.

Limits to Electoral Competition

If electoral change in regime is basic to political competition, another important element is ease of entry into the political game. The proportional-representation arrangements have facilitated the entering of campaigns and the founding of new parties. In 1977, twenty-two lists were on the ballot, of which nine received the 1 percent of the votes cast needed to enter the Knesset. Competition is limited, however, by the unequal distribution of economic and organizational resources, and by the laws for government provision of party finances,* for the allocation of nationally owned radio and television time during campaigns, and for the distribution of surplus votes in the allocation of Knesset seats.**

The Labor movement parties have always had reserve forces of election workers, such as kibbutz or cooperative members or Histadrut functionaries. Labor enterprises could help with financing, and the established party, particularly in Sapir's time, was able to raise substantial campaign contributions from business. Mapai had equity in many business enterprises, and valuable real estate used mainly for party clubs, while Herut operated a fund for small investors which eventually had serious financial difficulties. Indeed, in 1977 the Liberals and the DMC were the only important parties not deeply in debt.

The Jewish Agency contributes on a small scale to the "constructive" purposes of parties, that is, the building of social institutions. This is a vestige of the *parteistaat* era of the Yishuv. The complexity of municipal finance affords other avenues. The law provides for investigation by the State Controller of the use of public funds, but in practice there does not seem to be adequate supervision of municipal finance; nor is there legislation providing criteria for internal party democracy as a prior condition for the receipt of public support.

The close relation of institutions to parties is now less of a barrier to competition than it was in the earlier years when extensive politicization of ser-

---

*A 1968 Wage Protection Bill allowed automatic deductions of party contributions from wages, although opting out is permitted. From 1969 there has been public funding of elections, and from 1973 public finance of ongoing party activity, in both cases on the basis of the existing party strengths in the Knesset. Election grants are calculated on the basis of postelection results. The level of support is increased from time to time with inflation. An Israeli corporation may not make party contributions, but there are no limits for individuals.

**TV time is provided free of charge to the parties competing, but on the basis of their Knesset strength at the time of the campaign, which excludes new lists and discriminates against smaller old lists. Another advantage of large parties is the rule for the distribution of surplus votes. Under the Bader-Ofer Law, passed in 1975 with the collaboration of Labor and the Likud, the number of seats for each list is determined through iterations, in which, in step one, those not meeting the minimum for one seat (and the votes they received) are eliminated; initial allocation is made based on the total remaining votes divided by 120 as the votes needed per seat. Some seats (and votes) are still surplus; therefore in step two, for each list, a priority criterion of the total votes which the list received divided by one more than the number of seats already received is computed. The list with the highest result gets one seat; and the process is repeated until all 120 seats have been allocated.

vices blurred distinctions between politicians and the executive, especially in the perceptions of the clients of services, who could see little distinction between the agents of political recruitment and socialization and those of resource allocation.

Entry is far more difficult for an individual seeking nomination on a party list. Before the 1977 elections, nominations were generally made either by small inner committees or by elections within the governing bodies of the parties.* The classic of this genre is the system of the Labor Party, and the analysis in Chapter 1 shows how the economic and organizational dependence of members of the party's elected forums combined with the nominating procedures to restrict internal party democracy.

Coalitions and Cabinet Crises

Within the framework of the legitimacy and power relations which the elections allocate, the specifics of changes in power and office are often the outcome of postelection bargaining and of the impact of subsequent national events or Cabinet crises. Some crises have led to advances in the scheduled dates of elections. Others have left the Cabinet roster unchanged, but with somewhat different relations prevailing among the coalition partners.

Although by 1981 there were ten Knesset elections, no less than twenty-two cabinets had been formed.** As has been shown, many planks of the election platforms, especially those of minor partners, are altered in the bargaining through which coalitions are established, in this way setting aside the wishes of voters. In the list-voting procedure, voters have in any case little individual choice except for candidates at the top of the lists. While the candidates at the top of the list attract the voters, the floating vote that they capture decides which of each party's marginal candidates will be elected. Another way the voter is bypassed is the provision by which ministers can be appointed directly from outside the Knesset or even as defectors from a party not in the coalition. During the negotiations with the DMC after the 1977 elections, the Likud made such proposals to individuals in the DMC, unsuccessfully. A more extreme example was Begin's appointment of Moshe Dayan as Foreign Minister, although he had been elected to the Knesset from the Labor Party.

To those participating, coalition forming involves relations within and among elites rather than an attempt to carry out the mandates of the elec-

---

* Requirements for approval of individual candidates mainly began in 1977, perhaps stimulated by the example of the DMC primary. The Liberals and Labor now require a candidate for a third Knesset term to be approved by a special vote in the party central committee. The Herut Central Committee decides on the general rank order of candidates, and Labor continued to assign the rank order in a closed committee, to be voted for *en bloc* by the Central Committee.

** Shown in detail in Appendix C.

torate, whose next opportunity is in any case several years away, and whose influence, after the elections, is felt only indirectly through the relative strengths of internal party groups and the possible impact of the grave displeasure or disappointment of the factions involved.*

Interparty and interpersonal competition continues once a Cabinet is formed. Smaller parties need to defend issues which are their *raisons d'être* and which provide their individuality, while the dominant party seeks to maintain collective responsibility and Cabinet and party discipline. Many crises of the past were created or accentuated in the process of developing or enforcing such constitutional relations as collective responsibility, confidentiality, and the authority of the Prime Minister in his relations with Cabinet colleagues. This is particularly true of the early period, seen in the crises of 1955, 1957, and 1959. The tests of strength and individuality of the smaller parties in 1957 and 1959 were concerned with these questions.

A smaller party is always in danger of losing its public identity if it does not know when to put its central beliefs on the line in a Cabinet test. This was an important factor in the decline and fall of the Independent Liberals in 1977, and of the DMC thereafter. Mapam's solution for electoral survival was its agreement with Labor to maintain a fixed ratio of Knesset seats in the Alignment lists. Still, in joining a Cabinet the small party must give up many cherished ideas, in return for which it can hope to preserve a "core" principle, as in the case of the religious parties and the *status quo*. There is also always the hope of increasing or maintaining legitimacy in the eyes of the voters, due to sharing executive sovereignty, or of exerting personal influence on specific issues. There are organizational and economic resources to be developed from the ministries under its direction and from the public image which the minister can project. The opinion of a party's members and of the electorate can limit the extent of its concessions or its support for the government in a crisis. A party can resign at will, but leaving a Cabinet can be traumatic, and it is a step not easily taken.

Occasionally, the approach of an election brings Cabinet differences to a head, and a crisis can advance the election date.** Ideology *per se* has rarely been directly involved, however, and then mostly as an adjunct or rationale for questions more related to authority. Party followers and electorates, inured over the years to pragmatism in politics and often lacking alternate

---

* Examples: (a) The strength of Dayan and the former Rafi leaders within Labor was increased by fear that they might defect to the right. (b) The practice, when Labor was in office, was to rotate the Ministry of Agriculture between the *moshav* and kibbutz movements. Appropriately, in the first Likud Cabinet, the Minister of Agriculture was a private farm owner, Ariel Sharon.

** Before the 1977 elections, the Mafdal ministers chose the occasion of the first delivery of F–15 airplanes not to support the government in a vote of no confidence. The first airplanes arrived late on the afternoon of a Sabbath eve. Prime Minister Rabin used the opportunity afforded by the Mafdal vote to force a crisis, "seeing the Mafdal as having resigned from the government" and then resigning himself, thus advancing the election date by several months. Impending elections were also important in the Cabinet crises of 1955 and 1959.

political homes, will allow leaders to deviate widely from stated ideals. The broadening of the spectrum of party legitimacy with the first inclusion of Gahal in the Cabinet after 1967, and the potential, still unrealized, for a broader liberal center, may tend to limit the extent to which followers and voters can be ignored. At the same time, the conglomeration of Labor and the Likud and the near eclipse of the small liberal center parties reduce the extent of practical voter options.

The Effectiveness of Protests

Protest actions have changed social policies, and they have stimulated concern for the needs and sentiments of Arab Israelis, (as in the "Day of the Land" in 1976).[11] They have helped to crystallize decisions on Cabinet changes, and pressed the issues of Judea and Samaria settlement and peace initiatives.*

Riots in the immigrant camps were important in the chain of events leading to the 1953 legislation for parallel religious and nonreligious public schools. In 1959, Wadi Salib showed that immigration did not, in itself, lead to integration and equal opportunities. Dramatizing the feelings of social distance and discrimination, the riots signaled the need for positive action, and were followed by increased efforts to diminish income disparities, and on schooling. The Panther demonstrations of 1970 showed that despite the resources allocated for social purposes, children who grew up in Israel could see themselves as being alien to the society. The result was to move social questions much higher on the national agenda.

The 1967 war awakened dormant ideological debates on how to achieve peace, and on the territorial concepts of Zionism. Some proponents of annexation of Judea and Samaria forced the issues, settling without prior government approval. The town of Qiryat Arba next to Hebron was built with official approval after a religious activist settlers' movement first settled without permission in rented Hebron quarters.

When Golda Meir was in office, there were protests on a small scale advocating greater initiatives toward peace from several ideological points of view. The government saw them as important mainly because many of the protests came from intellectuals, educated youth, and those close to Labor ideology.** Protest and settlement initiatives sharpened and focused the ideological debate and emphasized internal Cabinet differences.[12]

* Social protests are discussed in Chapter 6. For the "Day of the Land" see Chapter 3.
** An example: In 1970, Nahum Goldman, president of the World Jewish Congress (who disagreed with the Israeli government's policy), received through a string of intermediaries what he believed was an invitation from Nasser for a meeting, providing the government would approve. (The invitation later turned out not to be an actual one.) When the Cabinet did not approve, fifty-four high school seniors, including the sons of Yitzchak Sadeh, a famous socialist underground defense leader, and of Victor Shemtov, a Mapam Cabinet minister, signed a letter of protest, saying that the government "was not trying seriously for peace." If this were true, they

Much more rarely, protests have influenced Cabinet changes. Popular and party demands led to the appointment of Moshe Dayan as Defense Minister on the eve of the Six Day War, and to the broadening of the Cabinet to include the Herut and Liberal parties. During the three-week waiting period before the war, while the Egyptian Army massed on the southern border, demand for preventive action flowed through hundreds, perhaps thousands, of links to the leaders of all parties; and at the crucial point of decision as to whether Prime Minister Eshkol should give over the defense portfolio to Allon or to Dayan, there were pro-Dayan demonstrations, not very spontaneous, in front of the headquarters where the Mapai secretariat was meeting. Another important instance was the protest which accelerated the resignation of Mrs. Meir's Cabinet in 1974.

The prevalence of direct popular action is not surprising. To the tradition of the Yishuv's struggle against the Mandatory power—through "illegal" immigration, newspaper strikes, clandestine settlement, and even armed action—is added frustration with what are frequently seen as closed parties and bureaucracies insensitive to needs. Labor had from the first established and generously used the right to strike. Cultures in which the strong verbal expression of aggression is common exist along with ineffective parliamentary opposition, while the closeness of national concerns to an individual frequently adds to the psychological burden deriving from personal and family concerns. Political leaders are accessible, media coverage is wide, and government reaction has been swift. These encourage protesters, who sometimes also enjoy the tacit or covert actual encouragement of political leaders.

Most protests have been brief, local, and of transitory interest, and we have therefore mentioned those which propelled a question to the head of the national agenda, at least temporarily, or led to important personal or policy changes. What the different incidents have in common is a belief that only by going outside of the usual political organizations could change or even a serious hearing be achieved. The issues were known before the protests, but their sensitivity and salience were never fully appreciated until the incidents occurred. Another characteristic is that demonstrations have been against the establishment rather than an attack of one group on another, and "ethnic" protests, such as Wadi Salib and the Panthers, have been against the government or police, not against Ashkenazim *per se*.[13] *

"doubted their willingness to fight in the army." (Eventually most of them served with distinction.) See also the account of Mrs. Meir's discussion with intellectuals on the return of the former inhabitants to the villages of Biram and Ikrit, in Chapter 4.

* Exceptions are local altercations, as when orthodox groups try to keep traffic from entering a largely orthodox neighborhood on the Sabbath. Specific group demands are frequent. Examples are the long sit-down strike of the Bene Israel, a group from India whose Jewish religious observances had become greatly modified over the years. A strike achieved for them official recognition as Jews and thus the rights to be married under Jewish law. Another was the use of force by Georgian immigrants in the Ashdod port, to prevent being laid off at work as those "last in," which is the general Histadrut rule.

The comprehensive role of government and the centralization of administration focus and stimulate protest, as do the low efficacy of local governments or of the Knesset in obtaining redress. Centrality and top-down operations have caused "horizontal" cooperation in the solution of problems to lag, impeded the growth of a participatory culture, and increased the frequency of frustration.

In the close-linked community, reactions to protests have often been rapid, but seldom well thought out. In most cases, neither the protest movement nor the response has been enduring. The form of reaction was a function of who was protesting and of the kind of issue—that is, the perception by the government of the extent to which the protest was representative, symbolic, or of real substantive content. Sensitivity has been great on questions which touch the leaders' own images of the society and of their own roles. They were often defensive, like parents who feel that they have done whatever was in their power for their children and who look back at the early years when resources were much more meager and everyone had to sacrifice. Social protests lead to particularly strong feelings by threatening the unity of the society and questioning its success in the integration of immigrations. A natural tendency of the establishment has been to try to defuse an issue politically and to coopt and absorb protest leaders, although not in serious political roles. The legitimation, with time, of more extreme groups can be seen as a marginal part of this cooptation process. The extent of extraparliamentary political action served to sharpen and polarize some central issues and occasionally led to important changes. It should, however, be seen in proportion. Competition continues after the elections, largely within the organized, institutional frameworks. In Israel as elsewhere, however, the growing importance of the populist mode, in which political leaders relate directly to most of the people, leads to doubts regarding the efficacy of the existing arrangements for representative government.

The Character of Pluralism

Electoral change is the focus of political competition in reallocating the roles at the top of the political hierarchy. But the feasibility of organized opposition and the presentation of alternatives in the Knesset, through the media and protests, are also essential elements of competition, though not sufficient. After elections have set the overall power arrangements, the subsequent allocation of economic and social values is determined by interactions throughout the society (including, of course, the bureaucracy), and the relations thus developed eventually react on the subsequent electoral struggles.

For these reasons, the nature of pluralism is important both for democracy and effectiveness.[14] An important factor in political pluralism is the degree to which adherence to social or religious beliefs, cultural or ethnic association, and economic and organizational interests do or do not overlap. The questions are, to what extent do those of different persuasions or cultural associations live in different worlds or in separate social conditions, and to what extent are the political organizations which compete for benefits and for values congruent with these social divisions? The converse of congruence would be a situation in which there is extensive cross-cutting, that is, in which political allegiances cut across lines of belief and class.

Congruence of political and social divisions could involve separation of the elites of the several groups from their supporters. Cartelization of the elites and a substantial amount of secrecy in the practice of government could result, as the leaders from all groups had in common a search for stability, and a desire to control competition lest it get out of hand and upset delicate balances. The greater the congruence, the larger the number of issues which are kept from appearing on the open agenda in order that consensus or coexistence may continue.

Further, congruence of political organizations and social divisions can make it difficult and often impossible for a society to resolve its major differences and embark on a course of action, or "for men and women with competing interests and goals to create a social order."[15] If crosscutting is limited, a society can become more of a consortium or a set of group alliances than a coherent whole, and its integrity can come to depend on vulnerable agreements between relatively independent sectors. Even if these agreements work, they limit competition.

Limited congruence and extensive dispersal can be expected to improve public debate and to temper the authority of the center. The possibility is increased that an issue will be fought out or decided on a substantive basis, since the outcome can be seen to have a more tenuous relation to the sets of interests and beliefs which the participants have regarding other questions. Those most active may tend to be those with an interest or special knowledge of the particular issue. Restraint of the government is furthered because its political followers and the institutions which they lead need the cooperation of other sectors and groups in order to function. This broadens and strengthens the base of participation and restrains the dominance of the political majority of the moment.

Another advantage of such pluralism is an increase in the opportunities for the circulation of elites and for communication with leaders. Within the different areas of life in which he functions, an individual can relate to several hierarchies. In conditions of limited congruence, there can be more independence of choice, since the adoption of one value does not make it mandatory to adopt a whole series of others. The probability that alternatives will be considered is increased, and competition is made more productive of substantive advance. The analyses which were made of the organization of the economy and in other policy areas illustrate the nature of Israeli pluralism.

The Economy

A study of the political economy shows that complex organizational relations result in considerable dispersal and pluralism, and this despite the predominance of central control. To recapitulate briefly some relevant points, in Chapter 5, "The Political Economy," it was shown that central direction of the economy in the Yishuv grew out of a combination of sectoral organization in political and settlement movements and a process in which the political center directed the inflow of national capital.

These characteristics could work against a crosscutting pluralism. In the state, the central role was reinforced by the national government's budget and fiscal authority, with local governments acting as funnels for the national funds which provide most of their budgets. The resulting mode was allocative rather than regulatory, and few bureaucrats or sectoral leaders could readily conceive of the existence of virtually independent bodies within the political economy. In the prevalent political culture there was no great concern to maintain competition or to avoid situations with a high probability of a conflict of interest; or to protect the consumer. Thus inequalities in the distribution of resources for competition were preserved. Producers were ahead of consumers, those representing interests more than principles, and the demands of workers in critical roles and of other strong veto groups, ahead of broader public needs. Economic dependence also served to dampen parliamentary opposition, and it came to be assumed that the government is responsible for the economic security of an enterprise, especially where a social or political goal is explicitly involved, such as sustaining a failing enterprise on which a development town depends for employment.*

The Tempering of Economic Centralism

Despite all of these factors, there is pluralism in the political economy. Among the causes are the degrees of independence of government ministries and the prevalence of bureaucratic politics within the government and its subsidiaries, of competition among subsectors and regions in agriculture, and the participation of private, government, and Histadrut sectors in industry and finance. The Histadrut is found to be far from monolithic. Its links with the

* The persistence of this attitude can be seen in the reaction of the Manufacturers Association in 1977, when the Likud government relaxed foreign-exchange controls and ended export subsidies. The first reaction of the president of the Association was to ask for help for those branches which would be in a weakened position because of the end of subsidies. Subsequently, industry came to accept the new order. After 1974 the government greatly reduced its emphasis on growth, largely because of foreign-currency deficits. As a result, industry lost much of its risk-taking propensity and its mood went from ambition for growth to a concern for survival and to hesitance and inaction.

430   ISRAELI DEMOCRACY

government are tenuous, even when Labor is in power. Pragmatism weakens the power deriving from the linking of ideologies and interests.

Within the government, the dominance of the Ministry of Finance is somewhat limited by coalition politics and by complex distribution of organizational and political resources. Faced by the demands of multifarious interests, the minister needs the support of many constituencies to make policies of restraint effective in practice.

When there is no longer "something for everyone," formal sources of authority are not enough. The interdependence of patrons and clients, the decline of direct party influence, and the mixed structure of the economy work toward pluralism. Large public economic groupings developed, managed by professional bureaucracies, whose relation with the government became interdependent and not merely dependent. There are, in effect, several economies—defense, other government corporations, banking-related conglomerates, medium-sized industry organized mainly within the Manufacturers Assocation, agricultural sectors, the Histadrut enterprises, and thousands of small independent concerns.

There remains the question of how it was that other sectors received substantial encouragement at the height of Labor's dominion. One reason was Labor's inability, in periods of rapid growth, to find the needed management and entrepreneurship within its own ranks. This limited government discrimination in favor of Histadrut enterprises. The weakness with which doctrinaire socialist beliefs were held faciliated the placing of national above sectoral concerns. Organizational behavior is another source. Within the Histadrut itself, there were centrifugal forces of the divergent aims of the different Histadrut enterprises.

The economy is characterized by strong interests and strong government, but neither of these is a monolithic power. Diversity of interests, interdependence, and functional decentralization temper central control and provide a higher degree of pluralism than the formal organization and the centrality of the channels through which resources flow would imply.

Other Policy Areas

Analysis of other policy areas reveals differences among them, deriving from historical sources and from organizational demands inherent in the problems. There are also common characteristics which affect the extent to which plural public choices are available in all areas. An educational system with vast resources is centrally managed, and almost half of the population is involved as parents, teachers, or students; yet its scope and consequent inertia, and local idiosyncrasies, make it difficult to focus issues or to change behavior. In welfare, weak clients have faced dispersed authorities, and while there is competition among those responsible for providing services, this has not afforded an effective choice between conceptual approaches to the more serious problems. In defense, I have shown how the knowledge and policy-making capabilities of the civilian branches of the Defense Ministry have not been equal to those of the military, and the difficulty of developing alternative defense policies outside of the Defense Ministry.

The system does not perform adequately in developing and debating alternatives. The resources needed to compete in the advocacy and execution of programs are unequally available; and the urge to be doing combines with the paucity of resources to create pressure to act. These factors have a stronger influence than the encouragement of open debate given by an independent press and by the distribution of authority inherent in the Cabinet system. Another impediment to pluralism is a fear of the implications of disunity, which sometimes lead to a search for an appearance of consensus, to the detriment of confrontation between differing ideas and policies.

Consensus and Conflict, Unity and Division

Without an adequate measure of consensus and unity on basic values, a political system is unable to resolve questions on which opinion is strongly divided. Yet attempts to impose consensus where it does not naturally arise can perpetuate a party's rule and reduce the openness and effectiveness of the system by keeping important value differences off the agenda. Consensus in Israel gives cause for satisfaction and concern on both scores.

In discussing political integration in Chapter 3, I mentioned factors which unite and divide. There are many reasons, *a priori*, for division. The country is united and pluralist, oriented to national goals and concerned with group and particularist demands; divided in beliefs and ideology yet capable of coherent action. Israel is socialist and capitalist, religious and secular, particular and universal, basically egalitarian and frequently stratified and deferent. The infinite variety of the population comprises the native-born and people born in more than a hundred other countries and separate cultures — Jews, Christian and Moslem Arabs, and Druze, members of kibbutzim or producers' cooperatives, investors, speculators, and pioneers, with a host of social and political beliefs. Moreover, immigration frequently changes the composition of the people, and even the boundaries of the country vary.

Belief in the integration of Jews from all countries and in a common heritage and destiny gives an "overarching value of solidarity."[16] Outside threats, national memories, and the will to survive make patriotism much more than the refuge of scoundrels, and its symbols are convincing. The meaning of left and right has blurred. There is no pervasive memory of class warfare, no earthquake fault in the aftermath of revolution. Sectoral and ideological intolerance of earlier years declined as sharp distinctions of ideologies were blunted.* Time has reinforced the traditions of electoral and parliamentary supremacy. Well-developed institutions serve as forums and meeting grounds, providing roles to which people can be coopted or elected and in which they interact and develop a common political language. That the country began with a well-developed and functioning center has been essential to the degree of unity achieved.

Also important is the small size of the country, in many ways a large city-state. Extensive interaction and community feeling persist despite growth. The press, radio, and television are national. Most people have at one time or another seen the national leaders face to face, and large strata of society interact with them personally. Many experiences, especially military service, are held in common.

With this, there are obvious divisions on questions of religion and the state and on future boundaries, and differences of advantage and culture among ethnic groups. Some of these potential lines of cleavage threaten the effectiveness and development of the political system—nearing but not crossing the limits of danger.** The reasons include both the natural dispersal of interests and beliefs among different groups, and artificial barriers resulting from the means which the political elites of the different parties use in a form of politics based both on competition and consensus. These two aspects are considered in turn.

The overlapping of lines of division is sufficiently limited and the extent to which political allegiances cut across lines of ethnic groups, class, and beliefs is sufficiently great so that there is reasonably effective political competition on a great many issues. At the same time, the effectiveness of competition is limited by the inadequacy of the integration of the very orthodox minority which maintains separate institutions and largely lives in separate enclaves; and on a much larger scale, by the difficulties of political integration of the Arab Israelis.

Among the great majority of Jewish Israelis the congruence or overlap of political beliefs with class, religious and ethnic group was found to be noticeable, but its extent and impact were limited by many factors.*** The greater religiosity of Asian/Africans did not lead them to give unusual support to the religious parties; nor did their stronger desire for more aggressive response to the threats of the Arab states and more prevalent social dissatisfaction lead to overwhelming identification with the Likud, although their votes furnished the Likud's margins of victory in 1977 and 1981.

---

* On the eve of the Six Day War, Herut finally became *hoffähig*, or "acceptable at court," joining the National Unity government. In the early years of the state, Ben Gurion had refused to talk to Begin. Changes in ideological differences and the reasons for their decline are discussed in Chapter 1.

** This discussion applies only very partially to the important relations with the Israeli Arabs, with whom there is genuine political cleavage. See Chapter 3, "Political Integration."

*** These limits are discussed in Chapter 3, "Political Integration."

Views on relations with the Arab countries on the future borders and on the way to peace and security were distributed, albeit unevenly, throughout the different groups in the society. The dispersal of views was most general among the broad political center. Other smaller groups with strong religious or ideological convictions were more singleminded.*

Religiosity is highly correlated with a belief that the national home should comprise the whole of the historic homeland. The political expression is most prominent in the younger groups of the National Religious Party. An exception to this is Agudat Israel, which does not advocate territorial considerations, and concentrates on advancing the goals of a *halachic* state, on preserving the way of life of its electorate, and in gaining resources for the educational and religious institutions it represents, while ensuring their autonomy. The membership of the "Peace Now" movement is strongly secularist, in contrast with the orthodoxy prevalent in Gush Imunim, a group determined to settle in Judea and Samaria as the land of the fathers promised to Abraham. Since 1967, and particularly since 1973, the Mafdal has moved toward belief in retention of Gaza, Judea and Samaria, broadening its political scope from the original single religious purpose. Beliefs in capitalism and socialism as ideologies are weakly held and widely dispersed among groups, even though, as in the case of religion and the state, there are enclaves in which there is considerable unity and even intensity of opinion.

One of the reasons congruence of lines of division is limited is the extent to which there is consensus on a broad range of issues, or at least on the *processes* for resolving differences. There is, however, sufficient division so that consensus is often felt to be tenuous. This can lead political leaders to seek consensus as a value, often in ways that limit political competition. An "artificial" enhancement of consensus politics is due to the modes of political leaders. Sensitive and divisive issues are characteristically avoided, as are those which might lead to drastic changes in political and party allegiances if forced to open confrontation. Some very basic questions have thus far been beyond resolution of the political system, which at best could hold at bay and reduce the friction caused by such problems as those of religion and the state, or of the fuller social and political integration of the Israeli Arabs or the social role of the Histadrut. Decades-long arrangements with the Mafdal, and sometimes with the Aguda, recognized that the religious question is not ripe for clear definition or resolution by a majority.** Despite recurrent skirmishes, conclusion is not pressed, and large issues are broken into problems which are smaller, more marginal, and more capable of solution.

* The different views within the Labor Alignment and the Likud are analyzed in Chapter 1.

** Not all would agree. Yishayahu Leibowitz, a leading (and maverick) religious scholar decrying what he calls the "sacred cow of national unity," says, "Anything of value was gained only through the toughest internal struggles." "Unity is principally attainable in secular politics, where a division of spoils is the issue." (Quoted in Hedda Bossem, "The Last of the Learned," *Ha'aretz*, September 26, 1976.)

Desire for consensus is particularly strong *within* a party. Fearing that forcing decisions on sensitive questions could lead to important realignments in the parties or even in the larger society, party leaders try to confine the debate on issues which involve the underlying values of important groups to elite forums.[17] One means is to control the agenda, using the hierarchical party structures, thus preventing the occurrence of sensitive debates on big central issues within the larger party forum where the results may be unpredictable. Still, nearly all views and interests find expression, if not resolution, at least in the press and to a great extent in the Knesset. Protests and the extraparliamentary action of more extreme groups sharpen issues and ensure their expression within the parliamentary system.

A different aspect of consensus politics is its role in strengthening the hold of a party in power, or of a group within a party. In a small country, frequent personal interaction enhances the importance of personal hostility or affinity, and leads to the avoidance of confrontation. Many rivals find that they depend on each other for organizational support or services, and this tends to limit or restrain competition. Finally, there is a wide acceptance of the need for effective and legitimate rule, so that the party elites seek agreements which provide at least the image of consensus and conciliation. Another limit to effective competition, however, is a fear of "being left out of things." This makes it easier for dominant parties to draw smaller ones into the compromises, sometimes far-reaching, which are needed in order to enter and remain in the government.

Because of these conditions, pluralism in the organization and execution of ongoing affairs makes less of a contribution to political competition than do the elections. The existence of many simultaneous challenges and external constraints reinforces the tendency to consensus which is inherent in a small country. This situation is relieved, however, by the operation of a mixed economy, by competition within the coalition and the bureaucracy, by the beginnings of regional and local political development, and by a vocal press and a critical public. More important still are the limits which exist to the congruence of the values on which the society is divided by class, ethnic group, and ideological or religious association.

Deference and Authority in the Political Culture

As in other working democracies, the Israeli political culture includes and accommodates contrasting elements: oligarchy and elitism, with populism; deference as well as the disregard of authority; central power and pluralism; competition and polyarchy. There are strong proclivities for freedom of action, self-expression, and scofflaw behavior, yet also for diffused deference to members of the political elite. The coexistence of these elements affords authority to govern as well as freedom and participation; but it is the modes of behavior in this coexistence which determine the cultural limits to authority, limits which are unusually important because of the degree to which government is centralized. Extensive formal electoral, parliamentary, and legal provisions for democratic participation and control are in part countered by many hierarchical arrangements and attitudes. Deference is reinforced when party and government roles are occupied by the same person, by the reliance on central authority which developed in many areas, and by longevity both in office and of elite-level membership characteristic of the decades of Labor rule and of the nomination system. Not of least importance is the identification of many of the political leaders with the national symbols and with the independence of the state and the aspirations of the Return.

Attitudes toward authority reinforce the organizational arrangements. Awe of large organizations and those who run them is strengthened when an organization is seen to symbolize or embody an ideal. State authority is very often viewed as necessary for the solution of problems, and a common recommendation of public committees set up to solve a policy question is that a new government department or even a ministry be set up to work on the particular problem which they were asked to study. There is a general desire for strong leadership, and it is assumed that those who have been given authority will use it. At the same time there is a demand for checks and balances of individual power—hence the requirement of committee approval of decisions; or, in many commercial firms, that two managers sign financial documents or contracts. In some quarters, sensitivity to process and individual rights is not always very highly developed.* As we have seen in analyzing the economy and the environment, people and groups whose main endowments are authority or resources have more influence than those representing principles, and there is often more deference to power than to learning. Sensitivity is increasing to situations in which there is potential conflict of interest, but these are often tolerated as inevitable because of the country's small scale.

There is, however, a considerable ambivalence toward elites and authority and a sensible decline of deference. These have historical roots. The Diaspora left a habit of defiance of the secular law, and in the communities there was often the propinquity and familiarity of an extended family, whose members often have difficulty in taking relatives completely seriously.** A critical spirit and a feeling for the limits of mortal authorities moved the Jewish minority. There was always some ambivalence about the worth of those who know—and those who have and donate. Oligarchies of the learned

---

* Israelis, for example, have not protested, as have citizens of some other countries, against the requirement of individual identity cards, or against possible excesses in the use of the rights of police search. In the detention of suspects while under investigation Israel seems to be more liberal than Western European countries, but the courts are far less liberal in this regard than are those of the United States.

** In 1948 a mechanic said, "Serving in the Israel Air Force is like working for your uncle." It is doubtful that one could hear that today.

and wealthy were under popular surveillance and control, and their authority was limited by belief in the existence of a higher law.

The Israeli, for all of his seeming passivity in the face of the authority of the bureaucracy and of other misuses of power, is sensitive to the limits of authority. Like de Tocqueville's American, he is restless at heart and has a natural taste for independence from regulation. From long sojourns among the nations, he knows that there are limits to power and that there are more enduring values.* But these feelings lie deeper in the consciousness than the more obvious manifestations of authority. What is operationally more important, they have yet to find very much expression in institutions or organized voluntary movements and are still relatively weak in comparison with authority relations.**

Factors which could lead to change are the greater economic independence of firms, *moshav* farmers, self-employed artisans, and skilled workers, and the growth of the professional middle class. Organization of the national civil service decreased patronage in public employment. There was a continuing decline of the structure and power of machine politics within the Labor Party. These developments created new opportunities and needs, but their impact was limited by the persistent characteristics of the culture of deference and authority. Feelings of independence have not yet developed to levels commensurate with the new realities; and while individualism is becoming more prevalent, its expression in organized cooperation for action has not yet developed serious countervailing forces.

The sources of a dependent culture include the importance of the party machine in the decades of Labor dominance, the instrumental and dependent socialization of immigrants and the tutelary relations on which it was based, and the dependence of local governments and party branches on the center. The newcomer was initially a dependent client; established politicians related to him in this way, and the human resources of the political movements were inadequate to teach either the new youth or their elders much beyond the elementary machinery of voting and client participation. Older institutions of political recruitment, such as the youth movements, and the political institutions in general had neither the people nor the flexibility of content and organization which were needed to transmit effectively the basis of social ideals of cooperative endeavor from which the institutions had developed.

Attitudes of deference and authority frequently combined extensive bargaining with a more pervasive "bureaucratic political culture." In that culture, at an extreme,

> Relations are perceived more as administrative or hierarchical than as entrepreneurial or market-oriented. Status has greater effect on decisions

---

* Most thinking Israelis would probably prefer Kipling's "Recessional" to "If."

** A phenomenon which of course is not unique to Israel. For example, see Maurice Duverger, *Political Parties*, 3d rev. ed., London, Methuen, 1965.

than do market or bargaining operations, and people's expectations and their orientation toward decisions and authority is "vertical." They look both up and down from their own imputed positions, rather than horizontally.

Attitudes to authority tend to oppose change. Status gives a substantial claim on continuity. This characteristic is related to a fear of losing office. The alternatives open to leaders at all levels are seen to be small, and politics is a zero-sum game.

Promotion and entrance into political life or into positions of economic or social authority tend to be hierarchical or administrative, that is, based on some kind of protégé system rather than on free competition for election or selection. The political system, therefore, tends to be closed to newcomers.

The role of ideology becomes the support of social and political groups and existing establishments rather than a driving force in new program development.

Bargaining processes tend to be more secret than open. (At least they are intended that way; but the facts rapidly become known.)

The opinions of scientists or experts are sought more often because of status and legitimacy than because of knowledge.

Political Parties and Authority

Political parties, preceding the state, had a great influence on the culture of authority. Each party has its own historic sources of internal deference. In Mapam the source is Marxist "democratic centralism." Labor, in the Mapai organizational tradition, depends (or rather, could depend, in the past) on loyal followers, or *omrei hein* (those who assent), and Herut expresses the secrecy and loyalty to the leader derived from the underground days. The culture of Labor was perhaps the most influential and pervasive, and most of this section refers to the Labor movement.

In Chapter 1, the evolution of the Labor Party structure and some of its implications were analyzed. At every level in the party, small groups, to an extent self-selected (although their election followed an accepted process), made the decisions and controlled the proceedings by methods I will presently describe. Members of lower-level groups depended on the leaders at the higher levels not only for political advancement but often for appointive jobs from which they earned their livelihoods. Much of the acceptance of authority, however, was a diffused deference, hard to assign specifically to a concrete form of patronage. Indeed, many factors kept the organization in line: the elementary economics of jobs, and a more diffuse fear of possible future sanctions against dissidents; awe of the complexity of the problems faced by the party and the nation, and deference to leaders who could cope with them;

unity of the party and the group as a higher value; and the needs for association and a leader to whom one could turn.

Bargaining normally takes place between groups or rather among the leaders of groups, while within a given group discipline and hierarchical relations often prevail. It is not unusual to encounter group, institutional, or party leaders who are champions of freedom and representation when acting in the arena outside of their organizations but are exemplars of authority within them.*

There is a clear sense of the hierarchical levels of party institutions, the deciding groups becoming rapidly smaller as the pinnacle, or *tzameret*, is approached. By the time the power of the Mapai machine reached its peak in the early 1960s, even higher ranks became filled with gray organization men who awaited the word of the leaders on questions of policy. The typical Mapai *askan*, or politician in the classic mode, has thus been caricatured by an old hand:

> His skin is that of an elephant, often more than an inch thick.
> As he sits at the conference table, he waits to see what the leadership is going to do. Since he is reasonable and sees both sides of the question, he can readily vote the way the leaders vote.
> He knows that public opinion does not really count very much and that party leaders need to guide it. On the other hand, he is greatly influenced by what is written in the newspapers, although still waiting to see what the leadership does about it, if anything.

Interestingly enough, deference to leaders did not depend only on specific achievements. As leader of his party, Ben Gurion achieved large pluralities in the national elections, but never a majority, and until the Rafi split in Mapai, open conflict in Labor over the leadership succession was avoided. Begin remained the leader of Herut through eight losing electoral campaigns. He was not replaced, and survived to become Prime Minister. At another level, there seems little direct connection between a minister's success in running his office and his political fate—except at the extremes of success or failure.

How Leaders See Their Roles

Until the Rabin Cabinet of 1974, the heads of the Labor Party were people who were already at the higher political levels even in the Yishuv. While their

---

*Conversely, it is hard for leaders to understand the phenomenon of an independent, or "leaderless," person. Shortly after I came to Israel during the War of Liberation, Ben Gurion asked me, during a first meeting, "Whose man are you?" He was mainly trying to place me, in that period of confusion. Twenty-five years later I told this story to a young Labor minister, one of the "young Turks" who publicly decried "the old ways." I intended it to be a humorous anecdote, but the minister showed no sign of amusement. "Well," said he, "whose man *were* you?"

individual personalities had an important influence on people and policies, much of their common attitude to authority derived from spending most of their political lives, in some cases decades, as members of a small group at or near the top of the hierarchy. The younger leaders who followed have many of the characteristics if not the style of those who preceded them—but without much of the simplicity of style or the faith.*

The classic attitude of the veteran leaders was paternal and tutelary; they saw themselves as embodying the ideals. Indeed, there can be little question of their devotion, of the simplicity of their personal lives, of their belief and directness of manner. Much of this continues, symbolically, as in the use of the term *pe'ilim*, or "activists," as a euphemism for "party leaders" and in avoiding the use of ministerial titles in the conduct of internal party meetings. Yet the leaders saw themselves as part of an *avant garde*, with the duty of teaching and leading the flock, and the role of the movement's aides and press was to aid them in the task. Thus Ben Aharon, as Secretary-General of the Histadrut, expressed great public anger at Hanah Zemer, editor of the Histadrut daily *Davar*, when the paper criticized his support of a strike of the Ashdod port workers.**

This self-image often caused overreaction to criticism. Attacks on policies could be seen as personal, and personal attacks as a questioning of the ideals and beliefs and as threatening a hard-won national consensus. "Look at how much we have done!" was Pinhas Sapir's natural reaction to criticism of social policy in the early 1970s. Sensitivity has been particularly great to criticism from those whose support and approval are highly valued, such as intellectuals or youth-movement members, but this did not greatly increase the probability that their advice would be taken. The realization that broad segments of the population see things differently came frequently as a shock, yet seldom led to a deeper understanding or a rethinking of basic policies and values. For example, after the Yom Kippur War, insensitive to the spread of protests, the parties' leaders put before the voters the Knesset lists, unchanged, which had been chosen on the eve of the war. Nor did they seem to understand the changes under way in the Arab sector. Old-style traditional patronage was attempted, and clan bosses who were no longer representative were renominated to the Labor-allied Arab Knesset lists in 1977—and suffered a conspicuous setback. A lack of responsiveness to local branches, their

---

* For the flavor of things as they once were, consider an incident of 1953. Moshe Sharett, the Foreign Minister, had some time before purchased a small and modest apartment in Tel Aviv. As Foreign Minister he was given the free use of a Jerusalem apartment. Azriel Karlebach, the editor of *Ma'ariv*, appealed to Sharett's public conscience, and as a result the private apartment was sold.

** For all his authority, Ben Gurion was a better listener than many of his successors. For instance, he once refused to address the opening of a Teachers' Union convention, preferring to sit in the hall throughout a regular session in order to get a feel for what the members were saying. Many believe, however, that Ben Gurion's ability to give authoritative dicta contributed a great deal to mental laziness within the organization.

needs and candidates, and to intellectuals was also characteristic. After the 1977 elections, an appeal was made to intellectuals to join in rejuvenating the party, but with only modest success at that time, in the dark days of the party's prospects.

Continuity in office has been seen as a right, and as related both to the correctness of policies and the legitimacy of the leadership group as a group. "One does not depose" is commonly heard, and above a certain rank an officeholder could be seen as invulnerable to forced resignation. One source of this feeling is self-preservation. "Don't throw the rascal out—the next rascal may be yourself."[18] A corollary is the feeling that in politics you either win or lose completely. Those who are out, for example in the opposition in the Knesset, are seen by many voters as well as leaders as being semiretired, for when politics is a vocation, putting someone out is like depriving him of the right to practice his profession.

How authoritarian, in effect, is the culture of the leaders? Less than it appears, yet more so than the way the leaders see it. There is a respect for procedures, and for bringing matters to the final decision of appropriate forums, even though the methods of nomination and election to these forums may be authoritarian in themselves. There is a demand for loyalty, especially for its public expression, except in situations and under conditions where a deliberate scope is given to debate and contest.

There are ways of indicating disagreement, such as saying, when voting for a leader-favored measure, "I will vote according to the caucus decision, but I personally think otherwise," or staying away from a meeting. Still, the effective ways to disagree are either those of an administrative hierarchy (that is, privately, as a close adviser), or publicly (as representative of a political constituency, such as the *moshav* or kibbutz movements, or, more rarely, possessing convincing populist appeal). Influence, in such cases, can be a function of the perceived threat to party unity or to the leaders' positions.

Collegeality

The coherent small group of leaders was at the heart of the system. Collectivity prevents open conflict, but it also can result in "group-think," in which preconceptions are reinforced and unpleasant or threatening outside stimuli are rejected.[19] In an uncertain world, also, it is reassuring to work with "people you know." There is a drive in all aspects of Israeli life not only to socialize with a small, known group but also to work with them. This is even more acute in politics, where the tensions of sizing up new people can be substantial.

The other face of the small group is the possibility of interpersonal friction and deep rivalry. Many party splits and great debates were due to personal relations and animosities. As one veteran politician put it, "I hope that the new generation will do it better. In my generation and in the one before it, we didn't know only discussions of ideas and issues. Our arguments always incorporated within discussions of issues personal attacks and personal elements. I know of no one in our movement who has not been a victim of this weakness of ours."[20]

One meaning of collegeality is that one supports the continuance of colleagues in office. Part of this is self-protection, but more important is the feeling that in numbers there is strength, that together the group can stand against the tide, or indeed direct its course. Some of these reactions come from the feeling of loyalty to each other within the small leadership group, which stimulates a defensive closing of the ranks as a reaction to public demand for change.* An example of "hanging together" was the reaction to public protest and internal party demands for the resignation of Moshe Dayan after the postwar 1974 elections. The former Rafi members of the Labor Party essentially said that if Dayan went, then the whole government should go, which eventually is what happened. One of the motives, apparently, for Golda Meir's resignation was the feeling that "the group was breaking up." But for the leader, the agreement to remain in office only because of the pressure has been a way of strengthening his influence and buttressing his authority as an indispensible man. Reluctantly accepting the "judgment of the movement" (din hatnua), a leader can say, "I am not a free man, and when the party imposes an obligation, I must obey."** A similar concept, now in decline, is that you do not run for office. The office seeks you out, as it did King Saul among his father's sheep.

Resignation and the creation of a crisis can be successful if one holds the right cards. If a leader is successful in overcoming a crisis of personality or policy, he gains in authority, the hierarchy is restored, and peace and order again prevail. But brinkmanship in resignation can seldom be used, and not by everyone. A former Mayor of Beersheba, David Tuviahu, was surprised

* The case of the former Minister of Justice, Ya'akov Shapiro, and a nationally owned oil company, Netivei Neft, is an example. Shapiro, in private life a wealthy corporation lawyer, belonged to Mrs. Meir's inner circle in the Labor Party. While he was Minister of Justice, in 1972, the manager of the Netivei Neft Company was accused of misusing his position for personal gain, of gross mismanagement, and of condoning corruption. Despite public outcry, Shapiro, as the Cabinet's legal expert, postponed formal inquiry for a long time, until eventually the Cabinet was forced to appoint a committee of inquiry. While there seemed to be damaging evidence, the committee voted 2:1 that they found no basis for criminal charges. The public felt that justice had been cheated. To add insult, the minister agreed that exorbitant legal fees be paid for the conduct of the manager's defense, thus offending the egalitarian ideology as well. While Mrs. Meir backed the minister, he resigned in the face of public and party clamor. Soon thereafter, Mrs. Meir used her prerogative (the informal but acknowledged right of a Prime Minister to choose colleagues from his own party) and brought Shapiro back as a most trusted adviser and Minister of Justice. She decided to let him go only after the 1973 war, when he violated group solidarity by publicly accusing Dayan of failure.

** Quoted, not from an Israeli Labor Party leader, but from Stalin's rebuttal to Trotsky at the Central Committee Plenum in 1927. Stalin had asked the committee to release him from his post as Secretary-General, but it refused.[21]

when one of his resignations (his last of many) was promptly accepted. "What is the country coming to?" he asked. "You can't resign any more." A classic early "resignation" was that of Ben Gurion in 1948, when he had to threaten to leave office before both the generals and the political parties accorded him the complete authority over the appointment of commanders, which he felt he needed as Minister of Defense.

A related tactic is the appeal to party unity, emphasizing the dangers inherent in possible disunity. The colleagues are asked to rally around the leaders or to forego the confrontation of issues—thereby making them nonissues—in order to preserve the higher value of the unity and survival of the group.

Consensus, unanimous decisions, and the avoidance of open voting confrontations can be sought in order to preserve group solidarity. Fear of dissent is reinforced by the history of party splits. One result is that organizational rather than electoral policy considerations gain priority. Another is the encouragement of extralegal and extralegislative arrangements, of negotiations and accommodation—or logrolling within the small group—which goes on in parallel with the formal legislative structure and can guide and supersede it. Recurrent examples are seen in postelection coalition bargaining and in the ongoing Cabinet inner circle, where ministers can forego the advocacy of their own policies in the interest of solidarity and the support of the leader. Despite strong rivalry and conflict, for years understanding and compromise, "joining them" rather than "fighting them," were the intragroup norms. Unanimous, agreed-upon decisions naturally enhanced control within and without the group. This is no longer the case.

A Mixed, or Guild, Democracy

The resulting authority relations are those of a controlled party democracy, based on very extensive and highly developed institutions. Thousands of people are members of works committees, workers' councils, the national Histadrut institutions, party branch councils and committees, political party forums at several levels, party and alignment caucuses of Knesset delegations, and formal and informal committees of ministers. Each of these organizations has procedures, constitutions, and bylaws, frequent meetings, debates, and periodic elections. Yet the nominations of candidates, the determination of agendas, and the outcomes of deliberations show, at most levels, the exercise of considerable oligarchic authority, made possible by the system and by extensive deference. How do the small executive groups at each level of the political hierarchy exercise this control?

Methods frequently observed include:

The use of collective responsibility and small-group solidarity

Controlling nomination procedures *

Controlling the procedures in the larger forums after the principal decisions have been made in smaller groups, and the understanding use of
rituals and symbols

Convincing followers and the public that there is no alternative to a specific policy (or leaders) because of exogenous situations or practical political constraints; appeals to unity

The uses of dependency and patronage

Cutting off the dissidents' resources

In times of ferment, change, and protest, leading a mass party is like the
proverbial ride on a tiger—it is almost impossible to stay on and fatal to get
off. In quieter times, control is easier, but still requires great skill and effort. If
one were to write a tactical manual for party leaders based on Labor Party
modes, one of the first sections would be devoted to procedure and the uses of
ritual.** A consensus on procedure is important for control and unity, and it
is important for the popular learning of parliamentary and electoral ways. It is
true that much of what takes place in larger meetings is symbolic and that the
decisive power of a meeting is inversely proportional to its size. But the larger
meetings can allow factions and proponents of policies to feel out potential
strengths and weaknesses, and provide rituals which enhance leadership and
hold together groups and individuals of diverse views. Procedural examples
include the practices of debate, questions on the agenda, and conflict on
ideological terms followed by a show of majority feeling, even though the
decision taken may be made by an elite minority on pragmatic grounds.

A second important rule, in parallel with the procedures and rituals, is to

* The DMC used a direct national primary, open to all, with all members voting for all candidates, rank-ordering their choices in a transferable-vote system like that of Ireland. Many later
blamed the system for producing a Knesset delegation made up of disparate individuals, and
perhaps less representative than that which would have resulted from the old methods. In the
Likud and the Mafdal, the contests for nomination took place within the groups at the top, and
the final list represented the outcome of coalition bargaining, between the groups within the Mafdal, and in the Likud, between its component parties and factions.

** Observing the 1969 Labor Party convention, Myron Aronoff contrasted the roles of the small
group of top leaders, who were stage-managing, from a distance, the standing committee, composed of more than 100 politicians of the second rank, and the convention plenum of more than
3,000 delegates. The standing committee was seen performing a ritual of open debate on sensitive
issues, with some criticism of the top leadership. Ritual aided control, defused sensitive issues,
and advanced factional unity by consolidation at the second level of politicians, who subsequently influenced their clients among the much larger number of convention delegates. But
Aronoff emphasizes the creative effect of ritual on the individuals, in helping to bridge over
the differences of their actual and real roles in the face of both the facts of intraparty power
and the growing gap between the Labor ideology and self-image and the society and its perception of the Labor politicians: "They were pioneers—but people saw them as party hacks; . . . the
party was democratic—but they were involved in and were the victims of oligarchic manipula-
tions. . . ."[22]

control the agenda, and whether an issue on the agenda will be brought for decision or will merely have a general and inconclusive general debate. Since pluralism can threaten the *status quo*, it should be confined to issues and arenas where it is controllable. Third, sensitive issues can be kept off the agenda of larger groups until the elite can reach a compromise. Attempts to democratize proceedings by broadening group membership have usually been self-defeating. When the numbers in a given forum are increased under pressure, as usually occurs, the principal actors simply move the real action elsewhere.

A fourth, most essential method is to control nominations. The classic Labor Party procedure is that at each level, a small nominating committee prepares a slate, which is voted for *en bloc* by the specific electorate. There are provisions for modification—for example, a provision that a certain proportion of the Knesset list be chosen by the local or regional organizations. But these can be ignored. In the 1977 elections, nominees chosen by the large Tel Aviv, Haifa, and Sharon regions were given places low on the list and thus unrealistic chances of election even by the optimistic pre-election Labor calculus.*

These means in no way exhaust the arsenal. There remain the many second- and third-rank politicians who have the vote in the several levels of organizations—who are on the payroll of the Labor movement, the Jewish Agency, or municipal or other public organizations. For them, politics is a vocation, and for many years the center had the ability to withhold resources from dissidents and to appoint the leaders of the bureaucracies in the party, Histadrut, and other Labor agencies. Information is used as a coin, and a secondary leader's authority is greatly enhanced when he is the source of information for his immediate henchmen. Finally, there is the simple predominance of forceful and compelling personalities. It is not easy to forget Golda Meir's direct gaze or her pungent remarks in summarizing a debate or putting a motion to an open vote. Israeli political leaders have no hang-ups about face-to-face relations. Indeed, they demand them and thrive on them.

Public Responsibility

Institutional and constitutional controls over power are needed, since cultural restraints are essential but not sufficient. Although elections can be effective, they occur at intervals of several years, and affect mainly the overall

---

* Broader forums, such as party central committees, are gaining more of a say in nominations, in voting for specific candidates (and not an *en bloc* list) at some point in the nomination procedure. In 1965, the nominating committees chose nearly all of those elected. In 1969 and 1973, central committees voted for one-quarter of the Knesset members, and in 1977 for two-thirds, in addition to the 15 DMC members nominated by a vote of the whole party membership. Except for the DMC, the final order of candidates was still arranged in smaller groups.[23]

regime and the personal responsibility of only a few leaders. Between elections there is some response to changes to a minor extent in anticipation of the reactions of the electorate and to a greater degree in response to the demands of internal party groups or particular sectors. But this response, in itself, does not meet the need for more specifically defined public responsibility.

Institutions and processes afford relatively weak accountability. Individual responsibility is diminished by the absence of individual elections to the Knesset and by the way in which collective Cabinet responsibility obviates the need for individual Cabinet members to keep the approval of the Knesset. The coalition-forming process creates marked divergences between election platforms and agreed government programs, and sanctions are infrequent. While the Cabinet form of government deprives the executive of the excuse of legislative blockage of its programs, it also means little separation of powers. The important role of the Supreme Court in furthering common-law constitutionalism and the separation of powers to a moderate degree have been analyzed in Chapter 2. Yet, although the court is one of the stronger links in the chain of public responsibility, there is a good case for more formal constitutional guarantees, for statutory requirements for party democracy, and for legislation which would ensure the rights of individuals and groups operating within the framework of intermediate or secondary institutions (such as the cooperative movements or agricultural producers' groups) whose authority is backed by the government.

Local government, whose straits have been described in Chapter 3, is a much weaker element. Dependence for resources on the national government and common ineptitude often make its direct responsibility to its citizens meaningless, although there are local authorities that govern very well. A less frequently observed impediment to national public responsibility is the influence of extrapolitical groups on party decisions. An example of these is the dependence of Agudat Israel's leaders on a council of the "Great Men of the Torah" for important policy decisions, such as the joining of the Begin coalition in 1977. The council is a self-perpetuating body of elders, responsible to its own conscience. This is an extreme example, but the responsiveness of parliamentary and elected executives to extrapolitical associations and interests is, of course, not confined in Israel to the orthodox or, indeed, to Israel. Yet common deficiencies in party democracy can be more critical in Israel because of list voting and government financial support of parties, and because the parties choose the members of the Cabinet.

Marked priority of the executive was continued from the Zionist movement and the Mandatory government. Although it is needed to enable coalition governments to have authority, collective Cabinet responsibility creates ambiguity regarding the degree to which the individual minister is answerable for his ministry. It reduces the independence of the Knesset, which must bring down the whole Cabinet in order to change a single member. Nor is the individual minister answerable hierarchically to the Prime Minister, who is rarely able to discharge a minister, although he can usually prevent the appointment of someone who is to him *persona non grata*, especially if the person is from his own party.

The Cabinet, as has been shown, is in many ways an upper house of the legislature as well as the executive whose decisions bind the coalition Knesset parties, an arrangement which severely limits the practicality of parliamentary supervision; yet wide media coverage helps make the Knesset an effective platform from which the broad spectrum of public conscience and criticism are expressed.*

In obtaining and disseminating information on what the executive is doing, however, the press leads the Knesset. During the Labor regime, the independent, or nonparty, press, which has the bulk of daily circulation, often played the role of an opposition. The press was spurred to efforts to find and expose error by the extent to which information is concentrated and often secreted in government hands, and by the lack of Knesset or opposition-party facilities for policy analysis or data gathering. Indeed, the press is often a source of the legislator's knowledge and thus indirectly the instigator of questions in the plenum or in committees. As has been shown, the freedom of the press is supported more by cultural norms and the legal tradition than by statute, and a more open and guaranteed approach to information affecting the public is needed.

Of another character is the occasional formal, even *a priori* reliance by the government on professional or expert opinion to decide questions which have considerable value content and political implications. The presence of the Chief of Staff at many Cabinet meetings, the increasingly frequent appeals for opinions to the Legal Adviser to the government, which began during the Rabin Cabinet and became usual under Begin, and the referral of such questions as tax reform to outside bodies of experts, as in the Ben Shachar Committee in 1975—these are all examples of the devolution of responsibility to the "expert."

Bureaucrats and Responsibility

The Israeli bureaucracy has unusual powers which derive from the centralization and scope of government, from the primacy of the executive, and from the diffused responsibility of individual ministers. Two aspects in particular are worth attention. The political cultures of the politicians and the higher civil servants are not as different from each other in Israel as they have been found to be in other countries, and the active intervention of ministers and their occupation with the ongoing details of policy is somewhat greater than would be found in other Western democracies.[24] Higher civil servants are

* These relations are analyzed in Chapter 2, "The Search for a Constitution."

more exposed to the public and the media than their British counterparts, and are as attuned as the politicians to public or political implications—although they may, for professional and value reasons, arrive at different conclusions.

The way in which decisions are made most often depends on the place in the hierarchy which the bureaucrat or politician occupies at a given time. The most senior bureaucrats are often closely associated with a leader of a faction or party, even though they are not usually active in politics during their government service. In the early years, bureaucratic service was the way to a political career to a greater extent than it is today; and the roles begin to diverge as decision processes become more technical.

The advocacy of the specific causes of individuals and interests, which is so much the task of members of the United States Congress, or British M.P.s, is largely absent in that form. Appeal is more usually through personal acquaintance, where the plaintiff or his attorneys have this opportunity—or through party leaders. In most cases, the relation between the individual citizen and the bureaucracy is one of bargaining, usually on very unequal terms. That is, the citizen or firm, if weak, lacking connections or knowledge of the law, or not part of an organized group with political influence, faces a hierarchical and authoritative bureaucracy which seems little concerned to solve his problem, or which applies regulations in ways that serve the advantage of the government rather than that of the citizen, on a time schedule and in a manner that are at the bureaucracy's convenience. There are a great many devoted and helpful civil servants, but the culture of the system, the loads upon it, and the quality of organization are such that the citizen feels a lack of efficacy in a great many cases where the matter is not of adequate scope to reach litigation, or where an important firm or group is not involved. On larger or more vital questions, the Supreme Court, sitting as a High Court of Justice, permits unusually rapid and inexpensive appeal. The State Controller also investigates complaints, in his capacity as Ombudsman and as part of an ongoing check on the working of the government, whose results are published a considerable time after the events. The Controller's extensive studies have an important deterrent effect, but there is little evidence of timely redress in specific cases. In newsworthy cases, resort to the press can speed tardy attention.

The overall record of the bureaucracy in providing specific public services, the application of policies, and the procurement of goods and services leaves something to be desired, both in its service aspects and in public responsibility. Unless he fears litigation, charges of illegality, or interference from the ministerial level, the senior bureaucrat sometimes shows little responsibility for keeping commitments or preventing undue waste of the citizens' or firm's time and energy. The public is somewhat responsible for these relations, because of the "subject" approach which developed.[25] There are signs that acquiesence is declining. Civil servants who were anxious to improve the system, however, were impeded in developing effective management by the overly detailed central control of the Budget Department and the Civil Service Commission. Indeed, the foregoing criticisms apply more to the attitudes of those charged with financial control or administration. Civil servants in substantive roles are very often active champions of their client's cause and work very hard to achieve their department's aims, but they do not have adequate freedom to organize so as to manage effectively the resources at their disposal.

Public responsibility is affected by the differences in the relations between interested groups, the bureaucracy, and political leaders which are found in the several policy areas. In defense, responsibility can be actual only to the extent that there is real political control of policies. This control was seen to be limited by the lack of organizational arrangements which could encourage the development and advocacy of independent and contending strategies or technological approaches, or independent civilian capabilities to evaluate them. Usually, but not at all times, the political support for ministerial control has been present, but not always the knowledge, civilian staff or independently sponsored alternatives. Cultural factors, however, have been consistently on the side of the acceptance of civilian leadership, so that at most times the undoubted bureaucratic strength of the military has been held in check. The civilian focus of responsibility in the defense system is thus clear.

The relations of economic policy were found to be far more complex. A strong and centralized bureaucracy undertakes control over an economy in which there are strong if dependent clients, veto groups of workers in essential services, and a trend toward decentralization to surbordinate financial centers of power. Responsibility for macroeconomic policy can be specified; far less so that for its outcomes, or for the many more specific developments which the Treasury tries to control.

The social services are operated mainly by local government, using national funds. In this dependent relation, local governments pass the onus onto the central government.

Indeed, the degree to which nearly all sectors are supported and are dependent has made it difficult to specify the locus of public responsibility. Because of this, and because of the other system characteristics (particularly the degree of detail of Ministry of Finance control), many earnest civil servants, and even ministers, often feel that they have responsibility without authority.

Effectiveness

As observed at the beginning of this chapter, effectiveness can be evaluated according to the abilities to sense and understand challenges, learn from experience, and set out a relevant agenda; to define goals, develop strategies, and make decisions; and to carry out decisions through mobilization, organization, and authority. Using these criteria, the analysis of the several issue areas shows that achievements are substantial and that government works better in many ways than the observation of its arrangements would lead one to expect, but less well than circumstances demand.

Limits are found in the compartmentalization of the national government and the frequent ineptitude and diffused operation of local authorities; in the limited extent to which thought on domestic problems is of a strategic nature; in the self-insulation of the bureaucracy against outside participation in policy making; and in the rigidities of an organization which has successfully resisted three decades of attempted reforms. Beyond these specifics, however, I would argue that effectiveness could best be improved through extending and improving the relations of responsibility, authority, and competition—that is, that many of the requisites for democracy are identical with those for effectiveness. Deficiency in the process of goal formulation through the consideration and confrontation of alternatives is a more serious drawback than a lag in formal analysis, and far greater impediments are found in the inadequacy of competition and backwardness in the use of adversary procedures than in organizational duplications or ambiguities. The following are some of the findings in specific areas.

Constitutional Arrangements

The rights of individuals are usually well observed in practice, but the law is not yet fully adequate as a formal yardstick for legislation and for court decisions, or to induce the courts to face up to the basic social implications of many decisions.

The supervision of the executive by the Knesset and the responsibility of individual ministers are limited by dependence of members, because of the party nominating systems; collective Cabinet responsibility, which obscures the responsibility of individual ministers and which binds Knesset delegation votes; the absence of Knesset committee staffs; the frequently cavalier treatment of Knesset questions; and the potential influence of Cabinet members who were appointed to their Cabinet posts without being first elected to the Knesset.

The Cabinet has only limited effectiveness as the executive committee of the government. It is frequently more of an "upper house" than an executive. Coalition separatism can deter the formation of coherent policies; the Cabinet's size impedes deliberation; and it lacks resources for policy analysis. Security issues keep many other questions off the agenda of the full Cabinet.

Responsibility of the bureaucracy to the Knesset and the public is weakened by the problem of the individual minister's responsibility and by lack of formal guarantees of freedom of information. Access to public information, the independence of the broadcast media, and the freedom of the press are reasonable in practice but have inadequate legislative guarantees. The Broadcast Authority is insulated from direct executive control, but its board is nominated on a partisan basis and it depends on the Knesset Finance Committee for its budget.

Defense Policy

There has been a lag, as has been shown, in relating political goals and military plans and capabilities, both for the long range and in a crisis, and in improving the mutual reinforcement of the social condition, economic development, and national security. Elements outside of the defense system have not been much involved in the development of strategies.

The asymmetry of forces and resources between Israel and the Arab countries has encouraged military planning based on the concepts needed to ensure immediate and medium-term survival. As has been shown, there is a great inequality in civilian and military defense expertise, and civilian staff departments lack the resources needed to develop alternatives. The organization for the meeting of unexpected crises, when deciding how to react, works better for the specifically military questions than it does in applying political considerations. In the allocation of resources between defense and other purposes, there is inadequate consideration of the ways in which security can be advanced through social and economic policies, or of the social implications of defense resources and the way they are used.

Economic Policy

Among the principal impediments have been the ineffectiveness of the controls for managing the economy, including the budget itself and the oversight of the Knesset through its Finance Committee; the organization of the economy; the quality of strategic planning and, related to it, the ability to carry out policies. Although government intervention is massive, neither the management systems nor the uses of market mechanisms or regulation are sufficiently sophisticated. As has been shown, the system led to dependence more than to enterprise. And despite centralization, there is political weakness in enforcing policies which would restrain strong groups and permit carrying out strategic measures involving restraint when there is not "something for everybody." In labor relations, the process of resolution is not fully developed, and despite formal mechanisms, relations are periodically subject to major trials of strength in which the public services are especially vulnerable to the sanctions of groups having critical functions.

Social Policy

More than in other areas, social policy has lacked an effective focus for decision, a condition aggravated by its lower place on the agenda. Execution has been impeded by the multiplicity of local and national agencies. In the larger sense, the formation of social policy has suffered because it was developed separately from economic considerations, and is derivative from them.

The benefits of pluralism could be real, but they are not readily achieved. Social debate has often been more on jurisdiction than on substance, and policy evaluated more by inputs than results. Approaches are embodied in the institutions which advocate them. Evaluation is inadequate, and much experimentation is sporadic. On the other hand, the readiness to experiment and innovate is great.

The longer-range social goals are in their nature difficult to achieve. Most of the major provisions of a welfare state, such as health and disability insurance and minimum income maintenance have been achieved. More equal opportunity, qualities of community relations, and local and individual initiative and responsibility remain as major challenges.

Effectiveness in Policy Formation

Learning is often partial or tardy. Satisfaction with past success lingers, dulling the capability for learning, self-criticism, flexibility, and innovation; and to this the quality of defense policy is particularly vulnerable. Many of the important problems which are sensed are not given a relevant place on the agenda, and they are often driven out of mind by the continuing predominance of international relations or by impending crises. Alternatively, problems are avoided as being not yet capable of resolution because of inherent contradictions or because it is feared that the forcing of a decision might lead to social schism. When events which shock the core of the national self-image arouse issues which have been neglected or ignored, a typical reaction is to *do something*,* to strike at symptoms rather than at more underlying or structural causes. This is not unusual among governments, which find it easier to allocate money or take specific action than to attempt to intervene in more basic social processes or to overcome vested organizational rights which inhibit change. To this common nature is added a considerable Israeli skepticism regarding the benefits of addressing the problems of the long run, and

---

*In 1868 Henry Adams wrote of the "new Americans" as follows: "They had no time for thought. . . . Above all, they naturally and intensely disliked being told what to do and how to do it, by men who took their ideas and methods from the abstract theories of history, philosophy or theology. . . . They knew enough to know that their world was one of energies quite new." *The Education of Henry Adams*, New York, Modern Library, 1931, p. 239.

about the efficacy of organizational or other formal arrangements, having faith in informal relations, and in synthesis more than in analysis.

Once it is addressed, how well is an issue handled? Academic criticisms of Israeli decision processes plead for more "rationality," citing inadequate use of formal policy analysis, mistrust of planning and planners, and deterrence by coalition government of the coordination of policy and the rationality of organization. Decision modes are criticized as being pragmatic, incremental, and based on compromise.[26] Such characteristics are, perhaps, more noticeable in Israel than in other democratic polities, but they are inherent and needed in democratic political choice,[27] and other problems of policy-making deserve more emphasis.

The simultaneous striving for several major objectives—security, economic growth, immigration, social services and equality—is a principal source of difficulty in the formulation of goals and the development of effective strategies. Political and social goals have continually demanded resources far greater than those which were in prospect. Because of multiple and heavy loads on the system, the adoption of clear priorities or an overall plan could well entail a serious downward revision of the aims or the abandonment of some of the goals. To make matters worse, each goal might be associated with the program of a specific faction or party. Procedures which would require the explicit confrontation of such alternatives have, therefore, instinctively been avoided.

The professional knowledge and experience of civil servants and politicians is much higher now than in the earlier years, and it is advancing the quality of the policy discourse. But if the governmental mind is improving, it is still not an open mind. Agencies often adopt the stance of a beleaguered porcupine when faced with new and different ideas propounded by outsiders. An agency which feels that it is responsible for a policy area will try to ensure that the development of possible activites for that area is kept within its hands. There is seldom an organizational responsibility to present alternatives, and where there is, the resources and the contests are manifestly unequal. Within the executive, bureaucratic politics thus fails to make the contribution to alternatives and debate of which it is capable.

The attention to policy outside of the bureaucracy is seldom persistent, organized, or effective. In the Knesset, the lack of staffs which could obtain and analyze current knowledge makes committees weak in formulating programs or legislation, which are left mainly to the executive. On the eve of an election, when platforms are needed, parties convene task forces, but these usually disperse as soon as practical coalition negotiations begin. Much of the available talent is not used effectively. Independent policy organizations are deliberately discouraged by lack of support. Despite the exhortations of professors, the universities have not developed any serious teaching program in policy analysis.

On another dimension, there are many reasons why analytical or "rational" policy processes are a very secondary mode. While analysis is no panacea, its absence impedes the profitable confrontation of ideas and the consideration of alternatives. In earlier chapters we saw some of the reasons why historical developments of the administrative culture deterred the development of formal proceedings or decision processes.

For much of its early history as a party in the state, Mapai had no formal official party leader, no clear-cut representative procedure, and very informal leadership and decision rules.[28] Although the party's growth led to trends away from the control mechanisms which communities and families can exercise, the adherence to formality and systems lagged. One outcome of this discrepancy was a frequent exacerbation of personal relations as situations grew in complexity.

The culture which developed was one of bargaining and personal achievement, in which personal and group relations were central, with complex interconnections which, like an omelette, could not be separated into their components. To the outsider, there was often organizational chaos, or a *balagan*, characterized by politicization, the dependence on "people you know," and a belief in the ability of sheer will or of champions of ideas to overcome obstacles. The dire prognoses of planners and experts were most often proven wrong, and getting things done took priority over efficiency. Those who could thrive in a state of confusion and high entropy succeeded. Others, more adapted to system and order, often withdrew or avoided challenges.*

The organization is further influenced by the feeling that getting things done requires the direct control of resources and authority more than it does cooperation, and that the real influence is that of the doers. For these reasons, the tendency is to organize so that planning is not separate from execution. If in theory advantages are seen in arm's-length relations, in practice these are felt to be outweighed by the gains in authority of execution provided by the concentration of power. The seeking of operational authority, as well as its centralized and personal nature, is part of the reason for a general neglect in the thinking about implementation of policy by means of community and individual behavior rather than on the basis of government management or hierarchical relations. This condition is not peculiar to Israel, as witness the ease of organizing space programs in the United States, compared, say, to those for urban improvements. Uncertainty and exogenous forces make planning seem hazardous, while compartmentalized executive authority leads to sectoral planning, without adequate coordination between sectors.**

* Giora Josephtal, whose personality was in many ways a classic example of the orderly and systematic German immigrant, is reported to have turned down an appointment as Minister of Finance, before the job was offered to Levi Eshkol, on the grounds that he could not succeed in such a hard task under the conditions of a *balagan*.

** A problem more acute, perhaps, in Israel than in many other places; but see Richard M. Cyert and James G. March, *A Behavioral Theory of the Firm*, Englewood Cliffs, N.J., Prentice-Hall, 1963, on the frequent inabilities of management, even within a firm, to integrate policy across subunits.

Effectiveness in Execution

The transformation of goals and overall policy into specific, coordinated, and effective programs is on a continuum with policy formation and is not separable from it. Many programs which are launched and approved in words or even in law change directions or become ineffectual because of the inability to overcome webs of inept organization, because of the objective problems inherent in many enterprises, and because of competing demands and public and bureaucratic opposition which develop when the program is already supposed to be under way. Originally honest intentions thus can later give the impression of having been lip service.

The nature of governmental organization is an awesome impediment to effective execution. Programs initiated or agreed upon at the ministerial level are often delayed or blocked within the bureaucracy. Almost as serious is the general neglect, when planning, of the future problems of implementation, to which little attention is given during the legislative process. Even when the needs of execution are considered, the importance of support and of the role of public behavior in determining the outcome is seldom kept in mind. Programs which depend to a great extent on the operations or enforcement of local governments often fail because of municipal incapacity.

Starting at the top, at the Cabinet level there is considerable feudalism and the counterproductive preoccupation of ministers and civil servants with the guarding of their turfs. As the action moves to the regional and local level, the several agencies continue their parallel and separate operations, addressing the problems of a given locality with the aid of differing standard operating procedures and criteria for the delivery of services, and with differing approaches to decentralization and central control. The several specific systems, each of which could be effective if acting on its own, often fail to meet goals when the coordinated application of thought and resources and closely related timing are needed.

There are several ways in which execution differs from national policy formation. The lower the level of a decision, the more firm and detailed are the procedures. Routine services to citizens become overburdened with paperwork and delays, while at the ministerial level, major directional changes can seemingly be made offhand, or without benefit of analysis. A second difference is that, where the question is *how* to carry out a specific project, there is more widespread use of developed decision techniques than there is in deciding *what* should be done. Quantitative approaches are better understood and more widely used than those with behavioral aspects. Staff departments at the national level are often unable to differentiate between policy and management. As a result, scarce staff resources are wasted in trying to control what goes on in the field, instead of being spent in developing concepts and strategies, or in teaching. One reason is that national officials fear that only by continued presence at the local level can they prevent their rivals from taking over.

The civil service system is inflexible, unsuited to the challenges of meeting unexpected needs, recruiting and developing the best people, and giving their initiative full scope. Rewards and punishments and both the incentives and the opportunities for excellence are constrained. Attempts at order and meritocracy and detailed supervision may have limited inequities and excessive politicization, but they have also led to a pseudo-rationalism which injures the performance of the system and the incentives to individuals to express themselves.[29]

Authority-responsibility relations, both for ministers and for civil servants, are out of balance; that is, there can be a preponderance of one without the other. Ministers can feel—as do many presidents of the United States, for different reasons—that they have the responsibility without the authority. Democratic politics necessarily involves waste motion, the expenditure of large efforts for small gains; yet the difficulties of the Israeli minister in getting a firm grasp on the direction of policy can be imagined when it is noted that the civil service structure formally limits the extent of discretionary or political appointments to the minister's immediate office staff (which is far smaller than that of a United States Senator) and to the director-general of his ministry, who is subject to Cabinet approval. In practice, there is usually more discretion; but a minister taking office in a ministry which formerly was in the charge of another party finds that he has inherited a staff which, however competent, includes permanent incumbents who were politically appointed. At another level, this is a reflection of the Prime Minister's lack of authority to determine the membership of the Cabinet, especially where ministers from other parties are concerned.

The remedies do not lie, mainly, either in "taking operations out of government" or in "rationalization." Clearly definable operating services, such as telephones and transportation systems, can indeed be expected to operate better within the greater flexibility of corporations; but even these soon find that a change of form is not the heart of the matter. Policy, however, remains a responsibility of government which it can not devolve onto others for decision.

The Tensions of Democracy: A Summary

The polity as a going concern is more impressive in its democracy than in its effectiveness in formulating policies and carrying them out; and it is characterized more by the interest and knowledge of the public than by arrangements which ensure the responsibility of government to the public. Public responsibility, often ambiguous, is weakly felt, in large part by politicians' anticipation of possible election results and reaction to them. Coalition-forming agreements, the predominance of the executive, and the dependence of all sectors on the center all make for inadequate accountability.

A program to improve effectiveness and responsibility could result from the following aims of inquiry:

> To clarify the responsibility of individual ministers, and to secure for the Knesset the capabilities needed to oversee the work of the government.

> To enable the Cabinet and the higher civil service to develop policies conceived across the boundaries of ministries and disciplines, and therefore become more coherent; and to consider decisions in the light of plural sources of information and evaluation and of more adequate analysis.

> To improve the effectiveness of public management by enhancing the independence in operation of local government, in particular, and of public services in general; in so doing, to free the staffs of the ministries to concentrate on policy, as contrasted with ongoing management.

The picture of democratic and nondemocratic trends is mixed; but the balance is in favor of democracy, using the criteria of participation, political competition, and the character of authority relations.

Interest in public affairs and knowledge of them are widespread. Voting participation is high, yet political activity between elections is largely limited to the elites. Voluntary organization can be very active in times of crisis, but shows little continuity of action in the long pull under more normal conditions. Participation for most people is generally in the roles of spectator or voter. Where the large national questions are concerned, this condition is possibly useful in limiting the importance of extraparliamentary politics. For more specific or local questions, however, much can be lost because of the lack of perserverance or feeling of efficacy of voluntary groups, whose countervailing challenge to authority is generally inadequate.

Political competition, initially restrained, developed to the point where a change in the parties in power took place. The change was facilitated by the loss of Labor's monopoly of national symbols, progressive social and economic development, and a decline of a feeling of dependence on parties and their machines. There is considerable pluralism and public debate, yet the influence of adversary proceedings in determining goals and presenting alternatives is small. The congruence of interests, associations, beliefs, and social roles is sufficiently limited that pluralism has a positive and useful form. These limits, however, approach a borderline beyond which competition would only with difficulty be democratic. This threat is visible in the islands of separatism, in the political force of religiosity, and in the correlation of class and ethnic association. Although there is a national consensus regarding the importance of procedure, competing interest groups often prevent the resolution of issues.

Deference to high office and status is ambivalent, and its effects are mitigated by the traditions of community control of local oligarchies and the familiarity deriving from face-to-face relations. Within parties, hierarchy and a bureaucratic political culture are still prevalent, in a guild form of democracy.

The relations and modes we observed are those of the first decades of the state. These were not static. Many of the earlier characteristics of the polity persist, but there have been significant changes. Competition for the national leadership became more open. No longer was there one dominant party around which every coalition would be formed, and legitimacy became widely distributed. The historic partnership of Labor and the National Religious Party ended, and the religious parties actively intervened in secular issues. Many more people began to feel free from the need for party allegiance and favor, as education and economic advance increased their independence and the importance and professionalization of the bureaucracy grew. Populist modes and the ability of pressure groups to appeal to and work directly with the government reduced the role of the parties as intermediaries. Information became more widely available and contact with political leaders through the media encouraged the populist trend. The principal parties became conglomerates, representing broad and increasingly pragmatic interests, and their role was increasingly electoral rather than the advocacy of an ideology, the seeking of utopias, or the arbitration of policy.

The analysis shows Israel to be a working democracy, but one with much unfinished business. This is as it should be in a society that, hopefully, has most of its development ahead of it. The question, therefore, is how to address the future.

CHAPTER 10

Epilogue

THIS STUDY ENDS with the elections of 1977. The events between 1977 and the elections of June 1981 are now sketched in very brief outline. The feelings and developments of that period are recounted in order to improve the perspective of the past and the agenda for the future.

Winning a large plurality in the 1977 elections, Menachem Begin formed a government based on the Likud and the Mafdal in the Cabinet, and having the Knesset support of Agudat Israel. Although elected on the Labor Alignment List, Moshe Dayan left the Labor Party to become Foreign Minister as an independent. In the fall of 1977 the DMC joined the coalition, giving the government a Knesset majority of 76 out of 120.

By January 1981, the majority decreased to between 61 and 65, depending on the issue involved. Moshe Dayan had resigned as Foreign Minister, Ezer Weizman as Minister of Defense, Yigal Hurwitz as Minister of Finance, and Shmuel Tamir as Minister of Justice. The Minister for Religious Affairs, Aharon Abuhatzeira, was charged with bribery. The coalition thus became fragile and the authority of the Prime Minister was eroded. The press actively denigrated the government, when it was deserved and when it was not.

Internal Cabinet dissension and the likelihood of a no-confidence vote in the Knesset forced Begin to ask for elections to be held in June instead of at the appointed time in November. Opinion polls at first predicted an overwhelming Labor victory, perhaps even a majority. In the following months this lead disappeared. The Likud gained an inconclusive victory, 48 seats to Labor's 47, and formed a narrow coalition of 61 members with the NRP (Mafdal) (6), the Aguda (4), and the Movement for the Tradition of Israel, (Tami), (3).*

The feelings of frustration and anxiety characteristic of much of the 1977–81 period were not relieved by the inconclusive election. Indeed, the campaign had instigated and sharpened feelings of class-ethnic congruence. The atmosphere which resulted from the new coalition agreement with the religious parties (who enjoyed concessions not earned at the polls) accentuated the gap between the constitutional concepts of orthodoxy and the liberal majority, and threatened the *modus vivendi* which had been achieved. But there were other reasons for concern, of broader import. The signing of the peace treaty with Egypt, the outstanding event of the period, was followed by a malaise stronger than the hopes which were aroused. Some of the causes were fear and doubt regarding the impact of the Camp David agreements on Israel's long-term security; an inflation which well exceeded 100 percent a year; frequent public dissension among Cabinet ministers; and the disappointment of hopes that deep-seated social problems could be corrected in short order. Things were seen through a glass darkly; yet periods of gloom have not been unusual.** The causes in 1981 lay not only in the appearance of the domestic and international situations. More fundamental reasons derived from problems which had existed before 1977, and from the stage at which the Zionist endeavor found itself.

Dilemmas after Camp David

In late 1977, Anwar Sadat made a surprise request for an official visit to Jerusalem, where he addressed the Knesset. This set in train intensive negotiations, leading to the Camp David agreements in the fall of 1978. Two levels of action were specified: Israeli withdrawal from Sinai and the normalization of the relations of Egypt and Israel; and the granting of administrative autonomy to Judea, Samaria, and Gaza, whose ultimate political future would be decided after a period of five years.***

In this agreement, Israel paid a very substantial price, giving up, in the Sinai withdrawal, three major airfields and oil resources which had supplied nearly one-third of Israel's oil needs and bid fair, one day, to provide them all. The large forces deployed in Sinai were withdrawn into the Negev, requiring a tremendous investment in new roads and installations. Also given up was the

---

* For the Tenth Knesset election and its results, see Appendix B.

** For example, of 1952 it was said: "It was a situation in which everyone had the impression of living in a confused twilight of ancient history and future promise; in which everything seemed possible and still so unattainable. It was an endless battle for survival."[1]

*** The text is in Appendix A.

wholly new city of Yamit and the settlements founded since 1967 in the Rafiah area south of Gaza. In addition to the loss of strategic depth, the withdrawal created financial burdens that could cripple the economy for a long time to come and, in so doing, increase Israel's political dependence.

Despite the beginning of normalization with Egypt, there was little ame-lioration of the overall conflict, and the needs of defense grew. Syria remained intransigent, effectively occupying most of Lebanon, which the PLO used as its base. Jordan and the PLO both rejected the Camp David agreements, and West Bank leaders, leaning either to Jordan or, more strongly than before, toward the PLO, did what they could to counter the autonomy proposals. In-cidents of violence on the West Bank became more frequent. The Israeli government began to see some features of the autonomy proposals as leading to an independent Palestinian state, and took steps to ensure long-term Israeli control through encouraging settlement, mainly on the high ground in Samaria. This was in contrast to the previous emphasis on the Jordan Valley, as in the original Allon plan.[2]

The settlements were a focus of disagreement within Israel and of criticism of Israel abroad. The bounds of the issue were set by groups with strong ideological commitments—principally the Shalom Achshav, or "Peace Now," Movement, which opposed all settlement and Gush Imunim, a religious-nationalist group which tried to settle actively, with or without gov-ernment sanction.* The settlement actions and the protests contributed to a feeling of polarization. Some jurists saw an increase in unilateral popular in-itiatives (as in a few of the settlements and on such issues as housing or Sab-bath enforcement) as inimical to the rule of law, since they applied pressures and "created facts" outside of the parliamentary system.[3]

Settlement questions had been pressed in similar ways before 1977.[4] The Labor Alignment, however, did not have the internal tensions of the 1977-81 Begin government, which had come to power endowed with the territorial ideology of the Revisionist movement and with the electoral support, *inter alia*, of Gush Imunim and its sympathizers. The very large concessions of the peace process alienated those who believed in the congruence of Zionism with the ancestral territories and those who feared the defense implications of the withdrawals, but they did not satisfy those who believed that an opportunity for a broader peace was at hand and should be seized, even though this meant, in the case of withdrawal from Judea and Samaria, a considerable military risk, as well as giving up parts of the land of the fathers. Yet retaining Judea and Samaria could, some feared, lead to a binational state with an eventual Arab majority.**

---

* The Peace Now Movement later became dormant as its leaders sought places on party election lists. Some of the firm opponents of Camp David and other territorial concessions formed the Tehiya (Rebirth) Party, which gained three Knesset seats in the 1981 elections.

** The questions of Judea and Samaria, following the 1967 war, are discussed in Chapter 1, pages 48-50, and their defense implications are considered in Chapter 4, pages 169-70.

Settlement, however, was clearly not the sole or principal obstacle to peace. Despite Sadat's views, much of the Egyptian intelligentsia and bureaucracy was cool to the normalization of Egyptian-Israeli relations. The Arab states which opposed accommodation emphasized the Palestinian question. It was an issue that could serve them as a proxy and as the national focus of the more general conflict.[5] Yet it was the rejection and mistreatment of Palestinians in the Arab countries which led Palestinian Arabs, particularly after 1967, to seek their own Palestinian nationality.[6] In the European Common Market, and the UN the legitimacy of the PLO grew, despite its terrorist activity. The other Palestinian voices were not heard. Israel felt its own world image and legitimacy decline. In the United Nations, the opposition of Third World countries was to be expected, but the espousal of the PLO by European countries eager to import oil and export arms and capital goods was demoralizing. In the autonomy talks the United States sought to advance an overall settlement, and was often seen as pressing for concessions which could impair Israeli security or compromise the future status of Jerusalem. For the overwhelming majority of Israelis, Jerusalem is a united city, the capital of Israel, and therefore outside the scope of the autonomy negotiations. The Iranian revolt, the Russian invasion of Afghanistan, and Syrian control of Lebanon added to the feeling of isolation.

Arab wealth and technology grew, and the military balance of forces worsened as the United States armed Egypt and Saudi Arabia and the Soviet Union modernized and expanded Syrian forces. In 1980 it was announced that France had supplied Iraq with nuclear technology and materials. In a few years this could lead to nuclear weapons in a country formally at war with Israel and which was vying with Egypt for leadership of the Arab world. A sophisticated Israeli air raid destroyed the Baghdad reactor in June 1981, but resupply by France and others was feared. Time had been gained, but not long-term freedom from nuclear threats.

The peace treaty with Egypt was a momentous event, a breakthrough toward the legitimacy of Israel in the Arab world. It was too early to tell, however, whether this acceptance would spread to the other Arab countries; whether the decline in Israel's image abroad could be checked and reversed; and whether, in the long run, the agreements were the beginning of progress toward a secure peace, or rather a tactical move which gained the withdrawal of Israel from Sinai.

The Economy: Dependence, Inflation, Stagnation

A critical economic condition was at least partly related to the withdrawal. Inflation soared, industrial investment grew very little, and domestic and foreign debt rose. In 1977 there was a massive, one-step devaluation of the lira. The exchange rate was then allowed to float, and many of the formal foreign-currency restrictions were removed. While easing bureaucratic requirements for international transactions, the policy produced little noticeable economic gain. No really new economic strategy emerged.

Linkage to the cost-of-living allowance of wages, transfer payments, government bonds, insurance, and pension plans reduced much of the tension caused by inflation. In its turn, however, linkage pushed up costs, encouraged purchasing demand rather than saving, and acted as a palliative, feeding the inflation as well as ameliorating many of its effects. Because of the rapid decline in the real value of budgeted funds, the timing of their release for expenditure actually determined priorities. This timing was controlled by the Ministry of Finance, seriously weakening the Knesset's control of policy through the budget.

Restraint was clearly inadequate. In the fall of 1979, the Minister of Finance, Simcha Ehrlich, was replaced by Yigal Hurwitz. Government employment and budgets were curtailed with a strong hand. Subsidies on essential commodities or services were eliminated or greatly reduced. Despite its economic rationality and budget saving, this measure also raised prices, at least in the short run, and adversely affected those with the lowest incomes, who were partially compensated by increases in transfer payments. Because the government had not made improvements in the system of public management which it had inherited, the overall effectiveness of budget cuts was reduced, and they often impaired important staff work or services. The limited ability of fiscal and monetary policy to stem inflation became evident, and budget deficits continued. The government was unable to reach agreement with the Histadrut to restrain wages, prices, and profits.

In January 1981 Finance Minister Hurwitz resigned when the rest of the Cabinet would not accept the further cuts which he considered essential. His successor, Yoram Aridor of Herut, rapidly changed direction, restoring subsidies and cutting excise taxes and import duties, particularly on consumption items. Price rises were thus checked and consumers' spending power rose, at least temporarily. The price of the resulting budget deficit and of increased consumer demand would have to be paid after the elections.

Social Policy and the Democratic
Movement for Change

Two electorates which had been particularly important in the victory of the coalition parties were subsequently disappointed: more highly educated voters who had supported the DMC, and voters in development towns and poor urban areas who supported the Likud.* In 1977, although many of the

---

* Even in 1981, however, many of these associated Labor with the establishment. In many places, kibbutzim and the Histadrut were large employers, and the legend and the memory of the dif-

elements of the welfare state were in place, there still remained gaps in education, housing, and life opportunities in general and, more important politically, the feeling of not having had a fair share. Although the DMC had a strong impact on social policy, it failed to achieve its constitutional aims, or in having an influence proportionate to its Knesset strength.

Social policies emphasized security, notably in laws enacted to guarantee income, and to insure the medical and income needs of the helpless and chronically ill. The Law for the Guarantee of Income aimed to eliminate the involvement of social work with welfare payments, thus allowing concentration on guidance and questions of employment. Support payments, in concept somewhat resembling a negative income tax, were to be linked to a readiness to work. Free education through high school was added. A bill for a national health organization was introduced, but made little progress. At the same time, continuous efforts were needed to maintain the real incomes of the poor in the face of inflation. Social policy was on the defensive, trying to catch up with the impact of economic decisions arrived at independently, and of budget and personnel cuts in the social services. The Cabinet Committee on Society and Welfare still lacked budget authority, and therefore had little more authority than in the previous Cabinet.

It did, however, sponsor a major new program, Project Renewal, which attempted combined physical and social advance in disadvantaged neighborhoods. Going beyond the aims of the legislative program, which would complete the structure of the welfare state, Renewal was aimed at advancing social integration and weakening the dependency relations that were at the heart of the social question.[7] By 1981 comprehensive programs were in operation in 69 of the poorest neighborhoods.

The overall aim was to help and encourage the people of the neighborhoods in their efforts to advance and to make the neighborhood a good place in which to live and bring up children. Strategies, plans, and priorities to this end were initiated by the neighborhoods, rather than by the national government. The belief was that community development, leading to full resident participation in assessing needs, planning, and taking responsibility for execution, was essential for lasting improvement in a neighborhood and in the life opportunities of its people. The focus on a defined geographic area and on the confrontation of the totality of problems within it permitted an unusual degree of decentralization of decisions, and provided a framework in which community development could take place.

Neighborhood steering committees were the locus of decision and debate, and a training ground in procedures and leadership. National policy was developed by an inter-ministerial professional committee in the office of Deputy Prime Minister Yadin. Unlike the Ministers' Committee for Society

---

ficulties of the immigrations were kept very much alive. These, the Likud pointed out, took place when Labor was in power.

and Welfare, the professional committee decided budget allocations, and in so doing developed working methods across ministries and disciplines, as did many local steering committees.

There were, of course, many problems. Attempts to focus initiative in the neighborhood were superimposed on a highly centralized ongoing system of public management. New resources were added at the same time that ordinary budgets for education and social services were cut, giving rise to temptation to use Renewal funds to maintain operating levels, rather than to innovate or catalyze organizational improvement. The comprehensive consideration of a neighborhood's social condition often revealed the backwardness of the arts of social intervention. Community development proved to take longer and to be more difficult than anticipated; national and local elections threatened politicization; and it proved much easier to involve residents in making decisions than in taking on the responsibility and footing, increasingly, the costs of neighborhood programs. Yet even in these there was considerable progress; and the growth of neighborhood and ethnic pride and feelings of efficacy was notable.

Social policy was largely under the aegis of the two Democratic ministers who remained in the Cabinet throughout—Yigael Yadin as Deputy Prime Minister and Chairman of the Ministers' Committee for Society and Welfare, and Israel Katz, Minister of Labor and Welfare. Ironically, social measures were almost the only part of the original DMC platform that was carried out. Abundant press criticism of these programs was more an expression of disappointment with the original DMC and later with the Democrats (mainly because they did not resign from a Cabinet which would not enact the DMC program) than it was a critique of specific policies. The DMC had expressed the protest and the search for a new politics of many in the educated middle class, but most of the announced goals were out of reach, given the coalition forces as the DMC found them, and with a DMC Knesset delegation lacking cohesion and teamwork. Very galling to many was the failure to achieve a constituency Knesset election system.

After it joined the government, the DMC rapidly declined as a political force. Its Knesset delegation recurrently split, until by 1980 the Democrats in the coalition represented a Knesset strength of only four members. Yadin retired from politics in July 1981, and the Democratic movement dissolved.

The Democratic ministers made important individual contributions, raised the level of Cabinet debates and decisions, and tempered the government's international stance. But to hold fast to most of the original platform, they would have had to go into opposition. The more than 200,000 who had voted for the DMC were disillusioned, not only with the Democrats and with Shinui, which split off from the DMC, went into opposition in 1978, and gained two seats in 1981. More important for the 1981 elections, they despaired of the possibility of reforming the system from the outside without the organizational resources of the major blocs. Some of the professors who three years earlier had joined enthusiastically in helping to write the DMC platform now sought to proffer their advice and services to the Labor Alignment.

The Crowded Agenda

Clearly, the relations of power and the styles of the leaders changed under the Likud. The Prime Minister's role was more authoritative, and party forums were far less important in policy decisions than when Labor was in office. The ability of the government to impose its will was initially more limited than Labor's had been. In their decades in opposition, the Liberal Party and Herut had not developed the cadres of experienced people, depth of organization, or voluntary organizations comparable to those which provided Labor with the social networks, patronage and loyal cohorts that could further effective implementation or provide the leaders with a constant, informal flow of information. The Democrats, as though on principle, built no machine at all. In such circumstances, more attention was paid to formal and legal sources of authority. Likud political appointments began in 1977, but it was only after the 1981 elections that Likud leaders announced that they would try to bring their own people into the key roles in the bureaucracy, and began to do so in earnest.

Beyond the forms of authority, however, it appeared that long-standing, underlying questions predominated, although some now appeared in a sharper form. Among these were the meaning of a Jewish state and of religion in a free society, the integration and equality of the non-Jewish minority, the search for economic independence, and, not least, the practical meanings of equality, free enterprise, and socialism; of individualism and cooperation, of the nature of the social revolution in Jewish life, and of the relation between the society and the state.

The answers could be sought, effectively, only if there was to be a serious advance in the ways the government reached decisions and carried them out. In these there was little improvement, and lack of method continued to limit progress. But this was not the greatest impediment. The watershed of the 1967 war had reopened basic territorial questions of Zionism. The problems of security and of accommodation in the region, and particularly of the future boundaries and population hung over all. These major unresolved questions limited the ability of the political system to organize effectively to address the other issues which would determine the quality of the society.

The developments after the 1967 war also led to an attenuation of Israel's legitimacy abroad. Israel saw itself as a socially progressive, natural ally of other democracies, and of people everywhere who work for social advance and the dignity and rights of the individual. Much of the Third World, however, could see Israel as an imperialist agent. The West no longer considered Israel to be an underdog, or even a haven of refuge. The Holocaust was no longer very meaningful for most young Europeans, and democracy was not everywhere admired or an article of faith. A way was sought to explain at home and abroad that Israel has a *raison d'etre* in making important contributions to democracy and to the quality of society.

In the 1970s investment and enterprise seemed to stall, although there was a promising growth of industrial research in proportion to output and of high-technology exports. A reconsideration of economic strategies and of the structure of the economy was needed, so that the human potential in knowledge and enterprise could be realized.

Equality of educational attainment was growing and could lead to full political integration. Along the way young, educated persons of Asian/ African origin could feel and show frustration as the advance in status and power their education had promised materialized more slowly than expected. The base of educated people which was forming and its entry into politics and government (for example, in the new generation of mayors in development towns) showed a clear trend. The direct, personal election of mayors made them the only elected officials chosen by direct popular vote, enhancing their legitimacy and opening the way to national politics.*

Whatever the many frictions and the persistent strength of ethnic feelings and frustrations, the attainment of equality of opportunity and of integration among Israeli Jews of all origins was to be achieved through general rather than ethnically oriented policies. This, indeed, was the overall verdict of the voters, the three Knesset seats gained by Tami in 1981 notwithstanding. The political integration of Arab Israelis was a much more difficult question. It too depended on the general social advance, and, even more, on the form and timing of Israeli accommodation in the area. There was all the more reason to give the needs and aspirations of the Arab Israelis the policy consideration which they deserve.

A Jewish State

The meaning of a Jewish state remained a principal source of division. At one level a Jewish state is a haven to which Jews can come as a right and not on sufferance. At another, it is a country where the Jewish faith and culture can flourish and find expression, considering Judaism not as an abstract religion, but one whose beliefs are integral to society. In this there are divergent streams. One of them sees the religious traditions as embodying many of the

---

* Eight serving mayors were elected to the Tenth Knesset. Six were of Asian/African origin, one born in Israel of European/American ancestry, and one Arab. They were from five development towns, two small settlements and the town of Nazareth. One of those elected, Moshe Katzav, resigned as mayor of Kiriyat Malachi on being appointed Deputy Minister of Housing, in charge of Project Renewal.

answers to a better society, if they can only be discovered, understood, and carried out within the framework of a free, liberal society. The other sees the Jews as the subjects of religious law and the means of carrying out God's will. It is the law and the observances which count, preserving the people and the faith. Most of those espousing the latter view would have the laws of the state preserve the authority of the *Halacha*, or religious code—and thus of the established rabbinate which interprets it—over a great many aspects of the lives of its Jewish citizens.

In 1977, the decades-old alliance of Labor with the NRP (Mafdal) ended. Trends within the younger Mafdal toward Herut's beliefs and Begin's own sympathy for religiosity made the transition seem natural. Not so the new partnership of the Likud with the non-Zionist Agudat Israel, the strongest proponents of the *Halachic* state. Ironically, given Begin's passionate Zionism, the Aguda did not really see the state, or Jewish social change, as having any positive role in the destiny or contribution of the Jews. Important in prolonging the 1977-81 government, Aguda support was crucial in the formation of the 1981 Knesset majority of sixty-one, and most of the clauses in the coalition agreement were concessions to its demands. These included matters not only of religious observance but of resources and privileges as well.

The atmosphere that ensued was of more consequence than the specifics. While the historic alliance of orthodoxy with Labor had impeded constitutional development, its arrangements were largely concerned with religious observance. Those in the Mafdal who sought a *Halachic* state seemed prepared to wait until a majority would accept it, and to see in the Zionist endeavor the turning point in the modern history of the Jews.

In 1981 this delicate balance seemed to be in danger. Not only was a liberal constitution in question, but also the hope of creating, beyond a haven, a spiritual center with close ties to a Diaspora where Judaism has several legitimate forms. Separatism in institutional and geographic enclaves also became more acute and worked against social cohesion and development. The size of the liberal majority and the strength in the culture of the rule of law indicated that, given considerable vigilance, there would be little real danger to a liberal constitution. The greater problem was how to permit the religious tradition, within a free society, to have its full imprint on the development of Jewish life.

The New Society

As a central aim of the Zionist endeavor, social renewal has proven more elusive than any other goal; yet the development of the new society may be the principal source of strength and ability to face the difficult and crowded agenda.

After independence, intensive efforts in political education and self-selection of immigrants to the Yishuv gave way to the imperatives of the in-gathering of the exiles, and hundreds of thousands of post-independence im-migrants came to Israel out of sheer necessity. Their beliefs did not, in most cases, include self-work, cooperative living, voluntarism, or present denial for the sake of the future any more than do those of most people in other modern societies. They were introduced to democratic politics by party bureaucracies. Their numbers were very large in relation to the number and quality of veteran settlers spared from other national tasks to help them, and impeded effective political socialization. As the government took over responsibilities, the roles of voluntary or sectoral groups and even of local government declined, while many of those in office were too busy trying to solve pressing current problems, or to advance careers, to pursue visions of the future.

The growth of large organizations in government and business created a new environment in which groups committed to cooperation and equality found themselves surrounded by a dominant and challenging unbelieving world. As the country became a modern industrial state, the ideals of cooperation, equality, and of volunteer pioneering were confronted by the differentiation of function and rewards common to modern industries and bureaucracies.* Pioneering, physical work, and cooperative enterprise sur-rendered their primacy to the goals of economic growth. Self-work as an ideal declined with the growth of managerial functions, the emphasis on economic enterprise, and the immigration of people with less developed occupational skills. The danger grew that the Jews might largely stop being their own hewers of wood and drawers of water. One reason is that the country needs to perform management and intellectual tasks comparable to those of much larger countries. Another is the imbalance of payments, which means that in-dustrial labor for many goods is performed outside the country. Since the 1967 war, tens of thousands of Arab workers have commuted daily from Gaza, Judea, and Samaria, meeting much of the need for unskilled or semi-skilled labor.

When the social condition is compared with the aspirations of the genera-tion of the founding fathers of the several streams of the Zionist movement, and much of the advance toward a revolution in Jewish society seems to halt or reverse direction; when Israel fails to attract the immigration of the Jews of the advanced countries of the Diaspora; when the magnitude of the problems is contrasted with the means used to attack and resolve them, then the task ahead seems very large indeed.

Yet at this stage of the endeavor, the society can be likened to the cylinder of an engine in which the piston is at dead center, at the top of its stroke. Just before it begins to move down and turn the crankshaft, it seems momentarily stalled, without power or progress. In this impasse there is resort to nostalgia

---

* In 1974 agriculture provided only 6.5 percent of the GNP and about 7 percent of employment.

on the one hand, or to disillusion with the power of ideas and ideals on the other.

The many contradictions and pressures often lead to a nostalgia for a past when, as seen from a distance, there were few doubts about where to go or even how to get there; when there was little inequality and immigrants from even the most backward lands integrated rapidly; when challenges were answered by spontaneous volunteering, and ideologies and their symbols served as guides.* While there is much truth in this, that is not exactly the way it was.** Scholars now question some of the legends of the period of the Yishuv, finding, as might be expected, that the pioneers were flesh and blood, that ideologies often served interests and power, and that there were nondemocratic and bureaucratic elements in the political culture.[8] Such analyses are useful in understanding the continuities in the political culture, in the search for way to bring ideals and reality closer together; and they place present struggles in better perspective. But more detrimental than nostalgia is a surrender to current pragmatism, for observation of the role of beliefs in past achievements should encourage endeavors to renew the dream.

The achievements are impressive: a sovereign state, which can allow the free expression of the Jewish spirit in an independent society having a Jewish majority; the rebirth of the Hebrew language; the normalization of Jewish life through the performance of all the occupations of the society; a broad range of cooperative enterprise and innovative social institutions; and the symbolic encouragement of Jewish life in the Diaspora, which Israel provides. A working parliamentary regime maintains its democratic character through wars and economic crises.

The heritage is rich and the possibility of success is real. Equality, if it has declined in practice, remains a cultural ideal, for which the history is favorable. As in the United States, independence in Israel did not have to destroy a feudal structure or reform large landholdings or historical concentrations of great wealth; and views based on ideological principles, such as national ownership of land, have slowed the process of concentration of capital. There are inequalities in wealth, but they are minor compared to those in most other parts of the world. Today there is still a vast amount of cooperative activity, and equality and simplicity in manner and life style.

Intellectuals and practical people, however, question the present usefulness of beliefs in understanding problems and setting goals. Israel is, in a

---

* Golda Meir and Shimon Peres were astonished to hear workers say that they did not want "to build the country" but—as William Greene said of U.S. labor—that they wanted "more and more." When Professor Aharon Katzir visited the University of Beersheba with Mrs. Meir, they wept to hear students complain about the extra advantages given to immigrants, and asked, "Aren't we here in Israel so as to absorb immigrants?"

** At the beginning of the *History of England*, Macaulay says, "Those who compare the age in which their lot has fallen with a golden age which exists only in their imagination may talk of degeneracy and decay; but no man who is correctly informed of the past will be disposed to take a morose or desponding view of the present."

sense, between ideologies. Seeing the gap between the old ideals and the current realities, young and old are skeptical of social faiths. In fact, the country is far different because of beliefs than it would have been without them, for without the peculiar combination of Zionism and social beliefs, of the search for the unique and the universal, it would have been difficult if not impossible to mobilize and overcome the odds.[9] The broad nature of the goals set by the leaders of the Yishuv enabled many to move together in the same direction, even while marching to different drums. The result was a strong social base expressed by institutions that are still viable today, but whose ability to make unique contributions has greatly diminished.

Indeed, the form which the new society might take, and the ways to achieve it, are not readily conceived. The old philosophies do not now seem to answer to the complexities of industrial society, the questions of regulation and competition, of technology and society, of economic growth as against the quality of the environment or of city life. Nor do other countries seem to offer examples of a system of beliefs which could effectively answer the new challenges as well as the early pioneering ideology met the problems of the Yishuv. There has been as yet no A. D. Gordon to propound an ideology of work which seems realistic for an urban industrial or postindustrial society. Today's generation may be right in feeling that there are no specific utopias, no ideal future static conditions. In this case, the answer lies in the way the struggle is conducted. But if the complexities of the present and the future do indeed demand unusual ability to analyze and to organize, more than this is required, and the goals go far beyond the immediate problems. As Justice Zilberg wrote in the Shalit case: "We did not take on ourselves the great and very heavy burden of spreading Zionism among the Jews of the world . . . in order merely to set up a small democracy, *poor, grey, and speechless*, with nothing *of its own* to say."[10]

Because Israel sees itself in a unique role, the problem of ideals and realities becomes more poignant, and beliefs more important. Beliefs have helped restrain developing pragmatism, giving meaning and direction to compromises, limiting the roles of special interests, and keeping principles and interests in tenuous balance. Over the decades, overarching goals have given Israelis the content of a strong faith and larger values and long-range goals that can still move people to strive against huge odds.

Without an orientation to the future there will not be the hope needed to search for and find creative solutions. A central question now is how initiative can once again be directed toward development of the society. Many of the original goals of Zionism have been achieved, but others still seem out of reach. The state has solved the problems of many Jews, but there are still the remnants of communities, as in Syria, or large numbers, as in Russia, who need help. Military victories have not brought peace or made it easier to have effective deterrence. Economic growth and a rising standard of living have not brought the hoped-for degree of social cohesion or cultural development, nor have industrialization, unusual agricultural success, and high technological capability brought economic independence. The ingathering of the exiles did not *in itself* lead to integration and the disappearance of differences which had developed during generations of life in vastly different cultural milieus, nor did the *sabra*, because he was born and brought up in Israel, almost effortlessly emerge as the new Jew in the new society. After decades of striving, Israelis are learning that instead of having arrived, they are in the middle of the journey.

Appendixes

Documents

Declaration of Independence
of the State of Israel, 1948

In the Land of Israel the Jewish people came into being. In this Land was shaped their spiritual, religious, and national character. Here they lived in sovereign independence. Here they created a culture of national and universal import, and gave to the world the eternal Book of Books.

Exiled by force, still the Jewish people kept faith with their Land in all the countries of their dispersion, steadfast in their prayer and hope to return and here revive their political freedom.

Fired by this attachment of history and tradition, the Jews in every generation strove to renew their roots in the ancient Homeland, and in recent generations they came home in their multitudes.

Veteran pioneers and defenders, and newcomers braving blockade, they made the wilderness bloom, revived their Hebrew tongue, and built villages and towns. They founded a thriving society, master of its own economy and culture, pursuing peace but able to defend itself, bringing the blessing of progress to all the inhabitants of the Land, dedicated to the attainment of sovereign independence.

In 1897 the First Zionist Congress met at the call of Theodor Herzl, seer of the vision of the Jewish State, and gave public voice to the right of the Jewish people to national restoration in their Land.

This right was acknowledged in the Balfour Declaration on November 2, 1917, and confirmed in the Mandate of the League of Nations, which accorded international validity to the historical connection of the Jewish people with the Land of Israel, and to their right to reestablish their National Home.

The holocaust that in our time destroyed millions of Jews in Europe and proved beyond doubt the compelling need to solve the problem of Jewish homelessness and dependence by the renewal of the Jewish State in the Land of Israel, which would open wide the gates of the Homeland to every Jew and endow the Jewish people with the status of a nation with equality of rights within the family of nations.

Despite every hardship, hindrance and peril, the remnant that survived the grim Nazi slaughter in Europe, together with Jews from other countries, pressed on with their exodus to the Land of Israel and continued to assert their right to a life of dignity, freedom and honest toil in the Homeland of their people.

In the Second World War the Jewish community in the Land of Israel played its full part in the struggle of the nations championing freedom and peace against the Nazi forces of evil. Its war effort and the lives of its soldiers won it the right to be numbered among the founding peoples of the United Nations.

On November 29, 1947, the General Assembly of the United Nations adopted a resolution calling for the establishment of a Jewish State in the Land of Israel, and required the inhabitants themselves to take all measures necessary on their part to carry out the resolution. This recognition by the United Nations of the right of the Jewish people to establish their own State is irrevocable.

It is the natural right of the Jewish people, like any other people, to control their own destiny in their sovereign State.

Accordingly we, the members of the National Council, representing the Jewish people in the Land of Israel and the Zionist Movement, have assembled on the day of the termination of the British Mandate for Palestine, and, by virtue of our natural and historic right and of the resolution of the General Assembly of the United Nations, do hereby proclaim the establishment of a Jewish State in the Land of Israel—the State of Israel.

We resolve that from the moment the Mandate ends, at midnight on the Sabbath, the sixth of Iyar 5708, the fifteenth day of May 1948, until the establishment of the duly elected authorities of the State in accordance with a Constitution to be adopted by the Elected Constituent Assembly not later than October 1, 1948, the National Council shall act as the Provisional Council of State, and its executive arm, the National Administration, shall constitute the Provisional Government of the Jewish State, and the name of that State shall be Israel.

The State of Israel will be open to Jewish immigration and the ingathering of exiles. It will devote itself to developing the Land for the good of all its inhabitants.

It will rest upon foundations of liberty, justice, and peace as envisioned by the Prophets of Israel. It will maintain complete equality of social and political rights for all its citizens, without distinction of creed, race, or sex. It will guarantee freedom of religion and conscience, of language, education, and culture. It will safeguard the Holy Places of all religions. It will be loyal to the principles of the United Nations Charter.

The State of Israel will be prepared to cooperate with the organs and representatives of the United Nations in carrying out the General Assembly resolution of 29 November 1947, and will work for the establishment of the economic union of the whole Land of Israel.

We appeal to the United Nations to assist the Jewish people in the building of their State, and to admit the State of Israel into the family of nations.

Even amidst the violent attacks launched against us for months past, we call upon the sons of the Arab people dwelling in Israel to keep the peace and to play their part in building the State on the basis of full and equal citizenship and due representation in all its institutions, provisional and permanent.

We extend the hand of peace and good-neighborliness to all the states around us and to their peoples, and we call upon them to cooperate in mutual helpfulness with the independent Jewish nation in its Land. The State of Israel is prepared to make its contribution in a concerted effort for the advancement of the entire Middle East.

We call upon the Jewish people throughout the Diaspora to join forces with us in immigration and construction, and to be at our right hand in the great endeavor to fulfill the age-old longing for the redemption of Israel.

We trust in the Rock of Israel, we set out hands in witness to this Declaration at this session of the Provisional Council of State, on the soil of the homeland, in the city of Tel Aviv, this Sabbath Eve, the fifth day of Iyar 5708, the fourteenth day of May 1948.

David Ben Gurion	Herzl Vardi	David Zvi Pinkas
Daniel Auster	Rachel Cohen	Aharon Zisling
Mordekhai Bentov	Rabbi Kalman Kahana	Moshe Kolodny
Yitzchak Ben Zvi	Saadia Kobashi	Eliezer Kaplan
Eliyahu Berligne	Rabbi Yitzchak Meir Levin	Abraham Katznelson
Fritz Bernstein	Meir David Loewenstein	Felix Rosenblueth
Rabbi Wolf Gold	Zvi Luria	David Remez
Meir Grabovsky	Golda Myerson	Berl Repetur
Yitzchak Gruenbaum	Nachum Nir	Mordekhai Shattner
Abraham Granovsky	Zvi Segal	Ben Zion Sternberg
Eliyahu Dobkin	Rabbi Yehuda Leib	Behor Shitreet
Meir Wilner-Kovner	Hacohen Fishman	Moshe Shapira
Zerach Wahrhaftig		Moshe Shertok

The "Status Quo" Letter by David Ben Gurion

The following letter was written by David Ben Gurion, in his capacity as Chairman of the Jewish Agency Executive, to Rabbi J. L. Maimon, leader of the Agudat Israel in 1947:*

The Executive of the Jewish Agency was informed by its Chairman on your request with regard to Personal Status Law, the Shabbat, Education and Kashrut in the future State of Israel. The Chairman of the Executive had already informed you that the Jewish Agency or any other body has not the authority to determine now the Constitution of the future State. The establishment of the State needs the United Nations Resolution, and it is doubtful if freedom of conscience would not be guaranteed to all citizens. It is also important to make clear that our purpose is not to establish a theocracy. In the future Jewish State we shall also have non-Jewish citizens and it is our obligation to guarantee their equal rights, and not to use coercion or to discriminate in religious or other matters. We were happy to hear that you understand that at this time it is impossible to have an authoritative body that will determine the future constitution, and that the future State will be free in certain matters to determine its Constitution and the regime as will be decided by its citizens.

At the same time the Executive values your demands, and knows that they are a matter of concern not only to Agudat Israel but also to other Orthodox groups that are members of the Zionist Organization as well as to known partisans. The Executive understands your demand to be informed what is the Executive's attitude in those matters, and what it intends to do. The Executive invested the authority in the hands of the undersigned to respond to your demands on:

a. *Shabbat:* It is clear that the official day of rest of the Jewish State will be on Shabbat; naturally the Christians and other religions will be granted the Shabbat on their days.
b. *Kashrut:* All necessary steps will be taken to guarantee that any State kitchen for Jews will be kosher.
c. *Personal Status Law:* The members of the Executive understand the importance of the question and the problems involved. All the bodies which are represented on the Executive will do all to satisfy the religious needs of the Orthodox, to prevent the division of the people.
d. *Education:* The autonomy of the different educational systems (as now exists) will be guaranteed. No coercion from the authorities in matters of religion, and religious conscience will be applied. Naturally, the State will determine minimum studies in Hebrew, mathematics, history, etc., and will supervise them, but they will have the freedom to run the educational system according to their belief.

* Zionist Archives S/25/1446. Translation by David Sommer.

The Camp David Accords—
A Framework for Peace in the Middle East

Mohammed Anwar al-Sadat, President of the Arab Republic of Egypt, and Menachem Begin, Prime Minister of Israel, met with Jimmy Carter, President of the United States of America at Camp David from Sept. 5 to Sept. 17, 1978, and have agreed on the following framework for peace in the Middle East. They invite other parties to the Arab-Israeli conflict to adhere to it:

Preamble

The search for peace in the Middle East must be guided by the following:

The agreed basis for a peaceful settlement of the conflict between Israel and its neighbours is U.N. Security Council Resolution 242 in all its parts.

After four wars during 30 years, despite intensive humane efforts, the Middle East, which is the cradle of civilization and the birthplace of three great religions, does not yet enjoy the blessings of peace. The people of the Middle East yearn for peace, so that the vast human and natural resources of the region can be turned to the pursuits of peace and so that this area can become a model for coexistence and cooperation among nations.

The historic initiative by President Sadat in visiting Jerusalem and the reception accorded to him by the parliament, government and people of Israel, and the reciprocal visit of Prime Minister Begin to Ismailia, the peace proposals made by both leaders, as well as the warm reception of these missions by the peoples of both countries, have created an unprecedented opportunity for peace which must not be lost if this generation and future generations are to be spared the tragedies of war.

The provisions of the Charter of the United Nations and the other accepted norms of international law and legitimacy now provide accepted standards for the conduct of relations between all states.

To achieve a relationship of peace, in the spirit of Article 2 of the U.N. Charter, future negotiations between Israel and any neighbour prepared to negotiate peace and security with it, are necessary for the purpose of carrying out all the provisions and principles of Resolutions 242 and 338.

Peace requires respect for the sovereignty, territorial integrity and political independence of every state in the area and their right to live in peace within secure and recognized boundaries free from threats or acts of force. Progress toward that goal can accelerate movement toward a new era of reconciliation in the Middle East marked by cooperation in promoting economic development, in maintaining stability and in assuring security.

Security is enhanced by a relationship of peace and by cooperation between nations which enjoy normal relations. In addition, under the terms of peace treaties, the parties can, on the basis of reciprocity, agree to special security arrangements such as demilitarized zones, limited armaments areas, early warning stations, the presence of international forces, liaison, agreed measures for monitoring, and other arrangements that they agree are useful.

Taking these factors into account, the parties are determined to reach a just, comprehensive, and durable settlement of the Middle East conflict through the conclusion of peace treaties based on Security Council Resolutions 242 and 338 in all their parts. Their purpose is to achieve peace and good neighborly relations. They recognize that, for peace to endure, it must involve all those who have been most deeply affected by the conflict. They therefore agree that this framework as appropriate is intended by them to constitute a basis for peace not only between Egypt and Israel, but also between Israel and each of its other neighbors which is prepared to negotiate peace with Israel on this basis.

With that objective in mind, they have agreed to proceed as follows:

A. West Bank and Gaza

1. Egypt, Israel, Jordan and the representatives of the Palestinian People should participate in negotiations on the resolution of the Palestinian problem in all its aspects. To achieve that objective, negotiations relating to the West Bank and Gaza should proceed in three stages.

(A) Egypt and Israel agree that, in order to ensure a peaceful and orderly transfer of authority, and taking into account the security concerns of all the parties, there should be transitional arrangements for the West Bank and Gaza for a period not exceeding five years. In order to provide full autonomy to the inhabitants, under these arrangements the Israeli military government and its civilian administration will be withdrawn as soon as a self-governing authority has been freely elected by the inhabitants of these areas to replace the existing military government.

To negotiate the details of a transitional arrangement, the government of Jordan will be invited to join the negotiations on the basis of this framework. These new arrangements should give due consideration to both the principle of self-government by the inhabitants of these territories and to the legitimate security concerns of the parties involved.

(B) Egypt, Israel, and Jordan will agree on the modalities for establishing the elected self-governing authority in the West Bank and Gaza. The delegations of Egypt and Jordan may include Palestinians from the West Bank and Gaza or other Palestinians as mutually agreed. The parties will negotiate an agreement which will define the powers and responsibilities of the self-governing authority to be exercised in the West Bank and Gaza. A withdrawal of Israeli armed forces will take place and there will be a redeployment of the remaining Israeli forces into specified security locations.

The agreement will also include arrangements for assuring internal and external security and public order. A strong local police force will be established, which may include Jordanian citizens. In addition, Israeli and Jordanian forces will participate in joint patrols and in the manning of control posts to assure the security of the borders.

(C) When the self-governing authority (administrative council) in the West Bank and Gaza is established and inaugurated, the transitional period of five years will begin. As soon as possible, but not later than the third year after the beginning of the transitional period, negotiations will take place to determine the final status of the West Bank and Gaza and its relationship with its neighbours, and to conclude a peace treaty between Israel and Jordan by the end of the transitional period.

These negotiations will be conducted among Egypt, Israel, Jordan, and the elected representatives of the inhabitants of the West Bank and Gaza. Two separate but related committees will be convened, one committee, consisting of representatives of the four parties which will negotiate and agree on the final status of the West Bank and Gaza, and its relationship with its neighbours, and the second committee, consisting of representatives of Israel and representatives of Jordan to be joined by the elected representatives of the inhabitants of the West Bank and Gaza, to negotiate the peace treaty between Israel and Jordan, taking into account the agreement reached on the final status of the West Bank and Gaza.

The negotiations shall be based on all the provisions and principles of U.N. Security Council Resolution 242. The negotiations will resolve, among other matters, the location of the boundaries and the nature of the security arrangements.

The solution from the negotiations must also recognize the legitimate rights of the Palestinian people and their just requirements. In this way, the Palestinians will participate in the determination of their own future through:

1. The negotiations among Egypt, Israel, Jordan and the representatives of the inhabitants of the West Bank and Gaza to agree on the final status of the West Bank and Gaza and other outstanding issues by the end of the transitional period.
2. Submitting their agreement to a vote by the elected representatives of the inhabitants of the West Bank and Gaza.
3. Providing for the elected representatives of the inhabitants of the West Bank and Gaza to decide how they shall govern themselves consistent with the provisions of their agreement.
4. Participating as stated above in the work of the committee negotiating the peace treaty between Israel and Jordan.

2. All necessary measures will be taken and provisions made to assure the security of Israel and its neighbours during the transitional period and beyond. To assist in providing such security, a strong local police force will be constituted by the self-governing authority. It will be composed of inhabitants of the West Bank and Gaza. The police will maintain continuing

liaison on internal security matters with the designated Israeli, Jordanian and Egyptian officers.

3. During the transitional period, the representatives of Egypt, Israel, Jordan and the self-governing authority will constitute a continuing committee to decide by agreement on the modalities of admission of persons displaced from the West Bank and Gaza in 1967, together with necessary measures to prevent disruption and disorder. Other matters of common concern may also be dealt with by this committee.

4. Egypt and Israel will work with each other and with other interested parties to establish agreed procedures for a prompt, just and permanent implementation of the resolution of the refugee problem.

B. Egypt-Israel

1. Egypt and Israel undertake not to resort to the threat or the use of force to settle disputes. Any disputes shall be settled by peaceful means in accordance with the provisions of Article 33 of the Charter of the United Nations.

2. In order to achieve peace between them, the parties agreed to negotiate in good faith with a goal of concluding within three months from the signing of this Framework a peace treaty between them, while inviting the other parties to the conflict to proceed simultaneously to negotiate and conclude similar peace treaties with a view to achieving a comprehensive peace in the area. The Framework for the conclusion of a peace treaty between Egypt and Israel will govern the peace negotiations between them. The parties will agree on the modalities and the timetable for the implementation of their obligations under the treaty.

C. Associated Principles

1. Egypt and Israel state that the principles and provisions described below should apply to peace treaties between Israel and each of its neighbours—Egypt, Jordan, Syria and Lebanon.

2. Signatories shall establish among themselves relationships normal to states at peace with one another. To this end, they should undertake to abide by all the provisions of the Charter of the United Nations. Steps to be taken in this respect include:

A. Full recognition,
B. Abolishing economic boycotts,
C. Guaranteeing that under their jurisdiction the citizens of the other parties shall enjoy the protection of the due process of law.

3. Signatories should explore possibilities for economic development in the context of final peace treaties, with the objective of contributing to the atmosphere of peace, cooperation and friendship which is their common goal.

4. Claims commissions may be established for the mutual settlement of all financial claims.

5. The United States shall be invited to participate in the talks on matters related to the modalities of the implementation of the agreements and working out the timetable for the carrying out of the obligations of the parties.

6. The United Nations Security Council shall be requested to endorse the peace treaties and ensure that their provisions shall not be violated. The permanent members of the Security Council shall be requested to underwrite the peace treaties and ensure respect for their provisions. They shall also be requested to conform their policies and actions with the undertakings contained in this framework.

For the Government of the   For the Government
Arab Republic of Egypt: of Israel:

Witnessed by:

Jimmy Carter, President of the United States of America

A Framework for the Conclusion of a Peace Treaty between Israel and Egypt

In order to achieve peace between them, Israel and Egypt agree to negotiate in good faith with a goal of concluding within three months of the signing of this framework a peace treaty between them.

It is agreed that:

The site of the negotiations will be under a United Nations flag at a location or locations to be mutually agreed.

All of the principles of UN Resolution 242 will apply in this resolution of the dispute between Israel and Egypt.

Unless otherwise mutually agreed, terms of the peace treaty will be implemented between 2 and 3 years after the peace treaty is signed.

The following matters are agreed between the parties:

a. The full exercise of Egyptian sovereignty up to the internationally recognized border between Egypt and Mandated Palestine;

b. The withdrawal of Israeli armed forces from the Sinai;

c. The use of airfields left by the Israelis near El Arish, Rafah, Ras-en-Naqb and Sharm-el-Sheikh for civilian purposes only, including possible commercial use by all nations;

d. The right of free passage by ships of Israel through the Gulf of Suez and the Suez Canal on the basis of the Constantinople Convention of 1888 applying to all nations; the Strait of Tiran and the Gulf of Aqaba are international waterways to be open to all nations for unimpeded and non-suspendible freedom of navigation and overflight;

e. The construction of a highway between the Sinai and Jordan near Eilat with guaranteed free and peaceful passage by Egypt and Jordan; and

f. The stationing of military forces listed below.

Stationing of Forces

A. No more than one division (mechanized or infantry) of Egyptian armed forces will be stationed within an area lying approximately 50 kilometres east of the Gulf of Suez and the Suez Canal.

B. Only UN forces and civil police equipped with light weapons to perform normal police functions will be stationed within an area lying west of the international border and the Gulf of Aqaba, varying in width from 20 km. to 40 km.

C. In the area within three kilometres east of the international border there will be Israeli limited military forces not to exceed 4 infantry battalions and UN observers.

D. Border patrol units, not to exceed 3 battalions, will supplement the civil police in maintaining order in the area not included above.

The exact demarcation of the above areas will be decided during the peace negotiations.

Early warning stations may exist to insure compliance with the terms of the agreement.

UN forces will be stationed:

A. In part of the area in the Sinai lying within about 20 km. of the Mediterranean Sea, and adjacent to the international border, and

B. In the Sharm-el-Sheikh area to insure freedom of passage through the Strait of Tiran; and these forces will not be removed unless such removal is approved by the Security Council of the UN with a unanimous vote of the five permanent members.

After a peace treaty is signed, and after the interim withdrawal is complete, normal relations will be established between Egypt and Israel, including: Full recognition, including diplomatic, economic and cultural relations; termination of economic boycotts and barriers to the free movement of goods and people; and mutual protection of citizens by the due process of law.

Interim withdrawal

Between 3 months and 9 months after the signing of the peace treaty, all Israeli forces will withdraw east of a line extending from a point east of El Arish to Ras Mohammed, the exact location of this line to be determined by mutual agreement.

For the Government of the   For the Government
Arab Republic of Egypt: of Israel:

Witnessed by:

Jimmy Carter, President of the United States of America

Annex to the Framework Agreements— United Nations Security Council Resolutions 242 and 338

Resolution 242 of November 22, 1967

The Security Council,
Expressing its continuing concern with the grave situation in the Middle East,
Emphasizing the inadmissibility of the acquisition of territory by war and the need to work for a just and lasting peace in which every State in the area can live in security,
Emphasizing further that all Member States in their acceptance of the Charter of the United Nations have undertaken a commitment to act in accordance with Article 2 of the Charter,

1. *Affirms* that the fulfilment of Charter principles requires the establishment of a just and lasting peace in the Middle East which should include the application of both the following principles:

   i. Withdrawal of Israeli armed forces from territories occupied in the recent conflict;
   ii. Termination of all claims or states of belligerency and respect for and acknowledgement of the sovereignty, territorial integrity and political independence of every State in the area and their right to live in peace within secure and recognized boundaries free from threats or acts of force;

2. *Affirms further* the necessity

   a. For guaranteeing freedom of navigation through international waterways in the area;

b. For achieving a just settlement of the refugee problem;

c. For guaranteeing the territorial inviolability and political independence of every State in the area, through measures including the establishment of demilitarized zones;

3. *Requests* the Secretary-General to designate a Special Representative to proceed to the Middle East to establish and maintain contacts with the States concerned in order to promote agreement and assist efforts to achieve a peaceful and accepted settlement in accordance with the provisions and principles of this resolution.

4. *Requests* the Secretary-General to report to the Security Council on the progress of the efforts of the Special Representative as soon as possible.

Resolution 338 of October 22, 1973

The Security Council

1. *Calls upon* all parties to the present fighting to cease all firing and terminate all military activity immediately, no later than 12 hours after the moment of the adoption of this decision, in the positions they now occupy;

2. *Calls upon* the parties concerned to start immediately after the cease-fire the implementation of Security Council Resolution 242 (1967) in all of its parts;

3. *Decides* that, immediately and concurrently with the cease-fire, negotiations start between the parties concerned under appropriate auspices aimed at establishing a just and durable peace in the Middle East.

Exchanges of Letters

All letters from Mr. Carter are dated September 22, 1978, all the other letters are dated September 17, 1978.

The President
Camp David
Thurmont, Maryland

September 17, 1978

Dear Mr. President:

I have the honor to inform you that during two weeks after my return home I will submit a motion before Israel's Parliament (the Knesset) to decide on the following question:

If during the negotiations to conclude a peace treaty between Israel and Egypt all outstanding issues are agreed upon, "are you in favor of the removal of the Israeli settlers from the northern and southern Sinai areas or are you in favor of keeping the aforementioned settlers in those areas?"

The vote, Mr. President, on this issue will be completely free from the usual Parliamentary Party discipline to the effect that although the coalition is being now supported by 70 members out of 120, every member of the Knesset, as I believe, both of the Government and the Opposition benches will be enabled to vote in accordance with his own conscience.

Sincerely yours,

Menachem Begin

His Excellency
Anwar Al-Sadat
President of the Arab
    Republic of Egypt
Cairo

September 22, 1978

Dear Mr. President:

I transmit herewith a copy of a letter to me from Prime Minister Begin setting forth how he proposes to present the issue of the Sinai settlements to the Knesset for the latter's decision.

In this connection, I understand from your letter that Knesset approval to withdraw all Israeli settlers from Sinai according to a timetable within the period specified for the implementation of the peace treaty is a prerequisite to any negotiations on a peace treaty between Egypt and Israel.

Sincerely,

Jimmy Carter

Enclosure:
Letter from Prime Minister Begin

His Excellency Jimmy Carter
President of the United States

September 17, 1978

Dear Mr. President:

In connection with the "Framework for a Settlement in Sinai" to be signed tonight, I would like to reaffirm the position of the Arab Republic of Egypt with respect to the settlements:

1. All Israeli settlers must be withdrawn from Sinai according to a timetable within the period specified for the implementation of the peace treaty.

2. Agreement by the Israeli Government and its constitutional institutions to this basic principle is therefore a prerequisite to starting peace negotiations for concluding a peace treaty.

3. If Israel fails to meet this commitment, the "framework" shall be void and invalid.

Sincerely,

Mohamed Anwar El Sadat

His Excellency
Menachem Begin
Prime Minister of Israel

Dear Mr. Prime Minister:

I have received your letter of September 17, 1978, describing how you intend to place the question of the future of Israeli settlements in Sinai before the Knesset for its decision.

Enclosed is a copy of President Sadat's letter to me on this subject:

Sincerely,

Jimmy Carter

Enclosure:
Letter from President Sadat

His Excellency Jimmy Carter
President of the United States

September 17, 1978

Dear Mr. President:

I am writing you to reaffirm the position of the Arab Republic of Egypt with respect to Jerusalem.

1. Arab Jerusalem is an integral part of the West Bank. Legal and historical Arab rights in the city must be respected and restored.

2. Arab Jerusalem should be under Arab sovereignty.

3. The Palestinian inhabitants of Arab Jerusalem are entitled to exercise their legitimate national rights, being part of the Palestinian People in the West Bank.

4. Relevant Security Council resolutions, particularly Resolutions 242

and 267, must be applied with regard to Jerusalem. All the measures taken by Israel to alter the status of the City are null and void and should be rescinded.

5. All peoples must have free access to the City and enjoy the free exercises of worship and the right to visit and transit to the holy places without distinction or discrimination.

6. The holy places of each faith may be placed under the administration and control of their representatives.

7. Essential functions in the City should be undivided and a joint municipal council composed of an equal number of Arab and Israeli members can supervise the carrying out of these functions. In this way, the city shall be undivided.

Sincerely,

Mohamed Anwar El Sadat

The President
Camp David
Thurmont, Maryland

17 September 1978

Dear Mr. President:

I have the honor to inform you, Mr. President, that on 28 June 1967—Israel's parliament (The Knesset) promulgated and adopted a law to the effect: "the Government is empowered by a decree to apply the law, the jurisdiction and administration of the State to any part of Eretz Israel (Land of Israel—Palestine), as stated in that decree."

On the basis of this law, the government of Israel decreed in July 1967 that Jerusalem is one city indivisible, the capital of the State of Israel.

Sincerely,

Menachem Begin

His Excellency
Anwar al-Sadat
President of the Arab
   Republic of Egypt
Cairo

Dear Mr. President:

I have received your letter of September 17, 1978, setting forth the Egyptian position on Jerusalem. I am transmitting a copy of that letter to Prime Minister Begin for his information.

The position of the United States on Jerusalem remains as stated by Ambassador Goldberg in the United Nations General Assembly on July 14, 1967, and subsequently by Ambassador Yost in the United Nations Security Council on July 1, 1969.

Sincerely,

Jimmy Carter

His Excellency
Jimmy Carter
President of the United States
The White House
Washington, D.C.

September 17, 1978

Dear Mr. President:

In connection with the "Framework for Peace in the Middle East," I am writing you this letter to inform you of the position of the Arab Republic of Egypt, with respect to the implementation of the comprehensive settlement.

To ensure the implementation of the provisions related to the West Bank and Gaza and in order to safeguard the legitimate rights of the Palestinian people, Egypt will be prepared to assume the Arab role emanating from these provisions, following consultations with Jordan and the representatives of the Palestinian people.

Sincerely,

Mohamed Anwar El Sadat

His Excellency
Menachem Begin
Prime Minister of Israel

Dear Mr. Prime Minister:

I hereby acknowledge that you have informed me as follows:

A. In each paragraph of the Agreed Framework Document the expressions "Palestinians" or "Palestinian People" are being and will be construed and understood by you as "Palestinian Arabs."

B. In each paragraph in which the expression "West Bank" appears it is being, and will be, understood by the Government of Israel as Judea and Samaria.

Sincerely,

Jimmy Carter

Knesset Election Results

The Election of 1981 and Its Outcome

In the campaign, an overconfident Alignment at first lost valuable time and public confidence through internal struggles for the future Cabinet roles. Only on the eve of the election did desperation lead to the appointment of Yitzhak Rabin as Defense Minister in the shadow Cabinet. No new direction or appeal came forth. The top-down, guild-type process of candidate selection continued as before, and reinforced Labor's historic lack of appeal or effective contact with the disadvantaged and less educated. For example, the Asian/Africans on the Alignment list were *appointed*, not *elected* by the Party Central Committee as the Herut candidates were. Even so, the Alignment list, despite the human resources available, seemed to be the lackluster result of group maneuvers.

Overconfidence led to a tactical error of holding the Histadrut elections in April. In these, the Likud polled more than 26 percent, close to the 1977 result, showing overall strength and continued appeal in the *shechunot*, or city neighborhoods, and the development towns. Late in the campaign attempts were made to disrupt Alignment rallies by force, Peres was greeted with fierce chants of "Begin! Begin!" and in one place he was forced to withdraw. The Alignment's reaction was to show itself as "the better Israel," and it seemed to be aiming its campaign at the better-educated. This served to widen the gap between Labor and the masses.

Peres did an impressive job of putting the party organization back together after the 1977 debacle, but the Likud had the campaign initiative. It capitalized on the historic memories of disaffection, and to many Likud supporters, the Alignment was still the establishment even though in opposition. Of all of the factors, Begin's populist mass appeal, nationalism, and confidence that he had the answers were predominant.

Events and government actions were also very important. With the dissidents gone, the Cabinet seemed united. National feelings were strengthened by a crisis in Lebanon, in which Syrian helicopters, used in attacks on Christian forces, were shot down by Israel, following which Syria introduced antiaircraft missiles. Chancelor Schmidt of Germany offered arms to Saudia Arabia, and was publicly chastised by Begin for "forgetting the Holocaust," as was the French government for espousing the PLO. In June, a raid on the Baghdad atomic reactor and a summit meeting with Sadat reinforced the image of a strong leader. The political wars seemed to restore Begin, like Golda Meir before him, to robust health and boundless energy.

Much of the Likud vote was ascribed to the actions of its new Minister of Finance, Yoram Aridor, who increased the public's spending power and slowed inflation, for the short term, by restoring subsidies and cutting import duties.

The composition of the Tenth Knesset in 1981 was, for the government, Likud, 48; NRP (Mafdal), 6; Aguda, 4; and Tami, 3. Supporting the government on most issues was the Tehiya (Rebirth) Movement, 3. In opposition were Alignment, 47, plus the Citizens Rights Movement, 1, altogether 48; Telem, 2; Shinui (Change), 2; DFPE (formerly Rakah), 4.

The new lists were Telem, Moshe Dayan's party, whose central plank was the initiation of autonomy in Judea, Samaria, and Gaza on Israel's part alone, without dependence on reaching an agreement with Egypt; Tehiya, which aimed to cancel the return of Sinai under the Camp David agreements and to intensify settlement; and Tami, a religious-ethnic list formed at the last minute by Aharon Abuhatzeira, Minister of Religious Affairs. Shortly before the deadline for filing, Abuhatzeira was acquitted on charges of bribery for lack of evidence, but with judicial expressions of opprobrium regarding the ministry's administrative arrangements. When his request for a higher place for himself and his associates on the NRP list was refused, he formed a list aimed at religious and ethnic support, mainly of North Africans, hoping to draw Asian/African Mafdal supporters. The results of Tami and Telem (Dayan) fell far short of expectations. The Shinui (Change) descendant of the DMC gained two seats, while the Democrats dissolved, as Yigael Yadin retired from active politics.

The DFPE (formerly Rakah) lost one seat, winning four, as more Arabs voted for the Alignment, for the first time in thirty years. Due to Abuhatzeira's split with the NRP leadership, a party with principally ethnic appeal won Knesset seats (Tami, 3). Other ethnic lists failed to gain any seats, their combined vote equaling much less than 1 percent. The small parties apparently lost heavily in the last days before the elections, as the Zionist left and many supporters of the center and a good part of the floating vote swung to the Alignment, hoping to stop the Likud (indicated by a longitudinal analysis of opinion in 1980–81 by the Israel Institute for Applied Social Research, reported in the *Institute Bulletin,* No. 55, August 1981).

Arab voting participation dropped from 74 percent in 1977 to 68 percent in 1981. This is ascribed partly to the timing of the election, at the harvest season, and partly to the exhortation of extreme groups to boycott the elections. The estimated results were: Rakah, 37 percent; Labor Alignment, 29 percent; Likud, 6.4 percent; NRP (Mafdal), 3.4 percent. (References: Ra'anan Cohen, *The Elections to the Tenth Knesset in the Arab Sector* (Heb., mimeo), Tel Aviv, The Israel Labor Party, 1981; and *Leket* No. 6 (Heb.), Jerusalem, Adviser on Arab Affairs, The Prime Minister's Office, 1981)

Rakah's loss was ascribed to several factors; the lack of new leaders or message, and a rigidity of doctrine and organization; although "radical" (it opposed the peace with Egypt, and was endorsed by the PLO), Rakah was injured by the abstention from voting of more extreme university students and graduates. The Labor Alignment appealed directly to Arab voters, no longer supporting "affiliated" Arab lists, and Arab candidates were included in the Alignment list and those of other "Zionist" parties.

TABLE B. Knesset Election Results by Parties and Broad Ideological Groupings

Knesset / Year	I 1949	II 1951	III 1955	IV 1959	V 1961	VI 1965	VII 1969	VIII 1973	IX 1977
Noncommunist, left of center									
Mapam	19	15	9	9	9	8	—	—	—
Ahdut Ha'Avoda	—	—	10	7	8	— (brace)	— (brace)	— (brace)	— (brace)
Mapai	46	45	40	47	42	} 45[9]	} 56[1]	} 51	} 32
Rafi	—	—	—	—	—	10	—	—	—
State List[2]	—	—	—	—	—	—	4	—	—
Citizens Rights Movement	—	—	—	—	—	—	—	3	1
Sheli (the Camp of Peace for Israel)	—	—	—	—	—	—	—	—	2[6]
Labor-affiliated Arab lists	2	5	5	5	4	4	4	3	1
Total seats	67	65	64	68	63	67	64	57	36
Percent of vote	(52.1)	(54.5)	(53.9)	(54.9)	(52.3)	(54.6)	(52.8)	(45.1)	(28.8)
Center parties									
Democratic Movement for change	—	—	—	—	—	—	—	—	15
Liberals[3]	7	20	13	8	} 17	—	—	—	—
Progressives (later Independent Liberals)[10]	5	4	5	6	(brace)	5	4	4	1
Total seats	12	24	18	14	17	5	4	4	16
Percent of vote	(9.3)	(19.6)	(14.6)	(10.8)	(13.6)	(3.75)	(3.2)	(3.6)	(12.8)
Center-right									
Herut	14	8	15	17	17	— (brace)	— (brace)	— (brace)	— (brace)
Herut-Liberals (Gahal)	—	—	—	—	—	} 26[3]	} 26	— (brace)	— (brace)
Free Center[4]	—	—	—	—	—	—	2	— (brace)	— (brace)
Likud (from 1973)	—	—	—	—	—	—	—	} 39	} 45[8]
Total seats	14	8	15	17	17	26	28	39	45
Percent of Vote	(11.5)	(6.6)	(12.6)	(13.6)	(13.7)	(21.3)	(22.9)	(30.2)	(35.3)

Knesset Year	I 1949	II 1951	III 1955	IV 1959	V 1961	VI 1965	VII 1969	VIII 1973	IX 1977
Communists									
Israel Communists	4	5	6	3	5	1	1	1[5]	—
Rakah	—	—	—	—	—	3	3	4	5
Religious parties									
Mizrachi and Poalei Mizrachi[7]	}16	10	11	12	12	11	12	10	12
Agudat Israel		3	}6	}6	}6	4	}6	}5	4
Poalei Agudat Israel		2				2			1
Total seats	16	15	17	18	18	17	18	15	17
Percent of Vote	(12.2)	(11.9)	(13.8)	(14.6)	(15.4)	(14.1)	(14.7)	(12.1)	(13.9)
Other lists	7	3	—	—	—	1	2	—	1

1. In 1969, 1973, and 1977, the Alignment included Labor and Mapam.

2. The State list, which became ideologically closer to the right, comprised mainly former Rafi members who did not join Labor. Ben Gurion led the list in 1969, and it has for that year been included in the left-of-center category. In the 1973 and 1977 elections, it was part of the Likud (in 1977 within La'am).

3. In 1965, the Independent Liberals (the former Progressives) left the Liberal Party, which joined with Herut in forming the Gahal Alignment. The parties in Gahal and the Likud continued their separate organizations. From the time the Liberals joined with Herut, we have included them in the center-right group.

4. The Free Center split from Herut to run separately in 1969. In 1973 it was in the Likud, and in 1977 many of its members joined the Democratic Movement for Change. Others, together with the Land of Israel Movement and Rafi, formed La'am within the Likud.

5. Moked was a union of the Israel Communists (the predominantly Jewish party) and the Zionist-Socialist (but noncommunist) Blue and Red Movement. Since the Knesset representative of Moked and its political leader, Meir Pa'il, was from Blue and Red, it could be included in the noncommunist left.

6. Sheli, or The Camp of Peace for Israel, is a union (from 1977) of Moked with the group formerly in Labor headed by Lova Eliav and Uri Avineri's Olam Hazeh—New Force.

7. The Mizrachi and Poalei Mizrachi united in 1956 to form the National Religious Party, called by its acronym, Mafdal.

8. Includes the two seats won by Ariel Sharon's list, which joined the Likud as members of Herut after the elections.

9. In 1965, Mapai and Ahdut Ha'Avoda ran on a joint list. (See Figure 1.2.)

10. In 1961, the General Zionists and Progressives ran as the Liberal Party. From 1965, the Independent Liberal and Liberal parties were separate. (See Figure 1.3.)

Cabinet Coalitions

TABLE C. Coalitions: 1949–81

Year	Prime Minister	Coalition Membership	Size of Knesset Delegation Support
1949[E]	Ben Gurion	Mapai * (48), Religious Front (16), Progressives (5), Sephardim (4)	
1950	Ben Gurion	Mapai (48), Religious Front (16), Progressives (5), Sephardim (4)	73
			73
1951[E]	Ben Gurion	Mapai (50), Mizrachi + Hapoel Hamizrachi (10), Aguda (8), Poalei Aguda (5) + Sephardim (2)	67
1952	Ben Gurion	Mapai (50), Mizrachi + Hapoel Hamizrachi (10), General Zionists (20), Progressives (4)	84
1954	Sharett	Mapai (50), Mizrachi + Hapoel Hamizrachi (10), General Zionists (20), Progressives (4)	84
1955	Sharett	Mapai (50), Mizrachi + Hapoel Hamizrachi (10), Progressives (4)	64
1955[E]	Ben Gurion	Mapai (45), Mizrachi + Hapoel Hamizrachi (11), Ahdut Ha'Avoda (10), Mapam (9), Progressives (4)	80

TABLE C.   Coalitions: 1949–81 (con't.)

Year	Prime Minister	Coalition Membership	Size of Knesset Delegation Support
1958	Ben Gurion	Mapai (45), Mafdal (11),** Ahdut Ha'Avoda (10), Mapam, (9), Progressives (4)	80
1959[E]	Ben Gurion	Mapai (52), Mafdal (12), Ahdut Ha'Avoda (7), Mapam (9), Progressives (6)	86
1961[E]	Ben Gurion	Mapai (46), Mafdal (12), Poalei Aguda (2), Ahdut Ha'Avoda (8)	68
1963	Eshkol	Mapai (46), Mafdal (12), Poalei Aguda (2), Ahdut Ha'Avoda (8)	68
1964	Eshkol	Mapai (46), Mafdal (12), Poalei Aguda (2), Ahdut Ha'Avoda (8), Independent Liberals (5)	73
1966[E]	Eshkol	Alignment * (49), Mapam (8), Mafdal (11), Poalei Aguda (2), Independent Liberals (5)	75
1967	Eshkol	Alignment (49), Mapam (8), Mafdal (11), Poalei Aguda (2), Independent Liberals (5), Rafi (10), Gahal (26)	111
1969	Meir	Alignment (60), Mafdal (12), Independent Liberals (4), Gahal (26)	102
1970	Meir	Alignment (60), Mafdal (12), Independent Liberals (4)	76
1974[E]	Meir	Alignment (54), Mafdal (10), Independent Liberals (4)	68
1974	Rabin	Alignment (54), Civil Rights (3), Independent Liberals (4)	61
1974	Rabin	Alignment (54), Mafdal (10), Independent Liberals (4)	68
1977[E]	Begin To October 1977	Likud (45), Dayan (1), Mafdal (12), Aguda (4)	62
	From October 1977	Likud (45), Dayan (1), Mafdal (12), Aguda (4), DMC (15)	77
1981[E]	Begin	Likud (48), Mafdal (6), Tami (3), Aguda (4)	61

[E] Formed following an election.
* Includes allied Arab lists.
** Mizrachi and Hapoel Hamizrachi united to form Mafdal (NRP) in 1956.

Cabinet Crises

The term "crisis" is used for the resignation of a Cabinet or of the Prime Minister (which automatically means that the Cabinet as a whole has resigned). Some crises are "near misses," and the rift is resolved. If a Cabinet resigns at a time which falls between scheduled elections, the President then asks a member of the Knesset to form a new Cabinet, as he would do following an election. If this is not achieved, an election is called. The outgoing Cabinet continues as a caretaker government until a new Cabinet has been approved by the Knesset. New Cabinets have been formed in the following circumstances:

The First Knesset (1949–51)

The two crises in this period were over control and direction of the education of the large number of immigrant children. Both Labor and the orthodox sought as much influence as possible, while Ben Gurion himself wanted a unified national system. The religious parties defined true religious education as that under the control of the Mizrachi or the Aguda. Labor used its extensive political organization, together with the establishment of a "labor-religious" trend, to enroll as many children as possible in Labor movement schools. The coalitions of the first Cabinets were narrow, and could not last under these tensions. The *First Cabinet* ended its tenure in 1950, when the religious parties forced a crisis, ostensibly over a government proposal to reorganize the services of supply and rationing. After some compromise on education, Ben Gurion formed a very similar *Second Cabinet.* Shortly thereafter, in 1951, the Knesset brought down the government when the religious parties voted with the opposition to censure educational policy. Never since has a government actually resigned because of an adverse Knesset vote.

The Second Knesset (1951–55)

The *Third Cabinet*, 1951–52, was again a narrow coalition, after an initial Mapai–religious front agreement to a one-year moratorium on educational changes, during which policy would be reviewed. At the end of the year, the Aguda left the government when Mapai proposed to conscript orthodox girls for national nonmilitary service and to unify the several school trends. Ben Gurion then resigned, forming the *Fourth Cabinet* (1952–53) on a broad basis: the General Zionists, the Mizrachi, and the Progressives. Educational organization was resolved, and the new unified national system comprised both religious and secular schools. Soon thereafter the General Zionists used their new electoral weight of twenty seats to protest against a Mapai Central Committee resolution which favored the use of socialist hymns and red flags, if the parents wanted to, on such occasions as the First of May. The General Zionist threat to leave the Cabinet was withdrawn when Ben Gurion agreed to ignore the Central Committee recommendation. In this crisis the Mizrachi stood by Mapai—and from then until 1976 was Labor's faithful partner.

The *Fifth Cabinet* (1954–55) was led by Moshe Sharett as Prime Minister, after Ben Gurion unexpectedly retired (temporarily) to Kibbutz Sde Boker in the Negev. In 1955 Sharett resigned after the General Zionists refused to support the government against a motion of no confidence brought in the Knesset by Herut on the subject of the Kastner libel trial.*

Sharett's resignation was on the ground of collective Cabinet responsibility. The crisis immediately preceded a scheduled election, and both Mapai and the General Zionists seem to have had an interest in a crisis—Mapai, to

---

* Kastner, a Mapai activist, had negotiated with the Nazis over the rescue of Hungarian Jews in his capacity as the head of the Hungarian Zionist Rescue Committee in Budapest. In 1953 a Herut editor, Greenwald, published a broadside accusing Kastner of cooperating with the Nazis and aiding the Holocaust by lulling his compatriots into a false feeling of security. In a libel suit urged by Mapai leaders, not only Kastner but also the Labor leadership, which had been at the helm of rescue operations during the war, came under attack. Greenwald won the case on most counts, and Kastner was assassinated shortly thereafter. In 1958, the Supreme Court reversed the lower court's decision. Like the Lavon affair, the trial disturbed public faith in the establishment, since the leadership of Mapai had been prominent in the conduct of relations with the powers during the war.

enforce Cabinet responsibility and to become free, for the elections, of any stigma arising from association with the right (Ahdut Ha'Avoda and Mapam had just shown gains in the Histadrut elections); and the General Zionists, to emphasize their individuality as well as to draw votes from Herut. A *Sixth Cabinet* served as a caretaker until the 1955 elections.

The Third Knesset (1955–59)

After the elections, Ben Gurion returned as Prime Minister, leading a *Seventh Cabinet* (1955–57), which included Mapai, Mizrachi–Hapoel Hamizrachi, Ahdut Ha'Avoda, Mapam, and the Progressives. In 1957 a crisis arose when it was secretly proposed that Chief of Staff Moshe Dayan go to Germany to discuss the purchase of arms. At this time, Ahdut Ha'Avoda and Mapam were concerned with Ben Gurion's reported leaning toward a NATO involvement and also with his tendency to make security decisions without prior Cabinet knowledge. Shortly after the Cabinet had approved the mission by a narrow margin, the Ahdut Ha'Avoda daily, *Lamerhav*, published a thinly disguised report of the debate, referring to Dayan as a "high personage," and attacked the decision. Ahdut Ha'Avoda and Mapam threatened to resign unless the mission was canceled. Eventually it was, but at the same time Mapai accused Ahdut Ha'Avoda of putting factionalism ahead of national security and asked the Ahdut Ha'Avoda ministers to resign. Backed by Mapam, they refused; but there was broad public support for the Mapai position. Mapai proposals for a resolution failed of acceptance, including a proposal to give a Prime Minister the authority to discharge a minister if supported by a two-thirds Cabinet majority, and at the end of 1957 Ben Gurion resigned.

The *Eighth Cabinet* (1958–59) shortly took office, with the same membership, after the parties had agreed to a more stringent definition of collective responsibility. Cabinet proceedings would be secret, and coalition members would share collective responsibility, which included, unless permission were given to abstain, the voting support of their Knesset delegations.

The crisis sprang partly from Ahdut Ha'Avoda and Mapam opposition to the extent of the government's Western commitment in security policy, but it was even more a test of the degree of partnership and independence which they could achieve as coalition partners with Mapai. Ben Gurion was, above all, concerned with the constitutional question of a clearer definition of collective responsibility and with establishing strong Mapai authority over its smaller partners; yet he retreated from the demand for authority to discharge a minister.

The Eighth Cabinet was soon again in crisis. The Minister of the Interior, from Ahdut Ha'Avoda, had decided that for administrative simplicity, individuals would be registered as Jews by the Ministry of the Interior (for secular purposes) on their own declaration, whether or not they qualified under *Halachic* law. The government backed this clear division between the secular and religious authority, and between national origin and religion. The deeper political question was not "who is a Jew," but whether the rabbinic or the secular authorities should decide. The Mafdal left the Cabinet, remaining in opposition until after the 1959 elections.

Near the end of the Third Knesset's term in 1959, the Cabinet resigned in a new incident involving arms and Germany. When the German weekly *Der Spiegel* published an account of proposed Israel arms sales to Germany, Ahdut Ha'Avoda claimed that the question had never been put to the Cabinet. (It turned out that it had, some time before, but was approved in passing—not after a debate, but after a brief announcement by Ben Gurion to which no one had raised objections.) There were bitter charges and countercharges, and the Ahdut Ha'Avoda ministers refused Ben Gurion's demand that they resign, although they voted against the government in the Knesset. The Cabinet then resigned, and continued as a caretaker government until the 1959 elections.

The Fourth Knesset (1959–61)

After a large Mapai gain, to a peak of forty-seven seats, Ben Gurion formed the *Ninth Cabinet* as a coalition with the Mafdal, Progressives, Mapam, and Ahdut Ha'Avoda. In 1960–61 Mapai went through a major internal crisis over the Lavon affair; and Ben Gurion resigned in protest over the exoneration of Lavon by a committee of ministers, demanding a formal judicial inquiry instead. The Knesset set new elections for August 1961, which resulted in the *Tenth Cabinet* in the Fifth Knesset.

The Fifth Knesset (1961–65)

In 1963 Ben Gurion unexpectedly resigned for personal reasons, and an *Eleventh Cabinet*, headed by Levi Eshkol (1963–64), succeeded. In 1964 Eshkol resigned in the face of a deep split in Mapai on whether or not a judicial committee should investigate the Lavon affair. Eshkol opposed the inquiry and wanted the Cabinet to be the locus of decision rather than the Mapai Central Committee. After this tactic removed the Central Committee from the game, Eshkol formed an identical *Twelfth Cabinet*, which served until the scheduled elections of 1965.

The Sixth Knesset (1965–69)

The *Thirteenth Cabinet* was formed by Eshkol after the 1965 elections. In 1967, on the eve of the Six Day War, Gahal and Rafi joined, forming the National Unity government, or *Fourteenth Cabinet*. In 1968, Rafi, Ahdut

Ha'Avoda, and Mapai formed the Labor Party. After the death in office of Levi Eshkol, Mrs. Meir became Prime Minister.

The Seventh Knesset (1969–73)

Mrs. Meir continued as Prime Minister, heading a *Fifteenth Cabinet* of National Unity, until 1970. Then Gahal (Herut, Liberals) left the government, when the terms for the cease-fire in the war of attrition along the Suez Canal included an agreement to negotiate territorial concessions along the lines of the Rogers plan. The rest of the Cabinet, which now included Labor, the Mafdal, and the Independent Liberals, did not resign, and served until the post-Yom Kippur War elections of 1973, as the *Sixteenth Cabinet*.

The Eighth Knesset (1973–77)

Mrs. Meir formed the *Seventeenth Cabinet* in March 1974, to include Labor, the Mafdal, and the Independent Liberals, but it shortly resigned following protest movements and the publication of the Agranat Report on the war. Itzchak Rabin was chosen by the Labor Central Committee to form the *Eighteenth Cabinet* (Labor, Independent Liberals, and Civil Rights). After some delay, the Mafdal joined, leading to the resignation of the Civil Rights Party.

The *Nineteenth Cabinet* served until after the 1977 elections. The premature ending of its term was preceded by several near crises in which the Independent Liberals irresolutely threatened to resign on questions of principal (compulsory arbitration, free choice of health fund in the proposed health services law [see Chapter 6], government organization). In December 1976, the first F–15 airplanes to be delivered were welcomed at a ceremony which took place on a Friday afternoon at an hour which forced some guests to travel home on the Sabbath. Two Mafdal ministers (and the Mafdal Knesset delegation) did not vote to support the government on an ensuing motion of no confidence. Rabin took the opportunity to precipitate a Cabinet crisis. He declared the Mafdal ministers to have resigned, following which he resigned himself. The Cabinet thus became a caretaker government, from which the Independent Liberal ministers could not resign until a new Cabinet was formed. In the next tactical move, the elections were advanced from the fall to May by legislation.

The Ninth Knesset (1977–81)

After the resounding defeat of Labor in the May elections, Menachem Begin formed the *Twentieth Cabinet*, including the Likud, Moshe Dayan as a member of a one-man Knesset delegation, the Mafdal, and the Aguda. The Aguda were not actually willing to sit in the Cabinet, but agreed to support the government, receiving, *inter alia*, the important Knesset Finance Committee chairmanship. In October 1977, the DMC joined the Cabinet with four ministers: the Deputy Prime Minister, Justice, Labor and Welfare, and Transportation.

The Organization of the Government

The overall concept is shown on Figure E.

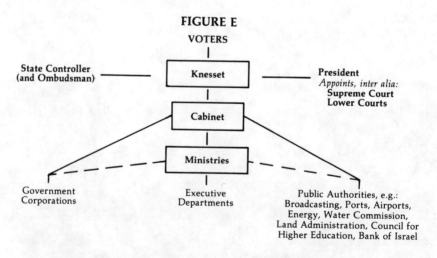

FIGURE E

VOTERS

Knesset

State Controller (and Ombudsman)

President
Appoints, inter alia:
Supreme Court
Lower Courts

Cabinet

Ministries

Government Corporations

Executive Departments

Public Authorities, e.g.: Broadcasting, Ports, Airports, Energy, Water Commission, Land Administration, Council for Higher Education, Bank of Israel

The Cabinet, or executive, retains office between elections, subject to the continuing approval of the Knesset or until it resigns. It exercises its authority through executive departments, government corporations, and public authorities. Some heads of authorities are independent of direct Cabinet control. Thus the President is elected for a five-year term by the Knesset, while a Knesset or Cabinet is normally limited to four years. The State Controller is appointed by the President, on the Knesset's recommendation, and also has a five-year term, as does the Governor of the Bank of Israel. Judges are under the administrative aegis of the Ministry of Justice, but they are appointed for life by the President, on the recommendation of a committee made up of three Supreme Court justices, two representatives of the Bar Association, the Minister of Justice and one other minister, and two members of the Knesset, elected by secret ballot. The Attorney-General has independent discretion in criminal proceedings and in the professional advice which he gives the government, which is of particular significance where elected officials or judges are involved. Each public authority is established by laws specifying how their governing bodies are appointed, the procedure of appointments, and which ministers have general political responsibility. Examples follow: *The Broadcast Authority* (see Chapter 2) is overseen by a plenum of thirty-one members, thirty of whom represent the public and are appointed by the President, and one of whom is appointed by the Jewish Agency. The authority for ongoing management, however, is an Executive of seven members, appointed by the Cabinet. Five of these are also members of the plenum and the other two are the chairman and vice-chairman. The *Land Administration* (see Chapter 8) and the *Water Commission* are the responsibility of the Minister of Agriculture. The Council of the Land Administration has eight representatives of the government and seven of the Jewish National Fund. The minister is chairman. The *Water Council*, with the Minister of Agriculture as chairman and the Water Commissioner (his appointee) as vice-chairman, is an advisory body of twenty-seven to thirty-nine members, two-thirds of whom are to represent the public, including consumers and suppliers. The *Council for Higher Education*, through its Budget Committee and its Accreditation Authority, develops the policy for the development of higher education and its budget priorities. Two-thirds of the Council are of standing in universities, and the rest represent the broader public. Some authorities, such as the *Ports Authority*, were formed to gain administrative and financial flexibility; others, such as the *Broadcasting* and *Higher Education Authorities*, are attempts to achieve broad public representation while removing professional activities from ongoing partisan influence.

The Cabinet

Recurrent proposals to reallocate ministerial responsibilities have been unsuccessful, due mainly to the defense of their territories by coalition or internal factional leaders and by the compromises arising during negotiations to form coalitions. During the 1977 election campaign, the Likud and particularly the Democratic Movement for Change promised to streamline the cabinet and its functions, and to provide for the coordination of major policy areas. Table E compares the proposals with the eventual reality.

TABLE E.   Ministries: 1973 and 1977

1973–77 (ACTUAL)	1977–81 (ACTUAL)	AN ORIGINAL LIKUD PROPOSAL, 1977*	ONE OF THE DEMOCRATIC MOVEMENT FOR CHANGE PROPOSALS, 1977**
Prime Minister's Office	Prime Minister's Office	Prime Minister's Office	Prime Minister's Office
Foreign Ministry	Foreign Ministry	Foreign Ministry	Foreign Ministry
Defense	Defense	Defense (defense industries in Commerce and Industry)	Defense (without industries)
Finance (incl. Energy Authority)	Finance	Finance	Economic Affairs, to include: Treasury, Commerce and Industry, Tourism, Agriculture, Communications, and Transport
Agriculture (incl. Water, Lands)	Agriculture (incl. Water, Lands)	Agriculture (without Water Commission or Land Administration)	
Commerce and Industry	Commerce, Industry, and Tourism	Commerce, Industry and Tourism	
Tourism			
Transportation	Transportation and Communications	Transportation and Communications	
Communications			
Labor	Social Welfare and Labor	Social Welfare and Labor	Social Welfare: Human Resources Development, Welfare Services, Income Maintenance, Health, Rehabilitation, Housing Policy
Welfare			
Health	Health	(National Health Authority)	
Immigrant Absorption	Immigrant Absorption	(A joint Authority, Government and Agency)	(A joint Authority, Government and Agency)
Education	Education	Education	Education

TABLE E.   Ministries: 1973 and 1977 (con't)

1973–77 (Actual)	1977–81 (Actual)	An Original Likud Proposal, 1977*	One of the Democratic Movement for Change Proposals, 1977**
Justice	Justice	Justice (to include religious courts)	Justice (to include religious courts)
Interior	Interior (incl. Police) (incl. Environment, Physical Planning)	Interior (incl. Police) (incl. Religious Services)	Interior (incl. Police) (incl. Religious Services)
Police	—	—	—
Housing	Building and Housing	Building, Housing Energy and Infrastr. incl. Water and Land Administration)	Environment (Environment quality, Physical Planning, Energy and National Resources, Government Building and Roads, Land and Water)
—	Energy and Infrastructure (incl. Council for R&D)		
Religions	Religions	—	—

* This Likud proposal (for twelve ministries) was prepared by a Committee for Transfer of the Regime, under Joseph Rom, M.K. By the time the Democratic Change Party coalition negotiations with the Likud reached "practical" discussions, the 1977 organization of sixteen ministries had been decided, reflecting demands of internal Likud parties and Likud-Mafdal relations.

** The DMC plan shown here is one of several. Another approach was to have a small Cabinet which would decide major issues and coordinate a larger number of ministries. Both approaches had the same end, to limit Cabinet size and coordinate economic and social policies.

The State Controller and Commissioner for the Public's Complaints ("Ombudsman")

Appointed by the President on the advice of the Knesset, the State Controller scrutinizes all government departments, corporations, and authorities, local governments, and any organization in whose management the government participates. It investigates whether the operation of the organizations is according to law and proper procedure, and is efficient and according to accepted standards of probity. The Controller reports to the Knesset. (The annual report is first presented to the Minister of Finance, who then sends it to the Knesset within ten weeks.) The Controller has considerable prestige but little or no authority, except for that of publicizing findings, to enforce recommendations. Since 1971, the Controller is also the Ombudsman, or Commissioner for the Complaints of the Public.

The Jewish Agency

Independent of the government, the Jewish Agency for Palestine was founded in 1929 to represent the Jewish people officially to the Mandatory power and to organize immigration and economic development with national resources. The Agency represents both members and nonmembers of the Zionist movement throughout the world. Before the state, it performed important governmental functions—foreign and Mandate government relations, self-defense, immigration, settlement, national investment. The state took over most of these, and the Agency's principal importance is now in new settlement, immigration, and education in the Diaspora. For these activities, the Agency continued to maintain a bureaucracy whose operations could lead to friction with government agencies. (See the section on the absorption of immigration in Chapter 6.) Its funds come mainly from voluntary sources, such as the United Jewish Appeal, and the policy for their use is decided by a Board of Governors, of whom 30 percent are designated by the United Israel Appeal (U.S.A.), 20 percent are from outside of Israel and the United States, and 50 percent are members of the Assembly, designated by the World Zionist Organization (the political parties' role is via the WZO). (The Assembly is a larger representative body, above the board, while the ongoing work is carried out by a small executive.) For the background of Zionist–non-Zionist relations in the Agency constitution, see Ernest Stock, "The Reconstitution of the Jewish Agency: A Political Analysis", *The American Jewish Yearbook*, New York, 1972.

NOTES

Introduction to Part I

1. Dan Horowitz and Moshe Lissak, *The Origins of the Israel Polity: Israel Under the Mandate*, Chicago, University of Chicago Press, 1978.

Chapter 1

1. References on the Diaspora communities include Salo W. Baron, *The Jewish Community*, Philadelphia, Jewish Publication Society, 1942; Salo W. Baron, *The Russian Jew Under Tsars and Socialism*, New York, Macmillan, 1964; S. M. Dubnow, *History of the Jews in Russia and Poland*, Philadelphia, Jewish Publication Society, 1920; Yehoshua Prawer, *The Jewish Community: An Historic Survey*, Jerusalem, International Conference of Jewish Social Service, 1978; and Mark Zborowsky and Elizabeth Herzog, *Life Is with People*, New York, Schocken, 1932. Also see the notes to Chapter 3 for references on the Middle Eastern and North African communities.

2. Jacob S. Raisin, *The Haskalah Movement*, Philadelphia, Jewish Publication Society, 1913, and Westport, Conn., Greenwood Press, 1973.

3. David Vital, *The Origins of Zionism*, London, Oxford University Press, 1975, p. 31.

4. Ezra Mendelsohn, *Class Struggle in the Pale*, London, Cambridge University Press, 1970; and Henry J. Tobias, *The Jewish Bund in Russia*, Stanford, Calif., Stanford University Press, 1972.

5. Shlomo Avineri, *HaRa'ayon Hatzioni Legvanav* (Varieties of Zionist Thought) (Heb.), Tel Aviv, Am Oved, 1980. Arthur Hertzberg (ed.), *The Zionist Idea*, New York, Athenaeum, 1973, Introduction.

6. Raisin, supra.

7. Jacob Talmon, *Israel Among the Nations*, London, Weidenfeld and Nicolson, 1970.

8. For the development of the Zionist movement, see Vital, *The Origins of Zionism*, supra; and David Vital *Zionism: The Formative Years*, Oxford, England, The Oxford University Press, 1982. Ben Halpern, *The Idea of the Jewish State*, Cambridge, Mass., Harvard, 1969, 2d ed.; and Walter Lacquer, *A History of Zionism*, London, Weidenfeld and Nicolson, 1972. For an anthology of basic writings in translation, with comments, see Hertzberg, supra. For an analysis in Hebrew, see Avineri, supra.

9. Vital, supra, p. 66.

10. Joel Cotton, *Leon Blum*, Cambridge, Mass.: M.I.T., 1966.

11. Vital, *The Origins of Zionism* supra, p. 373.

12. Berl Katzenelson, *Rashei Prakim LeToldot Tnuat Hapoalim* (Outline of the History of the Labor Movement) (Heb.), mimeographed set of lectures, November 1928.

13. Yonatan Shapiro, *Demokratia Be'Yisroel* (Democracy in Israel) (Heb.), Ramat Gan, Masada, 1977.

14. For development of the Labor movement and Yishuv political system, see Halpern, supra; Yosef Gorni, *Ahdut Ha'Avoda, 1919-1930* (Ideological Foundations and the Political Method) (Heb.), Tel Aviv, University of Tel Aviv and the Kibbutz Hameuchad, 1973 (emphasizes the development of beliefs, and their relation to political decisions); Yonatan Shapiro, *Ahdut Ha'Avoda; The Formative Years of the Israeli Labor Party*, London, Sage, 1976; emphasizes, for the 1920s, the role of considerations of power and bureaucratic politics; in Horowitz and Lissak, supra; Katzenelson, supra; Peter Y. Medding, *Mapai in Israel*, London, Cambridge University Press, 1972; and biographical works, such as: Anita Shapira, *Berl Katzenelson*, Tel Aviv, Am Oved, 1981.

15. Anita Shapira, *Hama'avak al Avoda Ivrit* (The Struggle for Hebrew Work) (Heb.), Tel Aviv, Hakibbutz Hameuhad, 1977.

16. Joseph Baratz, *A Village by the Jordan*, Tel Aviv, Ichud Habonim, 1960; and Katzenelson, supra.

17. S. N. Eisenstadt, *Israel Society*, London, Weidenfeld and Nicolson, 1964, p. 24.

18. Lincoln Steffens, *Autobiography*, New York, Literary Guild, 1931, p. 799.

19. The searching, experimental spirit of the early 1920's is reflected in David Horowitz, *Ha'etmol Sheli* (My Yesterdays) (Heb), Jerusalem, Schocken, 1970.

20. Zvi Y. Gitelman, *Jewish Nationality and Soviet Politics*, Princeton, 1972. Yonatan Shapiro, supra, and Anita Shapira *Berl Katzenelson*, supra, pp. 371-427.

21. Meir Avizohar, "Ideological Development and the Importance of Public Ownership," Paper presented at the Hevrat Ovdim Conference, Tel Aviv, May 1973.

22. Quoted in Amos Perlmutter, *Anatomy of Political Institutionalism: The Case of Israel*, Occasional Papers in International Affairs, No. 26, August 1970, Center for International Affairs, Harvard University.

23. D. Weintraub, M. Lissak, and Y. Azmon, *Moshava, Kibbutz and Moshav: Patterns of Jewish Rural Settlement and Development in Palestine*, Ithaca, N.Y., Cornell University Press, 1969.

24. Weintraub, supra.

25. An autobiography which illuminates the problems of developing Histadrut enterprises: Hillel Dan, *Baderech Lo Slula* (Along an Unpaved Road) (Heb.), Jerusalem, Schocken, 1963.

26. David Ben Gurion, *Me Ma'amad La'am* (From a Class to a People) (Heb.), Tel Aviv, Davar, 1933.

27. Avineri, supra.

28. Giora Goldberg, *Labor Exchanges as a Political Instrument in a Developing Country* (Heb.), unpublished M.A. thesis, University of Tel Aviv, 1975.; and Anita Shapira, *Berl Katzenelson*, supra, pp. 419–424.

29. Nathan Yanai, *Kera Batzameret* (A Rift in the Leadership) (Heb.), Tel Aviv, Lewin-Epstein, 1969. Also Y. Shapiro, *The Formative Years*, supra.

30. Myron Aronoff, *Power and Ritual in the Israel Labor Party*, Assen, Holland, Van Gorcum, 1977.

31. Shapiro, *Demokratia BeYisroel*, supra.

32. Medding, supra, p. 16; Perlmutter, supra, p. 33.

33. Medding, supra.

34. Occupational dependence of elected officials is shown by Medding, op. cit., on pp. 158–59. The work of the party machine, or Gush, is described in Medding and Nathan Yanai, supra, and its culture in Aronoff, supra.

35. Zvi Sussman, *Wage Differentials and Equality Within the Histadrut* (Heb.), Ramat Gan, Massada, 1974.

36. Harel Fisch, "Faith in Israel," *Commentary*, Vol. 47, February 1969, pp. 64–67.

37. David Sommer, *The Origin of the "Status Quo": Church and State in Israel—Its Development and Problems*, unpublished Ph.D. dissertation, New School for Social Research, New York, 1976.

38. Michael Kahan and Shimshon Zelniker, "Religion and Nascent Cleavages: Israel's Religious Parties," paper delivered at APSA Annual Meeting, Washington, D.C., 1972.

39. For a short bibliography on the Revisionists and Herut refer to: Joseph B. Schechtman and Yehuda Ben Ari, *The History of the Revisionist Movement, Vol. I, 1925–1930*, Tel Aviv, Hadar Press, 1970; V. Jabotinsky, *Baderech Lamedina* (On the Way to a State) (Heb.), Jerusalem, Ari Jabotinsky Publishing House, Ltd., 1953; Menachem Begin, *The Revolt*, London, W. H. Allen, 1951; Joseph B. Schechtman, *Rebel and Statesman, Vladimir Jabotinsky: The Early Years*, New

York, Thomas Yoseloff, Inc., 1956; Joseph B. Schechtman, *Fighter and Prophet, the Vladimir Jabotinsky Story: The Last Years*, New York, Thomas Yoseloff, Inc., 1961; Vladimir Jabotinsky, *Evidence Submitted to the Palestine Royal Commission*, Pamphlet, London, 1937. This chapter also benefited from conversations with Mr. Yehuda Ben Ari, Chairman of the Board of Directors of the Jabotinsky Institute, and Mr. P. Gani, who is in charge of the archives, Jabotinsky Institute, and a member of the Herut Party Central Committee.

40. Ahad Ha'am, "The Truth from the Land of Israel" (Emeth Me'eretz Yisroel) in *Nationalism and the Jewish Ethic*, Hans Kohn (ed.), New York, Herzl Press, 1960.

41. Vladimir Jabotinsky, *Die Tribuna*, Copenhagen, May 10, 1916, quoted in *Ma'ariv*, August 4, 1978.

42. Baer Borochov, *Katavim* (Writings) (Heb.), Tel Aviv, Mapai Press, 1955.

43. Chaim Weizmann, *Trial and Error*, New York, Harper & Brothers, 1949.

44. Berl Katzenelson, "On the Question of the Political Regime in the Land," in *Katavim* (Writings) (Heb.), Part IV, Tel Aviv, Mapai Press, 1946, pp. 150–67; "What Is Ahead," in *Katavim* (Writings) (Heb.), Part VIII, Tel Aviv, Mapai Press, 1950, p. 25.

45. For expressions of this latter view, see A. B. Yehoshua, "Yonim, Ka'an Ve'achshav" (Doves, Here and Now) (Heb.), *Ha'aretz*, November 1937; and Lova Eliav, *Land of the Hart*, Philadelphia, Jewish Publication Society, 1975. See also Shlomo Avineri, "Peace Making: The Arab-Israeli Conflict," *Foreign Affairs*, New York, Fall 1978.

46. Mahmoud Hussein, in Shaul Friedlander and Mahmoud Hussein, *Arabs and Israelis*, New York, Homes and Meier, 1975, p. 85.

Chapter 2

1. David Nahmias, "A Note on Coalition Payoffs in a Dominant Party System," *Political Studies*, Vol. XXI, September 1973, pp. 301–05.

2. Peter Medding, *Mapai in Israel*, London, Cambridge University Press, 1972.

3. Eliahu S. Likhovski, *Israel's Parliament*, London, Oxford University Press, 1971, p. 94 ff.

4. For the legal background, see Henry E. Baker, *The Legal System of Israel*, Jerusalem, Israel Universities Press, 1968; Melville Nimmer, "The Uses of Judicial Review in Israel's Quest for a Constitution," *Columbia Law Revue*, 1970; Likhovski, op. cit; Yehoshua Freudenheim, *Government in Israel* (Heb.), Jerusalem, Reuven Mass, 1973, 5th ed.; Amnon Rubinstein, *Hamishpat Hakonstitutzioni* (Constitutional Law) (Heb.), Jerusalem, Schocken, 1969.

5. Amitai Etzioni, "Alternative Ways to Democracy: The Example of Israel," *Political Science Quarterly*, LXXIV, No. 2, June 1959, pp. 196–214.

6. See Ben Halpern and Shalom Wurm (eds.), *The Responsible Attitude: The Life and Times of Giora Josephtal*, New York, Schocken, 1966, p. 228.

7. Tom Stoppard, *Rosencrantz and Guildenstern Are Dead*, New York, Grove Press, 1967.

8. From a legal opinion re the Agranat Committee Report on the 1973 war given by Minister of Justice Haim Zadok to the Cabinet (quoting Attorney-General Shamgar). Reported in *Ma'ariv*, April 11, 1974.

9. *Basic Law: The Government*, and *Basic Law: The President of the State*.

10. Quoted in Michael Brecher, *The Foreign Policy System of Israel*, London, Oxford, 1972, p. 379, from Moshe Pearlman, *Ben Gurion Looks Back*.

11. See Henry Baker, *Legal System of Israel*, op. cit, p. 200, for a summary of the Supreme Court's mandate.

12. The Judges Law, 1953. See Henry Baker, "The Selection of Judges in Israel," *Public Administration in Israel and Abroad*, Vol. 3, 1962, pp. 31–44.

13. *Mahdy Daoud et al. vs. Minister of Defense*, Bagatz 51/64, and *Mahdy Daoud et al. vs. Appeal Commission for the Security Zones*, 51/239.

14. *The Judges Law, 1953*, supra.

15. H.C. 98/69, *Bergman vs. Minister of Finance*, 23 Pskei Din (P.D.) (1) 693, 969, 1969.

16. References on Al-Ard cases are Case 253/64, *Sabri Jiris vs. District Court of Haifa*, 18 P.D. 673, 1964. H.C. Case 1/65, *Y. Yardor (Iredor) vs. Chairman of the Central Elections Commission*, 19 P.D. (III) 365, 1965.

17. H.C. 73/53, 87/53, *"Kol Ha'am" Company Limited vs. Minister of the Interior*, *"Al-Ittihad" Newspaper vs. Minister of the Interior*, 7 P.D. 671, 1 S.F. 90, 1953.

18. See Nimmer, op. cit., and "Felix Frankfurter, Mr. Justice Cardozo and the Public Law," Papers Dedicated to Mr. Justice Cardozo, *Harvard-Yale-Columbia Law Review, Fall, 1939*.

19. A. Rubinstein, supra, pp. 110–13.

20. *Rufeysen vs. Minister of Interior*, 16 P.D., 2428, 2446, 1963.

21. The law is the Registration of Inhabitants Ordinance, 1949; it provided for the inscription of "nationality" and "religion" in an identity card carried by each individual. For a summary of the legal relations, see Amnon Rubinstein, "Law and Religion in Israel," *Israel Law Review*, Vol. 2, No. 3, July 1967: and Freudenheim, op. cit.

22. Dina Goren, in *Sodiut, Bitachon, Vechofesh Ha'itonut* (Secrecy, Security, and Freedom of the Press) (Heb.), Jerusalem, Magnes Press, 1975, gives a convincing and useful analysis of these relations.

23. High Court Case 73/53; 87/53, "Kol Ha'am," supra.

24. High Court Case 243/62, *Israel Cinema Studios vs. Levi Geri and the Council for Film and Stage Criticism, Ministry of the Interior*, 16 P.D. 2407.

25. High Court Case 25/53, *"Kol Ha'am" Company, Ltd. vs. Minister of the Interior*, 7 P.D. 165, 1953.

26. Allan E. Shapiro, "Self Restraint of the Supreme Court and the Preservation of Civil Liberties," *Tel Aviv University Law Review*, Vol. C., No. 2, September 1973.

27. Uriel Gorney, "American Precedent in the Supreme Court of Israel," *Harvard Law Review*, Vol. 68, May 1955, pp. 1194–210.

28. Al-Ard cases, note 16, supra.

29. High Court Case 243/62, supra.

30. Interviews with Elihu Katz, the first Director of Television, and (1976) Itzchak Livny, Director of the Broadcast Authority. See also Elihu Katz, "Television Comes to the Middle East," *Trans-action*, June 1971.

31. The Criminal Law Amendment (Security of the State), 1957.

32. Zeev Schiff, "The Army Spokesman Announces", *Journalists' Year Book*, 1969, pp. 203–209.

33. Itzchak Galnur, "Transformation in the Israel Political System," mimeograph, paper presented at the January 1978 meeting of the Israel Political Science Association.

34. See Melville Nimmer, Allan Shapiro, supra; and Amos Shapera, "The Supreme Court as Guardian of the Individual's Fundamental Freedoms in Israel: A fortified Bastion or a Paper Tiger" (Heb., English summary), *Tel Aviv University Law Review*, No. 2, September 1973.

Chapter 3

1. C.B.S., *Society in Israel*, Jerusalem, 1976, p. 1; C.B.S., *Statistical Abstract of Israel, 1976*, Jerusalem, Prime Minister's Office, 1976, p. 19f. Figure 3.1, calculated independently, approximates Figure 2 in *Israel Society, 1980*, Jerusalem, 1981, reproduced by permission.

2. The following discuss the absorption of immigrants: S. N. Eisenstadt, *The Absorption of Immigrants*, Chicago, The Free Press of Glencoe, Ill., 1955; J. Shuval, *Immigrants on the Threshold*, New York, Atherton, 1963; A. Weingrod, *Reluctant Pioneers*, Ithaca, N.Y., Cornell University Press, 1966; C. Frankenstein (ed.), *Between Past and Future: Essays and Studies on Aspects of Immigrant Absorption in Israel*, Jerusalem, Henrietta Szold Institute, 1953; R. Patai, *Israel Between East and West*, Philadelphia, Jewish Publication Society, 1957; Eric Cohen et al., *Research on Immigrant Absorption in a Development Town*, Jerusalem, Department of Sociology, Hebrew University, 1962; Moshe Lissak, *The Political Absorption of Immigrants and the Preservation of Political Integration in Israel*, mimeograph, Jerusalem, Department of Sociology, Hebrew University, 1975; Deborah Bernstein, "Immigrants and Society—a Critical View of the Dominant School of Israeli Sociology," *British Journal of Sociology*, Volume 31, 2, June, 1980, pp. 246–64. (analyzes and criticizes the "absorption" analysis in Eisenstadt, supra); Louis Miller, "Migration and Social Identity," in I. Pilowsky (ed.), *Cultures in Collision*, Adelaide, Australia, Society for Mental Health, 1975; Phyllis Palgi, *Socio-Cultural Trends and Mental Health*, Ministry of Health, Government of Israel, 1969; "Cultural Components of Immigrants' Adjustment," in Henry P. David (ed.), *Migration, Mental Health and Community Services*, International Research Institute, Washington; Geneva, Switzerland, American Joint Distribution Committee, 1966; Sammy Smooha, *Israel: Pluralism and Conflict*, London, Routledge & Kegan Paul, 1978.

3. L. Miller, supra.

4. References on Jews of the Maghreb include Doris Ben-Simon Donath, *Immigrants d'Afrique du Nord en Israel*, Paris, Anthropos, 1967; Natan-André Chouraqui, *La*

Saga des Juifs en Afrique du Nord (Heb.), Tel Aviv, Am Oved, 1975; Michael Inbar and Chaim Adler, *Ethnic Integration in Israel* (a comparative case study of Moroccan brothers who settled in France and Israel, New Brunswick, N.J., Transaction Books, 1977; *Report on Wadi Salib* (Heb.), Jerusalem, Prime Minister's Office, 1959; Rivka Bar-Yosef, "Wadi Salib; An Analysis of the Status of Moroccan Jews in Israel" (Heb.), *Molad*, Vol. 17, 1959.

5. Nuzhat Katzav, *Hishtalvut shel Yotzei Iraq* (The Integration of Iraqis) (Heb.), Jerusalem, Ben Zvi Institute, 1976; Phyllis Palgi et al., "Typical Personality Disturbances in a Group of Iraqi Women in the Light of Their Cultural Background" (Heb.), *Megamot*, Vol. 3, July 1955, pp. 236–43; P. Palgi, note 2.

6. The conditions in the camps in the winter of 1951 are vividly described by Giora Yosephtal, then Treasurer of the Jewish Agency, in *The Responsible Attitude*, New York, Schocken, 1966.

7. A. Zigel, *Ehad-Esrei Shnot Klita* (Eleven Years of Absorption) (Heb.), Tel Aviv, Jewish Agency Absorption Department, internal memorandum, 1959.

8. For the experiences of the new *moshavim*, see Dorothy Willner, *Nation-Building and Community in Israel*, Princeton, N.J., Princeton University Press, 1969; Alex Weingrod, op. cit.; Dan Gileadi (ed.), *Moshavei Olim* (Immigrants' Moshavim) (Heb.), Tel Aviv, Moshav Movement Press, 1973.

9. D. Willner, supra, p. 18.

10. D. Gileadi, supra.

11. Ruth Zilberberg, *Population Dispersal in Israel, 1948–1972* (Heb.), mimeo, Jerusalem, Economic Planning Authority, Ministry of Finance, 1973.

12. C.B.S. Special Publications No. 348 *(Local Authorities, 1969–70)* and No. 387 *(Local Authorities, 1970–71)*.

13. Haim Kubersky, "Mutual Relations of the Local and Central Governments," *D'var Hashilton Hamekomi* (Heb.), June-July, 1972, pp. 7–10.

14. Myron Aronoff, "Party Center and Local Branch Relationships," in A. Arian (ed.), *The Elections in Israel, 1969*, Jerusalem, Academic Press, 1972.

15. P. Medding, *Mapai in Israel*, Cambridge University Press, 1974, p. 139.

16. Josephtal, *The Responsible Attitude*, supra.

17. Eric Cohen, as cited in note 2.

18. Rivka Bar Yosef, "Desocialization and Resocialization: The Adjustment Process of Immigrants," *International Migration Review*, 3, 27:45. See also Joseph Ben David, "Ethnic Differences and Social Change," in C. Frankenstein (ed.), *Between Past and Future*, Jerusalem, Henrietta Szold Institute, 1953.

19. See references in note 2—particularly, for a critique of predominant analysis, D. Bernstein and S. Smooha.

20. Harry E. Goldberg, *Cave Dwellers and Citrus Growers*, London, Cambridge University Press, 1972.

21. Interviews in Beersheba, conducted by Dan Keren.

22. Daniel Elazar, "The Local Elections," in A. Arian (ed.), *The Elections in Israel, 1969*, Jerusalem, Academic Press, 1972; and A. Arian and Sh. Weiss, "Split-Ticket Voting in Israel," in A. Arian (ed.), *The Elections in Israel, 1973*, Jerusalem, Academic Press, 1975.

23. Shlomo Deshen, " 'The Business of Ethnicity Is Finished?' The Ethnic Factor in a Local Election Campaign," in A. Arian (ed.), *The Elections in Israel, 1969*, op. cit.

24. H. Goldberg, supra.

25. Elihu Katz and S. N. Eisenstadt, "Some Sociological Observations on the Response of Israeli Organizations to New Immigrants," *Administrative Science Quarterly*, Vol. 5, 1960–61.

26. Nezer Menuhin, *Determinants of Immigrant Leadership: A Challenge to the System*, Unpublished M.A. thesis, Tel Aviv University, Department of Political Science, 1972.

27. Sammy Smooha and Yochanan Peres, "Ethnic Inequality in Israel" (Heb.), *Megamot*, No. 1, January 1974; Sh. Weiss, *Hapolitikaim* (The Politicians) (Heb.), Tel Aviv, Ahiasaf, 1973; Nuzhat Katzav, supra.

28. David Haniel, *Senior Civil Servants, Unified Rank System, 1968*, and *Senior Civil Servants, Academic Rank in Social Sciences and Humanities, 1969*, Jerusalem, Civil Service Commission, 1971.

29. P. Medding, *Mapai in Israel*, and S. Smooha, supra (note 2).

30. See Medding, op. cit., for a description of the Gush, or Tel Aviv and Central District Mapai machine; Chapter 1 of this book on party bureaucracies; Nathan Yanai, *Kera Betzameret* (A Rift in the Leadership) (Heb.), Tel Aviv, Lewin-Epstein, 1969.

31. Daniel Shimshoni, "Higher Education for Children of the Well-to-do," *Ha'aretz*, Tel Aviv, July 11, 1969; data from Ministry of Labor, *Manpower Planning Survey*, 1967.

32. For data useful in analyzing ethnic relations and opinions, see the following: Yochanan Peres, "Ethnic Relations in Israel," *American Journal of Sociology*, 76, 6, 1971; Elihu Katz and Michael Gurevitch, *The Secularization of Leisure*, London, Faber & Faber, 1976; Chava Etzioni and Rina Shapero, *Political Culture in Israel*, New York, Praeger, 1977; Institute for Applied Social Research and Communications Institute of the Hebrew University, Jerusalem, *The Current Situation Is Seen by the Public*, published periodically since 1967. Sammy Smooha, supra (note 2).

33. Katz and Gurevitch, supra (note 32), found education to be the most influential variable in predicting the choice of cultural activities.

34. C.B.S., *Annual Statistical Abstract, 1974*, Table iii/14.

35. S. Smooha, supra.

36. A. Arian, "Stability and Change in Israeli Public Opinion and Politics," *Public Opinion Quarterly*, 35, Spring 1971.

37. Lecture by Minister of Education Zevulun Hammer at Bar Ilan University, Spring 1979.

38. Jacob M. Landau, *The Arabs in Israel*, London, Oxford University Press, 1969; Ernest Stock, *From Conflict to Understanding: Relations Between Arabs and Jews in Israel Since 1948*, New York, Institute of Human Relations Press, American Jewish Committee, 1968; and Ian Lustick, *Arabs in the Jewish State*, Austin, Texas, University of Texas Press, 1980.

39. C.B.S., *Annual Statistical Abstract, 1976*, pp. 40, 47; and Yehiel Harari, *The Arabs in Israel—1973: Facts and Numbers* (Ha'aravim Beyisrael—1973: Uvdot Vemisparim) (Heb.), Giv'at Haviva, Center for Arab Studies, 1974.

40. Letter from Dr. B. Biltzky, Ministry of Education, Jerusalem, February 1976.

41. Shimon Shamir, "Changes in Village Leadership," *New Outlook*, March-April, 1962; and Abner Cohen, *Arab Border Villages in Israel*, Manchester, Manchester University Press, 1965.

42. Gabriel Ben Dor, *The Druzes in Israel*, Jerusalem, The Magnes Press, 1979.

43. Stock, supra, p. 41f.

44. Haim Kubersky et al, *Report of Committee on Problems of Planning and Building in the Arab Sector in the North*, submitted to the Prime Minister, 1976.

45. Eli Reches, *Survey of Graduates of Universities in Israel from the Minorities (1961-71)* (Heb.), mimeo, Tel Aviv, University of Tel Aviv, Shiloah Institute, 1973.

46. Matityahu Peled, *Doch Tzevet Hachinuch Ha'aravi* (Report of the Task Force on Arab Education) (Heb.), mimeo, Jerusalem, Ministry of Education, 1975.

47. Eli Reches, *The Israeli Arabs After 1967: The Problem of Integration Becomes More Acute* (Arviei Yisrael le'achar 1967: Hachrafat Haba'aya (Heb.), mimeo, Tel Aviv, University of Tel Aviv, Shiloah Institute, 1976.

48. Eli Reches, *The Israeli Arabs and Land Annexation in the Galilee, 1975-77*, Tel Aviv, University of Tel Aviv, Shiloah Institute, 1977; Moshe Shokeid, "Strategy and Change in the Arab Vote: Observations in a Mixed Town," in A. Arian (ed.), *The Elections in Israel, 1973*, supra.

49. Itai Zak, *Arab-Israel Identity and Readiness for Social Relations Between Young Arabs and Jews in Israel*, preliminary research report to the Israel Foundations Trustees. University of Tel Aviv, School of Education, 1976.

50. Interviews in Israel and Judaea and Samaria, 1973.

Chapter 4

1. For data on forces, see Nadav Safran, *From War to War*, New York, Pegasus, 1969; Avraham Tamir, "Eichut mul Kamut" (Quality Versus Quantity) (Heb.), *Ma'arachot*, 250, July 1976; Institute of Strategic Studies, *The Military Balance*, London, IISS, 1972 and subsequent years; *Aviation Week*, issues for 1973 and 1974; Luttwak and Horowitz, supra; Herzog, supra.

2. Bard O'Neill *Armed Struggle in Palestine* Boulder, Colorado, Westview, 1978.

3. B. H. Liddell Hart, *Strategy*, New York, Praeger Paperbacks, 1961.

4. Steven J. Rosen, *Military Geography and the Military Balance in the Arab-Israel Conflict*, Jerusalem, Hebrew University, Davis Institute, 1977, pp. 56-57, for Arab and Israeli losses in proportion to population.

5. For an overview of the campaigns: Luttwak and Horowitz, supra; Yehuda Wallach, *Ma'ariv*, May 26, 1974; Natanel Lorch, *Israel's War of Independence, 1947-49*, 2d rev. ed., Hartford, Conn., Hartmore House, 1968; Y. Allon, *Masach Shel Chol* (A Curtain of Sand) (Heb.), rev. ed., Tel Aviv, Hakibbutz Hameuhad, 1969; Jon and David Kimche, *Both Sides of the Hill*, London, Secker & Warburg, 1960; Zeev Shiff, *Knafaim Me'al Suez* (Wings over Suez) (Heb.), Tel Aviv, Ot-Paz, 1970; Herzog, supra; Shabtai Tevet, *The Tanks of Tammuz*, London, Weidenfeld and Nicolson, 1968; David Kimche and Dan Bawly, *The Sandstorm*,

London, Secker & Warburg, 1968; S. L. A. Marshall, *Sinai Victory*, New York, Morrow, 1967.

6. For discussions of Israeli strategic concepts, see Dan Horowitz, *Hatfisa Hayisraelit shel Bitahon Le'umi* (Israel's Concept of National Security) (Heb.), Jerusalem, Eshkol Research Institute, Hebrew University, 1973, and *Israel's Concept of Defensible Borders*, Jerusalem, Davis Institute for International Relations, Hebrew University, 1975; Michael Brecher, *The Foreign Policy System of Israel: Settings, Images, Process*, London, Oxford University Press, 1972; Yigal Allon, supra; Michael Handel, *Israel's Political-Military Doctrine*, Cambridge, Mass., Harvard University Center for International Affairs, Occasional Papers, No. 30, 1973; Israel Tal, "Torat Habitahon, Reka Umedini'ut" (Security Doctrine Background and Policy) (Heb.), *Ma'arachot*, 253, December 1976; and references on specific conflicts, supra. For the use of the indirect approach in the War of Liberation, see appendixes by Yigael Yadin and Natanel Lorch to B. H. Liddell Hart, *Strategy of Indirect Approach*, London, Faber & Faber, 1967; and Itzchak Rabin, "Hagisha Ha'okefett Bemilchemet Ha'aztmaut" (The Indirect Approach in the War of Independence) (Heb.), *Ma'arachot*, 43, April 1963; and Trevor N. Dupuy, *Elusive Victory*, New York, Harper & Row, 1978.

7. Lorch, supra; Tal, supra.

8. Daniel Shimshoni, Dov Peleg, et al, *Duach: Hava'ada Letichnun Chel Ha'avir* (Report, Committee to Plan the Air Force) (Heb.), 1949.

9. On armor, see Haim Laskov and Meir Zorea, "Vehaya ki Yetze le Milchama" (And When He Will Go to War) (Heb.), *Ma'ariv*, October 10, 1965; Yehuda Wallach, *Ma'arachot*, 197, January 1968; I. Tal, supra; and Shabtai Tevet, supra. On air in this period, see Ezer Weizman, *Lecho Shamaim Velecho Aretz* (For Yours Are the Heavens and the Earth) (Heb.), Tel Aviv, *Ma'ariv*, 1975.

10. Major-General Ariel Sharon, quoted in Luttwak and Horowitz, supra, Chapter 9.

11. Herzog, supra, pp. 5–12.

12. James F. Digby, *Precision Guided Weapons*, Adelphi Papers, No. 118, and Richard Burt, *New Weapons Technologies*, Adelphi Papers, No. 126, London, International Institute for Strategic Studies, 1976.

13. Dan Horowitz, *Israel's Concept of Defensible Borders*, supra; M. A. McPeak, "Israel: Borders and Security," *Foreign Affairs*, Vol. 54, No. 3, 1976; Yigal Allon, "Israel: The Case for Defensible Borders," *Foreign Affairs*, Vol. 55, No. 1, October 1976; Yuval Ne'eman, "Madua Hitpatarti Mimisrad Habitachon" (Why I Resigned from the Ministry of Defense) (Heb.), *Ha'aretz*, February 6, 1976; Rosen, supra.

14. Shabtai Tevet, *Moshe Dayan*, London, Weidenfeld and Nicolson, 1972.

15. Dan Margalit, *Sheder Mehaba'it Halavan* (A Message from the White House) (Heb.), Tel Aviv, Ot-Paz, 1971.

16. Michael Brecher, *Israel, the Korean War, and China*, Jerusalem, Academic Press, 1974.

17. Nadav Safran, *Israel, the Embattled Ally*, Cambridge, Mass., Harvard University Press, 1977.

18. Thomas E. Wheelock, "Arms for Israel: The Limit of Leverage," *International Security*, Vol. 3, No. 2, Fall 1978.

19. Abraham S. Becker, *The Superpowers in the Arab-Israeli Conflict, 1970–1973*, Santa Monica, Calif., Rand Corporation, Report P–5167, December 1973; Nadav Safran, supra; Walter Lacquer, *Confrontation: The Middle East and World Politics*, London, Abacus, 1974.

20. Yehuda Wallach in *Ma'ariv*, May 26, 1974.

21. Major-General George Keagan, Jr., "Camp David Dangers," paper presented at a conference of the National Committee on American Foreign Policy, November 1978; excerpts printed in the *Jerusalem Post*, March 9, 1979. Presents a clear summary of the military risks undertaken by Israel in the Egyptian peace agreement.

22. For analyses and "models" of civil-military relations: for "Praetorians," see Edward Gibbon, *The Decline and Fall of the Roman Empire*, London, J. M. Dent & Sons Ltd. 1916; for the "garrison state," see Harold Lasswell, *The Garrison State, American Journal of Sociology*, 46, 1941, and *National Security and Individual Freedom*, New York, McGraw-Hill, 1950; for the professionalized military, see Samuel Huntington, *The Soldier and the State*, New York, Vintage Books, 1959. For an example of the impact of the momentum of military needs, see David Halberstam, *The Best and the Brightest*, New York, Random House, 1971.

23. See the bibliographies and discussions in A. R. Horelick, A. R. Johnson, and J. D. Steinbruner, *The Study of Soviet Foreign Policy: A Review of Decision-Theory Related Approaches*, Rand Report No. R–1334, Los Angeles, Rand Corporation, 1973; Commission on the Organization of the Government for the Conduct of Foreign Policy, *Report*, Washington, U.S. Government Printing Office, 1975; David Owen, *The Politics of Defense*, London, Jonathan Cape, 1972; John Steinbrunner, *The Cybernetic Theory of Decision*, Princeton, N.J., Princeton University Press, 1974. See also State of Israel, *Recommendations of Yadin-Sherf Committee to David Ben Gurion*, July 1963: "(a) The Prime Minister needs the full information from the covert activities. . . . (b) The intelligence picture should be balanced, and on no account come from one source." Reported in State of Israel, *The Yom Kippur War Commission of Inquiry: Report*, Jerusalem, 1975.

24. See *Sefer Toldot Hahaganah* (The History of the Haganah) (Heb.), Tel Aviv, Ma'arachot, 1954, and additional volumes in subsequent years); *Sefer Hapalmach* (The Palmach) (Heb.), Tel Aviv, Hakibbutz Hame'uhad, 1956; Meir Pa'il, *Hitpatchut Hapikud Ha'elyon Shel "Irgun Hahaganah" mi 1920 ve'ad Hakamat Zahal be Mai-Juni, 1948* (Development of the Supreme Command of the Haganah, 1920–1948) (Heb.), mimeo, Tel Aviv, University of Tel Aviv, 1970. I am particularly indebted to Meir Pa'il, who made available research material from his Ph.D. dissertation. See also Dan Horowitz and Moshe Lissak, *The Origins of the Israeli Polity, Israel Under the Mandate* Chicago, University of Chicago Press, 1978. (Much of Pa'il's thesis was published as: *Min ha "Haganah" le Zva Haganah* (From the "Haganah" to the Defense Forces), Tel Aviv, Zmora, Beitan, Modan, 1979.

25. Conversation with the late Moshe Sneh. Sneh was a General Zionist leader at the time, and served as RAMA (Figure 4.3). He later was an M.K. as a leader of the Jewish Communist Party.

26. Lissak and Horowitz, op. cit.

27. See Chapter 1, "Ideals and Reality," and Menachem Begin, *The Revolt*, London, W. H. Allen, 1951.

28. Shimshoni, Peleg, et al, 1949, supra.

29. Joseph Aboudi, unpublished M.A. thesis in military history, University of Tel Aviv.

30. Agranat Report (State of Israel, *The Yom Kippur War Commission of Inquiry: Report*, Jerusalem, 1975).

31. Allan E. Shapiro, article in the *Jerusalem Post*, May 7, 1978.

32. Interview with Brigadier-General Menachem Aviram, *Ma'ariv*, 1976.

33. Letter from General David Elazar to Prime Minister Rabin, published in *Ma'ariv*, April 20, 1976.

34. Moshe Dayan "The Yom Kippur War: The Status of the Minister of Defense," *Ma'ariv*, November 27, 1981.

35. There has been little research in Israel on these more complex kinds of influences. For indications regarding the pre-Sinai period, see Moshe Sharett, *Yoman Medini* (Political Diary) (Heb.), Tel Aviv, Am Oved, 1958; Moshe Dayan, *Sinai Diary*, supra, and *The Story of My Life*, London, Weidenfeld and Nicolson, 1976; and Michael Bar-Zohar, *Ben Gurion*, Tel Aviv, Am Oved, 1977; Yair Evron, "Foreign Policy Dependent on the Army," *Ha'aretz*, November 5, 1965; and Yosef Aboudi, supra.

36. For accounts of political activity in the weeks preceding the Six Day War, see, *inter alia*, Michael Bar Zohar, *Hahodesh Ha'aroch Beyoter* (The Longest Month) (Heb.), Tel Aviv, A. Levin-Epstein, 1968; M. A. Gilboa, *Shesh Shanim, Shisha Yamim* (Six Years, Six Days) (Heb.), Tel Aviv, Am Oved, 1969; Shlomo Nakdimon, *Likrat Sha'at Ha'efes* (Towards the Zero Hour) (Heb.), Tel Aviv, Ramador, 1968.

37. Michael Brecher, *The Foreign Policy System of Israel*, London, Oxford University Press, 1972.

38. Quoted in *Ma'ariv*, August 3, 1972.

39. Ephraim Turgovnick "Election Issues and Interfactional Conflict in Israel," in A. Arian (ed.), *The Elections in Israel, 1969*, Jerusalem, Academic Press, 1972.

40. Dan Margalit, *Sheder Mehaba'it Halavan*, supra.

41. Graham Allison, "Military Capabilities and American Foreign Policy," in the *Annals of the American Academy of Political and Social Science*, March, 1973.

42. See Morris Janowitz, *The Professional Soldier*, New York, Free Press, 1960.

43. A 1971 questionnaire administered to serving senior officers showed them to be more liberal in their views on the occupied territories than the population mean. Reported by Yoram Peri, letter to *Ha'aretz*, November 27, 1974.

44. On the West Bank administrative policies, see Dan Bawly and David Jarhi, *Israel and the Palestinians*, London, Anglo-Israel Association, 1941; and Yakov Lifschitz, *Economic Development in the Occupied Areas 1967–79* (Heb.), Tel Aviv, Ma'arachot, 1970.

45. For example, David Ben Gurion in the Knesset on March 5, 1951, on the importance of agricultural training during military service. For the extended role of the Army, see Amos Perlmutter, *Military and Politics in Israel*, London, Frank Cass, 1969, pp. 69–79.

46. Amos Elon, *The Israelis, Founders and Sons*, New York, Holt, Rinehart and Winston, 1971, p. 270.

Chapter 5

1. Michael Brecher, "Images, Process, and Feedback in Foreign Policy: Israel's Decision on German Reparations," *APSR*, LXVII, No. 1, March 1973.
2. Sources of economic data and analyses of development include *Annual Reports of the Bank of Israel*, Jerusalem (published in English as well as Hebrew); Central Bureau of Statistics, *Statistical Abstract of Israel*, annual, Jerusalem, Prime Minister's Office; *The Economic Quarterly* (Heb., Rive'on Lekalkala), Tel Aviv; Nadav Halevi and Ruth Klinov-Malul, *The Economic Development of Israel* New York, Praeger, 1968; Howard Pack, *Structural Change and Economic Policy in Israel*, New Haven, Conn., Yale University Press, 1971; and Don Patinkin, *The Israel Economy: The First Decade*, Jerusalem, Falk Project for Economic Research in Israel, 1960. See also the ongoing publications of the Falk Foundation and the Research Department of the Bank of Israel, and special reports of the Central Bureau of Statistics, as well as the Budget Laws of each year and supplementary budgets, and reports published by the various government departments, the Economic Planning Authority, the Faculty of Agriculture at Rehovot, and the universities. For international comparisons, see the United Nations *Yearbook of National Accounts Statistics*, New York, United Nations, 1971 and later years.
3. Howard Pack, supra.
4. Ya'akov Lifschitz, "Mishkalan shel Hotza'ot Habitachon Bameshek Hale'umi Ubasektor Hamemshalti" (The Weight of Defense Expenditure in the National Economy and the Government Sector) (Heb.), in Nadav Halevi and Ya'akov Kop (eds.), *Iyunim Bekalkalat Yisrael* (Heb.), Jerusalem, Falk Institute, 1974.
5. *Bank of Israel Annual Report, 1975* (Heb.), p. 40.
6. C.B.S., *Statistical Abstract of Israel, 1978*, and *Bank of Israel Annual Report, 1977* (Heb.), p. 38.
7. See, for example, *Aviation Week* for November and December 1973 and again for January and February 1977. Data on export growth are from *Bank of Israel Annual Report, 1975*, p. 77.
8. C.B.S., supra, 1976.
9. Ibid.
10. Yuval Elizur in *Ma'ariv*, February 28, 1972, reports a speech by Dr. Pinhas Zussman, Chief Economist of the Ministry of Defense. For an analysis of some forms of technology transfer, see D. Shimshoni, "The Mobile Entrepreneur," *Minerva*, January, 1970.
11. H. Ben-Shachar, M. Bruno, Y. Ben-Porath, Sh. Ronal, and B. Nahir, *Hamlatzot Leshinui Bemas Hayashir* (Recommendations for Changes in Direct Taxes) (Heb.), mimeo, Report of the Committee for Tax Reform, Jerusalem, Ministry of Finance, 1975.
12. Conversation with Haim Zadok, later Minister of Justice, in 1973.

13. References on the budget process include Arnon Gafni and David Wainshal *Budgeting Systems in Israel: Report on Progress Submitted to the International Institute of Administrative Science;* manuscript of a lecture on the budget process, May 1973; M. Sandberg (Sanbar) and H. Stoessel, "Budget Preparation and Management in Israel," *International Review of Administrative Sciences,* Vol. XXXI, No. 4, 1965, pp. 330–46; David Wainshal, "Planning and Budgeting in Israel; Problems and Experience," *Public Finance,* No. 2, 1972, The Hague, pp. 196–204; Arnon Gafni and David Wainshal, *Open-End Budget and Block Allocation Strategies: An Integrated Approach,* mimeographed lecture, Jerusalem, Ministry of Finance, April 1973; Marver Bernstein, *The Politics of Israel,* Princeton, N.J., Princeton University Press, 1957. I am grateful for preliminary drafts of materials on the United States budget process, made available by J. P. Crecine.

14. See Gad Ya'akobi in *Ot,* Vol. II, No. 5, Tel Aviv, March 1968, and his "Intervention of the Government and Its Involvement in the Israel Economy" (Heb.), *Israel Economy Quarterly,* August 1972; David Kohav, "How the Israeli System Works," in Judd Teller (ed.), *Government and the Democratic Process,* New York, American Histadrut Cultural Exchange Institute; Itzchak Ben Aharon, "Planning," *Quarterly Banking Review* Tel Aviv Association of Banks in Israel, March 1968, p. 64.

15. Speech by Pinhas Sapir to the Economic Policy Task Force of the Labor Party at Beit Berl in June 1973.

16. A detailed analysis of the operation of the capital market is given in Haim Ben-Shachar, Saul Bronfeld, and Alexander Cukierman, "The Capital Market in Israel," in Pierre Uri (ed.), *Israel and the Common Market,* Jerusalem, Weidenfeld and Nicolson, 1971. Page 225 presents a detailed chart of the flow of investment funds.

17. *The Management of State Enterprises,* Jerusalem, Israel Association of Political Science, 1965.

18. The literature on the kibbutz and *moshav* is extensive. For an introduction, see, for example, S. N. Eisenstadt, *Israeli Society,* London, Weidenfeld and Nicolson, 1967; and Dorothy Willner, *Nation-Building and Community in Israel,* Princeton, N.J., Princeton University Press, 1969. For a simple but convincing description of the start of kibbutz settlement, see Joseph Baratz, *A Village by the Jordan: The Story of Degania,* London, Harvil Press, 1954. Don Gileadi describes the late-blooming economic development of cooperative agriculture in "Predominance of the Hityashvut Ovedet: Since Which Time?" (Heb.), *Social Research Quarterly* (Riveon Lemehkar Hevrati), Haifa, June, 1972.

19. Pinhas Zusman, *Power Measurement in Econometric Models,* Working Paper No. 7302, Center for Agricultural Economic Research, Rehovot, Israel. Zusman uses econometrics to measure "power relationships" between consumers (seeking consumers' surplus), the Ministry of Finance (minimizing subsidy costs), and producers (seeking producers' surplus), and finds a power relation persistent over time, with some advantage to the producers.

20. For an analysis of increasing "regionalism" in agriculture, see Daniel Rosolio, "In-

tercommunal Cooperation on a Regional Level," paper presented at the International Conference of Hevrat Ovdim, Tel Aviv, May 1973.

21. Nadav Safran, *The United States and Israel*, Cambridge, Mass., Harvard University Press, 1963, p. 127. For descriptions of the scope of the Histadrut, see also Margaret Plunkett, "The Histadrut," *Industrial and Labor Relations Review*, II, January 1950; and Aaron Becker, "The Work of the General Federation of Workers in Israel," *International Labor Review*, LXXXI, May 1960.

22. For discussions relevant to the internal politics and goals of the Histadrut, see Meir Avizohar, "Ideological Development and the Importance of Public Ownership," May 1973, paper presented at Hevrat Ovdim Conference, and *A Reverse Direction Pressure Group* (Heb.), Institute for Research on Work and Society, University of Tel Aviv, 1971; Amira Galin and Aharon Harel, *Hitpatchuyot Utmurot Bema'arechet Yachasei Avoda Beyisroel* (Developments and Changes in the Labor Relations System of Israel) (Heb.), mimeographed draft, Tel Aviv, 1977; Eli Ginzberg, "The Human Economy: The Balance Between Economic and Non-Economic Values," paper given at Hevrat Ovdim 1973 Conference; Aharon Harel, "Ways and Trends to Ensure Representative Democracy in the Histadrut," speech at the Central Committee of the Labor Party, February 8, 1973; and *The Organization of the Histadrut to Accomplish Its Mission* (Heb.), pamphlet abstracted from speeches of members in party forums and the conclusions of deliberating groups, Tel Aviv, Israel Labor Party, The Center, November 1972; Histadrut Eleventh Convention, *Decisions* (Heb.), stenciled summary (internal), Tel Aviv, December 12, 1969; Israel Keissar, "Power Structures in Israeli Unions and Their Impact on Collective Bargaining," paper given at Hevrat Ovdim International Conference on the Role of Cooperative and Public Economies in Democratic Societies, Tel Aviv, May 1973.

23. Galin and Harel, supra, and Histadrut Department of Organization:

24. F. Medding, *Mapai in Israel*, London, Cambridge University Press, 1972, pp. 128–29.

25. Aharon Harel, supra.

26. For processes of wage negotiations: Zippora Abel Lefkowitz "Wage Policy in Israel," unpublished paper for postgraduate Public Policy Seminar, University of Tel Aviv, 1973; J. Beilin, "Hashokolad Hamar" (The Bitter Chocolate) (Heb.), Tel Aviv, *Ot*, No. 66, August 3, 1972 (on the Elite strike); Gideon Ben-Israel, "Settlement of Labor Disputes in Non-Private Enterprises in Israel," paper given at Hevrat Ovdim 1973 Conference; Galin and Harel, supra; 1957 Law of Collective Agreements; Arieh Shirom, "On the Problem of Labor Relations in Israel" (Heb.), *Economic Quarterly*, Vol. 16, No. 64, December 1969, pp. 382–87.

27. Edward Tufte, *Political Control of the Economy*, Princeton, N.J., Princeton University Press, 1978.

28. Conversation with A. Harel, Director of Histadrut Organization Department.

29. A. Lerner and H. Ben-Shachar, *Kalkala Ye'ila* (The Efficient Economy) (Heb.), Tel Aviv, Amikam, 1969.

30. But see, as an exception, Bruno, supra.

31. Michel Crozier *The Bureaucratic Phenomenon*, Chicago, Illinois, University of Chicago Press, 1964.

Chapter 6

1. Zvi Susman, *Wage Differentials and Equality Within the Histadrut* (Heb.), Tel Aviv, Massada, 1974, p. 69.

2. For equality measures, see H. Ben Shachar and Moshe Sandberg, "Economic and Institutional Effects on Income Distribution: The Case of Israel," *Public Finance*, XII, 1967, p. 241f; David Horwitz (Chairman), *Report of the Committee to Investigate Developments in Income and the Social Gap* (Heb.), mimeo, Tel Aviv, 1971; Jack Habib, *The Reform of Taxes and Transfers: 1969–1973*, Discussion Paper 765, Jerusalem, Falk Institute for Economic Research, 1974.

3. Central Bureau of Statistics *Surveys on Family Budgets in Special Populations 1968/69: First Results*, Special Series 340, Jerusalem, C.B.S., 1971.

4. Israel Katz et al., *Report of the Prime Minister's Commission on Children and Youth in Distress*, Jerusalem, Prime Minister's Office, 1974, 2d ed.

5. Hanna Keren-Ya'ar and Miriam Souery, *Families with Children in Israel, 1968–78, Survey No. 28*, Jerusalem, National Insurance Institute, 1980; and, for parents' education, 1969, 1972; Jack Habib, *Children in Israel*, Preliminary Research Report No. 168, Jerusalem, Szold Institute, 1972; also I. Katz, supra. For 1976–77, educational data estimated from Mosheh Egozi, *Pupils in Primary Education*, Jerusalem, Ministry of Education, 1977.

6. Central Bureau of Statistics, *Statistical Abstract of Israel, 1978*, Jerusalem, Prime Minister's Office.

7. "Food Consumption and Nutrition of Old People on Welfare Who Live by Themselves," *Harefuah*, Vol. 62, 1967, p. 401. which recommended giving priority to public health, reported in *Public Health*, Vol. 3, No. 2, May 1960, pp. 98–118.

8. International Labor Office, Geneva, *Annual Report, 1978*.

9. Avraham Doron and Ralph M. Kramer, "Ideology, Program and Organizational Factors in Public Assistance: The Case of Israel," *Social Security*, 9–10 (Heb., English summary), December 1975.

10. Rose Zeitlin, *Henrietta Szold*, New York, Dial, 1952, p. 81.

11. C.B.S., *Statistical Abstract of Israel, 1975*, Jerusalem, Prime Minister's Office, 1975, pp. 91–102.

12. Arye Nizan, "Past, Present and Future in Israel's Social Security System," *Social Security*, No. 8 (Heb., English summary), March 1975.

13. C.B.S., *Survey on Family Budgets*, supra. J. Habib, supra.

14. Much information on the Panthers was supplied by Deborah Bernstein, based on her field research for an M.A. in sociology, Hebrew University, Jerusalem, 1974, and unpublished Ph.D. thesis, Sussex University, 1976.

15. For the prestate period, see Giora Goldberg, *Labor Exchanges as a Political Instrument in a Developing Country* (Heb.), mimeo of unpublished M.A. thesis,

University of Tel Aviv, 1975; Josef Gorni, *Ahdut Ha'avoda: 1919–1930, Basic Ideas and Political Methods* (Heb.), Kibbutz Meuhad, 1973; Yonatan Shapiro, *Ahdut Ha'avoda Hahistorit* (The Organization of Power) (Heb.), Tel Aviv, Am Oved, 1975.

16. Don Patinkin, *The Economy of Israel: The First Ten Years*, Jerusalem, Falk Center for Economic Research, 1965.

17. *Manpower Planning Authority Annual Report, 1967*, Jerusalem, Ministry of Labor, 1968.

18. See Chapter 1 for a discussion of *mamlachtiut*. Paltiel Khayyam Zev, *The Progressive Party* (Heb.), unpublished Ph.D. thesis, Hebrew University, 1963. Peter Y. Medding, *Mapai in Israel*, London, Cambridge University Press, 1972, pp. 231–33, and Goldberg, op. cit., propose contrasting reasons for Mapai's change on this question.

19. Medding, supra; Goldberg, op. cit.

20. Report by Ernest Kaiser, actuary, Jerusalem, Ministry of Labor, 1972.

21. C.B.S., *Statistical Abstract of Israel, 1975*, Table ii/17, Jerusalem.

22. A. Doron, "The Social Security System in Israel: Forms of Structure and Change" (Heb.), *The State, Government, and International Relations*, 13, Winter 1979, Jerusalem, pp. 63–81; and conversations with Israel Katz.

23. R. Roter and N. Shamai, "Patterns of Poverty in Israel: Preliminary Findings," *Social Security*, No. 1 (Heb., English summary), February 1971, pp. 17–28.

24. Eliezer Jaffe, "Welfare Issues in Jerusalem," *Journal of Jewish Communal Service*, XLLX, No. 4, Summer 1973; Jack Habib, "Poverty in Israel 1964–74 in the Light of the System for Income Maintenance," *Social Security*, No. 8 (Heb., English summary), March 1975.

25. C.B.S., *Annual Statistical Abstracts*.

26. C.B.S., *Survey of Young Couples*, Special Publication No. 375, Jerusalem, Prime Minister's Office, 1972.

27. A. Doron, "Health Services in Israel: Another Point of View" (Heb.), *Bitachon Soziali* (Social Security), Jerusalem, March 1979.

28. Peter Y. Medding, *Mapai in Israel*, op. cit., pp. 234–40.

29. The Committee for Comprehensive Health Insurance (Choushi Committee), *Report* (Heb.) to Minister of Labor and Minister of Health, including minority reports, Jerusalem, January 1968; and Letter to Minister of Health Victor Shem-Tov, January 18, 1972, from the Associated Health Funds (Ovdim Leumi'im, Maccabbee, Merkazit, Amamit, Assaf, Brit Kupot Holim).

30. K. J. Mann, "Summary of Recommendations of the Israel Medical Association Committee on the Organization of Health Services in Israel," *Journal of Medical Sciences*, Vol. 6, No. 1, 1970, pp. 168–75.

31. Some sources on immigration: interviews and conversations with those involved, including A. Zigel, long head of the Agency's Department of Klita; Lova Eliav, Leo Doltzin, and the late Louis Pincus; Yosef Geva, first Director-General of the Ministry of Absorption; and student seminar papers, particularly by Dvora Artzi and Yosef Beilin at the University of Tel Aviv.

32. See Chapter 3, "Political Integration."

33. Elad Peled et al., *Education in Israel in the Nineteen-Eighties* (Heb.), draft, Jerusalem, Ministry of Education, June 1976.

34. Aharon F. Kleinberger, *Society, Schools and Progress in Israel*, Oxford, Pergamon, 1969, pp. 125–26.

35. Moshe Smilansky, "The Social Test of the Structure of Education in Israel," *Megamot*, VIII, No. 3, July 1954.

36. The Prime Minister's Committee on Children and Youth in Distress, *Report*, Jerusalem, Prime Minister's Office, 2d ed., 1974.

37. Kleinberger, supra, p. 298.

38. For a summary of research and experiment in advancing the disadvantaged, see Chaim Adler and Rahel Peleg, *Ha'arachat Toza'ot Mechkarim Venisuim Betipuah Hinuchi* (Evaluation of the Results of Research and Experiments in Overcoming Educational Disadvantage) (Heb.), mimeo, Jerusalem, Hebrew University, School of Education, 1975.

39. J. Prawer, Chairman, et al., *Conclusions of the Public Committee on Extension of Free Compulsory Education* (Heb.), Jerusalem, Ministry of Education and Culture, 1965.

40. Dr. Elimelech Rimalt, Chairman, *Report of the Parliamentary Committee to Investigate the Structure of Elementary and Secondary Education in Israel, 1966–68* (Heb.), Jerusalem, The Knesset, 1971.

41. For discussions, see Kleinberger, supra, pp. 146–50; and Naftaly Glassman, "The Structural Change Proposal in the Israeli Schools: Conflict and Conquest," *Journal of Educational Administration*, VIII:1, May 1970.

42. Elad Peled, comments, and *The Hidden Agenda of Educational Policy in Israel*, unpublished Ph.D. thesis, Columbia University, 1979.

43. Y. Amir, Chairman, et al., the Public Committee to Investigate the Reform in the Israeli Educational System, *Report* (Heb.), mimeo, Jerusalem, Ministry of Education, 1979.

44. C.B.S., *Manpower Survey*, 1973, p. 182; *Yediot Bestatistika Hinuchit* (Information in Educational Statistics) (Heb.), No. 35, January 1971, p. 85.

45. M. Egozi, *Statistical Survey of the Educational System* (Heb.), mimeo, Jerusalem, Ministry of Education, 1978; and data supplied by Dr. P. Biltzky, Ministry of Education, July 1975. See also C.B.S. *Statistical Abstract*, supra; and Planning Department, Ministry of Education, *The Educational System Mirrored in Numbers* (Heb.), Jerusalem, Ministry of Education, 1974.

46. Letter from Dr. P. Biltzki, Planning Department, Ministry of Education, February 1976.

47. A. Minkovitch, D. Davis, and J. Bashi, *Evaluation of the Educational Achievements of the Elementary School in Israel*, Jerusalem, Hebrew University, School of Education, 1977.

48. Daniel Shimshoni, "Higher Education for Children of the Well-to-do," *Ha'aretz*, July 11, 1969. Data are from the Ministry of Labor *Manpower Planning Survey*, 1967.

49. For additional references on educational achievements, see Gina Ortar, "Educa-

tional Achievements of Primary School Graduates in Israel as Related to their Socio-cultural Background," *Comparative Education*, 4, 1967; Uri Litwin, *Allocation of Resources in Education in Light of Factors Influencing Pupils' Achievements in the Survey Tests* (Heb.), Jerusalem, Falk Institute for Economic Research, 1971, also in *Megamot*, December 1971. For a qualitative picture, see C. Frankenstein, "Schools Without Parents" (Heb.), *Megamot*, XII, No. 1, March 1962; and Aliza Lowenberg, "Bridging Two Worlds," in Jacob Landau (ed.), *Man, State and Society in the Middle East*, New York, Praeger, 1972, and *Chapters from Kiryat Shmonah* (Heb.), Tel Aviv, Schocken, 1964. For the level of parent's education, see Minkowitz, Davis, and Bashi, supra; and Moshe Egozi, *The Index Need for Advancement*, a condensed English version of *Pupils in Primary Education, by Father's Origin and Level of Education and by Family Size* (Heb.), Jerusalem, Ministry of Education, 1977.

50. *C.B.S., 1975*, supra, Table II/21, p. 47, and Table xxii/32, p. 627.

51. Y. Parush, "Differences in Consumption Among Population Strata" (Heb.), *Economic Quarterly*, No. 49–50, 1969.

52. Matityahu Peled, *Report of Arab Education Group* (Heb.), mimeo, Jerusalem, Ministry of Education, Project to Plan Education for the 1980s, 1975.

53. Baruch Levy, *A Comparative Study of Attempts to Formulate Social Policies at the National Level*, unpublished Ph.D. thesis, Brandeis University, Waltham, Mass., 1980.

54. Lotte Salzberger and Jona M. Rosenfeld, "The Anatomy of 276 Social Welfare Agencies in Jerusalem: Findings from a Census," *Social Service Review*, June, 1974, pp. 255–67.

55. S. M. Lipset, op. cit.; Interview material. See also Meir Avizohar, "The Sources of the Egalitarian Approach to Welfare Policy," *Social Security* (Heb., English summary), Vol. II, December 1971; and Gunnar Myrdal, *An American Dilemma*, New York, Harper & Bros., 1944.

56. See Nathan Glazer and Patrick Moynihan, *Beyond the Melting Pot*, Cambridge, Mass., M.I.T. and Harvard, 1963.

57. *Report* of the Prime Minister's Committee on Children and Youth in Distress, op. cit.

58. Richard M. Titmuss, *Commitment to Welfare*, London, George Allen, 1968, p. 135.

59. Daniel Shimshoni, *An Interim Report on Renewal*, mimeo, Jerusalem, Ministry of Building and Housing, August, 1981; and "Projects Progress," *Jerusalem Post*, August 9, 1981.

60. C. Frankenstein, op. cit.

61. Shmuel Eisenstadt, *Israel Society* (Heb.), Jerusalem, Magnes Press, 1967, p. 112.

Chapter 7

1. See, for example, David Greenberg, "Israel," *Science*, Vol. 168, April 24, 1970, pp. 446–51; S. Wald, *Industry, Science, University in Israel*, Jerusalem, NCRD,

Prime Minister's Office, 1972; and Daniel Shimshoni, "Israeli Scientific Policy," *Minerva*, III, No. 4, Summer 1965.

2. Joseph Ben David, "Scientific Endeavor in Israel and the United States," *American Behavioral Scientist*, 6.4, 1962.

3. On roles and on political culture, see, for example, Gabriel Almond and Sidney Verba, *The Civic Culture*, Princeton, N.J., Princeton University Press, 1963; Robert Putnam, *The Beliefs of Politicians*, New Haven, Conn., Yale University Press, 1973; S. M. Lipset and Asoke Basu, "The Roles of the Intellectual and Political Roles," in Lewis Coser (ed.), *The Idea of Social Structure*, New York, Harcourt, Brace, 1975; and Robert A. Dahl, *Modern Political Analysis*, Englewood Cliffs, N.J., Prentice-Hall, 1976. See also Chapter 9 of this book.

4. Quoted from a letter from Achad Ha'am to Weizmann, in Chaim Weizmann, *Trial and Error*, New York, Harper & Brothers, 1949, p. 237.

5. Conversation with the late Arthur Blok, Director of the Technion in the early 1920s, in London, 1963.

6. C.B.S. *Annual Report*, 1976, p. 611f. For data on the growth of higher education, see the C.B.S. Annual Reports and Special Surveys, Jerusalem, Central Bureau of Statistics, Prime Minister's Office.

7. Daniel Shimshoni, "Higher Education for Children of the Well-to-do" (Heb.), *Ha'aretz*, Tel Aviv, July 11, 1969, and Chaim Adler, supra, Chapter 6.

8. For science policy documents, see Shimshoni, 1959, note 14, and *NCRD Biennial Report*, 1963–64, Jerusalem, Prime Minister's Office, 1965; Ephraim Katzir (Katchalsky), *Report—Committee to Inquire into the Organisation and Administration of Governmental Research*, Jerusalem, Prime Minister's Office, 1968; and Itzchak Ya'akov (Chief Scientist, Ministry of Commerce and Industry), *The Policy of the Ministry of Commerce and Industry for Industrial Research* (Heb.), mimeo, Jerusalem, 1976.

9. For a concept of R&D strategy, see Robert Gilpin, *Technology, Economic Growth and International Competitiveness*, report to the Joint Economic Committee of the Congress, Washington, U.S. Government Printing Office, 1975.

10. Committee on Higher Education (Sherf Committee), *Report* (Heb.), Jerusalem, Prime Minister's Office, 1956.

11. *Proposed Law of the Council for Higher Education*, Jerusalem, Ministry of Justice, 1968.

12. Ben David, supra.

13. Internal memorandum by Prof. E. D. Bergmann, then head of defense research, 1961.

14. Daniel Shimshoni (assisted by Yael Rom), *Scientific Research and Technological Development in Israel* (Heb.), Jerusalem, Prime Minister's Office, 1959.

15. See Chapter 4, "The Nation in Arms."

16. See Chapter 5, "The Political Economy."

17. Israel Katz et al., *Report of the Prime Minister's Committee for Children and Youth in Distress* (Heb.), Jerusalem, Prime Minister's Office, 1975.

18. A. Doron, in Doron et al. (eds), *Welfare Policy in Israel*, Jerusalem, Academon Press, 1970.

19. The new PSSC high school physics program was explained to Israeli scientists by Jerrold Zacharias in 1960.

20. See Chapter 8, "The Physical Environment."

21. Don K. Price, *The Scientific Estate*, Cambridge, Mass., Harvard University Press, 1965.

22. See, for example, the discussion of Biram and Ikrit in Chapter 4, "The Nation in Arms."

23. Shlomo Avineri, interviewed on Israel Television, June 1977.

24. G. Almond and S. Verba, *The Civic Culture* (Princeton, N.J., Princeton University Press, 1963).

25. Richard Hofstadter, *Anti-Intellectualism in American Life*, New York, Vintage Books, 1962.

26. Lipset and Basu, supra.

27. See Medding, *Mapai in Israel*, supra, p. 263, re the Lavon affair.

28. Ralph Waldo Emerson, "The American Scholar," Cambridge, Mass., Harvard Phi Beta Kappa Address, 1837.

29. Patricia R. Harris in address to Kennedy School of Government Forum, 1979, in Kennedy School *Bulletin*, III no. 2, Cambridge, Mass., 1980.

Chapter 8

1. Alpheus T. Mason, *Brandeis: A Free Man's Life*, New York, Viking Press, 1946, page 457.

2. D. Shimshoni, M. Arens, L. Kestenbaum, D. Bardin, E. Posner, and A. Shapera, *Government Organization for Dealing with the Environment*, a report for NCRD, Prime Minister's Office, Tel Aviv, Advanced Technology, Ltd., 1973.

3. Central Bureau of Statistics, *Statistical Abstract of Israel*, Jerusalem, Prime Minister's Office, 1976.

4. A. Karin, *Policy of the Committee to Preserve Agricultural Land*, internal memo, mimeographed, Jerusalem, Ministry of the Interior, 1975.

5. Nathaniel Lichfield, *Israel's New Towns: A Strategy for their Future*, Tel Aviv, Ministry of Housing, 1970.

6. Erik Cohen, *The City in Zionist Ideology*, Jerusalem, Institute of Urban and Regional Studies, Hebrew University, 1970.

7. Yonatan Shapiro, *Achdut Ha'avoda Hahistorit*, Chapter 1, supra.

8. Unpublished note by Moshe Lissak, "The Impact of the Arab-Jewish Conflict on the Building and Integration of the Jewish Community in Palestine."

9. D. Weintraub, M. Lissak, and Y. Atzmon, supra, Chapter 1; E. Brutzkus, *Physical Planning in Israel*, Jerusalem, Ministry of the Interior, 1964; Shalom Reichman, "Three Dilemmas in the Development of Jewish Settlement" (Heb.), *Ir Ve'Ezor* (Town and Region), Second Year, Vol. 3, February 1975, pp. 47–56. Arieh Shachar, "Israel's Development Towns," *AIP Journal*, November 1971. E. Brutzkus, *Regional Policy in Israel*, Jerusalem, Ministry of the Interior, 1970.

10. Shimshoni, Arens, Kestenbaum, et al., supra; and Nissim Baruch, *Physical Planning in Israel: Organization of the Systems* (Heb.), report to the Interministerial Committee on Efficiency, Jerusalem, Ministry of Finance, 1971.

11. Haim Barkai, "Land and the Land Authority," in Nachum Gross (ed.), *Essays on Economic Policy in Israel* (Heb.), Jerusalem, Universities Publishers, 1975, p. 323f.

12. Shaul Amir and Reuven Shtraz, *The Nature Preservation Society: Potential for Intervention in Environmental Quality Protection* (Heb.), mimeo, Haifa, The Technion, 1974.

13. Lichfield, supra.

14. R. Zilberberg, *Population Dispersal in Israel, 1948-1972* (Heb.), mimeo, Jerusalem, Economic Planning Authority, Ministry of Finance, 1973. A. Berler, *Development Towns in Israel*, Jerusalem, Israel Universities Press, 1970.

15. Zilberberg, supra.

Chapter 9

1. Robert Dahl, *Polyarchy: Participation and Opposition*, New Haven, Conn., Yale University Press, 1971.

2. S. M. Lipset, *The First New Nation*, London, Heinemann, 1964.

3. Amitai Etzioni, "Alternative Ways to Democracy: The Example of Israel," *Political Science Quarterly*, 74, 1949, pp. 196–214.

4. Yuval Elizur and Eliahu Salpeter, *Who Rules Israel?*, New York, Harper & Row, 1973.

5. Peter Medding, *Mapai in Israel*, supra, and Nathan Yanai, *A Rift in the Leadership* (Heb.), supra.

6. Itzchak Ben Aharon, "Courage to Change Before There Is Catastrophe," *Davar*, Jan. 11, 1963. The article was widely believed to have been instrumental in advancing the merger of the Labor movement parties.

7. Yohanan Peres, Efraim Yuchtman (Yaar), and Rivka Shafat, "Predicting and Explaining Voters' Behavior in Israel," and Rachel Tokatli, "Image Modification and Voters' Behavior," both in A. Arian (ed.), *Elections in Israel, 1973*, Jerusalem, Academic Press, 1975.

8. Louis Guttmann, "Before and After the 1977 Election" (Heb.), *Yedion* (Bulletin), Jerusalem, Institute for Applied Social Research, 1977.

9. See the analysis in Chapter 3, "Political Integration."

10. Colonel (reserve) Arik Achmon, in conversation, 1973.

11. Eli Reches, *Arviyei Yisroel Vehafka'at Hakarka'ot Begalil* (Arab Israelis and the Appropriation [by eminent domain] of Galilee Lands) (Heb.), mimeo, Tel Aviv, University of Tel Aviv, Shiloah Institute, May 1977.

12. Rael Jean Issac, *Israel Divided: Ideological Politics in the Jewish State*, Baltimore, Johns Hopkins, 1976.

13. For strong ethnic and nonleft protest, see Yehuda Nini, "The Destruction of the Third Temple," *Shdemot*, No. 3 (Heb.), 1971, pp. 54–61, as more typical of the

Panther-type attitude. See also Deborah Bernstein, *The Black Panthers of Israel, 1971–72*, supra.

14. Arend Lijphart, *The Politics of Accommodation. Pluralism and Accommodation in the Netherlands* Berkeley, University of California Press, 1968; See also S. M. Lipset, *Political Man: The Social Basis of Politics*, Garden City, N.Y., Doubleday, 1960, and Ralf Dahrendorf, *Class and Class Conflict in Industrial Society*, Stanford, Calif. Stanford University Press, 1959 pp. 213–18.

15. Morris Janowitz, *Social Control of the Welfare State*, New York, Elsevier, 1976.

16. Harry Eckstein, *Division and Cohesion in Democracy*, Princeton, N.J., Princeton University Press, 1966, pp. 37, 76f.

17. Myron Aronoff, *Power and Ritual in the Israel Labor Party*, Assen, Netherlands, Van Gorcum, 1977.

18. Aronoff, supra.

19. Irving Janis, *Victims of Groupthink: A Psychological Study of Foreign Policy Decisions and Fiascoes*, Boston, Houghton Mifflin, 1972.

20. Itzchak Ben Aharon, in a seminar talk at Tel Aviv University, early 1970s.

21. Robert Tucker, *Stalin as Revolutionary*, London, Chatto and Windus, 1974.

22. Aronoff, supra.

23. Nathan Yanai, *Party Leadership in Israel: Maintenance and Change*, Turtledove Publishing, Ramat Gan, Israel, 1981.

24. In *The Beliefs of Politicians: Ideology, Conflict and Democracy*, New Haven, Yale University Press, 1973, Robert Putnam analyzes differences between politicians and civil servants in England and Italy, finding politicians to be concerned with major rather than incremental changes, sensitive more to political than to technical constraints, and interested more in goals and in political philosophy than in methods.

25. "Subject" as defined in Gabriel Almond and Sidney Verba, *The Civic Culture*, supra.

26. B. Aktzin and Y. Dror, *Israel—High Pressure Planning*, Syracuse, Syracuse Univ. Press, 1966, and Y. Dror in *Ha'aretz*, Sept. 8, 1977 and April 23, 1978.

27. Charles Lindblom, *The Intelligence of Democracy: Decision Making Through Mutual Adjustment*, New York, Free Press, 1965; Robert A. Dahl and Charles Lindblom, *Politics, Economics, and Welfare*, New York, Harper & Row, 1963.

28. Medding, supra, pp. 132–33.

29. Yaakov Reuveni, *Haminhal Hatziburi Beyisrael* (Public Administration in Israel) (Heb.), Ramat Gan, Masada, 1974, contrasts the stated aims of the civil service system with its administrative culture.

Chapter 10

1. V. D. Segre, *Israel: A Society in Transition*, London, Oxford University Press, 1971.

2. See Figure 4.1.

3. Attorney General Itzchak Zamir, "On the Rule of Law in Israel," *Ha'aretz*, June 23, 1980.

4. Rael Jean Isaac, *Israel Divided: Ideological Politics in the Jewish State*, supra.

5. Itamar Rabinovich, "Israel: The Impact of the Peace Treaty," *Current History*, January 1980.

6. W. F. Abboushi, "Changes in Political Attitudes in the West Bank after Camp David", in Emile A. Nakhleh (ed.), *A Palestinian Agenda for the West Bank and Gaza*, Washington, D.C., American Enterprise Institute for Public Policy Research, 1980, pp. 11–12.

7. Daniel Shimshoni, *An Interim Report on Renewal*, mimeo, Jerusalem, Ministry of Building and Housing, August 1981; "Project's Progress," *Jerusalem Post*, August 9, 1981; *Constitution of Neighborhood Steering Committees* (Heb.), Jerusalem, Office of the Deputy Prime Minister, July 1981; "The Rehabilitation of Depressed Neighborhoods in Israel," International Federation for Housing and Planning, *Papers and Proceedings, 35th World Congress*, 1980 Vol. II, The Hague, Netherlands, 1981.

8. Yonatan Shapiro, supra (notes to Chapter 1); Dan Horowitz and Moshe Lissak, supra (notes to Chapter 4); M. Aronoff, supra (notes to chapter 1).

9. "Ever since the beginning of the modern era," writes S. M. Lipset, "the revolutionary nationalism of new nations has tended to incorporate supra-national ideals." *The First New Nation*, supra, pp. 74–75.

10. Zilberg, supra (Chapter 1). Emphasis is in the original.

Name Index

Subject Index

536